"Approaching genius . . . Tosches's forages through American popular culture are that extraordinary. For the second time in his writing life, Tosches has walked through the American cultural garbage dump and found a great subject everyone else had thrown away. . . . Read *Dino: Living High in the Dirty Business of Dreams*. You'll see."

—*The Buffalo News*

"Memories, and memorable biographies are made of this."

—*Time*

"A true image of Martin's mind and background . . . Here are the rise, the glory and the fading into his own shadow of Dean Martin, an entertainer who won the world but lost all that makes the winning worth it. . . . Tosches's literary high jumps . . . set before us a hypnotically attractive, homegrown American monster."

—*Hollywood Reporter*

"Intriguing stuff . . . Nick Tosches has written a surprisingly readable book."

—*Cleveland Plain Dealer*

"Fascinating . . . [a] combination of meticulous research and speculative reverie . . . an impudent view of Martin's rise from his Italian immigrant family origins, his superstardom, and then his decline."

—*Booklist*

Dino

*L*IVING HIGH

IN THE DIRTY

BUSINESS OF

DREAMS

•

Nick Tosches

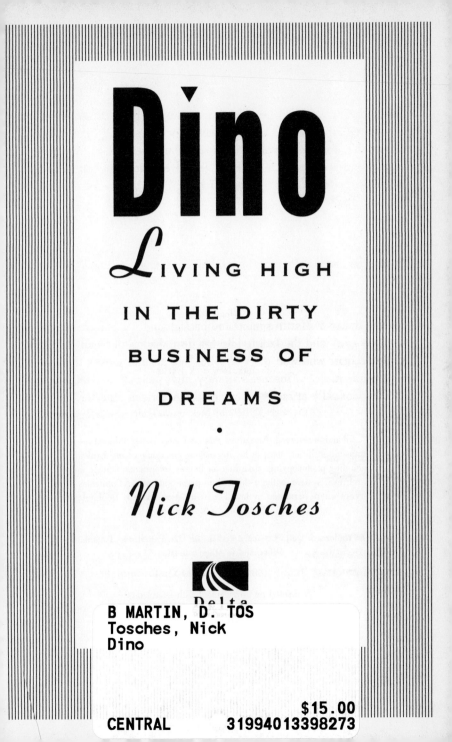

Delta

$\mathcal{F}$OR MY

FATHER

$\mathcal{A}$CKNOWLEDGMENTS

During the years of my work on this book, I tried to keep a running account of the many people who helped me in the course of it. Now, looking at those lists in the softer light of work's end, I can see two things clearly. One is the general kindness of people in taking time out from their own lives and work to help a stranger in his. The other is the true extent of my indebtedness to those people. I hope that in gleaning whatever worth or pleasure lies in these pages, the reader will bear in mind those here acknowledged. Theirs are the voices, memories, and labor underlying it all. Whatever fault lies in the weaving of what they gave is, of course, the weaver's own.

Susan Nadler proved invaluable in giving me the name and number of an acquaintance in Steubenville, Ohio, and then preparing my way in Steubenville with a few gracious words of her own. The acquaintance led me in turn to others, who led me to still others: those who had shared Dean Martin's early years. Through her hospitality and eagerness to help, Susan's acquaintance, who asked not to be named, lent optimism to the beginning of a long journey; and for that, as well as for her other help, I thank her. That journey would later take me to places, the barrens of fame, where people often spoke as if from scripts. So it is with a special fondness and appreciation that I remember those in Steubenville whom I here thank: Christopher Christ; Joe, Leo, and Martha D'Anniballe; Irma D'Aurora; Agon DeLuca; Ralph DeMarco; John DeSarro; Emilio Julian; Angie Kayafas and her mother, Agnes Synodinos; Minnie from the Federal Terrace Bar; Tim Paidousis; Paul Paolisso; Mike Pavlovich; Beans Pompa; Bob Sasso; and Anna Yannon. Mindy Costanzo, Mike DiNovo, George and Ann Mavromatis, Ross Monaco, and Mary Crocetti Vecchione were the most helpful of a helpful many. I should also like to thank the Jefferson County Historical Association, the clerks of Jefferson County Probate Court, Mrs. Jerry Manfred of the Steubenville City Health Department, the staff of the Schiappa Memorial Branch Library of the Public Library of Steubenville and Jefferson County, Helen Simmons of the Fort Steuben Area Council of the Boy Scouts of America, and Dora V. Iacune and Eugene M. Saggio of St. Anthony's Rectory.

Some of those with Steubenville memories were found far from Steubenville: Archie Crocetti in Las Vegas; the delightful Bernice Del Villan Sperduti in Cleveland; and in Atlantic City, Tony Torcasio, whom I likely would not have been able to meet without the aid of Mike Mavromatis. Like others named here, Gina Simera Pestian entrusted me with photographs.

Across the Ohio River from Steubenville, in New Cumberland, West Virginia, I want to thank Jane Mehaffrey of the Swaney Memorial Library Association; Jean Milton; and Eleanor Straight, the Hancock County Clerk.

For help in researching the Crocetti family background, in addition to several of those named above, the following were indispensable: Massimo Antinio and Giuseppe Di Luca of the Ufficio dello Stato Civile, Comune di Montesilvano, Provincia di Pescara, in Montesilvano, Italy; Robert L. Brown, district director, Immigration and Naturalization Service, U.S. Department of Justice, Cleveland; Carolyn Dettore; the Reverend Robert C. Nash, chancellor of the diocese of Wheeling-Charleston, West Virginia; and Georgia L. Weber of the Family Research Center in Salt Lake City.

In Columbus, I should like to thank Irene Clark of the Magazine and Newspapers Division at the Public Library of Columbus and Franklin County, as well as Pat Hall and the rest of the staff of the library's main branch; the staff of the Division of Vital Statistics, Ohio Department of Health; and Local Number 103, American Federation of Musicians. For help in Cleveland: William Becker, archivist, the Cleveland Press Collection, Cleveland State University Archives, and his assistant, Rob Moody; the staffs of the Cleveland Public Library, the Cuyahoga County Courthouse, and the Department of Vital Statistics; Downtown Joe (that's the way he likes it); Marge Duhigg of St. Ann's Parish; Robert Fatica of Primo Vino on

Mayfield Road; Henry S. George, president, and Jean Sibits, head of membership services, Local Number 4, American Federation of Musicians; Patti Graziano of the *Cleveland Plain Dealer;* John Lawson; Ann K. Sindelar, reference supervisor, the Western Reserve Historical Society; and Mark Stueve. One of the most valuable sources of information regarding the Cleveland years was found in Las Vegas: Merle Jacobs.

In the East: Bob Allen; the staff of the Atlantic City Library; the staff of the Federal Records Center in Bayonne, New Jersey; Gene Baylos; Alan Betrock; Al Bianculli; Tim Brooks; Sam Brylawski of the Motion Picture, Broadcasting, and Recorded Sound Division, Library of Congress; Nancy Evans; Jim Fitzgerald; Bob and Ron Furmanek; Jean Furukawa of City Travel; Herman Gollub; Peter Guralnick; Muriel Harris, public relations director of Bally's Grand, Atlantic City; Rocco Idone; Jerry Jerome; Sonny King; my buddy Mike McGovern and Faigi Rosenthal of the *New York Daily News;* Tracy Mercado, bankruptcy clerk, Southern District of New York; Frank Military; Billy Miller and Miriam Linna; Emil P. Moschella, former chief, and J. Kevin O'Brien, chief, Freedom of Information— Privacy Acts Section, Federal Bureau of Investigation; Frank R. Newett, chief of the Information Service Unit, Office of Enforcement Operations, Criminal Division, U.S. Department of Justice; Big Al Pavlow; Robert Policastro; Stephen Rubin; Mort Savada of Records Revisited; Victoria Shaw; Harriet Wright of Copa Girls; Jayne Young; and Renée Zuckerbrot. The wealth of material of every kind gathered from the various divisions of the New York Public Library serves to remind that the library and its senior staff are among the city's greatest assets.

In the West and elsewhere: Anna Maria Alberghetti; Dick Blackburn; Honor Blackman; Paul Bogart; Sharnette Bradley; Joe Broady; Sammy Cahn; Susan Clark; Don DeFore; Angie Dickinson; Joanne Dru; David Ehrenstein; Art Fein; Nina Foch; Anthony Franciosa; Abby Greshler; Skip Heinecke of Anson & Schwam; Christina Hopkinson of Capitol Records; Herman Hover; Geneva Hunt of the U.S. District Court; Cheryl Kagan of Rogers & Cowan; Mrs. Harry Keller; Arnold Laven; Erna Lazarus; Ruta Lee; the staffs of the Los Angeles Public Library, the Beverly Hills Library, the Los

Angeles County Records Center, the Los Angeles County Registrar-Recorder's Office at the Hall of Records, and the Beverly Hills Municipal Court; Andrew McLaglen; Mike McGreevy; Beverly Magid; Dorothy Malone; Daniel Mann; the staff of the Margaret Herrick Library, Academy of Motion Picture Arts and Sciences, Beverly Hills; Lori Nelson; George Peppard; Joseph Pevney; Thalmus Rasulala; Jack Rose; Albert S. Ruddy; Janice Rule; Michael J. Sargent of the Gaming Control Board of Nevada; Gene Sculatti; George Schlatter; Linda Starr; Stella Stevens; J. Lee Thompson; the late Richard Thorpe; Mort Viner; Ray Walston; and Woody Wilson of *Daily Variety*.

Without the help of Irene Forrest, I would not have been able to reach many of the movie stars who proved so helpful. I am lucky to know her, even luckier to have her as a friend. It is difficult for me to think of Los Angeles without thinking of two others I can always count on: Bob Merlis of Warner Bros. and my friend Richard Meltzer.

To Jerry Lewis and especially Jeanne Martin, for sharing with me what they had every right to keep to themselves, I owe deeply.

I could not have hoped for a better editor on this job than my man at Doubleday, David Gernert, a champ.

My agent, Russell Galen of the Scott Meredith Literary Agency, should by now know what he means to me, and how important he was to this book. So should Noni Watters, whose resourcefulness, dedication, conscientiousness, and brilliance as a researcher are surpassed only by equally rare, and to me far more valuable, qualities as a person.

I am thankful to those who brought to my attention and helped to correct several inaccuracies and oversights that have been amended in the present edition: Bob Gray, Jim Lowe, Greil Marcus, Jeanne Martin, Ted Martin, Frank Reda, Mary Vandecastle, and Timothy White. Sally Showalter did a remarkable job of plucking the elusive gnats of typographical error that escaped scrutiny in the first edition.

Of course, without Dean Martin, we would be holding about a pound of blank pages right now.

CONTENTS

THERE CAN BE NO QUESTION
THAT FORTUNE IS SUPREME
IN ALL HUMAN AFFAIRS.
IT IS A CAPRICIOUS POWER,
WHICH MAKES MEN'S
ACTIONS FAMOUS OR LEAVES
THEM IN OBSCURITY
WITHOUT REGARD TO
THEIR TRUE WORTH.

—SALLUST

Dino

*I*t was like the guys from the other side used to say: *La vecchiaia è carogna*. They were right: Old age is carrion.

He was only fifty-four; he would turn fifty-five a month from this day. But he felt like an old man, like the carrion those old men spoke of in those days of shadow and sunlight; felt as if he had skulked and staggered and stridden through three lifetimes, been wrung and wracked and worn down by them. Sometimes those days of shadow and sunlight returned to him. They brought a calmness laced with chill, like nighttime pond-water in the woods of a dream; and the voices of the old men from those days came too, like haunted breezes rippling across that dream-pond. But more often, as time passed, nothing came, nothing returned to him, and the chill calm and the haunted breezes, silent and voiceless, seemed to emanate not so much from the remembered days, from the shadow and sunlight of memory, but from some farther place, beyond where the shadows deepened and the sunlight dwindled to blackness; from some forbidding but mesmerizing thing, some final dark seduction: dread, death's inkling, swathed in lullaby. He could feel it now, standing there alone with nothing inside him. He muttered the words aloud: *"La vecchiaia è carogna."*

He raised his eyes, squinted into the desert sky, which had no color and was only a vast empty glare. He saw them up there, big and black, flapping in dirge against the glare. He snorted a bleak, bitter ghost of a laugh.

It was May 7, 1972, and he was in a place called Chama, in northern New Mexico; slouched there, in the middle of nowhere, wearing a toy gun and dolled up like Giovanni Mack Brown; stuck there, in the middle of nowhere, fifty-something years old, playing cowboy with fucking Rock Hudson; stuck there, in the middle of nowhere, like a fucking *cafone,* wondering why, after more than twenty-one years of marriage, he was throwing away his wife for a twenty-four-year-old piece of ass whose lies he didn't even believe; wondering what the fuck he was doing there, for a lousy twenty-five grand a week when he had more millions than he could ever live to spend; wondering what the fuck he had been doing all these years.

Fuck the twenty-five grand a week. Fuck the cowboy hat and the cap pistol. Fuck all this shit. It was time to go home, wherever in hell that was.

He closed his eyes, feeling that dark seduction, that inkling, like the reverberation of a tolling in emptiness. The sunlight had never even been real. He had imagined it. The sky of the old days had been a sulfurous pall. The shadows had been real, the sunlight dreamt. He saw himself, half a century ago—a vanished breath ago, three lifetimes ago; it was all the same, improbable and without meaning—moving through them, the shadows and the sunlight. The toy gun and the cowboy hat had suited him well then. He was, after all, Tom Mix, *nevvero?* And this was, after all, *l'America.*

I.

L'AMERICA

*I*t lay to the west beyond an ocean they had never seen, beyond where imaginings reached. To Gaetano Crocetti and his brothers, it was *la terra promessa,* the promised land.

They lived in a small town near the Adriatic Sea, a place shaded by the sylvan foothills of the Gran Sasso Mountains that gave the town its name: Montesilvano. It was there, in that little town in the province of Teramo, in the Abruzzi region of Italy, that their father, Giovanni Crocetti, had been born, in 1858; there that he had grown to manhood, and there that he had taken pretty Maria Focosa as his wife. It was there that the birth-cries of the five sons were swallowed by the familiar breezes that came easterly from the pines and westerly from the sea, that wove through crumbling medieval churches built on ancient crossroads where other gods had dwelt before. They were breezes that the old women, the mourning-ones, of Montesilvano knew by names. Some breezes carried the souls of the dead, others carried sickness, and others brought fortune. They were like a censing through the town, those breezes: an endless spectral waltz of sea-born Venus and Mater Dolorosa. It was the air those five brothers breathed, the only air under God they knew. Surely *la terra promessa,* cut from wilderness barely a lifetime ago, must taste sweet beyond this.

The country's golden new voices came from the Abruzzi. The poet Gabriele D'Annunzio, born not far from Montesilvano, in Pescara, believed that Italy could conquer the world, and that conquerors could do without freedom. Many young men of Italy, Mussolini and countless others whose names and faces would be lost in the shadow of his, took that voluptuous and bellicose voice to heart. Others followed the voice, also from Abruzzi, of the philosopher Benedetto Croce, who saw doom where D'Annunzio saw dawn. But for many more, especially in the Mezzogiorno, the South, which began in Abruzzi, there were no voices, only the old breezes under the gathering clouds of a new darkness.

Life grew poorer there each year, as the lira of the earth grew worthless against the lira of the factories. The South was languishing, becoming a forgotten land, a beggar at the gate of the North's flourishing industry and wealth. The exodus began with the agricultural depression of 1887. Southerners had migrated first to Brazil, the Argentine, and elsewhere in Latin America; then, especially after the United States depression years of 1893 to 1896, they came in greater and greater numbers to America. In 1898 more immigrants would come to America from Italy than from anywhere else. By the spring of 1915, when Italy declared war on Austria-Hungary, one in four of her sons and daughters would leave her to the poets and the politicians, the philosophers and the kings. Most of them would become part of that tide of immigrants—more than a million a year in six of the ten years from 1905 to 1914—to that western land, *l'America*.

Many of them would get no farther than the port of New York. There, those without family or friends to lead them fell thrall to the work-bosses who spoke their language. These bosses, their own kind, were their worst enemies, the dirt beneath the nails of *la mano nera*, the Black Hand, the nightmare at the end of freedom's dream, which extorted tribute from every level of immigrant society. Herding men together and dispatching them to do what awful dockside toil and offal-hauling others shunned, the bosses paid them cents from the dollars they collected for delivering them. These cents consigned them to shared penury in crowded tenement quarters, or worse: Seven cents bought a night's sleep on a strip of dirty sailcloth hung between two beams at the Old Bismark on Mulberry Street. The work-bosses who lured their *paesani* into servitude were known by a word connoting arrogance and maleficence entwined: *guappo;* in Sicilian, *guappu* or *vappu*. The lowly labor of that servitude itself came to be called *guappo* work, or "wop" work; and those who performed it were known as "wops." Jack London wrote in 1913 of a financial desperation that drove him years before to seek "work as a wop, lumper, and roustabout." But the word settled upon the Italians, from whose tongue it had come, and, in time, all of them in the new land would bear its malison.

Others discovered the land beyond East Harlem and the Lower East Side. The Crocetti brothers knew some of those from Montesilvano and the neighboring villages who had journeyed there, vanished into the beguiling embrace of America west of the Hudson. Their families received letters telling of good fortune and wonderment. There were photographs too, showing the journeyers in creased britches, starched collars, and cocked hats, transformed by the new land from *cafoni* to, as they called them in New York, *shports*. It did not matter that they all seemed to be wearing the same suit, standing before the same painted background.

Some had found their way, others had followed them, from New York to a place in the state called Ohio, a place with the odd name of Steubenville. It sounded *mezzo tedesco*, half German, this place, but possessed the hint of the familiar: *ville*, estates. Not for nothing, those back home reflected, envisioning this hamlet of Alpine manors, was that far land of promise called *crogiuolo*, the melting-pot. The letters said that every week brought new *paesani* from the homeland to what was becoming a real *comunità abruzzese*. They said that work was plentiful in the *acciaieria*, the steelworks, there, whose furnaces were the bellows of the new world's abundance, whose fire and fury were the glorious might of the new world's dominion. A cousin of the Crocetti brothers, Carlo DiPultro, was among the many who made their way there.

The brothers pictured it: the crucible at the heart of America, the tree-lined streets of commerce and pleasure, the river and the hills, the carnival of words, *abruzzesi e inglesi*, buoyant with the exhilaration of illimitable possibility. It had a name now in their minds, that *terra promessa*, an odd name, but a name nonetheless: Steubenville.

The first American steel rails were rolled in the smelters of Chicago in 1865. Throughout the Midwest, those rails of steel formed a growing network, bringing together by the power of steam with its monstrous fierce breath the ore and the coal needed to smelt that ore and turn it to steel. Much of that coal, the nation's richest deposits of anthracite, lay beneath the Appalachian Highlands and

the Ohio River Valley, where Pennsylvania, Ohio, and the new state
of West Virginia converged. This became the land of the mills as
well as of the mines, the heart of America's steel industry.

When President Lincoln's heart stopped on the morning of
April 15, 1865, it was a Quaker son of Steubenville, Secretary of
War Edwin McMasters Stanton, who gave an era its epitaph: "Now
he belongs to the ages." But it was Steubenville herself, and the
other steel towns like her, that were already making a new nation, a
nation of steam and of steel, a nation in which the mills thundered
on, and in which, amid that thunder, no one heartbeat could ever be
heard or missed. Steel had freed the nigger, raised him in the name
of God from chattel to wage-slave; brought the new nigger—the
donkey, the kraut, the polack, and the guinea: by 1870 he outnum-
bered the old—to his place in liberty's mine. It was Stanton's statue
that would someday stand in front of the Jefferson County Courthouse on Market Street, but it was steel money that in 1871 built
that courthouse and stretched the city limits.

Andrew Carnegie, the greatest of the steelmakers, had come as
an immigrant, had started out in 1848, at the age of thirteen, working in a cotton factory in Allegheny, Pennsylvania. Pittsburgh, the
city of Carnegie's fortune, the center of the continent's greatest
coalfield, was only thirty-six miles east of Steubenville, separated
by the northernmost sliver of West Virginia and the winding Ohio
River, which flowed from Pittsburgh and which both cities shared.
What the immigrant Carnegie had done in America defined the
dream of those who came later. True, they thought, he was a Scot,
and the Scots were cheap bastards who kept their purses where
their pricks should be; but they did not want millions, they only
wanted, as the Sicilians said, *fari vagnari u pizzu*, to wet their
beaks. After they were here awhile, the greenhorns learned the
truth. The inspiration of the dream and its nemesis were one, pro-
vider and destroyer. The enemy of the workingman was the one who
paid him, the one without whom he would perish. It was, after all,
the way of the world, the new as well as the old. No dream would
ever change it, no American Federation of Labor would ever turn to
true power the sum of the dreamers' impotence and insignificance.
They would damn their new homeland—*mannaggia l'America!*—as

they had damned everything, from their mammas to the Madonna, all their lives. Still, as they damned and complained—the work was hard, the wine was not like it was in the old country, the tomatoes were not the same—they knew they had never had it so good.

Giuseppe Crocetti, born in 1883, was the oldest brother, and the first to go. With a ticket paid for by his cousin Carlo, he sailed from Naples aboard the two-masted *Madonna* in the spring of 1907. Vincenzo followed him from Naples in 1910, arriving on the S.S. *Berlin* at the port of New York two months before he turned nineteen. Umberto and Luciano, who had good jobs, made up their minds in the end to stay where they were.

In 1900, Steubenville's industrial productivity had increased almost three-fold, surpassing the growth of any other city in the state. There had been barely fourteen thousand souls then in the town, less than two thousand of them foreign-born, less than eight hundred of them black. By the year of Vincenzo's arrival, the population of Steubenville had grown to about twenty-two thousand; and a good deal of the increase came from Italy. Ohio itself by then had the eighth-largest Italian-born populace of the forty-seven states.

Giuseppe had found work in Steubenville as a *giornaliero*, a day laborer, at La Belle Iron Works; and he had gotten Vincenzo work there as well. Located at the foot of South Third Street, at the site of the old Jefferson Iron Works, the mill was a branch of La Belle Iron Works of Wheeling. It was Steubenville's biggest employer and one of the largest iron and steel plants in the country, with ten fifty-ton open-hearth furnaces blasting forth everything from one-inch sheared and grooved rolled plates to thirty-gauge sheets of black galvanized and blue annealed steel. They worked, they slept, they ate, living together in a rooming-house with other laborers from the old country, in the Italian community, the *piccolo Abruzzo*, that had developed on the south side of town, near the steelworks and the river. They would never outnumber the original folk here of Welsh and Irish and English stock, or the Germans, whose blood was the most common everywhere in this new land. But they took care of their own, and they prevailed. The first of them here had found their God—an American version of Him anyway—

at the Holy Name Church on South Fifth Street, where they were allowed to hold services in the basement. By 1907, there were enough Italians to begin forming their own parish; and in 1910, when Vincenzo came, they had their own church, St. Anthony of Padua, at 711 South Street.

Some of the men had wives and families back home, whom they would send for when enough money was put aside. Others, like the Crocetti brothers, would find their wives here. Giuseppe, who had been the first to be born and the first to sail away, was also the first to marry. His bride, Giulia Porreca, was, like so many of the Italians here, also from the Abruzzi. Their first home, at 530 Slack Street, was in the heart of the Italian neighborhood; but they, like their neighbors, Americanized their Christian names. They were Joe and Julia now, *tutti americani.* Before long, the family name itself would become Americanized. The open Italianate *o* would become a closed *oh* sound, and the palatal *ch* sound of the *c* that followed it would become a hissing: *Crow-setti.* They themselves would come to say it that way.

Joe and Julia brought life into the world in June 1913: a daughter, Maria, named for Joe's mother. The letters young Gaetano got from his older brothers across the sea beckoned him to join them. Life was good in Steubenville, they told him; and besides, they said, he was now an uncle.

In 1913, Gaetano Crocetti, the most slightly built of the brothers, was nineteen and working as a farm laborer. Unlike his older brothers, he was *analfabeta:* he could barely read or write. The farmlands were dying, and the breezes of fortune grew more dire each day.

Giuseppe sent him twenty-five dollars and a steerage ticket; and what few things Gaetano had, he packed. His mother wept to see another leave, and this one, like Vincenzo, still so young, still more a boy than a man; and his father shook his head at the sad sundering folly of it all, of a dream that took men from their homes like a whore, and of a homeland that let it happen. Gaetano went by train to Naples, through country and through towns he had never seen and would never see again; and from Naples, aboard the fourteen-year-old *Hamburg,* he sailed on August 30, 1913, arriving at

Ellis Island in New York Harbor on the warm, breezy Thursday of
September 11.

Ellis Island lay in the shadow of Liberty's statue, the seaward-
staring woman of steel—"mighty woman with a torch," the tablet-
verse beneath her read; "Mother of Exiles"—who welcomed that
"wretched refuse" to this land of steel. From the great vaulted Reg-
istry Room of the main building on that twenty-four-acre landfill,
Gaetano descended to the ferryboat that delivered the huddled
masses to their freedom on that bigger island called Manhattan.

From Manhattan the Pennsylvania Railroad took Gaetano west,
like his brothers before him. The rolling lush countryside, not so
unlike the hills of home, gave way to the black bellowings of Pittsburgh, from where—it was all written down for him in his brother's
hand—the Pittsburgh, Cincinnati, Chicago & St. Louis would carry
him to Steubenville. He had never witnessed anything like these
bellowings before. He had never seen a sky so vast and ashen with
empty fury; had never heard such dire ceaseless rumblings and
deafening wails. It was as if misery, that most human of states, had
taken on the dimensions of an existence apart from humanity; for it
was not any sense of human misery he perceived here, nor any
misery of the heavens—there were no heavens—but rather a misery
of the elements themselves, of the earth and the coal-fires and the
dampness of the air. He had imagined the crucible at the heart of
America to be a great majestic gleaming in the sun, like the shield
of Aeneas in the storybook increased a hundredfold. He had imagined many things. As his father long ago had told him: Dream in one
hand, shit in the other, and see which hand is filled.

A barber's wage in America was a decent one, from eight to
fifteen dollars a week, and there were few long waits for a haircut in
the new land. Barbering was the trade most commonly professed by
Italian workmen arriving from Italy. During some years, from one-
half to two-thirds of them declared themselves *barbieri*. Gaetano
was not one of them. Yet in Steubenville, it became his profession.

Steubenville was a town for barbers. In 1908 there had been
twenty-three barbershops and more than a hundred saloons. Two
days before Christmas of that year, the saloons had been shut down

as Steubenville went officially dry, yielding finally to the local pro-
hibitionist forces of the Women's Christian Temperance Union. The
number of barbershops had continued to grow since then, in part
fulfilling the need for womanless sanctuary that had widened with
the closing of the bars. One of the oldest-established barbers from
the other side was Ambrogio DiBacco, who had been operating his
own shop on South Sixth Street since 1906.

DiBacco, whose first name had been transmuted to Ambrose,
lived with his wife, Maria, behind his storefront shop at 319 South
Sixth Street, just a few doors away from where Joe Crocetti and his
family, and with them newly arrived Gaetano, now lived, at number
303. It was there, under DiBacco's roof, that Gaetano found work.

The old-timer taught Gaetano the trade. He told him too about
the new law that had been passed just months earlier, the law that
said men must now pay tax on what they earned; and he explained,
as it had been explained to him, that they were among the more
fortunate ones as far as this new income tax went, for they were not
payroll workers like those in the mills; theirs was a business of
coins, which none but them tallied.

A good *barbiere*, Gaetano told himself, was his own man. He
could set up anywhere. Men the world over had hair. When they lost
it, new men took their places. A barber was like a priest. Men came
to him whether they wanted to or not, because it made them feel
clean, because it was something that one did. A haircut was a
sacrament, a ritual, a communion not with God but with other men.
The barber's shop served as a church of the true heart, where one's
sins were celebrated instead of shrived, where each had his turn at
ascending the cathedral throne, where the soft rhythmic sibilance
and click of the shears and the expert draw of the blade through hot
lather lulled each in his turn to that state of tranquil vanity that lay
beyond grace. Yes, he told himself, a good barber could find his
flock in any town. *Come croce, come palo.* The faithful came to the
spiraled pole as to the cross.

And it was under DiBacco's roof that Gaetano found his bride.

Angela Barra had been born in Ohio, in the nearby community
of Fernwood, on December 18, 1897, the first daughter of Domenico
and Josephine Miriglia Barra, both immigrants. Her family—there

were two older brothers, Michele and Antonio, and a younger sister, Anna—moved into Steubenville early in the century, to a small place on Kilgore Street. The Barra name by then had been clipped to Barr. They moved again, across the river to New Cumberland, twelve miles away, in West Virginia, where Domenic and Josephine opened a produce store, and where their youngest child, Leonard, was born.

Domenic Barr vanished. His fate would remain a mystery. And, as her children watched in fear, Josephine Barr's mind slowly unraveled, descending ultimately into madness. She was hauled away to the Ohio Institution for the Feeble Minded, a place on a hill on the western outskirts of Columbus, then to the adjacent acres of the Ohio State Hospital for the Insane, where she lived out her days. Mike, the eldest of the children, was sent to relatives in Italy; and in January 1910, across the river at the Jefferson County Courthouse in Steubenville, a man named E. DeMitt Erskine and a woman named Salvatora Vetella assumed legal guardianship of the remaining Barr children. Thus established as wards within the diocese of Columbus, the children were then transferred to St. Vincent's Orphanage in that city. There, under the care of the Sisters of St. Francis of Stella Niagara, Angela remained until 1913. She would remember the place as a "German nunnery" where she learned to sew.

Returning to Steubenville, she found work as a seamstress and came to live with Ambrogio and Maria DiBacco on South Sixth Street. Gaetano found her there when he began barbering for DiBacco. It was almost as if she had been awaiting him, diminutive and dark-eyed and still and alone, a new-world flower with the scent of the old. She spoke barely any Italian, he any English.

In 1914—the year that Mussolini was expelled from the Socialist Party back home—twenty-three-year-old Vincenzo married Maria Biandoria Febo, twenty, from the town of Castellammare in Teramo. They were James and Mary now.

Gaetano now was Guy. He turned twenty here, as big now as he would ever be: like his father, barely five and a half feet tall, barely a hundred and twenty-five pounds. Two weeks after his birthday came Angelina's sixteenth. He and she made a cute couple, people said; after all, they were both small and they both had noses like *cucuzze.* On the Sunday of October 25, 1914, at the altar of St. Anthony's, Father Luigi made them man and wife, *cucuzzone* and *cucuzzetta.* Guy moved out of his brother's place, and he and Angelina made their first home together, at 443 South Sixth Street. He became an uncle twice again in 1915. Joe and Julia had their second child, John, named for Papa Crocetti in Italy, on June of that year; James and Mary had their first child, Robert, in November. By then Guy knew that he would soon be a father too.

DiBacco moved his shop and residence a few doors up on South Sixth Street, and Guy and Angelina took over his old quarters. There, at 319 South Sixth Street, Guy opened his own shop; and there, Angelina gave birth to a son on the night of June 24, 1916. They named him Guglielmo: William.

Both Angela and her sister-in-law Julia Crocetti were pregnant again as that year flowed toward the next. Julia's child, her third, came first, on the seventh of May, a month after America declared war on Germany, joining the conflict—the Great War, they called it —that Italy had joined the spring before. They gave him the good Italian name of Alceo, which ended up as Alice on his birth certificate. In the end, everyone called him Archie.

The feast of St. Anthony of Padua came in June, transforming the South Side streets around the church into a carnival of games and fireworks and *dolci della festa* that would culminate on the feast day of the thirteenth. It was early in this feast week, at five minutes to midnight on June 7, at the little house at 319 South Sixth Street, that Angelina's child came. The delivery was premature. Guy could see the concern in the face of old DiLoretto, the neighborhood doctor who brought his son forth, scrawny and purpled, from the womb. But it was going to be all right, DiLoretto said; and it was.

Pater et Filius et Spiritus Sanctus. Dino Crocetti was baptized by St. Anthony's new pastor, the Reverend Joe Morello, on Sunday, September 16. His *comare* was Julia Crocetti's sister Marietta Porreca; his *padrino,* Guy's friend Giacomo Areshone.

It was the eve of an autumn that reddened the old country with the blood and disgrace of its sons. After more than two years of battling along the Isonzo River, at the Italian frontier of Austria-

Hungary, the Central Powers prevailed and broke through in October at Caporetto, driving the Italians to retreat southward, scattering into rabble beyond the Piave. Some were captured in their flight, more surrendered. Others deserted and others were killed. In the end, Italian casualties numbered more than two million. It was left for America, with her steel and her might, to rescue the Entente Powers. For Joe, Jimmy, and Guy Crocetti, and those like them, Italians living in America, it was a time of both sadness and glory. As Italians, they had been defeated. As Americans, they would win out.

Three months after the war's end, in February 1919, Guy Crocetti formally applied for citizenship, swearing his "bona fide intention to renounce forever all allegiance and fidelity to any foreign prince, potentate, state, or sovereignty, and particularly to Victor Emmanuel III, King of Italy," of whom he was still a subject. "I am not an anarchist," he swore; "I am not a polygamist nor a believer in the practice of polygamy; and it is my intention in good faith to become a citizen of the United States of America and to permanently reside therein; SO HELP ME GOD."

La Belle Iron Works was reorganized and rechristened in the spring of 1920 as part of the giant new Wheeling Steel Corporation, whose properties now stretched from Wheeling to Steubenville along the western shore of the Ohio, with the Steubenville plant the biggest of its operations. Joe Crocetti still worked there. Jimmy had taken a job driving a truck. They both lived with their families on South Sixth Street, as did Guy. Joe's daughter, Mary, who turned seven that year, was the oldest of the cousins and the only girl.

Less than two years separated the eldest of the five male cousins, Joe's first son, John, who was five that summer, from the youngest, Dino, who was three. The fathers remained close, as they had been in the old country, and the children grew together, more as siblings than as cousins, under the shared maternity of the women. In September of that year, when Julia Crocetti, cursed with a bad heart, went to her grave at the age of thirty-four, little Mary was taken in down the block by Guy and Angela.

In the spring of 1921, Giovanni and Maria Crocetti came from Italy to see their sons and their daughters-in-law and their grandchildren and the place that had claimed them. Giovanni could have stayed on, *padre e padrone;* but the old woman could not abide the strangeness of the place, its savorless *cucina* and its present without past and its breezes bleached of mourning. They were gone before long, returned to the old country, where Mussolini now was prime minister, where soon dictatorship would be proclaimed; there to die, shadows to their grandchildren faintly glimpsed and faintly re-called.

"Until I was five years old, all I spoke was Italian," Dino would later recall. But now those days of *abruzzese* were over. His mother had never liked them anyway. Her sons should learn to speak proper English; Guy should stop speaking to them in the tongue of the old country. This was America, they were Americans.

Grant School, built in 1869 at the corner of South and Fourth streets, was the first and oldest building of the Steubenville school system. It was there, in that dilapidated twelve-room schoolhouse, in September 1922, that Dino Crocetti commenced the years of his academic misery. For him the countenance of knowledge and that of his teacher, Miss Lulu Mulliman, the principal's sister, would be-come one.

"Mine isn't really Italian," Dino would say of that lapsed tongue of his childhood, that language that would linger within him for the rest of his life. "It's a dialect from Abruzzi, and I speak it badly." And he would remember the days of his schooling: "I don't speak good English, either."

By now the difference between Dino and his brother, William, was plain to see. They looked like brothers. Both had the wavy dark hair and brown eyes of their father, as well as his *nasone.* ("If you're going to have a nose, have a nose," he would say.) Both had the same gait and grin. But their natures were like night and day. William was a quiet boy, for whom the mastery of the words beneath the pictures in the little book at Grant School possessed a mystery, for whom the ritual articulation of those words, so unlike those of his father and his uncles, was like the billowy thrill of a sailing outward from this place. Dino, however, wanted none of it. An apple was not a handful of letters or a dumb-ass drawing in a moldy old book. An apple was something you ate. Spelling it had nothing to do with it. His father called it a *mela*. His teacher called it an apple. Sometimes his father called it that too, except it came out *un appla*. Whatever you called it, however you spelled it, it was all the same. The Antonucci brothers, who sold the damned things, likely could not spell them. Neither probably could the farmers who grew them. You could grow them, you could buy them, you could swipe them; but spelling them got you nowhere. Let William do the spelling. He himself would tend to the eating.

He did reluctantly learn the spelling end of things, as to not learn it only meant getting left back and not-learning it over and over again, which could only be more insufferable than learning it and forgetting it and moving on. And so it went, straight through to where you were not only spelling the apple but the worm that was in it; straight through to where you were plussing one apple with another and coming up with two, then dividing the two by two and coming up with the one again. It got to where when the nun at Sunday school started talking about Adam and Eve and the apple, he saw that apple as the one that had started all this spelling and adding and subtracting and dividing. He saw that as the sin, as the downfall. God had told them to eat whatever they wanted, but not that apple from the tree of knowledge. But, no, they were not satisfied just to eat; they wanted knowledge, those fools, wanted not just to eat but to spell what they ate, to divide it and add it and subtract it too. That was the original sin. And he was still paying for it, with all this spelling and arithmeticking five days a week, with all this Sunday-morning apple-talk to boot. That whole business back there in the Garden had so displeased God that he had transformed Eve's kind into a race of mothers, Mullimans, and nuns; had consigned Adam's kind to forever suffer under them; had made it hard to bite into an apple without tasting the bitterness of letters and plus signs and minus signs. It was horrible, really, when you thought about it, enough to shake your faith.

Now, Tom Mix: there was a man, a man who shot instead of spelled. Dino was eight years old when the majestic Grand Theatre opened in the old Griesinger Building on South Fourth Street, and the splendid Capital opened at Fourth and Adams; when he fell under the spell of the great man who roamed free and proud, the Westerner whose faithful horse, Tony, was the steed of righteousness. From *The Trouble Shooter* to *Riders of the Purple Sage* to *Outlaws of Red River,* he followed the flickering silent shadows of his hero's adventures in the appleless plains west of Eden. These Saturday matinees, these nickel flights into the prelapsarian six-gun dreamland where nuns feared to tread, brought that outward-sailing thrill that his brother found elsewhere. His uncles told him that the great man was a fake, that he was from east of Steubenville here, from Pennsylvania, that he lived in Beverly Hills, in a big fancy mansion that flashed his name in lights. They told him these things, but he paid them no mind, for he knew they spoke only from envy and jealousy. He saw himself at the campfire with the great man, eating spaghetti under the prairie stars. A lone wolf howled in the distance, or maybe it was one of those unspellable creatures, a coyote.

His cousin Mary would never forget the sight of it: him and her brother Archie, the two of them with their cap-pistols and felt cowboy hats, killing each other and whoever happened to stroll near the weeds of their endless deaths and resurrections. The Ohio River became the Red. The backyards and empty lots and shrubs of the South Side grew rife with rustlers and hombres. Beatty Park, where the Crocetti wagon-party often picnicked, was a wilderness where renegade redskins lurked behind every elm. To the west lay haunted Tombstone, which dudes called Union Cemetery. There was only one problem, the same problem again and again. One cousin alone could be Tom Mix. The other must be Hoot Gibson, or worse.

"It was real cute when they played," Mary remembered of those days, sixty-five years later, after the South Side of their make-believe had become a ghost town for real, after all the cousins had gone away—Dino and Archie, sure enough, ridden off into the West —or died, save her. "One had to yell it first, what they wanted to be. Archie was quick: 'I'm Tom Mix!' There was Tom Mix, Hoot Gibson, a couple of others. I'd stand on the side and watch."

Dino's childhood, if only in his own memory, was idyllic. He would never embellish it with romantic hardships. "I didn't have to peddle newspapers to help out. My father," he would say proudly, "was a very successful barber. We Crocettis had everything we needed. I had a bicycle. We had a car and good food. As a cook, my mother was the greatest."

Angela continued to take in sewing work. "She was the best in town," said Agon DeLuca, whose wife's bridal gown was made by Angela. "All the old-timers would take their stuff to her," a neighbor, Mike DiNovo, remembered. Guy was a quiet man and a thankful man and a meek man. He was not the master of his home, as men in the old country were; his wife was not his chattel, as wives in the old country were. She was a strong woman, who believed in toil and in stoic ways. And she instilled many of those ways in Dino, her son. Tears, she taught him, were the womanly water of disgrace. He should never bare what was within him if he was to be a man. Much less should he ever show weakness or cry. All those things that she secretly wanted but would never abide in her husband, she sowed in her son.

Guy Crocetti gloried in both his boys. His life was one of daily ceremony; of rising, eating, working, sleeping. He tended to his barbering tools with the sacral care of a priest tending to the implements of Mass. The shank and tang of his bone-handled razor were kept clean of any dirt, the pivot well-oiled and swift; the heel and shoulder, the back and head of the crocus-buffed blade, kept gleaming and bright, the point sharp and the wedge-ground edge— he preferred the wedge to the commoner hollow grind—well honed and stropped. The French shears, the German shears, the fancy Bressant clipper, received the same care. The teeth of the horn combs in their bain of alcohol and the bristles of the brushes and neck-duster arranged beside them on the shelf were free of any stranger's hair or scent; the shaving-brush, cup, and soap were allowed to gather no scum; the towels were always laundered and ironed, the headrest paper was always fresh. When business was slow, he stropped and swept, polished his mirrors and trim with Metalglas, arranged the rows of his sundry embrocations and tonsorial balms: the opal and cobalt stand-bottles of tonic-waters and witch-hazels, the amber jars of brilliantine, the long-necked jars of *acqua di Colonia* for the sports, the Osage Rub and the Wildroot, Auerbach's Million Dollar Tonic and Fitch's Tonique Superbe, the

Lilac Vegetal and the Love Me Dearie, the Baldpate and the Herpi-
cide, the canisters of mange remedy and talcum. Only then, when
all these things were seen to, would he allow himself to sit, and then
never in the great porcelained-steel and leathern-cushioned *pol-
trona* itself; no, that was reserved for those to whom he ministered,
those who paid. He would sit there on a chair in the temple of his
trade and he would smile to those who passed by the door, which
was open more often than not; and in work and in rest—a glass of
neighborhood wine now and then to lend the lie of sweetness to it
all, or a cold beer, which he had acquired a taste for here—the days
passed, and there were no hungry nights, none without *pane e pasta*
or the blessing of sleep. It was his sons who brought light to the
endless, unvarying ceremonies of his life. They were the wonder of
it, growing and flowering from the dead rock of it. Guglielmo, Guy
thought, was the smart one. He would become someday a great
uomo d'affari. He savored the sound of it in his mind: *il dottor*
Crocetti, *l'avvocato* Crocetti. Dino was more of an undealt card. He
was a *scuccia,* a ballbuster, true; but he was good. The undealt card
could be *una matta,* a joker, or *un re,* a king. Time would tell. In
any case, there was always the barbershop. Of that much in patri-
mony his sons could be assured.

The 1920s were years of continuing growth for Steubenville. A
new ten-story office tower now stood downtown; the building of the
Fort Steuben Suspension Bridge, connecting Steubenville to Weirton, West Virginia, was under way. Grant School was rebuilt, at a
cost of over half a million dollars. During the construction, Dean
and the others attended nearby Stanton School at Fourth and Dock
streets, another twelve-room schoolhouse dating to 1869, destined
to be torn down and rebuilt after the new Grant Junior High School
opened in 1927. On May 15 of that year, at St. Anthony's, Dean
made his first Holy Communion; and there, on April 30, 1928, along
with William and their cousins John and Archie, he was confirmed,
taking Paul as his name of confirmation.

Guy had taken in barbers to work the shop's second chair, just
as old Ambrogio DiBacco had taken him in. First there had been
Nick Norcio, then Pete Gillette. In 1925 he had gone into business
on the North Side, sharing the shop of E. J. Sickler on North Fifth

Street. A few years later he moved his family to the northern end of town as well, to 118 Brady Avenue. Twelve-year-old Dino transferred to the nearby Harding Junior High School on January 27, 1930.

The steel industry, which lay at the heart of Steubenville's economy, was hit hard by the coming of the Great Depression. The price of United States Steel common stock dropped from a 1929 high of 261½ to a 1932 low of 21¼. The common-stock price of Wheeling Steel, Steubenville's largest employer, fell from 112½ in 1929 to 18½ in 1931, when it ceased trading. A new fifty-dollar-par common-stock issue by Wheeling fell from 20¼ in 1931 to 5 the following year. The Pittsburgh steel baron Andrew Mellon was then serving as secretary of the treasury under President Hoover. Mellon, whose vast fortune no candy-ass Great Depression could dent, was an advocate of the fuck-it school of economic philosophy: "Liquidate labor, liquidate stocks, liquidate the farmer, liquidate real estate." Let the damned thing take its natural course, and to hell with handouts. "People will work harder, live a more moral life. Values will be adjusted, and enterprising people will pick up the wrecks from less competent people."

Dino by then had already begun to surmise that life was a racket with which morality had little to do. He had discovered gambling and was learning all about right bets, wrong bets, proposition bets, side bets, flat bets, point bets, come bets, don't-come bets, hard-way bets, come-out bets, and other such aspects of non-Mulliman enlightenment that served him well in the alley games of the older boys. Andrew W. Fenske, the manual-arts teacher at Grant, known as a strict but reasonable man, remembered him coming to shop class "with silver dollars in his hands." This was during the Depression; the kid was barely twelve. "He would show off the dollars and go out and gamble some more." Yet as the dice rolled, the shadow of Tom Mix, though far away and fading fast, could still be discerned, and the dream of spaghetti by the campfire still lingered. *Il richiamo della foresta*, the call of the wild, beckoned.

The Fort Steuben Area Council, Number 459, of the Boy Scouts of America had been established in 1927, and in May 1930 the

Cristoforo Colombo Lodge of the Sons of Italy on South Street sponsored the charter of a troop on the Catholic South Side. Dino, who turned twelve in 1929, met the requirement that "a Scout must be full twelve years of age." With William, Archie, and Robert, he became one of the thirteen original members of Troop Ten, which met each Monday at St. Anthony's with Scoutmaster Agon DeLuca and the Reverend Angelicus R. Iadone, the church's new pastor and troop chaplain. Dino was the troop's drummer.

DeLuca remembered taking the boys out on a bivouac one night to the Wintersville farmland, northwest of town. "I talked with a farmer, and he let me stay with my boys, put 'em up in the barn for the night. They had a lot of crab-apple trees around, and so I informed the boys not to bother the crab-apple trees. At that time, they were green, they weren't ripe yet. They'd get stomachaches. So I told 'em to stay the hell away from the trees. So, of course, Mr. Dean Martin, he was in his glory; he thought he was gonna eat an apple. Unfortunately, it stuck down his throat. We almost lost him. They called me, and I really, you know, put the pressure, the pressure to the chest, and out came the apple. The apple came out of his throat, and in an hour or so he was good. But it scared the hell out of the whole bunch of us."

All that spelling, adding, dividing, all that penance for the damned things; all that, and now, to boot, he had nearly been put under by one.

While keeping their ties to the old neighborhood and its church, the other Crocettis began moving to the tree-lined streets of the town's West End. Guy came to the new neighborhood in 1931, to 630 Grandview Avenue in Pleasant Heights, to a little brick house with grass and even a tree, a big old maple, out front. Once again Dino changed schools, transferring to McKinley, where he would attend classes, when compelled, until February of the following year.

Mary remembered playing card games with the boys, and family outings to the countryside, to City Park to the north, and to Beatty Park close by. "We always went on picnics, all of us." She remembered the Santucci family, Osidio and Agnes and their daughter, Anna Mary, who lived across from the Holy Name Church on South

Fifth Street; remembered how Anna Mary "used to teach Dean little dances. He'd put on acts. Sometimes William used to be in on the deal. All the kids." But most of all, she remembered Dean singing.

"Dean sang steady as a little kid. He lamented all the time."

She recalled sitting with his mother while the older woman sewed, the two of them hearing him, off in another room, singing— "lamenting," as she put it—and the mother saying, again and again, as she sewed, "If he's not going to be a singer, no one's going to be a singer."

He "wore a hat all the time, in the house." That is how Mary always saw him, the image of him she always kept from those days: "walking around with a hat on, singing."

That lamenting boy was soon to discover a world whose evil was its good. More and more he would enter his own shadow, and that world, or any other, would never truly know him. Eve, the naked bitch, would swoon, and all her sons would be fools for the taking. There would be apples, not those of the moon or of the sun or of any limp-dicked vain conceit, but those that were the sweetest of any fruit of any lush and ancient tree; those that grew along the river Lethe, which ran from hell into Ohio and meandered west to where the hat made the man and where those without shadows to cast or to enter paid to suck upon the shades of others. He would discover the soul of *l'America* and the secret passages that wound beneath its funhouse of troubled dreams like the maze of shafts that snaked under Steubenville. That funhouse, he would find, was one easy fucking joint to rob.

II.

DREAMLAND

*T*he funhouse was a vast and wonderful place of imaginings and greed. One entered for a nickel, the twentieth part of a dollar. Even in this century, the painted face of the laughing man on the great western wall, faded and excoriated by the seasons of a century and more, could still be discerned: the slick black hair parted in the middle; the eyes wide and transfixed as if in the throes of an ecstasy more terrible in its emptiness and endlessness than agony; the thin-lipped, rollicking cancerous grin of metastatic delights.

> *"And the worst part of it, Amos, 's Sapphire thinks it's culture."*
>
> —KINGFISH STEVENS

Italians built the first opera house in America, with money raised among them by Lorenzo Da Ponte. In Europe, where he had been an acquaintance of the elderly Casanova, Da Ponte had written librettos for Mozart's *Le Nozze di Figaro, Don Giovanni,* and *Così Fan Tutte;* and in America he taught the poetry of Dante at Columbia University, where he held the school's first, nonpaying professorship of Italian literature. Like most of those who came to America from Italy before the last part of the nineteenth century, he was a northerner, a Venetian Jew who converted to Catholicism. His Italian Opera House, which opened in downtown New York in the autumn of 1833 with Rossini's *La Gazza Ladra,* was a great failure, and was abandoned after eight months and a loss of nearly $30,000. Da Ponte died broke in New York in the summer of 1838. That was the year Alexis de Tocqueville's *Democracy in America* first appeared in an American edition. "In aristocracies," Tocqueville observed, "a few great pictures are produced; in democratic countries, a vast number of insignificant ones. In the former, statues are raised of bronze; in the latter, they are modelled in plaster."

Henry James foresaw in 1886 a coming "reign of mediocrity." But the world that James portrayed with such brilliant elegance was already decaying around him. The reign of mediocrity, democracy's flowering, had come. America respected James; but respect is cheap, and she did not buy his books. She bought Mark Twain's. His sentiments lent eloquence to feelings that long had been held back in diffidence. It was Twain's mockery of the classical European store of culture in *The Innocents Abroad* that established him in 1869; established him not merely as a writer but also, among those not given to books, as an entertainer, a vindicator of the mob's cultural suffrage.

But it was neither Twain nor James who was the voice of the age, but rather Johnson—George Washington Johnson, the Whistling Coon, the ex-slave who became America's first recording star. For the first time, a common man achieved fame, a fame greater than Twain's, greater by far than James's, a fame won through the supremely democratic art of whistling. The centuries of quarrying rock and hammering gold for the glory of gods and men were ended. Carrara marble gave way to linoleum, granite to concrete and Sheetrock. All was transitory, nothing built to endure. Eternity ceded to the moment, as gold to plastic.

It was what democracy had wrought. As the fate of Lorenzo Da Ponte's opera house showed, it was not edification the child sovereign craved. It was entertainment. *Panem et circenses:* bread and circuses. These, Juvenal had decried at the turn of the second century, were all that his fellow Romans had come to care about. The mobs had forsaken the glory and beauty of Catullus and Virgil, Horace and Propertius; had let tragedy and comedy perish of neglect, giving over the theaters to crass pantomime and farce. Young, thriving America, with no past, no Virgil or Horace to detain her course, was by nature from the womb a land of bread and circuses.

The culture of the American gentry—that is, the culture of Europe which it appropriated for lack of its own—would never become the culture of America. The few had the wealth. But the mob had the numbers, the loudest voice. And, as ever, the cry of that voice was the same. In whatever language, it was for bread and circuses. It would be those who were most rightfully heir to the dead centuries' spirit, those who had fled here from Europe while Henry James and his like sailed there to bask, whose tastes would become those of the nation. They were the ones, *analfabeta,* unlettered, who built her; they, and their children, were the ones whose song she would sing, stealing at last the vulgar words and colors and chords from her own native winds.

America was a land of machines, and it was through machines, the miraculous handmaidens of mob culture, that the muses of illiteracy brought America her voice and vision during the years of the immigrants' waves. Centuries ago, movable type had given literacy to the common man. Now, through these wondrous newer machines, he would give it back.

On July 18, 1877, at his laboratory in Menlo Park, New Jersey, Thomas Alva Edison noted on a worksheet that he had discovered the basic mechanism that would enable him "to store up & reproduce automatically at any future time the human voice perfectly." He applied for a patent the following Christmas Eve, and he got it in February 1878. Five days later, the Edison Speaking Phonograph Company came into being. Victor introduced its Victrola in 1906, and within a few years, by the time the last of the Crocetti brothers arrived in America, there was a machine for nearly every home, from the ten-dollar Victor Junior with its horn of black-japanned steel to the opulent four-hundred-dollar Victrola XVI with its vernis-Martin finish, enclosed sound-box, and gold-plated tone-arm and trimmings.

The polyglot sound of it all, the Babel of the mob, merged in the breezes. In a town like Steubenville in 1917, the year Dino Crocetti was born, one could hear it: "O Sole Mio" by Caruso, still in the air since its release the year before, the most popular of the various recorded versions dating back to Francesco Daddi's in 1902; "When Irish Eyes Are Smiling" by John McCormack; "Jägerleben" by Karl Jörn; "The Darktown Strutters' Ball," the first recording by the Original Dixieland Jass Band; "I'se Gwine Back to Dixie" by

Alma Gluck; and several versions of that wartime year's biggest hit, George M. Cohan's "Over There." (The world would have to wait until the following year for Caruso's multilingual version.)

This was the sound of America: Enrico Caruso and Alma Gluck gwine back to Dixieland by way of the Rhine to join Citizen McCormack 'neath the shamrock-spangled *bandiera* of the darktown Zion ball.

Drifting above it all on South Sixth Street in Steubenville, as other melodies prevailed above the Babel of other streets, there were "Marì, Marì" and "Mattinata," "Santa Lucia" and "Torna a Surriento." The last seemed to convey in the somber sweep of its melody and words the shadowing magic of those ancient breezes half-recalled.

> *Guarda il mare com'è bello!*
> *Spira tanto sentimento*
> *Come il tuo soave accento*
> *Che me, desto, fa sognar.*

Sixteen years after the patent of the phonograph, a man named Fred Ott sneezed in West Orange, New Jersey. Two days later Edison registered for copyright a forty-five-frame paper roll bearing the title *Edison Kinetoscope Record of a Sneeze, January 7, 1894.*

In April 1894, three months after Fred Ott's sneeze, the first kinetoscope parlor opened in what had been a shoe store at 1155 Broadway in New York City. There, entering beneath an illuminated dragon with electric eyeballs, one found two rows of five Edison machines lined along opposite walls. For two bits, an hour's wage, one could squint through the peepholes of either row, enjoying five separate shows lasting up to sixteen seconds each. Machines were shipped to Chicago, to Atlantic City. Soon the odd machines were everywhere, and soon enough came their greatest progeny—the moving picture.

Like the breath and shadows of ancient gods in older lands, sounds and pictures soon came to move through the air itself.

In 1922 the Radio Corporation of America began selling home

radio-receivers, priced at about seventy-five dollars, and in 1924 Americans spent more than $350,000,000 on home radios.

America within the span of fifty years had set in motion the wondrous machinery of mob culture. The low had superseded the high. Tin Pan Alley had eclipsed Vienna. *The Temptation of St. Anthony* had been transformed from a fifteenth-century engraving by Schongauer to a moving picture with tits and everything. "Amos 'n' Andy" had easily wrested the airwaves from Rossini and Leoncavallo. Television was by nature from the electric womb such a child of the mob that many regarded it as civilization's end. Even the word repulsed T. S. Eliot, who in 1942 declared it "ugly" and its welding of Greek and Latin roots a mark of "ill-breeding." The thing itself, he would warn in 1950, was a "habitual form of entertainment." But Eliot, who, like Henry James before him, became a British subject, was an outsider to his own culture, just as those at its heart, the immigrants to his homeland years before, had been outsiders to their own, which he and other Americans claimed as theirs. In the country of his birth, they had danced to "I Wish I Could Shimmy Like My Sister Kate" while he, across the sea, wrote *The Waste Land.* Like his fellow Missourian Mark Twain, Eliot did not shy away from recording, but his records were nothing to dance to, and no jukebox ever played them. He plied his craft on radio as well, but neither an Amos nor an Andy was he.

It was not the free verse of *The Waste Land* that informed the mythology of the mob. A literature of freer prose already had risen to serve them, beginning with *Photoplay* in 1911. The reign of mediocrity—democracy—was flowering full. Henry James had been to the movies. Furthermore, he had liked them.

America alone among nations had conceived of her destiny as a dream. The American Dream, she called it. Now dreams as well as steel were her industry. Hard-girdered reality and flickering, lilting fantasy were the inhalation and exhalation of her being. It was her dreamland stars, not her statesmen or poets, through whom she found expression.

Dino Crocetti, an immigrant barber's son, born under a steel-gray sky, was to be one of those dreamland stars. He would do what no other of them could. Recordings, movies, radio, television: He would cast his presence over them all, a mob-culture Renaissance man. And he would come to know, as few ever would, how dirty the business of dreams could be.

III.

SHADOWLAND

*T*here it was on the shelf in Guy Crocetti's barbershop, along with the other sheik-oils: Auerbach's Million Dollar Hair Tonic. It invigorated the scalp and lent the sensuous iridescent sheen of elegant nobility to the misbegotten crowns of greenhorn Valentinos. A cigarette angling downward with precise nonchalance between the lips, the eyebrow cocked like so—the effect was then complete. One could almost feel, like electricity in the air, the tinglings of desire in the women that passed. One could almost breathe it, like musky perfume in that air, the *succo di fica* that trickled unseen from those women who beheld them. Ah, yes, someday. It was only a matter of time. The courses of nature and sheik-oil would inevitably converge.

But Auerbach's was more than a mere invigorator of the scalp and subjugator of womankind. Unlike the other bottles with which it shared the barber's shelf, it represented something above and beyond itself. To those who knew its secrets, it was a symbol as meaningful in this land of dreams as any star-spangled banner or faggot-faced plaster Christ.

The first that America heard of what it would later call the Mafia was in newspaper accounts of certain events in New Orleans. In the spring of 1869, the *Times* of that city noted that the Second District had become infested by "well-known and notorious Sicilian murderers, counterfeiters and burglars, who, in the last month, have formed a sort of general co-partnership or stock company for the plunder and disturbance of the city." Emigration from southern Italy then was still largely to Brazil and the Argentine; New Orleans, with its busy port traffic to and from South America, was a natural destination for Sicilians, among them the mafiosi whose presence became known in 1869.

The Mafia was, and is, *una cosa puramente siciliana,* a purely Sicilian thing; and even in Sicily it was never a concerted, homogeneous force. One *cosca* might do business or conspire with another, but even when marriage brought them together they remained leery and covetous. They coexisted, but they did so *da lontano,* at a distance. Whenever that *lontananza* was breached, it was more often in hostility than in harmony. And as much as these men distrusted one another, so much greater was their animosity for outsiders. The purely Sicilian nature of the Mafia was sacrosanct. This idea of Sicilian purity—part Greek, part African, part Italian, part French, part Spanish: no matter; the Sicilian could tell an outsider at a glance—was ingrained as deeply as greed in the nature of the Mafia. A *cosca*'s business might extend to the Italian mainland, to the cities of the world beyond. But men who were not Sicilians would never be part of that *cosca;* they would never be mafiosi. It was a matter of blood pride; and a similar sense of exclusivity, superiority, and natural enmity governed the black forces to the north, the Camorra of the Campagna, the 'ndrangheta of Calabria.

Mussolini was the only man who succeeded in driving down the Mafia in Sicily. In 1926, when the first laws against the Mafia were decreed, sixty-four-year-old Don Vito Cascio Ferro of Palermo, the most powerful mafioso on the island, was seized and committed to the Ucciardone prison, where he remained until his death. Conspiracy charges were brought against his successor, Don Calogero Vizzini, in 1929; and the dark forces remained subdued under Il Duce's dictatorship throughout the decade that followed. But Mussolini's dream of power came to its end in the summer of 1943, and in Sicily the Allied Military Government of Occupied Territories set about its business of restoring order. Under AMGOT officers such as forty-year-old Colonel Charles Poletti, a former lieutenant governor of New York, the mafiosi who had been driven down by Mussolini's reign were placed in positions of sanctioned power. Sixty-six-year-old Don Calò Vizzini, whose indictment under Il Duce in 1929 had signified the suppression of the honored society, was in the summer of 1943 appointed mayor of his town of Villalba. He would remain the Mafia's patriarch until his death in the summer of 1954. Other honored men in other towns, victims and enemies of Fascism all, were placed by AMGOT in like positions. Poletti, the Harvard-lawyer son of northern-Italian emigrants to Vermont, was received by the pope and decorated in Rome for his work. After returning to New York in 1945, he founded his own law firm on Madison Avenue. The mercenary ease with which he moved from American law and Democratic politics to Mafia vassalage and back illustrates that the two spheres were not wholly dissimilar. In fact, long before the Italians arrived in America in any number, law and politics had done a fine job of organizing crime without them—and nowhere better than in Cleveland, the big city on Lake Erie, a hundred or so miles northwest of Steubenville.

What Boss Tweed was to the Tammany Hall Democratic political machine of New York, Mark Hanna was to the Republican machinery of Cleveland. Known as the Lord of the Great Lakes, he had built the first steel vessel to sail Lake Erie. The fleet of his Cleveland Transportation Company plied the shores with ever increasing tonnages of coal and iron ore. He took over the Cleveland Opera House, became the president of his own Union National Bank, ran the Cleveland City Railroad, and introduced the city's first electric streetcar system. By 1890, Hanna extended his grasp to politics, backing the Republican congressman William McKinley of Canton in his winning gubernatorial campaign. Cleveland newspapers quoted a Jewish immigrant from Russia who had been asked to describe the government of the new land: "Mark Hanna is king."

It was no secret to Hanna that the new governor of Ohio was heavily in debt. Convening with steel tycoons Andrew Carnegie and Henry Frick, and others willing to gamble on McKinley's political ascendancy, Hanna organized a $130,000 loan fund for the governor. In the presidential-election year of 1896 Hanna became the national chairman of the Republican party; and McKinley, babbling of manifest destiny while his younger opponent Bryan babbled of his Cross of Gold, emerged the victor of the contest. Hanna and his cohorts had their debtor-friend where they wanted him. While mak-

ing a show of refusing a cabinet position, lest it seem a reward for
his support, Hanna persuaded seventy-four-year-old Senator John
Sherman to take the state department so that he could have the old
man's seat in the Senate. As the chairman of the Republican National Committee, Hanna was the first prominent leader to openly
represent a union of politics and business. As the patron force
behind McKinley, he was the first industrialist to secretly guide
presidential policy.

When McKinley was assassinated at Buffalo in the fall of 1901,
barely six months into his second term, and vice-president Theodore Roosevelt assumed office, a Hanna-for-President movement
grew among those who shared the senator's hatred for the drugstore
cowboy who had fought Tammany Hall in New York and who now
declared war against the nation's "malefactors of great wealth."
Senator Hanna, however, died in February of the election year
1904. His legacy was the Ohio Gang, a group of Cleveland politicos
that embraced Hanna's ways to effect a manifest destiny of their
own.

By 1917, twenty-seven states had gone dry, and there were dry
counties in many of the others, including Ohio, which had become
predominantly dry since the turn of the century. The Volstead Act of
October 1919 defined prohibited liquor as any that was one-proof or
more; that is, any containing one half of one percent alcohol. The
Eighteenth Amendment went into effect on January 16, 1920. Prohibition, which lasted almost thirteen years, allowed the criminal
fiefdoms of America to amass wealth and power on a scale previously unimagined. The gangster—a word that seems to have first
appeared in an April 1896 issue of the Columbus, Ohio, *Evening
Dispatch*—was now as potent a force in America as the steelman, as
the moving-picture tycoon, a baron of democracy in his own malfea-
sant right.

Detroit's proximity to Ontario rendered its infamous Purple
Gang one of the principal suppliers of bootlegged Canadian whiskey
to Capone in Chicago and to Maranzano, Masseria, Luciano, and
others in New York, who in turn supplied the Purple Gang with
Scotch. It was a proximity shared by Cleveland.

Hanna's political heirs had backed another Ohio Republican,

Warren G. Harding, in his dark-horse rise to the presidency. Harry Micajah Daugherty, a Columbus lawyer, became the United States attorney general and placed his cohort Ray Haynes in the office of David Blair, an upright Quaker whom Harding appointed Commissioner of Internal Revenue as a gesture to the victorious Prohibition forces. Other positions went to others in the gang's circle: Will H. Hays, who had been Harding's campaign manager and would later become the lord of movie censorship in Hollywood was made postmaster general; a former county sheriff from Marion was made director of the mint. One of Harding's bodyguards, William J. Edick, would later sully the Secret Service's image by becoming part of a counterfeiting conspiracy. Harding had his own White House bootlegger, a man named Elias H. Mortimer, while the Washington meeting-place of the Ohio Gang, a little green house on K Street, operated as a gambling-hall and speakeasy for government officials and bootleggers alike. The gang had nothing to fear from the Bureau of Investigation, which was run by gang ally William J. Burns. Two of Burns's underlings, Gaston Means and Jess Smith, ran the gang's trade in B-permits, the warrants that allowed the withdrawal of alcoholic liquors from distilleries or bonded warehouses for medicinal purposes. The going price was from $50,000 to more than $300,000, depending on the nature of the permit, which came with an implicit guarantee of immunity from federal prosecution or conviction. In little more than two years, Smith and Means took in over $7,000,000 selling permits, protection, and confiscated liquor.

The Auerbach brothers, immigrant barbers of Cleveland, discovered too late that the Ohio Gang's protection was not fully underwritten by the federal government of their adopted land.

"THE MILLION $ TONIC IS ODORIZING THE COUNTRY," proclaimed the ads in *The Barbers' Journal* for this highly perfumed "deadly enemy of dandruff," which wholesaled for $7 a gallon to Guy Crocetti and others. Million Dollar contained alcohol, and when Prohibition came, the Auerbachs were legally entitled to procure what they needed through B-permits. Through the Ohio Gang, however, permits were obtained for far more than was needed, and the Auerbachs were able to buy at $6 a gallon and pass along to bootleggers at $26 a gallon some 80,000 gallons of alcohol. Diluted two-to-one, then flavored and colored with rye extracts, the 80,000 gallons became 240,000 gallons, sold by the quart at $64 a gallon. The Auerbachs surely were not alone in diverting alcohol in Ohio. At its ten-acre compound in Cincinnati, the Federal Products Company was producing its Velva Cologne Spirits, "distilled from grain U.S.P., 190 Proof," and God only knew what else. Nor were they alone in being busted. Abe Auerbach learned to read and write in the federal prison at Atlanta. Years later, convicted of another crime and working in the Ohio-penitentiary barbershop, he slit his own throat with a razor.

Under the mayoralty of the gang's Harry L. Davis, Cleveland's criminal interests, chiefly the Mayfield Road Gang in Little Italy and their Jewish counterpart, the Big Four, operated with little local interference. Davis became governor at the same time Harding became president, and the mayors who followed him until his return to the city office in 1933 were easily suborned.

The sheltering corruption of Cleveland allowed crime to flourish everywhere in eastern Ohio. But nowhere was that flourishing so sublime and so all-pervasive and—yes, the old-timers would long remember it as such—so beautiful as in Steubenville. Dino Crocetti would someday live on Mayfield Road; he would rise through the shifting dreamlands and shadowlands; would walk around with his hat on, singing, while the reigns of mediocrity and evil danced their endless slow dance on the grave of the promised land. But there would never be anything again quite like that town of churches and sin.

IV.

The
TEMPTATION
OF
ST. ANTHONY

*S*teubenville called itself the City of Churches. There were, in the 1930s, in that town of barely 35,000, more than forty temples of the Lord, representing some eighteen denominations among them, from the prevailing Methodists and Presbyterians to the Catholics and the Jews, from the Episcopalians and Greek Orthodox to the Reorganized Church of Jesus Christ and Latter Day Saints. But the Almighty was no match for the Prince of Darkness; and throughout the Ohio Valley and beyond, Steubenville was known by different names: Boys Town, Little Chicago. Sin as an industry was second only to steel, and it not only claimed much of the local steel purse but brought in far-flung wealth as well. The years of Prohibition, 1920 to 1933, the years of Dino Crocetti's youth, were the years of that industry's growth. Steubenville was a bootleggers' paradise. The pall of the mills over the Italian South Side and the Irish Fifth Ward was noisome with the smell of rotgut alchemy. When, toward the end of those years, an immense still blew up in a building across from St. Anthony's one Sunday morning during Mass, it was like a blast from hell—no one there would ever forget it—a peal of destruction that shook the stained glass in its leaden cames and overwhelmed the godly words and righteous delusions as if for once and for all.

Dino entered Wells High School in 1932, one of that year's enrollment of 1,155. The sixteen-room school, built in 1906 at North and Fourth streets, was known more for its football team, the Big Red, than for its academic standards. The star of the Big Red in the fall of 1932 was its black captain, George "Puck" Burgwin. One of Dino's boyhood friends from the Grant School days was a Greek shopkeeper's son named George Mavromatis. Though he was the same age as Dean, Mavromatis had advanced more expeditiously through the ordeals of Mullimanism, and he was already at Wells and on the Big Red team when Dean arrived. Like the team's captain, Mavromatis too had a nickname.

"You're a little small," the coach had told him when he went out for the team.

"Well, I'll grow," the kid had answered.

"No, you're a little runt. You're not ever gonna be big."

The coach assigned him to the inglorious duty of watching over the team's two footballs. When a guard named Simmons was injured, George was sent in to replace him, and eventually he became a starting player. But the nickname stuck. It was what most everybody, including Dean, called him: Runt.

Mavromatis, more than half a century later, would remember those football-mad days at Wells. "If you lost a game, the townspeople wouldn't speak to you. It was that bad." And he would remember Dean too.

"A tough little cookie," he would say; and the stroke that had long since incapacitated him could not suppress the light in his grin and in his eyes.

"He was a good kid. He could do everything good. He was a good dancer, nice dresser. He was a fair player. He was very mannerly. In the classroom, it was always 'Yes, ma'am' to the teacher. Good-lookin'. Jesus, was that kid good-lookin'. He had real black curly hair. I can see it now, shinin' all the time. He must've put pomade or somethin' in it. But he was tough. He'd fight at the drop of a hat. If you rubbed him wrong, or said something wrong to him, he'd fight ya. He fought a lot of street fights. And he came from a tough neighborhood. North End, and South Sixth Street. It's all black now, but in those days, it was all Italians there. And it was a tough neighborhood. You had to fight your way, literally, to school and back home. And he lived about four blocks north of Grant School. I can imagine what he had to go through to get there with somebody always challenging him. First you'd think he was a sissy, 'cause he dressed nice. But, boy, if you ever got in a beef with him, you'd find out in a hurry that he wasn't a sissy.

"To me he was just a heck of a kid. I liked him. He was the

kind of guy you'd want for a friend. What struck me was he was kindhearted. He'd say, 'Runt, you wanna go over to the confection-ery and get some candy?' Penny pieces of candy. Little chocolate caramels for a penny. Licorice sticks. I said, 'I ain't got no money. What the hell, I'm gonna go over there and watch you eat it?' He said, 'No, come on over with me.' So we'd go over there. He'd have a nickel, he'd say, 'You pick two cents' worth, what you want.' "

Mavromatis had discovered back at Grant that Dino could run and he could play ball and he could fight. "We used to play a game called aerial passes. It's a football game, only you use any kind of a ball. The quarterback throws the ball. And we'd always send Dino way out on the end, 'cause he had the speed, man, he'd just cut across—nobody could keep up with him—and score with it. That's how I met him, really, out on the playground all the time."

"He'd run like the wind. He didn't have finesse or technique or nothin'; he just had speed. Boy, and when he turned it on, *shoo*. He cut me in that hundred, it really hurt my feelings, 'cause I thought nobody could beat me on the track. He won the two-twenty. After he beat me, I went over to the two-twenty to watch him run again, to make sure, and he just smoked them guys at the two-twenty like they wasn't even there, standin' still."

But "Dean was never on any teams. He got wrapped up in music. Nothin' mattered to him but singin'.' "

After high school, Mavromatis went to work at his father's sea-food-and-poultry market on South Fourth Street. He played football with the Steubenville Pros for five dollars a game. The Pittsburgh Steelers signed him in 1942. He was with them for three months. The pay was somewhat better, seventy-five a game. The highest-paid Steelers at the time—the team's captain, Chuck Cherundolo, and Bill Dudley, the All-American back from the University of Virginia among them—got only five grand a year. Sitting on his family's front porch on High Street, he would watch the men on the road walking to and from their jobs at the mill. "I'd see these men going to work, real clean, walking real sprightly, carrying their buckets. Then I'd see 'em at three-thirty comin' home, dirty, bent-over, tired. And I said, I'm never gonna work in that mill." He joined the Marine Corps, and when he got out, in 1946, he joined the Steubenville police force, rising eventually to become chief of police in 1969.

By the time George Mavromatis became a cop, Dino was gone and most of Dino's other boyhood friends were on the other side of the law.

"I told him later," Mavromatis would say, with that light in his grin and in his eyes, of those schoolyard races and those days that existed nowhere now but in that very same obdurate and dwindling light; "I told him later, 'You know why you beat me, Dino?' 'Yeah, I'm faster.' 'No,' I said. 'You had more experience. The cops were always chasin' you.' "

Dino hung out—"loafed," as they said in Steubenville—at the same places the other high-school kids hung out. Jumbo milkshakes were a dime at Isaly's on North Fourth Street. Nearby, the Green Mill offered lunch for a quarter. The latest records could be heard and had at Donvito's Music and Italian Book Store on South Sixth Street—Crosby, the Dorsey Brothers; during that snowy Christmas season of 1932, Fred Astaire, drowning out with "Night and Day" the lament of "Brother, Can You Spare a Dime?" There were dances at the Capitol Ball Room on Adams Street, the Catholic Community Center on Fourth.

But Dino loafed as well in places where many of the other kids did not venture. There were more than a dozen poolrooms and cigar stores downtown—six of them between the Den at 320 Market and Turk Bertram's joint at 608 Market alone—all of which operated as *biscazze,* gambling-dens; and Dino already had come to know most of them by the time he started high school. His brother, Bill, excelled in his classes. His cousins John and Robert, as duly noted by the *Wells High Bulletin* of March 30, 1933, upheld the honor of the Crocetti name in a checker tournament sponsored by the Greek Club. ("The plan," the *Bulletin* obliquely revealed, "was suggested after the study of the Homeric days.") But Dino, spurning both books and checkers, Homeric or otherwise, took to the joints. It was in one of them, the Academy Billiard Parlor, that fourteen-year-old Dino met the Rizzo brothers, three kids from South Seventh Street with big ideas. John was the oldest. Then there were Frank, who was

known as Jiggs, and Michael, the youngest, known as M
was sitting around smoking, waiting for a live one to hustle
ball.

"Wanna make some real money?"

The next night, Dino and Frank Rosta, a childhood buddy from
South Eighth Street who now, in his worldly years beyond puberty,
was called Slick, found themselves riding with Jiggs Rizzo to deliver
ten cases of bootleg whiskey across the river to Canonsburg, Pennsylvania. There were other nights, other runs. Dino, Jiggs, and
Mandy became fast friends.

The Twenty-first Amendment, repealing Prohibition, was rati-
fied in December 1933. All with eyes to see had seen it coming with
the election of Roosevelt in the fall of 1932. But the end of Prohibition meant nothing but the end of a pretense in Steubenville. The
lush and fruitful garden of wickedness so lovingly tended to by the
prodigiously corrupt political machinery of the Democratic party
thrived all the more in the wake of repeal. It was, as Roosevelt said,
a New Deal. Gambling and prostitution, which had spread in Steubenville during Prohibition, now all but defined the soul of the
place itself.

The Democratic chairman was the overlord of all malfeasance:
Pinky Nolan at first, then his son and successor, Jackie, and
Jackie's partner and fellow attorney, Hugo "Nunzie" Alexander.
Then came the Jefferson County sheriff: R. B. Long, then R. D.
Bates. The mayor came next: James C. McMaster, Earl D. Apple-
gate, and other hollow figureheads after them. Then there was the
chief of police, R. H. Cunningham.

Pittsburgh, Youngstown, Wheeling, and other steel towns were
mines of corruption as well. Big Bill Lias, the rackets boss of
Wheeling, ran his downtown casinos year-round as openly as he ran
his steakhouse. And, with Elyria and Steubenville, these cities were
the centers of a white-slavery ring that kept the steel-town whorehouses stocked with fresh dumb meat from the outlying hills. But no
place was as wide-open or as wondrous in its venality as Steubenville, which in the years following Prohibition became the mecca
of greater damnation to which all steel-town sinners, suckers,

schemers, and love-starved soldiers were drawn; the vortex of every dirty dollar and dream.

Steubenville was the obscure nexus, the heart of the web that connected illegal gambling everywhere. Colonel Edward Riley Bradley—a Kentucky governor conferred the title on him—was then the most legendary figure in American gambling. Born across the river in Pennsylvania in 1859, Bradley, after working as a cow-puncher and as an Indian-fighting aide to government troops, had opened his first joint, the Bacchus Club, in El Paso in the early 1890s, and from there had gone on to own and operate the Beach Hotel in Chicago. In 1898 in Palm Beach, Florida, he opened what was to become the longest-running illegal casino in America, the Beach Club. A horse-owner as well as a gambler ("I am a gambler and will bet on anything," he told a Senate investigating commit-tee), Bradley, whose horses won over a thousand races, became in 1933 the only man to win the Kentucky Derby four times. The Beach Club by then was the most celebrated and classiest estab-lishment of its kind. Colonel Bradley's no-women policy had been eased, but admittance was still denied to Floridians, those under the influence of liquor, and men not dressed in formal evening attire. The nine roulette tables and the three dice of his one hazard game, along with his horses and other investments—among them his Idle Hour farm in Kentucky and the Hialeah Park racetrack in Miami; two other Palm Beach joints, the Embassy Club and the Oasis Club—rendered Bradley one of America's wealthiest men and most lavish philanthropists. It was to Steubenville that Colonel Bradley, like lesser casino men throughout the East and Midwest, turned for dealers and managers to keep the profits coming.

Bob Sasso of Steubenville was Bradley's greatest trainer and recruiter. The two men worked together until the end of Bradley's career, 1945, when, a year before his death, Bradley sold both the Beach Club and the Embassy. (The Oasis Club property had been donated in 1940 to the Institutum Divi Thomae, a Catholic cancer-research organization.) Under the name of Steve Manas, Sasso was registered as the president of the Academy Billiard Parlor and the co-owner of the Mayflower lunchroom, both on Market Street. The Academy, where young Dean met the brothers Rizzo, had gambling in its back room, but it was another Market Street establishment, a gambling-joint near M&M Hardware on Market Street, that was the true center of Sasso's operations, the breeding ground for those who would go on to Bradley's joints and to scores of other joints in scores of other towns. When Las Vegas opened wide after World War II— by then Sasso had moved his joint across the street and was operating above the Wheel restaurant at the corner of Market and Sixth— there was not a single casino operating without a key man from Steubenville. By the early fifties, some five hundred or so Steubenville families were represented there. Today almost three hundred of Steubenville's sons are active in the casinos of Atlantic City as well. When George Mavromatis went to the altar, people joked that his wife, Ann Vuceta, married him to protect her Nevada-bound brothers, Mitch and Tux, from indictment. George and Ann's son, Mike, would become an executive in Atlantic City.

"I sent them everywhere," Sasso, the oldest of the old-timers from that wide-open age, would say. "I sent kids to Bradley's, to New York, to Washington. My dealings was all out of town. I sent them everywhere. The kid—Dino Crocetti—I didn't know too much. He was a nice boy, as far as I could tell. He had a nice mother and a nice dad. He never worked with me or for me. He was a wild little kid I didn't want to handle. He was more or less with another outfit."

And, to be sure, Steubenville was a place for outfits. Al Schiappa, to whose widely disseminated clan Dean's late aunt Julia had been related through marriage, not only owned the Home Coal Company of Steubenville, but also held a monopoly over the slot-machine action throughout the county. Sasso and his partner, Money O'Brien, ran a bookmaking ring in town; Henry Barber, across the river in Weirton, handled action as well. Two other rings, built on the numbers action, were also in operation, run independently of one another, by Tommy Walker and Patrick J. Brogan, better known as Blinky. Action was taken on two numbers a day: the track-handle number and the stock-market number. Competition for the numbers action, in the finest free-market spirit of capitalism, led bookmakers to vie with one another in offering greater and greater payoff odds, from five hundred on a dollar, to six hundred, and even seven hundred. The runners themselves, those who delivered the action, got a respectable thirty-five percent. When the most heavily-bet number in town hit—632, the telephone number of the Butte Laundry Company, digits that loomed over Steubenville from the laundry's towering smokestack—it broke Walker and left Blinky Brogan boss of the numbers. Dean's uncle Tony Barr, who lived near Joe Crocetti's family on Rosswell Avenue, had quit the steel mill to work for Brogan. He dealt the wheel at the B. J. B. Company, the joint above the Market Street barbershop of Frank Mininni, in the back room of which Brogan had his headquarters.

"Three-chair barbershop," George Mavromatis remembered it. "There was a door. You open that door and you went back into a room. There were all kinds of guys countin' money. Coins, bills. They had them coin-counters goin'."

Did anyone ever get a haircut there?

"I think I saw a couple guys."

The Imperial Cigar Store, run by Money O'Brien's partner Harry Cooper and A. J. McGraw in the Hotel Imperial at Market and Sixth, the Smokehouse on Fourth, Star Cigar on Sixth, and many other joints served as drops for Brogan's operation, as the Academy Billiard Parlor served for Sasso and O'Brien's. The numbers racket was the bread and butter of every operation, but the big money was made in the back rooms. The *roccoli*, the pimps, who ran the whorehouses that flourished down on Water Street, High Street, and lower Market were mostly Italian; but gambling belonged to every race, color, and creed. There were Jews such as Harry Cooper, as big a gambling power as any; his brother, Benny, who ran an after-hours joint downtown; and the Greenburg brothers, Joe and Max, who controlled the first post-Prohibition beer-distribution company in town. Greeks ran the New York Restaurant, a gambling center on Market. The blacks had the Ionic Club and other joints in the one-hundred block of Market.

"It was a funny town," Mavromatis would say. "It really was. But you could walk the streets. In a way, it was a lot better place. These guys, Brogan and them, they were all cheaters, but they were all good joes. Sasso was a gentleman. A finer man you'd never meet in your life. They were gentlemen, and there was no trouble in town."

The *padrone* of Steubenville, the man who oversaw it all, the one to whom the Irish and the Jews and the rest paid tribute, was James Vincent Tripodi, whom no one ever described as a gentleman. Born in Italy in December 1899, Vincenzo Tripodi had established himself early and violently as the demon lover of the Democratic bosses, as the evilest dark breeze in that lush and fruitful garden. He lived at 638 Broadway with his wife. They called her Mae or Mabel, but her name was Amelia. She too had come from the other side, and was a girl of eighteen when Tripodi married her in 1926. There were semi-legitimate businesses: the J. V. Tripodi Restaurant on North Sixth Street, the beer distributorship that had grown out of a Prohibition monopoly. But Tripodi's sub-rosa interests were everywhere his will decided them to be. He knew others of his kind, men in Cleveland, Detroit, New York. They would come to his daughter's wedding and embrace him. But he neither sought nor cultivated their company, desiring no such shadow other than his own in the garden he held as his sacrosanct domain. He would end it many years later as he had begun it, with his hands and his will, blowing out his brains with a thirty-eight, alone in his garage, on a wintry afternoon in December 1987, eleven days before his eighty-eighth birthday.

Tripodi was the first of many such characters whom Dino would encounter in his life: men—America called them the Mafia—who sought to wet their beaks *(fari vagnari u pizzu,* as the Sicilians said) in the lifeblood of every man's good fortune. He shared many traits with these men, traits born of the old ways: the taciturn harboring close to the heart of any thought or feeling that ran too deeply; that emotional distance, that wall of *lontananza* between the self and the world; a natural, unarticulated belief in the supreme inviolability of the old ways themselves; a devout sense of Catholicism, based upon the power of its rituals and predicated on God's special forgiveness for the sins of those whose faith was founded in the ancient, sacred grain of the old ways' *moralità.* He shared these traits with them, but he did not share his money with them; and the more he came to

know them—and he came to know them as few would—the more he
hated them for the predators they were, and the more intent he
became on beating them at their own racket. It was not a matter of
bravado. He did not share that trait with them. It was a matter,
rather, of *menefreghismo.* Deep down, that, as much as anything,
was what he was, a *menefreghista*—one who simply did not give a
fuck.

By the time repeal came, Dino and his family had moved to
1210 Riverview Avenue, a small two-story gabled house with a
backyard overlooking the Ohio and the West Virginia hills beyond.
Guy was managing the beauty shop in the Hub department store at
Market and Fifth. And Dean by then had come to know most of
those with whom he would run through the end of his Steubenville
days.

Mindy Costanzo—most people did not even know the name he
had been christened with: Emmanuel—was from South Street. Two
years older than Dean, Mindy in 1933 was already working as a
clerk at M&M Hardware, the Market Street store his father, Michael, owned in partnership with a man named H. W. Master.

Ross Monaco, who lived with his widowed mother on South
Street, was the oldest of the bunch. He had graduated from high
school in 1928, and in 1933 was working for the Chicago Wall
Paper Manufacturing Company on South Seventh Street, running a
few numbers for Harry Cooper on the side.

Mike Simera lived on North Ninth Street. Joe DiNovo, five years
older than Dean, lived on North Third, where his father, Pietro, had
been selling cars and trucks since 1917: Stutzes and Moons and
Diamond T's, then Plymouths and Dodges and Dodge Brothers
trucks. Americo Sperduti, from South Sixth Street, had been named
by his father for the new land, *l'America,* but his friends had renamed him for a comic-strip character called Smuggles, and that
was the name that stuck: Smuggs Sperduti.

From Stewart Alley, the ponderous Tony Torcasio—Ape Head,
they called him—was younger than Dino and most of the others, but
he had come up harder. Never knowing his father, who died six
months after the infant Ape Head's birth, Tony was working three

newspaper routes by the age of seven. Hustling all the way, he made it to the top in Las Vegas and Atlantic City, rising eventually to become the casino manager, then the general manager, and finally chairman of the board of the Tropicana.

Demetrios George Synodinos, whom they called Jimmy, was born on September 9, 1918. His grandfather had come from the Greek island of Khíos to Steubenville in 1904 and founded the White House Meat Market, the butcher shop on Third and Market that Jimmy's father now ran. When he and Dino met at Grant School, Jimmy was living with his parents, George and Sultana, on North Street. In 1930 Jimmy moved with his parents to Greece. It was there that his twenty-nine-year-old mother was shot to death, along with his aunt Theano, by the love-deranged husband whom Theano had left. The spurned husband ended the bloodbath by firing into his own temple. In Khíos, Jimmy's father found a new wife. They returned in 1932 to Steubenville, to a new home on South Fifth Street. Jimmy's father reopened the White House Market on South Fourth Street; but Jimmy had no intention of following him into the family business.

Fourteen-year-old Jimmy began loafing with Dean at the Capitol Cigar Store and the Dixie Cigar Store on South Fourth, and at the Academy Billiard Parlor, where before long Jimmy was working as a runner, delivering bets through the back door to Money O'Brien. Soon he was spinning the Big Six wheel in the Academy's back room.

"Oh, they was good boys," Jimmy's stepmother, Agnes, would avow, holding the image of the two boys climbing the branches of her backyard pear tree. "Dino come to the house after school lotta times. One time they bring me a pool table inna house. I don't know where they find it, but they bring it. I have my mother-in-law with me, and my brother, and I say, 'Where I'm gonna put this table here? Nine people, six-room house; where I'm gonna put this?'

"But, really, they was good boys. No stealing. Dino came all the time. Lotta time I have the spaghetti, you know, sit down, eat. They was good boys. Come and go, come and go. Both of them, they go to Antonucci's place through the alley, spend the money, buy candy."

.   .   .

"It was for singin' that I quit school," Dino would someday say. It sounded right; after a while, he even came to believe it himself.

Dino did not so much quit high school, really, as fade from it. He was getting too old for that shit, anyway. He was sixteen. He had made it to the tenth grade. He had even read a book straight through: *Black Beauty*. Enough was enough. There was pussy out there, and money, and all sorts of things. When the Sons of Italy sponsored a basketball team, the Sons of Italy Juniors, in 1935, Jiggs Rizzo—Roozi, as he was now also known—was the captain and Dean was the center. As the team was to be drawn exclusively from the Wells student body, Dean played out the season as such. But in truth, as he and Jiggs waged league war against the lowly polacks of St. Stanislaus on the court of the Catholic Community Center, Dean's days of Mullimanism were then behind him. His increasingly rare presence at Wells had finally evanesced and left a vacant seat.

His schoolmates had never really known him. Even his loving family could not tell for sure what lay within this kid who moseyed around among them with a hat on, singing. There was a pin-tumbler sidebar lock on his guts that no one could pick. That was just the way he was, and it was just the way he always would be.

Unlettered and rough-cut, Dino possessed both wiles and wisdom beyond his years—anyone trying to fuck with his mind or his body or his soul found this out forthwith. But the wisdom served by those wiles was an annihilating wisdom. It was the wisdom of the old ways, a wisdom through which the seductions of reason and love and truth and all such frail and flimsy lepidoptera would in their seasons emerge and thrive, wither and die. The sum of Dino's instincts had to do with the old ways, those ways that were like a wall, ways that kept the world *lontano,* as the mafiosi would say: distant, safely and wisely at bay. That was how he liked it: *lontano,* like the flickering images on the theater screen that gave him pleasure as he sat alone, apart from them and unknown to them, in the dark.

Those close to him could sense it: He was there, but he was not really there; a part of them, but apart from them as well. The glint in his eye was disarming, so captivating and so chilling at once, like lantern-light gleaming on nighttime sea: the tiny soft twinkling so

gaily inviting, belying for an instant, then illuminating, a vast unseen cold blackness beneath and beyond. The secret in its depth
seemed to be the most horrible secret of all: that there was no
secret, no mystery other than that which resides, not as a puzzle to
be solved or a revelation to be discovered, but as blank immanence,
in emptiness itself.

There was a picnic in Beatty Park. Roozi had gotten hold of an
eight-millimeter movie camera, and they were all going to be in
pictures. No one who saw that movie ever forgot it. The camera
captured the silent laughter of the Crocettis and the Barrs. It followed Dino's friends back and forth as they ran and fumbled, threw
and jumped in a makeshift football game. There was merriment
everywhere, but there was no Dino. Then the camera scanned to the
right, to a tree off in the distance, and there he was by himself
under the tree, away from it all, caught unawares and expressionless, abstractedly toying with a twig, sort of mind-whittling it. That
was Dino, all right; the Dino inside the Dino who sang and swore
and loafed and laughed.

He was born alone. He would die alone. These truths, he, like
every punk, took to heart. But in him they framed another truth,
another solitary, stubborn stone in the eye of nothing. There was
something, a knowing, in him that others did not apprehend. He was
born alone, and he would die alone, yes. But in between—somehow
—the world in all its glory would hunker down before him like a
sweet-lipped High Street whore.

Tony Torcasio would one day sit in a back booth in a place in
Atlantic City called the Irish Pub—"the kid who owns it, he's from
Steu'ville," he would say in the way of explaining his presence in
what was ostensibly a shamrock joint—and he would remember
what they used to say in Steubenville.

"They had a sayin' in Steu'ville, when you was born and you
was young and you was a kid, they'd say: Learn to steal, learn to
deal, or go to the mill."

Though Dino did all three, he had no more natural affinity for
work than he had for school. Years before, when they first came to
the new land, Giuseppe Crocetti had followed his older brother

Vincenzo into a life in the steel mill. The brothers were now in their
fifties. Vincenzo had found easier work, at the Steubenville Pure
Milk Company; and Giuseppe, following him once again, had quit
Wheeling Steel after nearly twenty years there, and taken a job
driving a milk truck. Dino, like his cousins, had occasionally
helped Uncle Joe on his delivery route. That, some adolescent
nickel-a-pop shoe-shining, and one summer of pumping gas at the
D&R Service Station at Sixth and South comprised the sum of firsthand knowledge that Dino possessed of that thing called "work."

Dino's brother, Bill, and his cousin Robert would pursue their
studies beyond high school. His cousins John and Archie would join
their father at the milk company. Mary, the eldest, was already
working as a hairstylist—a "beauty operator," as they said. Starting
out at Hook's Permanent Wave Shoppe, she had moved to the ritzier
La Rosella Wave Shop, and would go on to work as a manager for
her uncle Guy. Dino's father encouraged him as well to get into the
tonsorial racket. But Dino, who already knew how to cut hair from
watching his old man, would have nothing to do with it.

Prizefighting was big on both sides of the river. Regular
matches were sponsored at Rex Hall in Weirton by the Weirton
Steel-Tin Mill Security League. In Steubenville, there was a gym
above the Knights of Columbus hall on Fourth Street, a makeshift
sparring-ring above M&M Hardware, and fights were held at both
the Catholic Community Center on South Fourth and Trombetti Hall
on South Seventh. It did not seem like a bad proposition to young
Dino. He had beaten up his share of kids in the Grant School
playground. "Gutty. Wasn't afraid of nothin'," remembered Mike
Pavlovich, who later ran a joint called Mike's Cafe near the Wheeling Mill. Why not get paid for doing it professionally? Lean and
under 147 pounds, he could fight as a welterweight. Barney Ross,
the new welterweight champ, did not look all that formidable to him.
And besides, when the time came for Dino to do to Ross what Ross
had done to McLarnin, Ross would be past his prime and poised to
fall. One of the back-room gamblers, regaling him with a fine line of
shit, offered to manage him. They would go places together. So it
came to pass that sixteen-year-old Dino Crocetti became Kid
Crochet.

Ross Monaco would remember Dino fighting "three or four matches at the Community Center," and Tony Torcasio, attesting that "Dino could handle himself pretty good," would recall "a few boxing matches." But Steubenville's only professional boxer was also the only one in town who would recollect anything more of Kid Crochet's ill-starred career. Emilio Julian, born in 1908, was, like Dino's father, an immigrant from the *abruzzese* province of Teramo. Julian, from South Street, fought in the twenties as Young Ketchell, a bantamweight. He left the game, took a steady job at Weirton Steel, and later became an assistant scoutmaster of Agon DeLuca's Troop Ten, which is where he first met the future Kid Crochet.

"I could tell ya, he's a hell of a nice guy," he would say of Dino, "but he was the laziest guy in the United States. Hell of a nice guy. No trouble. Just lazy, that's all. Oh, he was a good kid. If I ever had a kid, I'd want him to be like him. Respectful. He was good. Just didn't wanna work."

As a boxer? "Well, I wouldn't give him too much credit, now. He fooled around a little bit. He didn't have too many fights. Most of 'em was him gettin' the hell out the way from gettin' hit. After he got hit in the face a few times, why, he quit."

Dino would ever after bear the scar of the brow-cuts and the split lip that Kid Crochet incurred. "And my hands," he would say, "aren't exactly pretty. They weren't taped correctly—my manager knew even less about fighting than I did. He just looked forward to my dragging down a five-dollar watch, so we could sell it and split the loot. Big deal."

As George Mavromatis put it: "He fought amateur for a while. Wasn't bad. But he was too good-lookin' to be a fighter."

"I liked it, but I didn't last long," Dino would say. "I worked up to being paid about ten dollars a match, which was enough to buy my dad a watch or a fountain pen; then I blew the racket." That is what he would tell the broads, anyway. They ate that phony tough-guy shit like candy. To others, he would mention his twelve fights in 1936 with a wave of the hand. "Yeah," he would say, "I won all but eleven."

And so, it came to pass that Kid Crochet became once again Dino Crocetti, and got himself a job at the Weirton Steel Company.

It didn't seem so bad. Smuggs Sperduti and his brother, Pasquale, were already working there. Another of Dino's buddies, Richard Yannon, worked there too. Yannon made three dollars and seventy-two cents a day, and he had been able to buy his mother a fur coat. Dino got a job working with Yannon as a puddler, bundling hot coils, at Weirton.

"We had big platforms, half a block long," he would recall. "Hot coils of steel wire came down on them. They cooled as they came because there was water splashing on them. At a certain point, a buddy of mine and I would bang the end of a coil with a hammer; I'd pull a lever, and the coil would go into a boxcar." Dean rode across the Fort Steuben Bridge every morning with Dick Yannon in the company bus. Anna DeCarlo Yannon, Richard's widow, would remember Dean and her future husband almost getting fired for tapdancing on the big fresh sheets of steel that rolled from the mill.

In the spring of 1936, Dean and Ross Monaco decided to journey west. With California as their ultimate destination, they traveled first by rail to Chicago, where Ross had an aunt, uncle, and cousin. "Take good care of my teeth and make them look good," Dean's family dentist, old Dr. V. J. DeLuca, remembered Dean saying as a kid. "When I get big, I'm gonna be an entertainer." Now, in Chicago, Dino finagled himself some financially painless dentistry.

"My cousin, she was a nurse for this dentist out there," Monaco recalled. "Romeo Camino was his name. Real nice guy. He said, 'Sit around, Ross. I wanna hear about California. I gotta get to California myself.' Which he eventually did. So I'd sit and talk. 'Well, we're gonna go out there, bum around.' 'By the way, how's your teeth?' 'I guess they're all right.' 'Why'nt you sit around the office, one of the patients leaves, sit in the chair, we'll bullshit.' So he took care of me, a few fillings. Then he took care of Dino's teeth too. 'Hey, Doc,' I said, 'you know, we're short on money.' He said, 'Don't worry. When you get it, send it to me.' As luck would have it, the years moved by. I took care of him. I took care of Dino's."

They found Dean's uncle Leonard Barr in Chicago. While

Leonard's big brother Tony had become a dealer, Leonard, every bit
as ugly as Tony was good-looking, had gone into show business.
Known as Bananas, Leonard years ago had moved from the Steubenville mills to the mills of Cincinnati. In Cincinnati, he had taken
dance lessons at night. He had quit the mills in the twenties and
gone into vaudeville with a "crazy-legs" specialty act. He twice had
taken young Dino with him to visit New York, giving him his first,
fleeting glimpses of Broadway. With dancer Virginia Estes, Leonard
later would work up a team act, Barr and Estes, "Lunatics of the
Dance," that played throughout the country for years to come.

Another Steubenville journeyer, Joe DiNovo, was soon to pass
through Chicago as well. He had just gotten married to a girl named
Agatha in Canada, was already regretting his folly, and decided to
take Dean and Ross along with him and his wife on their honeymoon.

After visiting his new in-laws in Portland, Joe drove Dean and
Ross south to Los Angeles. The three of them checked into a small
motel near Santa Monica. "It was pretty cheap," as Ross remembered it. Joe was just along for the ride, but Dean and Ross shared
other delusions. Ross, looking up to Dean's uncle Leonard, wanted
to be a dance man; and Dean was still walking around singing.

Dean followed Santa Monica Boulevard one drizzly afternoon
into Hollywood. He stood by himself outside the gates of the Paramount Studios on Marathon Street. He saw Frances Dee walk past.
And that was it. The Paramount lot was vast. Hollywood Cemetery,
whose grounds and Paramount's ran together, was even bigger.

The vague fantasy of Hollywood vanished into the foggy gray of
something like reality, a gray as dead and dismal, glimpsed through
that motel window, as that which colored Steubenville itself. As
Ross recalled it: "Me and Dino loafed around out there about three
weeks. Then he said, 'I don't think I can hack it. I'm sorta home-
sick.' So he went back with Joe when Joe was ready."

Back home, most of the old gang were hard at work—hustling.

Jimmy Synodinos was doing the best of all. In 1934, when
Prohibition ended, Money O'Brien, Harry Cooper, and a third partner, Tom Griffin, had opened the Half Moon Nite Club. It was an
elegant joint overlooking the river a mile north of the Fort Steuben

Bridge on Route 7. The Half Moon offered two floor shows nightly and the finest food in Ohio, and the gambling casino in the back offered a plush and luxurious alternative to the back-room dives downtown. Jimmy, already working as a runner for O'Brien, had started out parking cars at the Half Moon for a dime a rap. Now, at eighteen, he was dealing craps in the back room.

"When he brought all this money home, my father thought he stole it," Jimmy's little half-sister, Angie, recalled. "That was the only time he ever smacked Jimmy."

Jimmy would travel to Las Vegas the following year. Returning to Steubenville, he would open his own office in the National Exchange Bank Building at 401 Market Street. The lettering on Jimmy's door would read B&F COMMISSIONER. The *B* stood for Baseball, the *F* for Football. With Tom Griffin as his partner, and with the benison of Democratic boss Jackie Nolan, Jimmy, hooked into the Amorita Club in Pittsburgh, would become the main oddsmaker and bookmaker throughout the Ohio Valley. Football betting switched from odds to the point-spread system in the early forties; and, by the time he stood as best man at George Mavromatis's wedding, Jimmy had established himself as one of the country's point-posting pioneers. Known as Jimmy Snyder, he would return eventually to Vegas to reign.

"No cops at my door," Agnes Synodinos Kayafas would proudly say of Jimmy's years as the B&F Commissioner of Steubenville. "When Jimmy the Greek is your son, that's good." She would pause, nodding deliberately, serenely. "I hate cops."

Most of the others, Ross Monaco discovered, were hustling at a new joint called the Rex. Some of them, like Smuggs, who still worked at Weirton Steel, were holding down straight jobs during the week and working the Rex on weekends. But Dino had gone in full tilt as a dealer.

The Rex Cigar Store was run by a character named Cosmo Quattrone. Born on the other side, Cosmo was a dark-haired man of average height but prodigious weight. He smoked Parodis, the cheap, gnarled little *toscanello*-style cigars, known as guinea ropes or guinea stinkers, that were manufactured across the river in Pennsylvania and were a common sight among Steubenville's gentlemen of Italian descent. But no one had ever seen anybody smoke a Parodi the way old Cosmo did, bringing it to and from his mouth with an upturned, vertical clasp of forefinger and thumb. Later, when World War II movies like *Hitler's Madman* and *The Master Race* showed the monocled bad guys of Hollywood's Waffen-S.S. smoking cigarettes in this same fashion, Cosmo's way of handling a Parodi—Nazi-style, they called it—would take on a new and sinister air among the moviegoers of Steubenville.

Cosmo lived with his wife, Mary, on Broadway. He had been a grocer, a poolroom operator, a bookmaker; but most of his money had been made as a bootlegger.

Cosmo opened the Rex Cigar Store, the cathedral of his back-room dreams, late in 1936. It was located at 523 Market Street, directly next door to M&M Hardware, which became an outpost of legitimacy between the Rex on one side and Bob Sasso's joint on the other. The front room of the Rex, the actual cigar store, was overseen by Tony Cresta, a man from nearby Mingo Junction. Cresta's end of the operation was taken over in time by a guy named John DeSarro, whom people in Steubenville knew as Stogie.

Stogie—who never smoked cigars; the nickname "goes back to when I started school, about six years old. DeSarro, then DeCigar, then Stogie"—was then in his early thirties. In his eighties, he would recall how he "put the pool tables in there" and generally gussied up the joint. He handled bets and oversaw things when Cosmo was not there.

"How I got hooked up with Cosmo is a long story," he would say. "I got hooked up with them guys back durin' the bootleggin' days. When I come home—well, I was in the can, ya got it? It was for bootleggin'—I bought this other guy out and I ran the cigar store. Cosmo owned it all the time. He had the joint in the back. When I got in there, the joint was goin', everything was goin'."

Mindy Costanzo, working next door for his father, would never forget the joint.

"The Rex was fabulous," he would say. "You walked in, Stogie had the cigar store in the front, there was a pool table. Cosmo had the back. There was a back entrance too. You could park back there; they had a parking-lot. Anybody could walk in. Come in off Market; off Sixth, down the alley, come in the back door.

"They built a cubbyhole in the back of the room with armor plate. A guy was up there with a shotgun all the time. In fact, I sold the guy the shotgun. He wanted a sawed-off shotgun, I said, 'Well, saw it off yourself.' The goddamn fool—he was from the toe of Italy —cut off the wooden stock. When he went out to shoot it, it kicked him back about ten feet. So I had to order him a new stock and tell him to saw the other end off.

"Boy, the action they had in that place. Day and night, seven days a week. They had the horses, the numbers. They had a poker game goin' all the time. Roulette. Two blackjack tables, two crap tables. They were two-deep, three-deep at them crap tables."

They even air-conditioned the joint. Mindy sold Cosmo the first air conditioner in Steubenville. That was in the summer of 1937, not long after Ross threw in with his friends and started working the horse book in Cosmo's back room. He came in at sixty-five dollars a week and worked his way up to a hundred and more.

Moses L. Annenberg was the man on whom every horse bookie in America ultimately relied. The circulation manager for the Hearst newspaper empire in the twenties, Annenberg owned *The Daily Racing Form* and controlling interests in the *New York Morning Telegraph, Radio Guide,* and *Screen Guide.* In 1936, for $15,000,000, he bought the *Philadelphia Inquirer.* His Nation-Wide News Service maintained telegraph and telephone wires at twenty-nine racetracks. These lines in turn serviced bookmaking operations in two hundred and thirty-three cities, each of which fed into operations throughout their regions. Until his indictment for income-tax evasion in 1939, Annenberg was the American Telephone and Telegraph Company's fifth biggest customer.

"We'd get all the races, from all over," Monaco said. "The wire was hooked into Hank Crowley's system. He had the horse books all through the valley, his system. A certain time, you would flip on the speaker and they would give you the morning line, about an hour, hour and a half, depending on how many tracks were runnin'. The California track, we didn't get any service, we just booked it cold.

We'd get the morning line at ten-thirty; we'd be through after mar-kin' it all on the board, maybe eleven-thirty, a quarter to twelve. The first race would be about one o'clock. We'd have lunch, work from one to about five-thirty. Sometimes, with the New Orleans track, about an hour's difference, we'd stay till about six. We got the New York tracks; Chicago, Maryland, you name it. We used to get 'em all. We'd get actual service—they'd call the whole race—at about seven tracks. The New York tracks got the most action. Mary-land. We paid track prices on the big races. We had a limit. The most you could get for a two-dollar ticket was thirty-two dollars."

The pay for Dino and the rest of the dealers was higher, for they put in more hours than those who worked the races. Like the horse book, the tables opened every morning at ten or ten-thirty, but they did not close until the last gamblers were done. Poker games some-times ran for three and four days on end.

"He was a beautiful dealer," Mike Simera would remember. "What hands!"

Dino learned how to stack and to palm; he even learned how to deal seconds; but he never used these skills to cheat the patrons of the Rex. "I was a damn good dealer," he said, " 'cause I never cheated, never." After all, he was kindred; most of what he made often ended up in some other joint's till. So he let the suckers be, and robbed Cosmo instead.

There were no chips at the Rex. Wagering and payoffs were all in silver dollars. Over the course of time, Dean became quite profi-cient—in the end, an expert—not only at slipping silver dollars into his pockets, but, more impressively, at surreptitiously firing them downward in a perfect sinking trajectory into the oversized loafers that served as his knock-down deposit-boxes. An extra five or ten bucks a night never hurt; and, besides, the cool silver helped to soothe a dealer's tired feet.

Cosmo caught his ass too. Walking through the feast of St. An-thony on a break one June day, Dino decided to take a ride on the loop-the-loop. As it spun high in its first wild overturning arc, a glittering heavy rain of silver dollars spun down to disperse in a clanking puddle amid the crowd.

"I hear you like to dance," Cosmo said to him a few nights later.

"That's what they tell me," he said, holding that Parodi in that way he had of holding it. "I'd like to see you dance," he said. "I'd like to see you dance in them shoes you got on there."

Like the other joints in town—except for the occasional token raid on one of the nigger joints—the Rex never got busted. In fact, one ran a higher risk in Steubenville of being collared for violating Section 436 of the city's Revised Ordinances, which outlawed barbering on Sunday, than for transgressing against Sections 450 and 451, which prohibited gambling, or Section 399, which forbade the keeping of a "house of ill-fame." As Mike Pavlovich would say, "Every time they elected a sheriff here, he left office after two or three terms. He never had to work anymore."

When George Mavromatis became chief of police many years later, he decided, just for the hell of it, to see if Dean had a record from his days at the Rex. "I got the Bertillon man, I said, 'Joe, I want you to go clear through these files here and see if you can find me anything on Dean.' Not even a traffic ticket. No record whatsoever."

Each winter and spring, the joints reciprocated with grace the understanding shown them by the city fathers. "It was a regular thing," Mindy Costanzo remembered, "twice a year, the grand jury, January and June; they'd close the casinos up a week or ten days, sometimes two weeks, while they brought in the indictments." When the joints closed for Satan's winter break, Dino, Smuggs, Ross, Mandy, and Jiggs would get hold of a car—sometimes there were more of them; sometimes, two cars—and drive south to Florida, to Miami Beach and Palm Beach.

Dino dealt blackjack and sometimes served as the roulette croupier; but his main job at the Rex was working craps. As at every joint, craps was the fastest-action, biggest-money game in the house. The so-called smart gamblers were quick to explain that of all casino games, bank craps had the lowest consistent percentage favoring the house, a frontline disadvantage of only 1.41 percent; but the speed of the game, the number of frontline decisions over the course of play, rendered those same crapshooters the house's biggest suckers. It was to this steady, overflowing, fast-rushing stream of dice degenerates that Dino ministered, covering bets and handling the stick, in hourly shifts of forty minutes on, twenty minutes off.

When he had first started working at the Rex, in 1936, Dino had trouble explaining the situation to his parents.

"My aunts said, 'Your son's gonna be a gangster. He's gonna die in the electric chair,'" he would recall.

"I talked to my mom and pop and said, 'I'm not a gambler. I deal, I work.'"

Earlier that year, the family had gone to the movies to see Ronald Colman in *The Man Who Broke the Bank at Monte Carlo*. Now he asked his mother, "Remember the guy with the stick? He wore the nice suit, the tie. He didn't gamble, he just worked. Well, that's me."

And Angela Crocetti told his aunts, "You're crazy. My son's gonna be a star."

This was not Monte Carlo, but, yes, Jimmy the Greek's mother would say of Dean's crowd, "They dressed nice." Her daughter, Jimmy the Greek's half-sister, Angie, would remember seeing them as a little girl: standing around, laughing, talking, smoking, in the fancy clothes they bought at Reiner's. "They always wore the pleated pants with the pegged cuffs and the chains, with a nice shirt." Ray Prologo, who was an eight-year-old shoeshine boy at the time, would never forget shining Dino's hepcat shoes. "I'll catch you later," Dino told him; *domani, domani, domani.*

They were sports now, all of them, and they prowled the night as such. Mindy Costanzo had the car, a big six-wheel Auburn.

"It was my old man's. I'd sneak it out at night. We'd cruise around to five or six in the morning. Every night. That was our life."

"Steu'ville," Tony Torcasio would say, "was a wide-open town. People from Pittsburgh and from all over used to come there. They used to come from hundreds of miles down to Steu'ville, 'cause Steu'ville had everything there."

They had all drunk since they were kids. "We always had our bootleg joints," as Mindy said. "We had our different spots to get the corn whiskey. We'd go buy a gallon for two dollars and a quarter and go to a dance. White corn, moonshine. These guys would bring it in

from the country. And there were distilleries all over town." After
Prohibition, it was a little harder for Dean and the others who were
under twenty-one. "They would arrest you if you were under-age.
The bars wouldn't serve you."

"Shit, we were drunk every night," Costanzo said. "We lived in
joints all our lives. There used to be about four or five after-hours
places. We closed every one of 'em up every goddamn night. It was
a party town."

Dawn often found them at the all-night Chinese-Italian restaurant in Miller's Hotel on North Sixth Street opposite Panhandle
Station. The Chinese chef at Miller's Restaurant was known for the
beansprout farm he maintained in the basement; the Italian chef, for
his daybreak specials of veal scaloppine and chicken cacciatore.
On other mornings, they went to Del's, a café on Sixth Street run as
a family business by the Del Villans.

Some mornings found them, with or without egg fu-yung or
sausage and peppers, at Cunningham Stables, just outside of town,
in Wintersville. They would ride through the countryside for hours.
Sometimes they toted rifles and stalked inanimate objects. And
there were mornings on the golf course at Belleview Park—Goat
Hill, they called it—nine holes for thirty cents. These were the days
and nights, the sultry illimitable whirl of sunshine and darkness, of
vague dreams and laughter and dirty desires, that they would never
forget.

A quart of decent booze in those halcyon days cost three bucks
or less. The miracle of love was even cheaper.

"It was a dollar straight; two dollars, a trip around the world,"
Costanzo would recall.

"A buck a crack!" Mike Pavlovich testified, like one who had
glimpsed Eden. "And I'll tell you somethin', they were the most
gorgeous girls you ever laid eyes on."

"The whorehouses," Pavlovich said, "were fantastic. All the
girls were examined. Nobody ever got any venereal disease; not that
I heard of, anyway."

The whorehouses had operated openly, on Water Street, High
Street, lower Market, for as long as Dino or any of them could

remember; had operated openly long before the gambling-joints. The whores, as Mindy said, "would line up; they'd be at the windows, like it was legal. They had twenty, twenty-five whorehouses, two hundred whores. Water Street, bumper to bumper comin' from Youngstown, Pittsburgh, Wheeling. Saturday night, you thought you were in Times Square in New York, all the joints goin'."

Jimmy the Greek's stepmother never forgot wandering unawares into the red-light district when she first came to this country. "I sold church tickets there. I didn't know. My husband's friend saw me there. 'What were you doing down there?' 'I sell tickets for the church.' 'Your husband know?' 'My husband know I sell tickets. But what? Why you ask me this question?' When he told me, oh my God. I sold so many tickets."

"There was a philosophy," her daughter said. "They really thought the streets were safer when they had houses of ill repute. That was their reasoning: The women were safe and the daughters were safe because men didn't have to abduct anyone, they could just go to these houses of choice. Two or three blocks of them. The girls would hang out on the porches."

"When I was a kid, I wasn't allowed to go down there," George Mavromatis said. "I learned to play football on the riverbank, and Water Street was the last street down. I was scared to go there anyway, because the bigger boys told me, they said, 'George, if you go down there, if you just walk down that street, them girls'll run out the house, they'll grab ya, and they'll pull ya in the house.' I said, 'What the hell they gonna do with me?' They said, 'They got great big pins, horse-blanket pins, that they'll pin your penis to your belly button.' They scared the hell out of me. So when I had to play football, I'd walk maybe three blocks out of the way, and then cut down."

In Steubenville, even smut seemed to pander to the gambling edge. "IT'S 100 TO 1 THESE DELINQUENT DAUGHTERS WILL GO WRONG! MIDNITE SHOWS ONLY. ADULTS ONLY. SEE CREATION OF BABY AND 3 DIFFERENT BIRTHS OF A BABY," cried the October 1938 advertisements for *Body of Beautiful* at the Rex Theatre, just a few doors down from the Rex Cigar Store, on Market Street.

Dino and the others had not known the fear of the horse-blanket pins, and had teethed upon the fairer sex as precociously as they had suckled at the rotgut fount. Dino, like most of them, had a sweetheart of sorts.

Irma DiBenedetto lived on North Seventh Street with her mother, Mary, and her father, Ralph, who was a foreman with the Pennsylvania Railroad. Dino had begun dating her in 1936, soon after his family moved in down the street from hers. She was a beautiful girl with black hair and dark southern-Italian skin. Looking into her laughing eyes, people said, was like losing oneself in those songs from the other side.

"Oh, they were very much in love," said Anna DeCarlo Yannon, whose memory of Irma was as "my best friend." Tony Torcasio saw it differently: "She was his girlfriend, but I don't think Dino was her boyfriend."

"He was serious at the time," Mindy Costanzo said. "She was so beautiful. They dated a good while. But, hell, he never took her anywhere. House dates."

"He had other girls too," his cousin Mary said. "He went with other girls. Here today, gone tomorrow. That's Dean." And Bernice Del Villan, Smuggs Sperduti's future wife, would remember Dino, with that way about him and that dark brown wavy hair: "He didn't have to chase women. They came."

Irma was a lovely girl, everyone agreed, "a real nice person," as Ross Monaco put it. "But, shit," as Mindy Costanzo recalled, "Dino used to fuck every human he could. The dealers he worked with, when they went on shift, he'd go sneak down their apartments and fuck their wives."

Years later, after Dean was long gone, Irma married Mindy's cousin Guy D'Aurora. "Right after she got married, she blew up to three hundred pounds," Mindy said. Half a century and more after Dino's last kiss, Irma DiBenedetto D'Aurora would still be found, with her husband and her ghosts, in that little house on North Seventh Street where Dino had first romanced her. People now spoke of her in strange tones. "Irma's real sick now," Mindy Costanzo declared. "She's huge," Dino's cousin Mary whispered. "She's big as a house. She very seldom goes out," Anna Yannon said.

And when asked about Dino and those long-ago days, Irma's voice would crack in anger: "I don't have nothing to do with him. I don't have nothing to do with him *anymore*. I'm married. I got a nice husband, and, uh, I did go with him and that's *it*. I quit! He was a dirty *bum*—that's all! Here—before he got up in the big time. Dirty liar—a bum."

So there were no fond memories, no lingerings of songlight in laughing spring-night eyes?

"No!"—de profundis—"Never!"

For Dino, there were other eyes, other songs.

V.

THE DIVINATIONS OF SORELLI

*T*he first time that Dino sang before a crowd was at Craig Beach in the summer of 1934. It was the summer that German Chancellor Adolf Hitler was first hailed as "Der Führer"; but there were no stormclouds yet to threaten the slow tidal magic of hot days and balmy nights flowing aimlessly to the melodies of Benny Goodman's "Moon Glow" and Bing Crosby's "Love in Bloom." Teenagers from Steubenville, as from other towns, converged by the daytripping carfuls at that resort on the northwestern shore of Lake Milton, not far south of Youngstown, in Mahoning County. There was a bandstand, music that wove through the breezes from the lake, and dancing every evening. The George Williams Orchestra did its best to cense the air with its cheesy aphrodisiac.

"Hey," Ross Monaco said to Williams one day, "we got a fellow here that sings. How about lettin' him sing?"

"Sure," the bandleader said.

Williams took seventeen-year-old Dino aside. "Okay, kid," he said, "what do you want to sing?"

That was a good question, and Dino mulled it over. The trouble was, as Ross said, "He didn't know too many songs at the time. Ballads. He never sang any peppy songs or anything like that. A couple of Italian things." But Williams played dance music. He did not know from that spaghetti-bender shit. Together he and Dino decided on "Oh, Marie," a sprightly, danceable Italian melody that even polacks knew.

Like Dino's family, the song had come from the other side and been Americanized. It was an old Neapolitan *canzone*. Brought to America and published in English by 1905, the song had been recorded more than a dozen times and, like "O Sole Mio," had become a standard beyond all ethnic bounds. Dino knew it by heart.

For him, as for many others, it evoked those *vergini Marie* of his life
—that trinity of Maria Crocettis: grandmother, aunt, and cousin—as
well as all those other, less virginal Marys that whirled in a dizzying
concentric ring of desire around them.

As his friends already knew, Dino was serious about singing. In
fact, as much as he loathed lessons of any kind, he was serious
enough to take voice lessons from the mayor's wife, Corrine Apple-
gate, who taught music on North Fourth Street. But Dino's greatest
teacher was Bing Crosby, whose voice he emulated until he found
his own.

"When a Bing Crosby movie ever came to Steubenville, I would
stay there all day and watch. And that's where I learned to sing,
'cause it's true I don't read a note," he would say. "I learned from
Crosby, and so did Sinatra, and Perry Como. We all started imitatin'
him. He was the teacher for all of us."

In the 1933 movie *College Humor,* Crosby sang "Learn to
Croon," a Harold Arlen song from the Broadway show *You Said It.*
His Brunswick recording of it became a hit that summer, and with
it, Crosby's way of singing, slow and low and cool, became known
irrevocably as crooning. Many years later, there would be fancy talk
of Crosby's "discreet use of appoggiaturas, mordents, and slurs,"
and the *New York Times* would describe him as "a bel-canto baritone whose art disguises art." But back then, it was crooning pure
and simple. He worked the microphone as if it were a broad, weaving songs whose melodies seemed magically to merge with his natural breath. Young Dino was not alone. No singer who came after
Crosby would ever approach a microphone or a song without passing through his shadow.

Crosby switched radio networks in 1935, moving from CBS to
host the Thursday-night "Kraft Music Hall" on NBC. One of the
most powerful of the NBC stations was in Ohio. Broadcasting at
50,000 watts, WLW of Cincinnati had as much juice as any network
station in America. It was the station that in the late twenties had
launched the Mills Brothers, the Piqua, Ohio, teenagers who had
gone on to record with Crosby and become the most popular vocal
group of the era, the forebears of every black singing group to come.
"The Tom Mix Ralston Sharpshooters," premiering over NBC in the

fall of 1933, had come to radio a bit too late for Dino, for whom the call of the coyote had been drowned out by the greater call of soft-rustling silk-stockinged legs. But the music those legs moved to was everywhere, from the mighty WLW to Steubenville's own WIBR, operating out of the Sinclair Building at Market and Fourth.

Minstrelsy was still a going form of entertainment in the late thirties, and when the Theta Chi Alpha Fraternity on South Street—"Greek letters, but it was all Italian fellas," Archie Crocetti explained—presented a three-night minstrel show at the Grant School auditorium, Dino took part as a blackface singer.

There were dances every week—at the Capital Ball Room, the Catholic Community Center, the Florentine Ball Room, the Polish Hall; the Colonial Ball Room in Weirton. By the time he began working at the Rex, in 1936, Dino, urged on by his friends, was becoming a familiar presence onstage at many of those dances. "Dean would go to all of them, or most of them," remembered Christopher Christ, a former Grant School classmate, who was at the Capitol when Dean sang with Al Arter's orchestra and others. "Everyone knew that he had a pretty good voice, and he would always be enticed to get up and sing. After a while, all the orchestras knew him, and they welcomed it, because he did have a good voice." Christ saw what everyone close to Dean saw: "He wanted to sing more than anything else." And, as Christ said, "all the fellows from the cigar store were very supportive of him."

There was a blue law that forbade stage shows in Pittsburgh on Sundays. The big acts that played the Stanley Theatre there would often come across the river on the Lord's day to perform at the Capitol Theatre in Steubenville. One Sunday night, after playing the Capitol, Glenn Miller and a few of his bandmembers went upstairs to the ballroom. Dean was singing with Al Arter's group, and somebody asked Miller what he thought of the music. Archie Crocetti would never forget Miller's response: "Well, the music is pretty good. But that singer'll never make it."

"We used to cruise around," Mindy Costanzo recalled, "and Dino would sing in the car; we'd cruise around until four, five, six in the morning."

They went everywhere, especially where there was dancing, for "anyplace with dancin'," as Ross Monaco said, "was good for meetin' girls." They followed the music, even to the Ionic Club and other *tizzun'* joints, where few white boys ventured. "We used to hit 'em," Costanzo said. "They used to have nigger singers in 'em." There was music everywhere: at the Red Horse Tavern on Third Street, at the Venetian, which also operated after-hours, on Market. There was the Hy-Hat, Tony Lamantia's joint on North Fourth, where musicians from Pittsburgh would congregate on Saturday afternoons: drummer Mickey Scrima, who joined Harry James in 1939; pianist Dodo Marmarosa, who would later play with Gene Krupa, Charlie Barnet, Tommy Dorsey, Artie Shaw, and Charlie Parker.

They hit the high-class joints too: the Rainbow Gardens, out on Sinclair Avenue in Wintersville, and the Half Moon Nite Club. The Rainbow Gardens, owned by Tony Tarmano, then Al LaMann and others, was one of the places where Helen O'Connell got her start. By the time she moved from the Rainbow Gardens to the fancier Half Moon, Dino and the rest of them were all dying to get close enough to the blond singer to see if her cuffs, as they said, matched her collar. Jimmy the Greek, who was dealing there, was the worst of the bunch. "He would give her a corsage from Hawaii every goddamn day," Costanzo said. But she was gone before they knew it. In December 1938, Jimmy Dorsey heard her singing at the Village Barn in New York, and by February she was recording and touring with Dorsey.

Dino would later sing at the Half Moon as well. But it was at the downtown joints, the ball-and-beer boîtes, where he really spread his wings. His repertoire grew around the old standards and the Italian songs and the succession of hits from Crosby's pictures: "June in January," from *Here Is My Heart*, in 1934; "It's Easy to Remember," from *Mississippi*, in 1935; "Pennies from Heaven," from the picture of the same name, in 1936; "Sweet Leilani," Crosby's first million-selling record, from *Waikiki Wedding*, in 1937; "I've Got a Pocketful of Dreams," from *Sing, You Sinners*, in 1938. Dino saw *Sing, You Sinners* at the Paramount on North Fifth Street that autumn. It struck an ironic chord of recognition: Crosby, in his first substantial dramatic role, portrayed an irresponsible young gambler adrift amid his loving family's concern for him.

Typical of the places Dean sang in was Walker's, where, as Mindy Costanzo remembered it, "you could go, drink a beer for a dime, see a floorshow. They had a floorshow every night." Ross Monaco, who had emboldened Dino at Craig Beach, did the same at Walker's and the other joints as well. "I used to egg him on. I'd say, 'Why don't you take a shot, what d'ya got to lose?' That he kept at it was a surprise to me. Because he'd had some rough times."

George Mavromatis remembered Walker's as "a real tough bar. It usually wound up in a brawl in that place. Dino would go down there in the evenings. You buy him a beer, he'd sing what songs you want. They had a band there. Never was in tune. I never drank, to this day, and I was embarrassed to go in there, but I'd go in there with a couple buddies of mine because I wanted to hear him sing. He wasn't bad really. But that band, oh, Jesus."

One of the bands that played regularly at Walker's in the late thirties was a quintet called the Star Liters, whose piano player, Leo D'Anniballe, recalled Dean telling him, "There are only two people that really believe in me. That's my mother and myself." And he remembered Dino years later when he began coming into Walker's on Washington Street during his late-night breaks from the Rex.

"Even then, he had a great rapport with the audience. He had a mike technique even then. He always went over. It was more than just a local guy singing. He had a way of communicating with an audience, and they took to him. He was a very charismatic person."

Leo's brother Joe, a sax player, recalled Dean as "a little cocky and all, but well liked. He clowned a lot, but, I think, deep in his heart, he was serious. He liked to sing, and I guess that's why he stuck it out."

In the spring of 1939, Dino got work at the Mounds Club outside of Cleveland, a club owned by the Mayfield Road Gang, which had been involved in an ever-widening, shifting network of gambling joints since Prohibition days. Located near Chardon in the beautiful maple-grove country of Lake County, east of Cleveland, the Mounds was the Mayfield Road Gang's idea of paradise, a fabulously appointed joint that offered its patrons the biggest names in entertainment, fine dining, and a butt-fucking that left them broke and moaning for more.

Mike Simera, Smuggs Sperduti, Tony Torcasio, and others from Steubenville found work at the Mounds, where the money more than made up for the long ride back and forth. Dino went along for the ride more than once, and it was through the Mounds that the Mayfield Road Gang set him up as a singing croupier at another of their joints, the Jungle Inn, midway between there and Steubenville. He would be paid to deal, but he would sing for free. The experience, the exposure—the avuncular voices of Mayfield Road reminded him —these, of course, were things that one could not put a price upon. He also sang in Youngstown at the Merry-Go-Round Club, a joint run by Nick Constantino, one of the big brothers of the Mayfield Road Brotherhood Club, headquarters of the Cleveland mob.

"You ever get sick of this shit and want to lay in some real scratch, I'm here," Constantino told him in the spring of 1939.

"Doin' what?"

"Things."

Ernie McKay, a chubby, goofy-looking sort of guy who lived on Neil Avenue in Columbus, was the city's best-known bandleader. This renown, however, was less than great. The air-conditioning at the Club Gloria was given top billing not only over Bea Wain's All-Star Sepia Revue ("Harlem at Its Hottest"), but also over him, the great white rockin' rhythm man himself.

On a swing through Youngstown that summer, McKay caught Dino's act at the Jungle Inn. There was a big world out there, McKay told him. Columbus was already his. It was only a matter of time before that big old world beyond spread its jitterbugging legs as well. There was room in the outfit for an up-and-comer like Dino. They would go places together.

Dino told the guys at the Rex that he had been offered a full-time job singing. They encouraged him to take it; they told him he would be a fool not to. There was a big world out there, they told him. But McKay was only offering forty dollars a week, he equivocated. This was, of course, well over the average weekly salary of the common American working stiff, but hardly enough for a *shport*.

"I can't live on forty dollars a week," he said. "I steal that much here, for Chrissake."

They told him not to worry about it. He could always come back. Hell, they would help him out; they would tighten him up themselves. They took up a collection for him when he left for Columbus. "In fact," Tony Torcasio recalled, "there's a few times we were sending our tips" to Columbus.

McKay had an enterprising imagination. Ted Weems had that kid, Perry Como, from Freddie Carlone's band. Until a few years ago—he was Pierino then, not Perry—he had been a barber across the river in Cannonsburg. Harry James had hired a wop singer too, just this past June: some punk from Jersey by the name of Sinatra. Maybe wops were the way to go. What was that other wop's name? The one the broads went crazy for?

Nino Martini was the one. Martini had almost become another Valentino. Born in Verona, Italy, Martini had emerged as a singing gondolier in an early talking picture, *Paramount on Parade.* He had a brief stint at the Metropolitan Opera Company and finally settled for becoming a heartthrob, singing his way through such forgettable pictures as *Here's to Romance, The Gay Desperado,* and *Music for Madame.* His career had begun to fade, but a vestige of romance still lingered in his name.

Nino. Dino. There had to be a way, McKay figured, of tying together these two rhyming wop monikers into a top-shelf package of foolproof greaseball allure.

And so it came to pass that the first time Dino Crocetti saw his name in print, in the *Columbus Evening Dispatch* of November 24, 1939, it was no longer his own:

"The State Restaurant will have its final Saturday afternoon football party this weekend as Ohio State closes its gridiron season with Michigan at Ann Arbor. The McKaymen, with their 'Singing Strings Trio' and vocalist Dino Martini, will entertain football stay-at-homes at the luncheon, dinner, and supper sessions."

Ohio State lost, but there was more to Columbus than college football; and, while learning to sing "The Sweetheart of Sigma Chi," Dino got around. The Little Italy Night Club on Barthman Avenue offered three floorshows nightly. There was the new Ritz Club, and the Arabian Supper Club over on East Broad. Valley Dale brought in all the big bands. There was golf at Twin Rivers, out past the Club Gloria; racing at Beulah Park in nearby Grove City; boxing at the Columbus Auditorium; twenty-five movie houses. Moreover, Columbus was a city for chop-suey joints. And the State Restaurant, Ernie McKay's main venue, was one of them.

Located upstairs at 63½ East State Street, the State was run by Louis, Paul, and Harry Yee, three brothers who advertised their restaurant as having "SMART ATMOSPHERE! SMART ENTERTAINMENT! SMART DANCE BAND!" Louis, the head Yee, must have thought this Dino Martini was pretty smart himself. By mid-December, anyway, he was no longer merely a vocalist; he was a "sensation."

STATE RESTAURANT
ERNIE McKAY'S
"BAND OF ROMANCE"
STARRING
DINO MARTINI
NEW SINGING SENSATION
Luncheons from 35¢•Dinners from 55¢
LUNCHEON• DINNER• SUPPER• DANCING
NO COVER• NO MINIMUM

Dino worked three shows a day with McKay at the State, at half a yard a week plus all the chop-suey he could eat. Beginning on Christmas, the three daily shows were expanded by Yee into full-blown revues. Now, in addition to McKay and his new singing sensation, there were the ballroom-dancing team of Wayne and Roberta, the high-kick specialist Billy Ware, an "expert contortionist" known as the Great Eugene, and—enjoying a brief reprieve, Dino would say, on their way to Yee's chow-mein pot—Terry's Six Wonder Dogs.

Dino got his picture in the paper on the last Friday of the decade. In its guide to "New Year's Week-End Entertainers of Note," the *Dispatch* showed him, grinning before a microphone in a rented tuxedo and bow tie, flanked by two other dapper and awkward-looking gents. "Walter Phleuger, Dino Martini and Frank La-

Rue," the newspaper identified them, "are the 'Three Well-Wishers'
novelty singing trio with Ernie McKay's 'Band of Romance' at the
State restaurant."

> *"Some of the greatest orchestras that came out of Cleveland*
> *came out of Chinese restaurants."*
>
> MERLE JACOBS

During Prohibition, when the Mayfield Road Gang and the syndicate of Dalitz, Kleinman, Rothkopf, and Tucker held Cleveland in
their grasp, Austin J. Wylie—the man known as the Paul Whiteman
of Cleveland—made the music to which the city and the devil
danced.

The importance of the chow-mein connection in American jazz
has yet to be explored. Much has been said of the Negro, precious
little of the Cantonese. Yet surely, in Ohio at least, the legacy of the
rice paddy looms as large as that of the cotton field.

The Sammy Watkins orchestra was a Cleveland institution, the
reigning big band at Cleveland's top supper club, the Vogue Room
in the swanky Hollenden hotel. Sammy Watkins, born Samuel B.
Watkovitz, was married to a singer from Columbus who went by the
name of Lee Ann Lee, and it was she who told Sammy about some
crooner whose act she had caught in a Chinese restaurant during a
hometown visit in the winter of 1939–40. His name was Dino Martini, she said, and he was about as hep and as smooth as they came.
Sammy figured it was worth a call.

"Dean sent me a record," Watkins would say, "and in those
days, records weren't what they are today. They were tinny and
wavy. But Dean's voice came through very well. More than that.
There was this wonderful, easy way of singing. He always was loose
as a goose. He was born with that."

The two men met in the summer of 1940. Dino was twenty-two
years old. Watkins, who was thirty-five, was already wearing a toupee. It ran in the family; Sammy's brother, Sidney, wore one too.
Sammy's toupee was a fine one, so fine that few noticed it. But still,
it was there. Dino had always been self-conscious of his nose. But
Sammy's—to use Merle Jacobs's phrase—"Jewish features" were

dominated by a schnozz so bountiful that few men would have borne it with a grin of cheer, as Sammy did.

Sammy was doing well at the Hollenden, but the excitement was dwindling. The Vogue Room's main competition, the Terrace Room at the Statler Hilton, was going the Cuban route, and there was concern that the Hollenden would lose its dance patrons to the rumba. Sammy could see that Dick Marsh, whom hotel owner Theo DeWitt had brought in from Kansas City to manage the Hollenden, was trying to liven up things somehow. Just weeks ago, in June, Nan Blakstone had been booked into the Vogue Room to sing with Watkins. Blakstone, a silvery-haired singer known for her lasciviousness, had backfired in Marsh's face. She had not been able, Glen Pullen wrote in *Variety*, "to gauge accurately the tempo or mood of this somewhat bluenose town." Her performances "were far too torrid for even this spot's rather sporty clientele."

Dino had what the Sammy Watkins orchestra needed: young blood and sex appeal with a touch of class. The wop name, however, would have to go. After all, this was America. Could Sammy Watkovitz have gone as far as Sammy Watkins did? This wasn't the opera. None of that Caruso shit worked here. Dino protested. But what about that new Tommy Dorsey record, "I'll Never Smile Again," with that guy named Sinatra? A freak shot, Watkins replied. If Mussolini had declared war on England and France a week earlier, they would have changed the kid's name to Frankie Williams. Anyway, everything Dorsey touched turned to gold. Well, what about that clarinet player Watkins himself had, that Archie Rosati? Hell, Watkins said, there was a difference between a reedman and a singer. Reedmen were *supposed* to be zoo animals. Singers were like gods. Them actors—these were your American gods. You want to be a god, you got to have a god's name.

And so it came to pass, in the early autumn of 1940, that Dino Martini, who had entered this vale of jive as Dino Crocetti, was reborn as a god in Cleveland.

There was a lot about Cleveland to remind Dean of Steubenville. The whores were only a buck a crack, just like home. Here you could get away even cheaper: fifty cents, if you didn't mind *la carne nera*. The Gillsy on Ninth, the Erie over near St. John's Cathe-

dral—these were class whorehouses. So was the Milner, just up
Chester Street from the Roxy burlesque. BE FOXY—GO TO THE ROXY
advised the advertisements.

There were more than a dozen golf courses nearby. There was
racing—not always fixed—out at Thistledown, where "Moe" Dalitz
and the Big Four owned a sixty-percent piece. Right across from the
track, on Route 8, there was the East Side Drive-In Theatre. When
Dean arrived in town, the drive-in was presenting "the greatest
moral story ever filmed":

DAMAGED GOODS
ONE MOMENT OF ECSTASY . . . A LIFETIME OF SORROW!
THE PICTURE THAT DARES TO TELL THE TRUTH ABOUT . . .
DAMAGED GOODS
ADULTS ONLY!
The Greatest MORAL STORY Ever Filmed
See it in the Privacy of your own CAR!
WOULD YOU MARRY DAMAGED GOODS?

The New York Spaghetti House was still down on Ninth Street,
but most of the Italians by now had forsaken the old neighborhood
for Mayfield Heights. The bars closed at two, but there were after-
hours joints—"sneak joints," they called them here; a phrase left
over from Prohibition. The Lighthouse, over near the county morgue
at Ninth and Lakeside, was the most popular. The Greek coffee-
houses on Bolivar Road all offered round-the-clock booze and gambling. There were all-night restaurants too: the Nickel Plate Grill on
Broadway, and others. There was the Kit Kat Klub on Hough, the
3700 Club on Euclid, featuring Dolores, the Gorgeous Bombshell of
Rhythm, and her Parisian Divorcées. But the classiest joint in town
was what *Variety* called the "ultra-modernistic, intimate" Vogue
Room.

In the last century, five United States presidents, as well as the
president-maker himself, Mark Hanna, had occupied the Hollenden's bay-windowed suites. Now, behind the Victorian stateli-
ness of its red-brick facade, the hotel, as the chosen haunt of the
Cleveland *malavita*, hosted newer powers. Tony Milano, brother of

Frank Milano, *padrone* of the Mayfield Road Gang, was a familiar presence.

"I'm still here, kid." The face was different, the voice the same.

"Yeah. Things."

"Just a shot away."

The Sterling Hotel, on Prospect and Thirtieth, was where the Mayfield Road Gang put up gunmen recruited from out of town. But the Hollenden was the place they took their wives and their families and their mistresses. It was located conveniently near the Continental Press offices in the Ninth-Chester Building and its rear entrance was next-door to the Theatrical Grill, the restaurant at 711 Vincent Avenue that Mushy Wexler, a casino troubleshooter, had developed into the favorite schmoozing-place of his superiors. Short Vincent, as the winding little street—less than five hundred feet in length—was known, was the Calvary road of every lowlife in town. Amid the bars and girlie joints that stood like stations of the neon cross opposite the sacred Theatrical, an alley led directly to the backstage door of paradise itself, the Roxy. A man could find anything in that alley, it was said.

Short Vincent had run red with gore more than a few times, but none of it was ever tracked in to sully the Hollenden. This was one of the reasons why, as *Variety* observed, in its finest remedial heptalk, "Besides being the hangout of political nabobs, track promoters and money-boys," the Vogue Room "manages to hold a good class trade."

On Friday night, the first of November 1940, that good class trade, for a buck-fifty minimum, was privileged to enjoy the fruits of many muses. To open the show, there was Sigrid Dagnie, the "Beauteous Ballerina." Glen Pullen, who was there that night for *Variety*, remarked on her "Andalusian song-and-dance bits" and the "neat gown of burgundy and chartreuse that reveals her oomphy chassis." Next came Floretta and Boyette, "Mental & Mystic," with "a potpourri of mind-reading, magic and broad gags." Rex Weber, still billed as the "introducer" of the 1932 song "Brother, Can You Spare a Dime?" performed his "standard routine of ventriloquistic singing." The pianist Marion Arden filled the lulls of passage between acts, while Sorelli the Mystic roamed the audience, offering what the Vogue Room advertised as "Tableside Divinations." None of these acts was new that night to the Vogue Room; and, of course, neither was the featured attraction, Sammy Watkins and His Orchestra. But the young man whom Sammy introduced as Dean Martin, the young man who stepped forward acknowledging that improbable name—he was new.

A few days later, Pullen's review in *Variety* gave him his first national notice. "Nostalgic semi-swing arrangements of old pop numbers are its longest suit," Pullen wrote of the orchestra. "For another asset, Watkins has acquired a new vocalist, Dean Martin, who backs a personable kisser with a warm, low tenor and an agreeable manner."

Watkins was paid $1,000 a week at the Hollenden. Ten percent of that went to MCA, his agency. The seven bandmembers on the payroll received from fifty to seventy-five each, depending on what Sammy thought they were worth. Dean started out at thirty-five dollars a week, plus a free room and a 50-percent discount on food at the hotel. His salary rose as his local popularity increased. By February 1941, he was a featured part of the billing.

SAMMY WATKINS
and His Orchestra
with
DEAN MARTIN
Vocalist

But some strange new shit was brewing in the jazz clubs of New York. John Birks Gillespie, who had assumed the name Dizzy and was in 1941 one of three trumpeters in Cab Calloway's orchestra, would give that strange new shit a name five years later, when he and his All-Star Quintet released a record called "Be-Bop." The music of Sammy Watkins—"delightful, danceable music," as the Vogue Room advertised it—was on its way out. Once a hepster himself, Sammy was now, to use a term officially sanctioned by the *Original Handbook of Harlem Jive,* a "square." Bing Crosby, whom Dean still emulated, would, like the Dorseys and Goodman and James, remain in a state of semi-hipster grace throughout the de-

cade, fading into the pantheon of nostalgia as the patina of tradition
and inert respectability accrued. Dean was an effulgence of the
warp between the square and the fashionably cool; and, as such,
somehow always would elude the fate of the cool, which invariably
was to become the square. His was a cool that was rarely au cou-
rant. It was a preternatural cool, as divorced from the passing modes
of the day as he himself was from the world that in turn embraced
and discarded them. In Columbus he had made "The Sweetheart of
Sigma Chi" sound cool. Those college kids had been singing that
cornball song since 1912; but Dean sang it as he would sing about
any broad, as if she were real, as if she had a scent to luxuriate in,
silk panties to be whispered out of. And he made "Guess Who" and
Sammy's other creaking fox-trots sound cool too. He did not do what
those jazzbos did. He did not take old songs and modernize them
with improvisation or contrived invention. Instead he sang them as
if they belonged to no time at all, as if—and was it not true, regardless of any jazzbo's pretensions or any talk of art?—they were nothing more and nothing less than the colors of those seductions of the
heart that wove through the breezes of the old ways' obdurate
woods. They were there. They lighted upon him. He could feel
them. But the colors he sang rarely left the shadows of those woods.
Underneath the feeling in his voice, underneath the weaving of
those colors, there was always *lontananza*. His was the voice of a
man who would bring the boys of Sigma Chi to sentimental tears,
then go off to sneak-fuck their sweetheart before vanishing into the
night. As Tony Torcasio said, "He pissed ice water."

The women loved him, and he knew it. "He was a bastard," one
of them would recall, "all wine and candlelight, then a pat on the
ass in the morning." No, women were never a problem. But Dean
also knew that it was the men at the tables who were paying the
checks, and that those checks were the measure of his worth. He
developed a style of presence that he would never abandon. He
sang to the men rather than to the women. He sang to them as if
only they could truly understand him. Other singers worked to seduce the women in the audience. To him, that came naturally. He
worked to seduce the men, winning them, bonding them to his side
with the illusion of camaraderie. It was them he wanted, them he

needed. And he got them. Night after night, they would come, without jealousy or intimidation, enjoying him as a man's man, while their wives and lovers sat moistening beside them.

Two special women came to Cleveland in 1941. Dean would never forget either of them. One was Zorita, who arrived at the Roxy that cold March accompanied by her snake. It was a boa constrictor, but the Roxy, suggesting more venomous thrills, advertised ZORITA AND HER RATTLER. The other, snakeless, was a Swarthmore girl named Betty.

Elizabeth Anne McDonald, the youngest of William and Gertrude O'Neill McDonald's three daughters, had been born eighteen years before in the town of Chester in Delaware County, Pennsylvania. Her earliest years were spent in Morton, a smaller Delaware County town of barely a thousand souls not far from Philadelphia, and at nearby Swarthmore, where her family moved when she was seven. There, excelling at lacrosse, Betty Anne graduated from high school with three athletic scholarships to choose from. Her sisters were attending Smith College, from which they would both graduate with honors and go on to receive master's degrees. Betty's scholarship choices were Strasburg, Temple, and Swarthmore; and she decided on the last one because she thought her parents would be pleased to have her attend college in their hometown. She did well at sports, but not at her studies. Swarthmore dismissed her after one semester. Her father did not get angry, as she thought he would. In fact, Bill McDonald, seeing how disappointed and upset she was, proposed taking her along on a business trip to get her mind off things. He was a salesman for Oldetyme Distillers, and the company was sending him to Cleveland.

"We stayed at the Hollenden hotel," Betty remembered. "The first night, we went downstairs, and there was Dean singing in the dinner club with the Sammy Watkins band. Dean kept looking over at us and talking to the trombone player. I learned later that the trombonist had said, 'Don't you know who that is? That's Mayor Lausche and his daughter. Come on, I'll introduce you.' Well, Dean was afraid to take him up on it, I guess, because he knew his friend really had no idea who we were."

She was gorgeous to behold: a rosy, Irish-eyed, wavy-haired

brunette with an innocent but game and playful grin that seemed to promise things untold. Dean, as he drank in her looks, figured he would never see her again. But on that trip, Bill McDonald was told that he was being promoted to district manager. He would be moving to Cleveland, where he would work out of the regional office on Euclid Avenue. Betty stayed on with her father while he shopped for a house. As the days passed and Betty became a familiar presence in the hotel, Dean began to follow her about, striking up small talk when he could. She was flattered and hot to trot, but she feigned annoyance. Sensing her bluff, Dean finally asked her out. Betty later said they fell in love on that first date.

Bill McDonald found a house in suburban Cleveland Heights. His wife and other daughters joined him and Betty there in the spring of 1941. By then, Betty and Dean were chasing butterflies in each other's eyes.

Dean brought Betty to Steubenville that summer. He took her first to the Rex. As she later said, "He had to get their opinion of me. I guess I passed their inspection, because later that night he proposed."

The seductions of the heart had glamoured him. He loved her, and when she said yes, it made everything right. Man, as Dean knew, was put on earth for one reason. He had to produce in this world. *Mettere su famiglia.* It was the oldest of the old ways, after all. It was almost a duty as well as a blessing. And the Italians and the Irish—hell, every midwife and doctor knew it—they made beautiful children together. He could introduce her now to his mother and to his father, as he had never introduced a woman before, as his *fidanzata,* his betrothed. His parents were filled with happiness. All that gambling nonsense, all those strange, distant ways. It was as if they finally knew him, as if a chill had been banished by the familiar warmth of the hearth. And Betty, who had delivered him thus, seemed like an angel to them. Angela embraced her, promising her the finest wedding dress she ever fashioned.

The Sammy Watkins orchestra was scheduled to go on tour for several weeks beginning in early October. The guys in the band could tell that Dean was really in love: He wanted to take Betty along. Of course, to do so without being married would be to pub-

licly invoke the curse of Damaged Goods. The trouble was, the
Catholic Church back then required the posting of banns for at least
six weeks before a wedding. Betty went to her parish priest, Father
John Powers, the pastor of St. Ann's Church in Cleveland Heights.
The reverend surmised that Dean, as a sweet-singer in the grasp of
a Jew, fought Satan daily and doubly; and that he was only trying to
do the right thing. Furthermore, the McDonalds were no slouches
when the offering-basket came around. He granted the couple a
special dispensation; and on the first of October, Dean and Betty
went to the Cuyahoga County Court House and got their license,
which bore the rightful name of Dino Crocetti. The following morning, at St. Ann's Church, on Coventry Road, Father H. N. McCor-
mick pronounced them man and wife. Dean's family, Betty's family,
Sammy, the boys in the band, they all were there. And in Sorelli the
Mystic's crystal ball, refracted like a little rainbow, the tears of Irma
DiBenedetto did fall.

Dean and Betty spent their wedding night at the Hollenden, and
in the morning were off in the Sammy Watkins touring bus, headed
south toward Louisville.

The band returned to the Hollenden in late November. Joy
Hodges, "singing star of stage and screen" (she had appeared five
years ago in a small role in *Follow the Fleet),* replaced Dean while
he took time off to settle in with Betty at their new home, a fur-
nished apartment at 2820 Mayfield Road in Cleveland Heights.
They went together to the new Bing Crosby picture, *Birth of the
Blues,* at the Loew's State; and they were together when they saw the
Plain Dealer headline on the eighth of December:

JAPS WAR ON U.S., BRITAIN;
BOMB HAWAII, PHILIPPINES;
CONGRESS TO HEAR F.D.R.

What Congress heard, and answered, was a call for the declaration of war against Japan. That same day, by executive order, all
Italian noncitizens—Dean's uncle Jimmy was one of them—were
designated as enemy aliens. Three days later, on December 11,
America was at war with Italy and Germany as well as Japan. A few

months earlier, *L'Araldo,* the Cleveland Italian-language newspaper, had praised Mussolini and hailed the alliance of Italy, Germany, and Japan as "the foundation on which future mankind will be organized." Now the Italian language itself was uttered only with caution.

Dean returned to the stage of the Vogue Room a few days later. He celebrated his second New Year's Eve with the band. In February, they hit the road again. This time, Betty stayed behind. It was not only because she was pregnant. The breeze between them was already cooling.

Back in Steubenville, Guy and Angela Crocetti had moved once again, to 2130 Sunset Boulevard. It was to that address that Dean's draft notice was sent in the spring of 1942. Mindy Costanzo, Ross Monaco, who, like Dean, was a married man now—they were already overseas, fighting. Jiggs Rizzo had received his notice as well, and they rode together to the induction center in Columbus.

"They don't want me," Dean told him. "I got a hernia."

He was right. They did not want him. And there was more in his abdominal cavity than he knew: It was a double hernia. He returned to Cleveland, classified 4-F.

Sammy Watkins and His Orchestra, however, were an important part of the homefront war effort, for Sammy had pledged to give a free show at any war-production plant that agreed to send a million cigarettes to the fighting troops. Through shows at General Electric Nela Park and other war-plant locations, the band proudly raised twenty-five million cigarettes for the boys overseas.

Dean turned twenty-five on the seventh of June, and twenty-two days later he became a father. At seven-thirty on the morning of June 29, precisely nine months after their wedding night, nineteen-year-old Betty gave birth at Evangelical Deaconess Hospital. Dean wanted to be with his wife when their child was born. But he fainted in the cab on the way to the hospital with her; and, as he sat and paced and smoked in the hospital waiting-room that morning, he came to the conclusion that womankind was meant to bear its blessed issue alone.

It was a boy, as Dean had hoped it would be. They named him

Stephan Craig Martin. The father's name on the certificate of birth
was registered as Martin as well. The *cognome* of Crocetti was *finito*.

The "Fitch Bandwagon" had been broadcast by NBC since
1932, when F. W. Fitch began marketing Fitch Shampoo nationally.
It was a half-hour Sunday-night show, and was carried in Cleveland
by WTAM, the 50,000-watt NBC station that was older than the
network itself. The "Bandwagon" held contests in various cities to
determine the most popular local bands, and performances by the
winners were broadcast nationally from their hometowns. That summer, while they were busy raising cigarettes for liberty, Sammy
Watkins and His Orchestra were voted Cleveland's favorite; and, at
half past seven on the Sunday evening of July 5, six days after the
birth of Stephan Craig Martin, the band gathered at the WTAM
studio on Superior Avenue.

For his coast-to-coast debut, Dean sang four songs. "What'll I
Do?" was an old Irving Berlin piece, recorded by Paul Whiteman
and others in 1924. "Sweet Leilani" was Crosby's big hit of 1937.
The other two were new wartime songs that Sammy had gotten from
publishers in New York and worked up especially for the occasion:
"A Boy in Khaki, a Girl in Lace" had been recorded only three days
before by Tommy Dorsey and His Orchestra; "So Long, Until Victory," by a songwriter named Frank Paul Forziano, would not be
copyrighted until three months later.

As America listened, announcer Tobe Reed closed out the momentous occasion: "You have been listening to the music of Sammy
Kaye!"

Stephan Craig Martin—he would grow up as Craig; the first
name would be forgotten—was baptized at St. Ann's on August 15.
Betty's parents had moved back to Pennsylvania. Dean's mother
and his brother, Bill, who was now working as a government inspector, came to Cleveland as godmother and godfather.

On the first of December, gas rationing, which had been in
effect in the eastern states since the previous spring, was extended
throughout the country. On the fourth, American airplanes bombed
Naples. There was no end to the war in sight. Dean, however, had it
good compared to most of the guys from the old days. Those of them

who were not overseas were still hustling. Poor Joe DiNovo was already gone, taken not by the war but by leukemia.

Dean had started out in Cleveland at thirty-five bucks a week plus room and board. By 1943 he was pulling down fifty every payday. He was well known in Cleveland. Advertisements for the Vogue Room featured a caricature of him.

THIS IS OUR CROONER,

DEAN MARTIN

EVERY SONG HE PUTS HIS

HEART-IN

HEART THROB DANCE MUSIC BY

SAMMY WATKINS

AND HIS ORCHESTRA

But, then again, Johnny Gallus, "the Jocular Juggler on the Jive Side," and Nella Webb, "Noted Reader of Horoscopes," were featured attractions too. Sometimes he felt as if he would remain forever in this glass-doored, ultra-modernistic, air-conditioned purgatorio, ending up with a toupee of his own, crooning "Guess Who" and "Sweet Leilani" to the ghosts of a dream gone wrong.

In the summer of 1943, a few days after he turned twenty-six, Dean told Sammy that he wanted more. Sammy had a contract drawn up. Signed by them on July 3, the contract stipulated that through June 30, 1944, Martin was "to render his best artistic services" to Sammy Watkins and His Orchestra, and, "as remuneration for said employment," Watkins was to pay "the sum of Sixty-five Dollars ($65.00) per week," except for those weeks when the orchestra was not active. In addition, the agreement gave Watkins a cut of any and all monies paid to Martin for outside work, as well as the right to renew the agreement every year for four years simply by giving Dean ten days' notice of his intention to exercise this option.

It was a contract that he soon wanted out of, for a month later a call came from New York. Frank Sinatra, the rage of the bobby-soxers, had canceled an engagement, but it was a relatively low-paying engagement at a chic Manhattan nightclub, the Riobamba, on East Fifty-seventh Street, and the club's managers, Linton Weil and Arthur Jarwood, were looking frantically for another headliner. They had managed to get Jane Kean, a singer and comedienne who was then starring in the Broadway musical hit *Early to Bed*. But they wanted another crooner, another wop wonder like that bastard Sinatra. Sinatra's agency, the powerful Music Corporation of America, had called its Cleveland office, run by Merle Jacobs. Jacobs, who represented Sammy Watkins, said he had just the singer the Riobamba needed.

Italy surrendered that September. Mussolini escaped into Abruzzi, to a hideout in the Gran Sasso Mountains, those mountains from whose shadows Gaetano Crocetti and his brothers long ago had escaped; escaped to this land of strange names and strange ways, this land where Giuseppe had become Joe, and Crocetti had become Martin, and men with names like Weil owned joints with names like Riobamba. It was hard to tell who or what was real, anywhere. Was the real Italy the one that had turned overnight to join the fight against Germany, the one that had gone to sleep singing "Faccetta Nera" and risen the next morning singing "God Bless America"? Or was it the one hiding in the *abruzzese* hills?

The September 26 Sunday edition of the *Cleveland Plain Dealer* contained the usual, weekly Vogue Room advertisement for Sammy Watkins and His Orchestra, "featuring DEAN MARTIN." There was also an advertisement that day in the *New York Sunday Mirror*, for the "bright, new revue" at the Riobamba:

SPECIALLY ADDED
DEAN MARTIN
THE NEWEST FASHION IN SONG STYLE

Before Cleveland knew he was gone, Dean Martin had proved that his word—*fuck everything*—was his bond.

VI.

*L*OVE AS A
RACKET

*B*efore he could open at the Riobamba, Dean had to sign an exclusive contract with MCA. And before he could sign an exclusive contract with MCA, he had to be released from the contract he had signed with Sammy Watkins.

On September 23, the eve of the opening, Watkins met in Manhattan with Dean, who had checked into the Astor Hotel at Broadway and Forty-fourth Street. Watkins brought with him a new contract, which, if signed, would annul the old and grant Martin the freedom he sought.

It stated that Watkins was "willing to comply with the request of Martin, but only upon the terms, covenants and conditions hereinafter set forth." In agreeing to those terms, covenants, and conditions, Martin would have to sign away to Watkins ten percent of all his gross income for the next seven years.

Dean signed, then proceeded to sign the MCA contract, which called for ten percent of his gross income as well. He was thus left with eighty percent of himself, before taxes.

"There's other ways," somebody, one of the shadows at the Riobamba, a voice reminiscent of Cleveland brotherhood, told him.

He opened at the Riobamba the next night, Friday, September 24. He was allotted only eight minutes on stage. The band, Charles Baum's Society Orchestra, was new to him.

He stood there and he smiled and he did what he had been doing for years, in the backseat of that Auburn and that chop-suey joint on State Street and the Vogue; and, yes, the people who sat there before him, aloof and in judgment, they were fancy people, the cream of society, but they were really only dolled-up, high-rent versions of all the smart-talking suckers who had ever passed before him, from the Rex to the Mounds to the clubs of Short Vincent. All

he had to do was fill the *lontananza* with those sweet colors of his,
those seductions, those lies that went so well with wine; all he had
to do was remember to sing to the men; the women, Irma
DiBenedettos in ermines and pearls, were already his.

Earl Wilson gave him a mention in his *New York Post* column
the following morning: "The Riobamba has a hell of a good crooner
in this new Cleveland boy, Dean Martin." Lee Mortimer's column in
the *Mirror* that Sunday was less kind: "In Sinatra's singing spot is a
chap by the name of Dean Martin, who sounds like him, uses the
same arrangements of the same songs and almost looks like him."
Least kind of all was the review in that week's *Variety*.

> Cleveland's entry in the swoon-stakes is Dean Martin,
> a thin-visaged, dark-haired baritone who's making his New
> York debut with this date. The New York competition is apt
> to be a little too tough.
> Martin, seemingly, would be lost without that mike.
> He's lacking in personality, looks ill-fitting in that dinner
> jacket and, at best, has just a fair voice that suggests it
> would have little resonance without the p.a. system.

But the crowd loved him, and, as he was held over again and
again at the Riobamba that autumn, the press changed its tune.
Variety saw him now as "a vocalist with definitely big possibilities"
and "a distinctive song stylist, with a casual type of delivery, which
seems surefire for stage, screen or radio." Lee Mortimer's *Mirror*
comparison of him to Sinatra was revised into a compliment. Dean,
he now said, "sings and looks like Sinatra—only healthier." *Billboard* praised his "easy and fluid delivery." Dorothy Kilgallen of the
New York Journal-American proclaimed him a "threat to Frank Sinatra." The *Herald Tribune* placed him "among the Top Nite Club
Singers of the Nation," and Nick Kenny of the *Daily Mirror* predicted that "Dean will be the biggest singing star of 1944."

Just as his name was not his own, so it was with his songs. His
showstoppers, his most requested numbers, were songs irrevocably
associated with others. "Sunday, Monday, or Always" had been

written by Johnny Mercer and Jimmy Van Heusen for the recent
Bing Crosby picture, *Dixie*. "Paper Doll," written by Johnny Black,
had been recorded in 1942 by the Mills Brothers. It had attracted
little popularity upon its initial release, but, reissued in the summer
of 1943, it had gone on to become, after Crosby's "White Christmas," the biggest hit of the decade. "My Melancholy Baby" had
been around for more than thirty years. George Norton and Ernie
Burnett had written it in 1911, and by the time Bing Crosby's version had come out, in 1939, the song, like the 1909 hit "I Wonder
Who's Kissing Her Now," another of Dean's early mainstays,
seemed to have been around forever, a mossy artifact from the
Urschleim of Tin Pan Alley sentimentality. Yet Martin, according to
Louis Sobol of the *Journal-American,* delivered the song "so beautifully" that Sobol extended him—ahem—"a standing invitation to
come to my house every night to sing it for me."

He had a gift for tapping into that Ur-slime, a gift for slipping
the songs of others, like so many silver dollars, into the oversized
shoes of his own nascent style.

He was held over at the Riobamba through Christmas, making
$150 a week. He sang as a guest that autumn on two afternoon radio
shows as well, "The Home Front Matinee," on WABC, and "Full
Speed Ahead," on WOR.

Dean and Betty moved into the London Terrace Apartments in
the Chelsea section of Manhattan. Dean was making good money,
but he was blowing more than he made. He had to turn to another
wayfarer, the comedian Gene Baylos, for money to buy a turkey and
other tidings to put on the table that Thanksgiving. "Yeah," Baylos
would recall almost forty years later. "I lent him twenty dollars. And
I went home on the subway to the Bronx."

Little Craig was eighteen months old that Christmas, and Betty
was six months pregnant.

They used to make love and laugh. Now they fucked and fought.
How long, after all, could butterflies live? Love was a racket. It was
like booze. It exhilarated you, it transported you, and in the end it
fucked you over and left you feeling like shit.

But God, in his infinite wisdom, had created chorus girls. Dean found one of the newest in town. Back in Beloit, Wisconsin, they knew her as Dora Fjelstad, but now, after coming in fifth in the 1943 Miss America Pageant, she was calling herself Gregg Sherwood, the name under which she danced in the line at the Latin Quarter and posed for *Beauty Parade* and other pinup magazines. Dean, who was as unknown then as she, was only a warm-up for what followed. Later, after an affair with Joe DiMaggio, Sherwood married Walter Sherwin, the box-office treasurer of the New York Yankees. Claiming to be an heir to the Sherwin-Williams Paint fortune, Sherwin lavished her with extravagance. After he was indicted for grand larceny and forgery, Sherwood found the real thing, and went on to become the fifth wife of the aging motorcar scion and besotted millionaire Horace E. Dodge II. New York was full of Dora Fjelstads. It was a city full of fresh, conniving, cock-fancying damsels; sweet *fica*, untainted by motherhood's holiness, ripe for the harvesting.

MCA arranged for Dean's picture to appear on the cover of *Billboard* in January 1944, as the agency sent him out of town on the Statler Hotel circuit, first to Buffalo, then to Boston and elsewhere. Betty went to stay with her parents, in Ridley Park outside Philadelphia. It was there, on March 16, while Dean was performing in Montreal, that Betty gave birth to a daughter, Claudia Martin.

Dean and Betty brought the kids to Steubenville that spring. Archie Crocetti, the cousin to whom he was closest, had married Violet Schiappa, and he and Violet had a place on Railroad Avenue. Dean, Betty, and the kids stayed there with them, as well as with Guy and Angela. They also spent a lot of time with Smuggs Sperduti and his sweetheart, Bernice Del Villan.

Bernice and Smuggs were coming out of a movie theater on South Sixth Street one afternoon when they saw Betty walking— stalking, really—toward them, a sole white glaring face amid a crowd of blacks. Two blocks behind her, they could see Dino.

"I'm so mad," Betty said. Her blue eyes were contracted points of cold sapphire wrath.

"What happened?" Bernice asked.

"I'm gonna leave him."

There had been an argument, uglier than usual, at Archie's place. Bernice walked her to the Pennsylvania Railroad Station. Betty, who had left the kids with Angela, borrowed ten dollars from Bernice and took the next train to Philadelphia. Later, Bernice told Dean what had happened.

"Ah, let her go," he said.

Steubenville held nothing for him now but the ghosts of memory, adrift in faint springtime sadness. One of those ghosts followed him back to Manhattan. It was the *citrullo* who had managed his ill-fated boxing career. Recently discharged from the army, with a few hundred bucks in mustering-out money, he proposed that he become the manager of Dean's new career. They would go places together. He knew people in New York, friends of friends back home. Nice people, Italian people.

Dean had never been good with money. Whatever came to him, he squandered. Back in Cleveland, his pockets and his pay had barely met. Almost every Saturday, he had hit up Sammy for a loan of an extra fin. The yard and a half each week at the Riobamba had gone the same way. He drank, he gambled; awhirl in a blue-mirrored neon dream of laughter and music and spermatobibulous showgirls, he threw it around as if he were *un pezzo grosso*, a big shot. The London Terrace was evicting him for nonpayment. He was behind on his commissions to MCA. Sammy had not seen shekel one from that mocky Magna Carta of his. There were tabs, bookies, shylocks, grocery bills. He had even tried driving a cab for a few weeks, to make a few bucks off the books. It was fucking ridiculous.

And so, for two hundred bucks, Dean sold another piece of himself. It was as if those apples from Grant School had come back to haunt him. He was dividing himself into oblivion. But like those Grant School apples, these percentages meant nothing to him. The *citrullo* decided that as Dean's new manager, he should have an all-American name too, just like his star client. Thus Dick Richards, setting up office at 1560 Broadway, became the personal manager of Dean Martin, under the direction of MCA Artists, Ltd. Dean moved into the Belmont Plaza Hotel on Lexington Avenue between Forty-ninth and Fiftieth streets.

The five-year contract Dean signed with Richards on April 25,

1944, entitled his new "exclusive manager" to ten percent of "all gross receipts over and above $300 and up to $750 per week," fifteen percent of everything between $750 and $1,000, and twenty percent beyond that. The arrangement was to be automatically renewed for an additional five years unless Richards decided otherwise.

One of the people whom Richards knew in Manhattan was a guy named Rario, who ran La Martinique, a nightclub at 57 West Fifty-seventh Street. Richards not only knew people, he had a way with words as well; and when Dean was booked into La Martinique in early June, he was advertised as:

THE DEAN OF THE 'VOICES'
DEAN MARTIN
The Boy with the Tall, Dark and Handsome Voice

Nightclubs went through hard times that spring. A new thirty-percent cabaret tax, enacted on April 1 and subsequently passed along to patrons as a surcharge, had led to a steep decline in business. On June 11, La Martinique became one of several nightclubs to temporarily shut down. Business began to rebound when the tax was cut to twenty percent, coinciding with the burgeoning air of celebration and optimism that came in the wake of D-Day. In late June, Dean was booked into the Harlequin on the East Side.

The reviews were good. "A tall, dark good-looking lad, Martin has one of the best deliveries heard in these parts for many a long day," wrote Bill Smith of *Billboard*. "Baritone voice is clear and steady and manner is calculated to make fem hearts pop." His rendition of "Melancholy Baby," said Smith, "had the gals applauding wildly and their boy friends joining in." Lee Mortimer of the *Daily Mirror* wrote that Dean, "as usual, swoons the dames and makes the guys cheer."

Not every guy cheered. Among those caught up in that summer's air of celebration, there were many who resented the fact that a young man—a greaseball, no less: just look at that fucking face; he wasn't kidding them with that "Martin" shit—should be standing around dolled-up on a stage, making fem hearts pop while other young men were off stalking through France popping krauts with bayonets.

"What are you, 4-F or somethin'?" one of them hollered one night from a ringside table at the Harlequin. There was laughter amid the disquiet in the room. Dean glanced away and let it pass. But the guy kept it up. Dean looked into his fat fucking cunt-eating face. He needed this drunken bastard like he needed another fucking hernia. He muttered something in Italian, the meaning of which was not understood but the wrath of which was sensed. The drunk reached into his pocket; Dean dove from the stage as the switch-blade emerged. They crashed down together, and the blade of that cocksucker's impotence fell aside, and Dean took that fat head like a melon between his hands and bashed it to the floor. Then other drunken bastards were upon him, and, swinging out, he lurched upright, and, swinging still, lunged through them to the door and out into the street, while the bouncer and others blocked the way behind him.

Dean made $200 a week at the Harlequin. The London Terrace Apartments, from which he had been evicted, had placed a $30-a-week lien on his earnings through MCA, to whom he also owed money for unpaid commissions. Under a special arrangement, the Harlequin paid him nightly in cash to help him evade the lien. Still, he managed to come out broke at the end of each week. And soon he would be without a home as well. Betty was traveling back and forth with the children between Manhattan and Ridley Park. In Manhattan, she would fight with Dean. In Ridley Park, she would fight with her parents. She had married a loser, her mother told her, a bum. She had never drunk much when she first met Dean. But Dean had liked to hang out. In his own odd way, he was far more sociable than she. Society, small talk, and drinks seemed to serve as a distraction for him. So she had begun to drink with him; and, as the years passed and they spent less and less time together amid that distraction, she would drink more and more alone to escape into numbness from the fights with her mother and the fights with him and the wailing of the kids, who had become her only happi-

ness in this whole fucking mess that her life, at the age of twenty-
one, had become. It almost made her laugh: Dean, out there in those
nightclubs, singing "Melancholy Baby" to a bunch of dopey young
twats, while she, who had once been one of them, sat there in
Ridley Park, drinking by herself; them wanting him, and she having
him, and this—nothingness, a certain anxious tightening in the
chest—being what having him came down to.

Lou Perry of the American Guild of Variety Artists had met
Dean through Arthur Jarwood at the Riobamba last fall, and the two
had gotten to know one another in the months since then. Perry,
who was in his late thirties, wanted to leave his job as a union
organizer and become a manager, and had set up his own office as
such in the AGVA building at 1697 Broadway. In the summer of
1944, while Dean was playing at the Harlequin, Perry began court-
ing him as a prospective client. In June, Dean moved out of the
Belmont Plaza and into the cheaper Bryant Hotel at Broadway and
Fifty-fourth Street, where Perry also kept a room. In early August,
after Dean ran up a bill at the Bryant that he could not pay, Perry
let him move in with him.

Perry's protégé Sonny King, another ex-boxer who had turned
singer and lost his rightful Italian name along the way, was already
sharing his room at the Bryant. Sonny was from Brooklyn, but he
was too proud to go home and admit that he was not making it as a
big shot in New York.

"There was a pullout couch that would sleep two," Sonny remembered of the accommodations in Room 616 at the Bryant. "One
week, Dean would sleep in the couch with Lou, and I would sleep
on the floor on the cushions from the couch. Next week, I would
sleep in the couch and Dean would have the floor. This went on for
about a year and a half."

Dean and Sonny routinely shared the fifteen-cent breakfast special at Nedick's on Times Square: a glass of orange juice, a doughnut, and a cup of coffee. "Dean would drink half the orange juice,
half the coffee, eat half the doughnut. I'd say something like, 'You
better go sign those contracts'; he'd say, 'Finish this for me.' "

Every once in a while, Dean and Sonny would put on a private exhibition match at the Bryant. "We did it for money," Sonny said. The admission was "five bucks a head." Those who paid, however, were too insistent on seeing blood drawn. Sonny had fought as a light heavyweight. "Dean felt that I should respect him because he was older than me. That meant that he could punch the shit out of me, but I shouldn't do it to him." Sonny almost got killed one day. His chest would bear the scars of that last exhibition match for the rest of his life.

"Dean knocked me out the window. I clung onto the metal blinds. If it wasn't for that, I would've gone down six floors."

There was no knowing Dean, Sonny came to realize. "Dean never trusted anyone or opened up to anyone." He was "always distant. Once in a while, he'd say to me, 'You're my best buddy,' but in such a manner that you wouldn't believe it. And Dean was even like that with Betty, and she was a wonderful girl."

There was a woman whose identity Sonny would never later reveal. "A very, very prominent girl. A gorgeous woman. She was living at a hotel for women. We would sneak up the fire escape at night. Dean was seeing her, I was seeing her girlfriend. We got nailed one night too." But Dean did not take her seriously either.

"The only one he ever took seriously," Sonny would say, "was himself."

Lou Perry took Dean golfing out at Oceanside, Long Island, several times that summer. To show Dean how much he could do for him as a personal manager, Perry helped him get his own radio show (although it was Richards who paid for the audition recording, $3.03 on June 26). It was to begin later that summer. Dean thought about it: Why the hell shouldn't he sign with Perry? Dick Richards, whoever the fuck he was, whatever the fuck he was, seemed to have run out of Rarios. Besides, maybe managers were like horsepower; maybe the more you had, the faster you got where you were going. So, late that summer, Dean agreed to sell a thirty-five-percent interest in himself to Lou Perry.

Frank Military was another who ended up at Room 616 in the Bryant. He was working as a receptionist at MGM Pictures when he first met Lou Perry, who came in every once in a while trying to arrange a screen test for Dean.

"What are you doing here at MGM?" Perry said to him one day. "Why don't you come with us? You'll learn the business. You'll be my partner. How much money do you have?"

"I have about four hundred in the bank."

"Give me the four hundred, you're my partner."

Looking back, almost half a century later, Military laughed. "I gave him the four hundred, quit my job, and went to work for him for no salary. Ended up sleepin' in the goddamn bathtub in the Bryant. But I had such fun, and I learned so much. Dean and I used to take walks down Forty-second Street at two o'clock in the morning. We'd go to the movies, talk to the screen: 'Watch out, he's comin'!' "

Military remembered Dean chasing after Janie Ford, a young singer from Texas whom Perry also managed. "Dean was always lookin' to make her," he said. Military's closest friends back then were a pair of Broadway bookmakers known as Johnny Buff and Peppi. Dean and Military would make the rounds with them as they went from one nightclub to another taking care of business.

"They were real tough guys. Johnny Buff was like my brother. And they were very close to Dean. He and I were out with them all the time. Every night, we went to five or six different clubs. The Copacabana. Tony Canzoneri's joint. Abe Attell's joint. The Carnival. The Latin Quarter. Wherever we'd go, we always had something. The reason we ate is that they used to take us out to eat."

Meanwhile, another player entered the scene.

Together since 1936, Bud Abbott and Lou Costello had developed since 1940 into one of MCA's biggest acts. Their NBC radio show was about to enter its third and most popular year, and their twelfth movie, *In Society*, was released that August. Costello was then thirty-eight. He had been stricken the year before with rheumatic heart disease, but it had not daunted him; and since the loss of his year-old son in November, he had been drinking more than before. He was making the rounds in New York one night with his manager, Eddie Sherman, when they stopped in at the Harlequin, where Dean was appearing. Both Lou and Sherman were impressed by the way Dean seemed to hold the women in the room in sway. Sherman, who had been a booking agent in Philadelphia, was later warned against Dean by his friend Jack Lynch, who ran the Walton Roof in Philly. "I want to give you a tip: steer clear of him. He's got thirty different managers and each has got a piece of him. And he drinks." Sherman told Lou what Lynch had said. But Lou, whose father had been an immigrant from Italy and whose real name was Cristillo; Lou, who had been baptized in St. Anthony's Church in Paterson, New Jersey; Lou, who drank and who gambled and who fucked around and loved his kids and his mother; Lou, whom Lucky Luciano called "a no-good prick"—Lou and Dino hit it off just fine. Twenty-five percent for a grand seemed fair. Costello's New York lawyer, I. Robert Broder, drew up the contract.

Menefreghismo knew no bounds. Without a home, heavily in debt, and with a growing family to support, he had now almost wholly divested himself of any interest in himself. Ten percent to MCA, ten percent to Sammy Watkins; twenty percent to Richards, thirty-five to Perry, twenty-five to Costello. That left him with five percent of himself; fifty dollars, before taxes, from every grand he made. But even that—before taxes, after taxes—meant nothing to him. He had not filed a return since leaving Cleveland.

But it was all only make-believe, *nevvero?*

Before Dick Richards got hit with the news, Dean let him take care of a few things for him: a down payment of $18.54 to Howard Clothes; a bill for $80 from the Belmont Plaza; one for $80.91 from the Bryant; $25 to the London Terrace; $12.38 to Bernstock Photos for publicity glossies; $2.22 to Cowan Music Supplies; and other odds and ends. And then there was the $250 to Dr. Irving B. Goldman, the $99.86 to Mount Sinai Hospital on August 16.

Dean was twenty-seven, and he had hated the snout that God had given him for as many of those years as he could remember. It was a curse. Costello, who was talking about putting Dean in the movies with him and Abbott, agreed. The melancholy babies loved him as he was. He had lipstick traces on his shorts to prove it. But the same broads who went gaga for him across a dark room would laugh if they saw that fucking *cucuzza* plastered across a movie screen. And look what they were calling him in the papers: "the schnozzola Sinatra."

In mid-August he looked in the telephone directory, and he found what he wanted.

FACIAL RECONSTRUCTION
Mis-shaped NOSES *of all Types,*
re-shaped and Corrected

It cost five hundred bucks for rhinoplasty to undo what the lord of snouts had done. But Dean ended up spending far more than that. None of it, of course, was his own. Originally, Lou Costello advanced him the money for the operation, but Dean squandered it instead. Dean then turned to Johnny Buff and Peppi, who agreed to front the money under one condition: They would pay the doctor directly, without a dollar of it passing through Dean's hands. The medical bills paid by Dick Richards that August would seem to represent the balance.

"Dean Martin's nose operation a big success," proclaimed the *Daily Mirror.*

Dean's WMCA radio show, "Songs by Dean Martin," had its premiere two nights later, on August 21. Relying heavily on recorded music, talk shows, and news programs, WMCA president Nathan Straus and musical director Jerry Sears envisioned Dean's show as an early-evening refreshment of live music: fifteen minutes of songs with the Sears Orchestra every weeknight at a quarter to eight. Dean's pay was $75 a week. Eventually the show would have a sponsor: Littman's Department Store. Sonny King would get a kick out of those few bars Dean had to sing every night: *"In her sweet little Alice blue gown . . ."*

Dean hired Sears as his arranger, promising him—what the fuck—ten percent of his income. He had now done the impossible. He had sold a hundred and five percent of himself, more of him than there was.

He was scheduled to return to La Martinique when it re-opened the following month. That engagement was canceled as Richards in his anger turned from fighting Perry to denouncing Dean himself. He ended up suing Dean for $15,000, settling out of court for a promise of $2,600. Jerry Sears would later settle as well, relinquishing his contract with Dean for a cash payment of a few hundred dollars. *The Billboard 1944 Music Year Book* had already gone to press. The full-page advertisement for Dean, who was still—albeit now unpunctuated—"The Boy with the Tall Dark and Handsome Voice" as well as "America's Newest Singing Sensation," not only pictured him pre-nosejob; it also listed Richards as his personal manager and plugged the aborted return engagement at La Martinique. Even *Billboard* would end up suing him, for an unpaid advertising balance of $954.10.

Perry and Costello, meanwhile, got along well. Through MCA, Perry booked Dean into the Glass Hat, the nightclub in the Belmont Plaza, where Dean had stayed during the spring. Then, together, Perry and Costello negotiated with MCA to buy out Dean's contract. Costello's clout at MCA, and the fact that Dean had brought more trouble than income to the company, facilitated the deal. While Perry and Costello announced to the press that it was a five-grand buy-out, MCA let Dean go for $545, only $200 plus the amount he owed in unpaid commissions.

"Top slotting" at the Glass Hat's new show on August 31 went, as *Billboard* put it, "to warbler Dean Martin and his new schnozz." Dean had been in New York for less than a year, but already there was a jaded and imperious edge to his presence. The Glass Hat was supposed to be a class operation, but the sound system was rotten, the waiters were noisy, and Frank Law, who managed the club, did not seem to give a shit one way or the other. He might as well be singing in a fucking chop-suey joint in Columbus.

"Hey, pallie, get your own microphone," he suggested from the stage to a customer whose voice he deemed too loud.

While noting—"a word of friendly warning to Martin"—that it was "weak showmanship to show impatience with payees when they make too much noise," Bill Smith of *Billboard* once again expressed praise for him: "Lad is one of the better stylists around town who can sing and sell a song with the best of 'em." Along with "Melancholy Baby," his versions of Bing Crosby's recent hit "San Fernando

Valley" and "Is You Is or Is You Ain't (Ma Baby)," which had just been released by Crosby and the Andrews Sisters, "won hefty mitts from those who could hear him."

Sharing the bill with Dean and Payton Re's orchestra at the Glass Hat were two dance acts, Vivian Newell and the team of Cappella and Patricia. There was also a comedian of sorts, a creepy-looking Jewish kid by the name of Jerry Lewis.

VII.

TIMES SQUARE

$\mathcal{D}$anny Levitch was going to be the next Al Jolson. But things had not worked out that way.

Born on Manhattan's Lower East Side in 1902, he had grown up in the Brownsville section of Brooklyn, working in his father's wine cellar. All he wanted, like that rabbi's blackfaced son, was to rock-a-bye the world with a Dixie melody. Like Jolson, he changed his name; and, as Danny Lewis, he found work singing. By the time he was twenty, and fame and glory were not forthcoming, he took a job as a song-plugger for the Manhattan publishing company of Fred Fisher, Inc.

The S. S. Kresge five-and-dime store on Market Street in Newark was among the places where Danny was sent to peddle Fisher's sheet music. There was a nineteen-year-old salesgirl there named Rachel Brodsky, whose job it was to demonstrate songs on the piano for customers. Like him, Rae was the child of Russian immigrants. He placed Fisher's "They Go Wild, Simply Wild over Me" in the stand before her, then sang into her eyes as she played along. What woman could resist? They married in January 1925, after a courtship of nearly two years. Danny pursued his singing career, and he was performing at the Empire Theatre in Newark fourteen months later, on March 16, 1926, when their only child, a son they named for Rae's father, was born in that city.

With Rae as his rehearsal pianist, Danny Lewis toured the burlesque circuit as a singer and baggy-pants comic. Rae had her own agent, and played piano in cocktail lounges around town. In the summer months, they were familiar figures at the resort hotels of the Catskill Mountains area in Sullivan County, New York—the President Hotel on Swan Lake, Grossinger's and Young's Gap in Liberty, the Evans in Loch Sheldrake, and others that comprised what came to be known as the borscht circuit. He was a regular at the President, where he sang, did comedy, and served as master of ceremonies; and it was at the President, at a Firemen's Association benefit in the summer of 1932, that six-year-old Joey Levitch made his debut, singing "Brother, Can You Spare a Dime?" to his mother's accompaniment.

Dino Crocetti had grown up into an emotional loner, a man of the old ways, beyond the pale and ken of tame psychology's parlor-game knowing. Little Joey Levitch, on the other hand, became a convoluted, colicky knot of clinical frays. His earliest childhood was one beset by fears of abandonment. His parents were often away. As he was passed from one relative to another, always seeming to come back to his grandmother Sarah Brodsky, those fears grew worse.

"All my life, I've been afraid of being alone," he would say. "Grandma Sarah was the only one who understood my loneliness." He felt that if his parents loved him, if they wanted him, they would not leave him so. He remembered running through Irvington one night as a child, seeking his mother in a desperate panic, overcome with the thought that she did not love him and might never return. He found her playing piano in a bar. "I got scared," he cried as she took him home. That panic returned to him in nightmares for decades to come. Loved-starved and insecure, he craved the mother's-milk of attention and would do anything he could to get it.

In 1937, while Dino Crocetti was working at the Rex, Joey Levitch was going to the Union Avenue School and the Hebrew school at the Avrom Buchom Cheldem Synogogue in Irvington. In May of that year, burlesque was banned in New York by Mayor Fiorello La Guardia, whose commissioner of police, Lewis Valentine, charged that the striptease was largely responsible for the rising wave of sex crimes. New York's loss was Newark's gain, and Danny Levitch did all right. He also found winter work at a small resort hotel that was closer to home than the Catskills, a place called the Arthur, in Lakewood, New Jersey. Charles and Lillian Brown, the owners of the Arthur, had a young daughter named Lonnie. She was about three years older than Joey, and she liked to while away the time singing along with phonograph records of

Edythe Wright and other big-band girl singers. She called it "practicing her records." In time, she let Joey watch her, if he promised not to laugh. He enjoyed it, but he thought it would be more fun if, instead of using her own voice, she made believe she was the person who was really singing. He showed her what he meant. He replayed the record she had sung to, "You're a Sweetheart" by Tommy Dorsey and His Clambake Seven, moving his mouth grotesquely to Edythe Wright's voice, falling to one knee, addressing the song preposterously to Lonnie's teddy bear. Lonnie thought it was pretty funny, and the two of them began lampooning their way through her record collection, each trying to outreach the other in absurdity.

At the nearby Brunswick Hotel, Red Buttons was working as a bellhop under his real name of Arthur Schwatt. On weekends, he was a comic at the Arthur. One Saturday night, he failed to show up at the Arthur, and Charlie Brown allowed Lonnie and Joey to do their little phonograph-record act. She did Edythe White, he did Jimmy Durante, and together they did Jeanette MacDonald and Nelson Eddy doing "Indian Love Call." They thought the applause was for them, but actually Red Buttons had finally shown up during their finale.

That was in early 1939. Joey was still doing the same act at the Glass Hat five years later.

After his grandmother Sarah died and he graduated from grammar school, Joey spent the summer of 1939 with his aunt in Brooklyn, and got a job in Manhattan as an usher at the Paramount Theatre. Bob Shapiro, the Paramount's manager, fired him—"Levitch, turn in your dickey!"—when he asked for a better-fitting uniform. He went on to usher at the Strand, the Loew's State, and other theaters before returning to New Jersey to enter Irvington High School in the fall. He was no longer so little. He was rising tall and lean beside his squat, burly father. People had never seen two people who shared the same face with such different builds as Danny and his son.

Charlie and Lillian Brown took over the Ambassador Hotel at Loch Sheldrake in the Catskills, and, in the summer of 1941, they hired Danny, who was now working as a team with comic Lou Black. And when they heard that Joey Levitch had made the Irving ton High baseball team, they hired him too, as an athletic director, paying him ten dollars a week to blow a whistle and lead a bunch of middle-aged women in calisthenics every morning. He lasted less than two weeks, then became a bellboy.

During that summer in the Catskills, the team of Lewis and Black performed at the Majestic Hotel. For more than two years, Joey Levitch had thought that he and Lonnie Brown had invented that record routine of theirs. But at the Majestic, Joey saw a comedian named Sammy Birch doing the same thing, only better. Sammy told the kid that it was old hat, that record acts had been playing all over Europe and America for about ten years now.

When he was five years old, Grandpa Levitch had given him a dime to see Charlie Chaplin in *The Circus* at the Loew's Pitkin in Brooklyn. The movie was already old by then; it had been around for a few years. But to Joey Levitch it was a whole new world, the first moving picture he ever saw. And when he saw Chaplin, he knew then and there that he wanted to be a clown. Now, at fifteen, he knew what sort of clown.

His mother gave him thirty dollars to buy a phonograph machine. He bought one in Liberty, along with a bunch of records: "The Sow Song" by Cryil Smith; Igor Gorin's "Largo al Factotum" from Rossini's *Barber of Seville;* "Dinah" by Danny Kaye; Louis Armstrong; Jerry Colonna; Kate Smith. He practiced in front of a mirror. The bellhop at the Ambassador, a balding, woe-faced over-the-hill comic named Irving Kaye, who had worked for the Browns at the Arthur, drove him to his first paying engagement, a five-dollar premiere at a run-down restaurant nearby called the Cozy Corner. Lonnie Brown came along as Joey's assistant, to alter the speed of the records and supply other effects. From the Cozy Corner, he brought his record act from hotel to hotel, billed as Joey Levitch and His Hollywood Friends. In the hours between his bellboy job and his evening shows, he would practice under the world-weary guidance of Irving the bellhop.

His father long had told him not to make the same mistake that he had made, had told him to get an education and forget about being a joker. But Joey wanted what he wanted. He quit school at sixteen. Irving Kaye, through a friend who packaged shows for the

Loew's circuit in New Jersey, got him an audition. Hired for a six-week run through Jersey at twenty bucks a night, he adopted the stage name his father had taken, and went from Joey to Jerry to avoid confusion with the comedian Joe E. Lewis.

He was playing the Ritz Theatre on Staten Island for seven dollars a night when a sickly-looking, whey-faced, dybbuk-eyed man entered the dressing-room and introduced himself. He was Abner J. Greshler, an agent. The following morning, accompanied by his father, sixteen-year-old Jerry Lewis signed a management contract with Greshler at his office at 1260 Sixth Avenue in Manhattan.

Abby booked Jerry straightaway into the Palace Theatre in Buffalo. It sounded like the big time. Arriving in Buffalo with Irving Kaye, he found that the Palace was a dilapidated burlesque house. The marquee lights were busted, the entrance stank of piss. There was an audience of perhaps a dozen men in the otherwise empty theater. They were scattered up front with newspapers and overcoats covering their laps. "Get the fuck off!" they yelled when he took the stage. "Bring on the babes!"

Slowly it got better. By the time he was seventeen, Jerry was making $150 a week traveling the Loew's circuit through Boston, Philadelphia, Baltimore, and other towns. The act grew more elaborate: there were wigs and props. Irving Kaye, a bellhop no more, was his full-time road manager.

Since the beginning of his act, one of the performers whose records he relied on was Louis Prima, whose jive glossolalia lent itself well to pantomime. Since 1939, Lily Ann Carol, a Brooklyn girl whose real name was Greco, had been singing with Prima. She was billed as Miss Personality of Song. Jerry met her when he was playing as an opening act for Prima at the Central Theatre in Passaic in 1943. He fell in love with her—he thought he did, anyway. But to her he was just a virgin kid. She was in her twenties and squeezing the banana of the great man himself.

"Jerry had this genius for mugging," Abby Greshler remembered; but "he was a scared kid with a high squeaky voice. He was afraid to talk, to express himself, and that was why he had been crazy to do a record act—he didn't have to speak; the record did it for him. I told him he had to talk if he wanted to make any money. I explained that if he did some emcee work as well as the record specialty, I had a better chance of getting him jobs in clubs."

In the summer of 1943, Danny and Rae moved into the Holland Hotel near Times Square, and Jerry and Irving moved in together down the hall from them. Danny's dream of becoming the next Al Jolson had died long ago. Now burlesque was dying too. His son was beginning to do better than he was doing. Greshler had succeeded in breaking Jerry in as a master of ceremonies, at the Gayety Theatre in Montreal; and in New York that October, Greshler got him his first nightclub job, at the Hurricane, a big jungle-motif joint run by Dave Wolper at Broadway and Forty-ninth. Jerry was one of the opening acts at the Hurricane for Duke Ellington that fall while Dino was playing farther uptown, at the Riobamba.

His draft notice came soon after his eighteenth birthday. A heart murmur and a punctured eardrum rendered him 4-F and free. He signed on for six weeks with the Camp Shows troupe of the United Service Organizations. Working "Der Fuhrer's Face" by Spike Jones into the act, he toured military bases and hospitals as the Great Impersonator.

Jerry was still thinking of Lily Ann Carol when he met Patti Palmer at the Downtown Theatre in Detroit in August 1944. He was a sixty-dollar-a-week intermission act there, performing while the headliner, Ted Fio Rito and His Orchestra, set up; and she was Fio Rito's singer. She sang with the Solidaires on Fio Rito's new record, "Mamalu," released that very month. But Fio Rito's glory days were over; he had not had a hit in years. "Mamalu" was recorded for an obscure St. Louis company, Premier, that few had heard of.

Patti was a diminutive dark-haired doll, a *krassavitseh*, a beauty. From the first glimpse of her ankle, he was hers, a child at the breast of all maternity, a boy in the lap of high-heeled love.

Her real name was Esther Calonico. She was the daughter of Italian immigrants who wound up in Cambria, Wyoming. Her father, a coal miner, drank a lot and beat her mother, and one morning, after her mother threw a butcher knife at her father and then threatened to kill herself, she and her brother moved with her to Detroit, where mama got a job in the Chrysler plant. The old man showed up, and, after more fighting, he hauled Patti and her brother off and boarded them on a farm in St. Charles, Michigan. Her mother remarried and brought them back to Detroit. Later a judge gave Patti to her mother, her brother to the old man. Her stepfather beat her mother even worse than her father had. Her pretty contralto voice had been her way out.

She told him all this on their first date. And he thought he'd had it rough as a kid. Like Lily, she was a shiksa. Like Lily, she was older than he was, six years older. But unlike Lily, she fell in love with him in return.

Fio Rito had helped make Hollywood stars of two of his previous singers, Betty Grable and Betty Hutton. He planned to do the same with Patti, and he told her that getting involved with this Jew was the last thing that she and her career needed. When the engagement in Detroit came to an end, Jerry returned to New York and Patti went on with Fio Rito to an engagement in New Bedford, Massachusetts. By then, Jerry had proposed to her and was pursuing her with letters and calls. Fio Rito threatened to fire her if she continued on with "that Jew." Patti beat him to the punch. She had heard that Jimmy Dorsey was looking for a new singer to replace Kitty Kallen. She sent him a copy of her record and a photograph, and now she was to join the Dorsey band in Pittsburgh. While in New York, playing one last date with Fio Rito at the Roseland Ballroom, she asked Jerry if he had told his parents yet. "About what?" he asked, knowing what she meant. "About us wanting to get married," Patti said. "I think it'll be better if I don't," he said, and he looked away when he said it. She understood what he was telling her.

She went to Pittsburgh, he stayed and opened the next week at the Glass Hat.

Jerry would never forget his first sight of Dean. It was in the lobby of the Belmont Plaza. Jerry was standing there, studying the billing card that had been placed on an easel to advertise the upcoming show. There was one of the new publicity glossies that Abby had gotten made. It pictured him in a suit and tie, smiling suavely and sporting a well-oiled pompadour. The white border at the bottom, which bore the legend JERRY LEWIS: SATIRICAL IMPRESSIONS IN PANTOMIMICRY, had been cropped. Instead, beneath the picture in a flowing script were the words JERRY LEWIS—*Sotto Voce*. That was what puzzled him. Later, Greshler would explain the joke: *Sotto voce* meant low voice, right? Jerry was using somebody else's voice, right? You couldn't get any more *sotto voce* than that, right? So, see, it was funny, right?

He was standing there, trying to figure it out, when the elevator doors opened. A group of elderly women stepped out, followed by a man who struck Jerry as tall, though in reality the man was no taller than he. He had wavy coal-black hair, and brown eyes that seemed to sparkle with blue. The only thing that blemished his looks was the fine line of a fresh but fading surgical scar down the bridge of his nose. Then he saw the shoes: carmine-red patent-leather uppers that gleamed beneath the lobby lights. He watched those shoes, and the man in them, walk to the front entrance; watched him pause to say something to the doorman, then continue on his way. He was blank to the fact that he had just seen this man's picture above his own on the lobby card.

"Who was that?" he asked the doorman.

"Dean Martin."

"He looks important."

"Could be. He sings on WMCA."

"No kidding. What program?"

The doorman shrugged and turned his palms upward.

As it turned out, they knew people in common. Jerry knew Gene Baylos from the Ambassador Hotel in the Catskills. He knew Sonny King from Leon & Eddie's on West Fifty-second Street. It was Sonny who introduced Dean and Jerry. He had tired of the fifteen-cent breakfast special and had gone to work as a longshoreman. Now he was back singing. He was walking down the street one day with Jerry when Dean came their way at Broadway and Forty-ninth Street. Dean and Sonny had not seen one another for a while. Jerry would remember listening quietly "while Dean and Sonny talked about everything from broads to singing and work, and back to broads again."

"Jerry Lewis fills comedy job to perfection," *Billboard* said of

the Glass Hat opening. "Set routine consists of recordings to which
Lewis mugs. Face is pliable and work gets belly laughs." As a
master of ceremonies, "the kid showed poise and assuredness." His
best bit, the reviewer wrote, was "Dinah" by Danny Kaye, "which
panicked them. A Rudy Vallee English madrigal recording also
wowed them. Unfortunately latter bit was marred by some blue gestures."

A few nights after the opening, Jerry found himself sitting in
Room 616 at the Bryant, rapt, as Dean spun tales of his misspent
youth. There was a bottle of booze and music from Sonny's pile of
records—Tommy Dorsey, Benny Goodman, Coleman Hawkins, Bil-
lie Holiday—to fill the lulls. When Dean drifted into silence, Sonny
would elicit another tale.

"You wanna hear that shit?" Dean would say.

Sonny had heard it all before, but the kid, Jerry, was visibly
enthralled.

From that very night, Jerry looked up to Dean. "I was in need of
a friend at the time," he would say. In Dean he foresaw a friend and
more. He found what he would call "a brother image," one who
possessed all the strength and security he so desperately lacked.
The distance, the *lontananza* that others found chilling, Jerry perceived as a sort of stole of nobility, an air of self-sufficiency and
self-assurance so profound that the dismal burdens of his own anxieties and fears seemed to lighten in its presence. Looking at Dean,
he saw what he wanted to see when he looked at himself.

And from the beginning, he was impressed as well by Dean's
innate sense of comedy. The world was a dirty joke to Dean, and he
seemed to perceive it anew in every breath he took. "His sense of
comic awareness was brilliant," Jerry said. "There are some people
born with that, the genius of time. And he had not just a sense of
humor, but he had a sense of humor that applied to anyone and
everything around him. And it was brilliant. It was right on the
money all the time. I was in awe of his ability to make you laugh."

Eddie Sherman, Lou Costello's manager, was loath to become
involved in handling Costello's new protégé, but nonetheless it was
through Sherman that Lou Perry and Costello booked Dean into the

Baltimore Hippodrome. Advertised as "New York's Latest Radio Singing Sensation," he opened there on September 21. It was his biggest payday yet, $540 for the week.

Jerry, billed as "The Gay Impostor," followed him into the Hippodrome the next week. Their buddy Gene Baylos, who had been playing there for years, would arrive a few weeks later.

In October, Patti Palmer came to New York to sing at the Capitol Theatre with Dorsey. While in town, she and Jerry eloped to Greenwich, Connecticut, where a justice of the peace married them. They honeymooned at the Arthur as guests of the Browns. When they returned to New York, Jerry confronted his parents at the Holland Hotel.

"What did I raise you for?" his mother cried. "To run off with a Catholic?"

His father glared at him and waved his hand violently. "Who needs you anyhow? Go! Get the hell out of here!"

Before Patti took off for a cross-country tour with Dorsey, she and Jerry found a two-and-a-half-room, second-floor apartment for sixty-five dollars a month on Lehigh Avenue in Newark. Patti, who made $125 a week with Dorsey, was doing better than Jerry, whose income, when he worked, wavered between thirty and eighty a week. After a January recording session with Dorsey in New York, Patti, who was then two months pregnant, left the band. In March, Jerry got another booking at the Glass Hat.

In April 1945, Patti suggested that Jerry might patch things up with his parents if she turned to the Torah. They discussed the situation with Grandpa Levitch in Brooklyn. He directed Patti to a rabbi. Later that month, on a Sunday afternoon, she and Jerry walked down the synagogue aisle to be consecrated beneath the *chuppah* according to the faith of Moses and of Israel and of the State of New York. The glass was broken underfoot, and Daniel and Rachel Levitch embraced their son and his lovely bride. Patti was six months pregnant at the time. A child, Gary Lewis, would be born on the last day of July.

In December 1944, Perry and Costello booked Dean into the New York Loew's State on a bill featuring the Lee Castle Orchestra.

Variety found Dean to be "a pleasing crooner, but he gets on and off the stage like a substitute halfback lumbering from the bench to the gridiron"; and the crowd's response to him was "only fair." He announced from the stage that he would be leaving town soon to make a picture with Abbott and Costello.

But it was not meant to be. Dean, who was still living for free with Perry, began charging clothes and other purchases to Costello through the office of I. Robert Broder, Costello's New York attorney. Costello got disgusted one day when Broder called him to report charges by Dean amounting to $2,000. "Get rid of him," Costello told him. So, by 1945, from amid a litter of contracts, Lou Perry emerged as Dean's sole manager, renegotiating their agreement on a straight ten-percent basis.

The WMCA radio show stood in the way of out-of-town work. By October, the show's schedule had been cut from five to three evenings a week, with singer Sid Gary taking over the time period on Tuesdays and Thursdays; and in mid-December 1944, Dean left the station and was replaced by a singer who shared the same last name, Ted Martin, a WNEW performer who recorded for DeLuxe Records over in Linden, New Jersey.

By November of 1944, Betty had gotten fed up with her mother and moved with the children to stay with Dean's parents in Steubenville. Joe Crocetti had already moved west, to Arizona, for his wife's health. In a few months, Guy and Angela would move west as well, to California.

Betty was six months pregnant that Christmas. Ohio Valley Hospital was just across the way from the Crocetti home, now at 1101 Cardinal Avenue. At four in the morning on April 11, 1945, she gave birth there to a six-and-a-half-pound girl. They named her Barbara Gail.

"Dean didn't have two pennies to rub together" when he came to Steubenville that spring, his cousin Mary remembered. "He didn't have any money. I would be over at their house when they lived over there at Cardinal Avenue; he'd walk in and ask his mother for fifty cents." Betty was a "beautiful girl," Mary said; "very nice, very sweet with us." But "she was an alcoholic."

Bernice Del Villan remembered Dean showing off his nosejob. He patted one side of it—"Five"—then the other—"hundred"—then the tip—"dollars"—then brought his fingers together to his grinning lips, kissing them: "Love that boy!"

The next time he came to town, he had a new tuxedo and fancy diamond ring, but again he had no money.

"Betty left him four times," Bernice would reflect. "Four fights, four kids."

Dean sang at the Half Moon, for old times' sake. But the old times were gone.

Dean, advertised as "America's Foremost Crooner," opened at the Chanticleer in Baltimore on August 9, 1945, the day Nagasaki was bombed. Jerry Lewis, a proud new father at the age of nineteen, had closed at the Chanticleer just the night before.

Jerry's record act had grown more elaborate. He did "Indian Love Call" now as a duet with himself, turning maniacally, back and forth, partly in drag, from Jeanette MacDonald to Nelson Eddy. He added to his repertoire of Igor Gorin, Kate Smith, and Louis Prima, whose "Please No Squeeza da Banana," released in May 1945, was a natural for the act. He did Sinatra. He alternated between Deanna Durbin's and Metropolitan Opera soprano Grace Moore's versions of "Il Bacio." There was Wilfred Pelletiere's "Poet and Peasant," a rendering in English of Franz von Suppé's 1854 "Dichter und Bauer."

He and Dean played many of the same joints at different times that year. As at the Hippodrome and the Chanticleer, their paths covered common ground, but they never quite crossed.

Guy and Angela Crocetti were living now in California, south of Los Angeles, in a little house at 1137 Gardenia Avenue in Long Beach, where Guy had laid down his razor and become a bartender. Betty was forced to return with the children to her mother and father in Ridley Park. She told Dean that she could not take it anymore. The children needed a home. They needed a father. She needed a husband.

As Christmas of 1945 approached, Dean was performing at the

Havana-Madrid, a joint in the basement of an office building at 1650 Broadway, near Fifty-first Street. "Martin remains a mike-romanticist," said *Variety;* "and while during the last couple of years he has gained poise and assurance, he still is just a mechanical crooner."

The Havana-Madrid was paying Dean less than two hundred a week, but Dean managed to beat its owner, Angel Lopez, out of an extra grand by selling him a five-percent interest in his career.

For a quick buck, Dean had for too long been signing anything set before him. Now he saw only one way out of the morass of debt, binding obligation, and lawful culpability into which he had so blithely descended. On January 23, 1946, he and Herman Siegel, Esq., a $120-a-pop Park Place lawyer, went to the federal courthouse at Foley Square. There, in the District Court of the United States for the Southern District of New York, he, Dean Martin, of New York, in the County of New York, did "declare himself to be unable to meet his debts and engagements and prayed to be a bankrupt pursuant to the provisions of the bankruptcy statutes." He estimated his personal property at $115—$100 in "wearing apparel," $15 in "cash on hand." "About $35" more, he said, was deposited in an account at the Fifty-fourth Street branch of the Corn Exchange Bank. It would take almost two years, but in the end it would work. Deliverance would come two days after Christmas of 1947, when it would be decreed "that the said DEAN MARTIN be, and he hereby is, discharged from all debts and claims."

Jerry was booked into the Glass Hat again in February 1946. He was making good money this time, a hundred and ten a week, and he took a room at the Belmont Plaza for Patti, himself, and the kid. Sonny King had just closed at the Havana-Madrid. Dean, in whom Angel Lopez believed he held an interest, was scheduled to open there again in March, this time for $350 a week. Now it turned out that Angel Lopez had cut a deal with Abby Greshler for Jerry to appear on the same bill.

The show also featured the flamenco team of Dorita and Valero, and a blonde named Betty Reilly who sang Afro-Cuban chants. In late January, before Sonny had played there, the safe at the Havana-

Madrid had been looted by safecrackers, and the subsequent investigation and arrests had been good publicity. The new show opened to a full house.

"Jerry Lewis, panto-record worker, has improved tremendously," said *Billboard*. Dean was "one of the most promising bary sellers around. His ease and delivery sell all the way." But, once again, his "habit of insulting inattentive customers" was criticized as "poor showmanship."

Something happened that March at the Havana-Madrid that would change the course of their lives, though they had no inkling of it then. They had grown closer, more comfortable with one another. They were performing as separate acts, but, as Jerry remembered it, "He would kibitz while I was on, and I'd kibitz when he was on, never knowing what we were gonna do ultimately." After a few nights, they were taking the stage together in the early-morning hours after the regular show was over. Using Pupi Campo, the Havana-Madrid orchestra leader, as a deadpan foil, Dean, without his songs, and Jerry, without his records, extemporized a sort of bareknuckles comedy in which Dean, as life's organ-grinder, and Jerry, as its monkey, yanked and bit at the rope by which fate bound them: Adonis and Stupidus out on the town.

That they might become a team was a notion they did not entertain. "No. Never even thought about it," Jerry said of those nights at the Havana-Madrid. "We were just screwing around."

The potential, however, was not lost on *Billboard*. "Martin and Lewis," noted Bill Smith, "do an after-piece that has all the makings of a sock act. Boys play straight for each other, deliberately step on each other's lines, mug and raise general bedlam. It's a toss-up who walks off with the biggest mitt. Lewis's double-takes, throwaways, mugging and deliberate over-acting are sensational. Martin's slow takes, ad libs and under-acting make him an ideal fall guy. Both got stand-out results from a mob that took dynamite to wake up."

Sonny King would sometimes join them onstage as a grotesque bass player. "I'd black out my front teeth, put my hair down on the sides, never crack a smile." The three of them would do an Ink Spots routine. Then Sonny got an offer for a three-month booking at the Tradewinds in Washington, D.C. "I really didn't think their act was gonna go anyplace except the Havana-Madrid," he said.

Once more, Dean and Jerry went their separate ways. Perry had booked Dean to open in Chicago as an added attraction at the Rio Cabana on March 15.

Milton Pickman, a New York executive of Columbia Pictures, had approached Lou Perry about Dean earlier in the year. Now, before Dean left for Chicago, Pickman produced a brief sample of him on film—a song and a few lines—at the Tenth Avenue studios of Twentieth Century-Fox, where Columbia and other companies rented space for Eastern screen tests. The test was sent with two others—of Blossom Plumb and Ruth Sitarr—to Columbia's fearsome president, Harry Cohn.

Cohn's dictated response to the screen tests Pickman sent him that winter was typically, tyrannically terse: "We have just seen the Dean Martin, Blossom Plumb, and Ruth Sitarr tests. They are a complete waste of time and money. Martin may have some ability in a night club, but he cannot talk at all."

That spring was not a propitious season for Lewis either. "Next booking mistake is Jerry Lewis in the comedy slot," commented *Variety* on his May appearance at the Gayety Theatre in Montreal. "He's obviously a seasoned guy with plenty of know-how on selling a punchline, but this just isn't his spot."

Perry was approached again, this time by Joe Pasternak of MGM, whose door Perry had been knocking at for years. Pasternak had recently produced *Anchors Aweigh*, with Frank Sinatra. Now he was looking for a new singer for his next production, *Till the Clouds Roll By*.

"Dean makes the girls sweat," he said after seeing him perform in New York.

Billed as "The Voice of Romance," Dean went over well at the Rio Cabana. The *Chicago Daily News* called him "an engaging Frank Sing-at-yuh type of croonster" with a growing and "insistent public." Held over through May at $750 a week, he made more in a fortnight than the average American made for the year. But he returned to New York with only sixty-five dollars, and borrowed twenty-five from Perry before leaving for a date in Baltimore. Dean was beginning to like Maryland. There was a girl down there in Cumberland who filled him with the song of songs, with love in all its splendor, whene'er she bent and whinnied.

Pasternak had asked George Sidney, the director of *Anchors Aweigh,* to screen-test Martin. In June, Sidney filmed him singing "San Fernando Valley"; then, having him strip to the waist, had him shadowbox a bit for the camera.

Later, that summer, viewing the test, Pasternak would tell Perry that he would not be producing *Till the Clouds Roll By* after all, that MGM was passing on Dean, and that the studio felt that besides already having Sinatra, it also already had a good-enough second-string Italian crooner in Tony Martin. And no, it did not really matter that Tony Martin was a Jew from Oakland named Alvin Morris; this was the movies. In the end, both Sinatra and Tony Martin appeared in *Till the Clouds Roll By,* produced by Arthur Freed. Pasternak told Perry that he would keep Dean in mind.

Dean turned twenty-nine in June. He was doing better than any Crocetti ever had, better than most men in America dreamed of doing, and he was doing it by singing. He had a wife, a family, a boundless sty of pussy on the side. But that old solitary, stubborn prescience, that desire that was as much a knowing as a craving; it was still there, unfulfilled, unabated, unsated. It felt sometimes as if the world had opened up to him only to reveal another, vaster and fancier Chinese restaurant, another cigar-store back room—an endless succession of them, through which he would have to hustle his way, song by song, silver dollar by silver dollar.

Dean had no way of knowing it as he signed the contracts that Lou Perry passed to him on July 19—they were for an upcoming engagement in Atlantic City; just another show—but that feeling, soon and suddenly and surely, was about to change.

Perry was fond of telling a story about two racket guys who came to his office on Broadway one afternoon. They brought with them a younger man, well groomed and strikingly handsome, and a copy of the young man's audition record, which they had subsidized. While the young man waited outside, his sponsors asked Perry to evaluate his potential as a singer. Perry told them that the kid was just another pretty face, that his voice was flat and expressionless.

"Ah, well," the one sponsor said to the other. "Fuck 'im, we'll make him a fighter."

There were a lot of characters like that in show business, but, as Perry knew, they all were not drawn so pleasantly from Damon Runyon as those two. Looking at the contracts that he and Dean signed in July was enough to remind him of that.

VIII.

Fate
IN A
FRUITED
TURBAN

*P*aul Emilio D'Amato: They called him Skinny. The Federal Bureau of Investigation would hound him for more than fifteen years, and would come up empty.

He was born on Willow Avenue in Atlantic City, New Jersey, on December 1, 1908, one of Willie and Mary D'Amato's brood of eight. Growing up in the neighborhood that came to be called Ducktown, he was known as Skinny. Now, almost six feet tall and 185 pounds, he was still known by everyone in town as Skinny D'Amato.

His father had run the Garibaldi Club, a Missouri Street café that served as one of the seats of power for the forces that ruled Atlantic City early in the century. Unlike that of most corrupt cities in America, the machinery of malfeasance in Atlantic City belonged to the Republican rather than the Democratic party. The town, with its two-mile Boardwalk by the sea, was a celebrated resort as early as 1880. By the turn of the century, there were some five hundred hotels and lodging-houses. As party boss Louis Kuehnle well knew, it took a lot of niggers to clean and wait on 20,000 rooms. And, as he also well knew, black folks voted Republican, the party of Lincoln. "If you were to take all the power ever exercised by Boss Tweed, the Philadelphia Gang, the Pittsburgh Ring, Boss Ruef of San Francisco, and Tammany Hall and concentrate it in one man, you would still fall a little short of Kuehnle's clutch on Atlantic City," said the Democratic *Sun* of New York.

Boss Kuehnle's thirty-year reign ended with his imprisonment in 1911, following the election of the Democrat Woodrow Wilson to the governorship of New Jersey. His protégé, Sheriff Enoch Johnson, succeeded him. Twenty-four-hour gambling, prostitution, drugs, and liquor were an important part of Atlantic City's tourism

industry, and "Nucky" Johnson controlled it all. As one of the original members of the East Coast bootlegging cartel known as the Big
Seven—the Meyer Lansky and Bugsy Siegel mob; the Joe Adonis
group; the New England mob headed by Charlie Solomon; the
Longie Zwillman and Willie Moretti group; the Philadelphia group
headed by Waxey Gordon, Harry Stromberg (alias Nig Rosen), and
Irving Bitz; the Luciano-Costello-Torrio alliance—Johnson maintained the Atlantic County shoreline as a landing-haven for the
shiploads of booze brought in from Canada, the Bahamas, and En-
gland. And it was Johnson who served as the host of the largest
malavita conclave in history. Gathered at the President Hotel in his
city in May 1929 were Joe Adonis, Albert Anastasia, Lepke
Buchalter, Al Capone, Frank Costello, Moe Dalitz, Frank Erickson,
Waxey Gordon, Meyer Lansky, Lucky Luciano, Louis Rothkopf,
Dutch Schultz, Johnny Torrio, Longie Zwillman, and others. The
Evening Journal of New York carried a photo of Johnson and
Capone strolling down the Boardwalk together.

By the age of fifteen, following the death of his father, Skinny
D'Amato was working at a gambling operation in the back room of a
cigar store on the corner of Missouri and Arctic avenues. He went
on to run a bookmaking ring, and dabbled in prostitution; but the
Depression and the repeal of Prohibition racked Atlantic City
throughout the thirties, and the money was not what it had been. At
the close of the decade, President Franklin Roosevelt, the man who
changed the party allegiance of black voters, was urged by William
Randolph Hearst to dispatch federal forces to clean up Atlantic
City. Roosevelt heeded his patron's bidding, and, in the summer of
1941, Nucky Johnson was convicted of income-tax evasion on his
estimated illegal income of more than half a million dollars a year.
He was sent to the federal penitentiary at Lewisburg, where Skinny
D'Amato was already serving time for a white-slavery conviction.

Johnson's successor was Senator Frank Farley, the chairman of
Atlantic County's Republican Committee and a practicing attorney.
Hap Farley worked closely with Mario Floriani, who was the boss of
the Fourth Ward Italian-American Club and the city's public-safety
commissioner. It was Floriani who served as the political minion of
the Philadelphia-based forces that now ran Atlantic City through

Farley. The ruler of those forces was Joe Ida, whose chief subalterns were Angelo Bruno of Philadelphia and Marco Reginelli of Camden, New Jersey. Reginelli, among other things, was the sub-rosa owner of a nightclub that stood where Willie D'Amato's café once had been.

The 500 Café had opened at 6 South Missouri Avenue in the golden days of 1918. Phil Barr, a former trolley conductor and boxing promoter from Philadelphia, ran the joint for twenty-four years. When Barr died, in June 1942, Reginelli brought in Irvin Wolf from Philadelphia to replace him. Skinny, who was then thirty-three and fresh out of prison, a friend of Floriani as well as of Reginelli, was given a piece of the operation along with Wolf. Affable and outgoing, Skinny was the one whose personality and presence the public came to associate with the 500 Café, or the 500 Club or the Fives as it was called. Under him, as Atlantic City bloomed, the club became the most famous and most popular joint in town, with a showroom that could seat a thousand and an illegal casino in the back room.

Nineteen forty-six was a year of various investigations and probes in Atlantic City. Though, when later questioned by FBI special agents, D'Amato insisted that he was the sole owner and operator of the 500 Club and its casino, the place was already under federal surveillance as a haunt of "known hoodlums," and Skinny had already been assigned FBI Number 1385288. A certificate of incorporation filed for the 500 Café in June of 1946 listed Irvin Wolf as the corporation's principal agent. Skinny's sister Antoinette Cohen and John Di Santi of his mother's family were also listed.

Skinny, beloved of all Atlantic City, cut the most striking figure in town, with his handsome dark looks, his custom-tailored suits, his London-made shoes, and his hand-colored silk ties. He was known to drink several pots of coffee and smoke between six and seven packs of cigarettes a day. The 500 Club, they said, was like his baby. He was always there, watching over it. The Bath and Turf Club on South Stanton, the Cliquot on North Illinois, the Copa Cabana on the Boardwalk opposite the Steel Pier, the Club Harlem on North Kentucky, the 22 Club, the Paradise ("The Oldest Night Club in America") with its 10 BEAUTIFUL CREOLE CHORUS GIRLS—

these were just the best-known of the joints that shared the action in
Atlantic City in 1946. But Skinny put the Fives in a class by itself.

Abby Greshler booked Jerry Lewis into the 500 that July, talking Wolf and Skinny into $150 a week. It was enough to allow Jerry
to bring Patti and Gary along. They stayed at the Princess Hotel, a
block from the Boardwalk.

There were three shows a night. Headlining was the singing
comedienne Jayne Manners, a Swedish-born former Ziegfeld girl
with a flair for creating scandal. She had been implicated, largely
through her own efforts, in the case of the 1930 disappearance of
Judge Joseph Crater; the press eagerly reported on her romances,
marriages, and divorces; and, most recently, just that March, she
had been banned in Boston after an off-color performance at the
Hotel Bradford Roof Garden. Jerry and his "satirical impressions in
pantomimicry" received second billing. Among the other lesser acts
was a singer named Jack Randall.

"The guy sings like his nuts are caught in a zipper," Jerry heard
Skinny say. During the third week of July, none too soon for Skinny,
Randall fell ill and left the show.

Thirty-five years later, in his autobiography, Lewis would say
that Randall, identified only as "the singer," was fired by D'Amato;
that he, Lewis, suggested replacing him with "my friend, Dean Martin," explaining that "we've worked together" and "we do a lot of
funny stuff"; and that D'Amato then called Lou Perry. Later still,
remembering the singer as Bill Randall, there was no firing: Randall "got sick the night I was appearing at the 500 Club, and I got
them to bring Dean in."

Abby Greshler's version was slightly different: "Wolf wanted a
boy singer and I recommended Martin."

Lou Perry's version was altogether different: "Lewis called me,
crying that Irvin Wolf was going to cancel him, and I could do
something about it." Perry called Wolf, who said he could not stomach Jerry's record act. Wolf and D'Amato had already expressed
their interest in Dean to Perry. Now, as an inducement to Wolf to
keep Lewis on, Perry said, he offered him Dean at $500, a cut from
what he was already getting. "That's how the whole thing came
about. If I hadn't made the phone call, it would've never happened."

A standard American Guild of Variety Artists contract, dated July 19, 1946, attested that Dean was to perform at the 500 Café for two consecutive weeks commencing July 25, and that he was to be paid $500, less ten percent to Perry.

In the week before he left New York for Atlantic City, Dean made his first commercial recording, for the Diamond Record Corporation. To date, Diamond's biggest star had been Nick Lucas, the singing guitarist whose last major hit was "Tip Toe thru the Tulips with Me" in 1929. Among the label's other artists were Jan August, who had played xylophone with Paul Whiteman, and the Brooks Brothers. Dean recorded four songs for Diamond. Two of them were new: "Which Way Did My Heart Go?" was copyrighted that April, and Irving Berlin's "I Got the Sun in the Morning" was from *Annie Get Your Gun*, which had opened at the Imperial that May. The first was coupled with "All of Me," from 1931; the latter, with "The Sweetheart of Sigma Chi." To back Dean on his recordings, Diamond had brought in pianist Nat Brandwynne and his twelve-piece salon orchestra from the Starlight Roof of the Waldorf-Astoria.

Dean's records were not yet released when he opened in Atlantic City, but he was nonetheless presented as a full-fledged recording artist.

Irvin Wolf Presents
3 SCINTILLATING REVUES
Last Show at 4 A.M.
STARRING THE UNPREDICTABLE
JAYNE MANNERS

ADDED ATTRACTION
Diamond Recording Artist
DEAN MARTIN
Romance in Song

Sensational Comic
JERRY LEWIS
"Satirical Impressions
in Pantomimicry"

Similarly, a photograph of Dean in the *Atlantic City Press* bore the legend: "DEAN MARTIN—Diamond recording artist and most recent Hollywood singing discovery, opens tonight at the 500 Café as an added attraction. He is making this appearance for a limited time before leaving for Hollywood. Martin will be seen shortly in a Joseph Pasternack [sic] film production."

Two days later, a brief piece in the *Press* described Dean as "Broadway's newest singing sensation," whose "debut here was just as successful as in New York." Describing the rest of the 500 Club revue, the piece went on to note that "the M.C. is that clever show stopping comedian, Jerry Lewis. His rise to stardom has been the most rapid of any young performer in many years due to the brilliant satirical impressions in pantomime which he presents."

"Skinny, Wolf, they were partners," Lewis said. "Wolfie was—it was nothing for him to get on the phone and get a guy to come over and break your legs; it was nothing. And Skinny D'Amato, who you'd think was with the Mafia, was the sweetest, nicest man. Defended us, protected us. Fought with Wolfie about us."

Dean did his act, Jerry did his. Then, as Lewis remembered it, Irvin Wolf came to him.

"Where's that funny shit you two were gonna do? If it ain't in the second show, you're both outta here tomorrow."

It was then, according to Jerry, feeling "that our job was at stake," that he "wrote a couple of routines, rehearsed Dean the next afternoon, and he walked onstage and embellished on it a thousand-fold."

"I had to write something," he said. "I had gotten them to bring Dean in under the guise of 'he's not just a singer.' I wrote the whole act. At least the bones of the act. See, all I had to do was to tell Dean I was gonna do such and such; that during one of his numbers I was gonna be a busboy in the audience. That's all I had to tell him; he went with me. I mean, we did one show one night that lasted over three hours. Three hours of 'Did you take a bath this morning?' —'Why, is there one missing?' That doesn't take three fuckin' hours. But we did things that I can't even begin to recall. If I started something, he'd pick up on it like a child goes after milk. And the wonderful thing was that no one ever knew when the cycle developed, when I was doing straight for Dean. No one ever knew it. We had that certain something that I wish I could say we planned. We didn't plan it. It was innate within us that out of the blue he was doing six, seven, eight minutes of comedy and I was straight for him."

Whether or not Dean's job at the 500 Club was ever in jeopardy —and it is very unlikely that it was; after all, he had a contract and was given featured billing from the start—it would become part of the apocryphal history of Martin and Lewis, perpetuated through the years by publicists, the media, and themselves. That adversity brought them fatefully together in the desperation of their common straits was a far more romantic story than their merely having expanded and elaborated at the 500 Café on the after-pieces they had performed four months earlier at the Havana-Madrid. Dean would be quoted years later as saying, "Jerry and I met when I was working the Club 500 in Atlantic City." Even Lewis in his autobiography would not mention those after-pieces, and would remember himself as arriving in Atlantic City on July 25, the apocryphal date of their fateful teaming, when in fact he had already been performing at the 500 the week before.

Popular culture breeds popular history. But one fact is irrefutable: Within days of Dean's opening at the 500, he and Jerry were the talk of Atlantic City.

"I knew it was happening," Lewis said. "The very first night, I knew."

Dean knew it too. One morning after the last show, just before dawn, the two of them lingered at the rail of the Boardwalk, breathing the salty sweet breeze and letting the sound of the waves and the gulls wash away the noise of the club that lingered in their ears. They watched the froth of the breakers turn a shimmering pale gold in the first hint of light. They did not speak. They just knew.

"Word of mouth, in less than three nights, you couldn't get near the club. It was unbelievable," Jerry said. "They never packed that joint like when we were there. First night, second night, third night, fourth night. Then Dean and I were layin' on the beach and I'd make believe I was drowning. The minute we had enough of a crowd around us, I'd jump up, Dean'd yell, 'First show's at eight o'clock,' and we'd run like hell back to the hotel."

Sophie Tucker, who was performing in Atlantic City at the Copa Cabana, and who remembered W. C. Fields pulling the same drowning routine on the same beach long years ago, became their first celebrity booster. Likening them to a combination of the Keystone Kops, the Marx Brothers, and Abbott and Costello, the Last of the Red-Hot Mamas predicted, "They will leave their mark on the whole profession."

Dean was held over, and, on August 8, replacing Manners at $750 a week, he became the star of the 500 Club's new midsummer revue. Jerry at the same time, retaining second billing, got a raise as well and became the "extra added attraction." They stayed through the end of the season.

Toward the end of August, Diamond released Dean's records. A half-page advertisement in *Billboard* proclaimed Dean as THE COUNTRY'S NEWEST SINGING SENSATION—EXCLUSIVE ON DIAMOND! And, as a more realistic enticement: "Dealers! Operators! 48$1/2$¢." But, even at that bargain rate, Dean's recording debut passed without notice. It was not that the records were not good. Dean's voice, imbued with the signature of a rich but deep and subtle vibrato, was full and vibrant and rode the music with the sultry natural ease of a summer wind. There was some Perry Como in that voice—Como's hit "Surrender" had pervaded the air when Dean was in the studio that July —and there was a shade of Crosby; but above all else, it was his own.

Abby Greshler came to Atlantic City that August. Pallid and cadaverous as ever, he moved beneath the summer sun like Death among the happy crowds. Angel Lopez wanted Dean and Jerry to return to the Havana-Madrid next month. He was offering $750 a week for Dean, less for Jerry. It was only business, a matter of arithmetic: Dean was worth more than Jerry, but, as a team, they would split one big price down the middle, and whoever managed that team would get his ten percent off the top. Lou Perry had already taken care of Dean's part of the Havana-Madrid deal. But Greshler had a feeling that there were a lot more deals like this to come.

When Perry heard from Irvin Wolf that Greshler had come to Atlantic City, he called Dean and advised him to be wary.

Greshler told Lewis that Dean was getting star billing at the Havana-Madrid, that Lewis was getting second-banana billing. "You can blame this on Perry," he said. He told Lewis that he would take care of it: "I'll get Perry in line. Leave it to me."

Angel Lopez tried something new that September at the Havana-Madrid. Instead of integrating the show as he had been doing, he put on all the Latin acts—Canelina, Carmen and Rolando, three-hundred-pound Sergio Orta—in the first half, and gave the second half to Martin and Lewis. Jerry opened their segment with his record act. "Guy's got stint down to perfection," *Variety* noted. As well as he should have had it down; he was still doing "Dinah" by Danny Kaye and "The Sow Song" by Cyril Smith, the records with which he had started five years ago in the Catskills.

"Martin," *Variety* went on, "then warms up his pleasantly smooth baritone on a group of pops. Young crooner is greatly improved since appearance at this club last winter. He still bounces around, jounces the mike and kids the audience but his completely relaxed manner builds up a nice intimacy with the crowd and he draws plenty of applause."

Lewis came back out, and he and Dean did the final twenty minutes of the show together. *Variety* described the act as "a bunch of zany routines, apparently following a set format but improvising most of the way along the line. The hoked-up gags, impressions, terping, etc., probably wouldn't go in the more sedate niteries but it's sock stuff here."

As the first days of September passed, Lewis had realized that he was seeing less and less of Perry, and that Dean and Greshler were spending more and more time together. Dean had moved his clothes out of Perry's room. He was doing well enough not to free-load, he said; and besides, he and Betty were getting their own place.

Dean and Greshler had already cut Perry's throat. In the first week of September, when Harry Steinman, the operator of the Latin Casino in Philadelphia, had approached Greshler about booking Jerry and Dean into his club that coming winter, Greshler had negotiated the deal without Perry: $1,200 a week for the two of them. He then had drafted a letter for Dean to sign and send to Perry. The letter was a notice of dismissal. It was an unorthodox and risky move, Greshler knew, but Dick Haymes had pulled it off a couple of years ago when he fired General Artists to sign with the William Morris Agency, and maybe that had set a precedent.

Perry, who had gotten the letter on the eve of the Havana-Madrid opening, sought justice through the arbitration committee of the American Guild of Variety Artists, filing charges against Greshler for booking dates and collecting commissions without authority.

Greshler's account of what had begun in Atlantic City and culminated in New York would later be plainly stated: "Martin pleaded with me to handle him." Greshler would also take credit for teaming Martin and Lewis: "Dean was foundering. I had the idea of putting him with Jerry, which I did. The rest is history."

Perry should have known better. He had methodically watched Dean fuck everybody else he had ever dealt with. But he had thought their deal was different. What he could not figure was what that fucking cutthroat wop thought Greshler could do for him that Perry could not. It was as if Greshler had sucked his cock, gone down on that fucking greaseball brain of his.

"Lou Perry would have gone to hell and back for Dean," Lewis said. "His loyalty was there from the start, but just when it looked as if the big payoff had finally come, he found himself out of the picture. To this day," Lewis claimed, "I don't know all the behind-the-scenes maneuverings that eventually put Abby Greshler in charge of the act."

One evening at the Havana-Madrid, Lou Perry walked up to Jerry and told him that he no longer represented Dean. He wished Jerry luck, then he quietly left.

After several indecisive AGVA hearings, Perry had agreed to let Martin go to Greshler for $4,000. "He went around showing everybody the check," Greshler said. "Then he wanted cash, so I took him to the Chemical Bank at Radio City. I cashed the check, and he said, 'Wow! Just like that, they cash a $4,000 check? You must be very good for the money.' Four thousand dollars was a dot to me. Perry and I were in different worlds."

"That was less dough than I spent on Martin while I was supporting him," Perry would say.

But Perry himself was no mere innocent, and what he never told anybody was that he had already agreed to sell out Dean to someone else before he sold him to Greshler. The buyer was Nick Constantino, the Mayfield Road Gang club owner who had known Dean since the Youngstown days.

Perry's partner, Frank Military, had been kept in the dark about the Constantino deal. "I had begged Lou not to sell Dean's contract to Abby Greshler," Military said. "I was crying. I was heartbroken. I would come to the office every day, but my heart wasn't in it." One day, the door opened, and in walked a man in a camel-hair coat with a wraparound belt.

"Lou Perry," he said.

Normally, Military would have asked "What is this in reference to?" or "What could I do for you?" But something about this caller in camel hair told him not to bother. He asked him to wait a moment, went into Perry's office, and in a hushed voice told him, "I think we've got trouble."

"Ah, send him in," Perry said, "we'll see what he wants."

But there was no need to do that. The door opened, and in he came. He strode up to Perry's desk and looked down at him.

"You Lou Perry?"

"Yup."

He punched Perry hard in the face. "Get Nick Constantino on the phone," he told him.

Perry dialed the telephone with one shaking hand and wiped at his blood with the other. The man grabbed the receiver from him.

"Yeah, Nick. You want this cocksucker out the window or what?"

"Let me talk to him first," Constantino said.

That was how Frank Military discovered Perry's secret deal. "Lou had sold Dean's contract to Nick Constantino before he had sold it to Abby Greshler. But it was never a formal deal. It was a handshake. He took the money and ran." The stranger in the camel-hair coat became a familiar presence, making sure that Perry made the weekly payments that Constantino had decreed. "We ended up gettin' friendly with the guy," Military said. "He was a gangster from downtown, the East Side. He wanted to be in show business. We took him to clubs with us. He started out threatenin' us, ended up protectin' us. And Nick used to come to town, we'd all hang out."

There would be no more separate billing now. They were in a car when they discussed what the billing should be, Lewis and Martin or Martin and Lewis.

"Let's not have an argument," Dean told him. "Let's just call it Martin and Lewis because it's alphabetically right."

"Alphabetically right? When the fuck did *M* come before *L?*"

"*D* comes before *J.*"

So it was settled. They were Martin and Lewis now; and Martin and Lewis they would remain, until they came to hate one another with a passion untold.

They opened for the first time as Martin and Lewis in New York, in January 1947, at the Loew's State. The deal, for $1,500 a week, included an option for an engagement at the Loew's Capitol for $1,750 a week and a second Capitol engagement within nine months for the same price.

Danny Lewis had wanted to be the next Jolson. Now his son was playing the State for more money than Danny had ever seen; and, ironically, the movie on the State program with Martin and Lewis was *The Jolson Story.*

The picture drew capacity crowds, which Abby Greshler stacked with servicemen at twenty-six cents a head, coaching them in their applause. Martin and Lewis performed for fifteen minutes, five or six times a day, before each picture-showing. Jerry's record routine was out. Dean sang while Jerry, in various roles—an addle-pated bartender, for one—drew him into take-offs on current stars. Together they worked over "That Old Gang of Mine," building to a finale in which Lewis, in the persona of José Disturbi (after the Spanish concert pianist José Iturbi), conducted the pit orchestra while Dean did an absurd hokum version of "Ol' Man River."

A review in the "New Acts" section of *Variety* concluded, "All in all, these two kids have themselves a fine act."

They were becoming valuable to Greshler. During the State engagement, he had them each take out a $15,000 New York Life Insurance policy naming him as the beneficiary. Seeking to enhance their value, he retained the services of publicist George B. Evans. At the age of forty-five, Evans was the most high-powered publicist in New York. He was the man who, in January 1943, had hired the bobby-soxers who screamed and swooned for Frank Sinatra at the Paramount. He had rehearsed the girls himself in the theater basement, had rented an ambulance to park outside, had notified the press that the ushers were equipped with emergency smelling-salts; had christened Sinatra "the Voice." His other clients included Glenn Miller, the Copacabana, Duke Ellington, and Louis Prima.

"He was as important to us as he was to Frank," Jerry said. "He *made* Frank. And he was just as important in selling us."

In March, they opened in Philadelphia at the Latin Casino, which had now been taken over by Jack Lynch, the Walton Roof operator who had warned Lou Costello's manager against any involvement with Dean. "The Anniversary Song," which Al Jolson and Saul Chaplin had based on Iosif Ivanovici's 1880 "Donauwellen," had been featured in *The Jolson Story*. That March, Jolson himself, Tex Beneke with the Glenn Miller Orchestra, Dinah Shore, and Andy Russell all had versions of the song on the charts; and Dean now made it part of his repertoire. He had also added Cole Porter's "Begin the Beguine," which Sinatra had revived the previous year; and was now once again singing "Oh, Marie." Phil Brito had included the song in his 1946 album, *Phil Brito Sings Songs of Italy*. His recordings in Italian were to have a lasting influence on Dean, who eventually adapted most of the songs on Brito's album to his own style.

Together they did a joked-up version of another, older Jolson song, "Sonny Boy." Lewis took the microphone on his own for "I'm a Big Boy Now," a turnaround on "I'm a Big Girl Now," a hit the previous year for Sammy Kaye and His Orchestra with Betty Barclay.

The massive infusion of gross comedy was already having an

effect on Dean's singing. He had never attached great importance to
it. That is, he knew that he was great, but to him singing by its very
nature was unimportant. Singers who viewed themselves in earnest
as artists struck him as fools, as pretenders, as prima donnas. The
comedy underscored that unimportance. Now when he sang alone it
was as a prelude to buffoonery, an interlude in a punchinello show.
When he sang with Jerry, the songs themselves became pas-
quinades. For a *menefreghista*, it was the perfect setup. When you
were onstage to fuck up, why should you, how could you, give a
fuck? As the *Variety* review of the Latin Casino show noted, "Martin, of the swoon-croon school, doesn't take himself too seriously."

Lewis knew exactly what they were about: sex and slapstick.
That was their secret formula. Consider the greatest of the stage
comedy teams. There were Olsen and Johnson, who had been
around since 1914 and were still at it. There were Wheeler and
Woolsey, whom Florenz Ziegfeld had brought together in *Rio Rita* in
1926. There were Abbott and Costello, who had transformed
Wheeler and Woolsey's routine about two towns named Which and
What into "Who's on First." Together since 1936, they were the
biggest comedy team in the country. But there had never been a
team like Martin and Lewis.

"You never had a handsome man and a monkey. Sex and slapstick. That's what we were," said Lewis. Though they were both six
feet tall, everybody referred to Jerry as "the little guy." He rein-
forced the impression by purposely crouching when they worked.
"The crouch came from the monkey, the thought of the monkey."
His presence must never diminish Dean's appearance of strength
and stature. And Dean, representing authority as well as romance
and sophistication, must never bend or stoop. "I'd say, 'Dean, if
something falls, if something happens, never bend down. Let me do
the bending.' And he understood that. Because he was the truant
officer, the authority, the bank manager, the leader, the boss, and I
was all of the other things that sat in that audience."

Olsen and Johnson had Olsen-and-Johnson fans; Wheeler and
Woolsey, Wheeler-and-Woolsey fans; Abbott and Costello, Abbott-
and-Costello fans. "But," as Lewis said, "who were Dean's fans?"
Men, women, the Italians. "Who were Jerry's fans?" Women, Jews,

kids. "Who were Martin and Lewis's fans? *All of them.* Incredible. You had those who didn't give a shit about who was Italian and who was Jewish. You had fans that didn't give a shit that Jerry was on or that Dean was singing. Because if Dean was singing, that was Martin and Lewis. If Jerry was goin' nuts, that was Martin and Lewis.

"There was a Dean Martin fan club in that audience. There was a Jerry Lewis fan club in that audience. And there was a Martin-and-Lewis fan club in that audience. How the fuck could you miss? When Jerry was off the stage and Dean was doin' love songs, he had that crowd and his group—and won a few of Jerry's. When Jerry was out there gettin' nuts, Jerry's group picked up a few of Dean's. And then Dean and Jerry's group were thrilled to death that the both of them were there. How could you miss? We had it all!"

From the Latin Casino, they returned in April to New York to open at the Loew's Capitol with Xavier Cugat. During their month-long stay at the Capitol, Greshler received an offer for them from the Copacabana. The offer was for $750 a week. Greshler asked for twice that, and when the Copacabana demurred, Martin and Lewis threatened to leave him. The Copa, after all, was the most celebrated nightclub in America. They had never heard of anyone turning down a chance to play there. George Evans, who handled publicity for the Copa as well as for them, agreed. But Greshler insisted that the Copacabana would be back to them in time, eager to pay that price and more.

In May, they went on to the Rio Cabana in Chicago, headlining for a month at $1,750 a week. Before leaving New York, Dean took out a $25,000 life-insurance policy naming Betty as beneficiary.

At the Capitol, they had worked up a version of "The Donkey Serenade," with sound effects by Lewis. In Chicago, *Variety* reported, it drove the crowds "into frenzy." It was in Chicago that Dean, summoning what he had learned watching his father work, cropped Jerry's hair into the crewcut that became his trademark.

In early June, they played the Stanley Theatre in Camden, New Jersey, then moved on to the Earle Theatre in Philadelphia. From there, they went to the 500 Club. On July 11, Dean commuted to New York for the creditors' meeting of his bankruptcy proceedings. The case had nearly been closed, but Dick Richards had now come forth with a new claim based on his October 1946, $15,000 suit against Dean, which was still pending in the New York Supreme Court.

"What are you, a singer?" asked Judge John E. Joyce, the referee.

"Yes, sir."

"How long have you been an entertainer?"

"About six years."

"What was your gross income during the year 1945?"

"I can't say right offhand."

"Did you file an income-tax return?"

"Well, we're working on that right now."

In late July, Dean and Jerry returned to the Loew's State in New York. During their engagement at the State, on August 5, they were guests on Barry Gray's Mutual radio show, "Scout About Town." Dean sang "Peg o' My Heart," the 1913 song that had resurfaced in recent months in three different hit versions. Afterward he almost blew one of his lines, thrown off by a polysyllabic verb: "Jerry, I wish you wouldn't excoriate my work." Lewis hurried in: "Excoriate! Ooh, what he said!" Their fellow guest, the soprano Dorothy Sarnoff, commented, "Dean Martin, you sounded just exactly like Bing Crosby." To which Dean responded, "Well, a lot of folks think that Crosby sounds a little like me."

In mid-August, they went south to the Capitol Theatre in Washington, D.C. There Dean ran into his old friend Smuggs, who was dealing at a private club, taking from senators and congressmen and rendering unto Caesar of the shades what they had taken from others. They were both doing good, each in his way.

Dean was now thirty. Fame and fortune lay a breath away. He could feel it. But other, darker things lay close at hand as well. He had almost forgotten about them: those who sought to wet their beaks—*fari vagnari u pizzu*, as the Sicilians said.

The Riviera was a fabulous joint. Designed by the architect Louis Allen Abramson, it had been built at a cost of a quarter of a million dollars by Ben Marden, who opened it in 1937. Its location in the Palisades section of Fort Lee, New Jersey—"Just Across the

George Washington Bridge," as Marden's advertisements said—placed it in the heart of the Bergen County mob domain of Joe Adonis, Albert Anastasia, Frank Erickson, and Willie and Sallie Moretti.

The Bergen County mob's main gambling operation was the Barn, which had originated, in 1937, as a crap game run by a local character known as the Baron in a Fairview, New Jersey, basement. The game got bigger, and the Bergen County mob took it from the Baron, moving it from Fairview to Cliffside Park and back to Fairview, to Little Ferry, to Fort Lee, then finally to a converted taxi-repair garage—the Barn—in Lodi. Employing four hundred workers and netting an average of $10,000,000 a year, the Barn was the biggest money-maker in the history of illegal gambling. It grossed more in a month than the Monte Carlo Casino grossed in a year. On its best night, the first of September 1946, the Barn took in more than a million and a quarter. The income from the Barn for New York mob boss Frank Costello alone was said to be $12,000 a week. Like Colonel Bradley's old Beach Club in Florida, the Barn refused admittance to local citizens. Limousine service ran regularly between it and the finer hotels in Manhattan. The Bergen County authorities were paid $2,000,000 a year to protect the Barn and other joints throughout the county. The most legitimate of those joints was the Riviera.

The Riviera was known for its food and its shows and its magnificent view overlooking the Hudson, but above all it was known for its gambling. Like the Barn, the Riviera casino was a multimillion-dollar-a-year operation. Martin and Lewis opened at the Riviera in the first week of September, following wire-service stories that Abby Greshler had reported Dean missing. The Riviera booking was the team's most prestigious nightclub engagement so far, and George Evans had concocted the disappearance to stir publicity. For Evans, it was a pleasant change.

Evans had been cultivating the image of Martin and Lewis as two freewheeling, fun-loving guys whose act was merely an extension of their everyday personalities and antics. Dean was supposed to be a sex symbol, sure. But sex symbols were not supposed to run around greasing every chorus girl in creation. It was charm and starry romance he was supposed to exude, not semen and saliva. Offstage, he was supposed to be far more interested in practical-joking and cavorting with Jerry than in playing hide-the-*salsiccia* in a succession of hotel rooms. Dean's philandering, however, had become increasingly brazen, and much of Evans's time and energy was spent suppressing the wrong kind of publicity rather than pro-moting the right kind. Now one of his melancholy babies, the dancer Miriam LaVelle, was in the show with them at the Riviera. Dean had first met Miriam when she was performing at Nicky Blair's Carnival on Eighth Avenue, one of the joints he hit making the rounds with Johnny Buff and Peppi. The pretty brunette had recently recovered from surgery on her leg, but there was no scar that nylon could not veil.

Martin and Lewis held the stage for almost an hour that first night at the Riviera. Jerry took the act out into the parking-lot, where he clowned as an attendant as the patrons arrived. Night after night, the crowds grew, and Riviera manager Bill Miller held them over, week after week, straight through to the end of October, at $2,250 a week.

During Prohibition, the young torch singer Helen Morgan made her way, via Chicago, from her native Danville, Ohio, to New York. In New York, she came under the favor and patronage of Lucky Luciano, who opened a speakeasy, Chez Morgan, in her honor. There, night after night, she would perch herself prettily atop the piano and sing "Can't Help Lovin' Dat Man," the song she made famous when she appeared in Ziegfeld's *Show Boat* in 1927. It was an old tradition: Louis Armstrong had started out at a joint called Matranga's, run by Henry Matranga, one of the brothers who had taken control in New Orleans after the Mafia war of 1890. Matranga "treated everybody fine," Armstrong remembered, "and the colored people who patronized his tonk loved him very much." Chez Morgan got busted before *Show Boat* made its way from Washington to Broadway, and Morgan was dead now—she had died broke—and Luciano was gone; but the symbiosis between show business and *la bisiness* was as strong as ever.

They had the gambling. They had the booze. Costello owned

Alliance Distributors, the sole American distributor for the Whiteley Company of Scotland, the makers of King's Ransom and House
of Lords Scotch. He also held the controlling interest in Whiteley's
parent company, J. G. Turney & Sons, Ltd., and, as an appointed
agent for Whitely, he received a commission of two shillings and
sixpence on every case of King's Ransom and House of Lords
brought into the country. These commissions amounted to some
$35,000 a month. Adonis, Meyer Lansky, and others, meanwhile,
had interests in Capitol Wine and Spirits, a major importer of European wines, Scotch, and Canadian whiskey.

Entertainers were like booze; they were like the slot-machines
and the rest of the shit in Longie's warehouse: just another way for a
joint to make money off the suckers.

Vito Genovese, one of Luciano's early cohorts, had fled to his
native Italy in 1934 to avoid trial for murder in New York. Brought
back in 1945, he had been acquitted in June of 1946. He had taken
his place then at the side of Frank Costello, whose power and fortune had eclipsed his own; and now he had embarked on wresting
and seizing that power and that fortune from within. It would take
ten long years, but he would succeed.

Heroin, *la bubbonia,* was the heart of Genovese's *imperium in
imperio.* But among his other burgeoning personal interests were
nightclubs. Eventually he owned several joints in Greenwich Village and on the Lower East Side: the Club Savannah, at 68 West
Third Street; the 82 Club, at 82 East Fourth Street; the Moroccan
Village, the 181 Club, and others. He held them in secret, placing
ownership in the names of others, such as his brother-in-law Tony
Petillo or Steve Francis, the escort and confidant of his lesbian wife,
Anna Petillo Vernotico, whom Genovese had widowed in order to
marry, in 1932. The Savannah, managed by Lou Taylor ("For Reservations, Call Smiling Lou"), featured a high-yellow chorus line of
"14 Beautiful Savannah Peaches" and shows produced by Clarence
Robinson, who had staged revues at the old Cotton Club. The 82
featured transvestite acts. There was money in this shit. People
craved entertainment like they craved dope. "Did you take a bath
this morning?" the *don giovanni* says. "Why, is there one missing?"

the *scimpanzè* says. *E fa 'n cul'*—it was true—*per questa merda pagavano,* for this they paid. And more handsomely than for his *caffelatte*-colored tootsies and his men in women's clothes.

"Nice boy, he work for me, he don't worry no more 'bout nothing," Genovese told Dean one night, like a shadow illuminated for one brief instant in the fulmination of a sudden passing moment. "Nice boy, he work for me, everything nice. *Come famiglia.*"

Dean, Jerry, and Greshler found themselves being courted by the vassals of Vito Genovese. With his *eroina* and his great displays of Catholic piety, with his drag queens and his strange little wife who had walked to the altar through the blood of her first husband, Genovese was the most violent, most grasping, and most treacherous of his breed. But there were others too, with nightclubs or connections or dreams of their own. On top of everything, Bill Miller, with the shadow of the Bergen County mob behind him, claimed to hold an unwritten option on future engagements. Greshler began receiving ominous visits and calls. Some of the callers he recognized. The ones he could not identify were even more disquieting.

"I have no comment on that," Greshler would say many years later when asked about those visits and calls. "I know every underworld character in the world, but I never had any problems with them. They kidnapped my kid once, but outside of that, it was quiet."

To make matters worse, Dean and Jerry had begun to argue, accusing each other of fucking up routines by trying to steal the spotlight. There were days when they refused to speak to one another offstage. And when they were getting along, they turned on Greshler, calling him to account for expenses and charging him with sly-fucking them. At one point, seeking a way out for himself, he offered to sell the act to the William Morris Agency. Asking for $17,500, he was turned down.

More and more, the strangers who approached Dean seemed to have that look that he had first come to know, long ago, in Jimmy Tripodi's eyes; that Mayfield Road *malocchio,* that look that boded no good. But there were other, more benevolent strangers who came to him that autumn as well.

Ike and Bess Berman, who operated the Rainbow Music Shop at

102 West 125th Street in Harlem, had started their little Apollo
Records company with two partners, Hy Siegel and Sam Schneider,
late in 1943. By early 1945, they had moved the company downtown to 615 Tenth Avenue. Apollo's first hit records, by blues
shouter Wynonie Harris and veteran jazz bandleader Luis Russell,
had made their mark in 1946. Moving to 342 Madison Avenue that
year, Apollo had begun to expand its horizons beyond the black
audience. The company's first album, released in May of that year,
was by Ray Eberle, formerly of the Glenn Miller Orchestra. In early
1947, Apollo had signed Gordon MacRae, Connee Boswell, and
other white singers, as well as Charlie Barnet and His Orchestra.
When Greshler read that an NBC staff conductor, Jerry Jerome, had
been appointed Apollo's music director, he invited him out to see
the show at the Riviera.

"So I came and saw the show, and it was hysterical," recalled
Jerome. "They were crazy, they were nuts. And I thought, Jesus,
Dean's got a pretty nice voice. I thought he'd be good to do some
nice, easy swing stuff, 'cause he was very loose, even in the way he
wore his hat and everything."

Dean was "very cordial," Jerome remembered. But, as it developed, he was also very "hard to pin down." When Jerome managed
finally to get him to the WOR Recording Studios later that October,
he found it odd that Dean, who had recorded professionally only
once before, evinced a sort of jaded, world-weary impatience rather
than the sense of eagerness and expectation that one might expect
from a young man enjoying the first exciting bloom of success.

Unlike Dean's idol Bing Crosby, with whom Jerome also
worked, Dean "was not a disciplined singer." He was very casual,
off-handedly funny, but "very impatient to get on with things," and
"he'd never do the same thing twice." He was cocky, assured. "And
he always used quite a bit of invective: 'Hey, why don't we forget
this fuckin' tune,' and 'Shit, fuck this,' and 'Hell, let's do it. I don't
care. Fuck it.' "

As a producer, Jerome found himself "treading carefully with
him. Because I wanted to get my work done. I didn't want to waste
time, and it cost money for the company."

Dean recorded two songs that day in the studio. In the first week of November, Apollo released them as a single: the 1930 Tin Pan Alley classic "Walkin' My Baby Back Home" and a blithe Italian version of "Oh, Marie."

Under his contract with Apollo, Dean was paid $150 for the two recordings. The contract held Dean to Apollo for a period of three months, with an option for a one-year renewal.

James Caesar Petrillo, the president of the American Federation of Musicians, had long been a crusader against what he called "the menace of mechanical music." Rightly foreseeing that recordings could someday wholly replace live music on radio, he had brought recording to a halt in the summer of 1942 by nullifying all AFM recording licenses. That AFM ban, winning out over antitrust complaints, had lasted for more than a year, and had not been fully settled, despite a plea from President Roosevelt, for more than two years. Now, in the fall of 1947, Petrillo was threatening another ban. Record companies, fearing the worst, rushed to stockpile recordings against that eventuality. Optimistically fearing that Dean's record might become a hit and that there would be nothing with which to follow it up, Apollo brought him back twice to record more songs in late November, once with the Hal Kanner Orchestra, once with a different, softer backing of vibes, guitar, sparse reeds, and a few timid organ-swells. By paying him the amount guaranteed under the option—$187.50 per side—rather than the price in effect under the original three-month period, Apollo also activated its hold on him for another year. Dean recorded four more songs, including another *napulitane* classic, Teodoro Cottrau's 1849 "Santa Lucia."

Amid continuing calls from the dark and Bill Miller's rising claims to the right of future commitments, Greshler had booked Martin and Lewis to open in Chicago on November 26, at the Chez Paree. Before leaving town, Dean brought Betty to New York. They fought and they fucked, and, in the end, Dean promised Betty that they would get their own place as soon as he got back from Chicago.

Established since the Prohibition days of 1932, the Chez was a much bigger and classier joint than the Rio Cabana, where they had performed before. At the Rio Cabana, they had shared the stage with Al Wheatley, doing business as Tung Pin Soo. It had been him, Charlene ("his sexappealing brunette assistant"), the pigeons that magically materialized nightly at the beckoning of the great Soo's wand, and them. At the Chez Paree, the act that preceded them, Paul Draper, danced, pigeonless, to Schumann's "Romance in F Major" and a Bach gigue. But, then again, the act that preceded him was a guy with two trained dogs.

"Martin's song styling is first rate," said *Variety*'s reviewer. His rendition of "Peg o' My Heart" had "femmes leaning forward for more"; his routines with Lewis elicited "yocks and salvos all the way."

Yocks were not commonly associated with the men who had taken over Al Capone's rule in Chicago. And yet, among the yocking hoi polloi, nearer the stage than most, unrecognized by Martin and Lewis, there they were.

"I made one mistake in Chicago," Jerry would later recall.

There was a man, about forty-five, seated with a group at one of the ringside tables. He was facing away from the stage, saying something to one of the men he was with. Jerry reached over and smacked him on the shoulder.

"Hey, pal, the show is up here!" he hollered in his mongoloid-from-hell voice.

The man turned and glared at him: "If you don't move away, right now, I'll blow your fuckin' head off."

Jerry was stunned. "Naive schmuck that I was, it flashed on me: I was in Chicago, who this guy might be, and what I had just done."

After the show, he gathered his courage and walked over to the man's table. "I said, 'May I please sit down a moment and extend my apologies?' I still don't know who I'm talking to. He says to this guy opposite him, 'Give him a chair.' I sit down. And he's dressed in a white-on-white shirt with a hundred-dollar white tie, with links. I mean, he *looked* like a don. He said, 'Go 'head, speak.' I said, 'Sir, there's no excuse for stupidity, but I'm young, I'm tryin' to do what I think is good on the stage, and I got carried away, and what I did was rude and disrespectful, and I'm really very sorry.' He says to me, 'After I tell you I'm gonna blow your fuckin' head off, you got the guts to come over here. You're all right.' Shakes my hand, says, 'My name is Charlie Fischetti.' I didn't know what that meant: Charlie Fischetti. But I can tell you now what it meant."

Charlie, whom the newspapers delighted in referring to as Trigger-Happy Fischetti, was Al Capone's cousin from Brooklyn. He had broken in Virginia Hill for Adonis, Luciano, and Siegel; had been Capone's right-hand man in the late twenties, and had risen beside Frank Nitti, Tony Accardo, Paul Ricca, and Jake Guzik to inherit the empire that Capone had left behind upon his imprisonment in 1932. Since Nitti's suicide in 1943 and the imprisonment of Ricca and others in 1944, the triumvirate of Accardo, Fischetti, and Guzik had ruled Chicago, alone and with the later benison and counsel of Ricca, that most gentlemanly of killers. Charlie's brothers, Rocco and Joe, were men of power as well. Rocco controlled gambling in Cook County under Charlie. Joe, who had befriended Frank Sinatra and other young celebrities, was a glamour boy of deadly sorts. But in Chicago, Charlie was the man. From his penthouse duplex at 3100 Lake Shore Drive, the city looked like his own vast cold garden. It was a view that Dean and Jerry came to know.

From that night at the Chez Paree—Jerry would cross his fingers tightly together as he said it—"I was like that with Charlie. I never went to Chicago without seeing Charlie. Rocky, his brother. Joe Fischetti, to this day. Very, very dear friends of mine. There's never been a telethon where I don't get very, very heavy-duty checks from that family, every year."

Martin and Lewis remained at the Chez Paree for more than three months. The average per-capita income in America for 1947 was $1,323; in 1948, it was slightly higher: $1,410. By the time they left Chicago, in February, Martin and Lewis had made more than $30,000. Midway through the engagement, on December 27, the United States District Court for the Southern District of New York duly adjudged Dean to be bankrupt and thereby "discharged from all debts and claims." By then, Betty Martin knew that she was pregnant again.

Back in New York, Martin and Lewis returned in March to the Loew's Capitol. The nine-month option from last April's Capitol date had expired, and Greshler was able to get them $2,250 a week for their month-long run. At the same time, Greshler had successfully negotiated a deal with the Copacabana. His asking price had risen to $3,000. Why, the Copa had demanded, was he seeking $2,500 elsewhere and $3,000 here? "Because I can't get a ringside seat here," Greshler had responded. In the end, the Copacabana had agreed to two weeks at $2,500 a week, plus a ringside table and unlimited house-tab for Greshler.

Dean kept his promise. He, Betty, and the kids moved into a ten-room apartment at Riverside Drive and West 106th Street. Dean dreaded elevators. Once, several years ago, he had been trapped in a stalled elevator for an hour or so. The experience had struck a nerve of fear that he had never known to be within him. The claustrophobic nightmare of that coffin-womb had not subsided, but had worsened, and he had not set foot in an elevator again. And so, while the preferred apartments in the Riverside Drive building were on the higher floors, Dean chose to live on the third and thus avoid the terror of that modern convenience that so attracted other renters.

"What I remembered most," Jerry said of the night Dean and Betty invited Jerry and Patti to their new home, "was that first look at Dean's bedroom closet, every square foot filled with handmade suits and tuxedos, racks and racks of shoes, ceiling-to-floor shelves containing imported silk shirts and cashmere sweaters."

Martin and Lewis headlined the Capitol show with Tex Beneke, whose twenty-eight-piece orchestra was one of the last of the actively touring big bands. The screen attraction, *The Naked City,* was one of the hits of the year, filling the theater, four times daily, close to its capacity of well over four thousand.

Variety reflected that the crowd of "action picture devotees being lured by the late Mark Hellinger's production probably isn't appreciative of the smooth, subtle and smart offerings of Tex Beneke's band." On the other hand, "Dean Martin and Jerry Lewis, whose comeuppance during the past two years has been considerable, do not wear out their welcome" in the course of their twenty-five-minute act. "Theirs is the type of act that throws everything at the audience, from impersonations, low comedy to straight singing. They're fresh and stuff is frequently original." Bill Smith, their longtime follower at *Billboard*, concurred: Beneke's half of the show "was monotonous," but the Martin-and-Lewis half "was terrific." They had "sharpened their timing" and had "a polish and an ease" that rendered the team "one of the top yock pullers in the business."

"They may hit name proportions with their date at the Copacabana, N.Y., next month," *Variety* remarked. It was a prediction that would soon prove true.

The Copacabana. This was it: the most famous joint in the world. It certainly was not Frank Costello's biggest money-maker, but it was his greatest showplace.

The Copa was a straight joint. There was no gambling. Yet the club had grown out of Costello's gambling operation upstate in Saratoga. In the second week of September 1940, after the close of the Saratoga racing season, the newly formed corporation of Copacabana, Inc., had leased the former location of the Villa Valle restaurant, a space of some twelve thousand square feet, at 10 East Sixtieth Street, in the Hotel Fourteen. The rent, payable to Hotel Fourteen, Inc., was slightly over $100,000 a year. Monte Proser, the Copacabana group's majority shareholder of record, was listed as the president, and it was his name that appeared, with his birthplace altered from "England" to "U.S.A.," on the license application. Forty-three-year-old Julie Podell, who fronted for Costello, did not present too immaculate a facade. He was a former bootlegger with a police record. In the summer of 1929, after being shot at the speakeasy he was running at 154 West Fiftieth Street, he was arrested for not cooperating with authorities; and, by the end of Prohibition, he had been arrested four times for Volstead Act violations and once for grand larceny. But Monte Proser, another front man, was clean. Walter Winchell helped to spread the illusion that it was Proser's place from the start, reporting in his November 2 *Daily Mirror* column that "Monte Proser's Copacabana opened last night."

Named for the resort hotel in Rio de Janiero, the four-hundred-seat room was done up in what Proser referred to as Brazilian decor. To complement the theme, there was dance music by two Latin bands, as well as by Nat Brandwynne and His Orchestra. Proser and his director, Marjery Fielding, developed a chorus line like no other. The Copacabana Girls, their hair upswept and dyed pink, green, orange, purple to match their sequined costumes, were, in the words of Walter Winchell, "the best girl show in town." The costumes themselves—besides the sequined outfits, there were mink panties, mink brassieres, and fruited turbans—were said to cost $4,000 for each girl.

The Copa had survived tax troubles and a 1944 investigation under Mayor La Guardia into its ties with Frank Costello. While the city sought to establish that "there were known racketeers or gangsters frequenting the Copacabana" as well as "persons interested or part owners who are disreputable persons engaged in unlawful enterprise," the Copa's attorney, Harold H. Corbin, indignantly declared that the Copacabana was "a national institution that everyone in the United States ought to be proud of." Costello himself was subpoenaed at his home at the Majestic Apartments, 115 Central Park West, eight blocks south of Meyer Lansky's new home at the Beresford. He refused to testify at the hearing on grounds that he had not been called in good faith; and, in the end, the Copacabana, while admitting no connection to Costello, agreed to render "completely terminated and severed" any connection that Costello "may now have or have had." The agreement with the city further stipulated that Jules Podell be dismissed. But the following year, Costello's man, Irish-born William O'Dwyer, was elected to take La Guardia's place as mayor. Now, in 1948, not only was Julie Podell still running the joint for Costello; people were calling it Jules Podell's Copacabana. The place was bigger now. It had built out onto a terrace. The showroom and bar seated over seven hundred. The number of girls in the line had been increased from six to eight. One thing had not changed: the menu specialized in Chinese food. To Dean, the Copa, for all its glamour, smelled like State Street in Columbus on a Saturday night.

They opened on April 8, billed second to Vivian Blaine, the twenty-six-year-old blond singer from Newark who had starred in several Twentieth Century-Fox musicals. The crowd, however, was there to see Martin and Lewis, to find out what all the talk was about, to be where the season's next-big-thing was about to enter café society from the outland of rumor and expectation. There were friendly faces at ringside: Betty was there, Patti's and Jerry's parents were there, Abby Greshler and Irving Kaye were there.

For two years, Dean and Jerry had been concocting their own routines. They had stolen bits and snatches here and there: Dean had lifted from the comedian Buddy Lester, with whom he had played the Rio Cabana and other joints, and who now, ironically, had teamed with Steve Condos in an act that was being compared to Martin and Lewis; his drunk persona, which grew more important over the years, was inspired by Joe E. Lewis. Jerry had taken from Gene Baylos, whose stumbling-jerk persona and Quasimodo movements had impressed him in the Catskills years ago, and from the Wesson Brothers, who until recently had been Greshler's biggest act. But most of their purloined bits and snatches served only as catalysts for their own interactive spontaneity. Uneasy about their Copa debut, however, Jerry had hired professional writers for the first time. Danny Shapiro, among them, was paid a grand. As the opening night approached, however, they had jettisoned it all. They went onstage and did what they had been doing all along, but with a new and wild adrenaline surge, borne by the precarious excitement of the moment, so irrevocable and decisive and yet so unreal.

Dean sang "You Won't Be Satisfied (Until You Break My Heart)," which Les Brown and Perry Como had released earlier in the year, "Oh, Marie," and "Rock-a-Bye Your Baby with a Dixie Melody." Jerry, replete with plastic buckteeth, took his idiot-waiter routine into the audience. Together they assaulted "That Old Gang of Mine." Dean did a few of the crazy-leg steps he remembered from his uncle Leonard Barr's routine.

"Although sub-billed to Vivian Blaine," said *Variety*, "Martin and Lewis are the real stars of the show—and will prove the real draw."

They remained onstage for fifty minutes, well over their allotted time. "They wouldn't let us off," Jerry said. "Nobody could have followed us." Vivian Blaine stumbled on the lyrics of what was supposed to be a funny song about the Kinsey Report. "She cut two numbers from her act and left the stage in tears."

Julie Podell, whose deep, rasping whiskey-voiced commands were often accompanied by the rapping of the great star-sapphire ring he wore, was not known for his delicacy of manner. Patrons trying to ingratiate themselves with him or impress their dates by greeting him in passing with a pat on the shoulder were likely to be countered with, "Get the fuck away from me, asshole." The acts were treated no differently: "Get off my stage, nigger!" he would bellow to Sammy Davis, Jr., when Sammy, against the order he was given, let his show run overtime; the singer Johnnie Ray, whom he could not stomach, would be locked by him in the club's freezer and stricken with pneumonia as a result. So, after that April 8 opening night, Podell came right out and told Vivian Blaine, point-blank, that he was making Martin and Lewis the headline attraction; and Vivian Blaine quit in humiliation.

In the nights that followed, it seemed as if all New York were gathering to get in. The minimum at the Copa was only three and a half bucks a head; but people, eager for ringside tables, were shake-slipping tens, twenties, even fifties, at the door. Joe Lopez, the maître d', was pulling down a grand a week and more in palm-money.

Once again, as at the Chez Paree, Jerry inadvertently fucked with the wrong man. It was between shows. Dean was shooting the breeze with Joe Lopez, while Jerry, as he often did, was drifting through the crowd, giving them a taste of mongoloid mayhem to come. He was getting laughs at the bar when he heard it: "Why don't you knock off that shit and shut the fuck up?"

The guy looked like a gorilla. Jerry was taken aback. He figured the guy was either kidding or too drunk to realize that Jerry was who he was. Remaining in character, he laughed idiotically, looked at the man, and threw off an old line: "That's what happens when cousins get married."

He saw Dean wince. Joe Lopez shook his head and raised his fingers to his temple.

The gorilla rose slowly. He stuck his forefinger toward Jerry's face. "That's not funny, you stupid sonofabitch. You open your mouth again, you won't have no teeth."

Jerry was silent. Dean was there now. "My partner's a little young," he said to the man, trying to calm him. "He didn't mean any harm."

The man glared at them for a moment, then turned away. Dean told Jerry to apologize to the guy. Jerry did as Dean said, and the man looked at Dean: "Okay. Only you keep the little bastard away from me. You tell him he's lucky I got a sense of humor."

The man with the sense of humor turned out to be a guy that they had long heard of but never encountered before, the guy the newspapers liked to call the Lord High Executioner of Murder, Inc.

"For your information, schmuck, that was Albert Anastasia," Dean told him.

Eventually, they met Frank Costello himself. They met them all. "Once they knew you, it was okay," Jerry said. "But they never, ever liked you to ruffle their dignity. Sunday nights at the Copa, at ringside, was the galaxy of the heads of the New York families. Sunday nights, with their wives. And after the show, when you were summoned to the table, you went so that they could introduce you to their children and their wives. Everything was very, very lovely and above-board. The next day, the same guy introducing you to his lovely two daughters pumps six shells into some poor sonofabitch on the Bowery, like nothin'. Tuesday, Wednesday night, you see the same guy with his broad. Now, the reason they put a trust in you—it's almost like they tested you—having played your cards right on Sunday night, having seen what you did on Wednesday night, then you're all right."

"Guys in the rackets," Jerry would say, "were very, very loyal, protective" of him and Dean. "But you had to be prepared to pay back. Like, for example, one of the daughters in one of the important New York families was getting married; the big favor, the big payback, was just to show up."

There was good, there was bad, and there was the world in which they lived. Men such as Frank Costello and Charlie Fischetti were gentlemen, but theirs was a gentility of the soul's deadliest night. "Charlie Fischetti," Jerry figured, "was guilty of more crimes in the city of Chicago than you could put in a book. And the good things these guys did didn't necessarily outweigh the bad things.

"But"—it came down to this—"if you're gonna have them in your life, there's nothing wrong with having them correctly. Because having them incorrectly, it ain't gonna be a long haul. It wouldn't take long."

The bigger and more valuable they got, the bigger the squeeze from all quarters of the dark. For every booking they took, it seemed there was "a hood who wanted us to play his nightclub instead of where we were going." Men such as Costello and Fischetti stood between them and Cerberus.

"You just have to know what calls to make."

Apollo Records had been right to prepare for an AFM recording ban. The ban had gone into effect on the first day of the new year. Dean's record, however, had done nothing, and Apollo had not released any of his other recordings. "The trouble with Apollo at the time," Jerry Jerome said, "was that while they spent money on getting artists and things like that, they really did not do a good job of promotion. They didn't spend. They tended to rely on knowing people behind the scenes, disc-jockeys and things, I guess a little payola here and there. And we just didn't spend enough money on Dean Martin. I thought it was a hell of a record." Now, in late April, in the wake of his success at the Copa, Apollo issued his bilingual "Santa Lucia" and "Hold Me," a song that had been done in the early thirties by Eddy Duchin, Ted Fio Rito, and others. Days after the record was released, Apollo entered a period of transition: Bess Berman, having inherited the company from Ike, was in the process of buying out her partners; and Jerry Jerome was leaving. Dean's new Apollo record, like its predecessor, sank unnoticed.

When the two-week engagement at the Copacabana neared its close, Podell was eager to extend. He held them over again and again, raising their pay to $5,000 a week to do so. They were given a suite above the nightclub in the Hotel Fourteen. It was a sanctuary where Dean could escape to explore the mink brassieres and fruited turbans of amore's balm while Jerry commuted dutifully back and forth to his family in Newark and Betty kept the homefire burning on Riverside Drive.

Spring became summer, and they were still there, headlining

night after night to capacity crowds. On May 14, between shows, they appeared at the Lambs Club Public Gambol; in June, they doubled at the Roxy Theatre, performing there for three weeks, hustling back and forth between the supper and midnight shows at the Copa. The Roxy, which was showing *Give My Regards to Broadway*, wanted something special that June to celebrate the unveiling of its new $80,000 ice stage. In addition to the ice-skating show, they had brought in the Andrews Sisters for their first Roxy appearance, and were paying $10,000 a week for New York's hottest new act. Toward the end of the month, Dean finagled Jerry and himself a respite from it all by pleading laryngitis.

RCA had marketed its first television receivers in 1939, and now, nine years later, there were still fewer than a million sets in America, and almost half of those were in New York. Those who had them had not been able to see much. But now those ugly little devices were beginning to hum and flicker with gathering gales of gray insect fury, joy and plague, mediocrity and madness, from that vast funhouse maw of metastatic delights.

NBC had first broadcast "Texaco Star Theatre," an hour-long television variety show, on June 8. Hosted by Milton Berle, with Señor Wences and Pearl Bailey as guests, the program was already easily the most popular attraction on television. Now CBS had hired the *Daily News* columnist Ed Sullivan, who had already worked as a radio-show host, to bring a similar variety show to its inchoate Sunday-night schedule. Sullivan's show, "Toast of the Town," premiered on June 20, broadcast at nine in the evening from Studio 44, the network's largest radio facility. The budget for that first show was $475, of which $200 went to Martin and Lewis for a six-minute bit.

Sullivan's show lacked the sparkle of the Texaco show, *Variety* said, "chiefly because Sullivan, as an emcee, is a good newspaper columnist." But the talent, which also included Richard Rodgers and Oscar Hammerstein II, "was standout. Tops were Dean Martin and Jerry Lewis with their zany comedics." The network was guilty, however, "of permitting them to give out with some blue material, okay for their nitery work but certainly not for tele."

The Sullivan show's band was the Ray Bloch Orchestra, one of radio's most ubiquitous groups, now making the transition to television. Abby Greshler, looking to both radio and television, hired the Ray Bloch Orchestra, along with writer Hal Block and radio singing star Georgia Gibbs, to make an audition record with Martin and Lewis for circulation among network programmers. The record cost $3,500 to make, and resulted in nothing. The essence of Martin and Lewis could not be conveyed by sound alone. Without the visual element, the comedy fell flat and lackluster.

On July 21, Martin and Lewis returned in triumph to the 500 Café in Atlantic City. There had been pressure from the Bergen County mob, which wanted them back there instead of down in Joe Ida's neck of the woods. Dean and Jerry, however, liked Skinny D'Amato, and they wanted to celebrate their success, and their second anniversary as a team, at Skinny's joint, where that success had begun two years ago this July.

"I called a certain friend of mine," Jerry said, "and, within twenty-four hours, the squeeze was off."

The Riviera got another Copa act, Henny Youngman, who came onstage in a leopardskin; and Martin and Lewis went south. Atlantic City was in full swing: Louis Jordan and his Tympany Five were at Orsati's, Louis Prima was at the Marine Ballroom, Peggy Lee was at the Steel Pier Music Hall. But the arrival of Martin and Lewis drew the crowds to Skinny's joint.

They did forty-five-minute shows, at half past eight, midnight, and three in the morning. There was less and less now of Dean singing straight and alone. His versions of the 1937 Tommy Dorsey hit "Once in a While," "My Heart Sings," and others were steered sideways by Jerry's presence among the musicians, taking the baton from bandleader Dave Ennis, playing the piano with two fingers, leading the band as a choir. They "bring down the house," *Variety* said, "and steal the show." But it seemed, as time went on, that it was becoming less a matter of "they" and more a matter of "the little guy." The monkey had begun to pull the chain on the organ-grinder.

They closed at the 500 Club on August 2. The next night, after returning to New York from Atlantic City, they made their second television appearance, on "Texaco Star Theatre," broadcast live from NBC Studio 6B at 30 Rockefeller Center. Less than a week later, on August 9, they arrived in Los Angeles for their West Coast debut.

> *"The guinea's not bad, but what do I do with the monkey?"*
>
> —LOUIS B. MAYER

Slapsy Maxie Rosenbloom was a colorful character around L.A., an ex-boxer whose sixteen-year career in the ring had left him eminently suited for portraying punch-drunk fighters in the movies. He had lent his name to Slapsy Maxie's Café, a nightclub at 5665 Wilshire Boulevard. The joint's real owners had driven it into the ground; and, in 1947, with the help of L.A.'s top bookie, Mickey Cohen, Sy and Charlie Devore, the clothiers, took it over, giving Cohen an office in one of the back rooms.

Mickey had his share of problems in 1948. His headquarters at 8800 Sunset was in an unincorporated part of Los Angeles, under the exclusive jurisdiction of the county sheriff. Known as the Sunset Strip, this unincorporated district was where every bookmaker in town had his office. And every one of those bookmakers paid $250 a week in juice to Cohen, who controlled the sheriff. Now Jack Dragna, who had held Los Angeles in the grasp of the Chicago forces since the days of Capone, had been assured by Al Guasti, the undersheriff of Los Angeles County, that, with Cohen out of the way, Dragna and the sheriff's office could easily take over most of the juice racket throughout the county, which was estimated at $80,000 a week. While Dragna prepared to dispose of Cohen, his emissaries were already working to lure Mickey's Italian henchmen over from the Magen David to the cross.

In the midst of the rising tension, Charlie and Sy Devore had told Cohen that they wanted to bring Martin and Lewis west to play Slapsy Maxie's. The trouble was that Abby Greshler wanted $4,000 a week plus three round-trip airfares for the twelve-hour flight. The Devores had borrowed from Mickey Cohen before, and they had always made good. "So," as Cohen would recall, "I put up the money to bring Dean Martin and Jerry Lewis in."

They opened at Slapsy Maxie's on August 9. Neither they nor

the Devores had ever witnessed anything like it. George Evans had gathered forth the most glamorous luminaries of make-believe.

"It was incredible," Jerry said. "People at the door fighting for tables. Jimmy Cagney, Fred Astaire, Loretta Young, Joan Crawford, Edward G. Robinson, June Allyson, Humphrey Bogart, Clark Gable, Jane Wyman, Gene Kelly, Gary Cooper—*fighting* for tables."

And sitting right there at ringside amid the stars were Guy and Angela Crocetti. They knew that their boy had been doing good. They had heard the tales of his success, and there had been money from him. The money had helped them move from their little place on Gardenia Avenue to a nicer home on Lemon Avenue. Now they had come in from Long Beach to share in the glory of their son. Twenty years ago and more, in those days when the breezes and shadow-scent of the old country still visited his sleep, Guy had sat alone in the afternoon quiet of his barbershop and wondered what would become of this *scuccia,* this undealt card of a son. Now here they were in Hollywood, *padre e figlio,* and the son stood above the father, and the royalty of this kingless land, this *terra promessa* of the father's boyhood dreams, were gathered to adore the son, in whose fortune the father saw what the others did not: the fulfillment of promise. Like the new land itself, it made little sense, but was still cause for rejoicing. As Gaetano looked around, he found himself slowly nodding in vague affirmation, saying words that had passed through his lips countless times before, at one time or the other bearing every tone in irony's spectrum: "Nice country, America."

There were two warm-up acts, the dancing Four Step Brothers and the singing Mack Triplets. Then Dean took the stage alone. The show would begin with him singing, and no bullshit. He did not want any laughs until later. And they heard him. "Martin, the straight man," *Billboard* reported of that opening night, "won ringsiders with his vocalizing even before the team went into comedy."

"Highest praise to be paid Jerry Lewis and Dean Martin," *Billboard* said, "is that they topped every word of advance build-up. Making their Coast bow, the gagsters had payers in their palms from the start."

"Filmites have been hearing for some time about Dean Martin and Jerry Lewis," said *Variety* of that night. "They weren't disappointed. A comedy team that more than lives up to advance billing, Martin and Lewis proceeded to tear the house down. High priced screen talent was draped all over the place laughing incessantly."

"They were really a hell of an act," said Mickey Cohen, who was also there that night. "I got a big kick out of them."

Ten nights later, Mickey got another sort of jolt. A sawed-off-shotgun blast from one of Dragna's men nearly finished him at his haberdashery on Beverly Boulevard. Mickey would survive the subsequent attempts by Dragna as well. He would be gunned down at a joint on Sunset, his house would be bombed. In the end, it would not be Dragna who was to put him out of business, but the Internal Revenue Service, which brought Cohen to trial in 1951. By the time Mickey was sent to prison, in 1952, Dragna's man, Al Guasti, had been removed from office. For Jack Dragna, it was already later than he knew. In March of the following year, Dragna, at sixty-four, would be placed under order for deportation to Italy. He would still be appealing that order three years later when he dropped dead of a heart attack in a Sunset Strip hotel room. Johnny Rosselli, Dragna's cohort since the twenties, would then take over on his own. Rosselli, who had been released from prison in 1947 following his involvement in the IATSE shakedowns, would present himself as a movie producer when questioned by the Kefauver committee in 1950.

"You had a lot of friends."

"I had a lot of friends, yes," Rosselli said.

"You had a reputation for being perhaps a tough guy?"

"I probably did during Prohibition."

"That reputation stayed with you, I suppose?"

"To my sorrow."

"I want a loud band," Greshler had told the Devores. What he had gotten was the Dick Stabile Orchestra, the regular house band. Like Jerry, Stabile was from Newark. Like Dean, he had been a Boy Scout drummer. After dropping out of high school, he had joined Ben Bernie's band as a clarinetist and alto saxophonist. He had left Bernie in 1935 to form his own orchestra, recruiting trumpeter

Bunny Berrigan to join the group for its first Decca session the following January. From a base at the William Penn Hotel in Pittsburgh, Stabile had gone on to tour extensively and establish himself in New York. His orchestra had developed into a band within a band, a fourteen-piece ensemble with a saxophone quartet, featuring himself and his younger brother Joe, at its heart. In 1946, before coming west to Slapsy Maxie's, he had worked with Frank Sinatra at the Waldorf, Copacabana, and Hotel Biltmore. In him, Martin and Lewis found the bandleader that would become their own.

During the long run at the Copa, several Hollywood producers expressed interest in Martin and Lewis. Among them was the veteran Hal Wallis, whose production company had a long-term deal with Paramount.

"I heard about them from several people," Wallis recalled in his memoirs, "and when I was in New York, I dropped by the Copacabana to see what the shouting was all about." Wallis did not much enjoy nightclub comedy of any sort, and his expectations had not been great. "They were strangely ill-matched. Dean, tall and very handsome, didn't look like a comedian and Jerry, equipped with a mouthful of oversized false teeth and a chimpanzee-like hairpiece, seemed grotesque.

"But even before they began their act, the audience was screaming with laughter. Never before or since have I seen an audience react as this one did." Wallis had known then and there that he wanted to sign them.

"I assure you, we're going to make a movie together. And soon," he had told them when Greshler brought him to their suite above the Copa after the show.

After their first night at Slapsy Maxie's, which Wallis attended, the others all rushed forth, as Wallis had known they would. Robert Goldstein from Universal Pictures was offering $30,000 but was insistent on an exclusive deal, under which Universal would authorize and control any outside work. Greshler would not capitulate, and Dean and Jerry, spread-eagled and panting for moving-picture glory, threatened to leave him and sign on their own. Meanwhile, Joe Pasternak and MGM director George K. Sidney had raised the bidding to $40,000. They too, however, were adamant on exclusivity, and again Greshler withdrew, and again Dean and Jerry threatened to quit him. When Pasternak countered with an offer for Dean alone, it appeared that the three of them—Martin, Lewis, and Greshler—were about to violently disperse and go their separate ways. Pasternak urged Greshler to talk to Louis B. Mayer before making another move. But instead Greshler met with Hal Wallis's partner, Joe Hazen. A series of further meetings ensued, and a screen test was arranged.

"When I ran the finished test," Wallis said, "I felt a shock wave of disappointment. Great on stage, the two comics were awful on screen: their timing was off; they were self-conscious and stiff. The charisma that live audiences responded to so enthusiastically disappeared in the transition to film. On the screen, nothing happened. Without saying anything to Dean and Jerry, I prepared another test. It was even worse than the first. They had lost the magic of their nightclub performances.

"Should I let them go? Suddenly it came to me. The reason they were terrible was that they were doing scenes written for them, playing characters."

Wallis set up a third test, telling them to just go ahead and do what they did onstage. "I had wanted to play down Jerry's slapstick humor with the wigs, masks, claw hands, and false teeth. I thought those burlesque routines would be too extreme for movie audiences, but I was wrong. The moment Dean and Jerry did their act exactly as they had done it on stage, they were fantastic. They burned up the screen. Everybody in the projection room was in stitches."

Wallis, Greshler, Martin, and Lewis were sitting together talking at Slapsy Maxie's one night. When Wallis left the table, Joe Pasternak came forward.

"If you take the Wallis deal, you'll never make another picture," he told them.

The next day, Greshler went with Pasternak to see Louis B. Mayer. Greshler brought Jerry along to see for himself that he was not being double-crossed.

According to Hal Wallis, Mayer had previously said, "The guinea's not bad, but what do I do with the monkey?" But now

Mayer told Greshler that MGM would pay whatever Wallis was offering. Once again, however, there could be no outside work.

Reflecting, as he later explained, that "nobody says no to
Mayer," Greshler told him he would think it over. That night,
Greshler suffered a nervous collapse and was taken to Temple
Hospital.

In the midst of all this, Greshler was playing Niles Trammel of
NBC and Bud Barry of ABC against one another for a network deal.
Of the record-company executives who came to Slapsy Maxie's that
August, Alan Livingston of Capitol was the most eager to offer a
contract: a one-year deal guaranteeing eight releases, straight recordings by Martin and comedy recordings by the team, with pres-
sings of 100,000 each.

Dean became a father again on August 19, when Betty gave
birth in New York to a fourth child, another dark-haired daughter.
Her birth certificate would bear the name Dina Martin, but she and
her family would always spell it differently: Deana. Late the next
afternoon, Dean and Jerry signed with Capitol Records.

Over the course of the next few days, Wallis and Greshler came
to terms. Wallis would have the right to make two pictures a year
with Martin and Lewis over the course of the next five years. Martin
and Lewis would be paid $50,000 for the first picture, $60,000 for
the second, $75,000 for the third, and so on, for a potential total of
$1,250,000. They would be permitted to make one additional pic-
ture each year on their own. They would be permitted to engage in
other outside work as well, except for nightclub appearances during
periods of film production, which were not to exceed ten weeks per
film. The deal was finalized and announced on the last day of the
month, along with the news that work on their first Hal Wallis production for Paramount, *My Friend Irma,* would begin in the fall.

Mickey Cohen, who took credit for bankrolling their trip to Los
Angeles, also claimed he helped get them their Screen Actors Guild
membership cards. There was a problem, he said, "because Lou
Costello put in a knock against them." But Costello was his friend,
"and I straightened the thing out and got them in the Guild." Lewis
considered Cohen's account of paying their way west to be plausible

but unlikely: "I doubt it." Regarding the Guild cards, however, he would say, "That's all bullshit."

Paramount. Dean remembered standing outside those gates on a gray spring afternoon twelve years and a world ago. That world, that dirty back-room dream, was ended. The kingdom of that nation east of Palestine, great Babylon, mother of all whoredom, was his.

Betty was stuck in New York. Newborn Deana had a congenital respiratory ailment. It would not prove serious, and Betty had already retained a housemaid to help care for the children, but she could not accept the idea of traveling without the baby. Dean commended and blessed her; and while she remained back east, he unzipped himself in Babylon. He was the darling of the moment in a land where all that was new and golden was adored; the gynecopia of starlet slutdom was his to savor at will. As always, the forbidden fruit, that from the loftiest bough, was sweetest.

Almost immediately, he took up with MGM's quintessential girl-next-door, June Allyson. On August 10, the day after Allyson attended the Martin-and-Lewis opening at Slapsy Maxie's, she and her husband Dick Powell took delivery of a two-month-old baby from the adoption agency that had long kept them waiting. It was the happiest day of their marriage. She told Dean so a few weeks later, on the night she first went to bed with him.

Jerry had begun picking up Dean's nasty habits early on in their relationship. He had started gambling in Atlantic City: twenty dollars on a baseball game, a trip to the track. Now in Babylon, the candyland of *loch* and *tsatskes*, his days as a faithful husband and nice Jewish boy were gone for good.

"Shit, yeah, we started knockin' 'em off. I think between us, we went through 'em all. Not something to be proud of, but true. The most beautiful broads went crazy for Dean. In truth, I fucked more than he did; but it was always like they wanted to burp me. When you take two six-year-olds and stick 'em in a candy store . . ." His voice would fade away.

Allyson was working that summer with Elizabeth Taylor and Janet Leigh in Mervyn LeRoy's new MGM version of *Little Women*. Twenty-one-year-old Leigh would remember Dean and Jerry visiting the set. By then Jerry was fucking around with June Allyson's friend Gloria De Haven, a big-band singer who had starred with June in *Best Foot Forward,* and who was married to the actor John Payne.

The four of them, Dean and June and Jerry and Gloria, were so bold in their public carryings-on that Hedda Hopper, at George Evans's request, warned them to be careful, lest they become the feast of less friendly columnists.

The money and the deals came down like sweet summer rain. Earl Ebi and Corning Jackson of the J. Walter Thompson advertising agency signed them for $2,500 to perform on an upcoming Thanksgiving radio special their client Elgin was sponsoring. Bob Hope, who had been with NBC for ten years with "The Pepsodent Show," was about to premiere his new NBC program, "The Bob Hope Show," sponsored by Swan Soap. After seeing Martin and Lewis at Slapsy Maxie's, Hope signed them as guests for the new show: $2,000 plus an option on five more spots at the same price.

On September 13, they made their first recordings at the Capitol Studio on Melrose Avenue. There were two songs recorded that day. One, "That Certain Party," by Gus Kahn and Walter Donaldson, had been recorded in 1925 as a comedy duet by the Happiness Boys team of Ernest Hare and Billy Jones, and had been recently revived by Benny Strong. The other, "The Money Song," from a stillborn musical by Harold Rome, had never been recorded before. Buddy Clark and the Andrews Sisters would follow Martin and Lewis with versions of their own.

The AFM ban that had commenced in January was still in effect that September, so Capitol had arranged to have the music for these recordings taped four days before in Mexico City by the nonunion musicians of the Mario R. Armengol Orchestra. The vocal tracks were then added. Through the further technical trickery of magnetic tape, Jerry's voice in "That Certain Party" was accelerated to absurdity while, simultaneously, Dean's retained its natural pace and pitch.

Martin and Lewis had a commitment with Jack Lynch to appear soon at the Latin Casino in Philadelphia. Sy and Charlie Devore had tried to buy out Lynch's contract, but to no avail. Dean and

Jerry returned east after the Capitol session. They were met in Philadelphia by Patti Lewis and three-year-old Gary, Betty and six-year-old Craig, four-year-old Claudia, three-year-old Barbara Gail, little Deana, and their nursemaid, Sue. The two men had not seen their families in well over a month; and Dean saw his new daughter for the first time then. Patti and Betty had stood by them through the years. Now it seemed, for one glorious autumn moment, that the dream had turned golden and the bad times were done. Betty would never have to listen to her mother's rantings again; Dean was making more in a month than Bill McDonald made in a year. And he loved her too, goddamnit, she knew it; in that one glorious, golden autumn moment, she knew it.

June Allyson and Gloria De Haven had followed their loverboys east and checked into suites at the Hampshire House, the luxury hotel on Central Park South where Frank Sinatra and Ava Gardner had set up house in Manhattan. On Sunday night, October 3, Dean and Jerry were to appear with Phil Silvers, the Russ Morgan Orchestra, and the Four Step Brothers on the premiere of NBC's "Welcome Aboard." Betty had fallen ill with pleurisy. There was no way that she would be commuting with Dean to New York for the show. Jerry persuaded Patti to remain in Philadelphia with Betty.

"Oh, Christ," Jerry remembered. "George Evans was our press agent, and he had fuckin' *migraines,* the way we carried on. We went arm-in-arm down Fifth Avenue. Two married men with the biggest stars in Hollywood."

In its review, *Variety* found Martin and Lewis "a little disappointing as TV fare. Somehow, this is one of those acts which gets across beautifully in the intimacy of a nightclub, but loses much of its flavor in televizing; the zanyisms don't register the same click in the living room." "Welcome Aboard" was a failure. The sponsor would pull out after only two months, and the show itself would die soon after. Nonetheless, Victor McLeod, the show's producer and director, was already committed to bringing back Martin and Lewis for the next two Sunday nights running.

Betty was still recuperating when Dean and Jerry prepared to return to New York for the second show, on October 10. This time, however, Patti could not be dissuaded. Jerry steered clear of Gloria.

But Dean—*che menefreghismo*—figured, fuck it. That half-a-*fi-nocchio* husband of June's, Dick Powell, didn't know what he was missing. Besides, Patti was Italian; she had been around; she ought to know what *state zitt'* meant.

Patti ratted him out as soon as she got back.

Betty had heard such things before about Dean, and she reck-oned they represented only an inkling of the truth she surmised. Was no illusion of happiness meant to last? "I was just going to ignore it, true or not," she would say. But a couple of nights later, she walked into Dean's dressing-room at the Latin Casino. Sue the nursemaid's husband, George, was standing there by himself with a piece of paper in his hand. "Without having any idea what it was, I took it and read it," Betty said. It was a confirmation copy of a Western Union telegram, addressed to June Allyson, that he had just sent for Dean. It said: "I'm still tingling."

Clutching the telegram, Betty rushed out in a fury to the edge of the stage. Dean and Jerry were doing their act. When he saw Betty angrily waving the telegram, he maneuvered Jerry to the right, be-tween himself and where she was standing. She moved to the other side of the stage; he steered Jerry back to where he had been. Somehow, the absurdity of Dean's desperation stirred laughter from her anger. The purblind desire to hold fast to that golden autumn's illusion conquered her. "I knew there was really nothing serious between Dean and June," she said. "So we made up, and I thought that was the end of it. Everything seemed fine between us."

As Jerry saw it, their philandering neither affected nor reflected their feelings for their wives. "Because, going home at night, we were going home to those that we loved. And what we were doing was playing in our little fucking fantasyland. I never had fifty bucks in my pocket at one time; now I'm walking around with thirty-five hundred in hundred-dollar bills, and I got a starlet on my arm. It's fantasyland."

Where does fantasyland end? When do the six-year-olds get sick of the candy store?

"It never ends."

The Capitol record was released in early October, toward the end of their run in Philadelphia. Performing "That Certain Party" at the Latin Casino and on "Welcome Aboard" did not much abet the record's mediocre sales. Even *Billboard,* far less critical a trade publication than *Variety,* was lukewarm toward it: "Martin is a pretty fine singer; Lewis is a zany guy. The combine turned out a pretty nice disking."

Capitol thus discovered what Greshler already knew: Martin and Lewis were an act whose effectiveness lay in both the eyes and the ears of the beholder. From now on, Capitol decided, Dean would record alone and straight.

Greshler had used the sensational success of the Copacabana run as bargaining power in booking the act far in advance for good money. He had committed them to a month, beginning November 26, at the Blackstone hotel in Chicago for $18,000. Now Greshler wanted out of the Blackstone deal, but the Kirkeby chain, which operated the Blackstone, insisted that it was a pay-or-play contract. A call to Charlie Fischetti helped straighten the matter out, and the Blackstone was placated by Greshler's promise that the act would play there next year at the same price. No sooner was that taken care of when Murray Weinger of the new Copa City nightclub in Miami Beach came forward claiming that Greshler had made a verbal agreement for Martin and Lewis to play his joint in December for $6,500 a week. Greshler, however, had gone ahead and booked them for more money into another Miami joint, Ned Schuyler's competing Beachcomber Club, directly across the street. Once again, Charlie Fischetti proved a valuable rabbi. Charlie owned an estate on Allison Island, Miami Beach; his wife, Ann, lived there year-round. His brothers, Rocco and Joe, were involved in the restaurant business and other family interests there as well. The Fischetti presence was nearly as powerful in Miami as it was in Chicago.

After the third "Welcome Aboard" TV show, they returned to Hollywood for "The Bob Hope Show." Dean made his first solo recordings for Capitol on November 22; and on the following night, he and Jerry returned for a second appearance on the Hope show. Two days later, on Thanksgiving, they performed on the "Elgin Holiday Star Time" show. This special NBC radio extravaganza, hosted by Don Ameche and also starring Jack Benny, Jimmy Durante,

Mario Lanza, the Mills Brothers, and André Previn, was broadcast in direct competition with the Wrigley "Thanksgiving Festival" on CBS, the network that until this year had carried the annual Elgin special. The Wrigley show, hosted by Gene Autry, featured Abbott and Costello, Amos 'n' Andy, the Andrews Sisters, Dorothy Lamour, and Marie Wilson, star of the hit radio show "My Friend Irma."

Hal Wallis had already obtained the movie rights to "My Friend Irma" from Martin Jurow of the William Morris Agency, and he had decided it was the perfect vehicle to launch Martin and Lewis. Thirty-three-year-old Cy Howard was hired to write a screenplay based on his radio characters; later, Parke Levy, whom he took on to write and direct the radio show, would join him. A budget of $500,000 was set, of which ten percent would go to Martin and Lewis. George Marshall would direct. Marie Wilson would star in the title role of the dizzy blond, Irma Peterson, that she had popularized on radio. Pretty, young Diana Lynn would take the part of Irma's sensible roommate, Jane Stacy, played on radio by Cathy Lewis. That left two leading male roles: Irma's slightly smarmy con-artist boyfriend, Al, played on radio by John Brown; and Jane's guy, played on radio by George Neise. Dean, Wallis figured, would star in the role of Jane's guy, rewritten as an aspiring singer named Steve Laird. But he now found himself echoing Louis B. Mayer's question: "What do I do with the monkey?"

"Desperate to play Al, Jerry fancied himself a handsome leading man," Wallis said. He placated Jerry at first by having Marshall screen-test him as Al. "Jerry, I'll be honest," Marshall told him. "It's a mistake to cast you in this role." As the casting proceeded— Don DeFore, under contract to Wallis, was screen-tested as Al; he did not want the role, and suggested John Lund, who had the same agent as DeFore and had worked last year with Marshall in *The Perils of Pauline;* Lund was cast as Al, and DeFore took the lesser role of Jane's rich boss, Mr. Rhinelander—Howard and Wallis invented a role for Jerry as Steve's bumbling sidekick. Howard gave the character his own true first name, which he loathed: Seymour.

"Jerry," Wallis recalled, "took one look at the script, stormed into my office, and had a screaming match with Cy Howard. Cy pointed out that he hadn't a hope in hell of having audiences accept him as Al. Jerry said it was Al or nothing, and that he would never play Seymour.

"We argued until well after midnight. I was so exhausted that I finally told Jerry I would have to drop him and the part of Seymour from the script entirely. He exploded again. I quietly pointed out that Dean would probably become a very big star in *Irma* even without him, looking him straight in the eye as I told him. Fond as he was of Dean, I knew he was jealous of his handsome face and figure. Jerry was very angry but he accepted the part of Seymour." As Jerry himself would later say, "I wasn't Al, and I knew it."

Dean's first solo Capitol record was released in early December: a version of Frank Loesser's "Once in Love with Amy," from the new Broadway musical *Where's Charley?*, coupled with "Tarra-Ta-Larra Ta-Lar," another new song, done recently by Bing Crosby, Johnny Desmond, Frankie Laine, Dinah Shore, and others. "Martin is not terribly effective on his debut crooner wax on this label," *Billboard* said in reviewing "Once in Love with Amy." And, of the flip side: "Same comment." *Variety* commented: "Capitol is building Dean Martin as a soloist as well as with his laugh-kick, Jerry Lewis. These sides won't help build him. Martin completely lost the flavor of 'Amy' and doesn't do too much with 'Tarra,' an adaptation of an Italian lullaby. Martin's singing is much superior to what he shows on this disking."

Abby Greshler, meanwhile, continued to pursue a network deal. NBC had dominated radio comedy since the early days of Amos 'n' Andy. The kings of radio comedy, all of whom owned their respective shows, paid very dearly for their success in income taxes. Now, however, CBS had shrewdly pointed out that if the comedians sold their programs as properties, they would reap windfall profits taxed at the lower, capital-gains rates while continuing to receive attractive salaries for the broadcast life of their programs. CBS, of course, was willing to purchase such properties as a capital investment—$2,500,000 for a twenty-year lease on "Amos 'n' Andy," for example—and NBC was losing more and more of its stars to that network's new scheme. In mid-December, running frantic in its search for fresh stars, NBC produced an elaborate audition recording of

Dean and Jerry doing a sample half-hour show before a studio audience. Lucille Ball and singer Ilene Woods were recruited as guests. Florence MacMichael was cast in the comedic—or so it was intended to be—presence of "the maid," envisioned as a running character.

"As you know, ladies and gentlemen, Dean Martin and Jerry Lewis are two young men who overnight have become the nation's comedy hit. But let's get on with the show. We take you now to the apartment of Dean Martin and Jerry Lewis, where we find the boys getting ready, somewhat nervously, to go to the NBC studios for their first radio show." Jerry's anxieties—"Everybody hates me!"—provided the basis for the first few minutes of comedy. Dean "rehearsed" his song "You Won't Be Satisfied (Until You Break My Heart)." The maid entered for a little more comedy. Passing through street-sound effects and a meeting with a couple of Dean's female fans, the pair arrived at the studio. With Woods, whose voice soon would become that of Walt Disney's Cinderella, Dean sang "You Was!," a new song that he had recorded just days before as a duet with Peggy Lee. Lucille Ball was introduced by Dean with a plug for her upcoming picture, *Sorrowful Jones;* Jerry joined them for some more comedy, and the three of them performed "The Money Song." Dean and Jerry ended up back at their apartment, in their adjoining beds, to be interrupted for one last brief bit with the maid.

On December 20, NBC signed Martin and Lewis to an exclusive contract, which insured that they would not be deserting to another network. They were to be paid $2,000 a week while the show was in development, $2,500 a week once it was on the air. Two nights later, NBC broadcast the preview show, then set out in search of a sponsor and writers who could collaborate with Martin and Lewis on a formula that worked.

Dean and Jerry moved their families west. Jerry, whose last lease had been for a $65-a-month two-and-a-half-room walk-up in Newark, rented the $1,500-a-month former home of the actress Maria Montez: a seventeen-room mansion with a swimming-pool and wooded grounds on Tower Road in Beverly Hills. Dean rented a less glamorous house, for $600 a month, farther west, at 850 Stone

Canyon Road, in the exclusive reaches of Bel Air. Angela Crocetti came up with Guy from Long Beach to help put the place in order before Betty and the kids got there.

Dean and Jerry were waiting at the train station when their families arrived together.

"I remember Dean taking me through the house," Betty said. "When we got to each room, he'd say, 'Now, Betty, close your eyes.'" Room after room, he "was like a little kid showing off his Christmas toys." Guy and Angela were there, overjoyed to have all their grandchildren with them at last. "I counted the rooms in the place," Betty said. "There was an extra bedroom and bath. I said to Dean, 'That's for mom and pop.' Well, he got tears in his eyes—he was so pleased about it. And, you know, they did move in with us."

The Stone Canyon home warmed with the sweet life of three generations; and Dean, as its heart and paterfamilias, *cuore della famiglia* and sun of the seasons of every loving dream, seemed to radiate a new and glorious quiet happiness, a contentment that Betty rarely had known in him. "It seemed," she said, "like the beginning of a beautiful life together in Hollywood."

Then, with a sudden cold breath, the light was spent.

IX.

BROADS AND MONEY

$\mathcal{D}$ean and Jerry were booked to bring in Christmas and the New Year at the Beachcomber Club in Miami, where they opened on December 23, 1948. They now had their own band-leader, Dick Stabile. They could afford him: The Beachcomber was paying them $12,000 a week.

As in the past nineteen years, New Year's Day was the high holy day of Miami's football calendar. Invited to compete that year at the Orange Bowl were Texas and Georgia. Twenty-one-year-old Jeannie Biegger of nearby Coral Gables did not much care for foot-ball, but this Orange Bowl, like last year's, was something very special. She was passing the scepter of her queenship.

Jeanne's parents were Midwesterners of Prussian stock. Her father, James Kenneth Biegger, was from Iowa; her mother, Marga-ret Kain, from Chicago. They had come south in the twenties to Florida, where, on March 27, 1927, their first child and only daugh-ter, Dorothy Jean, had been born. She was a gifted child, who by her late teens, as a student at the University of Miami and a copy-girl at the *Miami Daily News*, seemed likely to turn her youthful love of writing into a career. But she was gifted in beauty as well.

She was more than beautiful; she was marketably beautiful. Hers was the blond, blue-eyed beauty of the new American Venus. Another career, in modeling, had also begun in her teenage years, with work for the Alden's catalog while still attending Miami High. Since then, her picture had smiled forth from magazine covers, from the sides of express-mail trucks, and from barbershop posters as the Wildroot girl. Now she was about to be the new Dr Pepper calendar girl as well.

As an aspiring model, she had dropped the Dorothy and changed the Jean to Jeanne. And it was as Jeanne Biegger that, on

December 31, 1947, she had ridden and reigned, enthroned amid lacy valentines and a giant red heart, as the Orange Bowl Queen of Miami's 1947 King Orange Jamboree Parade.

Now, a year later, in the 1948 parade, to publicize their show at the Beachcomber Club, Dean and Jerry rode down Flagler Street and Biscayne Boulevard in a convertible amid the forty-one floats and twenty-eight bands and three thousand marchers and Sunkist gonfalons of King Orange's imperial retinue. It was Miami's coldest New Year's Eve in twenty-two years, and the most violent one that anybody could remember: The entire Miami police force was called out that night to put down what was termed "the most fantastic demonstration of mob fury ever seen in Miami"—thousands of teenagers setting fires and looting in the wake of the parade. That night, far from the rioting, Jeannie joined the new Orange Bowl Queen, Corine Gustafson, and others at ringside tables at the Beachcomber Club.

Jeanne was young. She had never really drunk. She was still dating boys she knew from high school, some of whom had gone on to college. She had never been to a Miami Beach nightclub before. "I lived with my parents and my brother, and knew nothing," she said, "of anything outside of Coral Gables." The glamour of Miami Beach itself was "like another world," and that New Year's Eve celebration was "kind of a big deal" for her, even though she had never heard of Martin and Lewis.

Dean saw her from the stage. Their eyes met. And that was it. Jeanne had heard of love at first sight, but until that moment she had never believed it happened in real life.

"We locked eyes, and I knew. I literally knew: This was it."

It made no sense. "He was certainly not anyone that I would have—I can't think of two people any more different. There's absolutely no reason in the world except that eye contact, be it kismet, or fate, or that it was supposed to be."

The spread was seven points: Texas, the unranked underdog team, beat eighth-ranking Georgia by a score of forty-one to twenty-eight. And on that same New Year's Day, Dean began to court his newfound American Venus.

"We just fell madly in love," Jeanne remembered it. "We actually did not know one single thing about each other. He never asked. I asked and got no answers. The attraction was just there."

Dean's second and third solo Capitol singles were released while he was in Florida. "Powder Your Face with Sunshine (Smile! Smile! Smile!)," which Dean had recorded on December 17, would become his most successful record thus far, selling well enough to remind Apollo of the unissued recordings that he had left behind. Two of them—"One Foot in Heaven" and Billy Rose's "The Night Is Young and You're So Beautiful," both recorded with the Hal Kanner Orchestra—were leased to Lew Gray's new little Embassy Record Company, which operated under Apollo's distributorship. Released in February, the Embassy record died as ignominiously as its Apollo predecessors.

While Dean and Jerry were headlining at the Beachcomber, Gene Baylos was performing nearby at the Five O'Clock Club, a smaller joint run by Sam Barken. When Baylos dropped by to see their show and congratulate them on their good fortune, he was enraged by what he saw. "He stole my body," Baylos would say of Lewis. "I asked Dean to tell him to stop, and he didn't. I didn't talk to Dean for five years. I made up to Dean. I still don't talk to Jerry now."

Dean and Jerry were to return to Slapsy Maxie's on January 21. "When he left Miami," Jeanne said, "he told me that he was serious. And I thought, sure, uh-huh, well, we'll see. I didn't even know that he was married."

On their first night back at Slapsy Maxie's, they packed the joint, remaining onstage for a full hour and leaving the audience screaming for more. "The humor," reported *Variety*, "is slick, sly and silly and it produces an almost unending laugh barrage. In a room where other comics have had to make a definite appeal to sophisticates, Martin and Lewis only rarely rely on tinted topics to derive a laugh. Neatly interlaced is Dean Martin's excellent singing with current stint giving him more vocalizing time than when the pair first opened here. With some Capitol disks coming up to make him w.k. in the non-night club set, Martin stands smart chance of becoming one of the country's top singing attractions."

Dean did not seem to be himself lately, Betty thought. But then again, did she even know anymore what that self was? Had she ever known? Had anyone? Then the little crates of oranges began arriving, addressed to Dean in a cursive, flowery hand. Betty asked him what in hell was going on.

"Have an orange," he told her. "They're good."

Jerry had been watching their marriage fall apart for years. "Betty was a lovely girl," he said. "Very, very lovely. They produced four gorgeous children. Betty did a good job with them.

"Betty had a drinking problem, but on the whole she was really a terrific dame. She was very, very much a good mother. And she was a good wife. But people fall out of love. I think Dean just fell out of love."

It was hard to keep track of Dean's kaleidoscopic love life. "He fell in love with Jeannie, and it was a storybook romance," Jerry would say. "We were playing in Baltimore, and he was driving all night to Cumberland, Maryland, where—wait a minute: have I got the wrong broad? I have the wrong broad. What the hell was her name? This was another chick he was goin' with that he almost married."

There was a song. Ivie Anderson had sung it with Duke Ellington back in 1936; it had been in the air that rainy springtime when Dean and Ross Monaco had come west with Joe DiNovo: "Love Is Like a Cigarette." Maybe that was what it came down to: a bad habit; a few drags of pleasure followed by a lousy taste. You put one out, you started another. Every once in a while, you coughed, you dumped the ashtray and said fuck it.

"No one ever got to know him," Jerry would say, "not even Betty."

In early February, Jeannie received a yes-I-want-to-marry-you telegram and an airplane ticket. Only after she arrived in Los Angeles and expressed her commitment to him did Dean tell her that he was married. "I guess that marriage was over," she would say, looking back, "and as long as he didn't have to tell me about it, that's what he did. Till he was sure I was committed."

Dean hid her out at the home of Dick Stabile. But it did not take Betty long to discover that Dean had proven her direst doubts about him to be true. Her howling flushed the birds from the trees, and their sundering came on February 9. Dean moved out and rented a small furnished house at 8800 Sunset Boulevard, in West Hollywood. Betty conferred with a Beverly Hills attorney, Jacques Leslie, who, on February 11, drew up a complaint for separate maintenance that sought the custody of their children along with the sum of $3,000 per month, "or one-third of the defendant's monthly gross earnings, whichever shall be greater." Toward justifying that figure, Betty listed her monthly expenses as $2,946, an amount that included $420 for servants and $500 for "incidentals." She stated that she had never been employed, and that she suffered from a "cardio-vascular disturbance." Her present net financial worth she estimated to be "nothing"; Dean's, "approximately $15,000 per month." The complaint further asked that Dean be ordered to pay Betty's legal costs of $2,500, and that he be similarly ordered to procure life insurance upon himself, naming Betty and the children beneficiaries, in the sum of $100,000. The complaint was filed in Los Angeles County Superior Court on Valentine's Day, the afternoon after Dean and Jerry closed at Slapsy Maxie's.

The next morning, in that same court, Sammy Watkins appeared with a complaint of his own against Dean. Since 1946, Sammy claimed, Dean had "earned and received large sums of money," of which Sammy was legally entitled to ten percent; but Dean, despite all entreaties, had paid Sammy only $1,000. His complaint sought an accounting of all monies earned and received by Dean since 1946 and the rendering forth of Sammy's ten percent thereof, along with the recovery of all legal costs incurred.

Betty's legal action and Dean's romance with Jeanne became public knowledge in a matter of days. When, on February 20, Dean suggested through his lawyers, Vernon L. Ferguson and Gavin M. Craig, that Betty change her complaint for separate maintenance to one of divorce, Betty's refusal was reported in Louella Parsons's syndicated Hollywood column the next day. "This precludes any possibility," Parsons wrote, "of Martin marrying the Florida girl, if that was his intention."

· · ·

My Friend Irma began filming at Paramount in late February. "From the beginning," Hal Wallis said, "Jerry was as hard to handle as Dino was easy." He apparently was still upset at not being seen as a leading man. Wallis would describe him as "sulking like a twenty-three-year-old spoiled child in his dressing room throughout the shooting."

Don DeFore, who was Dean's age and played his romantic competition in the picture, had appeared in one of the dismal Martin-and-Lewis screen tests, which he remembered as "not very funny." But he had seen them at Slapsy Maxie's too, "and, my God, they were hilarious. Just great." On the set, Martin and Lewis did not much mix with the others. "Their being a team, and being in an entirely different area of the theater than I was in, and also Lund and the rest of us, there was not too much camaraderie. Though I did enjoy being with Dean Martin. I'd go to lunch with him a couple of times. Very funny man, and an excellent voice, I thought."

Wallis kept a close watch on the production. "Wallis's moneyman, Hazen, came on the set too, to see what they had bought." Both Dean and Jerry, DeFore felt, were fortunate in having George Marshall as a director their first time out. Marshall was a consummate professional. His early experience of churning out more than sixty Mack Sennett one- and two-reelers a year had left him with a disdain for the new breed of directors who forwent the rigors of technical mastery in their sloppy pursuit of so-called art. He "knew exactly what he wanted out of his people," DeFore said, "how much a team should be together and how much they should be separated." Adolph Zukor himself, who had created the Zion of illusion known as Paramount, would see Martin and Lewis on-screen as "a throwback to the grand days of Mack Sennett comedies."

There was a scene in *My Friend Irma* where Dean and DeFore were to come to blows over Diana Lynn. "Well," Jerry recalled, "nobody told Dean about picture punches. You go by the chin, the camera's placed here, it looks like you've hit the man. Dean hit Don DeFore square on the fuckin' jaw and knocked a tooth out. It stopped production until the dentist could fix Don's tooth, and then we had to wait until the swelling went down."

The summons to respond to the Watkins suit was served on

March 9, when Dean went to Capitol to record "Dreamy Old New England Moon." It was a new song; one of its writers, the lyricist Max C. Freedman, would strike it rich a few years later with "Rock Around the Clock."

By then, Dean had succeeded in prevailing upon Betty to amend her petition. He would always love her, he said—it was a line from one of those songs he had sung; he could not remember which—and he would give her sixty grand in cash if she would just restore them both to their freedom. On March 23, her attorney drew up a new complaint that sought divorce on grounds of mental cruelty; and on the following day, Dean signed a separate agreement to the $60,000 settlement and $3,000-a-month support. The new complaint, filed in court on March 29, stated that during "the eight years, three months [sic] and seven days" that had elapsed from their wedding to their separation, "the conduct of the defendant toward this plaintiff has been cruel to the extent that she has been caused great grievous suffering and mental anguish." The new complaint mentioned no monthly payments, only that "the plaintiff and the defendant herein have entered into a property settlement agreement which provides for a division of their community property, and which makes provisions for the support and maintenance" of the plaintiff and the children.

NBC had spent over $100,000 developing "The Martin and Lewis Show." On March 10, the network announced that the show would finally have its debut at half past six on the Sunday evening of April 3, replacing "The Adventures of Ozzie and Harriet," which was moving to CBS on that same date.

The show was taped at NBC's Studio C on March 24. On Tuesday night, March 29, they went on "The Bob Hope Show" to plug their upcoming debut, for which Hope in turn had agreed to be the inaugural guest star. Then, on Sunday: "It's 'The Martin and Lewis Show'! The National Broadcasting Company brings you, transcribed, the new 'Martin and Lewis Show.' "

When "The Martin and Lewis Show" premiered, it was still without a sponsor; the only commercials were for U.S. Savings Bonds. Dean sang "Bye Bye Blackbird" as an opening theme with the Stabile orchestra. The routines that followed were a reprise of those from last December's preview show, with Florence MacMichael cast again as the maid. "Tell me," Bob Hope asked Jerry, addressing him as Bebop, "who does your hair, a Ubangi?" Dean's performance of "Tarra-Ta-Larra Ta-Lar" was prefaced by an exchange that had been worked up for *My Friend Irma:* "You take care of the singing and I'll take care of the conducting," Jerry said, inflecting the last word with a rising indecisive Yiddisher lilt: "con-*duct*ing?" "Why do you leave that last word up in the air? It's the end of a sentence. You're through with it. There's a period there. You don't need it anymore. You would say, 'I'm going to the corner,' not 'I'm goin' to the *cor*ner?' I mean, who talks like this?" "Well, you talk the way you want; I talk that way because *lis*ten?"

Hope managed to plug his own show's sponsor, Swan Soap, twice. Jerry turned serious to close the show with an appeal for Easter Seals.

On the following Saturday night, April 9, they appeared on a charity NBC-TV show for the Damon Runyon Memorial Fund, hosted by Milton Berle. It was the first telethon: the word itself entered the language through newspaper reports the next day.

The next night, they were back on the radio with their own show, this time with William Bendix, the star of the radio series "The Life of Riley," as their guest. Dean and Jerry repeated their "because-*lis*ten" routine from the previous week. Jerry did a trained-seal imitation, another bit that had been worked up for *My Friend Irma.* There was a Southern-colonel-and-darky routine, with Dean addressing Jerry as 'Lasses. For their third show, they got Jimmy Durante. The guest star on the following week was a surprising one: Dick Powell, the cuckold husband of Dean's side-slurp June Allyson.

"Potentially, the boys have got it," *Variety* remarked of "The Martin and Lewis Show." "But bridging the gap from a nitery visual assist into a strictly audio medium still remains a big 'but.' " There was praise for Dean's singing on the show, even "if the voice bears a striking resemblance to Bing Crosby's." The show itself, *Variety* said in closing, needed "plenty of work." *Newsweek* echoed *Variety:* "Jerry Lewis is a brash, squeaky-voiced kind of funny young fellow.

Dean Martin is a singer with a baritone voice more than casually reminiscent of an early-day Crosby. But the freshness of the Martin-Lewis humor, so evident on the night-club floor, was—on the air—a sometime thing." The *Newsweek* piece, their first notice in a main-stream national publication, incorporated the apocryphal story, fed by George Evans, of their having been brought together by fateful adversity in Atlantic City. A month later, *Time* magazine would repeat the tale, along with the sentiment: "radio cannot show the half of what Martin & Lewis have; they must be seen."

My Friend Irma finished filming in mid-April. After taping the show with Powell, Dean and Jerry flew east to open at the Copacabana on April 21, three nights before the show aired. "The return of Martin and Lewis brought out a mob reminiscent of the ones which packed the joint during the war boom," reported *Billboard*. "To say they made 'em laugh is an understatement. They made 'em howl."

The inevitable comparisons to Crosby were becoming more flattering, but no less tiresome. Dean, said the *Daily News* in its review of the Copacabana show, "sings as well as Crosby, or maybe better than the current Crosby."

Billboard did not agree: "Martin, looking handsomer than ever, a typical leading man, is now one of the best straight men in the biz. His singing, however, hasn't held up. He now goes in for too many voice tricks," wrote Bill Smith. "But Lewis is a sharply improved comic. His timing was marvelous; his bits bordering on the maniacal got hysterical returns."

For the first time, the monkey seemed to overshadow the organ-grinder. There was an eerie undercurrent creeping into the comedy. It was becoming sex, slapstick, and *psychomachia:* Seymour Agonistes emerging in darkness from the throes of "Melancholy Baby."

In *My Friend Irma*, Dean's character, Steve, under the shady management of Irma's fiancé, Al, got his big break when a chance came to sing at a Coney Island nightclub. Jerry's character, Seymour, under the impression that he was to perform as Steve's partner, discovered on the big night that he had been hired instead as the club's car-parking valet—an opportunity for Jerry to do in the picture what he had done in the Riviera's parking-lot. When Al arrived at the nightclub, Seymour confronted him.

"I'm supposed to be the show. Half, at least. Steve and me are a team. To me, this is not equal billing."

"Just be patient, Seymour, your time will come," Al told him. "On the next job, you will be the main feature. Steve will be nothing."

"That's the way I like to hear you talk. Remember, I am a great actor."

"Know it, son, know it. In the meantime, park the car."

It had been one of the last scenes they had done. Now, in New York, they taped a "Martin and Lewis Show" with Henry Fonda, who was starring in *Mister Roberts* at the Alvin Theatre. In one routine, following a visit to the theater to see *Mister Roberts,* Dean and Jerry went to a soda fountain, where Jerry fell down between two counter stools, prompting Dean to say, "Sometimes I don't know what I'm gonna do with you."

"What you're gonna do with me? Don't do anything with me, I'll get along by myself. I don't need you or the nightclub act or anything. I'll get a big dramatic job like Henry Fonda."

"We're partners, we're pals. You know we've always gone fifty-fifty on everything."

"Fifty-fifty on everything? Then why do I always get the ugly one? Well, I'm gonna have pretty girls running after me from now on. When I was sitting there watchin' Henry Fonda tonight, I said to myself: I shouldn't be a comedian, I should be playin' romantic leading-man parts like Henry Fonda."

"The Martin and Lewis Show" was not proving to be the success that NBC had hoped for. A proposed deal with Lever Brothers had fallen through, and the show was still without a sponsor. At the same time, its package price of $10,000 made it the most expensive of NBC's programs. In June 14, the network moved the show to Tuesday evenings at ten.

On June 25, Dean appeared without Jerry on NBC's "TV Screen Magazine," a magazine-style program hosted by John McCaffery. As throughout the filming of *My Friend Irma,* he seemed calm and happy. The divorce, which Betty still had not gone through with; the

Watkins suit, which was dragging on through defaults and postpone-
ments—none of it seemed to bother Dean. He moved into a new
house, at 9261 Warbler Way, on the northeastern edge of Beverly
Hills; a place big enough for him and his parents and Jeannie to
share.

Wallis and Hazen copyrighted *My Friend Irma* on July 19.
Previews were planned for early the following month. Betty did not
want to be around for the silver-screen apotheosis of the estranged
husband whom she had come to despise. She had left the children
with Guy and Angela, and traveled early that summer to Steubenville, as if in search of the ghost of that man she had once thought
she knew. Ross Monaco was working as a bartender for Stogie
DeSarro at the Hy-Hat, which Stogie had taken over from Mindy
Costanzo, when Betty walked in. She was already half loaded. Ross
had always liked her. He knew she was a jealous person, but he had
never thought of her as wild.

"Betty, why do you wanna divorce him?" he asked her. "He's
got a good buck. Stick around for the money, for the kids."

She just shook her head.

Earlier in the year, RCA-Victor and Columbia had begun making records out of polyvinyl instead of shellac: microgroove records
that were played at speeds of forty-five or thirty-three-and-a-third
revolutions per minute, rather than seventy-eight. The new, smaller
45-rpm singles would eventually overtake 78s; the new, ten- and
twelve-inch long-play recordings would replace the multirecord 78-
rpm albums of the forties even sooner. Glenn Wallichs, the president of Capitol, had announced in early February, even before
RCA-Victor issued its first 45s, that Capitol would begin releasing
singles in 45- as well as 78-rpm form starting in April.

This revolution in form coincided with a revolution in music
itself. Something, soon to be called rock 'n' roll, was happening.
Roy Brown, a black singer who idolized Bing Crosby, had recorded
"Good Rockin' Tonight" for DeLuxe Records in 1947. It had not
been a hit, but another version of it, recorded in December of that
year by blues shouter Wynonie Harris, had slowly but surely ascended the *Billboard* race-record charts to hit number one by June

of 1948. By then the wave was mounting: "We're Gonna Rock" by Wild Bill Moore, "Rockin' Boogie" by Joe Lutcher, and others had followed. In 1949 came Roy Brown's "Rockin' at Midnight." Later this summer, there would be Jimmy Preston's "Rock the Joint," Wynonie Harris's "All She Wants to Do Is Rock."

The industry establishment at first did not know quite what to make of the new music. Reviewing Johnny Otis's "Barrel House Stomp" in January 1949, *Billboard*, nonplussed, simply declared it to be "One of the loudest records ever made." A few months later, reviewing Wild Bill Moore's "Rock and Roll" and Louis Jordan's "Cole Slaw," *Billboard* had valiantly but awkwardly tried to adjust. Moore's record was "Another frenetic installment in the pounding 'good rock' serial. A potent new platter of its kind." Of Jordan's record, *Billboard*, donning its shades, had remarked, "Band really rocks." A month later, the term "race" had been forsaken by the cooler "rhythm and blues." By now it was becoming clear that what was going on was more than a "serial," as *Billboard* had suggested in the spring.

Dean's first 45-rpm single, "Just for Fun" coupled with "My Own, My Only, My All," was released in late July. *Billboard* called it "one of his best platters." Elvis Presley of Memphis was fourteen years old that summer; in several weeks, he would enter Humes High School. Five summers later, he would make his first recordings at Sam Phillips's little Sun Record Company. And not long after that, he would become the avatar of that wild brewing that was now in the air, of that thing, that nova, full-blown and raving, that came to be called rock 'n' roll. The strongest chains are wrought from the unlikeliest alloys: Elvis would transform Roy Brown's "Good Rockin' Tonight" into something new and apocalyptic, just as Roy Brown had forged his own fierce sound from Bing Crosby. And Elvis's favorite singer, the man he idolized, had passed through Crosby's shadow as well: Dean Martin. It was with "Just for Fun" that Elvis became aware of Dean. He would emulate Dean as Dean had emulated Crosby. In Dean's voice in "Just for Fun" lay the source of Elvis's own.

Paramount previewed *My Friend Irma* for the trade on August 8. "Radio's 'My Friend Irma' steps from the airwaves to celluloid in a not always graceful transition," reported *Variety*. But, while *Irma*'s "potentialities as film material are not fully realized upon, there's still enough frolicking and exploiting of the essentially funny character to rate a neat boxoffice payoff." The Howard-Levy screenplay was criticized for its "numerous story holes," but the director and actors were praised. The picture's "most notable value" was "the introduction of two nitery comics who prove they have film possibilities if used properly and backed with the right kind of material. They are Dean Martin and Jerry Lewis, and the emphasis is on the latter. He is a very funny man, a mugger of ability whose timing wallops over many a guffaw." And what of the organ-grinder? "Martin," *Variety* said, "is a handsome straight man singer and there are no complaints on his ability in that range. His voice is pleasant and easy, but his nightclub posturing needs toning down for films."

He had been barely noticed, and yet he should be toned down. The monkey bared its teeth and strutted. Seymour Agonistes was Seymour Invictus now.

Two days after the preview, Dean and Jerry renewed their contracts with Abby Greshler. The following Friday, Dean recorded his first ersatz-Italian song for Capitol. "Vieni Su (Say You Love Me Too)," with Italian and English lyrics by Johnny Cola and Jack Edwards, based on an arrangement by Walter L. Rosemont, was one of the songs included in *Phil Brito Sings Songs of Italy*, the 1946 album that had made an impression on Dean back in New York. He also recorded "That Lucky Old Sun," a song that sounded as if it had been around forever but in fact was barely six months old. Frankie Laine's recording of it for Mercury, released in mid-August, would become a number-one hit; and there would soon be versions by Sarah Vaughan, Louis Armstrong, Frank Sinatra, and Vaughan Monroe, who also covered Dean's recording of "Vieni Su" that fall for RCA-Victor.

Betty had finally resigned herself to the actuality of divorce. She had held out for another hundred bucks a week in blood money; that would bring her take to over $40,000 a year. In July 11, when Dean gave in and the settlement agreement was amended, she had gone to Las Vegas to fulfill the six-months-residency requirement necessary for a quick Nevada divorce. On August 24, represented by the counsel of Jones, Wiener & Jones, Betty appeared at the Clark County Court before District Judge Frank McNamee. Dean, who remained in California, was represented by an attorney, D. Francis Norsey. The claim that "the defendant has treated the plaintiff with extreme cruelty without just cause therefor" was duly accepted; and it was, "therefore, ordered, adjudged and decreed that the bonds of matrimony now and heretofore existing between the plaintiff, Elizabeth Anne Martin, and the defendant, Dean Paul Martin, be, and the same are wholly dissolved, set aside, and held for naught."

For naught: It sounded somehow so sweet; a frill, a chill, a wisp of finality in the passing breeze.

Two days later, he and Jeanne went downtown for a marriage license. Dean, who had turned thirty-two in June, stated his age as thirty; his occupation as actor. Jeanne, who was now twenty-two, had continued her career in modeling during her months in Los Angeles. But now that would end. Motherhood and the mysteries of marriage to Dean Martin had claimed her.

Guy and Angela Crocetti did not like the idea of their son's divorce. Betty had been a dutiful mother and wife, as far as they could see. Men could not change families as they changed their shirts and shoes, Guy told him. To marry once was the nature of man in his youth. To marry twice was the nature of a fool.

"I'm sure they were absolutely distraught at the idea of his remarrying," Jeanne said. "His marrying someone so young. Or just remarrying, period." But Angela "was just a marvelous woman. And she was wonderful to me. She was just as loving as my own mother."

A close observer of Dean in those days was Herman Hover, proprietor of Ciro's, the most successful nightclub in town.

"Ciro's did terrific," Hover said. "Everyone thought Howard Hughes was backing me, but there were no partners. I was getting the Haig & Haig from Kennedy. I was one of the few places serving real Scotch. It was impossible to get on account of the war."

There had been those who had tried to wet their beaks, but he had bluffed them away. "Well, I don't own this place," he would say. "People think I own it. I'm just fronting it. You know who I am? I'm a former lawyer with the federal government." It was true; he had worked for the U.S. Commerce Department in New York before going into private practice. "This place is owned by seven lawyers with the federal government. Anything you want, I'd have to call them." The assistant U.S. attorney general at the time was Irving J. Levy. Hover knew him from law school; they were close friends; Levy stayed with Hover whenever he was in Los Angeles. "You don't have to call all seven," Hover would say. "Just call Irving Levy at the Justice Department."

Ciro's got them all: James Roosevelt, the president's son ("he was my insurance man"), and his mother, Eleanor, whose close friend Mayris Chaney kept "a dinky apartment in the rear of Ciro's parking-lot"; Howard Hughes and his aide Johnny Myer ("he was in Ciro's every night of the week; he was by far the biggest customer I ever had; money meant nothing"); Frank Sinatra ("he was a cheap guy; I didn't dislike him, but he was a cheap guy"); General Jonathan Wainwright ("he used to sit there and make these strange yelping noises; I couldn't throw him out, he was a war hero and all that"); Mickey Cohen ("when he went to prison, I picked up a healthy tab for him; he was very grateful").

Hover lived at 606 North Bedford Drive in Beverly Hills, in a mansion that had belonged to Alfred G. Vanderbilt and Mary Pickford before him. It was where Howard Hughes conducted much of his business, and where some of the most celebrated after-hours gatherings of the era took place. There was a $40,000 supply of booze on hand at all times.

Both Dean and Jerry had become habitués of Ciro's; and Hover had grown especially close to Dean.

"Dean was known as a ladies' man, but he really wasn't," Hover recalled. The women chased Dean, not the other way around. "Ann Sheridan came in every night of the week, with a party of four, five, or six. Right down front, ringside. She'd be accompanied by Ross Hunter. He was a young actor and also a writer. And she was crazy about Dean. She said to me, 'If you can get me a date with Dean Martin, I'll fix you up with any girl in town. Anyone. You name it, I'll fix you up with her.'

"Lana Turner was crazy about him. In those days, there was a twelve-o'clock liquor curfew, so, frequently, when the joint closed, we'd go to somebody's house, mostly mine, but sometimes, like, Lana would say, 'Let's all go to my house.' There'd be about four or six of us, go up to her house, sometimes we'd bring the piano player with us, have an informal party. We really enjoyed it. I'd have parties almost every night at my house in Beverly Hills. And Lana was really stuck on him. I saw her pull some raw stuff with Dean, with her own husband, Bob Topping, right there. She went pretty far."

"He was a good sex man, but his big interest was golf." Did Hover think Dean would rather play golf than get laid? "Yeah, I would say that. If you played golf, you'd understand. It's like a disease. Look what Eisenhower did instead of sitting behind the desk at the White House."

Hover remembered that Dean "was not a great drinker, either. He never drank that much. Black & White mostly. Haig & Haig." Hover never saw him loaded.

"He was always joking, always kidding. I don't recall seeing a serious side. He was a rough guy. Uncouth. He was intelligent, not educated. I don't think he ever read a book. Jeanne was more educated. When I got married, she and my wife, Yvonne, became very friendly.

"Dean was a good guy. Very easy to get along with. He was always a very easygoing guy. Always ready to go up on the floor and do a show for you. Sing and joke. But Jerry didn't come in so often. Jerry was impetuous and took all the credit. Between the two, everybody liked Dean and practically no one liked Jerry."

It was at Herman Hover's home in Beverly Hills that Judge Charles J. Griffin pronounced Dean and Jeanne man and wife on the first afternoon of September 1949.

Divorce, tragedy, and lawyers—"they're the biggest swindlers and the easiest ones to swindle"—would leave Hover broke in the end. A scrapbook of yellowed clippings documenting his largess as a philanthropist and excesses as a millionaire playboy would be all that remained of his glory. Ciro's, the mansion in Beverly Hills, the $40,000 stock of booze: a memory. A jar of Cremora, a can of Raid, a copy of Theodore White's *America in Search of Itself* crowded together on a shelf in a cramped Hollywood apartment would compose the still-life of eighty-four-year-old Herman Hover's here-and-now. And he would sit there, while dog-eared America searched for itself behind him, and he would recall that wedding reception forty years before and more. It was a small and private but lavish affair.

"The garden was decorated with white gardenias," he would say. "I think the flowers cost me about ten or fifteen grand."

A few minutes later, he would apologize for his poor hearing. "Costs $900 to get a hearing-aid," he would explain. "You get an eye operation, the federal government pays. But if you want a hearing-aid, you have to pay it yourself."

Jerry was best man at the wedding. "You just got outa one marriage," Jerry said as Dean was dressing that day, putting a white carnation in his tuxedo lapel. "What the fuck are you rushin' for?"

"Jer, this is right. It's so strong."

They spent their wedding night with Jerry at Del Mar, Bing Crosby's racetrack, "Where the Surf Meets the Turf," north of San Diego. Dean liked to bet, but he never much cared to watch the horses run. Jeannie did not even care to bet. "I'll never forget," she said. "I don't know even to this day how we wound up there."

A week later, they were in Las Vegas, where Dean and Jerry were to open at the Flamingo, Bugsy Siegel's dream casino. "That's where I spent my honeymoon," Jeannie would remember.

The Flamingo had been Bugsy Siegel's dream, downfall, and death. Las Vegas, of course, had been nothing, a forgotten Pueblo wasteland that the white man had not even passed through until 1829. In 1911, when it was incorporated as a city, its population had been barely fifteen hundred. Gambling, which had been outlawed in Nevada in 1915, had been legalized again in 1931, the year that state legislation also eased divorce laws to increase state revenues. The first legal casinos, most of them located downtown in a two-block area around Fremont and Second streets, had drawn much of their profits from the paychecks of the workmen who were building the Boulder Dam southeast of town. It was Siegel who had believed that the little desert town in the middle of nowhere could become the air-conditioned Eden of every dirty dream.

In the summer of 1939, as the state attorney general of Califor-

nia, Earl Warren, had organized a fleet to crack down on the *Rex* and
other seaborne casinos that operated beyond the three-mile limit at
Santa Monica and Long Beach harbors. Siegel, who held a piece of
every west-coast gambling boat, had sent his henchman Little Moe
Sedway to reconnoiter the Nevada territory in the summer 1941.
Sedway, whose real name was Morris Sidwirtz, had been with Siegel
since the old days back in New York, and had been one of those
involved with the Copacabana in its early years. By the end of the
war, after Warren had become governor and renewed his crusade
against gambling, Siegel's Las Vegas interests, held in cahoots with
Frank Costello, Meyer Lansky, and others back east, had come to
include pieces of the Frontier Turf Club, the El Cortez Hotel, the El
Dorado Club, the Golden Nugget, and the Las Vegas Club. On September 13, 1945, a Las Vegas widow named Margaret Folsom had
quitclaimed her failed dilapidated motel and thirty acres outside of
town to Little Moe Sedway. Two months later, Sedway had quitclaimed the property in turn to Greg Bautzer, the young Hollywood
attorney who never tired of his tale of deflowering Lana Turner. ("I
didn't enjoy it at all," Turner would say.) Bautzer had then transferred the acquisition to an entity named the Nevada Projects Corporation, whose two major shareholders were Siegel and Meyer Lansky.
Among the others were: Frank Costello, through his representative
Morris Rosen, who also served as a manager, like Gus Greenbaum,
of Lansky's gambling operations in Havana and elsewhere; Samuel
Rothberg of American Distillers; Siegel's Los Angeles attorney, Joe
Ross; and Billy Wilkerson, the publisher of *The Hollywood Reporter*,
from whom Herman Hover had taken over Ciro's.

Ground had been broken in December 1945 for what Siegel
envisioned as the greatest gambling casino in the world. It was to
be called the Flamingo. "We thought up the name one day when
we were at the Hialeah Race Track in Florida," Lansky would recall. "There's a pretty, little lake there and in the evening you can
watch the flocks of pink flamingos rise in the sky. There's a local
legend that flamingos are a sign of good luck and anyone who
shoots the birds will have seven years of misfortune. So because of
the good-luck connection, Bugsy had the idea of naming our Las
Vegas project."

A budget of $1,000,000 had been set. Bugsy and his wife, Esther, had divorced in July 1946; he had agreed to pay her $32,000 a year. That fall, forty-year-old Bugsy had married thirty-year-old Virginia Hill. By then, more than $2,000,000 had been spent and the Flamingo was still unfinished. The hotel had remained largely unfurnished on the night of its grand opening, December 26, 1946. Siegel had relied on George Raft to round up some Hollywood glamour, but all Raft had been able to come up with were himself, Vivian Blaine, Charles Coburn, Georgie Jessel, George Sanders, and Sonny Tufts. There was music by Xavier Cugat. Jessel served as the master of ceremonies, and Jimmy Durante, who knew Siegel, Raft, and the rest of them from Prohibition days in New York, was the Flamingo's christening act.

The Flamingo had been a bust. Siegel had drained the Nevada Project's shareholders of roughly $6,000,000. In the casino's first weeks, its six bank-crap tables, six blackjack tables, three roulette wheels, and one hazard game had taken a beating for $774,000. By late January, there had been no choice but to shut it down. From George Raft and others, Siegel had raised the money to reopen the Flamingo on March 27, 1947. In May, the casino had cleared over $300,000, and things had been looking up for Siegel. But his days had been numbered since the previous December, before he had ever opened the joint.

There had been a meeting that December at the Hotel Nacional in Havana, where Frank Sinatra was performing as the Christmas attraction. They had all been there: Lansky, Costello, the exiled Luciano, in from Italy; Joe Adonis, Vito Genovese, Charlie Fischetti, and more. At that meeting, it had been decided that Bugsy had fucked them, and that he was wood. Charlie Fischetti had been entrusted with the job, and he had said he would take care of it through Jack Dragna in Los Angeles.

Siegel and Hill had spent the months of their marriage writing love poetry and screaming at one another, reading sweetly from their favorite romance, Mildred Cram's *Forever*, and smacking it out. One night in the spring of 1947, after a particularly brutal argument, Virginia stormed off to Paris. Siegel had flown to Los Angeles from Las Vegas on the night of June 19. A little after midnight, June 20, he had used the golden key Virginia had given him to let himself into her house on North Linden Drive in Beverly Hills. Her brother Chick was staying there while she was away. The following night, Siegel, Chick, and Chick's girlfriend, Jerri Mason, and a business associate, Allen Smiley, had gone to dinner together at a seafood joint called Jack's, in Ocean Park. When they had arrived back at the house on North Linden Drive, Siegel had cockled his nose and sniffed. He had smelled flowers. No one else could smell anything, and Chick had assured him that there wasn't a flower in the house. Chick remembered his and Virginia's grandmother in Alabama telling them long ago that when one smelled flowers where there were no flowers, it was a sign of death. Chick and Jerri had gone upstairs to bed. Siegel and Smiley had sat on the sofa by the living-room window. They were sitting there talking when the first of nine blasts from a .30-.30 carbine had shattered the window and Bugsy's face in one sudden instant.

Following the police to North Linden Drive, Florabel Muir, a reporter from the *New York Daily News,* had commented on the smell of the night-blooming jasmine that filled the living room from the bushes outside the sundered window. The shots had spattered the far wall with morsels of Bugsy. "From the jamb of the wide doorway," Muir had reported, "I picked up the sliver of flesh from which his long eyelashes extended."

Within twenty minutes of the carbine blasts, three men had strode through the lobby of the Flamingo: Little Moe Sedway, Morris Rosen, and Gus Greenbaum. They had gathered the casino staff and announced that the Flamingo was now under new management. In the year that followed, the casino showed a profit of over $4,000,000. Only the three Elohim of death and Meyer ben Samael's friends in New York knew how much profit there was that had been kept from showing. Bugsy lay in a mausoleum in Beth Olam Cemetery in Hollywood; but his dream, the Flamingo, was alive and well.

The Steubenville *Völkerwanderung* was already well underway. Tony Torcasio had been in Las Vegas since 1946. "Nothin' then but two hotels on the Strip, the El Rancho and the Last Frontier." He had fallen in with Wilbur Ivern Clark, a thirty-seven-year-old Midwesterner whose devious-cruising path as a professional gambler, café-owner, and casino worker had brought him to Las Vegas in 1942 by way of Reno, the Long Beach gambling-ship *Monte Carlo,* the Piping Rock Club in Saratoga, and the Mayfield Road Gang's joints in Ohio and Kentucky. Torcasio was with him when he had taken over the Players, a small bar and casino on the outskirts of town, and begun building it in May of 1947 into the Desert Inn. Money had run out, and the project had languished for more than two years. But now, in the summer of 1949, the Mayfield Road Gang had cut a deal with Clark. Directly and indirectly, the consortium of Moe Dalitz, Morris Kleinman, Tom McGinty, Lou Rothkopf, Sam Tucker, and others would bankroll him as their front-man in exchange for a seventy-four-percent interest. Dalitz would develop the Desert Inn corporation into a vast complex of diverse holdings, finding after 1955 an almost unlimited source of capital in low-interest loans from the Teamsters' Central States, Southeast and Southwest Areas Pension Fund, which his boyhood friend from Detroit, Teamsters vice-president Jimmy Hoffa, would create that year through a consolidation of local funds.

The Desert Inn was still several months away from opening when Dean and Jerry arrived in September 1949. The Flamingo was still the jewel of that stretch of Highway 91 that came to be called the Strip. The Rex Cigar Store, the Jungle Inn, the 500 Club, the Riviera—the great and gaudy neon cathedral of the Flamingo was all these joints exalted. Here, married by God and by state, anointed in the blood of Bugsy Siegel, *Unterwelt* and American dream lay down together in greed.

Martin and Lewis by now were among the beloved of that dream, embracing and embraced by the spirit of a post-heroic, post-literate, cathode-culture America. The Flamingo was the pleasure dome of the new prefab promised land: a land of chrome, not gold; of Armstrong linoleum, not Carrara marble; of heptalk, not epos or prophecy.

Martin and Lewis were the jesters of that land. *Time* magazine, then as always the cutting edge of lumpen-American mediocrity, the vox populi of the modern world, celebrated the dazzling appeal of their hilarity. The heart of their audience, the nightclub clientele whose reduction to a quivering mass of thunderous yockers *Variety* attested again and again, was sophisticated, white-collared, and well-heeled. The sophisticated, white-collared, and well-heeled *New York Times* itself, in an article published while Martin and Lewis were in Las Vegas, hailed their "refreshing brand of comic hysteria," their "wild and uninhibited imagination."

And yet, these few years later, the nature of that appeal is as alien and as difficult to translate as the language, syntax, and meter of Catullus. There are no films or tapes of their nightclub act. Only secondary fragments have survived to be judged: glimpses of routines reworked for pictures, such as the "Donkey Serenade" scene in *My Friend Irma,* and for pale renderings on radio; a few rare kinescopes of television broadcasts, none of them predating 1952. Those fragments convey almost nothing of the dazzling appeal of that hilarity proclaimed in contemporary accounts. And yet the howling laughter present in many of those fragments, in the radio shows and television performances, all done before live spectators, is unanswerable. Those spectators, who had lined up for free shows at network studios, were not the same urbane nightclub-goers who howled at the Copacabana or Chez Paree or the Flamingo. Their sense of yockery was perhaps homelier; but, on the other hand, it was less primed by booze. Jerry was right: Martin and Lewis appealed to everyone. But why?

"Let us not be deceived," the *New York Times* had declared in April 1947, while Dean and Jerry had been playing at the Loew's Capitol; "we are today in the midst of a cold war." Now, in September 1949, while they were in Las Vegas, President Truman, the first president to have a televised inauguration, revealed that the Soviet Union had set off an atomic-bomb explosion. A week later, on October 1, Chairman Mao Tse-tung would formally proclaim the Communist People's Republic of China. In January, Truman would order the development of the hydrogen bomb. Six months later, United States ground troops would invade South Korea. "Let us not be deceived"—but America wanted nothing more than to be deceived. Martin and Lewis gave them that: not laughter in the dark, but a denial of darkness itself, a regression, a transporting to the preternatural bliss of infantile senselessness. It was a catharsis, a celebration of ignorance, absurdity, and stupidity, as meaningless, as primitive-seeming, and as droll today as the fallout shelters and beatnik posings which offered opposing sanctuary in those days so close in time but so distant in consciousness.

Those days were the beginning of the end of timelessness. Homer's *Odyssey* spoke throughout the ages; Kerouac's American odyssey, *On the Road,* would have a shelf life, and would prove after a handful of years more outdated and stale than Homer after thousands. But like the detergent on the shelf in that other supermarket aisle, it was for the moment new and improved; and that is what mattered. And that is why the dead-serious pretensions of Kerouac today seem so droll while the comedy of that same neophiliac era seems so unfunny.

Dean, of course, had no use for any of this shit. He did not know the new and improved from the old and well-worn. Homer, Sorelli the Mystic: it was all the same shit to him. The Trojan War, World War II, the Cold War, what the fuck did he care? His hernia was bigger than history itself. He cared as much about Korea as Korea cared about his fucking hernia. He walked through his own world. And that world was as much a part of what commanded those audiences as the catharsis of the absurd slapstick; and it would continue to command, long after that catharsis, like a forgotten mystery rite, had lost all meaning and power. His uncaring air of romance reflected the flash and breezy sweet seductions of a world in which everything came down to broads, booze, and money, with plenty of linguine on the side. There was a beckoning to join him in the Lethe of the old ways' woods that appealed to the lover, the *menefreghista,* the rotten cocksucker, the sweet-hearted dreamer in everyone.

Mickey Cohen, a brutal killer who "got kind of friendly with him," said that "Dean would've been in the rackets if he didn't have the beautiful voice that he has. He probably would've wound up a gambling boss somewhere. I'd say Dean had the perfect makeup to be a racket guy, although he is a little too lackadaisical, if you know what I mean."

Love was Dean's racket. The traits he shared with the Fischettis and the Anastasias—that *lontananza,* that dark self-serving *moralità*—were never far beneath the surface of whatever sweet spell he meant to cast. Whatever talent he had, whatever effect he worked at, whatever was God-given and whatever manufactured, that much, that darkness beneath the spell, was immanent and intractable and ever-there.

Frank Sinatra, who had sung at the Nacional during the Havana yuletide gathering of 1946, was a *malavita* groupie, a scrawny mama's boy who liked to pretend he was a tough guy. He cultivated the company of, and catered to, men such as the Fischettis. But it was Dean, so aloof and yet seemingly so kindred, to whom those men themselves were drawn.

"They loved him," Jerry said. "But they knew that he wasn't the one to talk to on a business basis. He had his way of getting that clear to them. I would say he was the most brilliant diplomat I've ever known. I used to hear things like 'Talk to the Jew,' 'Talk to the kid,' 'Talk to the little one.' "

Las Vegas was a great place to play. "There's something you have to understand," said Herman Hover, who later became a part owner and entertainment director of the Frontier Hotel in Las Vegas. "Big attractions in those days were not that much interested in their salary. What they were interested in was money under the table—money that was not declared. Cash, off the books. So a contract might read for $2,500 and actually they might get an additional $1,000 or $1,500, on which they didn't pay an agent's commission or income tax." Dean and Jerry, he said, were making a lot of money under the table; and they were not alone. "Every attraction was getting it. They were getting it elsewhere, and that was our competition" at Ciro's. "In Las Vegas, it was very easy to get money under the table, because they had all that gambling money, which they didn't declare anyway."

Dean and Jerry were paid $15,000 a week at the Flamingo. By the end of their first week there, Jerry ran up a casino debt of $137,000. Moe Sedway, henchman of the late Bugsy, called him into his office.

"You realize you owe this hotel $137,000," he said.

"And you realize that you're running this hotel, and you're giving that kind of credit to someone that's getting $7,500 a week.
Doesn't that make you a fuckin' idiot?"

Sedway looked at him. "Well, yeah," he said, "I guess so."

"You guess so? I'm just a kid, and you let me run up a
$137,000 marker? Where the fuck do you think I'm gonna get that
kind of money from?"

"Well, that's just it. How *do* you propose to pay it?"

Jerry thought for a minute. He thought of Fischetti and those
guys back in New York, the ones with the good sense of humor, the
ones who had blown away Siegel and put Sedway here in this office
instead.

"Call New York and ask how I should pay it," he said. "And I
will follow those instructions."

That night Sedway came to him in his dressing-room. "You're to
pay it as you get it, however you can pay it, however long it takes.
But you're to pay it. Those are the instructions."

"What about gambling? Can I gamble to get even?"

"No. You're not to play anymore until you pay."

It would take Jerry a year and seven months to erase the debt.
During that time, he would lose gambling with Dean as well. "I
made train trips with him that were very costly. One time, we got on
the train, he owed me $600 for some bet or other. Three days later,
we got off the train in New York, I owed him $3,300. I said to him,
'You're a fuckin' dealer. Are you dealing me seconds? Would you do
that to me?' He looked at me and he said, 'Would I do that to you?'
And I said, 'No. But you keep fuckin' winning.' He said, 'You're an
unlucky Jew and I'm a good poker player.'"

Though Nevada law would later permit an annual Las Vegas
Gin-Rummy Tournament, gin-rummy gambling itself was illegal everywhere. That September, however, gambler Nick the Greek and
Ray Ryan, a young Texas oil tycoon, were engaged in a private high-
stakes gin marathon in one of the Flamingo's back rooms. Jeannie
Martin spent much of her honeymoon standing there watching them,
mesmerized. Ryan, who would later meet a violent end, was a notorious millionaire gambler whose partners in at least one petroleum-

lease venture included Frank Costello and Frank Erickson. Like so
many others, Ryan took a liking to Dean. But Dean, in this case,
took a liking as well.

The Hal Wallis deal permitted Martin and Lewis to make one
outside picture a year. That fall, Ryan put up the money that enabled them to found the York Pictures Corporation, their own inde-
pendent production company. Dean and Jerry held two thirds of
York. Abby Greshler, the president and executive producer, held
the other third.

From Las Vegas, Dean and Jerry traveled to New York, where,
on September 28, they were to open at the Paramount for the premiere of *My Friend Irma*. Ten years before, Jerry had been fired as a
Paramount usher; now he was returning in triumph to Zukor's fabulous temple of dreams, in the flesh and on the big screen, for $9,000
a week.

Dick Stabile led sixteen pieces at the Paramount, including the
key musicians the act always traveled with, pianist Lou Brown and
drummer Ray Toland. In Stabile, Dean as a singer had one of the
best popular bandleaders in America to work with. The effect at the
Paramount was noted by *Variety*, which reported "a medley that's
especially surefire for the dames." The comedy, however, was getting a bit out of hand, *Variety* said. "Though they remain the finest
young comedy team to come along in years," there were routines
now that seemed to have meaning only for Martin and Lewis, lines
that left "the audience wondering what it's all about." They "could
dispense with the couple of double entendres" as well. And Lewis
was going too far with "the nance stuff."

Bosley Crowther's *New York Times* review of *My Friend Irma*
found the picture to be lowbrow "nonsense about a female imbe-
cile." Though it had seemed that many at the premiere "would
expire in the Paramount yesterday, so severe were their merry con-
vulsions," Crowther "could find nothing in common with them." But
then came the *coup de grâce* of Seymour's revenge. Even Crowther
from his Olympus "could go along with the laughs fetched by a new
mad comedian, Jerry Lewis by name." His was "a genuine comic
quality." Though "meagerly used," he was by far "the funniest thing
in the film." There it was in black and white, in the *New York Times*,

the Talmud of newspapers, the intellectual borscht belt of the *balebatisheh yiden*. Even the caption of the review sang his praise: "Jerry Lewis, New Comedian, a Bright Spot in Silly Film." And Dean? He was Jerry's "collar-ad partner," and "as much as one may like" him, "one has to remark that he gives forth only standard glamour in this film."

In Steubenville, the picture's title alone evoked a special mirth. There it was up on the marquee, just a few blocks from where Irma DiBenedetto still lived and brooded.

The picture was a hit. Wallis would later claim that it grossed $5,000,000, ten times its cost; $3,000,000 would probably be closer to the truth. In any case, it made a lot of money. To Hal Wallis, that was all that mattered. He put Cy Howard and Parke Levy forthwith to work on concocting a sequel.

While in New York, on October 18, Martin and Lewis appeared again on "Texaco Star Theatre." When they had appeared on the show in August of last year, Morey Amsterdam had been the host, one of several who assumed that role in the show's first months. In September of 1948, Milton Berle, the first master of ceremonies of "Texaco Star Theatre," had become its permanent host. Berle's show had quickly become the most popular program on television. NBC that first season had paid him $2,500 a week. He had been making more on radio ten years before. By now, however, in the fall of 1949, Berle was commanding a salary of $25,000 a week from NBC, and the weekly production cost of "Texaco Star Theatre" itself had risen from $15,000 to $55,000. Jerry, who would regard Berle as "the master," remembered the Sunday-morning rehearsals for that Tuesday night's show. They were held in the Henry Hudson Hotel on Ninth Avenue and Fifty-seventh Street. Berle paced back and forth with a towel and corded whistle around his neck.

"What is this, a football game?" Dean said.

"We have a timed show here, boys," Berle told them. "Tighter than my aunt Jenny's corset. In other words, fellas, you must stick to eight minutes. Not ten. Not nine. I'm talking about eight minutes, on the nose. You got it?"

Jerry nodded.

"Good. No ad-libbing."

Jerry nodded.

"No extra shtick."

"We got it, Milton," Dean said. "Eight minutes."

But when Tuesday night came, at NBC Studio 6B at Rockefeller Center, they ignored the eight-minute warning. "Hold your horses, I'm not finished talking!" Dean hollered when Berle came out to introduce the next act. Jerry stuck his face into the camera: "Milton Berle! Big deal!" Berle hated it. The audience loved it. Berle loved it.

As for radio, NBC had learned the hard way what Abby Greshler and Capitol Records had already known, and what *Newsweek* and *Time* had pointed out: The magic of Martin and Lewis could not be conveyed through sound alone. "The Martin and Lewis Show" had been suspended in late August. On October 7, while Martin and Lewis were at the Paramount, NBC brought the show back, moving it to Friday nights. A month later, the show was shifted once again, to Mondays. By then, Dean and Jerry had left New York for Chicago and the Chez Paree.

Variety again expressed its disapproval: "It is surprising that two clean-cut lads like Dean Martin and Jerry Lewis need to resort to crude swish material plus foul words in foreign tongues. Also most of the opening night crowd was not the usual hep set and had come to see the comics on the basis of their picture, radio, and tele efforts."

Not long before Dean's wedding, Lou Costello had been in Ciro's one night when Dean and Jerry were there. Costello came in once in a while, Herman Hover said; "he gave me a tip one time on a racehorse that he owned; lost a lot of money." Jerry had come over to Lou's table that night, but Dean had ignored him.

"I'm gonna sue that bastard for breach of contract," Costello told his manager, Eddie Sherman, the next day.

"What are you talking about?" Sherman said. "I was with you when you told Broder to drop him."

"That don't matter. I still got a contract."

Sherman told him it would be an ugly, unwise move, that it would only be seen as jealousy.

"I don't care," Costello said. "Nobody's gonna slough me off. If he had just come over and sat down at the table, okay. But now I'm gonna make him pay."

While Dean and Jerry were in Chicago, Costello's suit, claiming breach of contract and seeking $100,000 in recompense, was filed in Los Angeles. "When I discovered Martin, he was unknown," Costello told columnist Louella Parsons. "He hasn't even bothered so much as to call me during the past five years."

Sherman eventually prevailed in convincing Costello to drop the suit, but Costello was persistent about drawing a few token drops of financial blood. That slight at Ciro's, he reckoned, was worth $20,000. Sherman suggested that he talk to Hal Wallis. When Costello showed Sherman a check from Wallis for that amount, Sherman said, "Now make yourself a big man and tear it up."

"Like hell I will," Costello said. He bet the $20,000 on a horse that did not even show.

It was in Chicago that Dean, Jerry, and Greshler found their first York Pictures property. *At War with the Army*, written by a Yale drama student named James B. Allardice, had been a success in New York earlier in the year, and had opened at the Harris Theatre in Chicago at about the same time Dean and Jerry opened at Chez Paree. In late November, soon after Greshler closed his deal with Allardice for motion-picture rights, *At War with the Army* folded, having brought in only $8,000 in five weeks at the Harris. Eight grand: pocket money, Dean reflected, glad that he wasn't in the play racket.

Ten years before, Dino Martini had rung in the new decade with Terry's Six Wonder Dogs at a chop-suey joint in Columbus. Now Dean Martin, sitting atop the world, closed his eyes and let those years, and all the years before them, wash away to where dreams and lies and truth ran together to the sea. He poured himself a drink, he poured himself another. He closed his eyes once more and grinned, a stranger even unto himself.

X.

The ORGAN-GRINDER AND THE MONKEY

$\mathcal{G}$eorge Evans, the master publicist who had helped to orchestrate the rise of Martin and Lewis over the course of the last three years, was felled suddenly by a heart attack at his New York home on January 26, 1950. He was forty-eight. Services were held two days later at Park West Chapel in Manhattan. Budd Granoff, who had worked under Evans since 1948, and Jack Keller, who had been Evans's West Coast partner, took over the handling of many of Evans's clients, including Martin and Lewis, who, like Sinatra, Mario Lanza, and others, paid $400 a week to be pimped to a public that was already theirs.

A few days later, on January 30, NBC once again suspended "The Martin and Lewis Show." At the same time, negotiations were underway between the network and Greshler to bring the act to television.

My Friend Irma Goes West began production at Paramount on February 1. This time around, the director was Hal Walker, a fifty-four-year-old Iowan who had been making pictures for Paramount since 1945. He was used to fast jobs—*Duffy's Tavern, Out of This World, The Stork Club,* and *Road to Utopia* had all been dispatched by him in the same year; and *My Friend Irma Goes West* would be a fast one indeed, barely seven weeks from start to finish. The screen story of *My Friend Irma,* such as it was, had ended on the morning of a double wedding, with Irma and Al, Steve and Jane about to be married. The screenplay for the sequel ignored that ending and opened with Irma and Al, Steve and Jane—played once again by Marie Wilson and John Lund, Dean and Diana Lynn—still affianced, brought west by misadventure to Las Vegas from New York. Wallis had cast the beautiful twenty-five-year-old French actress

Corinne Calvet as Yvonne Yvonne, a movie star whose advances try Jane's trust in faithful Steve.

"The picture is going to make you a big star," Wallis had told Calvet. "It's imperative that I get to know you better."

Calvet had suggested that he come to her house for dinner. She was married at the time to an aspiring actor named John Bromfield, who had appeared the previous year with her, Burt Lancaster, and Peter Lorre in *Rope of Sand*. Bromfield was also under contract to Wallis.

"Is the honeymoon over yet?" Wallis had asked.

Darryl F. Zanuck of Twentieth Century-Fox had promised to give her husband a career in exchange for moist favors. This little schmuck Wallis was almost as bad. "I had his destiny between my legs," she would say of Bromfield.

Her reaction to the screenplay had been one of angry dismay. "I could not believe that he would cast me in such a script. *Rope of Sand* had made me a valuable property. Doing this film would ruin my chances of rising higher as a dramatic star."

"How do you like the script?" Wallis had asked.

"I don't."

"Really? Why?"

She had told him. Her companion in the script was a chimpanzee in a leopard-skin pillbox hat. "I was," she would remember, "overwhelmed with the idea that my father would have a heart attack if he saw me in a film that insinuated that a chimpanzee was my boyfriend." That was only one of the things she had mentioned; she "could see no humor in the part." She then had broached the subject of Wallis's other current projects. Surely he had another role for her. He had stood then and started to feel her up, telling her it was a possibility. She had rebuffed him, and two days later had received notice that it was *My Friend Irma Goes West* or nothing at all. If she refused, Wallis and Paramount could place her on suspension for thirteen weeks without pay. Wallis also held paper on a loan that had enabled her to buy her house, and the loan could be recalled in full at any time.

"One picture like this won't do much to hurt you too badly,"

Wallis had told her; "but two or three of these kinds of parts and good-bye, stardom." Then she had felt his hand on her ass.

On the first day of filming, Wallis introduced her to Dean and Jerry and Pierre the chimpanzee.

"I found Dean friendly, a man of the world, self-assured and quiet," she said. "Lewis was the exact opposite, nervous, and trying to override his innate shyness by flattering and entertaining everyone around him. He seemed to be afraid of silence, to feel compelled to fill the empty spaces. I was sensitive to his great anxiety, his wanting to be liked by everyone."

The chimpanzee seemed deranged. He "followed me everywhere on the set, making obscene gestures and sticking his tongue in and out rapidly. His eyes would turn up in his head, his lips curl open, then close with a loud smack. I was mortified."

"What's the matter with him?" she asked the trainer.

"Well, miss"—the trainer hesitated—"could you be in your monthly cycle?" She nodded. "To him," the trainer said, "it's the time when the female is ready for reproduction."

"I don't understand."

"He's making sexual advances toward you."

"Make him stop."

"He won't understand. He'll stop as soon as your period's over."

The following days were a freakshow, with her simian Romeo straining at the leash to consummate his love on the set, and her husband giving her a hard time at home. For Bromfield, she said, sex was "an addiction he needed to satisfy in order to sleep," and "he resented my monthly period, because he felt it gave me the right to deprive him." Jerry, she said, made matters worse. He "couldn't resist the urge to imitate the chimp, and turned into a human monkey, harassing me without restraint. Controlling my mounting hysteria, I could do nothing but pretend to be a good sport about it."

Dean, watching her predicament, stepped in when he perceived that she was at her wits' end. He invited her to his dressing-room. No one would bother her there, he said, and he would appreciate her help with some lines.

"I hesitated a moment," she said. "But the choice was clear: Dean Martin or the chimp." It turned out that Dean was telling the truth. "He really did want me to help him with his lines. It made me feel important, so I took him under my wing the way Burt Lancaster had for me."

When the production moved to Las Vegas later in the month, Wallis canceled John Bromfield's contract.

By then, Greshler and Norman Blackburn of NBC-TV had closed their deal. The Sherman-Marquette, Bates agency was developing a weekly variety show for the Colgate-Palmolive-Peet Company. It was Colgate's plan to use a group of regular comic hosts, each serving once a month on a rotation basis. Martin and Lewis, hosting as a team, would be paid $95,000 to do ten shows.

It was a good deal for them. But it was an even better deal for Greshler, who had grown wilier with the passing of time. Though his contracts with Dean and Jerry restricted him to a ten-percent commission, that ten percent was enough to make Greshler a wealthy man. His house on Stradella Road in Bel Air had been gotten through that ten percent. Nevertheless, Greshler had hoodwinked them last year into signing papers that surrendered another ten percent of their income to his wife, Violet. A shell company, the Doe Corporation, had been set up with fictitious names—John Doe, Jane Doe, Richard Roe—to obfuscate the channeling of money Greshler handled as their fiduciary. When Dean and Jerry, who were making more money now than they could monitor, had discovered that an extra ten percent of it had been going to Greshler through his wife, Greshler had allayed them with double-talk, and had then reduced his skimming to a less noticeable five percent. Now Greshler had secretly made the Colgate deal contingent upon a separate deal between himself and NBC-TV. On February 13, when he concluded the deal for Martin and Lewis, he simultaneously concluded a deal for himself. He was to be paid $350 a week by NBC-TV. Ostensibly employed by the network as a program consultant, Greshler did nothing for the money but deliver forth Dean and Jerry, from whose $9,500 per show he would reap another $950 a month: a base-minimum take of $587.50 a week, for nothing.

Dean went into the recording studio twice that March. Lee Gillette, Dean's producer at Capitol, had decided to try something different. Paul Weston, Capitol's chief arranger and conductor, had been around. He had recorded in the twenties as a brass and string bassman, had arranged for Tommy Dorsey and Bing Crosby before coming to Capitol. His series of mood-music albums, begun in 1945 with *Music for Romancing*, was a success. His wife, Jo Stafford, who had sung with Sinatra as part of Tommy Dorsey's Pied Pipers, was one of Capitol's biggest stars; and Weston arranged all her hit recordings. But Dean's work with the Paul Weston Orchestra had not met with much success.

In April, Dean and Jerry opened at Ciro's for eleven nights. "Greshler would come down when they were playing, the place was jam-packed, and he'd get on the reservation phone and make all his long-distance calls. And he used to annoy the hell out of me," Herman Hover said. "But I couldn't offend him, because he had the hottest attraction in the country. Martin and Lewis were money in the bank." Greshler, Hover said, "was a guy you could never trust."

The day after they closed at Ciro's, Dean returned to the studio and recorded six more songs before leaving with Jerry for New York. One of these, copyrighted the previous October, was "I Don't Care If the Sun Don't Shine," by Mack David, the thirty-seven-year-old lawyer who had cowritten the songs for last year's Walt Disney hit, *Cinderella*. Released in May, "I Don't Care If the Sun Don't Shine" remained on *Billboard*'s "Most Played Juke Box Records" charts for more than two months, rising to number eight in late July, when the song appeared on the "Best Selling Sheet Music" charts as well. Elvis Presley would later record it, in September 1954, as the flip side of his second Sun single, "Good Rockin' Tonight." By June, Capitol had released six singles by Dean in as many months, and none of them had done much of anything.

When Dean had signed with Capitol, in August 1948, he was still under contract to Apollo Records in New York, and, technically, his contract with Capitol had been illegal from the start. Apollo had not wanted him back. If Capitol could not sell him, then surely Bess Berman's little Apollo could not either. But Apollo did want money. A breach-of-contract suit had been filed against Dean in New York Supreme Court, and now, on May 20, a jury decided in

Apollo's favor, and Judge E. Nathan, Jr., ordered Dean to pay $3,500 in damages plus interest and costs.

In October of last year, Greshler had booked Martin and Lewis into Chez Paree in direct conflict with a previous two-week booking he had made for them with the Latin Casino in Philadelphia. Harry Steinman, the operator of the Latin Casino, had taken his case to the local branch of the American Guild of Variety Artists, which had ruled that Martin and Lewis must either honor their commitment to Steinman or forfeit $12,000. Martin and Lewis, in turn, had filed a complaint with the national office of AGVA, claiming that Greshler had entered into the agreement with the Latin Casino without informing them and without their authorization. On the afternoon of June 13, several hours before the Berle show, Dean and Jerry attended the hearing of their case at the AGVA headquarters at 1697 Broadway.

"After careful consideration and deliberation," read the signed statement AGVA later issued, "it was the unanimous decision of the Arbitration Board that Dean Martin & Jerry Lewis are not obliged to play any date at the Latin Casino because they didn't sign any agreement to play any date at the Latin Casino." It was the board's verdict that the "burden upon Martin & Lewis was placed upon them by their agent, Abby Greshler, who presumed to commit the team to play a date at the Latin Casino without consulting them and without obtaining their prior consent. He exceeded his authority as agent." The board felt "very strongly that Abner Greshler, as agent, has embarrassed and inconvenienced the team and jeopardized their careers and that he also embarrassed and wronged the night club owner with whom AGVA has a Minimum Basic Agreement." It concluded by recommending "that immediate action be taken by AGVA against Abner J. Greshler for such conduct in violation of his franchise."

Greshler felt the heat. He would have to redeem himself somehow in Dean and Jerry's eyes. On the following Friday, June 16, Greshler managed to negotiate an amendatory agreement with NBC-TV, whereby he extended the promise of his clients' services to a period of five years in exchange for an increase to $20,000 per show. At the same time, he entered into his own amendatory agreement with the network, which guaranteed that his $350-a-week payments would continue for the span of those years.

A week later, Dean and Jerry returned to the Flamingo, where *My Friend Irma Goes West* was previewed for the press. Its opening at the El Portal Theatre, on June 26, was the first movie premiere in Las Vegas history.

It was Jerry's picture; the reviews last fall had given him the upper hand. Dean's presence was ghostly and undefined. *"Mamma mia!* Five hundred bucks a week!" was the only line he delivered with any life. The bizarre few moments in which he appeared singing "Santa Lucia" in a garish Western-swing outfit at a Las Vegas square dance were striking in their absurdity: They not only encapsulated the utter dumbness of the picture itself, but also offered an accidental glimpse of the mercurial, improbable, incongruous persona of Dean-Dino Crocetti-Martin *in statu nascendi* in the Hollywood alembic. The picture ended with Corinne Calvet forgetting about Dean and falling for Jerry, whom she decides to make her new leading man.

"Me? Is this on the level?" Seymour wonders.

"You will be wonderful," Yvonne gushes.

"I always knew I was a great actor." His voice changed, took on a new, Britannic tone. "Here, my boy, I shan't forget you," he says to Dean. "You shall be my stand-in, press my clothes, and do various small things around the studio. Yes, you shall all benefit. And you, my French beauty, I will love you and kiss you, love you and kiss you"—he embraces her. She swoons: "Ah!"

"Most of the laugh meat is tossed to Jerry Lewis," *Variety* noticed. The others, it seemed, were "around to help back up the footage play given Lewis." Calvet was pleasant but, the review predicted, "audiences will shudder at a couple of scenes showing her bussing the chimp." *Newsweek* dismissed the picture as "light-fingered malarkey."

Lew Wasserman had taken over from Jules Stein as the president of MCA. Even before the AGVA hearing, Wasserman had known that Martin and Lewis were dissatisfied with Greshler, whose factotum, Freddy Fields, had shared the secret with MCA vice-president Taft Schreiber in the hope of getting a job there. When they returned from Las Vegas, Wasserman asked Dean and Jerry to meet with him at his office, and to bring along a copy of their NBC contract.

The MCA building in Beverly Hills was a stately colonial white-brick structure, which Jules Stein owned and leased to the company. Wasserman's office, like many in the building—as in the MCA buildings Stein owned in New York and Chicago—was furnished with eighteenth-century antiques, of which Stein was among the world's foremost collectors. Amid the delicate richness of those antiques, the velvet drapes and dusky-rose carpeting, Wasserman, tall, lean, and well dressed, cut an imposing figure behind his big walnut desk.

"How could you have signed this?" he said, gesturing at the contract that lay before him on the desk.

"With a pen," Dean said. "Why?"

"The terms. A paltry sum." And, indeed, twenty-five grand a pop did seem paltry in that chamber of imperial elegance. "You've been hoodwinked, boys." Boys: he was barely four years older than Dean. "NBC's got you for peanuts."

Wasserman said that if they were free of Greshler, MCA would sign them and he himself would renegotiate the NBC contract. Furthermore, MCA, which six years ago had sold Dean for $545, would give them a good-faith advance of $40,000 upon signing.

Ray Ryan had brought together a group to form a company called Screen Associates, Inc. Centered in Beverly Hills, the company was set up to underwrite, and profit from, the movies Dean and Jerry made for York Pictures. On April 8, York Pictures and Screen Associates had entered into an agreement for seven pictures. The president of Screen Associates was Ralph E. Stolkin, a young entrepreneur who was involved with Ryan in several oil-drilling ventures. Stolkin had become a millionaire through his 1941 marriage to Ruth Koolish, the daughter of Abe Koolish, king of the punchboard racket. On July 5, *At War with the Army*, the first of the seven envisioned coproductions of York Pictures and Screen Associates, Inc., began filming at the Motion Picture Center in Hollywood, with a script by Fred F. Finklehoffe based on Allardice's play. Greshler was the executive producer.

The next day, before Dean went to Capitol to record a duet with Margaret Whiting, he and Jerry signed a letter to Abby Greshler. Though he was their agent and, as the producer of *At War with the Army*, would be seeing them on the set, they sent the letter by registered mail to his office at 324 South Beverly Drive.

There was a birthday party that night for Violet Greshler. Dean made an appearance, and showed no ill will toward either Abby or his wife. Quite the contrary, he "was the life of the party," Greshler remembered. "The next day, the letter came."

"Dear Mr. Greshler," it said. "For good and sufficient cause, we hereby cancel and terminate all agreements of any kind whatever which have heretofore been entered into between us, and we expressly revoke any and all authorizations for you to act for us as our agent or otherwise. Accordingly, you are no longer to represent us or to act in our behalf in any capacity whatsoever."

At the same time, through the Beverly Hills law firm of Pacht, Tannenbaum & Ross, they prepared a statement of claim against Greshler for the arbitration tribunal of the Screen Actors Guild. (N. Joseph Ross, the law-firm partner who handled Dean and Jerry personally, was the attorney who had represented Tommy Dorsey in his 1943 dispute with Frank Sinatra, and had afterward, in 1947, been retained in turn by Sinatra. He had also been Bugsy Siegel's lawyer at the time of Siegel's murder.) Contending that Greshler had been systematically sly-fucking them for years, the claim sought a sixfold judgment: that their letter of termination to him be declared "justified and proper"; that their contracts with him consequently be "declared ineffective and terminated"; that all money paid to Violet Greshler, estimated "to be in excess of $36,950," be restored; that Greshler "be required to promptly and fully account to the claimants for the moneys received by him for their account"; that a finding be made by the tribunal recommending "such disciplinary or other action as may be invoked"; that "such other relief as the arbitration tribunal may deem proper" be awarded.

Lew Wasserman, meanwhile, had been on the telephone to NBC in New York. They could forget about Greshler, he told them. They could forget about whatever contracts they had with Martin and Lewis as well. It was time to do business for real. It was only a

matter of days before Wasserman called Dean and Jerry to his office
to sign the new NBC contracts. The deal, he explained, was for five
shows, with terms to be extended or renegotiated thereafter.

"You do the first show for $100,000," he told them. "After that,
NBC will pay you $150,000 per show."

After MCA's cut, that came to $495,000, just shy of half a
million, for five shows. That cut, like every commission earned from
Martin and Lewis over the next two years, would be shared with
Abby Greshler, whose current, three-year contracts with Dean and
Jerry, signed last August, would be allowed to run out their course.

While Freddy Fields moved into his new office at MCA,
Greshler readied a million-dollar suit against MCA, accusing the
agency of inducing a breach of contract by "romancing and luring
away" his clients. Furthermore, he contended, the 1949 contracts
had an effective life of six years rather than three, as they included
options for automatic extension.

"I was not Lou Perry," Greshler said. "They ended up fighting
with Abby Greshler, and that's a whole different thing. James W.
Davis was my lawyer—40 Wall Street, four floors, four hundred
lawyers. It was a huge settlement. I'm not allowed to mention the
number, but you think of a lot of money and that's what it was. You
should retire on it, you and your family, and live well the rest of
your life. You're talkin' to a man with big assets. We have a villa in
Monaco. We bought the Frank Capra estate out here forty years ago;
we're still there. We just turned down $28,000,000 for the property.
I mean, that's me," explained the man whom Francis Coppola had
considered for the Meyer Lansky role that eventually went to Lee
Strasberg in *The Godfather, Part II*. "I'm that kind of a guy. Touch
wood."

Before signing with MCA, Dean had petitioned the court to
cancel his obligation to pay Betty the $3,400 a month she had been
getting from him since their divorce last summer. He maintained in
his complaint that these payments deprived him of from half to all
of his income, as opposed to the third he had foreseen upon agreeing to the settlement. On July 10, Judge William B. McKesson
turned him down.

At War with the Army finished production in August. At a final cost of $400,000, it had been a cheap picture to make. And it showed. Beyond the $40,000 taken by Dean and Jerry, there had been little money expended on actors. Polly Bergen, who had never been in a movie before, worked for close to nothing. Dick Stabile worked for even less. The storm between Greshler and Martin and Lewis had pervaded the production. In the end, *At War with the Army* emerged as a tortured attempt at comedy, more grim than funny. The poor technical quality of the film, from Hal Walker's disinterested direction to its dismal, hollow sound, from its poor lighting to the inferiority of the actual celluloid itself, gave it an almost funereal air of vaguely dreadful emptiness, foreshadowing the feel, if not quite the substance, of Samuel Beckett's work to come. The title under which it was shown in France even made it sound somewhat like a Beckett play: *Le Soldat Récalcitrant.*

Dean's recording of "I'll Always Love You," one of the songs from *My Friend Irma Goes West,* had been released by Capitol in May. Three months later, in the wake of the picture, that forgotten single began to sell. In the last week of August, it appeared at the very bottom of *Billboard*'s "Best Selling Pop Singles" chart, in the number-thirty position, directly beneath Frankie Laine's "Music, Maestro, Please." Four years to the month after his first record was released, he finally had a hit. Rising to number eleven in September, it remained on the charts for four months, straight through to Christmas.

In September, while accusations and cross-accusations between them and Greshler occupied their lawyers, Dean and Jerry traveled east. After playing the State Theatre in Hartford, they appeared at the Harvest Moon Ball Finals at Madison Square Garden. Four nights later, at eight o'clock on Sunday, September 17, they made their debut as hosts of "The Colgate Comedy Hour."

Broadcast from the Park Theatre, the Colgate show had premiered the previous week with Eddie Cantor hosting. The way it worked out, Colgate would sponsor the show three weeks out of the month; every fourth Sunday, as simply "The Comedy Hour," the show would be sponsored by Frigidaire and hosted by Bob Hope. This arrangement would continue through 1953, when Colgate took over the fourth Sunday as well.

WNBT, the NBC-TV key station, in New York, had sent out a news release promising "hilarious antics" from "Dean Martin, with his singing voice, and Jerry Lewis, with his squeaky falsetto." Dean and Jerry had spent three days preparing for this night with producer Ernie Glucksman and executive producer Sam Fuller. At one point, Glucksman had suggested to Dean that they should have lunch and get to know one another better.

"Nobody gets to know me," Dean told him. There was no smile, no anything; just those words.

At the final meeting on Saturday night, Jerry would remember, "the whole thing" had seemed "sensational and hopeless at the same time."

Marilyn Maxwell, the twenty-nine-year-old blond actress who had been one of their radio-show guests last year, sang one song. Dean had conned the producers into having his uncle Leonard Barr do one of his eccentric-dance routines. Other than those solo pieces, Dean and Jerry handled the entire hour.

The *New York Times* the next morning celebrated the show as "swell nonsense." *Variety*, in its review, drew upon that rarest of its lexicon's superlatives: "maximum yocks." Martin and Lewis, it said in closing, gave evidence "of video's maturity in the realm of comedy." Their little satire about the very mention of television creating a crisis in an empty movie theater struck such a response that they came forth a week later with a public apology to the theater industry. That same week, two of Dean's songs, "I Don't Care if the Sun Don't Shine" and his current hit, "I'll Always Love You," appeared on *Billboard*'s new "Songs with Most TV Performances" chart.

The ratings were better than Colgate had dared to dream. The sponsor knew it, NBC knew it, Dean and Jerry knew it: They had this racket by the balls.

A week later, they went on to the Stanley Theatre in Pittsburgh, while, back in Los Angeles, on October 4, subpoenas for deposition were issued to Abby and Violet Greshler. Jack L. Lande of Desser, Rau, Christensen & Hoffman, the law firm representing the Greshlers, drew up a demurrer to Dean and Jerry's complaint based on contentions of technical ambiguities and insufficiencies of fact. It claimed among other things that it could not be determined "how and in what manner, when and in what accounts and from whom and for what purposes and under what agreements, contracts or other arrangements," the money had been robbed.

Dean knew how it had been robbed: a slip of the hand, a silver dollar here and there. He remembered the way Cosmo had held that Parodi. *"I hear you like to dance."* That's what it came down to. No claims and counterclaims, no depositions, no arbitration; no half-assed-gonif shysters knocking you down for a dollar to win a deuce.

He remembered his uncles telling him how Tom Mix was a fake, how he lived in a big fancy mansion that flashed his name in lights in Beverly Hills. He had paid them no mind. Now he and Tom Mix were kindred. He told Jerry and Jeannie and Patti about Cosmo and that Parodi as they rode west from Pittsburgh into Steubenville on the Friday morning of October 6, the day the city of his birth had decreed to be Dean Martin Day.

Guy and Angela were already there. They had brought their eight-year-old grandson, Craig, with them. Guy drove around town in his new white Cadillac convertible. He would park it outside Alfonso Faieta's joint, the Three Steps Inn, on South Sixth Street in the old neighborhood. As Archie Crocetti remembered, "Uncle Guy liked to mess around in bars." The streets were changing. Things were different now. Guy and Alfonso would shake their heads as they drank: the *tizzun*'s, this, that, the other thing.

On Wednesday morning, the newspaper had taken Guy's picture for the afternoon edition: a little man with a pencil-thin moustache, standing in a dark suit and bow tie, smiling proudly amid a group of Kiwanians. Art D'Anniballe, who owned the gas station where Dean had worked, was one of them. In the photograph, he and Guy together held the stainless-steel key to the city that Dean was to receive.

The parade began at noon on Friday at the Fort Steuben Bridge. A cavalcade of fifty cars, the Steubenville High School and Catholic Central High School bands, and the marching, banner-bearing contingents of various fraternal organizations, the sponsoring Kiwanis Club foremost among them, wound their way south on Fourth Street, through the Adams Street business section—George Mavromatis was working the parade traffic as a cop; "Hey, Runt! What're you doin' out there?" Dean yelled to him—north on Fifth Street to Market Street, south on Third Street to the City building, where Mayor Walter C. Sterling gave Dean the key. From there, Dean and Jerry went to entertain handicapped children in the Sunshine Room of the Roosevelt School. At two, there was a press, radio, and television reception at the Fort Steuben Hotel, where they were staying. At four, they performed at the auditorium of the Steubenville High School, which had been known as Wells back when Dean quit it. At half past six, there was a testimonial dinner at the Fort Steuben Hotel ballroom; at nine, another show at the high-school auditorium. Leonard Barr and his partner, Virginia Estes, opened for them.

"It was quite a day," Jerry remembered. "I'm shakin' a guy's hand, he says, 'Hi, I'm Ape Head.' I said, 'I've heard about you, but I never thought I'd shake your hand.' Oh, God."

Jeannie loved it; her husband was King Orange and more. Everybody loved it. Leo D'Anniballe's wife, Martha Jane, who was running a dancing-school above the site of the old Rex Cigar store, helped choreograph the show. "It was fantastic," she said. Jimmy the Greek's half-sister, Angie, would never forget what she wore that day—"a gold corduroy suit. They picked four girls to be on top of a convertible in the parade, and I was one of the girls. We were just so thrilled."

The only one who did not enjoy Dean Martin Day, it seemed, was Dean. "He hated it," Jeannie said. "He loathed the whole thing." He had returned in triumph. The men at the mills were averaging $66.38 a week. He pocketed more on a single good night than they made in a year. Yet it all seemed to mean nothing. The adoring wife, the triumph, the money, the adulation: nothing. It was a fucking one-horse world, the whole fucking shebang. He had grown to hate this place. The sense of his own illimitableness had saved him and made him. Now the dreaming—yes, he knew now: that is what it had been; he was a fool like the rest of them—the dreaming was over, fulfilled, dead.

Late that night, he went out drinking with the ghosts of his past. Mindy, Ross, Jiggs, Smuggs, the rest of them: He still loved these

guys—especially Smuggs—like brothers. But it was as if they themselves, like those years to which they belonged, had washed away to
where he could not hear their downward rushing. They were translu-
cent: shades. Death for him was not a foreboding that lay ahead, it
was the Lenten damp grave of memory, of what lay behind. The past
had made him empty, and he had filled that emptiness with solitude, into which shades such as these would burrow. They were the
larvae of those seductions of reason and love, those burrowing
shades. He could feel them. They made his skin crawl, they unnerved him. Their precious memories were his cemetery earth. He
had never been happy in their way. He had never laughed in their
way. Their way was too close. His happiness, his laughter, were
apotropaic, a *mano cornuta* to keep the world at bay.

"You don't have time for me anymore," Jiggs Rizzo said to him
from across the table of glasses and ashtrays.

"What're you talkin' about? I'm right here. Whadaya want?"

What the fuck did they want, these men who needed the company of others to make a life, as he needed a woman to make
babies?

The *Herald-Star* the next day carried a picture of the parade on
its front page. An article captioned "Local Boy Makes Good" was
flanked on the left by an article on Senator Estes Kefauver's investigations into Charlie Fischetti's Chicago mob, on the right by a report implicating Frank Costello's man, the recently resigned Mayor
William O'Dwyer, in a New York grand-jury probe.

That weekend, Dean and a few others went golfing at the Steubenville Country Club. That was what he loved about golf: One
could be with other men but apart from them, in silence in the open
air. The driver clubface and that little white rubber-cored ball
barely met: 450 millionths of a second, that was it. It was the sort of
contact Dean liked.

He and Jeanne, Smuggs and Bernice, went for a ride in the
countryside in Smuggs's Buick convertible. Smuggs was a lot like
Dean, a quiet, private man of quiet, private knowing. That was why
they got along. Dean drove; Smuggs and Bernice, soon to be married, sat in the back. Bernice mentioned that she looked forward to
having a child.

"Me too," Jeannie said.

"You wanna try now?" Dean said, veering the car to the side of the road as if to park.

Bernice remembered Jeanne asking her again and again when the two were alone, "Put in a good word for me with Angela"; remembered herself telling Angela, "Oh, what a nice girl."

Bernice wore a sweater that autumn weekend. "Smuggs, you never told me about Bernice," Dean said, within the hearing of slight-chested Jeannie.

On November 14, two days after their third Colgate show, a verdict was finally handed down in the Sammy Watkins case, which had dragged on for over a year. Dean's attorneys had brought forth Dean's 1947 bankruptcy decree as an "affirmative, separate and complete defense to the cause of action sued upon herein." Watkins's attorney had gotten Jerry to corroborate that on June 1, 1948, when Watkins came to the Copacabana to see them, Dean had promised him: "I'll pay you all I owe you." While the prosecution contended that this promise nullified the defense of bankruptcy, Dean's attorneys had argued that, at most, it only extended Martin's indebtedness to the date of the promise and not beyond. Watkins sought an award based on the full, seven-year life of the contract— ten percent of Dean's income through September 1950. That income was estimated at $700,000, most of it derived since the verbal promise of 1948. Now, in state superior court in Los Angeles, Judge Allen W. Ashburn issued a thirty-six-page opinion that favored Dean, awarding Watkins $12,880, based on the contractual percentage of Dean's estimated income from the signing of the Watkins contract in 1943 through June 1, 1948. Dean's lawyers eventually got the figure down to a round $12,500 to help defray Dean's legal costs, Watkins got it up forty bucks to defray his, and that was that: $12,540, payable in $2,000 installments on the first of each month. "It was strictly a friendly suit," Sammy would later say.

Later in November, Sherrill Corwin of Screen Associates, Inc., finally closed a distribution deal with Paramount for *At War with the Army*, a deal complicated by the ongoing battle between Abby Greshler and the other two thirds of York Pictures. Dean and Jerry, through Joe Ross, had filed an amended superior-court complaint in response to the demurrer filed by the Greshlers' attorney. Their new complaint, naming Violet Greshler and the unknown principals of the Doe Corporation as defendants, declared that in the period from 1947 through their dismissal of Greshler, during which time Greshler had "enjoyed their full trust and confidence," they had earned "large sums of money, to wit, in excess of Six Hundred Thousand Dollars ($600,000), the exact amount of which is not known to plaintiffs but is known to the defendants and the said Abner Greshler," who with the defendants had "combined and acted in concert to cheat, mulct and defraud plaintiffs by various and sundry methods." The amount channeled through Violet Greshler, they said, was believed to be $36,950 "or thereabouts." That sum, "together with interest at the rate of seven percent (7%) per annum," was what they sought to recover. Greshler maintained that the claim against Violet had been established by their filing as separate from any claim against him, and that furthermore, they owed him $4,000 in commissions on the $40,000 they had been paid through York Pictures for *At War with the Army*. Subpoenaed to produce financial documents and answer deposition questions at the office of Pacht, Tannenbaum & Ross, Greshler arrived there empty-handed on December 14 with his attorney, Jack Lande. "In effect, upon the objections and pursuant to the instructions of his counsel, said witness Greshler failed and refused to testify." Subsequently, four days after Christmas, a subpoena duces tecum would be issued through the state superior court ordering Greshler to produce his financial records and account books on January 3. On the appointed day, it would be reported, "Greshler failed and refused to produce any documents as designated" and once again "failed and refused to answer questions." And so it would go, on and on, round and round. They could not get the bastard to dance. Six weeks later, on Valentine's Day, Greshler would win an AGVA judgment against them for $10,600 in back commissions.

In spite of all this, Greshler would state: "They didn't break up with me. We had contracts. We did not break up. I had no legal proceedings with them. My legal proceedings were with MCA."

"He took it all," Jerry would claim. "If I told you what we found him guilty of, you wouldn't believe it. I'm talking about millions."

Meanwhile, Dean had quit paying Betty, and she had succeeded in obtaining a court order of garnishment against him. Ten days before Christmas, his lawyers came forth pleading his poverty. All he had was life-insurance policies. As a dead man, he was worth $215,000. Alive, he owed $4,837.14 to Capitol Records on an overdrawn royalty account. In the end, he was made to dance, and the silver dollars came jangling from his shoes.

"I'll Always Love You" had been made with the Paul Weston Orchestra. The record had been enough to win Dean the next-to-last place that fall in *Billboard*'s annual ranking of the thirty "Top Vocalists," as well as the thirteenth place in the "Most Promising 'Newer' Vocalists" listing. But if Dean was to repeat the success of his first hit, it would have to be without Weston, who, along with his wife, Jo Stafford, had now left Capitol for Columbia. On the last day of July, working with Lou Busch and his orchestra, Dean had recorded four songs, none of which drew much notice. In early December, as "I'll Always Love You" began to ebb, Dean returned to the studio with Busch to record a song called "If." The song dated to 1934, but was little known outside of England. Its original London copyright had just been assigned to Shapiro, Bernstein & Company of New York, which was successful in placing the song with Dean, Jo Stafford, Perry Como, Vic Damone, Billy Eckstine, the Ink Spots, and others. Como's recording of "If" appeared on the charts at the end of the holiday season. Dean's version gathered attention in the wake of Como's, which it followed onto the *Billboard* charts two weeks later. Como's record would become the first number-one hit of the new year, displacing Patti Page's "Tennessee Waltz" in February and remaining on the charts through May. Dean's, rising only to number twenty-six and vanishing after a month, proved nevertheless that he was more than a one-hit singer.

His lawyers' claims aside, Dean was now well-off. He had wealth and he had fame. But his success as a singer grew ever more especially important to him, for, as far as Martin and Lewis went, it was now the monkey's show. Of their debut on "The Colgate Comedy Hour," the *New York Times* had said, "It is the Lewis half of the partnership who is the works." Of their November shows in Chicago: "It's Lewis, per usual," *Variety* had said, "who gets the laughs." *At War with the Army* had been previewed in Hollywood on December 7 and had premiered at the New York Paramount on January 24. Jerry had ended up doing as much singing as Dean in the picture. *Variety,* calling it "a cornball affair that cuts the cob down to the quick," had commented that its "production quality reflects the comparatively small budget." Beyond that, *Variety* had flatly declared, "It is Lewis' show." Noting the long lines that braved the rain outside the Paramount for the picture's opening, Bosley Crowther's colleague at the *New York Times* dismissed the picture as a "consignment of corn" that was redeemed only by "the masterful mugging of Mr. Lewis." The *Los Angeles Times,* denouncing it as "grubby fare," remarked that "Jerry Lewis is the funny member of the duo," while Dean "acts as if he thinks he is faintly superior not only to Lewis but also to most other people, including the audience. We do not care one way or the other what happens to him, but nothing much does." The *New York Daily News* called it a "static comedy," and took the opportunity to note that "Lewis, who gets second billing to Martin" was "really the team's drawing power."

Dean, with Jerry, was barely there: a *cafone,* a foil for the beloved Jew. So far, since 1946, he had made only one appearance without Jerry, on "Texaco Star Theatre" this past December 12. Only in the Capitol studio was he on his own, and only there, alone, as he had started out, walking around with his hat on, singing, could he be his own man.

Jerry perceived this: "Jerry this, Jerry that. The reviews: the silly one, the kid; Jerry, Jerry, Jerry. Now, I used to read those things, and I'd become incensed because they weren't looking at what we were doing. What made Jerry so funny but the guy next to him? And I can honestly say that I'd have been nothing without Dean. When he heard me telling him after a show, 'You did it again,' or, 'Thank God we got what we got,' and I'm the only one that's really seeing that? That's terrifying. If the tables were turned, I don't know that I could've handled it."

. . .

Work on their next Hal Wallis picture began on December 4, three days before the preview of *At War with the Army*. It was called *That's My Boy*.

By now, Dean and Jerry had developed very different relationships with the autocratic producer.

Wallis adored Dean, because, as Jerry remembered, "Dean never said anything but 'Hi, Mr. Wallis,' and he was on his way. He was wise enough never to get into anything with him. And Dean was wise enough never to play golf with him." But Jerry, who sought control over the films they made, was a thorn in Wallis's side: a thorn that Wallis loved as much as he hated. In young Jerry's budding passion for filmmaking, troublesome as it was, Wallis found a filial substitute for the son (Brent Wallis) who had turned against both the father and his pictures. As Jerry said: "He made me his kid."

That's My Boy, written by Cy Howard, directed by Hal Walker, told the story of a powerful, successful man—Jarring Jack Jackson, played by Eddie Mayehoff—who sends his weakling son, Junior Jackson, played by Jerry, to his alma mater, hiring the college football hero, Bill Baker, played by Dean, to recast the son in the image of the father.

"It was the Hal Wallis story," Jerry said. "Hal didn't know it, either. The writer, Cy Howard, was a good friend of mine. He and I knew the picture we were writing. I used to say to Cy, 'If you get this on his fuckin' desk, and he makes it, I'll be in shock.' But Wallis only saw one thing: dollar signs."

Wallis had begun work on yet another picture, *The Stooge*, while *That's My Boy* was being written and Dean and Jerry were making *At War with the Army*. As early as that July, he had announced the signing of the picture's leading lady, a slender blond singer whom he had discovered in Monte Carlo. Fred F. Finklehoffe, who had adapted James Allardice's play for *At War with the Army*, had devised the story for *The Stooge* with Sid Silvers. The screenplay, written by Finklehoffe and Marty Rackin, a former *Daily Mirror* and King Features journalist, departed from the pattern of the first three pictures. It was a comedy with dramatic undercurrents and a straight plot that embodied elements of the real-life story of Sid Silvers's years as a professional stooge with accordionist Phil Baker in the 1920s. It was also strangely evocative of the Martin-and-Lewis story itself, whose future it uncannily seemed to presage—in mirrored reverse. Dean portrayed Bill Miller, a singing, accordion-playing comic whose act founders until he acquires a stooge, played by Lewis, to work with him from the audience. Recently married—the wife, Mary, would be played by Polly Bergen, who had made her film debut in *At War with the Army;* the original star, Wallis's blond singing discovery, was fucked and forgotten—Miller would dump the stooge to become a star on his own. Failing, he would be reunited with the stooge, and they would achieve fame and concord together. Norman Taurog was the director of *The Stooge.* At the age of fifty-one, Taurog had been making pictures since 1928. He had won a 1931 Academy Award for *Skippy,* a movie based on a comic strip; his pictures ran the gamut, from *Boys' Town* to *Girl Crazy,* from *Young Tom Edison* to *The Hoodlum Saint.*

The Stooge began filming in mid-February and was done by the end of March. Wallis, however, would not release the film for almost another two years. There was something about it, that faint undertow of reality, that he did not like.

They opened at the Chez Paree on April 9, 1951. It was a black but busy night in Chicago. Just last week, after dodging the Kefauver committee's subpoena services for months, fifty-year-old Charlie Fischetti had surrendered secretly in Washington, along with his brother Rocco. Released on bond, Charlie had retreated to his Allison Island estate in Florida. There, on the morning of April 11, two days after Dean and Jerry opened at the Chez Paree, Charlie had dropped dead of a heart attack. His obituary in the *Chicago Daily Tribune* was unsentimental: "Fischetti was not liked and was never known to have done a kind deed or helped any of the less fortunate of his criminal associates." He was "a gunman, goon, and muscleman who stopped at nothing to acquire a dollar."

Now Chicago belonged to Tony Accardo and Jake Guzik, with old Paul Ricca still enthroned in the shadows. Guzik would be dead the following year. At the Chez Paree that spring, as Charlie Fischetti's body was laid to rest in his native Brooklyn, Dean and Jerry met the man who would eventually take power, five years later, under the aegis of Accardo and Ricca. He was one of Accardo's former bootleg drivers during the Capone days, the son of Sicilian immigrants, born in Chicago on June 15, 1908: Momo Salvatore Giancana. Everybody called him Sam.

Johnny Rosselli told Dean that Giancana was all right. Dean and Rosselli got along, *da lontano*. Rosselli, somehow, was different; it was as if there was a Rosselli that killed and a Rosselli that shared the same taciturn pleasures as Dean. They both went through a lot of the same broads, and thought along the same lines in many ways. But Dean would come to think differently about Giancana. He may have been all right as far as Rosselli was concerned, but in time Dean would come to regard him as the biggest pain in the ass of them all.

Dean and Jerry did their second "Colgate Comedy Hour" of the year on April 29, live from Chicago. During 1950, over six million television sets had been sold: almost twice as many as had been purchased throughout the entire decade of the 1940s. Now, in 1951, as the great umbilical cord of coaxial cable tied the East to the West, the number of televisions in America would increase to over fifteen million, and, for the first time, the industry would show a profit: $41,600,000, compared to a loss the previous year. That May, NBC signed Milton Berle to a new, thirty-year exclusive contract, valued at $6,000,000. He would receive $200,000 a year whether he worked or not. By now, the television popularity of Martin and Lewis was second only to that of Berle. Their Colgate shows were broadcast even in Europe, through the Armed Forces Radio Service. Leery of overexposure, they had now bound Colgate and NBC to terms that limited their appearances as hosts to between six and eight shows a year for a base pay of $1,000,000 a year.

When the show's original director, Kingman Moore, quit, Ernie Glucksman let young Bud Yorkin, who had started out as the stage manager, take his place. It was Yorkin who told Dean and Jerry about the disease his sister's son had succumbed to: muscular dystrophy. They, like most people, had never heard of it. One Sunday night, they gave the Muscular Dystrophy Association a plug on the show. It was the beginning of a long relationship between them and the MDA. The show also served as the starting point of a long relationship between Yorkin and one of the show's writers, Norman Lear. Together the two men would later form one of the most successful production companies in the history of television.

Lear remembered that Jerry's involvement was intense, that he strove for control, while Dean remained distant, almost disinterested in the process of developing material and putting together the shows. According to Lear, Jerry "couldn't stand it if Dean got any laughs. Dean could be insanely funny with a line. Any morning that Dean would come in and start being funny with the lines or do funny things, Jerry would wind up in a corner on the floor someplace with a bellyache. And a doctor would have to come. This was always true. Whenever Dean was very funny, strange physical things happened to Jerry. Sometimes he would go to the extreme of calling Martin Levy, who was his doctor at the time, to fly in from California to treat him."

They closed at the Chez Paree in May, then went east to the Copacabana. On the Fourth of July, a week after Truman ordered American forces into Korea, they opened at the Paramount. Their deal with the Paramount called for a guarantee of $50,000 a week, plus a fifty-percent share of all gross receipts over $100,000 a week. The record weekly gross at the Paramount, $135,000, had been set by Benny Goodman in March of 1946. Goodman had been playing with Hal Walker's Crosby-Hope hit *Road to Utopia;* Dean and Jerry were stuck with *Dear Brat,* a stiff sequel to *Dear Ruth* and *Dear Wife.* A total of 22,500 tickets were sold that first day. By Sunday, July 8, the Paramount's box-office figures showed that 119,000 people had paid $111,000 for tickets; and by the end of their first week, Dean and Jerry had broken the old Paramount record of five years' standing.

"There was always anywhere from ten to twenty thousand people outside the stage door," Jerry recalled. "They had to create another way for us to get out. They had a catwalk up high that led to the projection booth, and the projection booth had its own entrance that you took down to the Forty-third-Street side, the street that the

New York Times was on. That's the only way that Dean or I could get in or out of the theater with security." The *Daily News* reported that "it has been impossible to get through 44th Street or past the stage door worshipers. These little idiots massed tightly at the stage door for a glimpse of their beloveds and, whenever they got violent, an emissary from the lovable comedians came down with a handful of photos. The clutching hands of the faithful would come forth as though grabbing for the staff of life. There hasn't been anything like it since the great days of Sinatra."

After two weeks, Dean and Jerry had brought in $289,500, at a top ticket price of a buck and a half; and their own take came to $144,700. *The New Yorker*, noting their astounding success and the mystifying fact that they seemed "to have a frenzied following not only among the Copacabana set but among the Howard Johnson set" as well, reported the thunderous chanting that rose from the masses in the street toward the Paramount's dressing-room windows as "Martin, a medium-sized young man with dark hair," dumped armfuls of photographs to the crowd below:

"We want Jerry! We want Jerry!"

They returned to Chicago. There, on August 2, Jerry collapsed from what physicians diagnosed as nervous exhaustion.

On the following day, in superior court in Los Angeles, Screen Associates, Inc., filed a suit for violation of contract against York Pictures, Martin and Lewis, and Hal Wallis. *At War with the Army*, thrown together for $400,000, had already grossed a small fortune. It had done well not only in America but also abroad, even in the new Federal Republic of Germany, where it drew postwar yocks as *Kl'ach mit der Kompanie*. In time, its box-office take would surpass $3,300,000—more than realized by *All About Eve* and other respected pictures of the same year. Dean and Jerry, however, would see nothing of its profits; for, by the time the gross and then the ever-decreasing net passed through Paramount, Screen Associates, and then finally the hands of executive producer Abby Greshler, York—at least Dean and Jerry's end of it—was left with nothing. Now Screen Associates, claiming that it had a contract with York for seven pictures, and that York had only come through with one, was seeking $8,000,000 in damages from York and Hal Wallis, who, along with MCA, was named as a conspirator, and $2,000,000 from Martin and Lewis personally. Furthermore, the suit sought an injunction against their next Wallis production, which was scheduled to begin filming in four weeks.

When *That's My Boy* arrived at the Paramount in the first week of August, theatergoers got Danny Lewis instead of his famous son as an opening act. It was sort of *That's My Boy* in reverse. Describing him as a "singing refugee from the borscht belt," *Variety* looked down upon what he did: "Lewis pere is trading too much on his son's rep. Where once he made his own way with a voice resembling but not matching Al Jolson, he's doing the Jolie bit now only as an opener. Then he lets the audience in on his true identity and rides it into the ground from there."

Hal Wallis had cast Corinne Calvet to work with them again in their next picture, *Sailor Beware*. She was to play herself in the story, which revolved wobbly around a bet that Jerry's character, Melvin Jones, could manage a kiss from her aloof lips.

Calvet was hard up for cash and depressed. "Look, they're not even billing me above the title," she said to Edith Head, her dress designer for the picture. "I'm only a costar."

"It's not Wallis," Head told her. "It's because of Martin and Lewis's manager. Just like Hope and Crosby, they demand that they're the only ones above the title."

Their manager was now Herman Citron, a forty-six-year-old former New York City cop who had come west to work for MCA after the war. In addition to Dean and Jerry, he handled Alfred Hitchcock, James Stewart, and Norman Taurog, who had directed *The Stooge*.

Calvet and Dean were rehearsing a duet one morning when Wallis interrupted them by bellowing her name: "Corinne! I've told you, I don't want my actresses to wear falsies."

"I'm not."

"Go and take them out."

"Are you calling me a liar?"

She grabbed his hand and stuck it inside her dress. Dean was standing there grinning. "Bravo," he said. "That was magnificent."

A young James Dean "needed a day's work, and I put him on," Jerry remembered. All but one spoken line and a glimpse of him ended up as curls in the cutting-room trash.

Wallis had asked Jerry to write a sequence for the picture. It was a boxing scene. When Wallis asked him to sign release papers for the material, Jerry sent Joe Ross to tell Wallis that he would have to pay.

"Wallis was tighter than J. Paul Getty with a buck," recalled Lewis. "He thought if he could beat me, he'd beat me. And I said to my attorney: 'Tell him the following. It's gonna cost him $50,000 for the scene, and I want the check made out to the Muscular Dystrophy Association. I want him to know I'm not even getting it but *he* ain't fuckin' keepin' it.' It's now the first week in November and this picture's scheduled to open on New Year's Eve all over the country. Seven hundred theaters. And his picture isn't complete because he hasn't got my scene in it yet. Couldn't even cut it in the picture yet —and it's brilliant, it's a marvelous comedy sequence. He waited until the day the prints had to be finally cut, negative cut, called my attorney, said, 'I'll give him $45,000.' My attorney said, 'I'm not even gonna call Jerry. I'm tellin' ya, it's fifty, and I've got instructions for who the check must be made out to.' He finally capitulated. This was three weeks before Christmas. Comes Christmastime, he commissioned Paul Clemens, the artist, to do a picture of my children and paid him $100,000 for it. Same man, but that man was doing something for me and my family, outside of business. When I went to his office to thank him for the painting, I said, 'Hal, do you know what you put yourself through and me through for the last two fucking months over a $50,000 payment that goes into the budget of the picture, that's split by you, your partner, and Paramount, that doesn't come to a hill of beans; but you just took $100,000 out of your own pocket to give me a gift of the Paul Clemens portrait— don't you see this insanity?' He hated my bringing it to his attention. 'Well, what do *you* know?' he said. 'I been in this business forty years.' I said, 'You could've been in it wrong. The calendar doesn't make it right.' I didn't know it at the time, but I realized it later: through this he was getting everything he ever wanted from his son—confrontation."

For Dean, a house without children was not a home; a marriage without children, just a license to fight. A few minutes before seven on the evening of November 17, Jeannie gave birth to a baby boy at St. John's Hospital in Santa Monica. They named him Dean Paul Martin, Jr.

That birth and that bambino were special: a glorying not only of new life but of his own new life. For one brilliant, warm autumn moment, it turned rosy-gold and it meant something, all of it: the old ways, which his wife and his tiny pink-clenching son would never know, and the renewing of that breath of illimitableness that made sweethearts of wisdom and innocence, if only for a night. He felt it: the sombering sweep of that song from the other side, the shadowing magic, eros and death and joy, of those ancient breezes half-re-called in a dream that ran through the blood. And two days later, in the Capitol studio, he sang it, sounding more sincere than he had ever sounded:

> *Guarda il mare com'è bello!*
> *Spira tanto sentimento*
> *Come il tuo soave accento*
> *Che me, desto, fa sognar.*

XI.

BREAD AND CIRCUSES

*T*he early 1950s belonged to them. It was the age of television, of whitewalled, tail-finned mindlessness; a world gone mad with mediocrity. William Faulkner, the winner of the 1950 Nobel Prize for literature, would have nothing to do with it: "Television," he said, "is for niggers." Ernest Hemingway, who won the prize four years later, was a made-for-TV character. Soon it would not even matter. Like Dean and Jerry, most people would not even read. Ajax was no longer a Homeric hero; he was the "Comedy Hour" 's sponsor's foaming cleanser, no longer a contender with Odysseus for the arms of Achilles, but a consort of Fab, which had itself transplanted Melville's musings on "The Whiteness of the Whale" with the dictum "Whiter Whites without Bleaching."

Senator Estes Kefauver, riding Frank Costello and the others through the sideshow of his hearings, used the new medium to grasp the vice-presidential nomination from John F. Kennedy. Kefauver and Costello, running concurrently in 1951 with Martin and Lewis, tied the myth of the American Mafia into a network package ripe for sponsorship. By September of that year, Kefauver's investigator Rudolph Halley was hosting "Crime Syndicated" for CBS. By November, Kefauver himself had a stage act. Humphrey Bogart introduced him at the Los Angeles Philharmonic, where his presentation "Crime in America" was advertised as "ENOUGH EXCITING MATERIAL FOR 100 MOTION PICTURES."

By then, disc jockey Alan Freed was broadcasting his "Moondog Rock and Roll Party" over WJW in Cleveland. C. A. Swanson & Son introduced the first TV dinner in January 1952: frozen turkey, $1.09. The first hydrogen bomb went off the following November; a wave of 3-D movies followed. Bill Haley's "Crazy, Man, Crazy" hit the pop charts in May 1953. That December, *Playboy* brought forth the American sterility goddess, airbrushed Aphrodite, from the phosphate foam. In January 1954, the first atomic-powered submarine, the *Nautilus,* was launched. In April, as Major Donald Kehoe of the U.S. Marine Corps appeared on "The Betty White Show" to accuse the Air Force of a flying-saucer cover-up, Atlantic Records released Big Joe Turner's "Shake, Rattle and Roll." A month later, RCA introduced its $1,000 CT-100 Compatible Color TV, and, as Amos 'n' Andy approached the end of their first quarter century with NBC, the Supreme Court ruled that racial segregation in public schools was unconstitutional. In August 1954, Elvis Presley's first record appeared on the Memphis country-and-western charts. Disneyland opened on July 17, 1955; a few days later, Zenith unveiled its Flash-Matic remote-control TV sets.

Through it all—polyvinyl history: the American dream gone gaga—Martin and Lewis reigned as the jester-kings in a land where even laughter, freeze-dried and hollow, would soon be canned.

Jerry Lewis said it all: "Can you pay two men $9,000,000 to say 'Did you take a bath this morning?' 'Why, is there one missing'—do you dare contemplate such a fuck-and-duck? Yet that's what we did. We did that onstage, and they paid us $9,000,000."

"I feel the reason we are knocking down all this coin is that the public doesn't have to reach for our stuff," Dean would venture. "Certainly it's not our routine, because we don't have one."

They could not get any bigger than they already were in 1951; they could only get richer. Jerry and Patti had adopted a second son, Ronnie Guy, in December 1949. In October 1950, they had moved into a twelve-room ranch house on North Amalfi Drive, near the sea in the Palisades section of Brentwood Heights—"a dream house, with toddler swings in the backyard, a swimming pool, lemon and orange trees." They had a butler, a maid, a cook. Eventually, Jerry would buy the Beverly Hills home that Louis B. Mayer had built. Dean and Jeannie lived at 1317 Londonderry Place, in the quiet hills north of Sunset. They would move in time to a bigger home, near the Los Angeles Country Club, at 654 Woodruff Avenue in Westwood; then, finally, to their wood-and-fieldstone dream house, with three servants, six cars, a swimming-pool, a tennis court, at 601 Mountain Drive in Beverly Hills. The old man was right: Nice country, *l'America*.

By 1952, the year Dean and Jerry were included in the new edition of Who's Who in America, their drawing power was fail-proof and incontestable. Such was their fame that in October 1951, NBC had brought them back to radio. Produced and directed by Dick Mack and written by their television writers, Norman Lear and Ed Simmons, the new, Friday-night show even had sponsors: Chesterfield and Anacin. "In their initial attempt in '49 to penetrate the network Nielsens," *Variety* said, "Martin & Lewis were a dismal flop." Their new show, however, "with productional refinements that bespeak the hepness of producer-director Dick Mack," was "one of the most hilarious 30 minutes in radio." The radio show would last through April 1952, then would return in September for one last go-round on Tuesday nights. It was on radio, during the glory days of "The Colgate Comedy Hour," that Dean's *menefreghismo* truly shone through. They owned television. Who needed radio? He started lapsing into Italian. "My name is Dino Antonio Giuseppe Angelo Pietro Garibaldi Crocetti. I'm Italian," he said, introducing himself in a "Dragnet" take-off with Jack Webb. "Hey, *guaglione!*" he called to Dick Stabile in the same show. Another night, bringing out Ann Sheridan, the actress who had tried to get Herman Hover to set her up with Dean, he beheld her with the exclamation *"Maddon'!"*

Their renown alone was enough, both *Variety* and *The Hollywood Reporter* had predicted, to ensure the success of *Sailor Beware*. That success was enhanced by the reviews that followed the picture's New York opening, at the Mayfair Theatre, on January 31, 1952. The *New York Daily News* gave it three and a half stars. "The more you see of the average comic on the screen, the unfunnier he becomes," Kate Cameron wrote in her review for the paper. "But, with Dean Martin and Jerry Lewis, the reverse is true. These two zany comics grow more amusing with each picture," and this was "their best yet." The first-person-plural Bosley Crowther of the *Times* was still nonplussed: "Frankly, we do not get it." But the first-person singulars seemed to, as even Crowther perceived: "Whatever it is that Dean Martin and Jerry Lewis have got that makes people howl with laughter and toss with rocking frenzy in their chairs, there must be plenty of it in their new picture, 'Sailor Beware.' For this coolly objective reviewer is duty bound to report that people were doing plenty of both things at the Mayfair Theatre yesterday."

On March 15, they hosted their first telethon, a project that had been in development since December. Involving the work of six directors and fifty engineers under executive producer Budd Granoff and producer Ernie Glucksman, it had been the brainchild of fund-raiser Arthur Konvitz and philanthropist Martin Tannenbaum, both of whose parents had died of heart disease. Begun at midnight and broadcast by WNBT through four-thirty the following afternoon, the show raised pledges of $1,148,000 toward the construction of the proposed New York Cardiac Hospital, with an undisclosed percentage going to Dean and Jerry's chosen charity, the Muscular Dystrophy Association. Dean and Jerry were able to enlist the services of an all-star cast the likes of which television had never witnessed: Milton Berle, Sid Caesar, Cab Calloway, Nat King Cole, Perry Como, Ella Fitzgerald, Jackie Gleason, Erskine Hawkins, Gabby Hayes, Gene Krupa, Mel Tormé, Sarah Vaughan, and Henny Youngman. There were also Leonard Barr, Sonny King, and Danny Lewis, who brought his son a birthday cake. Connee Boswell sang from her wheelchair. Even Vivian Blaine, driven from the Copacabana by their success four years before, performed as a guest. So did Frank Sinatra, who had seen them back then at the Copa, but until now had never worked with them.

The telethon bought publicity that money could not buy. "In the metropolitan area there was almost a mass hypnosis in watching the entertainment world's most successful act of the moment stay on its feet night and day," reported the *New York Times*. "Tired as they were, the two performers never once were curt or abrupt as they accepted pledges over the telephone or received cash donations from an endless succession of children in the studio audience." The telethon was not only "tremendously entertaining" but "also brought out another side of Martin and Lewis that may be remembered even longer. Within the framework of their amusing slapstick art and their relish for the non sequitur, they gave an astonishing demonstration of patience, understanding and personal dignity." There was more: "Their modesty, thoughtfulness and good manners were faultless and instinctive. Aside from being capital performers, Martin and Lewis are very genuine human beings." Their telethon was "a unique example of concentrated Americana in the television age."

They were not only rich and famous, they were fucking saints. And it was tax-deductible too.

Two weeks later, they were scheduled to start another picture, *Scared Stiff*, with director George Marshall. On March 31, the day filming was to start, they refused to appear for work. The next day, it was rumored that they did not want to make the picture because they regarded it as simply a rehash of *The Ghost Breakers*, a picture that Marshall had made some years before with Bob Hope and Paulette Goddard. This was true, but it was hardly the whole truth. They wanted out of their original deal with Wallis. A million and a quarter had seemed like a lot to them in 1948. Now it seemed like nothing, and they did not want to wait until the end of next year for their contract to run its course.

They were scheduled to open at the Copacabana for a month on the first of May. Fuck that too, they figured: it was just so much more penny-ante shit. The deal, made a year ago, was for $6,000 a week; they already had taken a ten-grand advance on signing. Assistant manager and bouncer Jack Entratter, their friend at the Copa, would be moving soon to Vegas; Frank Costello was in prison. Dean and Jerry decided they would rather pay the Copa what the Copa had contracted to pay them, plus the ten-grand advance. Jules Podell, however, wanted them, not the $34,000. He lodged a complaint with the American Guild of Variety Artists; and the union demanded that Dean and Jerry explain themselves at a hearing in New York on May 19. Dean and Jerry told the American Guild of Variety Artists to bring the hearing to them.

On May 20, they got their way with Wallis. A new, seven-year contract was signed, putting them on straight salary, obligating them to Wallis for only one picture a year, and allowing them to make any outside pictures they pleased. The new contract, effective January 1, 1953, guaranteed them $1,000,000 a year. Ten days later, on the first of June, *Scared Stiff* started filming with a screenplay revised by Walter De Leon, Norman Lear, and Ed Simmons.

Dorothy Malone, who played a femme fatale named Rosie in the picture, was twenty-seven then and had been in more than twenty movies since 1943. "It was a wild time for me," she recalled, "because I had just lost the dearest brother in the whole world, by lightning. I always felt—I may have been wrong—that either Dean Martin or Jerry Lewis—I rather imagine, after knowing them, that it was Dean Martin—had said, 'Let's have her for the part, to get her back into the work,' because I was just devastated. I hadn't known them before. Of course, I was a big fan of theirs, but I hadn't known either one of them. Dean Martin was so thoughtful. I remember the contrast between them. I was driving a little car, a little convertible named Sunshine, that I thought was darling, and the first thing that Jerry Lewis said was, 'Good Lord, get rid of that trash-heap,' or whatever. Here I'd just lost my brother; I mean, who cared about the trash-heap? And Dean Martin was just so gentle. He never said much to me, but he just sort of guided me in my little scene. I never saw the finished picture, but I can still remember the way he touched me to guide me into the telephone booth in that scene. He just was thoughtful and sweet and gentle."

The way Malone remembered it, Dean and Jerry "didn't seem to get along. It hadn't gotten bad yet, but there was no cordiality or anything; just a strange aura on the set."

"I had a slight crush on Dean," she said. "I guess every woman in the world did."

Scared Stiff would include the last film appearance of Carmen Miranda, who died of a heart attack at forty-one two summers later. In a scene that drew upon his old record act, Jerry, who already had appeared in drag in *At War with the Army*, would don fruited headgear and platform shoes to mimic Miranda in her final role. Dean, who was still carrying his uncle Leonard on the road with him, got his uncle Tony Barr a bit part, and threw a reference to Steubenville into the picture.

On the first weekend in August, they opened in Chicago at the Chez Paree. They broke all attendance records, bringing more money into the club than in any two-week period in its twenty-year history. Dave Halper, who ran the joint for its shadow-owners, stopped taking reservations after the first week; more than two hundred people were being turned away at the door every night.

In June and July, during the production of *Scared Stiff*, Dean had recorded eight songs for Capitol. One of them was "You Belong to Me," the work of Chilton Price, Pee Wee King, and Redd Stewart, the team that had written "The Tennessee Waltz" in 1948. Copyrighted in April, "You Belong to Me" had gone directly to the pop market. Joni James, in her MGM recording debut, had been the first to do it. Jo Stafford's recording of it for Columbia, appearing on the charts in the first week of August, would become a number-one hit; a version by Patti Page, whose recording of "The Tennessee Waltz" had hit number one in 1950, followed Stafford's record onto the charts in the third week of August; and Dean's record made the charts a week later. The Dick Stabile Orchestra had been accompanying Dean on all his recordings since the spring of 1951; and it was Stabile's alto-saxophone work that made "You Belong to Me" one of Dean's finest recordings. The record remained on the charts for ten weeks, rising to number ten—the least successful but by far the best of the three hit versions.

Dean was vacationing at the Flamingo in Las Vegas, golfing and blowing money in the casino, when "You Belong to Me" hit the charts. When singer Kay Star, the Flamingo's headliner, fell sick and a fill-in was needed until Dick Haymes arrived to replace her, Dean eagerly accepted the rare opportunity to perform without Jerry.

Jerry purposely never played golf with Dean. "Dean was good at it," he said. "He had the kind of freedom out there that a recluse enjoys. It fell right into his pattern, because the game *demands* silence. It *demands* no communicating with the other guy if that's what his bailiwick is. It was marvelous for him. I didn't want to get into it with him. I can't do anything halfway, and whatever I pursue, I usually do very well. I would never touch golf for fear that I'd play better. And that would be dangerous. I was afraid of that, plus it was something that was all his." Perhaps in appreciation of that, Dean presented Jerry that September with a golf bag bearing an inscribed plate: *To the Happy Hebrew from the Nasal Neapolitan.*

In October, while "You Belong to Me" was on the charts, Dean and Jerry opened for sixteen days at the State Fair of Texas in Dallas: twenty-four performances for a guarantee of $100,000 against a percentage of the gross. After that, they went east for a string of one-nighters that started in Washington, D.C., and ended in Newark, New Jersey. With a guarantee of ten grand a night against sixty percent of the box-office gross, they took down close to $200,000 in ten nights. When they left New York on November 2 aboard the Twentieth-Century Limited for Chicago and a flight the next day to Los Angeles, they had made over $300,000 in less than a month, not counting their income from NBC and Paramount, or Dean's royalties from Capitol.

Inez Wallace, a Cleveland reporter who remembered Dean from the Hollenden days, took a few minutes of Dean's time that fall. She thought perhaps she would get a fond reminiscence or two for the *Plain Dealer*. But, for Dean, there were no good old days. "I sang for three years with Sammy Watkins's band in the Vogue Room," he told her. "Folks came in there, heard me warble my ballads, but they paid no attention to me. Now they would give a fortune to handle me, but when I stood in their very midst, they never gave me a tumble. Take yourself. Many times you visited the Vogue Room and clapped your hands politely after my songs but that was all."

The Stooge, previewed for the trade on October 1, was at last scheduled for release. There was only one new song in the picture; the rest were dusted-off classics from the years 1929–35. With arrangements by Nelson Riddle and Gus Levene, Dean recorded the bunch of them with the Dick Stabile Orchestra on November 20. They would be released together as Dean's first, ten-inch album.

Early on the morning of November 20, they began work with Norman Taurog on another picture. *The Caddy*, in which Dean got to play an Italian, was the first York Pictures production since *At War with the Army*. For $850,000, Dean and Jerry had bought their way out of their deal with Screen Associates, whose principals, led by president Ralph Stolkin, had been preoccupied in late September with taking over RKO from Howard Hughes. A series of exposés in *The Wall Street Journal*, recounting Stolkin's shady career and Ray Ryan's ties to Frank Costello, had already, barely a month later, resulted in the hasty resignations from RKO of Stolkin and his father-in-law, Abe Koolish, along with Ray Ryan's representative on the board, William Gorman, and Sidney Korshak, the Chicago-mob attorney who served as labor-relations consultant for the studio. Screen Associates had now entered into television production; and Abby Greshler's one-third interest in York became the holding of attorney Joe Ross and Paramount Pictures. Dean's brother, William, who had moved into Guy and Angela's house on Lemon Avenue in Long Beach, was put on the payroll as York's business manager. Henceforth, every York production, done in union with Paramount, would deliver seventy percent of all net profits to Martin and Lewis. Their gross income for the fiscal year 1952–53 would amount to more than $3,000,000. In years to come, it would surpass $8,000,000.

On December 15, the Sands opened for business on Highway 91 in Las Vegas. No other casino ever represented interests as far-flung. Sub-rosa owners of the Sands included men from the shadow-lands of New York and New Jersey, Miami and New Orleans, Boston and Detroit, Cleveland and Chicago, St. Louis and Los Angeles, and elsewhere. The man with the biggest piece was Doc Stacher, a Polish-born confederate of Longie Zwillman from Newark. The president was Jake Freedman, a Russian emigrant who controlled gambling in Houston and Galveston. The vice-president, representing Frank Costello's interests as well as his own, was Jack Entratter from the Copacabana.

Martin and Lewis severed their ties with the Flamingo for the Sands. "He was our love," Jerry said of Entratter. "We wouldn't go anywhere in Vegas but where Jack was. The performers that played the Copa—Sinatra, Lena Horne, Tony Bennett—he got them all to play the Sands."

Dean's album was released, plugging *The Stooge* on its cover, in late January 1953. "His partner's hilarious antics and his own droll quips may make you forget that Dean Martin's tall and dark and handsome, and that his voice is a full, rich baritone," read the liner notes of *Dean Martin Sings*. "With smiling ease and nonchalance, he's become a vital half of one of the greatest teams in entertainment history. But Dean hasn't lost his individuality, his warm and winning personality. You can hear it in his voice and in the songs he sings—the romantic ballads, the charming Italian airs from his childhood days, and the light bright tunes of Tin Pan Alley."

On February 4, the week after the album came out, *The Stooge* finally premiered. The *Los Angeles Examiner* declared it to be "absolutely, completely wonderful" in every way. The *New York Daily News* gave it three stars. But it also received praise from unlikely quarters. *The Saturday Review,* for one, declared it to be "in marked and laudable contrast to previous Martin and Lewis entertainment."

Seven days later, on February 11, Jeannie announced that she and Dean were separating.

Jeannie's first years of marriage to Dean had passed in a frenzy. "Those were such incredibly exciting, glamorous days in our lives," she would say. "They were golden boys." Socially, the Martins and the Lewises were not close. Jerry had told Patti that Ole Olsen and Chic Johnson, still together since 1914, had advised him that their comedy partnership had prevailed "because we cut out the social stuff and kept our wives apart." Only "very rarely," Patti said, did she and Jerry "join the Martins for dinner and dancing at Ciro's." Otherwise, "for the good of the act," distance between the couples was "strictly observed." Jerry agreed that he and Dean purposely kept their wives apart to avoid discord. "We never let them get together much. We never socialized with the wives for that very reason." The way Jeannie saw it, "we just moved in a different circle."

For Jeannie, those early years with Dean were magical. She had stepped from Coral Gables into the realm of fantasy. "At that young age," she said, "the first welcome was from the Bogarts and the Gary Coopers, people who loved Dean's work and knew he had it. We were very close to the Coopers and the Bogarts and the Eddie Robinsons. Dean adored George Raft."

Unlike most of the famous figures in Hollywood, Raft had a background and a manner that were similar to Dean's. "I don't think we ever saw George more than maybe four times," Jeannie remembered. But Dean saw much more of him than that.

"As a kid, I guess I'd seen every picture he ever made," Dean recalled. Now he never missed an opportunity to visit Raft's home in Coldwater Canyon. He was awed by it. "It was like the temple of a brothel. The most gorgeous women in town would be there. It wasn't just sex. They would swim nude in the pool, or we would sit around and talk. George would lounge all day in his silk robe at poolside. He never swam. In fact, the only exercise he ever had was with broads or shuffling a deck of cards. Dinner was a special event. When the girls would unfold their dinner napkins there would either be a hundred-dollar bill or some expensive earrings, or, for special broads, a brooch or a bracelet. George had class."

Raft was then in his late fifties. His great roles—Gino Rinaldi in *Scarface*, Stacey in *Each Dawn I Die*, and the rest—were behind him. Maxie Greenburg, alias Mack "Killer" Gray, the former boxing-manager Raft had known since Prohibition days in New York, had been Raft's personal assistant, confidant, and valet since 1932. Gray was forty-six in 1952, when it became obvious to both him and Raft that circumstances could no longer allow for Gray's services. Gray was willing to stay on for room and board, but Raft would not allow it. So, that year, Mack Gray assumed for Dean Martin the same duties that he had for twenty years so devotedly fulfilled for Raft. Soon Gray was joined by another at Dean's side: Jay Gerard. An Italian from New York whose real name was Gerardi, he was a studio extra who had worked as Dean's double as far back as *My Friend Irma*. Gerard became Dean's wardrobe attendant and man Friday. He and Mack Gray were buffers, keepers of *lontananza,* between Dean and the world.

Mack Gray would also keep Dean from the world in another way. As the songwriter Sammy Cahn recalled, "Mack Gray had a permanent migraine. I never saw Mack Gray when he didn't have his finger pressed to his head. He was always in pain." Gray's solution to his pain was Percodan.

Manufactured by Du Pont Pharmaceuticals, Percodan is a powerful drug whose principal ingredient, oxycodone, is a semisynthetic narcotic affecting the central nervous system and muscular organs in a manner similar to morphine. And like morphine, it is addictive and potentially lethal. Legally prescribed as a painkiller, Percodan is usually restricted to a dosage of one tablet, containing four and a

half or five milligrams of oxycodone, per hour. But Mack Gray
"would take Percodan like they were Tic-Tacs. Just flip them into
his mouth." Over the years, Dean began popping them as well. In
time, like Gray, he became a junkie.

"If we went to any party," Jeannie said of those early years,
"there was Dean next to the hostess, because he was certainly the
most beautiful man, and funny, amusing, and willing to stand at the
piano and sing a song. Things were wonderful."

But as Dean grew increasingly withdrawn, things became less
wonderful. More and more, Dean's private life seemed to shut her
out. Sometimes it did indeed seem that, as Dorothy Malone said,
"every woman in the world" had a crush on Dean. "A more handsome man never walked the earth," Jeannie said; and he had "this
gift besides"—this presence, this ability to command and to seduce,
to fill the air with those warm, sweet, lying colors of song and
illusion. Dorothy Malone was a beautiful girl, but she was a stand-
up broad as well. What of all the others, the grovelers, the vicious
ones, the ones out to stab their own husbands and every other
woman, the naive ones and the scheming ones, the fake mothers of
mercy and the star-struck nymphets? Dean would wipe his dick
almost anywhere. Sex for him was about as sacred an experience as
blowing his nose. He had always been that way. But the women who
sought to suck the gilding of fame from his *fallo* were now countless.

And there was much more to it than that. Dean's nature held
him absolutely, unwaveringly, infuriatingly incommunicado. "The
important thing to say about my husband is that I don't understand
him," Jeannie would say. It was a statement she would hold true
forever. Dean never revealed himself. "He *cannot* communicate.
Let's put it that way. He's one of the rare human beings who's not
comfortable with communicating. He's just not interested." Everyone saw Dean as a man's man, as someone who liked to run around
with the guys. But the men who claimed to be his friends were just
deluding themselves, attempting in their own way to suck the gilding. "He never had a male friend," Jeannie said. He was close to
Mack Gray, to Sammy Cahn, to Sinatra, to others. But he did not
need friendship. Men who did were probably looking to take it up

the ass. "Yeah," he told a reporter who asked him about that other golden guinea, "Frank is my dearest, closest friend. In fact, we slept together last night."

"Dean doesn't have an overwhelming desire to be loved. He doesn't give a damn," Jeannie would say. "He doesn't get involved with people because he really isn't interested in them."

Maybe that was why he and Johnny Rosselli got along. The two of them could sit there together, saying nothing, savoring the darkness of one another's solitude, letting those darknesses entwine in a silent interchange more comfortable, and in a way more expressive, than conversation.

Jeannie could not broach Dean's *lontananza*. She would describe him as "cold, calculating," as "an impersonal man." She had the feeling that she "bored Dean," that she was invisible. "He'd come home, I'd say, 'What happened today?' He'd say, 'Nothing.' I'd look at the news, and there would be the king and queen of England visiting the set and meeting Dean Martin. It just simply didn't faze him. No one, nothing impressed him deeply."

She would love him as a man, as a father; but she would never figure him out. "I don't know him," she would say. "He's either the most complex man imaginable or the simplest. There's either nothing under there or too much." He was "like a lunar lab, he was just from another planet." He and his brother, William, his own flesh and blood, "were just absolutely day and night." There was something that had settled deep within him long ago—"something disturbed him," she said; "something in him that is unreachable"—but what it was, she would never know. What she did learn was that one either accepted him or lost him, for there was no changing him.

Jerry agreed: "Dean was Dean. Dean didn't adjust or change. He had a wonderful way of putting up a facade, and that kept people at bay. And the thing that I loved about him was that he let people know, in front: This is how I am, and here's how you gotta take me; I'm taking you with whatever your foibles, whatever the good and the bad is, and I'm asking you to do the same with me. He really didn't want any phony bullshit. Dean was known to sit and watch fuckin' Westerns while he had a party of eight people at the house. Well, of course, you don't do that. He did! And if you loved him, you would look and say, 'Mind your fuckin' business. Let him.' "

He did not care about this world. "I don't even believe in television," he would say. "And those rockets. Do you believe these guys gonna go to the moon? What for? I don't like it."

"He used to love comic books," Jerry said. "We'd get on a plane and he'd get a kick outa reading 'em. Why? 'Cause you can escape with them. He didn't like to read that the Russians were moving on the cold front. He didn't want to know. I used to buy most of them for him, because he wouldn't go to the fuckin' newsstand. I thought that was cute. I loved it. I loved the fact that he got a kick out of that. What the fuck is wrong with that? He wasn't a closet queen, he read 'em in the presence of anyone. And he loved cowboy movies. If there was one on and there was company in the house, he'd excuse himself and he'd go and watch it. There are people who would look down their noses at that kind of shit, and I would say to them, 'Then don't go there. He's not being rude, he's not being discourteous; he's being what he is. I think it's goddamn admirable. You want him to sit with you and smile with a phony smile: "Oh, what a joy it is to be with you"? Fuck you! I'd like to do what he does.' How many nights, I had a party at my house, I would say to them, 'I think I should rest my eyes,' and what I was saying was, 'You're a fucking boring bunch of people.' He was an extraordinary man. Extraordinary."

As Jerry saw it, Dean and Jeannie had "a good marriage—as good as you can tell by not goin' behind the bedroom door. She and I had a couple of little fracases. Only because I was so protective of him. If she said something like, 'Well, he's not all that attentive,' I would get very protective and I would lean on her a little, and then she would tell him that I got fresh with her. Those little things happened. But I cared a great deal for her, more so than she knew, because she gave him so much pleasure."

The separation did not last long. Dean spent the nights with Killer Gray, drinking at Ciro's, dining at La Rue, a chic Sunset Boulevard restaurant where he and Jeanne more than once saw each other in passing. In mid-March, columnist Louella Parsons revealed that Jeannie was pregnant but had kept her pregnancy "very much a secret because she did not want it to influence Dean to return to her after the separation a month ago." Parsons said that Jeannie wanted to reconcile with Dean "more than anything in the world—that she is more in love with him now than when she married him." She quoted Jeannie describing herself as a small-town girl who perhaps "didn't understand Dean's problems. He and Jerry went to the top so fast. It takes mature mental adjustment for young people to remain happy in the glare of sudden success. I think now we could work out our problems." A day later, on March 20, Parsons reported that Dean and Jeannie were together again: "If I really played Cupid in the Dean Martin reconciliation, as Mrs. Martin says, all I can say is I am very happy. Dean went home to Jeanne after he read my story that his wife expected a baby in September. But that isn't what took him home. He went because he wanted to go." She quoted Jeannie again: "The important thing is for Dean to get everything settled in his own mind, and I'm sure he has now. We've both had a lesson, but we love each other and that's the important thing."

She came to accept the fact that, as she would later express it, "Dean was not and is not, nor will he ever be, the ideal husband."

There would be moments of revelation. "I'm going to ask you something, and I want you to tell me the truth—or just don't answer. Who is really in command between us? Who is really the stronger one?" she would ask him, and she would remember the way Dean looked at her when he answered:

"I am."

His thoughts would remain forever inward. There would be few confrontations between them. "As long as he came home at night and was attentive, and tried at least to be a good husband when he was with me, then that was fine," Jeannie said. "What he did during the day, what he did on the set, or whatever, I never in my entire life popped in on him anywhere. I always respected his privacy."

When they reconciled, Jeannie was a week away from turning twenty-six. She was young, but she was strong, and she saw the world for what it was.

"Dean was too beautiful, too handsome. The women, I mean. One had to accept that."

• • •

In March of 1953, when Capitol signed him, Frank Sinatra at thirty-seven had been written off as washed-up. No other company wanted him; Capitol itself took him only with reluctance and without an advance. His last Top Ten hit, a whitebread cover of Paul Williams's "The Hucklebuck," had been in 1949. His last picture, *Meet Danny Wilson*, had been a stiff. He had sung onstage at its opening at the Paramount a year ago, and he had not even been able to draw enough people to fill the balcony. His luck, however, was about to change. Alan Livingston of Capitol had assigned producer Voyle Gilmore to him. Gilmore would bring him together with Nelson Riddle, who had arranged Dean's album. Riddle, with whom Sinatra would produce his best work, would revive his recording career within a year with the hit "Young at Heart." And *From Here to Eternity*, which began filming that March, would do the same for his movie career.

Dean and his new fellow Capitol recording artist grew close in the years to come. There was a "twinkle" they had when they were together, Jeannie would say; the two of them had "a chemistry" that was "so Peck's-Bad-Boy," it was "wondrous to see it." But like all of Dean's relationships, it was more one-sided than reciprocal. Sinatra was enthralled by Dean. In his eyes, he saw the man he himself wanted to be. The racket guys sucked up to Dean, not the other way around. To Sinatra, who always seemed to be crying or killing himself over one broad or another, who always seemed to be dispatching others to do his dirty work, whose *mammismo* relationship with his mother was that of a little boy—to Sinatra, Dean was *la cosa vera*, the real thing, with *la stoffa giusta*, the right stuff.

Martin and Lewis by now had outgrown the boundaries of national success. In June of 1953, five weeks after finishing their tenth film, *Money from Home*, they sailed east across the Atlantic, toward that maternal bosom of culture of which they were the cathode-crackling idiot-bastard heirs. Passage aboard the *Queen Elizabeth* for their entourage of three musicians, five writers, two secretaries, a road manager, an attorney, an accountant, and assorted others came to $52,000. It was a lot, but they stood to gross $3,000,000. Dean got a good start: He took down $1,200 in the ship's casino.

On June 16, they arrived at City Hall in Glasgow, where it had been arranged that they be welcomed by Lord Provost T. A. Kerry. They were late in getting there. An official informed them that they had shown a "grave discourtesy" toward the lord provost and that he refused to receive them. It was a harbinger.

Things went well enough at the Empire Theatre in Glasgow that night and the nights that followed; and things went well enough in Liverpool too. There was nothing to prepare them for what happened in London.

America, fulfilling its destiny as the chrome-crowned glory of post-literate, polyvinyl civilization, had gone mad; Martin and Lewis were proof of that. But that madness had turned ugly. The anti-Communist witch-hunts of Senator Joseph McCarthy and his subcommittee were then at their most zealous, extending even to Europe, to which McCarthy had dispatched his chief gunsels, Roy Cohn and G. David Schine, on a "fact-gathering" tour. Cohn and Schine had passed through London on April 21. Though they denied that they were there to scrutinize the politically suspect affinities of the British Broadcasting Corporation, their presence had inspired a wave of anti-American sentiment that had been gathering with the British awareness of McCarthy's inquisition. That wave had not yet subsided when Dean and Jerry opened at the London Palladium on the night of June 20.

Several weeks before, two youthful readers of the *Daily Worker*, Cecil Bryant and Alan Hobbs, had organized an anti-American disruption of Vivian Blaine's opening in the London premiere of *Guys and Dolls*. The same pair were back as ringleaders at the Palladium for Dean and Jerry's opening.

The show went wonderfully until the end. The *Daily Herald* later reported that their act "was greeted throughout with ecstatic shrieks of applause," but when Jerry stepped forward to say how pleased they were to be in England, the hecklers erupted with shouts of "Go home, Martin and Lewis."

The incident was blown up in the tabloids, most of which had little good to say about the show itself. Dean and Jerry were stunned. They had not been aware of what Cohn and Schine had wrought. "I think it must be something to do with the execution of the Rosenbergs," Jerry told reporters backstage. What could you expect from these fucking people? Dean figured. With all their fucking airs, they had been living in caves until the Italians stopped off at their fucking island to take a shit. Dean found distraction, *all'altezza della fica,* in the twenty-one-year-old actress Pier Angeli, who was also in town. At the time of the reconciliation, it had been announced that Jeannie would accompany Dean to England; but he had left her behind with her parents, visiting from Florida, to keep her company. Angeli was engaged at the time to Kirk Douglas, who was crushed by the reports of their consorting.

Though they had broken all house records at the Palladium, Dean and Jerry were still pissed off when they arrived in France two weeks later. Talking to Art Buchwald, then a columnist for the *Herald Tribune,* Jerry said that the British "were just sore because we made £7,000 a week and they were making £6 a week. Is that our fault?"

"The British are a bunch of two-faced people," Dean put in. "Don't get us wrong. We thought the British public was great," he amended himself. "It's the British press that stinks." And "Don't forget to say we liked Scotland."

Sailor Beware, the first of their films to be dubbed into French, opened in Paris, as *Fais-Mois Peur,* during their tour of American air-force bases, which began at Orly on July 7 and took them to Laon, Fontainebleau, Orléans, and Suresnes. They continued to bad-mouth England at every opportunity, and as news of their comments reached America, Paramount and Hal Wallis grew uneasy. Wallis felt that they were showing bad business sense. *The Caddy,* after all, their next picture to play England, was their own production. It had taken a long time for them to break the British market, and now they were jeopardizing themselves.

They arrived back in New York aboard the *Liberté* on July 22. They told the waiting reporters that they would never set foot in England again. Dean characterized the British press succinctly: "They drink up all your booze, and then they turn on you."

Hal Wallis told Dean that he disapproved of his behavior. The Korean War Armistice had been signed while they were abroad. Trying to make light of his censuring of Dean, he suggested they effect an armistice with the British press. But Dean would not re-lent. "I still stick by what I said," he told a reporter. "I still say those critics stink. They didn't review our act, they criticized our nationalities." Then he threw in a shot at Wallis. When the reporter asked him about the upcoming "Comedy Hour" season, Dean re-sponded, "They'd like us to do twelve TV shows a year; we'll only do five. Look what happens to those comedians who go on every week. We figure people look forward to seeing us because we aren't on every week. It's like making too many pictures a year. Wallis would like to put us in anything, like the way Abbott and Costello make pictures. But we want to sustain our popularity by making better movies." *The Caddy*, he said, was their best so far.

Scared Stiff had opened in America while they were in London —an "overworked batch of songs, screams and gibbering nonsense played with the volume turned up to catch every overtone of the Lewis whine," complained the *New York Herald Tribune*—and it was making a fortune. The picture recycled the song "I Don't Care If the Sun Don't Shine," which Dean had recorded back in the spring of 1950. (Whether or not Elvis Presley already had that record, Dean's performance of it in *Scared Stiff* made an impression on him that summer. He recorded it himself the following summer, for release as his second single.)

The trade preview of *The Caddy* had been held on July 27, just three weeks after *Scared Stiff*'s premiere; and on August 13, Dean recorded two of the songs from the picture for release as a single. The movie's songwriters were Jack Brooks, an Englishman, and Harry Warren, of Italian descent (his real name was Salvatore Guaragna). Warren and Brooks had written an update of the conven-tional Italian pop ballad, called "That's Amore." To Dean, it sounded ridiculous, the bit about the "moon in your eye like a big pizza pie." But, then again, he was by now used to singing ridicu-lous songs in ridiculous pictures: "Tonda Wanda Hoy," "The Sailors' Polka," "The Parachute Jump"—these were songs beneath the dignity of Louie Yee's chop-suey joint.

At the end of the month, Dean and Jerry went east. On August 25, in Albany, their five shows drew the largest gross in the twenty-three-year history of the Fabian Theatre: $13,650, at a top ticket price of a buck-fifty. Two nights later, they opened at the Paramount in Manhattan, where, this time around, they would take a straight seventy percent of the gross. At the end of their first week, that came to $98,000. In September, they taped a radio commercial for *The Caddy:*

"Oh, hi, everybody, this is Dean Martin."

"And Jerry Lewis."

"We'd like to tell you all about our latest and funniest picture for Paramount."

"Of course, you mean *The Caddy.*"

"Oh, of course. You know, Jerry, I don't remember the last time I had so much fun makin' a picture."

"Boy, I'll say. How about that scene when I wreck the department store that I'm workin' in?"

"Yeah, and what about the scene when I come home and find a strange, and I do mean strange, man in my bed and it turns out to be you?"

"Tell 'em about the terrific game of golf I play. Go on, tell 'em."

"Terrific? I've never seen golf played that way before. Crazy, man, crazy."

"I hate to brag, folks, but I think *The Caddy* is the funniest picture we've made. No kidding, it's got ninety riotous minutes of howls, gags, fun, and more heartwarming entertainment than you and the family ever saw."

"You'll love Jerry and me in *The Caddy.*"

"Take my word for it. *The Caddy* is the most hilarious picture we've ever made. Come on and join the fun. See Paramount's *The Caddy.*"

"Yeah. *The Caddy.*"

After a pause, the voices were no longer so heartwarming.

Dean: "Was that all right, ya cocksucker?"

Jerry: "How was that, ya shit-heel?"

Dean: "Without reading it?"

From the sound booth: "I'm with you."

Dean: "Okay."

"Next. Ya still rollin'?"

"Still rollin'?"

"All right. Start."

"You can cut that bit out."

From the sound booth: "I will."

"Okay. This is Dean Martin."

"And Jerry Lewis, asking you to see our newest and funniest picture to date."

"Of course, you mean *The Caddy*."

"You bet I do. *The Caddy* is filled with ninety hilarious minutes of howls, gags, fun, and heartwarming entertainment that the entire family will enjoy."

"Crazy, man, crazy."

"No doubt about it, Dean, this is the funniest picture we've ever made. No kidding, folks, we're sensational. Take my word for it. Come on and join the fun. See Paramount's *The Caddy*." Another pause, another shift in voice. "It'll make ya shit."

Another pause, a shift in Dean's as well: "Cut out 'make.' Ya ready? He ain't doin' a fuckin' thing, he's just standin' there." Then the sweet voice again: "This is Dean Martin."

"And Jerry Lewis, uh, I, uh, hmm—ya cocksuckers."

Dean, shift: "Wait'll this guy with TB gets through here. Ready?" Shift. "Now, this is Dean Martin."

"And Jerry Lewis, with a reminder to see our newest and funniest motion picture ever, *The Caddy*."

"Oh, he's right, folks. Come on and join the fun in the most ri-tuous ninety minutes of howls—"

"*Ri-tuous!* Where the fuck do you see 'ri-tuous'? That's 'riotous,' ya greaseball. Ri-tuous. What is this, a religious picture?"

"I don't know." Shift. "This is religious Martin and Jerry Lewis." Pause, shift. "What is this? Five fuckin' lines and we can't get through it." Shift. "This is Dean Martin."

"And Jerry Lewis, with a reminder to see our newest and funniest motion picture ever, *The Caddy*."

"Ah, he's right, folks. Come on and join the fun in the most wonderful ninety minutes of howls and gags you ever saw."

"We'll be seeing you in Paramount's *The Caddy*."

"Yep, *The Caddy.*"

"With a big cock on it."

At a quarter past ten on the night of September 20, at St. John's
Hospital in Santa Monica, Jeannie gave birth to her second son,
Ricci James Martin. Dean called on Ray Ryan to be the boy's
padrino. Jerry's family would soon grow as well. He and Patti would
adopt a daughter, Sally Mae, that fall.

A few days before Ricci's birth, Paramount had released *The
Caddy* and Capitol had released "That's Amore." The *New York
Daily News,* usually fond of their pictures, said *The Caddy* "fails to
score a par for the course Paramount long ago laid out for Dean
Martin and Jerry Lewis." The newspaper gave it only two and a half
stars. "Other than a couple of new songs which are pretty good, the
production gives the fellows nothing fresh." In its review of Dean's
single the following week, *Billboard* called "That's Amore" a "cute
ballad with an Italianate flavor." It was sung "affectionately" and
"could attract sales loot with the plentiful exposure it's likely to get"
through the "current flicker."

Dean's comments about the British obviously had not hurt him,
as Hal Wallis had feared they would. His recording of "Kiss," released in America unsuccessfully in 1952, appeared on the British
pop charts now, in the fall of 1953, to become a number-five hit
throughout England.

On Sunday, October 4, Dean sang "That's Amore" on the first
"Colgate Comedy Hour" of the season. The next day, looking forward to a Christmas release, he recorded a new song, "The Christmas Blues," by Sammy Cahn and David Holt. It looked like a
comer; *Billboard* was enthusiastic in its issue of November 7: "This
tune has lyrics that pack a real impact and is something of a novelty
in the seasonal flood of cheerful music." Then, the following week,
in the chart of "Best Selling Singles" for the week ending November
7, there it was, at number fourteen, beneath "Istanbul" by the Four
Lads and above "Crying in the Chapel" by June Valli: "That's
Amore."

Though Dean was the singer, it was Jerry who chose the musical
director for their new picture, *Living It Up.* Walter Scharf's work on

Samuel Goldwyn's *Hans Christian Andersen* had been nominated for an Academy Award the previous spring. He had been sitting with other nominees at the ceremony when Jerry approached him.

"If you do our next picture," he said, "you can write your own ticket."

Not even Goldwyn talked that way; "but that business about writing my own ticket had a certain appeal," Scharf remembered. "So I joined the team."

With the permission of NBC, Dean and Jerry had in late October, during the production of *Living It Up*, entered into arrangements with ABC-TV to present a national Thanksgiving-eve muscular-dystrophy fund-raising special on that network. ABC, the weakest of the three big networks, recently had completed a strengthening merger with the Paramount theater chain. Unlike their March 1952 telethon, there would be no telephone pledges. By arrangement with the National Association of Letter Carriers and the United States Post Office, pledge forms were to be distributed and collected by postmen. Eddie Cantor opened the show with praise for Dean and Jerry, "who have taken this cause to their heart, who have taken three and a half years to make America aware of this dread disease of muscular dystrophy." Jerry spoke of Dean's "sharing the thrill with me of having his first real big hit"; and, of course, Dean sang it, but with a different touch, an uptempo break before the final bars. Bing Crosby had sung the song on his radio show; Perry Como had done it twice on his CBS-TV "Chesterfield Supper Club." Dean returned the favor this Thanksgiving eve by singing Como's current hit, "You Alone." He also sang "Christmas Blues," with Sammy Cahn playing piano, and "I Don't Care If the Sun Don't Shine," in its original Dixieland arrangement. Though the show lasted only two hours, there was the de rigueur telethon loosening of bow ties midway through. *Variety* did not care for the show at all: "they fluffed it." The production values were poor, the guests were not at their best, and "there was a little too much of Martin's singing."

Dean thought about it: "a little too much of Martin's singing." Now, what the fuck was that supposed to mean? Was he a singer or what? Were three songs—five, counting the couple that Jerry fucked up—"a little too much" for a singer to sing in two fucking hours? He had one of the biggest hits in the world now. Was he still supposed to fade into the background as Jerry's *citrullo?* That *Herald Tribune* review of *Scared Stiff* had been an anomaly. Not that it had held forth a kind word for Dean—it had not. But it had found Jerry unbearable. And that is the way Dean now found him: an overbearing egomaniacal obnoxious fucking Jew who was pushing thirty and still playing a thirteen-year-old palsied monkey and seeing it as fucking genius. Now he was a fucking artist. Somebody had put a Brownie camera in his hands, and he had gotten the idea that he was another Charlie Chaplin. He had started making those fucking home movies of his three years ago: *Watch on the Lime; Fairfax Avenue; The Re-Enforcer*—he had conned Dean into playing Joe Lasagna ("Send up-a da broads") in that one; *A Streetcar Named Repulsive*, with Janet Leigh doing Vivian Leigh and Jerry doing Brando; *Come Back, Little Shiksa*, in which Dean once again had deigned to appear. Home movies? He was spending thousands upon thousands of dollars on these sixteen-millimeter handjobs. He even gave his backyard film company a name: Gar-Ron Productions. Now the whole fucking world was his backyard. And Hal Wallis and the rest of them went right along with it, indulging his every fucking whim. Dean was disgusted when he saw the opening credits of *Money from Home:* "Special Material in Song Numbers Staged by Jerry Lewis." The "special material" was just another tired take on that same old fucking record act he had been stumbling along with at the Glass Hat ten years ago, adapted for just another tired comic variation on the Cyrano-Christian balcony bit.

Fuck it. Things were as they once had been, as they always should have been. He did not need the monkey. The week before Christmas, "That's Amore" was featured as the number-three song on "Your Hit Parade," the NBC series that brought the weekly *Billboard* charts to middle America. Dean's record would never hit number one; it could not dislodge Tony Bennett's "Rags to Riches" or its successor, Eddie Fisher's "Oh! My Pa-Pa." But it made it to number two, during Christmas week, and it remained on the charts for more than five months, featured every Saturday night on the "Hit

Parade" straight through the first weekend of March. In England,
where it appeared on the charts in January and remained through
April, it made it to number two as well.

The venom was rising. It was only a matter of time. On February 17, 1954, they began work on the picture that would sunder the
bond between them. Jerry called that bond friendship, Dean did not
call it anything; soon it would not matter, not one way or the other.

"When we were together," Jerry would say, "we were unbeat-
able. When we were together, we were a fucking solid-steel unit. If
any third faction got between us, it created problems. It was not just
the years of Jerry getting all the attention. Deep down, he knew that
for what it was worth. And I maintain his discipline as a performer
and as a man was great enough that we could have gone another
twenty years. But he had outside factions telling him that he's nothing. He had all these poison-droppers. Guys at the country club.
These shit-stirrers. A guy that couldn't cut a deal with me, wanted
to do a real-estate thing with me, and I knew he was a fuckin'
hustler on a golf course. Well, he happens to play golf with Dean.
When I turn him down and he can't get the $500,000 from me, he's
gonna tell Dean I'm a swell fella? No, he's gonna tell Dean, 'Hey,
how come *he* gets all of it?' It was that kind of shit."

Don McGuire was a young actor and screenwriter who had first
heard of Martin and Lewis from Frank Sinatra: "The dago's lousy,"
Sinatra had told him in 1948, "but the little Jew is great." Jerry had
cajoled a hard-up McGuire into writing a screenplay, based on
Jerry's idea, for one of his backyard pictures. It was called *How to
Smuggle a Hernia Across the Border.* Jerry, who knew about Dean's
wartime hernia, played a fag army recruiting officer in it. McGuire
had gone on to a bigger job at Universal, writing *Meet Danny Wilson,* the 1952 picture Sinatra starred in before making *From Here to
Eternity.* When asked by Hal Wallis if he had any ideas for Martin
and Lewis, McGuire told him about a story he wanted to write. It
was inspired by a newspaper item that he had read about studying
lion taming under the GI Bill.

When McGuire's script went into production that February in

Phoenix, where Wallis had cut a deal with the Clyde Beatty Circus for the use of its facilities, the picture was called *Big Top*, a title that eventually was changed to *Three Ring Circus*. Dean had noticed something odd about the script: His character, Pete Nelson, did not appear until after the first twenty pages. And there were also only two songs. Jerry, whose character was named Jerry, was the whole schmear. And that schmear had taken a decided turn away from their usual farce, a decided turn toward pathos. It was supposed to be pathos, anyway. It was really bathos: a dumb, sickly-sweet mélange of *schmerz* and schmaltz that was little more than a gaudy showcase for Jerry's gross clown-that-cried pretensions.

At a meeting in Wallis's office, Jerry had held that he also did not like the script. They were supposed to be partners.

Wallis knew that they were not getting along. "You mean, you don't meet soon enough in the script? Is that what's wrong here?"

"You bet your ass, baby," Dean said.

"Okay," Wallis said. He held up the script, leafed through the first part of it, ripped away a handful of pages, and threw what remained down on his desk. "There. You've *met!*"

Dean was used to whiling away time with a club and balls between scenes on the sets of their movies. But this was ridiculous. When it was finally time to sing his first song, halfway into the picture, he was not even given a broad to sing to. He had to stand there like a *cafone* singing to a bunch of stinking fucking animals.

Walter Scharf, the arranger and conductor, was Jerry's man. Don McGuire, the screenwriter, was Jerry's man. Jerry had even put his old gofer Irving Kaye in the picture. Now—Dean at first could not believe it—Wallis had let Jerry choose the director.

At thirty-three, director Joseph Pevney, a former stage actor, had directed mostly crime dramas. McGuire's *Meet Danny Wilson* had been one of them. It was Jerry, he remembered, not Wallis, who asked him to come over from Universal to direct the circus picture.

"Jerry had seen a picture that I did at Universal with his friend Tony Curtis. He was blind or something. Blind fighter. Deaf fighter. I don't remember. But it was a good little movie until about the third act. And Jerry was crazy about the picture, and he wanted me to direct his next movie. So he went to Hal Wallis and insisted that I be given the job."

It turned out to be something different for Pevney in more ways than one. Twentieth Century-Fox had copyrighted the CinemaScope process last year; the first picture to utilize the new wide-screen gimmick, *The Robe*, had already been released, and other studios were coming up with their own wide-screen variations. Paramount had VistaVision. *White Christmas* would be Paramount's maiden release in the new format; *Three Ring Circus* would be the second. VistaVision presented no trouble for Pevney. Hal Wallis, and the growing tension between Dean and Jerry, did.

"It was a very difficult situation. I was always of the belief that a director is the director. But Wallis didn't work that way. He owned the picture and it had to be done his way or else. With that film, he did with it what he damned well pleased.

"When we first started work, we were only using one circus ring. Well, for a director, that presents a lot of problems. How do you change angles? How do you show depth? So I went to Wallis with the conception of utilizing the Clyde Beatty Circus to its fullest —all three rings. And he said, 'Jesus, it will take so much more time.' And I said, 'Not that much more, but you'll at least have some production value in your picture. Shooting one ring, you get nothing.' He didn't give a damn what the production values were. Put Martin and Lewis on the screen, let 'em clown, let Jerry make his funny faces, and get off. That was his idea of a movie. And it came through all the time that way. Well, anyway, I sold him on the idea of using three rings, so the next thing you knew it was called *Three Ring Circus*. He was going to exploit it that way.

"I don't claim to have done any magnificent work in my career, but I wouldn't point to *Three Ring Circus* with any great deal of pride, and neither would anyone else. I don't know how it did at the box office. They all made money, because they didn't cost anything to make. I guess the budget of this one was a little over a million."

Pevney was right: They all made money. Wallis in the fifties began to build an art collection around the impressionist pieces his wife, Louise Fazenda, had gathered: Degas, Monet, Cassatt,

Pissarro, treasures of an age. He would serve for twenty years as a
trustee of the Los Angeles County Museum of Art. Yet in his work,
especially with Martin and Lewis, he remained a schlockmeister to
the end. *Sailor Beware,* their biggest hit, had cost under $750,000
to make but had done $27,000,000 in worldwide box-office business
at a time when a movie ticket cost a quarter or fifty cents. *Three
Ring Circus* brought Wallis and Paramount close to $4,000,000 from
domestic theater rentals—more than Wallis and Paramount made
from *Come Back, Little Sheba* and other more prestigious films. Like
That's My Boy, The Stooge, Scared Stiff, The Caddy, and *Money
from Home,* which was released while they were filming in Phoenix,
Three Ring Circus made more money than *Dial M for Murder, High
Noon, Stalag 17,* and other so-called classics of the same decade.
"What's more to be said of such nonsense?" Bosley Crowther wondered in his *Times* review of *Money from Home.* "It either makes you
laugh or it does not." And, as Crowther well knew, it did make a lot
of people laugh. *Living It Up,* released that coming summer, made
more than *Singin' in the Rain, An American in Paris, On the Water-
front, Love Me Tender, The African Queen, The Man with the Golden
Arm, Love Is a Many Splendored Thing,* and *Jailhouse Rock.*

But the schlockmeister's golden boys, worth more to him than
any impressionist master, were soon to reap their final yocks.

"Dean was very pleasant to work with," Joseph Pevney said.
"He was a lot of laughs, and he was a good guy. He was a worker.
He did his job, and that was it. But I inherited a very poor situation.
The guys were not happy. The germ of the warfare was already
present when I took over.

"Jerry wanted to make the movie, because he wanted to play a
clown. I don't think Dean was terribly happy with doing the movie.
He was much too talented for this. So he was out golfing as much as
he could."

The last time Dean had been to Steubenville it had been to visit
Smuggs and Bernice, who had finally married. He had joined them
for dinner at their home, right behind where old Cosmo and old
Tripodi lived. Smuggs traveled from town to town as a big-money

dealer. He worked in Florida, in Washington, at the Mounds and the Mayfield Road Gang's other casinos throughout Ohio and Kentucky. During the Kentucky Derby, he worked at French Lick, Indiana. He made out all right, Smuggs did, and Dean was happy for him. At dinner that night, he had thought that he had never seen two people more in love than Smuggs and Bernice. Smuggs was not jealous of Dean's success, either. In his quiet way, he was proud of Dean, happy for him, as Dean was happy for them. Bernice liked Dean. She never saw him mad. His attitude, she said, seemed to be: If I can do something about it, fine. If not, I'm not going to worry about it. But to her, Smuggs was much more handsome, and—it was their secret—he could sing better too.

Now, two days after filming began in Phoenix, Dean received word that Smuggs Sperduti had died suddenly of a heart attack. Bernice would never forget the sprays and sprays of roses that Dean sent to fill the funeral parlor that winter day. If Dean had ever had a friend, he had lost him now. Watching that fucking loudmouth little prick with his clown suit and his Hollywood tears made him want to puke.

"Dean kept blowing his top at me and everyone else," Jerry said. "It got pretty hairy. There were days when I thought Dean would ditch the whole package. It almost happened. One morning he arrived an hour late on the set and stared daggers at me."

But only Jerry would recall Dean's anger. To Pevney, "Dean was fun to work with." He was "a lot of laughs" and "a good guy." Joanne Dru, who starred as the circus owner, would say, "I just really loved him. He was just so funny and so wonderful. He was an original." Dean and thirty-one-year-old Dru lunched together frequently during the filming. "He used to have fried eggs and a martini. It used to make me sick. But we got along beautifully. He was sweet, kind. Utterly, utterly pleasant. He was just a darling, just always such a gentleman. I really liked him a lot."

No, the anger, the daggers, were for Jerry alone.

"Anytime you wanna call it quits," Dean told him one morning, "just let me know."

"What the hell would I do without you, anyway?"

There was no answer. "He grunted. Then a disgusted wave of
his hand and he strode toward his trailer. It developed into psychological warfare for the balance of the picture."

Walter Scharf, the music director, could see it: "Dean was *always* in the background. Jerry was *always* in the foreground,"
Scharf said. "At one point, I turned to Hal Wallis and said that I had
no doubt whatever that Dean wouldn't take much more of it. He had
more talent than he was being given credit for." Wallis disagreed
and told Scharf to mind his own business. But in time, Wallis began
to show concern. "As long as they don't kill each other, I'd be
happy," Scharf remembered him saying.

On March 12, there was a meeting at the MCA offices in Beverly Hills. Lew Wasserman and Joe Ross mediated between Dean
and Jerry, explaining to both of them that, prudence aside, they
were bound together by contractual responsibilities—to Hal Wallis
Productions, to NBC, to their own York Pictures—that they themselves had knowingly and willfully entered into.

One scene in the picture struck eerily true: Jerry and the troupe
plan to do a benefit show at a local orphanage, but Dean, who has
taken over the circus, is coldly adamant about moving on to the next
town. "You ain't nice anymore," Jerry tells him, in a natural voice,
in a natural way.

Back in California, they went to the McKinley Home for Boys in
the San Fernando Valley to film the orphanage-benefit scene, the
picture's finale, in which Jerry, failing to bring laughter to a pig-
tailed girl in leg braces, begins to weep. "Look at him. He's crying,"
the little crippled orphan girl exclaims. "The clown is crying." She
embraces him, giving him the compassionate laughter that alone
could stanch the repellent flow of lachrymal VistaVision emotion.

By then, rumors of a feud between Dean and Jerry had found
their way to print. On the day before they began filming the orphanage scene, their press agent Jack Keller had released a statement,
signed by Jerry and cosigned by Dean, that tried to make light of
those rumors:

"We had a disagreement. Well, it wasn't exactly a disagreement,
it was a fight. It started when Dean called me a dope. I got mad and
told him to prove it, and that's what we fought about. We are going

to split up the team. We have even picked the date—July 25, 1996, which will be our golden anniversary as a team. We figure by that time we will have enough kids between us to keep us supplied with wheel chair grease and bifocals."

In April, Dean and Jerry went to the Capitol studio together for the first time since 1948. Jerry's own recording career was a bust. Since hiring Walter Scharf, however, his attempts at singing had taken on a more serious tone, as if he now wanted to consign Dean to the shadows even in song. In *Living It Up*, he had sung a more or less straight rendition of "How Do You Speak to an Angel?," a melancholy counterversion of Dean's own performance of the song. In *Three Ring Circus*, Dean was joined by Jerry both times he sang "Hey, Punchinello." Now, three days before the preview of *Living It Up*, they recorded "Ev'ry Street's a Boulevard in Old New York," a duet from that picture, for release by Capitol as part of a five-song, extended-play soundtrack album, which would also include Jerry's solo performance of "Champagne and Wedding Cake." Dean did not need this shit. He needed more hits. Jerry's voice on a record was the kiss of death.

Two days later, Dean returned to the studio alone. One of the songs he recorded that day was called "Sway," a new adaptation, with English lyrics, of a *bolero mambo* by Pablo Beltrán Ruiz that had been a hit some months ago in Mexico under its original title of "¿Quién Será?" That same day, the Internal Revenue Service announced that liens had been filed against both him and Jerry. Dean and Jeanne, the government said, owed $20,222.35; Jerry and Patti, $56,533.

On May 2, on "The Colgate Comedy Hour"—the Treniers, one of the wildest of the early rock-'n'-roll groups, were their guests that night—Dean and Jerry put on happy faces to celebrate their eighth anniversary as a team by "recreating" their first appearance together at the 500 Club. They closed out the show by joining the Treniers for a berserk performance of the band's new record, "Rockin' Is Our Business." Few knew what to make of it. Elvis Presley was still two months away from making his first record, and most colored folk were still watching radio.

"Sway" appeared on the pop charts in mid-July, the week Dean

and Jerry traveled to Atlantic City for the premiere of *Living It Up*.
It was more than a premiere. Atlantic City, celebrating its centen-
nial year, had proclaimed July 15 to be Martin-Lewis Day. At seven
that morning, they appeared with Dave Garroway, who had brought
an NBC-TV mobile unit to broadcast the "Today" show from the
Boardwalk. At noon, they left their beachfront suites at the Traymore to greet busloads of arriving reporters at Bader Field. They
returned with the reporters in a thirty-car motorcade, past the 500
Club to the Traymore, where Colgate-Palmolive products, Scotch,
cigarette lighters, cuff links, and other gifts awaited the reporters in
their rooms. There was an afternoon of free booze, followed by a
banquet at six, attended by party-boss Senator Frank Farley and
Mayor Joseph Altman. At eight, a roller-chair parade of drunken
reporters proceeded down the Boardwalk from the Traymore to the
Warner Theatre, followed by Dean, Jerry, costar Janet Leigh, and
Skinny D'Amato in an open Cadillac convertible. As a crowd of
fifteen thousand gathered outside the theater at dusk, a nearby
Boardwalk bench, "on which they joined their talents," was officially dedicated with a bronze plaque. Leigh appeared onstage with
them and the Stabile orchestra before the premiere. At midnight,
there was a private show and party at the 500 Club. The party lasted
until early daylight. There was a breakfast banquet at the Traymore.
The reporters were hauled away that afternoon to deliver the publicity in time for the picture's national opening next week, while Dean
and Jerry remained in town for a ten-day run at their old friend
Skinny's joint.

On August 19, they were scheduled to open at Ciro's. Jerry had
told Hover that they would perform for him because they liked him,
just as they had done for Skinny at Atlantic City. He told Hover to
offer MCA $7,000 a week for two weeks; "If they say to pay more,
say 'Go fuck yourself.'" Hover had called MCA, and a half hour
later, Larry Barnett, MCA's vice-president, had called him back: "I
don't know what you've got on Jerry, but he says to get the contract
signed. Any price you stipulate."

Now, when opening night came, Jerry failed to show up. "The
place is jam-packed, I'm getting fifty dollars a person cover-charge,
and at the last minute I get word that Jerry is sick, he can't make it.

"Jerry and I were still friends then, and I was stupid enough to believe that friendship had a certain value. But it had no value whatsoever. The reason he did this was because he wanted some cash money. He wasn't sick."

Dean came through for the commitment Jerry had made. On August 30, Jerry took out a full-page advertisement in *The Hollywood Reporter* explaining the high fever that prevented him from appearing at Ciro's and offering his thanks and apologies to all involved. He was suffering, he said, from jaundice and nervous exhaustion.

"Sway," which became a number-fifteen hit, remained on the charts through autumn. At the end of September, Dean began work on his second album, a Dixieland-style collection called *Swingin' Down Yonder*. The liner notes would say it all: "The collection of Southern songs in 'Swingin' Down Yonder' takes on a new dimension when rendered in the modern Neapolitan stylings of Dean Martin. . . . To the great songs of the South, Dean Martin brings an artistry as fresh and imaginative as a breakfast of black-eyed peas and pizza pie."

In mid-October, he and Jerry went to work on another York picture with producer Paul Jones and director Norman Taurog: *You're Never Too Young*, a screenplay by Sidney Sheldon that was the latest incarnation of a story by Fannie Kilbourne. Nina Foch, whose most recent movie was *Executive Suite* with June Allyson and William Holden, played one of the two female leads with Diana Lynn, who had been Dean's girl in the *Irma* pictures.

Foch remembered that Dean did not appear happy. "He was drinking. I didn't like lying in his arms being sung to, smelling that vodka." One day, Foch was overcome by a whimsical notion. "I thought: How exciting it would be if Dean and Jerry did *The Importance of Being Earnest*, that it would make a hell of a property for them to work with. And so I went to D. A. Doran and said that to him. And he chuckled a little bit and said, 'Why don't you talk to them about it?' I got Jerry in the dressing-room, and I said, 'What about doing *The Importance of Being Earnest?*' I could see he didn't know what that was. So I said, 'Here, I'll get it for you.' He said, 'No, don't bother. I won't read it. You know, I don't read books. But my analyst says it's all right. I'm learning from life.' Illiterate and proud of it. Decent fellows, just not my sort, that's all."

It was not only Foch whose role *Variety* found wasteful. "Martin does his best," it said, "but he is hampered by the undeveloped character provided him by the scripter. He gets the girl at the end, in this case Diana Lynn, but it's Lewis who gets the audience." To state it plainly: "This is Lewis' show."

Dean, Jerry remembered, "now seemed like a stranger." Maybe it was "because in his heart he knew *he* was the reason we were successful."

You're Never Too Young was finished by the time *Three Ring Circus* opened across America for Christmas. In its review on Christmas Day, the *New York Times* was moved by Jerry's orphanage scene: "He really comes into his own toward the close as the wonderful clown he basically is, even managing a Pagliacci note in the affecting scene where he doggedly woos an unsmiling crippled moppet." Martin and Lewis, "at long last, are beginning to relax," said the *Times*. "Whether or not this presages better comedies to come, Merry Christmas, boys."

Wallis and Hazen saw Martin and Lewis coming apart before their eyes. They had a contract, and they were intent on having its terms fulfilled. Their next picture, *Artists and Models,* went into production in March 1955. In May, when it finished filming, Jerry received a call from Charlie Brown in the Catskills. It had been over fifteen years since Jerry and Lonnie Brown had first done their little record act at the Browns' place, the Arthur, in Lakewood, New Jersey, a decade since he had worked for Charles and Lillian Brown at their hotel in Loch Sheldrake. Jerry's father, Danny, had by now quit show business; Jerry's wife, Patti, had abandoned Judaism and returned to the religion of her blood. He was going through hell with Dean. Let David Ben Gurion have his Israel. There were no record acts in Tel Aviv. For Joseph Ben Levitch, the Catskills were Zion: his sanctuary and the mount of his triumph. Together Jerry and Charlie came up with the idea of premiering *Living It Up* at the Brown Hotel in Loch Sheldrake.

Jerry brought the idea to a meeting at York. "Line producer Paul Jones, director Norman Taurog, the Paramount publicity chief, and Jack Keller were all there. I told them that Charles and Lillian Brown would give us the royal treatment." Everyone, including Hal Wallis, liked the idea; everyone but Dean, who glared at Jerry the next day when the idea was laid before him.

"You should have consulted me first," Dean said.

"I'm consulting you now."

Dean drew a long disgusted breath. "Actually, Jerry, I really don't care where we hold it."

The premiere was scheduled for June 10. There would be a dedication ceremony that Friday night for the hotel's new Martin and Lewis Playhouse. Dean and Jerry would re-create their old single acts, then perform together. After the press preview, there would be a reception in the hotel's Brown Derby Club.

On June 5, they did the Colgate show together. Eighteen hours later, on the eve of their planned departure, Jerry was visited by Killer Gray.

"Your partner isn't making the trip," Gray told him.

"What—are you putting me on, Mack?"

"Look, Jerry, I'm relaying this straight from Dean's mouth. He said he's tired; he's going to take Jeanne on a vacation to Hawaii."

That night, Dean met with Herman Citron of MCA to discuss the possibility of developing his own television show. The next day, as Jerry and his family traveled east by rail, Earl Wilson of the *New York Post* spoke with Dean, who was preparing to leave for Honolulu with Jeannie.

"Outside of back east," Dean told him, "who knows about the Catskills?"

He told Wilson of the previous night's meeting. "I want a little TV show of my own, where I can sing more than two songs in an hour," he said. "I'm about ten years older than the boy. He wants to direct. He loves work. So maybe he can direct and I can sing."

Jerry and his family arrived at Penn Station on June 9. The swarm of reporters had few questions about the picture, or about Jerry's ties to the Browns and the Catskills. All they wanted to know was why Dean had backed out. "No comment," Jerry told them.

They spent the night at the Hampshire House, where, years ago, in that first wild flush of stupid glory, Jerry and Gloria De Haven had hid from Patti's knowing. The next day, riding north along Route 17, he gazed numbly at the roadside billboards proclaiming the arrival of Martin and Lewis at Brown's Hotel.

Sonny King joined him onstage. Patti sang "I Got a Man Who's Crazy for Me." The weekend passed.

Dean and Jerry did not speak to one another for the next two months. They seethed and they brooded, and, while they seethed and while they brooded, the Internal Revenue Service came down on them with a claim for $650,000. They did not have the cash. The mansion that Dean had bought at 601 Mountain Drive was costing him $225,000. In mid-July, Jerry went for help to Young Frank Freeman, the sixty-four-year-old Paramount vice-president who, with president Barney Balaban, vice-president George Weltner, attorney Paul Raibourn, and old chairman Adolph Zukor himself, was one of the five-man group that effectively ran Paramount. Freeman had the air of an old-school Southern gentleman. He wrote out a check to Jerry for the amount needed, drawn on the personal account that he and his wife had at the Bank of Atlanta. "Just tell me when I'm gonna get it back," he said.

The September issue of *Photoplay* went on sale the first week of August: "The future of Martin and Lewis is at stake," it proclaimed. "Can the faith and small prayers of their millions of fans heal the breach between them?"

"To me, this isn't a love affair," Dean told a United Press reporter on August 3. "This is a big business. I think it's ridiculous for the boy to brush aside such beautiful contracts." The reporter called Jerry, who gave him only two words: "No comment." Five days later, on August 8, there was a meeting at Y. Frank Freeman's office. Present were Dean, Jerry, Lew Wasserman, Hal Wallis, and Joe Ross. At issue were an estimated $20,000,000 in contractual commitments and the fact that Dean Martin and Jerry Lewis hated one another. Wallis wanted another picture; his contract with them was good through 1960. The new NBC-TV season was nearing. "The Colgate Comedy Hour" was now a group of four different shows presented under the banner of "The Colgate Variety Hour." One of those four shows was "The Dean Martin & Jerry Lewis

Show," which was produced by York, and in which Paramount and Wallis held a vested interest.

When they came out of that meeting, they still hated one another. But Jack Keller, their publicist, painted a rosy picture for the press. Their differences were resolved. They would return to NBC on September 18; their new picture, *Where Men Are Men,* would begin filming that fall. The *New York Daily News,* reviewing *You're Never Too Young* after its August 25 opening at the Criterion, called them "indefatigable, indestructible, irrepressible." On August 31, they posed together, smiling and embracing, for NBC photographers. "PEACE!" declared *The Hollywood Reporter* the day after their first Colgate show of the season. "At 8 o'clock last night Dean Martin and Jerry Lewis signed a peace pact in public view over several million TV screens after a feud that almost caused the destruction . . ." It really did seem more momentous than the Warsaw Pact.

Jerry had his Beverly Hills psychiatrist, Dr. Henry Luster. Dean had himself, *il dottore dell'io.* Airs, waters, and places had conspired against him. There could be no happiness but in waving away the world; none but in being apart, unthinking, unfeeling. He had heard of Dante and the *Commedia,* of the hundred cantos that rose toward a paradise of light, love, and reason with the breath of a woman at their heart. *Pura luce, piena d'amore.* But what was all the light and love in the world compared to a single good blowjob? That was what women did to men, turned them into fucking *pazzo* poets. And what the fuck did Dante know about hell? Dante Alighieri and Jerry Lewis. Nine years of listening to that *mortucrist'* wail and whine—then he really could have written a fucking *Inferno.* Fuck it all. Fuck all that love, light, and reason shit. Fuck Beatrice where she breathed. Fuck the moon in your eye like a big pizza pie. It was a racket, all right. You sang your song, you wrote your poem: a crust of bread, a jug of wine, and thou. It sounded so sweet. But a million bucks, a bottle of Scotch, and a blowjob—that's what it came down to. It was like the clown in the opera said: *La commedia è finita!*

Jeannie left him on October 13. She took the kids with her to a rented house in Palm Springs; he stayed behind in their new dream house. There were no immediate plans for divorce, she told Louella Parsons. "There is no other man or woman involved," she told another reporter. "Dean and I simply appear to be incompatible." Talking to the press through Mack Gray and Jack Keller, Dean said that he preferred a quiet homelife, while Jeanne was a more social person; that he had seen the conflict was undermining his wife's health, and had decided that a separation was for the best.

There was a moment of recoil. Sammy Cahn and his wife were about to go visit Jeannie in Palm Springs. Before they left, Sammy had dinner with Dean at Patsy D'Amore's Villa Capri. Dean looked terrible.

"Dean, look at you. What are you doin'?" Sammy said.

"I just came from church. Please, please talk to her."

He was "drained emotionally," Sammy said. "He was crying, really crying."

But the remorse did not last.

Two weeks later, Dean recorded a song called "Memories Are Made of This." Dean knew his racket well. His latest single, recorded in April and released in September, was "In Napoli," another ersatz Italian song, whose author's pseudonym of Carmen Vitale cloaked one real-life Ada Kurtz. It was manufactured in the style of "That's Amore," but it had stirred none of the earlier song's magic. He needed something new, something different. "Memories Are Made of This" was pure romance; and Dean, who hated memory itself, whose marriage had once again turned to shit just two weeks before, wove it into a lie of gold.

The $650,000 they had borrowed from Y. Frank Freeman had been paid back in September, as Jerry had promised Freeman it would be. In October, Freeman had told Jerry that he was serving as the committee chairman for a children-of-poverty benefit that the *Los Angeles Times* was sponsoring at the Shrine Auditorium on November 10. Would Dean and Jerry be willing to make an appearance? Jerry had assured him that they would; that it was the least they could do. He told Dean about it, and Dean told him it was all right. But when the night of the benefit came around, it was fuck

Jerry, fuck Freeman, fuck the *Los Angeles Times,* and fuck the poor little *mulagnan's.*

Where Men Are Men, a Sidney Sheldon knockoff of an old Crosby picture, *Rhythm on the Range,* was called *Pardners* by the time it went into production that November under the direction of Norman Taurog, who had also directed the Crosby picture nineteen years before. The female lead was twenty-two-year-old Lori Nelson, a pretty blonde who had appeared the year before in *Destry.* The production took them from the Paramount lot to Arizona and back. Dean began romancing Nelson before they left for Arizona. Jeanne and the children had returned to the house; Dean had taken an apartment on Sunset Boulevard.

"I was crazy about him," Nelson remembered. The trouble with Jeannie, the trouble with Jerry—none of it seemed to bother him. "He was very happy-go-lucky. And lots of fun. I think that Jerry was frantic at that point, trying desperately to do the movie and to be funny and to be more of what he'd always been. And Dean seemed to have the confidence to just sit back and relax. He was a very natural, laid-back person by nature."

They visited Ray Ryan, who owned a restaurant in Palm Springs and a ranch in North Ridge. Ryan gave them horses to ride. They kept to themselves. Dean was not drinking much. He did not drink in the morning; had only perhaps three or four drinks all day.

"He talked about marriage with me and everything, but he had all those kids, and he was considerably older than I was. He said, 'You know, she wants me to come back.' I had a tremendous conscience in those days, and I said, 'Well, go back. Talk to her about it. You have kids to consider, and I don't know, as young as I am, if I'm prepared to be a stepmother. So go back, talk to her, and see what's going to be happening.' And he said he didn't want to."

Capitol's advertisement for Dean's and Sinatra's new records in *Billboard* said it all: "Profits are made of these!" The company by now had been taken over by the British EMI conglomerate. The new, thirteen-story Capitol Tower rose at 1750 North Vine Street. Dean's recording of "Memories Are Made of This" appeared on the *Billboard* charts at the end of November. In January, it would displace Tennessee Ernie Ford's "Sixteen Tons" to become the number-one hit in the country. It would stay at number one for six long weeks, giving way finally to the Platters' "Great Pretender." In the end, it would remain on the pop charts for six months, emerging as one of the best-selling records of 1955–56. Colgate, meanwhile, following the second "Dean Martin & Jerry Lewis Show" of the season, broadcast on November 13, three days after Dean's no-show at the Shrine benefit, had decided to end its sponsorship of the "Variety Hour" on Christmas. The network planned to continue the Sunday-night series as "The NBC Comedy Hour," and in any event wanted to keep Martin and Lewis under contract. In mid-December, a new, five-year deal was worked out between them and NBC: $7,500,000 for a minimum of four television shows a year. Between the forthcoming advance from that deal and the royalties that were due from "Memories Are Made of This," with another wife down and a new blond baby on the line, the new year looked like a good one. "Maybe next time," Bosley Crowther had remarked a few days before Christmas in his *Times* review of *Artists and Models,* "Hal Wallis, this film's producer, will let Miss [Shirley] MacLaine and Jerry go it together, without Dean or anyone to get in their way." Yeah, Dean thought, maybe next time. Good fucking idea.

The movie magazines portrayed Dean as repentant and love-lorn. "I didn't make Jeannie part of my life," *Photoplay* had him say; "and I was wrong." *Motion Picture* produced a similar mea culpa: "It's my fault. But I'm going to win her back."

"At one point, after the picture, he did go back to his wife," Lori Nelson recalled. "We didn't see each other for about a week. We talked. Then he left her again, and we continued to see each other."

On January 24, Jeanne announced that she would seek a divorce. In early March, Dean returned again to Mountain Drive. "The Dean Martins," announced Earl Wilson in the *New York Post,* "are back together again." Wilson went on to say that "Dean and Jerry Lewis are also extremely harmonious now."

"And then, all of a sudden," recalled Lori Nelson, "it came out that she was pregnant. He said, 'What do you want me to do? I don't really want to go back.' And I said, 'Well, you really don't have much choice at this point. Obviously, you have to go back; she's going to have another baby.' So we saw each other a time or two after that. He was very, very depressed one night when we were together. And he said something like: 'It always seems like I'm just destined to never, ever get what I really, really want.' He was a very sweet, gentle, romantic man," and "a very remarkable man."

"Dean and I never slept together," she said. "I was very virginal in those days, which is kind of hard to believe for somebody in show business. To show you the kind of man he was, he respected that, and if that was the way I wanted it, he was not about to press me on that. It made me love him all the more."

When Dean returned to Jeanne in March of 1956, Nelson said, "he called me almost every day, and he was very depressed. He seemed to be very unhappy. But I guess he worked it out."

She saw him only once again in the years to come. "There was a golf tournament. I was one of the hostesses at the tournament, and I remember talking to him for a few minutes. He still seemed very unhappy, not the old happy-go-lucky Dean I had once known."

Dean and Jerry opened at the Sands in Las Vegas that March, but offstage the two men spoke only tersely and coldly. In April, they began work on another picture—their last.

Erna Lazarus had written a script called *Beginner's Luck*, the story of two strangers, a man and woman, who win a car with identical tickets at a theater lottery drawing. Hal Wallis had optioned it for a Shirley Booth picture. Now, as *Hollywood or Bust*, it had become a Martin-and-Lewis project instead. They had been filming *Pardners* when Wallis gave them Erna's screenplay.

"I read your script last night," Dean had said to her in the Paramount commissary one day.

"Yes."

"It's very good."

"Oh, I'm very glad, Dean."

"Of course, you know, it's no *Rose Tattoo*."

"Well, you're no Anna Magnani."

Since that first laugh together, the two of them had gotten along wonderfully. "I can't say the same for Jerry," she remembered. He was "a very, very strange, unpredictable man."

Lazarus was on the set of *Hollywood or Bust* a great deal be-

cause she was working for Wallis on a script called *Rodeo,* which
was to be Elvis Presley's next picture. As it turned out, *Rodeo* never
got made; instead, Wallis and Presley began their long association
with *Loving You.*

A day or so before production was to begin on *Hollywood or
Bust,* Lazarus had heard Jerry declaiming to one of the grips.

"This is nothing against you, or to do with you," he had said,
"but I intend to make it as difficult as possible for everybody connected with this picture."

Wallis swore Lazarus to secrecy. She was not to let anyone know
that this was the last Martin-and-Lewis picture, the end of Dean and
Jerry as people knew them.

Unwilling to confront Dean directly, Jerry turned his wrath toward others. When Slapsy Maxie Rosenbloom was given a small
part in the picture as a character named Bookie Benny, Jerry humil-
iated him on the set by mimicking a punch-drunk boxer. He yelled
orders to director Frank Tashlin, as if he himself were directing the
picture. His tantrums disrupted the shooting-schedule again and
again. Tashlin finally could take no more of him, and in May, he
halted production.

"I want you off the set," he told him.

Jerry looked at him and snorted. It had to be a joke.

"I mean it, Jerry. Off! You're a discourteous, obnoxious prick—
an embarrassment to me and a disgrace to the profession."

Jerry felt himself flush. "Hey, Tish, calm down." He was almost
stammering. "When did you get the right—"

"Jerry, as director of this picture, I order you to leave. Go. Get
your ass out of here and don't come back."

He went home sobbing. Later he begged Tashlin to let him
back. On May 18, a few nights after he went back to work, Jerry
served as the toastmaster at a Screen Actors Guild testimonial dinner for Jean Hersholt. Later that night, he experienced nausea and
chest pains. After taking an electrocardiogram, his doctor, Martin
Levy, rushed him to Mount Sinai Hospital. He was diagnosed as
suffering coronary strain from nervous exhaustion.

He hated Dean, but he was afraid of going on without him. That
fear, the ambivalent knot of his dependency, unnerved him. "I had

to break out of it," he said; "otherwise, I knew, it would eventually kill me."

Jerry likened it to a divorce: "The animosity was that of two people that loved one another very much, that split up, that did what they had to do. We did what we had to do and hated that we had to do it. See, I don't believe in the man and woman who say, 'Hey, we're great friends even though we're not married anymore.' Horseshit! That's horseshit. You know what that says to me? That says they didn't have love in the first place. See, if you love hard, you hate hard."

At the end of May, Jerry approached Dean. Melancholy had for a moment overwhelmed the anger and the manic anxiety and the depression. He wanted to say something, but he was not quite sure what it was. "You know, it's a hell of a thing," he began to say. "All I can think of is that what we do is not very important. Any two guys could have done it. But even the best of them wouldn't have had what made us what we were."

"Yeah? What's that?"

"I think it's love. I think it's how we still feel about each other."

Dean half-closed his eyes and said nothing. Then he looked dead-straight at Jerry:

"You can talk about love all you want. To me, you're nothing but a fucking dollar sign."

While at the Sands, Jerry had asked Don McGuire to write another screenplay for him and Dean. He would arrange this time for McGuire to direct, he said. McGuire had come up with a story, called *Damon and Pythias,* in which Jerry would play a lost kid and Dean would play the cop who takes him under his wing. As Jerry was McGuire's mealticket on the project, he had purposely underwritten Dean's part. Nevertheless, Jerry felt that McGuire had given Dean too much. It did not matter, for when Dean read the script, he came to Jerry in a rage.

"A fucking cop, hey?"

"That's right. A cop."

"I'm not playing a cop."

"Then we'll have to get somebody else."

"Start looking."

Hollywood or Bust wound toward its end. "We didn't talk. It was murder," Jerry said. "See, the beauty of what Dean and I had was pure truth, and that picture was pure fuckin' lie. To this day, I've never seen it. Never. Nor will I. It's just too painful."

On June 7, there was a birthday party for Dean at L'Escoffier. Jerry was not invited. Eight days later, *Pardners* was previewed at the Circle J Ranch in Newhall. Jerry showed up for the preview; Dean begged off with a bellyache.

The picture ended with the two of them singing the title song: *"You and me,"* they sang, *"we'll be the greatest pardners, buddies, and pals."* Then—"We're not ready for the end yet!" Jerry exclaimed—they shot apart the end titles.

"We have something to say to you, right, Dean?"

"We sure do, Jer. We want you folks to know we sure enjoyed workin' for you and we hope you enjoyed the picture."

"Yeah, and we hope you keep comin' to see us because we like seeing you."

"So long."

"Good-bye."

With a big cock on it.

In its advance review, *Variety* commented that, "As a team, Martin & Lewis come across strongly."

Jerry wanted to go ahead with the McGuire project; Dean had been asked to star opposite Doris Day in the Warner Brothers movie version of *The Pajama Game*. Jerry by now, through Y. Frank Freeman, had formally requested Paramount's permission to dissolve his partnership with Dean. Both he and Dean already had asked the same of Hal Wallis, and both of them had asked Herman Citron of MCA to renegotiate their deal with NBC as two separate deals. On Friday, June 16, the day after the *Pardners* preview, they were called to a meeting at Paramount. Freeman told them that Barney Balaban, the president of Paramount, was granting them the freedom they sought. Wallis was loath to do the same. A clause in his contract with them stipulated that they must work as a team in pictures regardless of who produced them. At Freeman's urging, Wallis relented, but only slightly. He would let them make one picture each apart. Aside from that, he insisted that they fulfill their contractual commitment to make three more pictures for him as a team. If they wanted to be released from that obligation, Wallis said, they would have to pay him $1,500,000 plus ten percent of their income from the last two pictures.

NBC proved to be a problem as well. The network maintained that its deal with York was for Martin and Lewis as a team. Only after York filed a breach-of-contract suit against NBC would the network yield. A revised five-year, $5,000,000 contract between York and NBC would call for thirty-four one-hour programs to be produced by York for the network through August 31, 1961, half of the programs to feature Martin, half to feature Lewis. In time, Dean would sell out his one-third interest in York and renegotiate his own NBC deal. And, in time, Wallis would accede: They would be permitted to meet their responsibilities to him individually. On June 18, both Dean and Jerry publicly confirmed that they were breaking up. *Hollywood or Bust* finished filming the next day.

Hate, fear, guilt. "Scared to death: What am I gonna do by myself?" Jerry said. "Worse than that: What will the public think? Remember, we took something away from the public that they loved. They grew up with Dean and Jerry. And the public is a strange duck. They'll turn on you."

They made one final trip east, flying separately, the following weekend. *Pardners* was premiering in Atlantic City, and they played ten nights there at Skinny D'Amato's 500 Club; they owed him that much. At the end of the month, they did a twenty-one-hour muscular-dystrophy telethon, broadcast by WABD from Carnegie Hall: their last television appearance as a team. On Friday, July 13, they opened at the Copacabana for their farewell engagement. They gave their last show on the hot Tuesday night of July 24, ten years to the week after their first show together at Skinny's joint.

"I hit the stage and glanced at Dean. His face was a mask," Jerry remembered. "He would play it cool even if it killed him." They finished with the closing crescendo from "Pardners": *"You and me, we'll be the greatest pardners, buddies, and pals!"* Dean threw his arm around him, pulled him toward him, hugged him. The joint was in an uproar. It was the biggest night in the club's history.

There was no encore. Dean took one aisle away from the stage, Jerry took the other.

Later, in bed in the early-morning hours in his room above the Copa, Jerry had the hotel operator put him through to Dean's suite. He had taken some tranquilizers; all he could think of was that handful of minutes, ten summers ago, just before dawn, when they had lingered at the Boardwalk, letting the sound of the waves and the gulls wash away the noise of the club that lingered in their ears, watching the breakers' froth turn pale shimmering gold in the first hint of light. He could smell it, hear it, see it. Dean, in his bed, smelled and heard and saw differently. Her name was—well, it was whatever it was.

"Hello, pallie," he said when he heard Jerry's voice. "How're you holdin' up?"

"I don't know. We had some good times, didn't we?"

"There'll be more."

"Yeah, well, take care of yourself."

"You too, pal."

And that was that. It was over.

XII.

*W*ORKS

AND DAYS

*A*merica entered into a new age. What Martin and Lewis were to the first lustrum of the 1950s Elvis Presley was to the latter. *"Man, she's the rockin'-'n'-rollin' best,"* Dean sang of a scantily-clad Pueblo dancer in *Hollywood or Bust.* The juxtaposition had been poetical: Presley's new picture being concocted on the sidelines of Martin and Lewis's last. Wallis had even inserted a reference to the Presley picture into the Martin-and-Lewis script. The age of white-man rock 'n' roll had come.

Jerry was right: The public was a strange duck. *Hollywood or Bust,* which opened for Christmas at the Loew's State, was their least successful picture of the decade. The public resented their breakup: the shattering of illusion, the truth. Illusion-deprivation, as always, took its toll at the box office. But there was more to it than that. The American spirit, in its continuing will to escape, had entered a further incarnation: one that pretended to a greater orgiastic expressiveness. The land of whiter whites belonged to Elvis, whose first picture, *Love Me Tender,* had opened at the Paramount in November, playing concurrently with, and just blocks away from, Martin and Lewis's last. Of course, the machinery was the same. As with Martin and Lewis, it was the big-business dreamworks that delivered America to Elvis in 1956: CBS with the Dorsey Brothers' "Stage Show" and "The Ed Sullivan Show," NBC with "The Milton Berle Show," RCA-Victor with "Heartbreak Hotel," Twentieth-Century Fox with *Love Me Tender.* Paramount had brought forth *At War with the Army* in 1950; in 1960, it would bring forth Presley's *G.I. Blues,* produced by Hal Wallis and directed by Norman Taurog. The more things changed, the more they stayed the same. From Zukor's Crystal Hall to the great Paramount temple, from "Love Is Mine" to "That's Amore" to "Love Me Tender," the nickel-in-the-slot wonderment of electric sound and moving pictures remained the philter of America's soul. Seventy years earlier, Henry James had foreseen a coming "reign of mediocrity." From another century, Jolson had answered him: "You ain't heard nothin' yet."

With Elvis, the paradigm of hep shifted. He bought his britches from Sy Devore, just like Dean, just like Sinatra. But he wore those britches differently. Dean and Sinatra, each along enough in years to be his father, now were the old guard. Of course, it meant something that Dean was Elvis's idol. There was a continuum there. But Elvis, twenty-one in 1956, was the voice of youth, the Dionysus of spring, the incendiary fire to their laid-back *vecchia guardia* candlelight.

Don McGuire's screenplay, which had precipitated Dean and Jerry's final breakup, went into production, with McGuire directing, on September 6. It was now called *The Delicate Delinquent*. Jerry, as the film's producer, had gotten Darren McGavin to play the cop role that had so angered Dean. Also in the picture was Hal Wallis's new wife, Martha Hyer. In July, Dean had turned down the proposed part in *The Pajama Game*—it went to stage singer John Raitt, whose first and last picture it would be—and had signed instead to star in an MGM production called *Ten Thousand Bedrooms*. Joe Pasternak, who had screen-tested and rejected Dean in 1946 and tried to sign him in 1948, was the film's producer. "We'll get the go-ahead signal after they've chosen a leading lady. It's sort of a satire on the Conrad Hilton hotel chain," Dean had told columnist Hy Gardner on the day of the final Copacabana show. "I may sing one or two songs in it, but it's definitely not a musical." Gardner had wanted to know if it was true that Dean had been told to stay out of Chicago because "the mob boys in the Windy City have vowed to get nasty" to avenge their disappointment at the breakup. Dean had shrugged: "Ridiculous." Where did they find these guys?

On September 11, five days after *The Delicate Delinquent* began production at Paramount, *Ten Thousand Bedrooms* started filming in Rome. Dean brought Jeannie with him to Italy. She was six months pregnant, and she loved it.

Young Anna Maria Alberghetti, who had been chosen to star

opposite Dean, recalled the production as an easy one. She would remember Dean as most of those who acted with him in the years to come would also remember him: as a consummate professional, who knew not only all his own lines and cues but everyone else's as well, who at the same time overwhelmed the set with an air of artless, natural relaxation that turned work to pleasance. "Dean was a lovely man," she said. "Just a really nice guy." (In August, the *New York Enquirer* had asked Dean to write his own obituary. "He was a nice guy," he said, would be just fine.) If he was at all apprehensive of venturing into his first picture without Lewis, "you would have never picked it up," said Alberghetti.

The film's director, Richard Thorpe, who was then sixty, had been working with Pasternak since *Two Girls and a Sailor* in 1944. The last musicals they had done together—and the four songs written by Sammy Cahn and Nicholas Brodszky for *Ten Thousand Bedrooms* qualified it as a musical, regardless of Dean's impression going into it—were in 1954: *The Student Prince* with Mario Lanza and *Athena* with Vic Damone. Thorpe too found Dean a pleasure to work with. "He was great," Thorpe would say. "We had no problems whatever."

Thorpe, who had gone from Mario Lanza to Dean Martin, would move on in his next picture to Elvis Presley. Was there any difference between directing Dean and Elvis, any difference between *Ten Thousand Bedrooms* and *Jailhouse Rock?*

"Jesus," he would say. "It's all work. It's just all work."

Dean's final child, a fourth daughter, was born at St. John's Hospital at twenty-six minutes past one on the morning of December 20, 1956. They gave her an Italianate rendering of Jeannie's name: Gina Carolyn Martin. That Christmas, Dean heard something he had never thought he would live to hear.

In early August, after the breakup, Jerry had filled in for Judy Garland at the Frontier in Las Vegas. He had gone over well and had closed the show with Garland's own finale, "Rock-a-Bye Your Baby with a Dixie Melody." By then, he was no longer under contract to Capitol; and it was he himself who had paid later that month when he went into the Capitol studio to record a semi-straight,

semi-freakish version of that song and three others. He had subsequently offered the recordings to Capitol, but the company had
passed. Decca, however, had taken them and released "Rock-a-Bye
Your Baby with a Dixie Melody" in November. Now it was a Top
Twenty hit. Dean himself had not had a hit since last spring—
"Watching the World Go By"—and it had barely made it to number
eighty-three. It was worse than that. Dean had never had a hit
album. *Jerry Lewis Just Sings* burst onto the LP charts the week
Gina was born, and in the weeks to come it would hit number three.
Was there a God, was there a St. Anthony in heaven?

On January 22, 1957, the new issue of *Look* magazine carried a
story by Jerry Lewis. It was called "I've Always Been Scared," but
there did not seem to be much fear in it:

"As early as 1949, things began to be different. Dean divorced
Betty and married his second wife, Jeanne, and suddenly our families weren't friendly any more. As time went on, I grew to believe
that Dean wasn't the strong, self-reliant character I thought he was,
but, if anything, felt even more insecure than I. We both discovered
that we were completely different in temperament and in our out-
look. I don't blame Dean for his thinking—it probably developed
out of his tough childhood—but he never was as warm and outgoing
as I hoped he'd be."

That Jerry should shoot off his mouth like this in public, in the
guise of humble honesty, was something that Dean found offensive.
But what really infuriated Dean was his dragging Jeannie into it.

"Jerry was jealous of Jeanne," Dean told the press. "He was
happy when Jeanne and I split up." The *Look* story had gone too far,
he said. "I respect other wives. I could talk about Patti and Jerry
knows it, but I wouldn't."

The next day, eight-year-old Deana Martin, a student at Rose-
wood Elementary School, was hurt when the school bus she was
riding in was swept broadside by a truck at the intersection of
Harper and Melrose. Her mother, Dean's ex-wife, Betty, by now had
become a somewhat notorious figure. "Today, she's one of the hardest drinkers in all Los Angeles," *Confidential* magazine had scan-
dalized the previous autumn. The home at 12812 Sunset Boulevard
where she lived with her four children was a place of drunken

partying. The police had been to the house on several occasions, once to arrest a man for violation of parole on a statutory-rape charge. "The kids?" *Confidential* had pontificated in its "memo" to Dean. "Well, they could tell you plenty about what goes on there. They could tell you about living on a pot of spaghetti for as long as a week at a time, while Betty tosses champagne binges for her hoodlum friends on the $3,500 a month you give her."

On January 28, Dean began work on a new album, *Pretty Baby*. That night, via a remote switch to a party he was attending at the Beverly Hilton Hotel, he appeared on Jack Lescoulie's new NBC-TV show, "Tonight! America After Dark." Drunk, he seized the opportunity to spit some venom Jerry's way. Asked if it was true that he had objected to Jerry's desire to inject "pathos and heart" into their work, Dean said he would not have objected "if he knew how to do it." The *Look* story, he said, was "full of lies." Columnist Dorothy Kilgallen commented that Dean's late-night words "hit the bad taste gong with quite a noise," while metaphor-skewing Barry Gray predicted, "Dean Martin will live to rue the day he took the 'curves' pitched by a Hollywood television interrogator, and worked his ex-partner Jerry Lewis over the coals with a hot baseball bat."

Jeannie's voice was also heard: "Jerry's been on an 'I-hate-Jeanne' kick for eight years. I can fight a woman being jealous, but I can't fight the jealousy of a man. Jerry's resentment would have been directed against anyone taking Dean's affection. It's not me— it's any third party.

"I wasn't happy about the split," she said. "They were like magic together, especially in nightclubs. It was awe-inspiring, and just seemed it was meant to be. This is not all Jerry's fault. Dean is older, and he had to prove to himself that it wasn't Jerry carrying him."

She did not know what the future held. "Now that Jerry's too fat and old to play the kid, I don't know what he'll do. I'm not rooting for Jerry's failure. I'm rooting for Dean's success."

Dean and Jerry's years at the height of their fame were "the five loneliest years I've ever known," she said. "Now I've got a husband."

The public acrimony between Dean and Jerry dissipated that

spring. Dean got the last licks. "I'm getting a little tired of being the heavy in this thing," he told Dan Jenkins from *TV Guide*. He had gotten sick of Jerry and "this pathos stuff"; that was all there was to it. "I get the reports. Jerry has stripped his house of every picture of me, all my records he used to have on the wall. Now isn't that pretty silly? I've got pictures of him all over this house. My kids have got Jerry's clown pictures in their rooms. Why shouldn't they?" The scandal magazines tried to keep the dust from settling. *Rave* explored Dean and Jerry's "deep latent homosexual attachment"; *Uncensored* condemned Dean as a philanderer and praised Jerry as a faithful husband. *On the QT* hinted that Patti Lewis had been Dean's lover before Jerry met her.

Ten Thousand Bedrooms was previewed at the RKO Pantages Theatre in Los Angeles on February 13. It premiered at the Loew's State in New York seven weeks later, on April 3. The picture almost killed Dean's acting career in one fell swoop. *Variety* was kind: Dean's first solo performance proved that he was "an affable leading man" who had "an easy way with a song." So was *The New Yorker*. The picture, its reviewer said, "does have the negative virtue of presenting him without Jerry Lewis." The picture was a stiff. *The Delicate Delinquent*, which had been finished before *Ten Thousand Bedrooms* but held up until now for release, fared far better.

On March 6, between the preview and the premiere of *Ten Thousand Bedrooms*, Dean had opened, for $25,000 a week, as a single at the Copa Room of the Sands. Long, loose shows had become the trend in Vegas. Dean was on and off in thirty-eight minutes, ending with "Memories Are Made of This" and leaving the crowd hungry and howling for more while he went out to deal blackjack in the casino. Later that night, Jack Entratter had presented him with a five-year deal.

After the farewell engagement at the Copacabana last July, Dean and Dick Stabile had gone their separate ways. Dean had begun recording with the Gus Levene Orchestra. At the Sands, he had used Antonio Morelli's seventeen-piece house orchestra, with the addition of pianist Hal Borne. Dean, however, had already taken steps toward hiring a new bandleader in February, when he had instructed his business manager, Eddie Traubner, to call Ken Lane.

Lane had started out as a vaudeville pianist. He had worked with Frances Langford, the original Betty Boop, and others. After a stretch in the army, he had been hired as Frank Sinatra's musical conductor. Dean knew him not only through Sinatra but through Paramount, where Lane served as a vocal coach for Martin and Lewis and others. Lane would begin working with Dean this spring; and the two would continue to work together until the end.

"If audience reaction is any criterion," *Variety* had said in its review of the Sands opening, "Martin will be around long and strong as a single cafe entertainer and headliner." He would always be able to sing for his dinner, there was no doubt of that. Twenty-five grand a week was nothing to sneer at. The average American per-capita income was still under two grand a year. And he had his NBC deal in the works as well. Still, *Ten Thousand Bedrooms* was a blow. There was no room, he knew, for "an affable leading man" who had "an easy way with a song." They had Elvis for that. If he was going to make it alone in the pictures, it would have to be as an actor. He could act, all right. What was an actor but a pretender, a con man? He had been conning the skin from snakes all his life. But in the wake of *Ten Thousand Bedrooms,* there were no serious takers.

There had been Hollywood interest in Irwin Shaw's novel *The Young Lions* almost immediately after its publication in the fall of 1948. The interest, however, had remained undeveloped over the years. Now film-industry pioneer Al Lichtman was finally about to put *The Young Lions* into production for Twentieth Century-Fox. A budget of $4,000,000 had been set; Edward Dmytryk would direct. Marlon Brando had been cast as the morally ambivalent German officer Christian Diestl. Montgomery Clift signed in April as the Jewish-American soldier Noah Ackerman. The part of the third male lead, that of Michael Whiteacre, a raffish would-be draft dodger caught up in the actualities of war, was set to be played by Tony Randall.

The start of production was only weeks away when Herman Citron of MCA approached Dmytryk with a plea to consider Dean for Tony Randall's role. Dean, he said, could do what Sinatra had done opposite Clift in *From Here to Eternity.* Dmytryk then mentioned Dean to Montgomery Clift, who knew of him only as Jerry Lewis's partner in schlock.

"Good God, no!" Clift exclaimed.

That night, in New York, Clift, who knew less of Tony Randall than he did of Dean, went to see Randall in a picture called *Oh, Men! Oh, Women!* The next morning, he called Dmytryk:

"If it's still all right, I'll go with Dean Martin."

The way the story circulated, MCA, which represented both Brando and Clift as well as Dean, had bullied Buddy Adler, the boss of Twentieth Century-Fox, into taking Dean or losing the two stars. This version found its way to print in *The Hollywood Reporter,* and was later repeated in a *Fortune* article on MCA's power in the industry, as well as in a *Confidential* exposé. By then, Buddy Adler was dead; but at a subsequent antitrust hearing involving MCA, Dmytryk testified that his own account of the matter was truthful, and that the rumors of blackmail had been propagated by Tony Randall's agent. And, as it turned out, Tony Randall's agent was Abby Greshler.

Dean accepted $20,000 to star in *The Young Lions:* less than he made in a week at the Sands, less than he had been paid to appear in *My Friend Irma,* his first, trifling picture, back in 1949. It was the biggest crapshoot of his career.

Meanwhile, Martin Tannenbaum and Arthur Konvitz, who five years ago had organized the first Martin-and-Lewis telethon, for the New York Cardiac Hospital, had recruited Dean for their new fundraising project. The City of Hope, begun in 1913 as a tuberculosis sanatorium in Duarte, California, had become a national free-care medical center in 1946, and in 1956 had entered into a new era of far-reaching scientific research. Now the City of Hope was seeking funds to establish the first free-care hospital and research center devoted exclusively to cancer and related blood disorders. Dean's nineteen-and-a-half-hour "Parade of Stars" telethon, broadcast by WABD from the Belasco Theatre in New York on the last weekend in May, raised $804,000 toward its founding. Dean's assortment of guests was an intriguing one: Captain Video and Tammany Hall boss Carmine DeSapio; Sammy Davis, Jr., and Ethel Waters; Ed-

ward G. Robinson and Perry Como; Floyd Patterson and Jackie
Gleason; a rock-'n'-roll contingent that took over early Sunday
morning under disc-jockey Murray Kaufman. Columnist Dorothy
Kilgallen described the telethon as "a mélange of third-rate acts,
bad taste and bad grammar that got worse as it went along" and
wondered, "Is leukemia an excuse for vulgarity?"

Ten days later, Dean opened, with Ken Lane conducting, at the
Twin Coaches in Pittsburgh. It was a disarming feeling: the dice in
the air, alone again, back in the Ohio Valley under the pall of the
mills. Mindy Costanzo, Ross Monaco, Mike Simera, and others from
the old days drove across the river to see him. Simera left wearing
Dean's fancy sport jacket. Hell, Dean still owed him a yard from the
old days; the jacket evened the score. Leo D'Anniballe remembered
Dean talking with anticipation to them of his upcoming role in *The
Young Lions.* Leo was impressed by something that happened at the
Twin Coaches. "Someone in the audience made a crack about Jerry
Lewis, and Dean said something to the effect that, 'Sir, I want you to
know that even though we've broken up, I have the greatest respect
for Jerry.'" It was not only a show of class; it won him the audience
in an instant. Leo's brother, Joe, remembered, "A lot of us around
here thought Jerry Lewis would do better than him at that point.
Because, well, he was Jewish, and they had the tie on entertainment
and all that. So I thought maybe he might be hurtin'. But one of the
fellows around town, he's an attorney now, he said, 'Oh, no, don't
sell him wrong, because he's got the looks.'"

Dean put on a more leisurely show than he had at the Sands.
"Martin," *Variety* said, "has everything it takes—looks, personality,
poise, charm, friendliness, ease and, of course, a voice. The relaxed
manner isn't pushed; on him it looks perfectly natural and is becoming. There's a feeling that he's up there for only one thing, to
entertain, and that he does, in spades, without any monkey business, pretense or side show. The impact's there," *Variety* concluded.
"Martin has it made."

Dean himself was not so sure of that as he prepared to leave for
France a month later to begin location work for *The Young Lions.*
Sammy Cahn had dinner with him at La Scala in Beverly Hills the

night before he left. Cahn had never known Dean to reveal himself as he did that night.

"I'm so scared," Dean told him. "I'm so scared."

He opened his shirt and showed Sammy his chest, which was broken out in a rash from nerves.

"Dean, please listen to me," Cahn said. "I beg you to listen to me. Do you know what Marlon Brando and Montgomery Clift would give to be able to do what you do? Walk out on a stage and charm an audience out of their skin? Dean, you're a champ. You're a rare, rare champ. These fellas have to do what a director tells them to do. You are in charge."

Dean, Brando, and Clift were quartered at the Hotel Raphael for the weeks of filming in and around Paris. There would be filming in Germany as well.

Dean's only scene with Brando came at the close of the picture when, walking with Clift toward a concentration camp in Germany, Martin encounters Brando and guns him down. It was a nice change: "All I ever killed in my other movies was time," he said. Brando himself, whose presence consumed much of the picture, was something of a problem to Dmytryk. Truman Capote had gotten him drunk on the set of his last picture for a *New Yorker* profile that had so upset him that he had quit drinking. But he was taking amphetamines and Seconals like candy to rise and cool out, and he often required from forty to sixty takes before finishing a scene. When Brando, who Clift felt was "using about one-tenth his talent," wanted to overdo his death scene, falling with arms outstretched like Christ on the cross, Clift threatened to walk off the job. Aside from that, the three stars got along well. Brando and Dean joked about how Samuel Goldwyn had suggested Dean for the part of Sky Masterson in the 1955 film version of *Guys and Dolls;* about how Joseph L. Mankiewicz had scoffed at the idea and given the singing role to Brando instead. And Dean was with Brando the morning he burned his balls. They were talking together at the bar of the Hotel George V, and Brando was making himself a cup of tea when Liliane Montevecchi, one of the female leads in the picture, brushed past, upsetting his arm. The scalding water poured into his lap and blistered his penis so badly that he had to be hospitalized.

Montgomery Clift adored Dean. Dean nicknamed him Spider; took care of Clift when Clift was too drunk or doped-up to take care of himself. "I would put him to bed, 'cause he was always on pills," Dean would recall. And Clift, whom Brando regarded with a touch of awe, coached Dean through their most dramatic scenes together. To both Clift and Brando, Dean seemed a natural.

While Dean was in Paris, an interviewer from *Melody Maker* in England reached him by telephone. "The Dean can't abide the tortured outpourings of today's best-sellers," the interviewer later wrote. "He named no names, but vehemently classified the whole school of rock-'n'-roll singing as 'disgusting.'

" 'Thank heaven it is on the way out,' he said with the urgent sincerity of a man who likes a good ballad sung as it should be sung."

Back home in August, he told reporters that he had not cared for France. "I despised every minute of it," he said. "The French don't like us and I don't like them. I liked Italy and Germany and England and I don't mind going back to those countries to work." But Paris had been so dull that "I'll never go to France for any reason without taking my wife." What about the food? "Barney's Beanery in Los Angeles has better food. The French make a big fuss over their food, but you can't eat fuss." Had he visited the Louvre? "I had a guy once who did my house in two days, was a better painter than those guys."

Perhaps Dean's aversion to France was instinctive. In just a few years' time, after Jerry Lewis began his directing career with *The Bellboy*, France would embrace the new *auteur du yock* as an American genius. His *Ladies' Man* would be analyzed by *Cahiers du Cinema* as "*un authentique chef-d'oeuvre burlesco-surréaliste.*" There would be much intellectual discussion of *le cas Lewis*, of "*une profondeur du rire.*"

When Dean arrived home in August, he was served with a subpoena to testify for the defense in the state of California's case against *Confidential* magazine. If Dean would affirm the truthfulness of the magazine's story about Betty, it would help to establish a standard of integrity in the face of libel charges that had been brought by a number of subjects of unflattering articles, including

Maureen O'Hara, Robert Mitchum, and Mae West. Dean never appeared to testify, and the suits were settled in a court agreement that effectively put *Confidential* out of the movie-gossip business.

At ten o'clock Saturday night, October 5, NBC broadcast "The Dean Martin Show," the first of Dean's one-hour color specials, produced and written by Cy Howard, sponsored by Prestone. His guests were fellow Capitol artists Louis Prima and Keely Smith, and James Mason and his family. He had tried to get Elvis, but Colonel Parker, Presley's manager, had wanted $75,000. Dean and Prima sang "Oh, Marie" together. In commenting on "Mr. Martin's leisurely and unhurried manner," the *New York Times* no longer compared Dean to Crosby: "Mr. Martin's singing style is very much his own." The *Daily News* called him "a creamy singer of pleasant sounds." Dean did more television work for NBC early the following month: "The Perry Como Show," "The Giselle MacKenzie Show," and "Club Oasis," a half-hour biweekly Saturday-night show that sponsor Liggett & Myers had named for its new Oasis cigarette brand.

On November 18, three days after having an infected cyst removed from his hip at Cedars of Lebanon Hospital, Dean filed for custody of his four children by Betty.

She had lost the house. Despite the $325,000 Dean had paid her in alimony and child support, she had no home, no bank account, no belongings; she was in hock to one Dante J. Dente, the owner of Dente's Carmel Market, for booze, food, and cash. Claudia, Gail, and Deana had been delivered to Dean's Mountain Drive door by Betty's sister, Ann Berry, on November 4, the eve of the first NBC show. Betty had been back and forth to fetch and return them sporadically since then. Fifteen-year-old Craig was living in a one-room guest house behind the home of Betty's friend Louis Graves on Hortense Street in Van Nuys. It was as much Jeannie's idea to file for custody as it was Dean's.

In her affidavit, she stated: "I live with my husband at 601 Mountain Drive, Beverly Hills, California. The home is large, containing four bedrooms and a large dressing room upstairs, a den-

Steubenville Boy Scout Troop Ten, 1930. Drum-bearing Dino Crocetti stands in the front row, above Scoutmaster Agon DeLuca, seated. Troop committee elder Dr. V. B. DiLoretto, the physician who delivered Dino thirteen years before, stands in the second row, flanked by Dino's cousin Archie Crocetti. Standing behind Archie is Dino's brother, William; behind William is cousin Robert Crocetti. (COURTESY OF THE *STEUBENVILLE HERALD-STAR*.)

California-bound, with Joe DiNovo, 1936.
(COURTESY OF MIKE DINOVO.)

At age seventeen. (COURTESY OF JEANNE MARTIN.)

*W*ith Sammy Watkins, Cleveland, 1942
(COURTESY OF THE *CLEVELAND PLAIN DEALER*

*H*epcats out West, 1936. Dino, with leg cocked, shows that the hat makes the man. (COURTESY OF MIKE DINOVO.)

*A*t the Havana-Madrid, New York, 1946. Standing, from left: Dean; comedian Alan King; bandleader Pupi Campo. Seated, from left: Jerry Lewis; Dean's manager Lou Perry; former boxer and nightclub frontman Abe Atell; unknown; entertainer Pat Rooney; Leon Enkin of Leon & Eddie's; singer Sonny King. (COURTESY OF FRANK MILITARY.)

Skinny D'Amato and his bride.
(*ATLANTIC CITY PRESS.*)

*A*tlantic City, August 1946.

*T*he organ-grinder
and the monkey.

*D*ean and Betty, 1948.
(*PICTORIAL PARADE.*)

*M*ickey Cohen, August 1948, the month Martin and Lewis came to Hollywood. (*PICTORIAL PARADE.*)

*J*ohnny Rosselli, 1950.
(A. P./WIDE WORLD PHOTOS.)

Golden boy.

*J*eanne Biegger, Dean's future wife, at twenty-one. She gave a copy of this modeling-agency picture to Dean after meeting him in Miami in December 1948. (COURTESY OF JEANNE MARTIN.)

*A*t the Hotel Flamingo, Las Vegas, March 1950, during the filming of *My Friend Irma Goes West*. Left to right: John Lund, Marie Wilson, Dean Martin, Diana Lynn, Jerry Lewis, Corinne Calvet. (COURTESY OF JERRY LEWIS.)

*W*ith Hal Wallis, 1950.
(COURTESY OF JERRY LEWIS.)

*C*harlie Fischetti, not long before his death,
in 1951. (A.P./WIDE WORLD PHOTOS.)

Sam Giancana, 1949.
(COURTESY OF SAMUEL M. GIANCANA.)

The first muscular-dystrophy telethon, with Dick Stabile, November 1953.
(COURTESY OF JERRY LEWIS.)

*W*ith Marilyn Monroe, Milton Berle, and Averell Harriman, c. 1954.
(COURTESY OF JEANNE MARTIN.)

*S*tanding, from left: Tony Curtis and Janet Leigh; Dean Martin; Marie ("the Body") McDonald.
Seated, from left: Jerry and Patti Lewis; Jeanne Martin. (COURTESY OF JEANNE MARTIN.)

*W*ith Sammy Cahn, on the set of *Pardners*, 1955. (COURTESY OF SAMMY CAHN.)

*A*t the Twin Coaches, Pittsburgh, June 1957, with Mindy Costanzo (standing, left) and others from the old days across the river. (COURTESY OF GINA SIMERA PESTIAN.)

*W*ith Marlon Brando and Montgomery Clift, during the filming of *The Young Lions*, summer 1957. (COURTESY OF JEANNE MARTIN.)

*T*he Martins at home, summer 1958.
Left to right: Craig, 16; Deana, 9;
Barbara Gail, 13; Dino Jr., 6; Ricci, 4;
Claudia, 14; Jeannie, with Gina, 1;
Dean. (COURTESY OF JEANNE MARTIN.)

*Y*awning in the studio, with Sinatra
conducting, October 1958.
(COURTESY OF JEANNE MARTIN.)

*J*ohnny Formosa: "Let's show 'em. Let's show those asshole Hollywood fruitcakes."

*T*he Rat Pack, 1960.

*W*ith Mack "Killer" Gray. (GLOBE PHOTOS.)

Standing, from left: Tony Curtis; Eddie Fisher;
Sammy Cahn; Dean Martin; Frank Sinatra;
Martin Tannenbaum. Seated: Mack Gray.

*W*ith Sinatra, 1963.

"*T*he answer, my friend, is blowin' in the wind."
The protest movement comes to Vegas, where they
too had a dream. (COURTESY OF JEANNE MARTIN.)

*C*elebrating his parents' fiftieth wedding anniversary, October 1964. Left to right: Craig; Jeannie; Ricci; Claudia; Deana; Gina; Angela and Guy Crocetti; Gail; Dino; and Dino Jr.
(A.P./WIDE WORLD PHOTOS.)

*B*obby Kennedy, Dean, Jeannie, and, with her back to the camera, Billy Wilder's wife, Audrey, address the issues of the day in their respective ways.
(COURTESY OF JEANNE MARTIN.)

*M*aking hits.

Sneaking a drink in the summer of love, August 1967, American Collegiate Golf Dinner. To the right: Francis Cardinal Spellman, Jeannie Martin, Bobby Kennedy's empty seat. (RON GALELLA, LTD.)

"*T*he Dean Martin Show":
"I always plays to de common folk."

*W*ith Gail Renshaw: Pebble Beach Golf Course, January 1970. (RON GALELLA, LTD.)

*D*ino, Jr. and Dino,
March 1970.
(RON GALELLA, LTD.)

*A*pril 1973. (GLOBE PHOTOS.)

*E*ndless love, take sixty-two: February 1979,
with Joni Anderson. (RON GALELLA, LTD.)

*S*ummer 1983.

*T*wilight of the gods: New York, September 1983. (RON GALELLA, LTD.)

bedroom-living room combination downstairs, as well as a large living room, dining room, breakfast room, den and kitchen. The house also has spacious grounds. My husband and I employ a full time Governess to assist me in caring for our three children.

"I am willing to and desire to have the four children of my husband's prior marriage to Elizabeth Martin reside with us. I wish to accept them into our home and treat them as if they were my own children."

When Dean returned to the Sands for Thanksgiving, he took the kids with him. On December 11, Judge Allen T. Lynch awarded him the custody he sought.

Dean had not had a Top Ten hit since "Memories Are Made of This." Capitol had tried to sell him to the rock-'n'-roll market, advertising his December 1956 single "Just Kiss Me" as "FOR TEEN-AGERS ONLY." The song, written by Jesse Stone, the author of "Shake, Rattle and Roll" and other classic rhythm-and-blues hits, was a good one; but Dean's recording of it left much to be desired. Such attempts to cash in on rock 'n' roll were by now quite routine. In January 1955, before landing Elvis, RCA-Victor had issued a cover version of Gene and Eunice's "Ko Ko Mo" with the exhortation: "DIG PERRY IN ACTION ON A GREAT 'ROCK-AND-ROLL' RECORD." As for Columbia's Tony Bennett: "HE SWINGS!! HE ROCKS!! HE GOES!!" On January 23, 1958, Dean recorded a song called "Return to Me." It had been written recently, in Italian and English—its copyright bore the parenthetical Italian title of "Ritorna a Me"—by Carmen Lombardo and Danny Di Minno. Carmen, who was Guy Lombardo's brother, had cowritten the 1948 hit "Powder Your Face with Sunshine (Smile! Smile! Smile!)." Released in late February, while Dean was performing at the Americana in Miami Beach, "Return to Me" appeared on the pop charts at the end of March. It would remain on the charts for more than five months, reaching number four.

"If there's still any doubt that Dean Martin can make it as a single, cast the doubt aside," said *Billboard* in its review of his Miami Beach opening. Now, on April 2, the week that "Return to

Me" appeared on the charts, *The Young Lions* opened at the newly refurbished Paramount Theatre in New York. For Dean, it was a golden spring.

His performance in *The Young Lions* had already drawn attention from *Variety* after a preview in mid-March. "It's inevitable," that bellwether review had said, "that his performance as the happy-go-lucky, dame-chasing Broadway character will be likened with what 'From Here to Eternity' did for Sinatra." The movie itself, *Variety* had declared, was "a blockbuster" and "easily one of the standout pictures of the year and one destined to remain a highlight in the annals." As it turned out, *The Young Lions* became one of the most acclaimed hits of the decade. In the end, it made barely more money at the box office than *Sailor Beware*. But it brought Dean what money could not buy: respect and credibility as an actor.

Dean, it seemed, was everywhere during those early months of 1958: nine television appearances alone from January through May. He did his second "Dean Martin Show" for NBC on the first of February, with a new producer-director, Jack Donohue, a new writer, Martin-and-Lewis screenplay author Herb Baker, and a new sponsor, Liggett & Myers. Frank Sinatra was his guest star; together they took a shot at "Jailhouse Rock." In April, with "Return to Me" in the air and *The Young Lions* in the theaters, he played the Cocoanut Grove. "It might be cheaper," *Billboard* remarked, "to give singer Dean Martin a piece of the business, because the next time he works at the Cocoanut Grove, it's a cinch his asking price will soar astronomically. Such was the devastating effect of the Italian street singer on the opening night, ropes-up showbiz audience at the Grove." *Billboard* reported with a straight turn of phrase what Dean told the audience: that his latest album was called *Ballads for B-Girls*. In early June, he opened in Lake Tahoe; two weeks after that, he returned to the Sands. Back in Los Angeles, on July 14, he recorded a song that had swept from Italy to America a few weeks before. The song, copyrighted in Milan in January as a *"fox moderato"* by a young Apulian named Domenico Modugno, was called "Nel Blu Dipinto di Blu," the title under which Modugno's original recording was released in America by Decca. It translated as "Blue Painted on Blue." Dean took another word from the lyrics, the Italian infinitive for "to fly," as the title of his version: "Volare." Both Modugno's original and Dean's "Volare" appeared on the American charts in the second week of August. Amid a slew of other cover versions—Jesse Belvin, Alan Dale, Rosa Linda, Umberto Macato, the McGuire Sisters, Katina Ranieri with the Riz Ortolani Orchestra, and Nelson Riddle were among those who recorded the song—Modugno's and Dean's broke into the Top Twenty, Modugno's record became a number-one hit; Dean's reached number fifteen and remained on the charts through November.

It was more than a golden spring. It was the beginning for Dean of a golden decade. He had done what no one before him had been able to do: prevail simultaneously as a star of stage, movies, television, and records. Sinatra came close, but television was Sinatra's curse. Dean was now in a class by himself.

He even had his own joint now. There had been a restaurant and bar at 8524 Sunset Boulevard called the Alpine Lodge. In the summer of "Volare," Dean and a partner, Maury Samuels, bought a fifty-percent interest in the Alpine from its owners, Harvey Gerry and Paul and Alex Wexler. The Alpine became Dino's Lodge. When "77 Sunset Strip," the ABC series that defined West Coast made-for-TV hip in the late fifties, premiered in the fall of 1958, Dino's became a national symbol through its appearance in the show's weekly opening credits; one of the show's characters, Kookie, was even supposed to be a parking-lot attendant there. Though Dean himself rarely appeared at the joint, his association with it made it a mecca for huddled masses of would-be hipsters yearning to bask in the aura of the great pizza pie that transcended all knowing. In August 1959, retaining a thirty-two-and-a-half-percent piece of the operation, Dean would strike a new agreement with his partners. His brother, Bill, was to become the general manager of the joint, and Dean himself was to receive an additional $1,000 a month for the continued use of his name and likeness.

That fall of 1958, he also sold his name and likeness to Liebmann Breweries in New York: " 'You may need good luck on the links,' says the famous crooner, 'but not at the nineteenth hole. You always score with Rheingold Extra Dry.' " He was now in the company of Ernest Hemingway, who, six years before, had put his name to the immortal advertising prose: "I would rather have a bottle of Ballantine Ale than any other drink after fighting a really big fish." A few months later, a "Playhouse 90" production of Hemingway's *For Whom the Bell Tolls* shared a television evening with "The Dean Martin Show." One New York reviewer found the former "hopelessly confused, pretentious, dated"; the latter, with "no pretenses at art or esthetics," on the other hand, "was thoroughly pleasant." Beaten now by Dean in both the literary and television arenas, Hemingway spent his final two years on earth in a slow, sad march to the grave.

Dean returned again to the Sands in October. The year had been even busier for him than nightclub-goers or television-watchers or record-buyers knew. By November 22, when he did his last television show of the year—and what a combination of guests: Bing Crosby and the Treniers—he had completed a new picture, was finishing a second, and was scheduled to begin yet another.

Some Came Running, the first of those pictures, was based on the novel that James Jones had written as a sort of sequel to his 1951 *From Here to Eternity.* Dean's pal Sinatra, who had won an Academy Award for his role as Maggio in the film version of the earlier novel, played the main character, Dave Hirsh, in the new picture. Hirsh was a Jones-like figure, a disillusioned war veteran and writer returned to small-town life in 1948 Indiana. Dean played Bama Dillert, a dying professional gambler composed in equal parts of wisdom, drunkenness, and hopelessness. Martha Hyer played Gwen French, a respectable teacher whom Hirsh falls in love with only to forsake her in the fateful end for Ginny Moorhead, a sweet, dumb floozy played by Shirley MacLaine. *Some Came Running* was the first hands-on production of fifty-five-year-old Sol C. Siegel following his takeover as production boss at MGM. Directed by Vincente Minnelli, largely on location in Madison, Indiana, the picture was supposed to exude melodramatic naturalism. Most of that naturalism came through Dean, who, with MacLaine, carried the picture. If there was a lot of him in *The Young Lions,* surely there was even more of him in *Some Came Running.* As he said, the role of Bama "was a snap for me. I just played cards and talked Southern." He already spoke with a drawl in real life. God only knew where it came from, that added growth of obscuring kudzu he had cultivated around the wall of *lontananza* that kept the world at bay. No one else from Steubenville ever talked that way. Yet, like the Stetson he wore in the movie, it somehow fit him.

"You ain't really gonna marry this broad? Even she knows she's a pig," he says to Sinatra toward the end, sounding more real than actors sounded in those days. Sinatra told him about loneliness, about the need to help and to be helped. "Yeah," Dean says, "but the fact remains, she's still a pig." It was Dean's first role without a snatch of song. (In a party scene in *The Young Lions,* he had sung some lines of "How About You?" and "Blue Moon.")

Some Came Running premiered at the Hollywood Paramount on December 18 and opened a month later at Radio City Music Hall in New York. It was, *Variety* said, "certainly one of the most exciting pictures of the season." Of Dean's performance: "It is not easy, either, to play a man dying of a chronic illness and do it with grace and humor, and this Dean Martin does without faltering." Even the first-person-plural Bosley Crowther of the *Times* was moved: "You're no more surprised than were we!" he exclaimed of Dean's performance. The picture emerged as one of the ten biggest box-office hits of the year, directly after *The Young Lions.* That placed Dean in two of the top ten films of 1958.

There he had been, thirty-five years ago and more: the Ohio River had been the Red; the backyards and empty lots and shrubs of the Italian South Side had stirred with the shadows of the West, with the dream of spaghetti by the campfire. Now here he was in Tucson, Arizona, on the set of *Rio Bravo,* directed by the legendary Howard Hawks.

Hawks's 1948 *Red River,* in which he had given Montgomery Clift his first role, was considered by many to be *the* classic Western picture, and with *Rio Bravo,* based on a short story by B. H. Mc-Campbell, he was making a rebuke to Fred Zinnemann's award-winning *High Noon.* Hawks had hated it. He hated the whole idea of a sheriff begging for help rather than relying on his own resources and a few close allies. For his sheriff hero in *Rio Bravo,* he had hired John Wayne, who had played the bad guy for him ten years before in *Red River*. For the part of Wayne's deputy, Dude, a booze-debased bum piecing together the shards of self-respect after a two-year drunk, Hawks had considered another *Red River* actor, Montgomery Clift. When Clift declined, MCA had suggested Dean.

"I hired him," Hawks remembered, "because an agent wanted me to meet him. And I said, 'Well, get him around here at nine o'clock tomorrow morning.' The agent said, 'He can't be here at nine.' So he came in about ten-thirty, and I said, 'Why the hell couldn't you be here at nine o'clock?' He said, 'I was working in Las Vegas, and I had to hire an airplane and fly down here.' And that made me think, 'Well, my Lord, this guy really wants to work.' So I said, 'You'd better go over and get some wardrobe.' He said, 'Am I hired?' And I said, 'Yeah. Anybody who'll do that ought to get a chance to do it.' He came back from wardrobe looking like a musical-comedy cowboy. I said, 'Dean, look, you know a little about drinking. You've seen a lot of drunks. I want a *drunk*. I want a guy in an old dirty sweatshirt and an old hat.' And he said, 'Okay, you don't have to tell me any more.' He went over, and he came back with the outfit that he wore in the picture. He must have been successful because Jack Warner said to me, 'We hired Dean Martin. When's he going to be in this picture?' I said, 'He's the funny-looking guy in the old hat.' 'Holy smoke, is that Dean Martin?'

"Dean did a great job. It was fun working with him. All you had to do was tell him something. The scene where he had a hangover, which he did in most of the scenes, there was one where he was suffering, and I said, 'Look, that's too damn polite. I knew a guy with a hangover who'd pound his leg trying to hurt himself and get some feeling in it.' 'Okay, I know that kind of guy,' he said. 'I can do it.' And he went on and did the scene with no rehearsal or anything."

"You have to have good people to play a drunk. Because you could get some people to play a drunk and it nauseates you," Hawks said.

Dean himself described *Rio Bravo* for a reporter that June: "I play a sodden, drunken bum. My hands shake so I can't hold a cigarette. I have no self-respect. It was a woman and I can't get over her. Then along comes Duke Wayne with a big problem and I start pulling myself together. The whole thing is kind of a horse-opera love affair between Wayne and myself."

Jeannie remembered her husband during the making of those first, important films of his newborn career. "His biggest stretch was not *The Young Lions*," she would say. "His biggest stretch was *Rio Bravo*." Of his role in *The Young Lions* Dean himself had told people: "Hell, I just played myself: a likable coward." His role as Bama in *Some Came Running* was "a snap." But in *Rio Bravo*, he had to portray from scratch.

Dean had Marlon Brando read the script for him. "He didn't tell me how to act the part. He just told me what to think about. I play a drunk with DTs. I'm fighting the bottle, the bad guys, and John Wayne, the sheriff who makes me his deputy." As Dean recognized, it was "a very good role, more dramatic than anything I've ever done."

The moment in *Rio Bravo* that proved the hardest for him was a scene that called for him to break down in tears. He had trouble doing that. Even pretending to cry was something that unnerved him; even as make-believe, it was *contra naturam*. Hawks seemed to sense this in Dean, and he put off the scene until the final day of shooting, and he helped him through it, for which Dean was grateful.

"I was willing to do almost anything," Hawks said, "because he was so nice to work with and so good at what he did." The way Hawks saw it, "He could do anything you wanted him to." But he saw another side of him too: "Dean's a damn good actor, but he also is a fellow that floats through life. He has to be urged. He has to get some kind of a hint, something going; otherwise, hell, he won't even rehearse in some of his shows. He wants to get on and play golf."

Dean and Wayne got along well, having fun teasing their costar Ricky Nelson, who had just become a teen idol with his number-one hit single "Poor Little Fool."

Nelson turned eighteen during filming and perhaps to show what they thought of his acting, or of his singing, or maybe because he just looked too damned pure, Dean and Wayne presented him with a three-hundred-pound sack of steer manure. The contents were emptied to the ground in a heap. Dean took hold of one arm,

Wayne took hold of the other, and together they heaved him into his gift.

Twenty-five-year-old Angie Dickinson was hired by Hawks to play Wayne's sweetheart, Feathers. "It was my first big movie," she remembered. "It was difficult only because I was inexperienced. I was scared. I wanted to be good. I talked too fast." The film ended in disappointment. Hawks had signed her to an exclusive contract. "I thought, gosh, I was gonna be molded into this great star by Hawks and do another movie with him." But Hawks only wanted to run up her value with *Rio Bravo*. He sold her afterward to Warner Brothers. "Which pissed me off," Dickinson said. But Dean "was wonderful. He was just divine. Actually, I think I would have fallen for him if I hadn't been involved, very much in love, with somebody else."

In Las Vegas, the casino era was entering its years of greatest glory, and though the city's murder, rape, robbery, and burglary rates were higher than those of New York—and its suicide rate was the highest in America—the veil of illusion prevailed.

It was the holy city of old-guard cool. There, Elvis was still a provincial, without *civitas*, without *imperium*. There, as the consuls of cool, Dean and Sinatra reigned supreme. Their *praetorium* was the Sands.

Humphrey Bogart had been close to Sinatra as well as to Dean and Jeannie. Sinatra had admired Bogart and coveted his wife, Lauren Bacall. With Judy Garland and her husband Sid Luft, David Niven, Nathaniel Benchley, Jimmy Van Heusen, and others, Sinatra had been a part of the drinking group, known as the Holmby Hills Rat Pack, that had gathered round the Bogarts. Bogie was dead now, and Sinatra—"I don't think Frank's an adult emotionally," Bogart had said of him—wanted to hold court himself. His group— Joey Bishop, Sammy Davis, Jr., Peter Lawford, Shirley MacLaine— were called the Clan. Dean, whose company Sinatra constantly pursued, was not one to play the sycophant. He liked Sinatra, but he knew him for what he was: a half-a-mozzarella that never grew up. Bishop, Davis, and Lawford were nobodies. They needed Sinatra, he did not. Sinatra had given him and MacLaine their parts in *Some*

Came Running; but they likely could have gotten the parts without him. Maybe MacLaine, Frankie's quondam *comare,* wanted to be one of the guys; he did not. He watched Sinatra call Davis "a dirty nigger bastard" when Davis told an interviewer that Sinatra was capable of being impolite; he had watched Davis beg to be returned to his good graces. Dean neither gave nor took that kind of shit. Sinatra could be a pain in the ass in other ways too. Little more than a year earlier, at Romanoff's on the Rocks in Palm Springs, Dean had had to drag him bodily away from Bill Davidson, a journalist who had written negative things about him. Why he even read the shit that people wrote about him was beyond Dean; that he let it get to him was ridiculous. He took it all so fucking seriously. He thought he was a fucking artist, a fucking god. But, again, at the same time, he liked Frank. Their families had grown close. They drank together. They gambled together. They laughed together. If people wanted to call him part of Sinatra's Clan, so be it, fuck it; it made no difference.

The so-called Clan, Frank and Dean's consulship of cool, came into national prominence during that January of 1959. On January 2, at the Capitol studio, Sinatra conducted the orchestra for *Sleep Warm,* Dean's new album. *Some Came Running,* with the trio of Sinatra, Martin, and MacLaine, was in the theaters; and, on January 28, Sinatra joined Dean for the first time on the stage of the Sands.

"Martin," *Variety* said, "a heavyweight who appeals to both distaffers and their gaming escorts, sparks casino activity even if he doesn't double as stage performer and blackjack dealer—which he usually does. First-nighters got an extra added attraction—Frank Sinatra joined his Great & Good friend onstage, and the pair put on one of the best shows ever seen at the Sands."

In time, Sinatra stopped calling it the Clan. It was too evocative of that other Klan, and he discouraged writers from using the term. It was politically incorrect: Senator John F. Kennedy, Peter Lawford's brother-in-law, the kid old Joe Kennedy's money had made, had his eye on the presidential nomination. Sinatra, who lusted to rub against any power greater than his own, threw himself fully into Kennedy's campaign. Reverting to the Bogart days, the Clan became the Rat Pack, the sideshow of Kennedy's privileged Democratic dream. Kennedy was a glamour boy. He enjoyed being around celebrities, as Sinatra enjoyed being around power. The two of them waxed dreamy-eyed round each other.

Dean and Jack Kennedy, who was barely two weeks older than him, had first met back in the winter of 1947–48. Martin and Lewis had been playing the Chez Paree in Chicago, staying at the Ambassador East Hotel. Kennedy, then in Congress, had been in town to give a speech at the Executives Club, and was also staying at the Ambassador East. Jerry and Kennedy had gotten on well together. But the young congressman from Massachusetts had made no impression on Dean. His father had given him a country to play with the way other fathers gave their sons toy trains. The dirty greed of the world had glimmered in the father's eyes; in the son's, there was only women, ambition, and the idealism that came from growing up rich and protected. He was just a Lord Fauntleroy version of Pinky Nolan gone big-time. Dean had had no use for him then; he had no use for him now.

"Dean paid no attention to John Kennedy," Jeannie would remember. "I mean, he thought—"; then she would only laugh and sigh.

The Clan, the Rat Pack, the New Frontier. It was all a bunch of meaningless shit, a bunch of newspaper reporters and magazine writers and television commentators jerking off in a circle around a can of fucking Sterno. Even the frontier was like Fab now, new and improved.

After closing at the Sands, Dean began work in late February on a new picture, which brought him back to Hal Wallis and Paramount for the first time since the breakup. The picture was an obligation for Dean, not a choice. Wallis was calling in Dean for a picture at $75,000 under the old Martin-and-Lewis contract.

Based on a 1957 off-Broadway play by James Lee, who also wrote the screenplay, *Career* was essentially a three-character tale of show-business vicissitudes. Dean played a director, Maury Novak; Anthony Franciosa, a struggling actor whom Novak befriends and abandons; and Shirley MacLaine, the drunken daughter of a dirty-rich producer. The first picture to be derived from off-Broadway theater, *Career* was a small movie with big overtones; and were it not for Dean's restraint and underplaying, the whole thing might have been sucked off into that particular stratosphere of Serious Art where beatnik poets and semiologists relate to weeping clowns. As it turned out, *Career* was one of those respectable little melodramas that got better with age.

"I thought Dean did an excellent job of acting in it," Franciosa said. "I was very impressed with what he did. He never revealed how hard he was working. He always tried to make it seem like he was doing it off the back of his hand, like he was putting no effort in it. He made it seem like it was kind of an effortless thing, and he was very relaxed about it. I knew he'd put a lot of work into it, but he never let it show. He knew his lines better than I knew mine. I remember we had a very long scene in a restaurant. The set was packed with a lot of extras; and I remember, at the end of the scene, the extras got up and applauded him. Which was a very rare thing for extras to do."

On March 2, *Sleep Warm,* the Martin-Sinatra consulship-of-cool album, was released in—but of course—"full dimensional stereo."

Menefreghismo was beginning to leak through the television tube. With its last program of 1958, "The Dean Martin Show" had switched from a live-broadcast to a videotape format. When the show returned, with a new sponsor, Timex, on March 19, it seemed to have switched to a nonrehearsed format as well. "Dean Martin may be a devil with the ladies, a roisterer with the boys and a real demon down at the poolroom," columnist Harriet Van Horne chided nasally, "but on America's home screen he can sometimes be a rather offensive young man.

"Watching his special color show last evening," she wrote, "I had the feeling that this pretty laddie with the careful ringlets and roguish grin would take great pleasure in spitting in the eye of the audience. His offhand air, his apparent lack of rehearsal and his highly personal ad libs all bespeak a faint contempt for his work."

On the other hand, Van Horne found the CBS production of *For Whom the Bell Tolls* to be "a massive accomplishment."

But for every Van Horne there were thousands of others who loved what Dean was doing. He was not spitting at them; he was spitting for them. His message was clear: All this fake-sincerity shit that was coming through television—not only through television: the newspapers, the pictures, every politician's false-faced caring word and grin—it was all a racket. It was a message that appealed to the *menefreghismo* in every heart: Fuck it all; eat, drink, and be merry, for even Sorelli the Mystic knew not what tomorrow might bring.

Rio Bravo had opened at the Roxy Theatre in New York the day before the NBC show was aired. "It looks as though Dean Martin can start calling himself an actor," said the *Daily News*. "Hardly recognizable in 'Rio Bravo' as a drunken derelict hiding behind a facade of whiskers and defeatism, he commands unprecedented respect in a difficult characterization deftly realized. Dean has come of age in a profession which held him a long time in bondage as a singer and straight man for a comedy duo." The *News* gave the picture three and a half stars. The *Times*, not so impressed with *Rio Bravo* itself—it was "well-made but awfully familiar fare"—praised "Dean Martin, as the alcoholic who conquers the demon rum and regains his self-respect under fire." The *Times* may have missed the point regarding *Rio Bravo*. What, after all, was any good Western but a retelling and reaffirming of archetypal, and by nature awfully familiar, myths? Then again, one could read too much into the archetypal angle too. One scholarly study of *Rio Bravo*, analyzing the scene in which Angie Dickinson shaves Dean while Wayne looks on, saw: "Chance (ego), Dude (shadow), and Feathers (anima), and with a mandala-Centric object (the Self) in the silver hatband among them (with Dude's fine anima-aspected clothes, and two lanterns figuring as well)." Hawks and Warner Brothers saw something more profound: money. *Rio Bravo* was one of the biggest hits of the year. Only one other picture that year made as much money for Warner Brothers: *The Nun's Story*, which, ironically, was directed by Fred Zinnemann, whose *High Noon* Hawks had set out to nullify.

Dean was back on television, with Mae West as a guest, on May 3. "It seemed like something from outer space. You watched it but you didn't believe it," *Variety* said. "The spectacle of a big star," said the *Daily News*, "undoubtedly the idol of an awful lot of young people, virtually building a show on the fact he gets plastered with frequency is trying. And in utterly miserable taste."

Since 1953, the year of her first separation from Dean, Jeannie had expended her social energies on SHARE (Share Happily and Reap Endlessly), the children's-foundation charity group that she had started that year with several other show-business wives. Their first annual benefit affairs, called Boomtown Parties, had been held at Ciro's. Herman Hover had been forced to shut down his nightclub on New Year's Eve, 1957; the following August, Ciro's had been sold at federal auction to satisfy bankruptcy claims. In May 1958, Dean hosted the SHARE Boomtown party for Jeanne at the Moulin Rouge, where he was lowered to the stage seated astride a white saddle on a chandelier. Sinatra showed up. He embraced Sammy Davis, Jr., onstage to show that the "dirty nigger bastard" was absolved; together they sang "The Lady Is a Tramp." There was a chorus line of Gary Cooper, Robert Mitchum, Jack Benny, Tony Curtis, Peter Lawford, Jack Webb, and other broads-for-a-night. By the morning hours, auctioning off Gypsy Rose Lee's bathing-suit and other curiosities, they raised $100,000.

That same month, Dean began work with Tony Curtis and Janet Leigh on a new picture, *Who Was That Lady?*, a comedy closely based on a recent Broadway play by Norman Krasna. George Sidney, who had screen-tested Dean for Joe Pasternak back in 1946, was Krasna's director and coproducer for the film. Dean's movie price now was set at $200,000 a picture. With an average filming schedule of eight weeks, that amounted to the equivalent of his nightclub pay: $25,000 a week, not counting his NBC and Capitol income. His ex-partner was not faring poorly either. In June, Lewis signed a seven-year, fourteen-film, $10,000,000 deal with Paramount—the biggest deal that Paramount had ever made with any actor.

Dean's last, minor Capitol hit appeared on the charts in July: "On an Evening in Roma," a rendition of Sandro Taccani and Umberto Bertini's "Sott' er Celo de Roma" with English lyrics by Nan Fredericks. Later in the summer, he recorded an album called *A Winter Romance*, designed for yuletide release. In August, his next picture, another $200,000 payday, went into preproduction.

Judy Holliday had made her musical-comedy debut in *Bells Are Ringing*, which had been written for her by her friends Betty Comden and Adolph Green with the musical collaboration of Jule Styne. The show had opened on Broadway at the Shubert Theatre in November 1956 and had run for nearly a thousand performances, winning Holliday both a Drama Critics Circle and a Tony award. Previously, Holliday had turned her Broadway-comedy role in *Born Yesterday* into an Academy Award–winning movie role, and it was hoped—though she was now thirty-seven and overweight—that she might do the same reprising her part as Ella Peterson in the MGM production of *Bells Are Ringing*. Dean, as the male lead, Jeff Moss, would be working once again with Vincente Minnelli, who had directed *Some Came Running* the previous year. As always, everyone involved with *Bells Are Ringing* found Dean a pleasure to work with, though he let it be known that he thought the role of Jeff Moss was a waste of his time and talent. Holliday, who was sick, depressed, and prone to crying jags throughout the production, liked Dean but had doubts about whether he was the right choice for the part. She was afraid that he was just walking through it.

Career was released in early October, while *Bells Are Ringing* was in production. Crowther of the *Times* did not care for it. He found that Lee's story had "lost too much of its intimacy and insight in its transfer to the large, conglomerate screen." Anthony Franciosa's "repulses and curious misconnections don't make satisfactory sense. Dean Martin is oddly loose and airy as an on-and-off director-friend, and Shirley MacLaine is as soggy as a dishrag." Other reviewers disagreed. The *Daily News* called it "a forceful dramatization distinguished by a realistic approach, ease of communication, the many superb performances and a presentation so impressive that it establishes almost total recall. Every sequence bears the mark of master craftsmanship." To the *Herald Tribune*, it was "fresh, vigorous, exciting," and "loaded with electricity." In terms of box-office take, it was the least successful picture Dean had made aside from *Ten Thousand Bedrooms*. It was a movie actors liked, but not the people who paid to see them.

On October 19, Dean joined Bing Crosby for "The Frank Sinatra Timex Show" on ABC. The three of them sang "Together." Dean sang "Wrap Your Troubles in Dreams," crossing his legs to reveal the words EAT AT DINO'S on the sole of his shoe. It was announced

that Dean, Crosby, and Sinatra would soon—"in the very near future"—be making a movie based on the life of Jimmy Durante.
Durante himself came out to join them for their finale. The movie,
however, was a project, dear to Frank Capra, that would never be
realized.

It was Crosby who, with George Jessel, had formed the Friars
Club twelve years earlier. Both Dean and Sinatra were members;
and Sinatra was among the many—Joey Bishop, George Burns,
Sammy Cahn, Tony Curtis, Kirk Douglas, Jimmy Durante, Judy Garland, Dinah Shore, Glenn Wallichs of Capitol, and over a thousand
others—who gathered to honor Dean at a Friars Club testimonial
dinner at the International Room of the Beverly Hilton Hotel on
November 8. In tribute to Dean, Sinatra sang "You're the Wop,"
lyrics written for the occasion by Sammy Cahn to the tune of Cole
Porter's "You're the Top":

He's the wop! Unlike any other!
He's the wop, who's a mother's mother.
When they split, rumors started spinning;
Full of shit! Dino's just beginning!
He's the wop, with real golfing power!
He's the wop, a guinea Eisenhower!
He's the kind of nut who will miss a putt and moan;
He likes golfball-thumpin' like I like humpin'—to each his own!
He's the slob, twice went to the altars;
Has a lob that never falters!

And so on. Later Cahn would write lyrics for Dean to sing at the
Friars' tribute to George Jessel:

I've grown accustomed to his face;
It was no simple thing to do.
A girl said, "He's my baby's father," and it came as quite a shock.
If he is, he used that big cigar and not his cock.
Although I know it sounds like bullshit, there's no doubts that he's
    the tops;

Once I heard him speak, and even I said, "Fuck the wops!"
I've grown accustomed to his toups . . .

The $300,000 raised by the dinner went to several charities, including the City of Hope, SHARE, and the Eddie Cantor Summer Camp for Underprivileged Boys. Supervisor Ernest Debs, on behalf of the Los Angeles County Board of Supervisors, presented Dean with a plaque commending him for, as the press release said, "his many charitable activities and also as an outstanding member of the community." A pillar. A fucking pillar.

In December, when *Bells Are Ringing* was finished, he returned to the Sands. Another decade, washed away in dreams and lies. He could feel it coming on: a song from the other side. It was time to throw the dice again, this time toward the shadows. Soon the pillar of the community would have an FBI file all his own.

XIII.

ARISTEIA IN SHARKSKIN

*S*inatra and Martin: There was something about them that brought out the biggest gamblers. What the Sands paid them, they brought back in spades. It was common knowledge: "Dean Martin is back in the Copa Room," said *Variety* in December 1959, "and the casino execs are happy—because Dino pulls in the same type heavy player as does Frank Sinatra, another of Jack Entratter's surefires."

It was not just the dirty-rich *giovanostri* and *padroni* who were drawn to them, to their glamour, to the appeal of darkness made respectable. The world was full, it seemed, of would-be wops and woplings who lived vicariously through them, to whom the imitation of cool took on the religiosity of the Renaissance ideal of *imitatio Christi*. The very songs that Sinatra and Dean sang, the very images they projected, inspired lavish squandering among the countless men who would be them. It was the Jew-roll around the prick that rendered them ithyphallic godkins, simulacra of the great ones, in their own eyes and in the eyes of the teased-hair lobster-slurping *Bimbo sapiens* they sought to impress.

Both Dean and Frank owned stock in the Sands. By the summer of 1961, Sinatra would hold a nine-percent piece of the operation. Of the other sixteen licensed Sands stockholders, only Jack Entratter, who had succeeded Jake Freedman in 1958 as president, with twelve percent, Freedman's widow, Sadie, with ten percent, and the Sands' vice-president and casino manager, Carl Cohen, with nine and a half percent, owned larger shares; one, Russian-born Hy Abrams, who had been a partner of Bugsy Siegel in the original Flamingo and moved to the Sands in 1954, held an equal, nine-percent piece. Dean, who was granted a gaming license on July 20, 1961, was one of three one-percent owners. His privileged price for that percentage was $28,838, which by then was less than a week's pay.

Despite their immense popularity and the success of Sinatra's albums, neither Dean nor Frank was selling many singles as the decade drew to a close. Sinatra had done well with "Witchcraft" in 1958; Dean had done better that year with "Volare." Since then, neither had broken into the Top Twenty. Sinatra's best-selling record of 1959, "High Hopes," had risen only so far as number thirty. On January 2, 1960, at a news conference in the Senate Caucus Room, John F. Kennedy announced his candidacy for the Democratic presidential nomination. "High Hopes," with new lyrics tailored by Sammy Cahn, would become Kennedy's campaign song. Along the way, it would become the anthem of a time's dumb optimism.

High hopes were what Sinatra had. He envisioned Kennedy, somehow, as his man. He envisioned too an empire of his own—his own casino, his own record company, God only knew what else. And Dean was along for the ride.

JFK and the Rat Pack: These were the symbols, image and spirit, of that carefree time. Even their smiles were alike. In January, while Kennedy got his campaign formally underway, the Rat Pack made the movie that would become its most celebrated legacy.

In 1956, Peter Lawford had been told an idea for a story about a precision-timed robbery sweep of the Las Vegas Strip. Sinatra had bought the rights to the story, with Lawford retaining a share, and hired Harry Brown and Charles Lederer to write a screenplay from it. As it developed, *Ocean's Eleven* became the tale of eleven World War II army buddies reunited for one last maneuver, a multi-million-dollar five-casino heist. Sinatra, who made the picture through his own Dorchester Productions, played ringleader Danny Ocean. They were all in it: Dean, Sammy, Lawford, Joey Bishop. Angie Dickinson played Danny Ocean's wife. Richard Conte, Henry Silva, Akim Tamiroff, and Buddy Lester had key roles. George Raft showed up as a casino owner. Shirley MacLaine had a cameo scene with Dean.

"I used to be Ricky Nelson," Dean tells her. "I'm Perry Como now."

Lewis Milestone, who was already a seasoned professional when he made *All Quiet on the Western Front* in 1930, was hired to direct.

"They say this is hard work, this acting. What bullshit," Dean said. "Work? Work my ass."

Dean and Richard Conte—Nick Conte, as those close to him knew him—got along well. Conte's background at the fringes of Jersey City's *malavita* was not dissimilar to Dean's; and both were the sons of old-fashioned Italian barbers. The production and the partying flowed together. From January 26 through February 16, the Rat Pack filmed by day and took the stage of the Sands by night. To Jack Entratter, the sign outside—it would appear at the closing credits—was like a dream come true:

FRANK SINATRA

DEAN MARTIN

SAMMY DAVIS JR.

PETER LAWFORD

JOEY BISHOP

The newspapers had been full of the upcoming Paris summit conference being planned by Eisenhower, Khrushchev, and De Gaulle. Well, Sinatra declared, they would have their own summit conference of cool. Newspapers across the country began publicizing it as the Rat Pack Summit. By the night they opened, every hotel room in Las Vegas was booked for the duration. Entratter was more than happy to go along with their setup: At least one of them would perform every night; sometimes two or three or four of them, sometimes all five.

Even Kennedy himself showed up at ringside one night. Sinatra introduced him from the stage. Dean came out: "What did you say his name was?" Then Dean picked up little Sammy and held him out to Sinatra: "Here. This award just came for you from the National Association for the Advancement of Colored People." Later, Kennedy joined the Rat Pack upstairs for drinks. Lawford took Davis aside and whispered to him:

"If you want to see what a million dollars in cash looks like, go into the next room; there's a brown leather satchel in the closet. It's a gift from the hotel owners for Jack's campaign."

There were broads that night as well: blowjobs on the house, all around, for the New Frontiersman and his Democratic crew. One of the women Sinatra introduced to Kennedy was a twenty-five-year-old would-be starlet named Judith Campbell. Sinatra had been fucking her for a while. So had Johnny Rosselli, the West Coast's lord of darkness. Now Campbell would begin a two-year affair with Jack Kennedy. Sinatra liked the idea: the two men bonding their friendship through a woman.

Most mornings, they would come offstage at half past one or a quarter to two, drink till dawn, and begin filming.

"It wasn't that it wasn't professional," Angie Dickinson said of the moviemaking; "but you'd have to look hard to find a camera to prove to you that they weren't playing. They really had fun together. The director was very easy. He knew exactly who was signing his check."

On their closing night, old-time movie-gangster Jack LaRue was introduced in the audience among a crowd of other celebrities. "Why don't you come up here and kill somebody?" Dean called out to him. Later, when he stumbled on a sentence, he remarked, "I got my nose fixed, and now my mouth doesn't work." He urged the audience, "On your way out, please buy a copy of my latest book, *The Power of Positive Drinking.*"

They took the train to Los Angeles that night, and resumed filming at Warner Brothers the next morning.

Ocean's Eleven was completed on March 23. Three weeks later, *Who Was That Lady?* opened at the Criterion in New York. In it, *Variety* had noted, "Martin strengthens the false impression that he isn't acting at all. It should be so easy!" The *Times* did not much care for it—these were the days when the paper of record found Jack Kerouac's *Pull My Daisy* "truly arresting"—but did declare that "Mr. Martin, especially, is fine." On May 9, with André Previn conducting, Dean recorded the soundtrack album for *Bells Are Ringing.* A day later, with Nelson Riddle, he recorded "Ain't That a Kick in the Head," the song that James Van Heusen and Sammy Cahn had written for *Ocean's Eleven.* In mid-June—they could not draft him now—he underwent an operation on his hernia at Cedars of Lebanon Hospital. *Bells Are Ringing* opened at Radio City Music Hall on June 20, two days before he was released from the hospital.

The *Daily News* called *Bells Are Ringing* "a knockout, even better entertainment than it was on the stage." Dean, as Holliday's "partner in singing, dancing and romancing," was "a perfect choice."

High hopes. That summer, the Rat Pack sang "The Star-Spangled Banner" to open the Democratic national convention in Los Angeles. The delegates from Mississippi loudly protested Sammy Davis's presence on the stage. But Mississippi had the lowest average income level and the fewest television sets per capita of any state. Jack was not playing to them. His bleeding heart went out to the downtrodden of that state, but only through the wonder of television could they truly experience the integrity of that heart and the probity of the sharecropper's friend. As every black man in Hyannis Port knew, young John Kennedy was a man whose sense of justice was real. Television conveyed that reality, as it conveyed all realities.

Dean, who earlier in the year had brought the realities of Fabian and André Previn together on his NBC show, found himself becoming more involved in the shadow play that surrounded Sinatra's infatuation with the prince of the New Frontier. Jack Kennedy's kid brother Bobby, a worse spoiled brat than he, was chief counsel to the McClellan Senate committee's investigations into labor racketeering. Bobby's holy war against Jimmy Hoffa and the Teamsters had stirred trouble far and wide. It seemed that the little rabbit-mouthed *irlandese* was out to crucify not only the new head of the Teamsters but every wop in America along with him. One of those who had been called before the committee in 1959 was Sam Giancana, boss of the Chicago mob, whom both Dean and Sinatra knew from his earliest days of power following the death of Charlie Fischetti. Wearing sunglasses and a cheap hairpiece, Sam had sat there holding a three-by-five-inch card bearing the words of the Fifth Amendment, whose protection he invoked in response to every question Kennedy put forth. The heat had not diminished, and it came to be believed that the only way to get Bobby Kennedy's nose out of everybody's business was through Jack. The Teamsters, of course, could not publicly endorse Jack, though Hoffa himself became one of the believers in the hope of his intercession. But, through Giancana, a large donation to Kennedy's presidential campaign was drawn from the Teamsters pension fund and passed to Jack beneath the blind eyes of his brother Bobby, who took time out from his wop-hunting to serve as Jack's campaign manager. There were also disbursements from the campaign fund made through Sinatra to Skinny D'Amato in Atlantic City. Under Giancana's guidance, D'Amato was to purchase the influence of several West Virginia election officials known to him through the 500 Club.

Giancana, cheap hairpiece and all, was far from a fool. He led Sinatra to think that the donation in support of Kennedy, as well as the influence-buying in West Virginia, was prompted to a great degree by the faith in Kennedy that Sinatra had expressed to him. By giving the impression that he was relying on Sinatra's judgment and that he was doing Sinatra a favor—Sinatra would be able to further ingratiate himself to Jack by taking credit for the donation and newfound support—Giancana rendered Sinatra beholden to him. Not only, Giancana figured, would he now be able to use Sinatra as a money-maker toward his own ends, Sinatra would be able to deliver that other one, that aloof bastard, that unreachable *menefreghista*, toward those same ends as well.

The McGuire Sisters, the three singing daughters of an Ohio minister, had risen to national prominence with a string of hits in 1954, the year that Sam Giancana had become a widower. Sam, who knew the act from the Chez Paree, had run into Phyllis McGuire in Las Vegas in early 1960, about the time that Kennedy announced his candidacy. She was twenty-nine, recently divorced, drinking, and gambling heavily; the days of the McGuire Sisters' big hits were past. She became Giancana's lover. Not long after they began their romance, Sinatra introduced Giancana to Judy Campbell, the woman who was now Kennedy's mistress. Again, he liked the idea. Now the three of them, Frank, Jack, and Sam, were sharing the same *braciole*.

High hopes: a casino of his own. Elmer "Bones" Remmer, the

San Francisco gangster who owned the Cal-Neva Lodge, at Crystal Bay on the Nevada side of Lake Tahoe, had gotten in trouble with the Treasury Department, trouble that went deeper than the $800,000 he owed the Internal Revenue Service. Control of the Cal-Neva had passed to Bert "Wingy" Grober, who had his problems too. In June 1960, there was talk of Grober's reducing his stake in the troubled casino. On July 13, 1960, the day Kennedy won the Democratic nomination in Los Angeles, it was announced in Carson City that a group of four men had applied for permission to take over a fifty-seven-percent, majority interest in the Cal-Neva Lodge. Those four men were Frank Sinatra, Dean Martin, Sinatra's longtime friend, piano player, and legbreaker, Hank Sanicola, and Skinny D'Amato. Under the plan, Wingy's interest would be reduced to eighteen percent. Sanicola would hold sixteen percent; D'Amato, thirteen; Dean, three. Sinatra's proposed twenty-five-percent inter-est, the largest piece, would be shared in secret with Sam Giancana, whose behind-the-scene machinations had enabled the four men to strike an above-board takeover price with Wingy of only $250,000.

On that same night of July 13, as Kennedy's nomination was being announced, Dean opened at the Sands.

"I'd like to tell you some of the *good* things the Mafia is doing," he said. There was a momentary hush, then a long, slow wave of rising laughter.

His singing had begun to take on a new tone. He was no longer merely selling the lie of romance. Stabbing sharply and coldly here and there into the songs with lines of wry disdain, he was exposing his own racket as well, selling the further delusion of their sharing in the secret of that lie itself. It was an elaboration on his tried and true style of singing to the men rather than the women, of singing to them as if they alone could truly understand him. It was also a natural emanation of the way he felt. He simply no longer cared. He began more songs than he finished, dismissing most of them with a wisecrack partway through. Some, with the help of lyricist Sammy Cahn, were simply reduced to gross parody.

"If you think I'm going to get serious, you're crazy. If you want to hear a serious song, buy one of my records."

In the first week of August, *Ocean's Eleven* was previewed at the

Fremont Theatre in Las Vegas. The *Los Angeles Examiner* declared it "something you should keep your children away from." *The New Yorker* dismissed it as "an admiring wide-screen color travelogue of the various effluvia—animate and inanimate—of Las Vegas." But *Variety*'s prediction proved true: despite "serious weaknesses in both material and interpretation," it would "rake in chips, thanks to cast." *Ocean's Eleven* became the ninth biggest money-maker of the year, behind such formidable pictures as *Psycho, Spartacus, Exodus, La Dolce Vita, Butterfield 8,* and *The Apartment.*

On September 13, the Nevada Gaming Control Board issued a recommendation for approval of the Cal-Neva takeover. Dean by then had finished another film: *All in a Night's Work,* produced by Hal Wallis and directed by Joseph Anthony, who had done *Career.* Shirley MacLaine once again had the female lead; Cliff Robertson played a romantic ringer in the background. As in *Career,* Wallis found MacLaine "difficult," but Dean "was never a problem." *All in a Night's Work,* as *Variety* later put it, was an "essentially predictable, featherweight comedy," excellently directed and with a strangely classical score by André Previn. "Never for one moment," *Variety* said, "is Martin believable in the role of the youthful publishing tycoon, but his easy-going manner and knack for supplying the comedy reaction gets him by."

On November 1, Sinatra joined Dean on "The Dean Martin Show," which was presented as "Honoring Frank Sinatra." Seven days later, John F. Kennedy was elected president. It was close: a plurality of only 118,574 votes, the narrowest presidential victory of the century.

"Listen, honey, if it wasn't for me, your boyfriend wouldn't even be in the White House," Sam Giancana would tell Judy Campbell.

"Frank won Kennedy the election," Skinny D'Amato would say.

But it was television that won it for him. It was Nixon's poor appearance before the debate cameras that gave Kennedy the votes he needed to scrape by.

The following night, November 9, Dean returned to the Sands: "I just talked to Jack this morning and he made me secretary of liquor." He was, *Variety* reported, "hotter than ever" and "one of the most potent lures for gamblers." He was also "more relaxed than ever—in fact he appears to be imitating his imitators."

Camelot opened in New York on December 3. The show was beloved of the new president, and his administration came to be known by its name: the Camelot years. Jack and Jackie became the fairyland royalty of the land of whiter whites.

High hopes: a record company of his own. Capitol's current contract with Sinatra's Essex Productions company, binding him to release his recordings exclusively through Capitol, would lapse to a nonexclusive basis in February. In early December, it was announced that Sinatra would then begin releasing his records through a new company of his own. On December 19, he made his first recordings for his new company, which now had a name: Reprise Records.

Dean saw what Sinatra was too blind to see: there was no place in Camelot for wops. Sinatra went all out organizing a gala at the National Guard Armory in Washington on January 19, the eve of Kennedy's swearing-in. Seeing him in his Inverness cape with red satin lining, his silk top hat, swallowtail coat, striped britches, and white kid gloves, Dean remarked, you would have figured it was him, not the fucking mick, who was being inaugurated. Sinatra gathered everyone he could to participate that night: Milton Berle, Leonard Bernstein, Joey Bishop, Nat King Cole, Tony Curtis, Bette Davis, Jimmy Durante, Ella Fitzgerald, Gene Kelly, Peter Lawford, Shirley MacLaine, Sir Laurence Olivier, Louis Prima, Anthony Quinn, and more. Sammy Cahn and James Van Heusen were brought in to write special songs; Jack Rose and Melville Shavelson, who had written *Living It Up* for Martin and Lewis, were among the writers engaged. Newlywed Sammy Davis, Jr., who had postponed his marriage to Mai Britt to avoid bringing down any aspersions on Kennedy during the campaign, felt it would be prudent, for the same reason, to stay away from the inaugural-eve celebration.

But even more conspicuous in his absence was Dean. He begged off with the excuse that he was busy making a movie.

The new president did not rein in his younger brother's anti-wop crusade. Rather, he appointed him attorney general; and, as attorney general, thirty-five-year-old Bobby Kennedy set out to write his own name large with the blood of Sam Giancana and his kind.

Meanwhile, Judith Campbell, who had gone from the beds of Frank Sinatra and Johnny Rosselli to those of John F. Kennedy and Sam Giancana, had taken a job working for Jerry Lewis at Paramount. In early 1961, Jerry was informed that he was about to be named as a respondent in a divorce suit filed by the husband of a young starlet named Judy Meredith. The detective hired by the cuckold husband was Fred Otash, the legendary Hollywood private investigator who had been retained by *Confidential*, Frank Sinatra, and other celebrated clients through the years. Judy Meredith, it seemed, got around every bit as much as Judy Campbell. Jerry Lewis was not the only man who would be named in the suit. Otash had gathered evidence of her adulterous affairs with several other famous men. Jerry's ex-partner, Dean, was among those men. So were Sinatra and John F. Kennedy.

"One of the great cunt men of all time," Lewis would say of Kennedy. "Except for me."

Unlike Dean and Sinatra, Jerry had not seen Giancana in years. When he was told of the impending suit, he asked Judy Campbell to have Giancana intercede. Giancana obliged, and, through the powers of Johnny Rosselli, the evidence that Otash had gathered was destroyed.

On Valentine's Day, 1961, a letter was sent from the Federal Bureau of Investigation headquarters at the U.S. Department of Justice in Washington to the FBI office in Newark, New Jersey. The subject of the letter was Skinny D'Amato, who was then preparing to go west for his first season as the manager of the Cal-Neva Lodge. "A case should be opened in your office," the director instructed, "and a preliminary investigation conducted to determine if D'Amato's activities justify considering him a top hoodlum."

Cal-Neva was no longer of concern to Dean. After realizing the extent of Giancana's hidden involvement in the operation, he had pulled out. He knew Giancana's kind far better than Sinatra ever would. Where that kind wet their beaks, others went dry. Rather than be Sinatra's partner at Cal-Neva, Dean would let Sinatra pay him to perform there. He would make out better that way.

In need of money in the fall of 1959, Lucky Luciano had signed a contract granting the rights for a movie based on his life. Now, in Rome, in late February 1961, sixty-three-year-old Luciano received a script and was curious to know who would portray him. He liked the idea of Dean Martin, and he said that he himself would get the script to Martin through his own channels. But Luciano would be dead within a year, and during his last months he would change his mind about going along with the movie deal, claiming that Meyer Lansky had strongly warned him against it.

On March 29, Dean opened at the Sands. "I'm the only singer around," he said, "who has ten percent of four gangsters."

All in a Night's Work had opened the week before to mediocre reviews and lackluster crowds. The picture he had just finished would fare even more poorly at the box office. It was called *Ada.*

Ada, based on a 1959 novel, *Ada Dallas,* by Wirt Williams and directed by Daniel Mann, who had just directed *Butterfield 8,* was the story of country-bumpkin political pawn Bo Gillis, a "nothin' candidate" who becomes the "nothin' governor" of a graft-ridden Southern state. There were similarities between the character Dean played and Jimmie Davis, the Louisiana governor who had sung his way into office for the Long machine in 1944 with his song "You Are My Sunshine," and who was now, in 1961, the governor again. Susan Hayward, whom Mann had directed in *I'll Cry Tomorrow,* was cast as his wife and lieutenant governor, the Ada of the title, a reformed whore. Hayward disliked Dean, she would later say, because "he's vulgar."

Dean and Danny Mann were brought together for the MGM project by Herman Citron, who was Mann's agent as well as Dean's. Mann had worked with many of the best and biggest actors of the day: Burt Lancaster and Shirley Booth in *Come Back, Little Sheba;* Anna Magnani in *The Rose Tattoo;* Marlon Brando in *The Teahouse of the August Moon;* Paul Muni in *The Last Angry Man;* Elizabeth Taylor in *Butterfield 8.*

But Dean was special: "He was a natural. He didn't go too deep, he didn't try to show you that he was full of emotion; he did things on the level of his understanding. I found it so rare, because a lot of people try awfully hard to be something that they're not. That's what bad acting is.

"Dean's complexities were different from Brando's. Dean was a guy who, on the surface, seemed to be easy-come, but he was much more complex than that. I think that he had a kind of basic insecurity about opening himself up, a fear of his own deep feelings about things.

"He never worried about the picture. I never had a feeling that he was worried about the picture. He was deeply concerned about what he had to do, and that was great. For a director, that's a pleasure. A movie should have one director, not four. And Dean did not need much direction. He was very professional. He was not a poseur. He was what he was. He always worked well. I'd come on the set, and he was ready to go. He was always up on his words, and he was always on time. He had a net fixed up on the stage; when he wasn't shooting, he'd be off there with his golf clubs, driving into the net. It relaxed him, and it helped him, and he enjoyed it. It was never an interference, it never got in the way of anybody's work. He was a nice guy. To me, he was a warm guy. But he was not a guy who really mixed with people."

"The Dean Martin Show" of April 25, 1961, with guests Andy Griffith, Tony Martin, and Tina Louise, was the last of the shows he owed NBC. While he would appear as a guest on other shows—on Danny Thomas's "Make Room for Daddy" in May, on "The Dinah Shore Show" in November—he chose not to sign a new contract with NBC or any other network. He was sick of television. "There's nothing left to do on TV," he would say. The shows he had done—"singing, joking, and sitting around—you get tired of them." That spring, he turned down the role that went to David Niven in *The Guns of Navarone*. He did not want to work in Europe.

On May 22, Capitol issued a new single by Dean called "Giuggiola," an Italian song by Nicola Salerno and Corrado Lojacono, with English lyrics by Sammy Cahn. As the Capitol press release said, "The unusual title comes from a feminine Italian first name."

What the press release did not say, what Capitol did not know, was that it was to be his last single for the label.

By then, Sinatra's first Reprise album, *Ring-a-Ding-Ding*, was on the charts and a new Rat Pack movie, *Sergeants 3*, was underway in Kanab, Utah: a Western reworking of *Gunga Din* with Sinatra, Dean, and Peter Lawford in the leads. Besides Sammy Davis and Joey Bishop, there were also roles once again for Henry Silva and Buddy Lester, and for Dean's old pal Sonny King. The female lead was played by Ruta Lee, whose part in Billy Wilder's *Witness for the Prosecution* had caught Sinatra's eye.

"*Sergeants 3* was one of the happiest experiences of my life, because I was the baby doll on the set with all of those guys," Lee said. "I had a wonderful time but, unfortunately, they all treated me like their kid sister. Dean was great fun to be around. They all sipped pretty good, but I never saw him sloshed. In fact, he taught me to drink beer on the rocks. And Frank taught me to drink champagne the same way.

"Somehow Dean could always keep calm. He was above it all. He floated like wonderful shit on the water. Nothing got to him. If it ever did, you never knew it."

That summer, Skinny D'Amato managed the Cal-Neva Lodge, which Sinatra planned to close down at the end of the season and reopen next year after extensive renovations. D'Amato had hired Ed Pucci, a two-hundred-and-fifty-pound former guard for the Cleveland Browns and Washington Redskins, as the casino's press agent. While at the Cal-Neva, D'Amato was visited by Joe DiMaggio, whom he had known since the Yankee days. Sinatra and DiMaggio had been friends for years as well. In 1954, when Frank's marriage to Ava Gardner and Joe's marriage to Marilyn Monroe had turned to shit at about the same time, the two had commiserated and drunk together. Now, during the summer of *Sergeants 3*, while Skinny and Joltin' Joe talked about the good old days, Frank was sleeping with Marilyn, who had divorced her third husband, the playwright Arthur Miller, on January 20, the day of Kennedy's inauguration. Dean himself had known Marilyn since early 1953, before Sinatra had met her, before DiMaggio had married her. It seemed that everybody—man, woman, and beast—wanted to fuck her. But her sexiness was only desperation. It had been in her eyes for years: death like a Valentine.

Both Dean and Sinatra were invited by Ambassador and Mrs. Joseph Kennedy to attend Princess Grace of Monaco's International Red Cross Ball on August 11. Dean sent Jeannie off to Monte Carlo with Janet Leigh, assuring her that he would meet her there. Sammy Davis entertained. Peter and Patricia Lawford were there. But neither Dean nor Sinatra showed up. "They were last reported in Germany," noted United Press International's coverage of the event.

Ada was released later that month. *Variety* found Dean "pretty hard to swallow as the guv"; the *Daily News,* on the other hand, said "Dean Martin gives an admirable performance." Moviegoers seemed not to care much either way, and the well-crafted little political soap opera passed with little notice.

On August 29, Dean filed two suits charging fraud and mismanagement against his three partners in Dino's Lodge. One complaint sought an order dissolving Dino's Lodge, Inc.; the other sought $24,000 the partners owed him under their August 1959 agreement. Acquiring Maury Samuels's stock, the other partners had gained majority control, fired Dean's brother, Bill, and begun stiffing Dean. The $24,000 would be paid him. His suits would be dismissed. But in January he would file another suit, for an injunction to prevent the further use of his name or image to advertise the joint. His petition would be denied; the joint, beneath his ire, would continue as Dino's for years to come.

On September 6, with producer Dave Cavanaugh, Dean began three days' work at Capitol on an album of Italian songs. Five of the songs were versions of songs from the 1946 *Phil Brito Sings Songs of Italy* album that had long ago made such an impression on Dean. "Dicitencello Vuie," a 1930 song by Rodolfo Falvo, was recorded now, as Vic Damone had recorded it in 1950, as "Just Say I Love Her." "Mattinata," written for the phonograph by the Neapolitan composer of *Pagliacci,* Ruggiero Leoncavallo, had been recorded by Caruso in 1904, by Nino Martini in 1935. "O Sole Mio" was done in its 1949 hit form, as "There's No Tomorrow." Composed in 1893, "O Marenariello," older even than "O Sole Mio," was recorded as "I Have but One Heart," the 1945 English-language version that both

Vic Damone and Sinatra had done in 1947, after Brito. "Vieni Su," a ringer by Jack Edwards and Walter Rosemont, had been recorded by Dean before, in 1949. Seven other recordings made up the album's dozen: "Arrivederci, Roma," from 1954; "Non Dimenticar," a minor hit for Nat King Cole in 1958; "My Heart Reminds Me," which had originated in Italy five years before as "Concerto d'Autunno"; new versions of "Torna a Surriento," "Ritorna a Me," and "Sott' er Celo de Roma"; and "Perdoname," one of Carmen Lombardo and Danny Di Minno's *mezzo italiano* counterfeits.

Dino: Italian Love Songs was a terrible album. The idea was great, some of the songs were great, Dean's voice was great. The liner notes explained the ruination of those factors: "Gus Levene's tasteful orchestral backing, featuring lush strings, mandolin, accordion, marimba, and a lovely chorus of voices, provides appropriate Mediterranean settings." This was Italian music made whiter than white. To hear Dean's 1951 version of "Torna a Surriento" was to feel a strange and timeless power; to hear his new version was to feel nothing—eros and death transformed into a pink-frosted pastry; the old ways, new and improved. His last album, *This Time I'm Swingin'*, recorded in 1960 with Nelson Riddle, produced by Lee Gillette, had been a wonderful failure. *Dino: Italian Love Songs*, released in February 1962, would be an abomination and a success.

Later in September, he was back at the Sands, with what *Variety* now called "his highly engaging 'somebody wrote this song so I might as well sing it' attitude." On October 6, while he was at the Sands, Jeannie entered Cedars of Lebanon Hospital for treatment of a pinched nerve. He flew in to see her and was back in time for the first show.

He still was not finishing the songs he began. Nor had he added anything new to his act—"and," as *Variety* said, "he doesn't have to, having become somewhat of a living legend in Vegas."

He was also becoming something of a legend in Chicago. He was the one who did not like to kneel, the one who refused to kiss the ring. The FBI had illegally bugged the Armory Lounge, Sam Giancana's hangout on West Roosevelt Road in the western suburb of Forest Park. On December 6, there was a conversation with Johnny Formosa, a henchman who oversaw operations in Lake

County, Indiana, and served as Giancana's emissary between Chicago and the West Coast. Giancana was by now rightly convinced that the whole Kennedy business had been a mistake. As Giancana would later say of Sinatra's political influence: "He can't get change for a quarter." The Kennedys were shit. Sinatra was shit. They were all shit.

"You see Dean," Giancana told Formosa. "You tell him I want ten days out of him."

"Ten days?"

"In other words, you get two weekends in."

"Where? At the Lake?"

"No, no. For a friend of mine."

"What if he says he's booked?"

"Find out when he ain't booked."

"All right."

"Right after, uh, January, about the tenth."

"In other words, you want ten days. Three days a week."

"January, February, March, and April."

"Ten days, three days each week."

"Yeah. You start on a Friday. Saturday, Sunday, Monday, Tuesday, Wednesday, Thursday, Friday, Saturday, and Sunday."

"Oh, that way?"

"Yeah, in other words, you get two weekends."

"Oh, I get it."

"January, February, March, around there. That'll give you a long time."

"I tell him this is a must, right? Tell him you said it. Tell him, 'Hey, Dean, this is a must. Sam wants you for ten days.'"

"Just put it to him for a couple weeks."

"Couple weeks. And if he says, 'Where?' I'll say, 'In Chicago.' He'll give me that date and then I'll get ahold of you. You'll give me more on it?

"Well, I better go west then. After Sunday, I'm free."

"Don't make a special trip. Call him."

"That fuckin' prima donna. You can't call him. I gotta go there and lay the law down to him, so he knows I mean business."

. . .

The week before Christmas, Dean made his final Capitol recordings, fulfilling his contract by laying in enough for another album. The last song he recorded, on December 20, was "A Hundred Years from Today," a song that Ethel Waters had recorded with Benny Goodman back in 1933, the year that Prohibition had ended, the year before seventeen-year-old Dino Crocetti had worked up the balls to get up onstage and sing.

Dean filmed a guest appearance late in the year, along with Sinatra, for the Crosby-Hope picture *The Road to Hong Kong.* His own next picture, *Who's Got the Action?*, a horseplayers' comedy based on a novel by Alexander Rose, went into production in January 1962 with Daniel Mann directing. For Mann, who in his ten years of moviemaking had concentrated on a more serious sort of picture, *Who's Got the Action?* was a drastic departure. Herman Citron had set the deal up with producer Jack Rose and Paramount so that Mann, like Dean, would be given a share in the picture's profits.

"I figured, Jesus, that's beautiful," Mann remembered. "I'll get away from something heavy and I'll do a little comedy, which I would love to do. My origins were in the borscht circuit. I was a musician. New York, the Catskills."

It was a pleasant experience. "Never any problems with Dean, never any problems in terms of temperament or bullshit or anything else. It couldn't have been nicer. We would go back into his dressing-room, instead of going to the Paramount commissary. Jay Gerard would organize some Italian food. We'd have a banquet, for Chrissake."

The picture was about gambling; but there was as much betting on the set as in the script. Dean and his co-star Walter Matthau had their own bookmaker on the Paramount lot.

"I wasn't betting," Mann said. "I didn't drink. I guess I was maybe even considered kind of square. It had nothing to do with morality. These were not things that gave me any pleasure. So, one day, this guy came on the stage, this guy that Dean and some of the others were betting with, and he said, 'Danny, there's a horse named Catcall, and it's gonna win.' And I said, 'Okay.' I dug into my pocket, the first thing I grabbed was a fifty-dollar bill. I said, 'Put this on the nose.' And I'm not a horse-bettor. Anyway, the end of the day, or the next day, in came this guy, and I was in the middle of a scene, and when the scene was over, he rushed up to me and handed me $750. That $750 cost me a couple of thousand."

Dean played Steve Flood, a lawyer whose gambling leads to problems. Lana Turner, who years ago, coming on to him, had done everything but stick it in Dean's face, played Melanie Flood, his wife. Turner, now forty-two and less lively, collapsed from exhaustion during a birthday party for her on the set in February.

On February 13, five days after Turner's collapse, Dean made his first recordings for Sinatra's year-old Reprise label. He began in Italian: "Senza Fine."

Herman Citron, Dean's agent at MCA, had pioneered profit-participation in 1950 by freeing James Stewart from his studio contract and winning him a percentage of the take from *Winchester '73*. Through similar deals for other stars—Dean was one of them—MCA became an important factor in the breakdown of the studio-contract system. Under Citron's guidance, Dean had formed Claude Productions, Inc., in 1960. *Sergeants 3*, now playing, was a joint production of Dean's and Sinatra's companies, Claude and Essex. *Who's Got the Action?* was coproduced by Claude Productions as well; and from here on, Dean, in addition to his acting pay, would participate in the profits of every picture he made, either through the direct involvement of his company as producer or through contractual arrangements with the studio involved.

In 1962, in the midst of taking over both Universal Pictures and Decca Records, MCA, seen as controlling a sixty-percent share of the entertainment industry, was brought to task by the U.S. Justice Department under Bobby Kennedy. When the government succeeded in forcing the dissolution of MCA's talent-agency division, Herman Citron formed his own firm, the Citron-Park Agency, with Arthur Park. There he would continue to ensure that Dean, along with Jimmy Stewart and the rest of his small but select clientele, would receive a percentage of every dollar of profit their films brought the studios.

And, beginning with Dean's first Reprise session, no record company would own the permanent rights to his recordings. Those rights would be retained by Claude Productions, from which the record company would merely lease them.

Sinatra continued to entertain delusions of his place in Camelot. The door of a guest room at his Palm Springs home bore a plaque with Kennedy's name on it. He had gone so far as to have a heliport constructed on his estate, in preparation for an anticipated presidential visit in March. Cottages were added for the Secret Service. There were extra telephone lines installed, a flagpole erected. It was fucking ridiculous.

On February 25, Dean and Sinatra appeared as guests on "The Judy Garland Show." Two days later, on February 27, Attorney General Robert F. Kennedy received a memo from Director J. Edgar Hoover of the FBI. During its investigation of Johnny Rosselli, the Bureau had been led to Judith Campbell, whose telephone records, in turn, had revealed several calls to President Kennedy's personal secretary at the White House, as well as to Sam Giancana in Chicago. Bobby advised his brother, increased his office's surveillance of Giancana, and called Peter Lawford, his brother-in-law. He explained the situation to Lawford: JFK would have to steer clear of Sinatra, who was obviously the catalyst in the Kennedy-Campbell-Giancana triangle. On his trip west in March, the president would stay at Bing Crosby's home. Lawford would have to break the news to Sinatra.

"Frank was livid," Lawford said. "He called Bobby every name in the book." When Lawford left, Sinatra's butler watched him go at the heliport with a sledgehammer.

The message and the messenger were one. As far as Sinatra was concerned, that was the end of Lawford.

Releasing Dean's first Reprise single, "Just Close Your Eyes," at the end of the month, Sinatra's company took out a two-page advertisement in the March 3 *Billboard,* "revealing a long-held, poorly kept, highly portentous secret: Dean Martin's on Reprise!"

Dean's first Reprise album, *French Style* ("Mfgd. by Claude Prod. Inc."), was released in April, by which time he was back at the Sands, billed as just Dino. "He alters his act slightly this time in

that he completes quite a few songs," *Variety* observed. A month
later, in May, the Capitol album *Dino: Italian Love Songs* became
the first of Dean's albums to appear on the Top LP charts. Its *reduc-
tio ad tritum* rendering of the ersatz dago-cool eidos was taken up
by the Dino-manqué masses as a sort of stereo Spanish fly.

By then, Dean was at work on a new movie, called *Something's
Got to Give*. The deal, between Twentieth Century-Fox and Claude
Productions, called for him to receive $300,000 plus seven and a
half percent of the picture's profits. His costar was Marilyn Monroe.
Under her contract with Twentieth Century-Fox, she would be get-
ting $100,000, only a third of Dean's price.

Dean had always been fond of Marilyn, who seemed more lost
now than ever before. Sinatra had dumped her and gotten engaged
to Juliet Prowse in January. In early February, not long before the
sundering of Sinatra's Camelot delusions, Peter Lawford had introduced Marilyn to Bobby Kennedy at a dinner at the Lawford home.
Now Bobby, the protector of his brother's moral image, was stricken
himself with one of Sinatra's hand-me-downs; and Marilyn had
fallen under the Kennedy spell. Bobby seemed even more of a punk
than Jack. It was an American Gothic imagining: Marilyn and
Bobby, coupling furtively, awkwardly, in the ulterior embrace of two
starfucking fools; the attorney general and the platinum-blond goddess.

Something's Got to Give was really nothing more than a rework-
ing by Nunnally Johnson of a 1939 Cary Grant comedy called *My
Favorite Wife:* a woman, long assumed dead after being ship-
wrecked, reappears on her husband's wedding day. Twentieth Century-Fox had fallen on hard times. The studio had suffered a
$22,000,000 loss for the previous year, and the draining folly of
Elizabeth Taylor and *Cleopatra* was felt daily. It was hoped that
Something's Got to Give, with the drawing power of Monroe and
Martin, would help pull Fox back into the black. But it was not
meant to be.

Dean liked Marilyn. He felt sorry for her in a way. But she
turned the picture into a nightmare. She had made demands, which
the studio had met. Dean had been cast at her insistence. Producer
David Brown had been replaced by Harry Weinstein. Director Frank

Tashlin had been replaced by George Cukor. Production had been scheduled to begin on April 23, but Marilyn did not show up for work until May, when, after one day, she vanished again. She put in another three and a half days, then, on May 17, flew off with Peter Lawford in a helicopter to the Inglewood airport. She appeared two nights later at John F. Kennedy's birthday celebration at Madison Square Garden, to which Dean had also been invited. Bobby was with his wife, but JFK was alone. She returned to work on Monday, May 21, for a nude-swimming scene. Instead of the flesh-colored bikini she was supposed to wear in the pool, she stripped naked, and much of the day's shooting was lost to a nude-photography session. On June 4, the Monday following her thirty-sixth birthday, she failed to show up for work.

"I can't stand an actor or actress who tells me acting is hard work," Dean told a *New York Times* reporter who visited the set. "It's easy work. Anyone who says it isn't never had to stand on his feet all day dealing blackjack."

Peter G. Levathes, the Fox executive vice-president in charge of studio production, had been in Europe contending with the *Cleopatra* debacle. He was scheduled to return by June 8. Anticipating his return, Monroe, on June 7, issued a statement that she "was ready and eager to go back to work Monday." By then, she had appeared for only twelve of thirty-four production days. Upon his arrival in New York, Levathes wanted to hear nothing of Marilyn's willingness to return to work. On the Friday afternoon of June 8, a few minutes before the superior-court filings closed, Twentieth Century-Fox registered a $500,000 breach-of-contract suit against her and told the press that she was being removed from the cast of *Something's Got to Give.* Later that evening, it was announced that she would be replaced by Lee Remick.

On the following morning, through MCA, Dean notified the studio that he was quitting. His statement to the press read: "I have the greatest respect for Miss Lee Remick and her talent and all the other actresses who were considered for the role, but I signed to do the picture with Marilyn Monroe and I will do it with no one else." He had not even wanted to do the picture, he told others; he had accepted only because "Marilyn wanted me."

Attempts by Levathes to dissuade him from his decision failed. On Monday evening, June 11, Fox announced that *Something's Got to Give* had been shut down. A week later, on June 18, the studio filed suit against Dean and Claude Productions. Charging that Dean had verbally promised to consider a replacement for Monroe, then declined in "bad faith" to do so, the action sought $3,339,000—the $2,339,000 lost on the aborted picture, plus $1,000,000 in "exemplary damages." A week later, on June 25, Claude Productions filed a countersuit against the studio for $6,885,550, charging his reputation had been defamed by "false, fraudulent and misleading statements." Both lawsuits would lumber on in superior court for nearly a year. In the end, they would come to nothing. And *Something's Got to Give* would finally be made, with Doris Day and James Garner, as *Move Over, Darling*.

Skinny D'Amato had returned in May to Atlantic City from Lake Tahoe, where he had overseen the $2,200,000 expansion and renovation of the Cal-Neva Lodge, undertaken with a $1,500,000 loan from the Bank of Nevada. The FBI had questioned him about the Cal-Neva in April. He told them all about the new dining-room that would seat nearly five hundred, the showroom that would accommodate over seven hundred, the new shops, and the redecorated rooms that would start at sixteen dollars a night. So far, all the federal agents had on him was 1,450 pounds of stolen beef he had bought for $362.50 in December of 1961. The FBI reports concerning the purloined beef duly noted that Skinny "stated that if he had suspected that the meat was stolen, he would not have purchased it." The special agent who interrogated Skinny in April reported: "He said that because of his acquaintances with people who are alleged to be in the rackets, his character has been ruined.

"He stated that he cannot deny that he knows many of these persons, most of them who have become known to him through his contacts at the 500 Club. He stated he cannot now tell them to go away."

Sinatra himself headlined the opening of the new Cal-Neva on June 29. Dean opened there a month later, on July 27. Marilyn Monroe came to Cal-Neva on both occasions. On the first, she overdosed on pills and booze. On the second, wandering around in a ghostly stupor, she spoke to Skinny D'Amato of things of which, as he told her, people ought not to speak. Dean knew what was wrong with her, beyond the pills, beyond the booze, beyond the whole endless lost-little-girl thing: She just could not handle the dirty knowledge into which she had wandered, the black forest of Sam Giancana and Johnny Rosselli and her darling scumbag Kennedys, that world that lay past the dreamland she had shared with those who paid to see her. She wanted back into the fairytale, but there was really no way back. Dean knew things that people would not believe, things about the government sucking up to men such as Rosselli and Giancana, dealing with them in death, while others in government persecuted them; things about the black knights and the white knights fucking the same broads, drinking from the same bottle, and sharing the same spoils and murderous plots. Marilyn had glimpsed these things through her own errant innocence, and they had terrified her. The great temptress had finally encountered a few wisps of what really lay in the garden of temptation. Dean could see it: She was not long for this world. If she did not shut her mouth, she would not even need the pills to take her where she was going.

On July 26, Bobby Kennedy came to Los Angeles to deliver a speech to the National Insurance Association. While he was on his way to the engagement, the Los Angeles office of the FBI received an anonymous call warning that "gangland characters" were planning to murder him. Was Monroe trying to warn him or scare him? Was it even she who made the call? There was no point in asking. These were things even Johnny Rosselli did not know. On July 30, after Kennedy had returned to Washington, Monroe made her final call to his office at the Justice Department. Less than six days later, on August 5, Monroe was found dead in her bedroom. Events surrounding her death that later came to light—reports of a visit to her Brentwood home by Bobby Kennedy the night before; of an ambulance that night that took her away breathing and returned her dead —would inspire endless conjecture. Marilyn would be joined beyond the grave by her dear Kennedys; the three of them would become the stars of an endless afterlife soap opera. From two sleazy little books in 1964, *The Strange Death of Marilyn Monroe* and *Who Killed Kennedy?,* a dreamworld industry would grow. Conspiracy was everywhere: new, improved, whiter than white.

"There is more to what happened than anyone has told" is all that Skinny D'Amato would say.

What he knew, others knew: about Monroe, about the Kennedys, about Sam Giancana; about the thread of dirty, gray truth lost amid the glittering, gulling lies and fantasies.

On August 16, J. Edgar Hoover sent a personal memorandum to Attorney General Robert F. Kennedy. It conveyed information Hoover had received from the FBI field office in Tampa: "Before the last presidential election, Joseph P. Kennedy (the father of President John Kennedy) had been visited by many gangsters with gambling interests and a deal was made which resulted in Peter Lawford, Frank Sinatra, Dean Martin and others obtaining a lucrative gambling establishment, the Cal-Neva Hotel, at Lake Tahoe. These gangsters reportedly met with Joseph Kennedy at the Cal-Neva, where Kennedy was staying at the time." Hoover's implication was that old Joe Kennedy had arranged the deal whereby Sam Giancana, Skinny D'Amato, and the others took over the Cal-Neva in exchange for their support of his son Jack's presidential campaign.

A day later, on August 17, two weeks after Marilyn died, Dean and D'Amato flew together from Los Angeles to Philadelphia, then drove together to Atlantic City. Dean opened the next night at the 500 Club. The FBI was never far from them: "DEAN MARTIN, friend of subject, appeared at 500 Club," reported a special agent from the Newark office.

D'Amato needed the business. Atlantic City was dying a slow, ugly death. "I'm here because Skinny is a friend," Dean told a reporter who visited him at his suite at the Claridge Hotel.

The reporter asked him if he noticed any changes in Atlantic City since the last time he was here, five years ago.

"All I've seen are the cops that escort me, and the club. I eat backstage between shows, do another show, and they escort me back here."

He looked to the sliding glass doors that led to the terrace. "Is that rain? I haven't seen rain in seven months."

Did he have anything to say about the death of Marilyn Monroe?

"No." He watched the rain awhile. "She was a wonderful girl." Enough was enough.

"This is the longest interview I've had in two years."

On August 23, Sinatra joined Dean in Atlantic City. A crowd of nearly a thousand huddled outside the 500 Club as Police Captain Mario Floriani delivered the two singers to the service entrance. They performed together for Skinny for three nights running. On the third night, Sammy Davis, Jr., joined them.

The following week, in Los Angeles, Dean recorded his second Reprise album, *Dino Latino*. On September 2, Dean and Sinatra opened for two nights together at the Cal-Neva. On September 5, Dean went on to the Sands, with Sinatra joining him there later in the week. Work on Dean's next picture, *Toys in the Attic*, began on September 19.

The film version of Lillian Hellman's play had been in development for almost two years, since soon after the play itself had opened at the Hudson Theatre on Broadway in February 1960. The Mirisch Company, which held the rights to it, had recently produced the enormously successful *West Side Story*, as well as Hellman's *Children's Hour;* with Dean's involvement, *Toys in the Attic* became a Mirisch-Claude coproduction. Forty-year-old George Roy Hill, chosen to direct, had made only one other picture, the film version of Tennessee Williams's *Period of Adjustment*. The news that Dean had been chosen for the widely coveted role of Julian, played on Broadway by Jason Robards, had stirred both astonishment and anger in so-called serious-acting circles. A *New York Times* writer who approached Dean on the set found him "quite aware that there are some who think he is not good enough for the part of the flighty, tormented, tragic young Southerner."

Who were these serious cocksuckers, these jerk-offs who approached moving pictures as if they were fucking reality, who wouldn't even know reality if it bit them on the ass?

"I never saw the play. I never read the play," he said.

The *Times* was aghast at the horror of his words. "Actually, Mr. Martin dislikes all plays," the paper reported. Furthermore, his "favorite method of learning lines is to have his caddie cue him on the golf course."

"I don't know why everyone made such a mystery about how I got the part," he said. "My agent did it. Herman Citron—he's been my agent for maybe fifteen years—saw the play and liked it. He told me I ought to do it. I think Herman has good judgment about movies. So I said okay. Herman bargained with the Mirisch Company and I got the part. That's all there was to it so far as I'm concerned."

The reporter fled to the dressing-room of Dean's costar Wendy Hiller, the British actress "whose career in the theater as well as in movies is long and honorable." But Hiller, who "put aside a collection of Henry James's works" to talk to the *Times,* had not a bad word to say for Dean or his work.

Walter Mirisch thought Dean was a fine choice. "I think his performance in it was really outstanding," he would say. "Unfortunately, the film came rather at the end of a cycle of Southern psychological films. I think it was a very good film, but it wasn't a very successful film."

Dean and Sinatra had become directors of Hancock Raceways in Massachusetts through a joint stock purchase arranged by the track's president, Salvatore Rizzo, whom many believed to be a front-man for Boston shadow-boss Raymond Patriarca. On October 12, both Dean and Frank, along with Rizzo, were named as defendants in a suit filed by Dr. Charles Furcolo, the father of the former Massachusetts governor Foster Furcolo. The doctor, whose Hancock stock had been held in the name of an accountant, charged that the stock, worth $500,000, had been sold without his knowledge to Rizzo for $150,000, and that Martin and Sinatra were guilty, with Rizzo and the accountant, of "conspiring to deprive" him of the stock in question. Representing Dean and Sinatra, the law firm of Gang, Tyre, Rudin & Brown maintained that their clients were no longer involved with Hancock, as the Nevada gaming laws prohibited casino owners from engaging in any gambling enterprises in other states. A subsequent probe by a Massachusetts state-legislature committee into unrelated goings-on at Hancock threatened to subpoena the two singers to testify. Neither Dean nor Sinatra—nor, it seemed, anyone in Massachusetts—knew what in hell was going on. Where the fuck was Kennedy when you needed him?

Sam Giancana, meanwhile, was breathing down their necks from Chicago. Dean had defied Giancana's request for a command performance earlier in the year. The way he saw it, Sinatra and Kennedy and Giancana could keep their bullshit to themselves. Giancana saw it differently: Sinatra owed him for Kennedy, and it was up to Sinatra to deliver Dean as well. A further exchange between Giancana and Johnny Formosa had been recorded at the Armory Lounge:

"Let's show 'em," Formosa said. "Let's show those asshole Hollywood fruitcakes that they can't get away with it as if nothing's happened. Let's hit Sinatra. Or I could whack out a couple of those other guys, Lawford and that Martin, and I could take the nigger and put his other eye out."

"No," Giancana said. "I've got other plans for them."

Located northwest of Chicago, on Milwaukee Avenue in Northbrook, Illinois, the Villa Venice was a roadhouse joint that Giancana had secretly owned since 1956. It was a place where he, Tony Accardo, Paul Ricca, and others met to drink and do business. In 1961, Giancana and his new front-man at the Villa Venice, Leo Olsen, decided to renovate the joint into a big-time nightclub. Now, in October 1962, the Villa Venice was about to have its grand reopening. Giancana had set up a Quonset-hut casino two blocks away, near the Flamingo Motel on River Road. There would be regular shuttle-bus service between the club and the casino. Johnny Formosa and Johnny Rosselli proved, in the end, to be quite capable booking agents. Sinatra, Dean, and Sammy Davis would perform together at the Villa Venice in November. For free.

On October 22, before they left Los Angeles, Dean and Sammy Davis recorded a duet of "Sam's Song." Coupled with a duet by Sinatra and Davis, Reprise issued it in a special picture sleeve on November 9, in time for their engagement at Sam's joint.

FBI agents visited the three of them after they checked into their suites at the Ambassador East Hotel. Sinatra told the agents that he was performing as a favor to the club's owner, Leo Olsen.

Dean just waved them away: more scumbags. They asked Davis what he was doing there.

"Baby, that's a very good question. But I have to say it's for my man Francis."

"Or friends of his?"

"By all means."

"Like Sam Giancana?"

"By all means."

Onstage at the Villa Venice, Sinatra asked for a stool. Someone in the wings threw one to him.

"I thought you owned some of this. And that's how they treat you," Dean cracked.

Later, he pointed upward. "Hold the noise down," he told Sinatra and Davis, "there's a gangster sleeping up there."

FBI surveillance on November 27 followed Dean and Sinatra in the company of Joe Fischetti, who had come in from Florida.

Between business at the Villa Venice and action at the Quonset hut, Sam took in an estimated $3,000,000 during the engagement. Sinatra had planned for himself, Dean, and Davis to make a buck as well. Mo Ostin, who ran Reprise for him, had arranged to record a live album at the Villa Venice—*The Mafia's Greatest Hits*, as Dean wryly referred to it. Those live recordings, however, would never be released.

On December 1, while Dean was in Chicago, *Who's Got the Action?* was previewed in New York at the Forum, one of the theaters where it was scheduled to open on Christmas Eve. *Variety* judged it a "fair comedy." The *Morning Telegraph*, a paper known for its racing pages, found that "the most intriguing performer in the whole picture is a huge, complex Univac calculating machine, through whose flashing bulbs and whirring buzzers Walter Matthau manages to keep track of a whole network of thousands of customers anxious to put down two bucks in the fifth."

That week, Dean made a fleeting appearance near the bottom of the pop-singles charts, his first since 1959, with "From the Bottom of My Heart (Dammi Dammi Dammi)," one of Danny Di Minno's new quasi-Italian confections. Returning later in the month to California from Chicago, Dean decided to try something new in the studio. If he could be a cowboy, he could be a country singer as well. He recorded a dozen songs. Some of them were country classics: "Room Full of Roses," a 1949 country hit by the Sons of the Pioneers; Hank Williams's 1951 "Hey, Good Lookin'" and "I'm So Lonesome I Could Cry," which Williams had recorded in 1949 but which would not become a hit until its reissue in 1966; Johnny Cash's "I Walk the Line," from 1956. Others were country in the same sense that Danny Di Minno's songs were Italian: Clint Ballard's "Ain't Gonna Try Anymore," Mitchell Torok and Ramona Redd's "Face in a Crowd."

From Lillian Hellman to Sam Giancana to Hank Williams: *l'America.*

Dean, Sinatra, and Sammy opened at the Sands together on January 23, 1963. A week later, an FBI teletype—"URGENT 1-30-63 3-22 PM"—reported the event to Hoover in Washington and the office in Newark: "IT IS NOTED FRANK SINATRA, DEAN MARTIN, AND SAMMY DAVIS, JR. ARE CURRENTLY PLAYING AT THE SANDS HOTEL."

Dick Powell, June Allyson's husband, breathed his last that month. As gladly as he had filled in for Powell in other ways in the past, Dean now gladly filled in as a guest host for the February 23 episode of the weekly NBC drama anthology "The Dick Powell Show."

Dean began work that month on his third and last picture with Danny Mann, another Jack Rose Paramount comedy, *Who's Been Sleeping in My Bed?* Dean's role seemed perfect. He played Jason Steel, a therapist who specialized in unhappily married broads. Elizabeth Montgomery played his fiancée; Jill St. John, *scappatella* to Dean since 1958 and now true love to Sinatra, played one of the neglected wives pursuing him; Richard Conte, one of the neglectful husbands.

There was a moment during the making of *Who's Been Sleeping in My Bed?* that Danny Mann would never forget, a rare glimpse into the mystery of Dean's inner demons. The scene in the script called for Dean's character, the therapist, to extrapolate his own anxieties on another analyst's couch. It was a scene that *Variety* would later describe as "disagreeable." Mann had never seen Dean have the slightest difficulty with a scene, had never known him to forget a line or a cue. He was not even revealing himself; he was playing a character who was revealing himself. It was only make-believe in a dumb comedy. But still it unnerved him.

"That was a tough scene for Dean to do. One of the problems he had was remembering the words. There was never any problem in any other scene."

Dean and Sinatra were soon at work on another picture together: *Four for Texas.* Directed by Robert Aldrich, who recently had done *Whatever Happened to Baby Jane?,* this second Sinatra-Martin production was a half-witted Western comedy with Anita Ekberg, Ursula Andress, and Charles Bronson.

Dean turned forty-six in June. All he seemed to remember were the colors of breezes. Long ago in a hotel room in Cleveland, a rainy early-autumn gust had come through an open window and stirred the curtains like sighing sullen ghosts; and he had felt something. Now his oldest boy, Craig, was a man. He had joined the army, been sent off to Germany, had met a Tucson girl named Sandy Pfiffer there. Now, on June 29, Craig's twenty-first birthday, they were marrying.

Other breezes, other nights: Claudia was nineteen now. She wanted to be an actress, a singer, something. Sinatra's daughter Nancy also wanted to be an actress, a singer, something. Her father was giving her a part in a picture, a half-assed plug for Pepsi-Cola called *For Those Who Think Young,* that Sinatra Enterprises was making with James Darren at Paramount. Dean talked to Frank and got Claudia a part. They would start filming in August. She was in love, she said. Some *guaglione* fresh from a fucking Juárez divorce: Gavin Murrell, a name like a character in one of these stupid fucking pictures. In July, she ran off and married him. That was bad enough. She divorced him just as suddenly. Dean sat her down and shut the door. She left the house in tears; and the two of them did not speak for months.

Sam Giancana and Skinny D'Amato were now both under constant surveillance by the FBI. Giancana had sued to enjoin the

federal agents from harassment, claiming that their continual presence was an infringement on his constitutional right to privacy.
Though the court had decided in Giancana's favor, the FBI did not
relent. Bobby Kennedy wanted his fucking guinea ass. The idea that
a common wop gangster without even a trace of Harvard in his
accent should enjoy the same prosperity and pussy as the president
of the United States, especially when that president was a Kennedy,
was an affront to democracy.

The McGuire Sisters were scheduled to open at Cal-Neva on
July 27. Giancana arrived there with Phyllis on July 17. The FBI
reported Sam's presence to the Nevada Gaming Control Board,
whose chairman, Ed Olsen, summoned Sinatra to meet with him on
August 8, eleven days after Giancana left Lake Tahoe. Sinatra at the
time was in Las Vegas, where Dean had opened at the Sands two
nights before.

Tony Curtis and Janet Leigh had gotten divorced. Mort Viner,
who now handled Dean with Herman Citron, had, together with
Jeannie Martin, introduced Leigh to a man named Bob Brandt. Now,
in Las Vegas, Dean was throwing a wedding party for them.

On his opening night at the Sands, Sinatra and Davis came
onstage for the now-predictable Rat Pack routines. Dean loved it; it
meant less singing for him. Nine days ago, on August 28, a civil-
rights rally in Washington had brought forth almost a quarter of a
million people.

"Sammy wanted me to march on Washington," he told the audience. "I wouldn't march even if the Italians were marching."

While the FBI had evidence of Sinatra and Giancana golfing
and dining together, Sinatra told Olsen that he had barely greeted
Giancana in passing outside of McGuire's cabin. On the afternoon
of September 1, Sinatra and Olsen spoke once again, this time by
telephone. "Don't fuck with me," Sinatra had ended up telling him.
"Just don't fuck with me."

Two hours later, a pair of control-board audit agents arrived at
Cal-Neva to monitor counts of the gaming-table drop-boxes. When
they returned two days later, Skinny D'Amato offered them a hundred bucks each. They declined the money and reported the attempted bribe to Olsen. On September 11, Olsen issued a complaint

seeking the revocation of Sinatra's gaming license on several grounds, including attempted bribery and the violation of state laws prohibiting known criminals from casinos.

The Cal-Neva trouble came at an importune time. In October, just a few weeks after the control-board complaint was issued, Joseph Valachi, the government's prized paid rat, began testifying before the U.S. Senate's Permanent Subcommittee on Investigations. Spectacularly orchestrated for the media by Bobby Kennedy, Valachi's testimony was used to corroborate the picture of organized crime that the government had devised in its own image, the only image that it could truly comprehend: that of an ordered, homogenous entity, an imagined ideal bureaucracy. Valachi's testimony popularized the Italian phrase *Cosa Nostra*. It carried an air of inside knowledge that the well-worn *Mafia* now lacked. It was new and improved. Valachi's testimony did something else: It named Sam Giancana as the head of the Cosa Nostra in Chicago, one of the twelve overlords of crime in America. It did not matter that Valachi had never even met Giancana. The script, after all, had been written by Bobby Kennedy. The sudden burst of increased notoriety for Giancana would draw too much attention to Cal-Neva and perhaps even expose his hidden interest in it. By the day Sinatra was scheduled to respond to the gaming board's complaint, it was announced that his ownership of Cal-Neva was being dissolved. It was a financial shot in the shorts. Dean had been right to pull out when he did.

Reprise Records changed hands as well that summer. *Four for Texas,* like *Ocean's Eleven,* had been made for Warner Brothers, which had been operating a record company of its own since 1958. Few real singers recorded for Warner Brothers Records. The label's first, small hit had been by Tab Hunter. Other would-be singers were drawn from Warner Brothers' stable of television actors: Edd Byrnes and Roger Smith from "77 Sunset Strip," Connie Stevens from "Hawaiian Eye." On the other hand, Warner Brothers Records also had the Everly Brothers, one of the biggest acts in the country, and comedians Allan Sherman and Bob Newhart had given the company five number-one albums between them. In a merger deal worked out with Jack Warner on August 7, Warner Brothers Records paid Sinatra $3,000,000 for Reprise, and Sinatra in turn paid

Warner Brothers $2,000,000 for a one-third interest in the new Warner Brothers Reprise Records. The merger became effective in September. John Maitland, the president of Warner Brothers Records, became the president of the new Reprise division as well. Mo Ostin, who had run Reprise for Sinatra, continued to supervise the company under Maitland, with Sinatra as a member of the board of directors. At the same time, Sinatra and Jack Warner worked out a parallel deal by which Sinatra's new production company, Artanis Productions, Inc., would become a part of Warner Brothers Pictures.

Toys in the Attic, meanwhile, had opened on the last day of July. The *Daily News* declared it "one of the distinguished dramas of the year," and the *New York Journal-American* said, "The performance of Mr. Martin is—there is no other word for it—great." But these were voices of the hoi polloi. Other reviewers were not so receptive. Many objected to the new artificial ending that had been imposed by screenwriter James Poe. "Hollywood has made even more of a wreck of Lillian Hellman's 'Toys in the Attic' than was made of it on the stage," wrote Bosley Crowther of the *Times*. And Dean became the *bête noire* of the season. "Dean Martin, who plays the brother, moves woodenly throughout—on the verge, one feels, of singing 'That's Amore,'" wrote Christopher Rand of *The New Yorker*. "The casting of Dean Martin," wrote Stanley Kauffmann in *The New Republic*, "is an offense." To an objective eye, these words represented not so much an honest reaction to Dean's performance in the picture, but rather a reaction to his very presence in it. They were protective lapdog yelps in defense of a dainty cultural territory where Dean simply must never be allowed to intrude. To them the nickel-in-the-slot racket was *le cinema*. Dean openly scorned their world. To admit that he could play-act with the best of them would be to admit that—well, it would be to admit that it was all merely a matter of play-acting. He was anathema.

Toys in the Attic was a turning-point. From here on, there would be no more "serious" pictures for Dean. He would avoid them. He had proved himself as an actor. He had gained the respect of Marlon Brando, Montgomery Clift, Howard Hawks, Daniel Mann. Their respect was more important than the respect of those who sat jerking off at typewriters in a penny-a-word dreamworld. From here on, his pictures would be anti-serious, anti-art. In its review of *Who's Been Sleeping in My Bed?*, previewed on November 19, *Variety* would speak of the picture's lapses into "tastelessness." But those lapses were nothing compared to what was to follow. Dean would become the personification of tastelessness itself, projecting the image of one in whose scales of aesthetics a single good tit joke would outweigh all of Sophocles, Shakespeare, and Allardice. The spectrum of artistic worth as it pertained to the nickel-in-the-slot racket would become a lurid monochromatic blur. The low and the high, slapstick and splendor: it was all the same shit. He would make the easiest pictures he could for the most money he could get, lending to none of them the lie of integrity that veiled the crass greed at the heart of the racket. To him, no picture was art. He himself no longer even cared for pictures, except to lose himself in a Western. He no longer even watched his own finished pictures; he wondered at those who did, wondered at those who watched any picture, let alone those who were driven to find meaning in it. The very notion of looking for art in movies was like looking for love in a whorehouse. For some, such as Brando and Clift, there was money in playing that angle; but not for him.

Dean's next picture—"a big, gaudy, gimmicky comedy," *Variety* called it—was *What a Way to Go!* Written by Betty Comden and Adolph Green, from a story by Gwen Davis, *What a Way to Go!* was the tale, told in flashbacks from a psychiatrist's couch, of a poor Ohio girl whose search for true love led her through a succession of marriages and widowings that left her the richest woman in the world. Former publicist Arthur Jacobs, who owned the property, had never produced before.

"He asked my company to do it with his company. So we did it," said J. Lee Thompson, the Britisher who directed the picture. "Originally it was going to be done with Marilyn Monroe. When she died, we went to Shirley MacLaine."

Dean, Paul Newman, Robert Mitchum, and Gene Kelly played the husbands. Each of them put in only a week's work on the picture. Thompson, who had seen Martin and Lewis at the London Palladium ten years before, described Dean as "very pleasant to

work with and a lot of fun." The only problem came when he wanted
Dean to wear a red hairpiece for his role. "He didn't take kindly to
that. The first day on the set was rather stormy. He threw the wig
across his dressing-room. That was the end of the wig. He was very
adamant that he would not wear the wig. I failed to convince him
that I saw the character with red hair."

"It was rather a gentle little comedy," Thompson would say of
What a Way to Go! "It was really conceived on a small scale, and
probably we made the mistake of pumping it up into a big star
picture. I feel maybe we spoiled something by making it rather a
glitzy Hollywood star vehicle." Twentieth Century-Fox disagreed
with him. *What a Way to Go!* was one of the biggest hits of the
sixties.

When Sinatra and Jack Warner made their deals in the summer
of 1963, one picture remained to be made under a previous agreement with Warner Brothers: *Robin and the Seven Hoods.* It was a
musical comedy set in Prohibition-era Chicago, directed by Gordon
Douglas, who by now had made every sort of second-rate picture
imaginable, from *Zombies on Broadway* with Bela Lugosi to *Kiss
Tomorrow Goodbye* with James Cagney to *Them!* with a desertful of
giant ants. Besides Dean, Sinatra, and Sammy, the picture had some
added attractions: Bing Crosby, a score by Nelson Riddle, songs by
Sammy Cahn and James Van Heusen, and even an appearance by
Edward G. Robinson, Little Caesar himself. Peter Falk, Victor
Buono, Sonny King, and old-time movie-gangster Jack LaRue had
parts as well.

On November 22, they were filming a graveyard scene, the
burial of Edward G. Robinson's character when Jack Kennedy was
shot and killed in Dallas. Now you could almost hear Giancana's
voice in the cool November air: "I'm gonna put a new part in that
cocksucker's hair."

The end of Camelot was the end of the Rat Pack encampment
outside its fairyland walls. The carefree days of high hopes and
partying were done. America became aware now of a place called
Vietnam. It was out there somewhere, farther than Vegas, farther
than Los Angeles.

. . .

On December 8, in Lake Tahoe, Frank Sinatra's nineteen-year-old son was kidnapped at gunpoint and held for three days. The ransom was less than expected: $240,000. At their trial, the kidnappers would claim that it was all a hoax perpetrated by Frank Jr. as a stunt to attract publicity to his stillborn singing career. "I think the whole world has gone nuts," Dean said.

A few days later, on December 15, there was an eleventh-anniversary celebration at the Sands. Dean and Sinatra flew in and performed together. They were still the consuls of cool. But cool itself seemed to have lost its meaning in this winter of America's shriving. Even Elvis seemed over the hill. He had not had a Top Ten hit in over a year; and that one, "Bossa Nova Baby," had sounded like one of Dean's rejects. "Witchcraft" had been the flip side.

Four for Texas and *Who's Been Sleeping in My Bed?* both opened for Christmas. This juxtaposition in Times Square of gross Western and tasteless comedy was an illumination of Dean's *métier du cinema* on the verge of fully ripened maturity.

The body was no longer what it once had been: excrescences, aches, and skin like brittling caul. Mortality's inklings grew deeper; the flesh became a stranger's. On the fourth day of the new year, at Cedars of Lebanon hospital, he had a cyst removed from his left wrist. On January 22, when he opened with Sinatra at the Sands, he felt like an old man. They were billed as Dean Martin & Friend. They had their own bar cart onstage. The drunk routine was becoming less of an act and more of a hoked-up burlesque of drab reality. For years, he had been a man of moderation: a few drinks during the day, a few more and maybe a sleeping-pill at night. Now the nights were getting darker. Look at Sinatra: this guy wanted to be a kid forever. What more could one ask of life than a bottle of Scotch, a blowjob, and a million bucks? And Dean Martin had it. Why then did he go on? He was not like Frank; he got no thrill from this shit, being onstage, hearing himself on the radio, seeing himself ten feet tall on a screen. But he did not wonder long. Maybe it was like the philosopher said: Life was but a dream betwixt the cradle and the grave, and the less one pondered, the longer and more soundly he abided. Something like that.

It was in late January that he first heard of them, along with just about everyone else in America. What a silly name: Beatles, with an *a*. "I Want to Hold Your Hand" appeared on the *Billboard* charts the week that he and Sinatra opened at the Sands. Their old label too: Capitol. Frank, Dean, Sammy, and Peter; John, Paul, George, and Ringo. Everything changes, nothing abides. Who ever thought the day would come when America would buy back its own sense of cool secondhand from England? The days grew strange.

On February 4, while he was still at the Sands, word came from Steubenville that death had taken his cousin John Crocetti. He had been barely two years older than Dean. The present was a curse as much as the past. Fuck these days, with their Beatles and their deathward tremblings.

There had been days so long ago that the color of their breezes were now only faded shimmerings; days when the world had been sweet with promises, thrillful as a woman's perfumed neck—what had her name been, that blonde who danced, the one with more sin in her beautiful fucking eyes than in Frank Costello's soul?—days when he had hungered for all that he now had. The way he had sung "Melancholy Baby" had—what did that guy from *Billboard* say?— "had the gals applauding wildly and their boy friends joining in." If the world was now a tired wife, he could still sense in rare breaths now and then the luscious bitch he once had so deliciously seduced.

On March 12, he began four days' work on a new album, sharing the studio with only four other musicians. "The Times They Are a-Changin'," sang Bob Dylan on his own new album, released some days before. But, as Dean knew, while times changed, there was really no new thing under the sun. He started his four days of recording with "My Melancholy Baby" and continued with such half-forgotten breezes as "I'm Confessin'," "Baby, Won't You Please Come Home?," "Fools Rush In," and "Blue Moon." As Dean sang them, they seemed not so much a bunch of old romantic songs as threnodies for romance itself.

Dean had decided on eleven of the dozen songs on the album. Ken Lane was at Dean's house when they were trying to think of a twelfth choice. Lane remembered a song he had written with Irving

Taylor more than fifteen years ago. He had been with Sinatra then, and the song had been copyrighted, in June 1948, through Sinatra's publishing company, Sinatra Songs. Frank had recorded it for Columbia. Others had done it as well. "Everybody Loves Somebody" had never gone anywhere, but Lane was still partial to it. He played it for Dean at the piano.

"His wife, Jeanne, came in the room and said that it had been her favorite song for years," Lane remembered. "It became the twelfth song on the album."

On March 23, Dean's footprints were ceremoniously added to the cement of immortality outside Grauman's Chinese Theatre. By then, he had begun work on a new movie. It would end up as the most perversely curious and intriguing picture of his career.

Kiss Me, Stupid could not fail. It seemed that way, in any case. As a director, Billy Wilder was golden. In 1964, he was on a twenty-year winning streak that showed no sign of ending. Wilder had come from Vienna by way of France. In 1942, he had directed his first American picture, *The Major and the Minor*—later remade with Martin and Lewis as *You're Never Too Young*. Two years later, he had made *Double Indemnity*. Since then, Wilder had directed some of the most commercially successful and critically cherished pictures in Hollywood history: *The Lost Weekend, Sunset Boulevard, Stalag 17, The Seven Year Itch, Witness for the Prosecution, Some Like It Hot, The Apartment*. His last picture, *Irma La Douce*, was the fourth biggest money-maker of 1963. At the age of fifty-seven, Wilder seemed to be at the height of his powers.

Kiss Me, Stupid was ultimately, and loosely, derived from Anna Bonacci's play *L'Ora della Fantasia*. The play had been a success in Paris in 1953. An American version of it, *The Dazzling Hour*, produced by Gilbert Miller and José Ferrer, and starring Olivia de Havilland, folded during a pre-Broadway tryout. In Bonacci's original, an organist in an English hamlet dreams of becoming a great composer. When a high-ranking magistrate comes to visit, the organist, with his wife's complicity, engages a prostitute to take her place, that he might gain the magistrate's favor through the pretense of sharing both wife and home with him. In Wilder's adaptation, it emerged as the story of two hick-town songwriters willing to sell

their souls to sell a song. One of the songwriters was a grease
monkey, the other an insanely jealous piano teacher. When a famous singer stops for gas on his way through town—Climax, Nevada
—the grease monkey disconnects his fuel line to strand him there.
Knowing of the singer's reputation as a womanizer, the piano
teacher torments his wife into leaving, hires a local slut to imper-
sonate a wife in her place, and then orchestrates a liaison between
her and the singer, hoping that between the excitement and guilt of
adultery, a song might be sold. "Sophia," one of the songs for sale in
the picture, was so bad that most who heard it thought it had been
written as a joke. Actually, it was a newly modified version of
George and Ira Gershwin's 1937 song "Wake Up, Brother, and
Dance."

Kiss Me, Stupid was as sordid an idea as had ever been proposed for a movie comedy. Wilder and his collaborator I. A. L.
Diamond had written *Some Like It Hot, The Apartment, Irma La
Douce*—pictures that were sexy in an insouciant, sweet sort of way.
But their screenplay for *Kiss Me, Stupid* was downright, leeringly
sleazy. Sex and venality lay at the heart of every dirty laugh. No one
but Billy Wilder would have been allowed by a major studio even to
attempt to pull it off.

For the part of the slut, Polly the Pistol, Wilder had envisioned
Marilyn Monroe, with whom he had made *The Seven Year Itch* and
Some Like It Hot. Now the role went to Kim Novak. Peter Sellers,
working in Hollywood for the first time, was to play Orville J.
Spooner, the piano teacher. Dean was cast in his own persona, as
Dino. He was to play himself: the singer of "That's Amore," consul
of cool, holy ghost of tastelessness. Unlike many actors, Dean had
never allowed himself to be intimidated by Wilder. In December
1961, when Wilder told the Hollywood Press Club that "stars don't
mean a thing today," Dean wrote him a letter attacking his air of
self-importance and arrogance. Wilder respected him for that, as
well as for his no-nonsense approach to acting.

The picture was being produced for United Artists by Mirisch,
Wilder's Phalanx Productions, and Claude. It began filming, as *The
Dazzling Hour,* at the Samuel Goldwyn Studio on Santa Monica
Boulevard. Dean got along wonderfully with Peter Sellers, whose

deadpan glances he found so irresistibly funny that the cameras had
to be halted several times on account of his laughter.

On April 6, Sellers, who was thirty-nine, suffered a heart attack
and had to be replaced. Later, in June, when Sellers returned to
England, he would denounce Hollywood and swear never to work
there again. In response, Wilder and his cast and crew would send
him a wire reviling him as an "unprofessional rat."

The actor Wilder chose to take Seller's place was Ray Walston
whom Wilder had directed in *The Apartment* and who was now in a
new CBS-TV series called "My Favorite Martian." The series was in
the last week of its first season when Walston read the script for *The
Dazzling Hour.*

"Both my wife and I sat down and read this script," Walston
remembered, "and I said when I finished it, 'It's not good. It's not
good.' But one doesn't say that about a Billy Wilder–I. A. L. Diamond script. The feeling was that they would repair it. As is always
the case with Wilder, they did not have the ending written, but they
had more than three quarters of the film on script and they were
shooting. But when I read it, I thought, holy mackerel, this is no
going to work; there's something wrong; it's not that funny. But a
the same time, I thought, who the hell am I to say?

"What they did when I went in was to just simply redo everything that had been done with Sellers, and that was practically
everything. So I went in with actors who'd had, so to speak, a great
deal of rehearsal. On the first day, Wilder was giving me some
instructions, and they were very extensive. Martin was leaning
against the wall, close to me, and when Wilder got finished and
moved back toward the camera, Martin said, in a voice that everyone could hear: 'Tell the cocksucker to go fuck himself. Do it your
own way.' He was always fucking around. Wilder controls a set
when he's on it like nobody's business. Constantly barking and
screaming and yelling. Very, very Teutonic, from that school of film-
makers who are, you know, just God on the set. He's in absolute
control. And to say that Dean Martin usurped that control in a very
funny, wonderful way would be putting it mildly. He had Wilder on
the floor most of the time. They were very close."

One day Dean himself was the object of one of Wilder's extensive lectures.

"Well, for Chrissake, Jesus Christ Almighty, what the fuck," Dean told him. "I mean, if you wanted an actor, what the fuck did you get me for? Why didn't you go get fucking Marlon Brando?"

For Walston, the picture was both a bad experience and a good one. "Several fuckin' things that I have never forgiven Wilder for. One of 'em was, I had a guy workin' for me on the series who drove me and was my stand-in. I ran into him on the Paramount lot, hired him at the beginning, never saw him before in my life. I was lookin' for somebody who would drive me, 'cause I lived way up in the hills and didn't wanna drive, and he was workin' as an extra; I got him a job as a stand-in on the series. The guy's a homosexual. I paid no attention to that. But—I didn't learn this till later, till after the film was done; and I learned it from a very close source to Wilder—he thought I was queer. And that really hurt.

"More bad memories than good. Especially the failure of the picture. And then to learn that they had thought, most of them, that I was a fag."

There were lines in the script that Walston did not believe Wilder would get past the censors. "There was that line of Dean's: 'I'd like to see her parsley.' Things like that became ugly at the time. And I had a line, when I first bring Kim Novak into the house: 'Well, it's not very big but it's clean.' And they wanted it done with a slight look from her as if it meant my cock."

"Hey, Ray," Wilder said to him one afternoon. "Vat are the keedies gonna t'ink about you ven this film is released?"

"What the fuck are you talking about?" Walston countered. "What are the people in the business gonna say about *you?* How do you think you're gonna get away with some of this stuff?"

"Remember," Walston later would say, "this was 1964. And he said to me, 'I tell you what. I feel very strongly that something is about to happen in movies the likes of which you've never seen. Movies are gonna take a big, long leap. And it's gonna be a big, long leap toward things on the screen you would never believe.' He was way ahead of his time. He foresaw what was gonna happen."

The good experience was working with Dean. "He was wonderful. A lot of fun. Not only that, he was very professional. While he was full of mischief and fun, when he was shooting a scene, you couldn't fuck around. He had a glass in his hand all the time. And I got to the point where I thought, 'This cocksucker's full of shit. He doesn't have anything in that glass except ginger ale.' It *was* booze. But he was extremely professional. As a matter of fact, I learned some things from the guy. He had a very wonderful ease in front of the camera. A lot of actors get intimidated, especially in close-up work. Not him. He just took it very easy."

The Beatles had by now had four number-one hits in as many months. All twelve-year-old Dino Jr. could talk about was the Beatles: the Beatles this, the Beatles that, she-loves-you-yeah-yeah-yeah. Dean got sick of it. "I'm gonna knock your little pallies off the charts," he told the kid.

The album of small-group recordings that he had made in March, *Dream with Dean,* was still unreleased. On April 16, three days after filming resumed with Ray Walston, Dean recorded a second version of "Everybody Loves Somebody," with a full orchestral arrangement that, for once, added vibrancy rather than sappiness. Dean's voice was rich and strong; Ken Lane's doo-woppy piano notes rode the swing and swell of the band; the backbeat of the drums was there to be heard; even the background voices seemed more human than android. Reprise released it as a single in May. It took a while, but in late June, it appeared on the charts. In mid-August, "Everybody Loves Somebody" knocked the Beatles' "A Hard Day's Night" out of the number-one spot to become the biggest record in America. Two weeks later, it appeared on the pop charts in the Beatles' homeland as well. Little Dino Jr. beheld the old man in amazement.

By June, Billy Wilder had an ending for his picture, and a new title, *Kiss Me, Stupid,* drawn from its final line. The film's opening—Dean onstage at the Copa Room of the Sands, and then leaving town as workers removed the letters that spelled DINO beside his caricature on the marquee outside—was shot in July during an actual engagement at the Sands. Like the Dual Ghia convertible he drove into Climax, which in real life was his own car, the sign outside the Sands was real as well. "For the first time in the history of the Las Vegas Strip," *Variety* observed, "a marquee contains only one word —Dino. Above it is a huge neon caricature of Sandstar Dean Martin."

This time at the Sands, Dean accompanied himself on guitar for a version of Hank Williams's posthumous country hit "Take These Chains from My Heart." His stay at the Sands was concurrent with a Las Vegas Warner-Reprise sales convention, which he closed out, on the night of July 20, with "Everybody Loves Somebody." In mid-August, when the single reached number one, both *Dream with Dean,* containing Dean's original version of the song, and *Everybody Loves Somebody,* a hastily-put-together album containing the hit version of the song, appeared on the Top LP charts. They entered the Top Twenty together. The latter, which reached number two and remained on the charts for forty-nine weeks, became the most successful album of his career. By September 1, when he made his debut at Harrah's at Lake Tahoe—Bill Harrah paid a hundred grand a week to bring him in—Dean loomed over America like a mob-culture Zeus: indomitable, ever-cool, and all-selling.

In 1963, Jerry Lewis had signed a five-year, multimillion-dollar deal with ABC to host a live, two-hour variety-talk show on Saturday nights. He had sunk $4,500,000 into taking over and renovating the El Capitan Theatre on Vine Street for the show. Premiering in September of that year, "The Jerry Lewis Show" had been one of the biggest disasters in broadcasting history. It had lasted only three months, and in January 1964, ABC had taken over and renamed the theater for a mid-season replacement show, "The Hollywood Palace." The show, which featured a different celebrity host each week, had grown quite popular. And Dean, who first hosted the show in March—"I want to thank Jerry for building this wonderful theater for me"—proved the most popular host of all. Hosting again in June, he introduced the Rolling Stones on the show.

Reprise had its own British rock band now, the Kinks. Their single "You Really Got Me" hit the charts in late September, the same week as Dean's new Reprise single, "The Door Is Still Open to

My Heart." Both would rise to become Top Ten hits; but Dean's would rise higher.

His old network, NBC, was after him now like a bitch in heat. He waved away every offer that NBC made. And every time he waved, the network raised its ante.

Production on his next picture, *The Sons of Katie Elder*, had been held up. The story the screenplay was based on had been brought to Paramount years ago by John Sturges, the director of *Sergeants 3*. It had lain forgotten until Sturges brought it to Hal Wallis's attention. Wallis had developed it for John Wayne. Sturges was by then busy with other projects, and Wallis and Wayne had brought in the veteran Henry Hathaway, who referred to himself as "a genial hack." Everyone was set to begin location filming in Durango, Mexico, when Wayne had called Wallis into his dressing-room. "Well, Hal," he had said. "I'm going to hit you with it. I've got the big C." A routine physical examination at Scripps Clinic had revealed dangerous lesions on one of his lungs. *The Sons of Katie Elder* would have to wait until the lung was removed.

Meanwhile, on October 30, there was announced "a mammoth nationwide talent search by Columbia Pictures to find a leading man virile enough—and ruthless enough—to play Matt Helm in Columbia's upcoming release, *The Silencers*." The nationwide search led to Dean, who ruthlessly agreed to become Matt Helm on the condition that producer Irving Allen, who held the rights to Donald Hamilton's Matt Helm novels, move over and make room for Claude Productions.

Dean's third hit single of the year, "You're Nobody 'til Somebody Loves You," appeared on the charts in the second week of December. Dean did not attend the preview screening of *Kiss Me, Stupid* held later that month in Westwood. Ray Walston did.

Midway through the film, people started walking out. In the lobby, after it was over, Billy Wilder told Walston, "You should be veddy proud of yourself." To Walston, it was a devastating remark. "If you've been in the theater a long time," he said, "you know that as the kiss of death."

The Catholic Legion of Decency classified films according to a five-grade system. The optimum rating was A-1: Morally Unobjectionable for General Patronage. Since the revision of its code in December 1957, not a single picture had been anathematized with the full Church condemnation of a C rating; the last had been *Baby Doll* in 1956. Now *Kiss Me, Stupid* became the first film to be condemned in eight years. The banning came just as the Museum of Modern Art in New York was honoring Wilder with a retrospective. United Artists removed its name from the film and released it through its subsidiary Lopart Pictures Corporation. When the picture opened in New York and Los Angeles during Christmas week, *Variety*'s speculation that the "wave of notoriety generated by one of the sharpest condemnations the Roman Catholic Legion of Decency has issued in many years might conversely benefit" it proved untrue, as theaters across the country canceled scheduled bookings under pressure from morality-minded community groups.

Brendan Gill of *The New Yorker* denounced it as "squalid." *Daily Variety* called it "a dirty sex exercise." The *New York Daily News* headlined its review "Sex, Smut, Little Else." *Life* called it "a titanic dirty joke." Only *Newsweek* and *Vogue*, it seemed, did not gag with repulsion. The woman who reviewed it for the latter found it "a profoundly effective picture, as witnessed by the number of people who walk out on it."

As the god-king of mob culture, he had blown aside the Beatles with the breath of his might. Now, banned for tastelessness by the Church itself, he stood aloft and alone among those who claimed fame as their whore.

It rained millions. The week after Christmas, he headed a consortium that purchased seven hundred and fifty acres of land adjoining Palomar Airport in Carlsbad, California, for an undisclosed sum, listed in trust deeds as $2,500,000 but reported as "several million dollars" by the Beverly Hills real-estate firm that handled the transaction. Grant deeds showed Dean and Jeanne as holding a thirty-five-percent interest, with Jack Entratter of the Sands among the other, smaller buyers.

Martin Luther King had a dream. So did Dean. The next day he played it, a hundred dollars straight: 753.

XIV.

A THIEF AT THE GRAVE OF DESIRE

*H*e had gumption, all right. He had been at this racket for more than a quarter of a century now. Gumption. Where the fuck was Elvis? "Do the Clam," *shit.*

After finishing *The Sons of Katie Elder,* he knocked off *Marriage on the Rocks,* probably the worst of the pictures that Sinatra had suckered him into yet. But what the fuck, it was a quick few hundred grand. Dean never saw the picture. Many thought that it might very well be one of the worst movies ever made. But what did that matter? Never do anything halfway. What was next? He had a list here somewhere. Right: the Matt Helm *stupidaggine.* Production of *The Silencers* would begin in July. Money. It used to be good for something. Now it was just there, like smoke in the lungs.

His daughter Deana, who was only sixteen, got a deal with Columbia Records in April. Claudia had done "The Donna Reed Show" and "My Three Sons" on television, and was set in June for another picture. It sounded like a real winner: *Pajama Party in a Haunted House;* it would end up as *The Ghost in the Invisible Bikini.* Fourteen-year-old Dean Jr. had his own band with Desi Arnaz's boy and a kid named Hinsche: Dino, Desi & Billy. Their Reprise single "I'm a Fool," released in June, was outselling Sinatra on his own label. It hit number seventeen that summer, the season of the Rolling Stones' "Satisfaction." Dean reminded him who was boss. On September 15, he recorded "I Will" for Reprise. It hit number ten.

Phil Karlson, whose glory days as the director of *Kansas City Confidential* and *The Phenix City Story* were now long behind him, made *The Silencers* in the same spirit of jaded proficiency that he had brought to Elvis's *Kid Galahad* a few years before. He filmed the picture at the Desilu studio. Stella Stevens, the leading lady of *The Silencers,* recalled that Dean's "eyes twinkled and he did have fun." He had by now developed an aversion to night work. "If you would go past seven-thirty in the evening," Stevens said, "Dean was a little bit too inebriated to put up with much, so he would be a little brusque." *The Silencers,* she remembered, "was the first time I had my dress ripped off in a film." Dean was "warm and wonderful and helpful"; but—she would laugh—"we never had an affair, damn it." Had he ever had an affair? He could not remember that thing he sang of: love, sweet love. He wanted to, but he could not.

He had made his deal with NBC. "The Dean Martin Show" premiered on Thursday night, September 16, 1965, the day *The Silencers* finished filming and *Marriage on the Rocks* was released. The director of the show, Greg Garrison, had been involved with NBC since early 1951, when he had taken over "Your Show of Shows." He had become Milton Berle's director in 1954, had been hired in 1957 by the McCann-Erickson agency to produce and direct "Club Oasis," and had resumed directing Berle's show in 1958. Garrison, whom Berle considered the best of his television directors, was used to well-planned and well-rehearsed productions. With "The Dean Martin Show," the planning and the rehearsing would have to be carried out without the central player. Dean's idea of doing a show was just that: a show, with no strings attached. Garrison became indispensable to him, building each weekly show around him, then preparing him for each taping as simply and quickly and effectively as possible. Their rapport was tremendous, and Garrison had to admit that Dean's way of doing the show, which could have been pulled off by no one else, somehow worked. With NBC's money and Garrison as his right-hand man, Dean ran the show like a tightly-held conspiracy. It was a Claude Production, with Mack Gray as musical coordinator and Ken Lane as musical consultant. Later he would get his oldest boy, Craig, on the payroll as an assistant producer.

On his opening show, Dean walked out singing "Everybody Loves Somebody." He abandoned it after a few bars. "No point in singing the whole song, you might not buy the record," he said. It was obvious that he had no expectations, that he could not care less if the show succeeded or failed. "You know, I'm already gettin' tired," he remarked, moving to the bar that Garrison had built for him on the set. When it came time to mention the network, "NBC" came out as a slurred jumble. Fuck it. "I want you to know," he said, "that this is going to be a family show. The kind of a show where a man can take his wife and kids, his father and mother, and sit around in a bar and watch." A blonde came on and flashed some sequined bosom. Dean sang one of his recent hits, "Houston," while doing some card tricks, showing more interest in the cards than in the song. Steubenville. The Rex. Was Irma DiBenedetto watching? Bob Newhart came out and did his thing. Diahann Carroll was a guest. He fucked up and called her Dinah. What did it matter, one name or another? Sinatra came out. They joked around awhile with a flock of broads. Dean called Sinatra "the chairman of the board." Joey Heatherton danced around. It was a change: a few minutes of buttocks and thighs instead of tits. He ended with a few more bars of "Everybody Loves Somebody," with Sinatra mimicking him. And that was it.

"If Dean Martin in his first show," said *The Christian Science Monitor,* "were any more relaxed, he'd fall on his face. Many of his opening remarks and jokes had to do with drinking. One wondered, watching Dean, whether this man cared whether his show went over or not."

But "The Dean Martin Show" was an immense and immediate success. His uncaring manner and good-natured boorishness endeared him to the millions who were sick of sincerity, relevance, and pseudosophistication. Dean was a man whose success and fortune no man begrudged him. He seemed somehow kindred, one of them but blessed beyond them by the Fates. In him, for one late hour before the final day of every workweek, the multitudes, tired and half-drunk and onward-slouching, found something of their own: lullaby and vindication, justification and inspiration, a bit of boozy song and a glimpse of gal-meat.

He returned in November to the Sands. "It's Dean Martin time again at the Copa Room," *Variety* reported. "Martin attracts the hippies and the hoedowners with his casual, perfectly-timed soft-pedaled comedy and song. And he's a pet of the pit bosses, because when he's around the money's around."

•   •   •

On February 19, 1966, while Dean was at work in Arizona on another Western, *The Silencers* premiered at the Chicago Theatre. "Mr. Martin," wrote Brendan Gill of *The New Yorker,* "is, I suppose, the worst and most self-confident actor in the world." The *New York Times* described *The Silencers* well: "loud, fast, obvious and occasionally funny." In the end, it grossed $12,000,000, ten percent of which went to Dean.

By March 6, when the last of the season's programs was taped, the Nielsen ratings revealed "The Dean Martin Show" to be in command of an astounding thirty-eight percent of the nation's television households. The show's devotees included seventy-four-year-old Henry Miller, whose *Tropic of Cancer* had been the subject of sixty separate court actions before the U.S. Supreme Court's 1964 ruling in favor of its right to constitutional protection under the First Amendment. Through Joe Gray, an ex-boxer who sometimes worked as a stand-in for Dean in pictures, Henry Miller was even able to meet the great man. For Miller, as for the masses of sub-literate and post-literate slobs who comprised the vast heart of Dean's viewership, Dean was the American spirit at its truest: fuck Vietnam, fuck politics, fuck morality, fuck culture and fuck the counterculture, fuck it all. We were here for but a breath; twice around the fountain and into the grave: fuck it.

A reporter working on a *Look* cover story about him visited the Hollywood set of the Western he was making. Michael Gordon, the director, explained, "Dean doesn't like acting, really. We set scenes up so that he only has to work in short spurts." Dean himself defended the spurt system over the Stanislavsky-method system: "Motivation is a lotta crap," he told the *Look* broad.

Dean had finished the new Western—it was called *Texas Across the River*—and was doing a second Matt Helm picture, *Murderers' Row,* this time with Ann-Margret as the lead sex object. Columbia had wanted to do the new Helm picture on location in Cannes; instead, he had them build what the *Daily News* would later refer to as "fake Riviera sets."

He had a brand-new record on the charts, something called "Come Runnin' Back." Sinatra was finally selling some records of his own again. "Strangers in the Night," also brand-new, would be his first number-one hit in twenty years. Yeah, Dean told him, it was a good one, all right. Frank liked to hear that sort of shit. Dean did not even listen to records anymore, his own or anybody else's. He had tired too of making them. Now he had his producer, Jimmy Bowen, record the songs without him; he came in later, like a ghost in an empty studio, and sang to the music that had been recorded.

"This Jimmy Bowen who I have, he put the beat and the choir, and, I don't know, sort of, it's a new rhythm, I don't know what it is," he said in slurred response to a question about his music. How many gold records did he have? "I had 'That's Amore' and 'Memories Are Made of This.' I got two for that. That sold over two million. And 'Return to Me.' 'Volare.' And 'Everybody Loves Somebody.' And this other thing is on its way, that 'Open the Door, Richard,' or something, what's it, I don't remember."

On June 7, the two of them, Dean and Sinatra, went out drinking to celebrate Dean's birthday. They ended up after midnight in the Polo Lounge with Richard Conte, Sinatra's friend Jilly Rizzo, and a few broads. The beautiful people regarded them like gods in their midst.

"If looks could suck cock, we'd be wilted by now in this fuckin' joint," Dean told Sinatra.

At a booth near their table sat Frederick R. Weisman, the fifty-four-year-old director of the board and former president of Hunt's Foods, and Franklin H. Fox, a businessman from Boston. The two men were about to become fathers-in-law through the marriage of their children, and they had come from dinner at Chasen's to have a drink together. They found the noisy vulgarity from the nearby table offensive. Weisman leaned over and commented to Sinatra that there were other people present in the room.

"You're out of line, buddy," Sinatra told him. Then Sinatra took a good look at him and, turning back to Dean and the others, muttered something about "this fucking Jew bastard." Weisman objected. The next thing Dean knew, he was pulling Sinatra off the fucking Jew bastard, who was now talking about dirty wops. When Dean heard that, he rapped him in his fucking Jew-bastard face with his dirty-wop fist. A table broke as Weisman went down. Then

Dean, Sinatra, and the others were out of there, while Fox tried to help Weisman off the floor.

Twenty-four hours later, Weisman was still unconscious in the intensive-care unit of Mount Sinai Hospital. On Friday, June 10, in critical condition and not expected to live, he underwent two and a half hours of cranial surgery to alleviate the effects of a skull fracture. He began to regain consciousness the following day.

"It was a typical barroom brawl," said the Beverly Hills chief of police, Clinton Anderson. "Of course," he added, "we don't have any barrooms as such in Beverly Hills." Chief Anderson, who had questioned Dean and Sinatra concerning the incident, reported Dean's contention that "he hadn't seen a thing." The investigation was closed on June 30, with no charges pressed.

Even the federal government saw the universality of Dean's charisma. In July, on the set of *Murderers' Row,* the second Matt Helm picture, he and the movie's director, Henry Levin, were recruited to make three U.S. Treasury Bond Appeal trailers.

By the end of August, he had taped six of his upcoming season's television shows. "I don't even breathe hard," he told a reporter. "I don't know why those other stars make such a big thing of television." He described his eight-hour television workweek. "I go to the studio at one on Sunday afternoon and I'm out of there by nine. That's all there is to it."

Not all of Dean's viewers were as verbally free-spirited as Henry Miller. After Dean told his guest Bill Dana to take it up the ass—*"fa 'n cul'"*—during a comedy bit on "The Dean Martin Show" of October 20, NBC received the most massive barrage of protesting calls it had ever experienced. The network issued a statement: "NBC will see that it never happens again." Henceforth, the network promised, all remarks uttered in Italian by Dean would be censored from the show. Dean's response to the network, the *Daily News* reported, was "not printable."

His daughter Barbara Gail had graduated from Darlington College in England and was back home working as a shoe salesman. Dean heard her singing one day as he passed her room at home.

"Hey," he said. "You got a voice." In April, as soon as her twenty-first birthday legally allowed her to do so, she made her nightclub singing debut, at Ye Little Club in Beverly Hills. She showed, in *Variety*'s words, "a natural ability, a plucky spirit, and considerable talent." But, *Variety* had added, "it will take some work." She had gone on later in the spring to play the Oak Room at the King Edward Hotel in Toronto. In her thirty-five-minute act, put together for her by Dean, Sammy Cahn, and Sinatra, she displayed, a reviewer wrote, "a sweet quality, a strong measure of talent for someone who has been on the professional stage for only seven weeks, and enough energy to win applause and attention from patrons." But the reviewer found it "unfortunate that she has to be subjected to overgenerous pre-show publicity." Dean put her on his October 27 television show. The *Daily News* found her "a good-looker with a fair voice." She seemed "somewhat hesitant in her manner—understandable under the circumstances," and was "far from being in her father's league." In December, Dean would bring his daughter Deana on the show. A few months later, he would have his daughter Claudia on as well. She had been engaged to another fucking winner: Lord Timothy Hutton, some *citrullo* limey disc-jockey. But his rock-'n'-roll lordship didn't seem to do much for her career, so daddy came to the rescue.

November 1966 was proclaimed Dean Martin Month by Reprise. Dean, according to the promotional material circulated that fall among salesmen, was "America's best-selling vocalist." In the two years from June 1964 through June 1966, he had sold over 3,415,000 singles and 2,899,000 albums. In the three months since then, he had already sold over $1,860,000 in products. *Texas Across the River* opened Thanksgiving week. It was, *Variety* said, a "boisterous western spoof with belly laughs galore and Dean Martin." *Murderers' Row* opened a month later, a few days before Christmas. "Mucho display of girls; not mucho display of originality, but big boxoffice prospects," *Variety* predicted. The *Daily News* gave both pictures three stars. *Murderers' Row* made good money—not as much as *The Silencers*, but good. It did better than *Blow-Up, A Man and a Woman, Harper, Fantastic Voyage,* and other pictures that year. *Texas Across the River* made money too. Both were among the sloppiest and most witless pictures of a sloppy and witless era.

Another Western was in the works, a dramatic one, in which Dean for the only time in his career would play the bad guy. Marty Rackin, who had written *Sailor Beware* and *The Stooge* for Martin and Lewis and had gone on to become the head of production at Paramount in 1960, now had his own company, Martin Rackin Productions. Rackin had acquired the rights to a pulp Western by Marvin Albert called *The Man in Black*. When he hired Arnold Laven, the director of *Slaughter on Tenth Avenue* as well as of *The Monster That Challenged the World,* Rackin had commitments from Universal, Dean, and George Peppard. It was Peppard who offered the most telling location story about this utterly forgettable project: "I was passing Dean's dressing-room one day. It was early morning, and we both had had quite a bit to drink the night before. And he was drinking a glass of milk. I looked at him, and he looked in my eye and he said, 'Don't tell anybody. It'll spoil my reputation.' "

During the making of *Rough Night in Jericho,* Dean said that the only reason he worked was to get away from home. "He used to kid about his wife," Laven said. "And I kid about my wife. We've been married now well over thirty years. I would kid about her in a way to show the affection that exists between us, and I thought that was how Martin would kid. But it turns out he fooled me in that sense, that there really was a certain discord between him and his wife. He never revealed what was going on in his mind."

Angela Crocetti, the woman who had taught her little boy Dino never to cry or to show his emotions, had lain ill through much of the year in the house that Dean had bought his parents on Doheny Road. Multiple myeloma: the words meant nothing to old Gaetano as he looked upon her. It had all begun so long ago, in an ancient place amid ancient breezes. He had forgotten them, the breezes that the old women, the mourning-ones, of Montesilvano had known by name. Some breezes had carried sickness, others had brought fortune, others had carried the souls of the dead. They had been like a censing through the town, those breezes: the smell of the sea and the piney shadow-scent and the myrrhy dank of that dream of death that seeped from iconed walls. Now he was back among them.

Angela passed her sixty-ninth birthday in darkness. A week later, in the fourth hour of Christmas Day, her heart gave out beneath the weight of that darkness, and she was gone.

Dean's brother, Bill, now an aircraft engineer at North American Rockwell, lived with his wife, Josephine, and their kids on North Bowling Green Way. For Bill, who took it hard, Angela's death was the death of a mother. For Dean, it was that and more: the death as well of all that tied him to the past.

Dean put his arm around the old man, feeling what was left of him. They stood together awhile by themselves in the wintry morning.

"It ain't the end of the world, Pop."

"No, Dino. For you, it's not."

But they both knew it. A world without maternity was a world without morality. When a mother's eyes closed for good, conscience became a man's weak sister.

He made a great offering to St. John's Hospital in Steubenville. The hospital commemorated him with a brazen plaque proclaiming that it did

HOLD IN GREAT ESTEEM
DEAN MARTIN
FOR HIS GENEROUS CONTRIBUTIONS
TOWARD
THE COBALT UNIT SUITE
IN MEMORY OF HIS BELOVED MOM
ANGELA CROCETTI

For ten years, Guy himself had suffered from some of that fancy doctor-talk: pulmonary fibrosis. He was a little man, but he was bigger than schoolbook words, and neither illness nor its mumbo-jumbo had vanquished him. But he was not bigger than the breezes, and he was not big enough, or foolish enough, to think that there was more of sweetness to this life than he had found in that little new-world flower with the scent of the old, that dark-eyed little orphan he had found, waiting there, still and alone, in this land of dreams he did not understand.

And Dean, the flesh of his flesh, in slow abdication, receded further into the shadow of his own unknowing.

His own wife had given up the hope of ever truly knowing him. The few men who were close to him saw only one or another facet of a cut obsidian stone in which no light shone. There were his golfing cronies at the Bel-Air Country Club: Nicky Hilton, the director and chairman of the executive committee of the Hilton International Company, the eldest son of Conrad N. Hilton and the first husband of Elizabeth Taylor; Fletcher Jones, a Los Angeles car dealer; Bill Ransom, a Beverly Hills realtor; Bill Bastian, a Los Angeles meat-packer known as the Corned-Beef King. There were his business associates and retinue: Herman Citron, Mort Viner, Greg Garrison, Jay Gerard, and Mack Gray. There were those, like Sinatra and Sammy Cahn, who considered themselves friends and bosom buddies. But to Dean, they were all "pallies." No one knew him. The smart ones took that for granted. To Nicky Hilton, Dean was like a beautiful poem that he loved but could never understand.

More and more, Dean seemed to be leading a life about which Jeanne knew nothing. When he was ordered to testify in a federal case against two San Fernando bookmakers, Dominic Mastrippolito and Quentin Howard, who had booked his bets during the previous baseball season, Jeanne knew nothing about it until she read the newspaper accounts of his written federal-court stipulation on January 5, eleven days after Angela's death. Yeah, he had told the feds, he had known Dom for six or seven years. He "often placed wagers with him," his statement said.

He went to work in January on some new piece of shit that started out as *Band of Gold* and would end up being called *How to Save a Marriage and Ruin Your Life*. Produced by Stanley Shapiro for Columbia, it was a throwback to *Pillow Talk, Lover Come Back*, and the other screwball sex comedies that Shapiro was known for. It was supposed to be, anyway. Dean's method of spurt-acting left director Fielder Cook with little chance to make the comedy he wanted to make. Dean resisted Cook's pleas for repeated takes, and when Cook took the matter to Columbia boss Mike Frankovich, he was told, "Shoot it Dean's way."

In February, "The Dean Martin Show" entered first place in the Nielsen ratings, with an estimated audience of fifty million. Those who crowded to attend the Sunday-evening tapings in Burbank often waited as long as sixteen months for tickets.

"I always plays to de common folk," he explained to *Newsweek*, which dubbed him television's King Leer.

When he opened at the Sands in March, *Variety* reported, "maitre d' Phil Goldman could have filled the room twice over for each of the two shows." Two of his albums from last year, *The Hit Sound of Dean Martin* and *The Dean Martin TV Show*, were still on the charts. So was *The Best of Dean Martin*, a collection Capitol had issued in October. Another collection, *Relaxin'*, was released by Tower, a Capitol subsidiary, in February. A new Reprise album, *Happiness Is Dean Martin*, was finished two days before he opened at the Sands and would appear on the charts in May. On April 13, a week after Dean closed at the Sands, production of a third Matt Helm picture, *The Ambushers*, began in Mexico.

His costar in *The Ambushers* was Janice Rule, a serious actress with a background at the Actors Studio in New York. "It was just sort of a lark," she remembered. "Nobody was embarrassed by it," and Dean "was great fun to work with." Once, after rehearsing a scene, she asked Dean if they might go through it one more time.

"Honey," he told her sweetly, "you can rehearse with the director, or you can study all you want at home every night. But one rehearsal is all you're gonna get out of ol' Dino."

Claude Productions was buying land everywhere: $500,000 for fifty acres in Camarillo; more than $2,000,000 for five properties, totaling almost a thousand acres, in Ventura County. On April 25, back in Hollywood to finish work on *The Ambushers*, Dean announced that he was building his own $15,000,000 country club and golf course on three hundred and thirty acres between Benedict Canyon Road and Coldwater Canyon Drive in Beverly Hills. The tops of ridges would be graded to raise the valley floor four hundred feet; altogether some ten million cubic yards of earth would be moved. He himself was supervising course-designer Robert Trent Jones in the engineering of the par-seventy course, which would have twenty-two holes: four duplicate par-three holes were planned to eliminate slowdowns on the shortest holes. Memberships in the Beverly Hills Country Club would be restricted to six hundred, at $25,000 each.

"I don't think we'll have any trouble sellin 'em. People come up to me every day and say they want in. But we're not just taking everybody. What we're looking for is young people on the go," he said. "They don't have to be billionaires, either. We're working it out with my advisor, Al Hart of City National Bank, where a fellow can pay $5,000 down and the rest over a period of years.

"The accent is going to be on youth. The trouble with most golf clubs is that they're filled with old guys sitting around playing gin rummy and waiting to die."

Dean's income in 1967 rose to $5,000,000 for the year. Of that, $1,600,000 came from "The Dean Martin Show": $40,000 for each eight-hour day he put in. Now that the show had become the most popular program in America, the network was eager to commit him beyond the single season that remained under the original 1965 contract. On June 13, six days after his fiftieth birthday, negotiations for a new three-year contract were completed. Dean emerged with a deal that shook the very foundations of dreamland greed. His pay for each eight-hour workday was increased more than sevenfold, from $40,000 to more than $283,000. In all, NBC agreed to pay him $34,000,000. That came out to $11,333,333 a year for the next three years, raising his annual income to well above $15,000,000.

Fifteen fucking million dollars a year. And that was just his pocket money. The value of his real-estate holdings and investments would soon overwhelm reckoning:

His home at 601 Mountain Drive.

Another Beverly Hills house, at 2002 Loma Vista Drive.

The Solvang Ranch in Santa Barbara, purchased from James Stewart.

The Hidden Valley Ranch in Ventura.

A seventy-five-percent interest in the capital and profits of Northpoint Investors, holding rental properties in San Francisco.

A seventy-percent interest in the Rancho La Sierra Joint Venture, holding property in Riverside County.

A sixty-percent interest in the Pierce Ranch Joint Venture, holding property in Ventura County.

A forty-five-percent interest in the Rancho Dos Vientos Joint Venture, holding property in Ventura County.

An interest in the Palomar Joint Venture.

The Ventura School and Trailer Park.

The Bradford Park Apartment Houses.

The Park Sovereign Apartment Houses.

The Neumann Ranch.

The Scholle Ranch in Camarillo.

Two hundred and seventeen acres in Moorpark.

One hundred and ten acres in Riverside.

Unimproved lots in Tarzana and at the intersection of Old Topanga Canyon Road and Mulholland Drive in Los Angeles, held through Dean Martin Properties, Inc.

Interests in the Buena Ventura and Ventura Pacific lemon-growers' cooperatives.

More than 256,000 shares of stock in NBC's parent company, RCA.

His piece of the Sands.

And on and on it went: trust-deed notes and cash accounts and variable annuities.

Thirty years ago, he had stood there with silver dollars in those oversized shoes of his, and Cosmo Quattrone had stood there, holding that Parodi of his in that way he had of holding it. "I hear you like to dance," Cosmo had said; "that's what they tell me." Well, now he had danced.

Guy Crocetti was lost and undone. For him, the dream of America ended in a nursing-home on Inglewood Boulevard. At three in the morning on August 29, his heart fell still; and three days later, Dean brought him to his place beside Angela in the mausoleum he had built to bear the Crocetti name in Westwood Memorial Park.

. . .

Andrew V. McLaglen, the son of actor Victor McLaglen, had directed James Stewart in *Shenandoah.* Now McLaglen was making another Western with Stewart, called *Bandolero!* Dean would play Stewart's brother.

"It was an original story by Stanley Hough, who was later married to Howard Hughes's widow, Jean Peters. He wrote this treatment," McLaglen recalled. "Dick Zanuck liked it, and he wanted Jimmy Stewart. Well, in those days, anything that Jimmy Stewart did, he wanted me to do and James Lee Barrett to write, because we started off that combo in 1964 doing *Shenandoah.*"

As written by Barrett, *Bandolero!* involved three months of filming in Texas, Arizona, and Hollywood. For McLaglen and Stewart, Dean forsook the spurt method, as he had for Arnold Laven and *Rough Night in Jericho.* McLaglen found him to be "without any doubt the most conscientious actor I have ever worked with."

In September, soon before he went to work on *Bandolero!*, Dean taped a special Christmas edition of "The Dean Martin Show." The show featured him, Jeannie, and Sinatra together with all their children. Singing carols around a tree, they were the very picture of warmth and harmony. Viewers on December 21 would see a happy family blessed by the spirit of Christmas.

It was part of the image: the faithful family man beneath the vulgar abandon of the carefree boozer with the philandering eye. It was what made him acceptable. It was what endeared him. He reaffirmed the traditional values while flaunting them. His marriage of eighteen years and his old-world sense of family comforted his viewers while his good-humored blasphemy captivated them. They felt that difference between him and Sinatra, in whom, as a man, there was little for them to respect. This Christmas show illustrated that. Both families were supposed to have gathered, but Sinatra had not even been able to produce his latest wife, Mia Farrow, a simpering little flower child who was younger than his own daughter.

But, of course, the spirit of Christmas that seemed to ring so true and warm was all an illusion. What people saw in December was fabricated in the heat of the California summer. And that picture of a happy family was a lie as well.

He had learned long ago how to stack and to palm and how to deal seconds—not only with a deck of cards, but in life itself. In the fall of 1967, after the taping of his Christmas show, he consented to the only in-depth interview he ever granted. The interviewer was the Italian writer Oriana Fallaci, who had been hired by *Look* to profile him for a cover story to be published Christmas week. The tapestry of honesty and illusion that he wove for Fallaci was one of pure seduction. With his mother and father gone, the dissolution of his past, the final renunciation of that hated haunting—memory—was complete. Soon, withdrawing slowly and irrevocably into his own shadow, he would wave away the rest of life as well. It was as if the long interview with Fallaci was his last, languid waltz with memory.

"I think of my father," he said, "who came all alone from Abruzzi to Steubenville, Ohio, to find his brother and his hope. He was so young, nineteen or so, and he didn't even know his brother's address. And he was just walkin' down the street, and he recognized Joe, and he said: 'Are you Joe, *tu sei Giuseppe?*' And Joe said: 'Yes, *sì*. Are you Gaetano, *tu sei Gaetano?*' And he said: 'Yes, *sì*, I am Gaetano. I am your brother.' "

It seemed as if he were recalling a dream. The whole interview had a strange dreamlike quality. His mother "was in a convent. She met my father, and fell in love at first sight." It was a dream that ended in death: "They just died, you know? Six months apart, this year. First, Mom. She got that bone thing, and she got smaller and smaller, and she said laughin': 'I'm gonna whip this thing if it kills me, Dino.' Then my father. It was his heart; and also, he was takin' pills because of Mom's death. What a terrible blow. You know? The two of 'em. Almost together. And I loved 'em so. I had got 'em a beautiful house in Inglewood, and I got 'em everything they wanted in the world. My mother had diamonds, a fur coat. My father had a car, and money. And you give 'em all this, and they die."

As for those dark breezes: "Success kills fears. Even the fear of dyin'. I'm not afraid to die. If the Good Lord up there says I'm gonna die, well, I'm gonna die."

Did he believe that strongly in God?

"Oh! So very much! Oh! Every night—I still have never missed a night without prayin'. And I have my Saint Christopher, and when

I get on the airline, I cross myself and pray to Him. I don't get on my knees, I pray in bed. Oh, yes, I believe in God."

Jeannie would later confirm this: "Dean does say his prayers every single night, and has every single night that I've ever known him. Absolutely. I don't say them every night. He does."

Jeannie could sense the change in him. He had never had much interest in this world. Now he was relinquishing what little he had.

"I'd like to tell myself there was a reason," she would say years later. "He was still so young. He had everything. And, perhaps, that's really the point. But somewhere in there, he lost interest. He became disenchanted with all of it. Our marriage came to an end at that point. I'm sure it was evident. I didn't see it."

The nickel-in-the-slot racket now stunk of patchouli and incense. There was a whole new breed of psychedelic suckers out there. The advertisements in *Billboard* forced the limits of gullibility:

> MAHARISHI MAHESH YOGI
> Exclusively on World Pacific Records
> The Beatles' spiritual teacher
> speaks to the world on love and the untapped
> power that lies within.

In March 1968, three Reprise albums were certified gold, signifying sales of over $1,000,000, by the Record Industry Association of America. One of them was Jimi Hendrix's first album. The other two were by Dean.

Elvis was still out there somewhere. After marrying Priscilla in 1967, he had moved into a new home in Bel-Air. He would skulk on his motorcycle past Dean's house, never summoning the courage to ring the bell.

Sinatra had broken away from the Sands in a drunken rage a few days after the taping of Dean's Christmas show. Dean's own contract with the Sands was due to expire within a year; and Sinatra figured that Dean, out of allegiance to him, would not renew—

especially since Jack Entratter's presidency of the Sands had ended with the takeover of Howard Hughes's regime the previous July. When Dean instead entered into new negotiations with the Sands, Sinatra took it as a personal affront. And when he fell ill that spring in Miami and did not hear from Dean—who neither wrote nor called anyone—his pouting knew no bounds. "The glorious long friendship between our modern-day Damon and Pythias is in the ash can," reported gossip columnist Sheilah Graham.

Could Dean care less? He opened at the Sands in May, after finishing work in Mexico with Robert Mitchum on *Five Card Stud,* a Western mystery directed by Henry Hathaway. "Now that Dean Martin is such a skyrocketing blockbuster," *Variety* said, "many of the Sands execs are hiding and screening their calls—because even the highrollers know that they might be left standing in line without 'juice' to get them in." On his opening night, he sang only three songs all the way through: "Everybody Loves Somebody," "That's Amore," and "Welcome to My World." The rest he wrung cheap jokes from and cast aside.

The Ambushers and *How to Save a Marriage and Ruin Your Life* had both stiffed. *Bandolero!,* which was previewed in May, would do better. But *Five Card Stud,* previewed in July, would prove disappointing. And the fourth Matt Helm picture, *The Wrecking Crew,* which began production in June, would be another stiff; a planned fifth picture, *The Ravagers,* would never be made, and the series would be abandoned. On July 23, however, the day he recorded the theme song from *Five Card Stud* for release as a single, he signed to do a picture that Ross Hunter was making for Universal. It was called *Airport,* and it would be one of the biggest money-makers of all time.

His daughters Gail and Deana both had their own personal managers now and were under contract to Reprise. Last March, Deana had appeared in an episode of "The Monkees"; Gail, that same month, had played the Persian Room of the Plaza in New York. Now twenty-three-year-old Gail was marrying a man named Paul Polena. At least this one was a lawyer; at least, even if he did have gray in his hair, he was Italian.

Dean's brother, Bill, had begun to suffer severe headaches and tremors. That summer of Gail's marriage, Bill's worst fears were confirmed. The cancer in his brain was malignant. Dean saw him recede into the quiet horror of his end. That end came on October 20.

Riviera boss Gus Greenbaum had been murdered ten years ago, but his estate in Phoenix had still held the biggest single piece of the Riviera when new forces took over in the sixties. Eddie Torres, the Riviera's new president, now held the greatest interest in the operation, with thirty percent.

Previously, Torres had been an owner of the Fremont, where his involvement had resulted in a federal indictment for skimming. He was a friend of Meyer Lansky, who remembered Jeannie as a sweet girl who had been kind to his crippled son years ago in Florida. Through Torres, Lansky always sent his regards and asked after her. Torres was also a friend of Jerry Catena, the New Jersey slot-machine king who had shifted allegiance from Zwillman and Costello to become one of Vito Genovese's gambling-bosses. And he was among Dean Martin's dearest pallies as well. Torres's closest business associates were Delbert Coleman, the Harvard-educated chairman of the Chicago-based Seeburg Corporation, and Sidney Korshak, the shadowy Chicago-L.A. lawyer whose clients had ranged from Capone-gang killers to Teamster bosses to movie stars. As counsel for the Associated Booking Corporation, he served as the mediator between many celebrity performers and the shadowland-owned casinos that employed them.

Dean knew Korshak but was able to deal directly with men such as Torres and Johnny Rosselli, who on the West Coast represented the forces Korshak served. It was Dean who had sponsored Rosselli's membership in the Beverly Hills Friars Club, where Rosselli had been caught and indicted earlier in the year for running a high-stakes card-cheating racket. And it was Harvey L. Silbert, the Riviera board chairman himself, whom Herman Citron called upon late in 1968 to negotiate a contract for Dean that would take effect when his contract with the Sands expired the following spring.

The Riviera was a gold mine: seventeen blackjack tables, six crapshoots, two roulette wheels, baccarat, three hundred and twenty-nine slot machines, keno, a wheel of fortune, an automatic horse-race machine and a Big Bertha. The contract that was worked out between Dean and the Riviera guaranteed him $100,000 a week to perform and a $20,000-a-month retainer as a "talent consultant." And, in "special consideration," Dean was given ten percent of the Riviera for the nominal fee of $80,000. A gaming-license application was filed in his name on January 14, 1969. A week later, *Airport* began production.

His brother, Bill, lay beneath the dirt in Holy Cross Cemetery; his parents, in their granite tomb. The world for him had changed, and was changing still. Nicky Hilton, only forty-two, died in his sleep of a bad heart on February 5. Dean's oldest boy, Craig, now twenty-seven, had divorced his wife after making Dean a grandfather twice over. On March 9, at the Little Church of the West in Las Vegas, Craig married Kami Stevens. She was one of the dancers from "The Dean Martin Show." This marriage would not last either, and Craig would end up married to Carole Costello, the daughter of the man who long ago had helped to pay for Dean's nosejob. On June 3, Claudia ran off to Santa Monica to marry a third husband, a young actor named Keil Mueller, who adopted Keil Martin as his stage name in homage to Dean. On June 14, at the Church of the Good Shepherd in Beverly Hills, Deana married Terence Matthew Guerin, an aspiring writer. They both made pictures that year: Claudia's *Ski Fever* had come out in April; Deana's *Young Billy Young* would be out in September.

On June 17, three days after Deana's wedding, Dean opened for the first time at the Versailles Room of the Riviera. The per-person table minimum for Dean's shows at the Sands had risen from two bucks in 1957 to ten a decade later. The minimum of $15.50 levied by the Riviera for Dean's opening was the highest in Las Vegas, fifty cents more than Caesars Palace now imposed for Sinatra.

A few days after his fifty-second birthday, he recorded a version of Merle Haggard's 1968 country hit "I Take a Lot of Pride in What I Am." Released in July, it would be the last of Dean's singles to appear on the American pop charts. Like Sinatra, whose "My Way" had made it only to number twenty-seven earlier in the year, he had finally been vanquished by the age. He was now a singer too old to pass through the gates of the Top Twenty into the domain of the young. His singles now would be consigned to the lumpen limbo of the easy-listening charts.

"Get that fag out of here," Jack Entratter had snarled when Wayne Newton was presented to him in the Sands coffee shop. But the day would come when Las Vegas would belong to Wayne Newton, as the day now came when it belonged to Elvis. Bill Miller, who had run the old Riviera in Fort Lee, New Jersey, was now handling entertainment for the new International in Las Vegas. When Elvis, who had failed miserably in Vegas in 1956, opened victoriously at the International on July 31, 1969, he effectively ascended to his kingship in that holy city of old-guard cool where Dean and Sinatra had reigned supreme for a decade and more. That fall, Elvis would have his first number-one hit in more than seven years. Of course, the holy city was no longer what it once had been. It was the common, tawdry vacationland mecca of everyman, whose God had created Wayne Newton in His own image.

It was the summer of the Manson murders. Sharon Tate, who had starred with Dean in *The Wrecking Crew*, met her early end amid the slashings of that horror. The intended target of Manson's myrmidons that night of Tate's killing was Doris Day's son, Terry Melcher, an old sweetheart of Claudia Martin who had become entangled with Manson's Family ways.

"The accent is going to be on youth," he had said, regarding his proposed Beverly Hills Country Club, which never came to be. He was now fifty-two. He had been married for twenty years. Now the days of family were done. The grave had taken his parents and brother; two-bit lords and lawyers and dancing girls had taken his brood. Whatever happiness marriage and family had brought him now belonged to the realm of memory, that hated thing.

Jeannie clung to the illusion of their marriage until even the illusion died. "As long as he came home at night and was attentive, a good father, and tried at least to be a good husband, you know, when he was with me, then that was fine. When that stopped, then I left."

He had never flaunted his philandering. Unlike Sinatra, who conducted his affairs—yes, he was like a broad that way: he had affairs; the long-stemmed roses, all that shit—in public, as if to proclaim to the world at every turn that his dick still worked, Dean was never a tabloid Romeo. He never sought the company of women. It was not company that he had ever wanted from them, any more than he had wanted it from those with whom he played golf. It was what it was. And he took it in private. Any broad who went public with what happened behind closed doors, well, as far as he was concerned, that broad had spent the last dollar of his that she would ever see and drunk the last ounce of his fame and spratz as well. He was notorious for that: His song of songs was a blowjob and a fare-thee-well. "You wanna talk, see a priest," he would tell the girls in Vegas.

Kathy McKee, a Vegas showgirl who became Sammy Davis's lover, remembered her first encounter with Sinatra and Martin. She was with Davis backstage at the Sands. "When the two of us walked into Sammy's dressing-room, Frank Sinatra was there. Sammy had to leave for a few minutes, and when we were alone, Sinatra told me Dean Martin was due at any moment. He suggested that, as a gag, I should strip down to my underwear to greet him. I was hesitant at first, but I thought I was being put to a test to see if I could play in the big leagues. So I slipped out of my black-and-white polka-dot jumpsuit and greeted Dean Martin wearing my black bra, matching bikini panties, and white go-go boots. 'Wonderful, charming,' said Martin, who told me to get dressed again, 'because Frank is an asshole.' "

He was a wise man. Wisdom had blessed him with a disregard for the worth of his own racket. Where others sought nobility in acting or art in song, he had known things for what they were, and that knowledge had set him apart. Wisdom too had blessed him with an understanding of human nature, and that understanding had set him apart as well. It had never been his own compulsion for *lontananza* or his own abhorrence of communication that had been a problem. The problem had been the pressure from others to change, to become more like them—to share, to relate, to confront, to lend the lie of meaning to all those meaningless verbs and more.

To him, the problem was theirs: they who could neither accept what they were nor live alone with it. Wisdom had given him the strength to do both. And wisdom, in its way, was leading him now to withdraw from the world in fact as well as in spirit. He no longer cared. He never really had. He simply had been driven to possess the world, to pluck those apples that had been the fruit of his own discontent and imagining. Now his belly was full. He had signed no new moving-picture deal. He had announced through Herman Citron that he had made his last recordings for Reprise. He became a ghost on his own television show. The opening show of the season listed nine writers; *Variety* said they "must have spent their time elsewhere." When he returned to the Riviera in October, he seemed "as if he were someone impersonating Dean Martin." He simply no longer cared. He had been at this racket for thirty years. He had what he wanted. Let them find someone else to play them for suckers.

But wisdom, as it served him, also failed him. "The accent is going to be on youth," the aging man had said. The hunter was about to be captured by the game. Youth. Young flesh, sweet and milky-rose, sang its song of love to a Percodan-soaked heart.

Gail Renshaw was a blond, blue-eyed, twenty-two-year-old divorcée from Falls Church, Virginia. She had been Miss Speedway, Miss Good Grooming, and Miss Snow Queen. In September 1969, in Baltimore, she became Miss World-USA. Bob Hope, who crowned her, gave her a small part a few weeks later on his television special "Roberta." Her crown bore the jewels of duty as well as glamour: As Miss World-USA, she also took on the responsibilities of "ambassadress of goodwill" for Frostie Root Beer, one of the pageant's sponsors. Her manager, pageant director Al Patricelli of Bridgeport, Connecticut, brought the ambassadress to Las Vegas in October to work a greeting-card convention before leaving for London to compete as the American representative in the Miss World contest. Dean was at the Riviera. Dropping Bob Hope's name, Patricelli called the Riviera's press agent, Tony Zoppi, in the hope of having his client photographed with Dean. "Bring her backstage after the show," Dean told Zoppi on October 13. That night, wearing a dimestore crown and a MR. WONDERFUL-U.S.A. banner, he sat for a few pictures with her. "The least you can do now is have dinner with me," he said to her after the photographer left.

When they went to dinner that first night, Dean brought along his daughter Gail, who was two years older than the ambassadress. After that, they met alone. The ambassadress telephoned Ma and Pa Renshaw at their home in Alexandria, Virginia. "You won't believe this," she told her mother, Edna, "but I'm in love."

Gail Renshaw left in November for London, where she placed second to Miss Austria in the Miss World pageant. Before they parted, she and Dean agreed to rendezvous in Los Angeles upon her return. Meanwhile, Dean told Jeannie that he wanted a divorce. He left home and moved into the Beverly Hills Hotel.

During the first week of December, there was a rumor abroad that Dean, in a deal organized by Mort Viner, was about to buy the Los Angeles Rams football team from Dan Reeves for a reported $19,000,000. Sightings of Dean at the Beverly Hills Hotel stirred other rumors, and on December 10, those rumors were confirmed. As Dean flew off with Renshaw to Las Vegas for the Riviera's four-teenth-anniversary celebration, Jeannie issued a statement to the press through their family attorney, Arthur Manella.

"It is painfully difficult for me to announce the end of our marriage," she said. "My husband informed me several weeks ago that he had met and fallen in love with someone, and he asked me for a divorce. I assured him I would comply with his wishes. Proceedings will begin immediately. My deepest concern at the present is for our children. It is my hope that all concerned will make every effort to see that their lives are kept within as normal a pattern as the situation will permit. The children have always felt great love for their father, and I fully intend that it remain so."

As newspapers noted, "the identity of the other woman was not disclosed." But by December 12, the night of the Riviera party, Gail Renshaw's name and picture were everywhere.

"I haven't met her, but evidently all the children have," Jeannie told Earl Wilson of the *New York Post*. "All I know is that he asked me for a divorce—which surprised me—but I wouldn't want to live with a man who's not happy with me.

"I really have nothing to complain about. I am fortunate to have seven children that love me. I have no financial problems. I'm in good health. I just had my fortieth birthday. I've had twenty marvelous years with him.

"Now he's free, which is good. Now he can hide, which is what he does best."

A picture of Renshaw published in the *Post* showed her in bathing-suit and crown. Beneath were the words *The bride to be*.

Onstage at the Riviera, Dean joked that he had not had to pack for this trip to Vegas. "My clothes were already on the sidewalk." Jeannie, he said, would get the house. "But that's all right. I never could find it anyway."

One intrepid reporter called Ma Renshaw. "I've spoken to Mr. Martin on the phone many times now—he sounds just like he does on TV—and I'm sure he's going to make Gail a fine husband," Edna Renshaw said. "Certainly, she deserves the best. She's always been a sweet child. Never caused us a minute's trouble."

Dean took her to Elvis's show at the International on January 26, 1970. Seeing him at ringside, Elvis, elated, sang "Everybody Loves Somebody" in his honor.

As Dante, his Beatrice; so Dean, his Frostie Root Beer girl. Never under heaven had there been a truer love. His wealth and fame were as nothing; the beauty of his soul was all she craved. In the name of amore, she abdicated; in the name of amore, he bowed the knee of fealty to romance and eternal youth.

It lasted about three months. He waltzed around until March that way: like a fucking *cafone* with love-dust in his eyes. Then it got worse.

XV.

The
BREEZE

rthur Hailey's junk novel *Airport* had spent more than a year on the bestseller lists by the time that Ross Hunter's film version of it was released in March 1970. Written and directed by George Seaton, who had written and directed *The Counterfeit Traitor* in 1962, the picture was as mindlessly compelling and overblown as the book: a big gaudy melodrama with the well-worn but effective cheap trick of a madman's bomb sewn into the lamé of its plot. Dean starred as pilot Vernon Demerest, the adulterous brother-in-law of airport manager Mel Bakersfield, played by Burt Lancaster. Jacqueline Bisset played Dean's pregnant stewardess mistress.

Variety called *Airport* a jet-age *Grand Hotel:* "a handsome, often dramatically involving epitaph to a bygone brand of filmmaking." *Variety* doubted, however, that there would be "the kind of stampede necessary to bail out Universal's investment of around $10,000,000." The doubt proved false. Vincent Canby, writing in the *New York Times,* was more prescient. The picture was, he said, "an immensely silly film—and it will probably entertain millions of people who no longer care very much about movies." In the end, *Airport* became one of only half a dozen pictures made in the twenty years from 1950 to 1970 to take in more than $45,000,000.

By the time *Airport* was released, Gail Renshaw was back in Virginia, where she ended up as a part-time bartender.

On June 3, Claude Productions entered into an agreement of merger and plan of reorganization with NBC. As part of the deal, Dean and Jeannie, as the former owners of all Claude's capital stock, would receive 124,293 shares of RCA common stock, down considerably from its 1969 high of $48 a share, but still worth about $4,000,000.

By then, love had smiled anew upon Dean.

She was a twenty-three-year-old blonde named Catherine Mae Hawn. Like Dean, she was originally from Ohio, where she had been born, the daughter of Jim and Colleen Conatser Baxes, on November 5, 1947. In California, as a teenager in the sixties—she was Kathy by then, with a candied *K*—she had married a hairdresser named Michael Charles Hawn. At nineteen, in July 1966, she had given birth to a daughter, Sasha. In May 1970, she and Hawn had divorced. She accused him of beating her, drinking to excess, taking drugs, and knocking up another girl and paying for an abortion. He accused her of fucking around for months with a nightclub singer named Bobby Dee. When Dean met her, she was working as a receptionist in Gene Shacove's Beverly Hills beauty salon. The person who introduced her to Dean, at the Candy Store discotheque, was Frank Calcagnini, a small-time singer who soon began dating Jeannie Martin.

There was a testimonial debauch for Joe E. Lewis at the Riviera on September 12. Lewis had long ago served as an inspiration for Dean's happy-drunk persona. With Lewis, as with Dean in recent years, the persona had become reality. Only the happy aspect remained a sham. Beholding Lewis—and literally holding him upright that Sunday night, maneuvering him in and out of a wheelchair and into bed—Dean could glimpse in him one possible future. The old comedian was a wreck. He would be dead in less than a year. The loss of most of his liver, diabetes, ulcers, and a stroke had reduced him in his continuing drunkenness to a falling-down, incontinent, incoherent booze-ghoul. Dean already had the ulcers. He also now had his own private bar and lounge at the Riviera, Dino's Den, which was off-limits to all but him and his personal guests. The two of them, Dean and old Joe, along with a few other hangers-on, ended the night there, drinking together in opposite corners of the room.

Contrary to Herman Citron's announcement, Dean had not stopped recording for Reprise. The sweet inspiration of blonde amore seemed to have revived his interest. In January 1970, he had recorded Smokey Robinson's old hit "The Tracks of My Tears." In May, he had recorded a new album, *My Woman, My Woman, My Wife;* another, *For the Good Times,* in September; and in January

1971, he signed a new, three-year deal with Warner-Reprise, for ten albums at $150,000 per album plus a percentage of the profits. Jimmy Bowen, who had left Reprise in 1968, continued to produce all of Dean's recordings, as well as Sinatra's, through an arrangement between Reprise and his own Amos Productions company.

Dean's refusal to make the planned fifth Matt Helm picture, *The Ravagers,* had led to a court case involving Columbia's withholding of $299,940 from his share of the profits from *Murderers' Row* in compensation for losses the studio claimed his abandonment had caused. Now, concurrent with his renewed willingness to record, Dean also entered into a new movie commitment, his first since the *Airport* deal in 1968.

Something Big was yet another Western, written by James Lee Barrett and directed by Andrew McLaglen, the team that had made *Bandolero!* Written originally as a farce for Peter O'Toole, the story had been reworked for Dean, whose high price CBS was willing to meet in an attempt to save its National General motion-picture division. Dean's leading lady in *Something Big* was Honor Blackman, the forty-four-year-old British actress who had played Pussy Galore seven years before in *Goldfinger.*

"I went to the picture with some qualms," she remembered. "Based on his reputation in England, all one knew was that he was a great drinker and so forth. So there was a little trepidation." But her reservations faded once production began in Durango.

"I found Dean absolutely astonishing inasmuch as he was so relaxed and so lovely and so funny and knew every comma of everybody's lines," she said. "And he used to put his feet up on a chair and tip his hat over his eyes and just sing divinely. He was a funny man. A very warm man. A lovely, cuddly man."

Blackman remembered Kathy Hawn's weekend visits to the set. "I didn't like her awfully, is all I can say." Dean and Kathy would go off to a nearby house that had been rented for Dean. "I don't think anybody participated in his private life."

That spring, in Durango, Dean shared his vision of happiness with a reporter. When his NBC renegotiated contract ran out in 1973, he said, he was going to retire and drink every day until he died.

. . .

Nineteen-year-old Dino Jr. seemed at this point to have more brains than his old man. His precocious rock-'n'-roll career was behind him now; he was a premedical student at UCLA and a rising tournament-tennis player. On April 17, at a private chapel in Las Vegas, he married Olivia Hussey, the young English actress who three years before, at the age of seventeen, had starred in Franco Zeffirelli's *Romeo and Juliet*.

"I don't know him very well," young Dino would later say of his father. "We have never had a tremendous heart-to-heart conversation."

"He's a funny guy, keeps so much to himself," he would say on another occasion, to his brother-in-law, Deana's husband, the aspiring writer Terry Guerin, who tape-recorded a conversation with him for *Interview* magazine. "He's semi-retired. He has his golf, his girlfriend, and he keeps to himself."

In July, Dean publicly aligned himself with the organization known as Californians for Reagan, a renegade Democratic group that supported the Republican governor in his campaign for reelection against the Democratic challenger, Jesse Unruh. Through shows in Los Angeles and San Francisco the month before the election, Dean, along with Frank Sinatra, John Wayne, and others, would bring in more than $200,000 to Reagan's fund. A less successful attempt to raise money in San Francisco by Jesse Unruh featured a poetry reading by the black actor William Marshall. "Ronald Reagan can have Las Vegas dropouts," announced Senator George Moscone, the master of ceremonies at the Unruh affair. "I'll take William Marshall—and that's saying something for an Italian." Reagan would win. William Marshall would go on to star in *Blacula*.

On September 16, "The Dean Martin Show" began its seventh season. The sixties supposedly had been a baptism of liberation for America. Free love and free speech had sold well. But after all the Day-Glo debris, swami shit, and dead flowers were swept away, the puritan ethos emerged unvanquished. Beneath her new tie-dyed skirt, her whiter-than-white cotton panties remained undefiled. Now, however, her prudish tyranny governed not in the name of God and morality but in the name of sensitivity and liberty. That was the true legacy of the sixties' ideological boutique: censorship in the name of freedom. Just as other publicity-hound Baptist ministers, crying Satan, had tried to ban Elvis, so the Reverend Jesse Jackson, crying racism, would try to ban the Rolling Stones. Even the Ku Klux Klan was careful not to offend: "Every klansperson in Texas is invited," one Klan titan announced, eschewing sexism. Forced to tread gently among the myriad delicate whining *isms* of New Age sensitivity, the American language at last began to fulfill its promise as the world-voice of post-literate mediocrity. Amos Jones and Andrew H. Brown were Afro-Americans now. There was even an Italian-American Civil Rights League. Its Unity Day rally in June 1971 had served as the occasion of New York civil-rights activist Joe Colombo's murder. The Afro-American who deprived Colombo of his civil rights that day had been assured by his Italian-American brothers that he would be safely spirited away in the wake of his deed, but, alas, his civil rights too soon lay in a puddle in the street. "The Dean Martin Show," now in decline, and Dean himself, seemed more tasteless than ever amid the bloom of partisan sensitivity. The stage-set bar, suddenly deemed unwholesome by NBC after five years, had been removed from the show at the start of the 1970 season. But there were moves to compensate for such lapses in tastelessness. The twelve sex objects, the Golddiggers, whom Dean had introduced in the spring of 1968, were now replaced, in September 1971, by the even more offensively named Ding-a-Ling Sisters. The first show of the season, on which the four Ding-a-Ling Sisters made their bump-and-grind debut, also featured a hot-pants dance routine by Liberace and Art Carney, as well as a cue-card girl with the script written on her belly. In one routine, Dean and Richard Castellano, soon to portray Clemenza in *The Godfather*, played monks who had taken a vow of silence. The joke centered on waiting twenty years to find out where the toilet was.

And then there was *Something Big*, released in January 1972, the month of the Dean Martin–Tucson Open golf tournament. While not a commercial success—its distributor, National General, was on its way out by then—*Something Big* did much to resuscitate Dean's renown as a tasteless slob. *Variety* described it as: "An American-themed film which glorifies criminal behavior, makes fun of law and order, milks humor from hedonistic brawling, physical abuse of dead bodies and the antics of two nymphomaniacs, and is climaxed by the dramatically-excessive slaughter of dozens of people by a machine gun." Looking down its editorial nose, the review remarked that the picture might "find okay b.o. responses in general redneck situations." Tsk-tsk, that word—*redneck*—soon would have to go. Jimmy Carter, who sinned only in his heart, was a-coming to town.

The fact of Dean's narrowing mainstream popularity was well illustrated on October 5 at the Boston Garden. Liberace had sold out the Garden's fifteen thousand seats on Labor Day Sunday. Tickets for Elvis's upcoming concert on the tenth had nearly sold out overnight. Yet when promoters lured Dean to the Garden for a guarantee of $100,000, more than half the seats remained unsold. He stayed onstage for barely thirty minutes, then flew back west with his hundred grand.

In December, onstage at the Riviera, he fell silent a moment as if in thought.

"I hate guys that sing serious," he said.

Jeannie still did not want to believe that it was really over. She had done nothing to legally dissolve the marriage that had ended more than two years earlier. On Valentine's Day, 1972, Dean himself filed for divorce.

"I know it's the gentlemanly thing to let the wife file," he said. "But everybody knows I'm no gentleman."

The ultimatum that Dean presented to the Riviera was unheard-of in the history of Las Vegas: From now on, he would do only one show a night. His friend Eddie Torres, the president of the Riviera, could not go along with him. The board found Dean's demand preposterous. The very idea was unthinkable.

"You know who runs this town," Dean was told. "You can't fuck like that with these guys."

His answer was a whisper: *"Va 'n figa di tua madre."*

So it came to pass that Dean, standing hard, never performed at the Riviera again. Seven days after he filed for divorce, he accepted the Riviera board's offer to purchase his ten-percent interest, while the still-unopened MGM Grand Hotel and Casino negotiated with the Riviera to acquire Dean's performance contract, which was not due to expire for two more years.

He had committed himself to one more Western. *Showdown* was to be produced and directed for Universal by George Seaton, who had done *Airport* for the same studio. John Ford had told Seaton that he would never really be a director until he had made a Western. This was his Western. Dean would play a train-robber named Billy. Rock Hudson would play the boyhood friend who now, as Sheriff Chuck, must hunt him down. Susan Clark would play Kate, the Love of Both Their Lives. They began filming, in Chama, New Mexico, on April 11.

His mind was set on it. He would marry Kathy Hawn and live happily ever after, drinking chilled champagne and popping Percodans at the nineteenth hole of fellatory bliss, gazing out in the rosy-golden dusk across the rolling limitless manicured lawn of eternal youth.

But all was not right. There were moments of lucidity when he could see the snakes.

"He seemed not fully there," said Susan Clark. "He kept very much to himself. We all lived on a reserve outside of town. It was like a lodge, I guess, where they came and hunted and fished in the fall, and it was very outdoorsy; and he chose to live in this little tiny town of Chama. And even though he was playing this Western person, he was clearly not comfortable in the wilderness. He was very gracious and polite, but rather vague. He was always charming to me. He was, you know, the Italian gentleman. But he didn't seem real happy to be there.

"He was bored. I was still young, and most everybody else was quite pleased to have a job, and it seemed funny to be working with a man who was not as excited to be there as everybody else. I don't know why he did the movie.

"I think what he was suffering from was burnout. Just exhaustion and burnout. He seemed to be losing memory. He had trouble with lines.

"He wasn't awfully fond of Rock. It was disappointing that the two men didn't really hit it off. Perhaps Dean disapproved of Rock. I don't know. Rock had fun. Dean was tortured, because he was not a happy person doing that picture."

Dean had not been paid the money due him from *Airport*. On April 21, his lawyers filed suit against Universal seeking immediate payment of "not less than $1,000,000."

As Susan Clark realized, Dean did not want to be there. But it went beyond that: Dean did not want to be anywhere.

La vecchiaia è carogna.

He did not want to be anywhere, yet there he was, in the middle of nowhere, wearing a fucking toy gun and dolled up like fucking Giovanni Mack Brown; stuck there, in the middle of nowhere, fifty-something years old, playing cowboy with this Rock Hudson; stuck there, in the middle of nowhere, like a fucking *cafone*, wondering why, after more than twenty-one years of marriage, he was throwing away his wife for a twenty-four-year-old piece of ass whose fucking lies he didn't even believe; wondering what the fuck he was doing there, for a lousy twenty-five grand a week when he had more millions than he could ever live to spend; wondering what the fuck he had been doing all these years.

When his eighteen-year-old horse, Tops, dropped dead, he told Seaton that he was through. He was taking the carcass back to California to bury it.

Fuck the picture. Fuck Kathy Hawn. Fuck the world where it breathed. It was time to go home. On May 8, Dean left Chama.

"No goddamn fucking actor is going to blackmail me," hollered Lew Wasserman, the head of MCA, which owned Universal. "Shut down the production." A week later, Universal filed a suit against Dean for $6,000,000.

After Dean finally returned to work, there was another long delay in production. Rock Hudson drove a steam car into an adobe wall on a set in Santa Fe and was hospitalized for eight weeks with broken ribs.

"This is the longest picture I've ever been on since I stopped working with Montgomery Clift," said Seaton.

Dean told people that if he ever did another picture, he would produce it himself. There would be none of this long drawn-out shit. "There's an easier way," he said. "I'll shoot it like I shoot television." No one knew if he was serious or not. "I'd really like to find me a good gangster part. I think I could do something with it. I don't mean a *Godfather,* either. I didn't like that picture. I didn't like what they did to the Italian people. There was no call for that. I know a lot of gangsters and they're not Italians. They're guys with briefcases—an Irishman, a Jewish guy, and an all-American type."

Meanwhile, there was trouble with "The Dean Martin Show." At the start of the previous season, *Variety* had observed, "This variety show should be around as long as Dean Martin remains standing, because the basic booze-broads-and-boys-in-drag comedy formula is in such relief of the general sitcom antiseptics that a viewer can actually laugh out loud." But New Age sensitivity had its voice as well. In April, *Life* had taken a look at what it called "the witless reign of King Leer." It had seen "Deano, slumped inside his neon suntan, a cigarette hanging out of his mouth like a fuse." It had been repelled by "the drinking jokes" and "the mammary gland jokes." The show's sexual humor was one of "calculated degradation." It was "pathological—anti-woman and anti-man, too." It could be *"entertaining* only to monsters or to people wholly incapable of love." In conclusion, "Deano's systematic sniggering diminishes all of us, and if the radical feminists want to picket next Thursday night, I'll join them if they'll have me."

In May, at a Los Angeles meeting of NBC affiliates, the local stations had sided with *Life*—and, they claimed, an increasing number of their viewers—in expressing their concern to the network. They complained that "The Dean Martin Show" was "too suggestive" and in "questionable taste." NBC had taken their concern to heart, and in June, Greg Garrison announced to the show's writers and production staff that things would have to be cleaned up and toned down for the upcoming season.

Herminio Traviesas, the NBC vice-president in charge of censorship—"broadcasting standards" was the network's euphemism—stated that many of the letters of complaint that the affiliate stations had received came from young people. When Kay Gardella, the television editor of the *New York Daily News,* criticized NBC's dec-

laration of "war on our favorite television star," readers responded
with puritanical indignation. Gardella's defense of "The Dean Martin Show" "was as nauseating a column as I've ever read." The show
was "a cheap, bawdy production." Dean was a "dirty old man." One
reader was "disappointed that anyone can condone the garbage that
Dean Martin has been dumping into our living rooms. Martin's
steady routine of jokes concerning homosexuals has become disgusting. And those concerning the opposite sex have become a little
too risque to enjoy."

On July 28, Dean announced that he and Kathy Hawn would
marry as soon as Jeannie cut him loose. And yes, he said, it was
true, he would retire when his NBC contract expired. "Where am I
going?" he said. "I've done everything. I've made plenty of money. I
might as well play golf."

His silvering hair was dyed a strange reddish-brown. He
claimed he had been pressured into it by NBC out of concern for the
younger market. "I'm going to do something about it, though," he
said.

Two weeks before "The Dean Martin Show" began its eighth
season, Greg Garrison announced that he had decided to defy
NBC's mandate. The show's staff, he said, "had been living in a
monastery." They were "going back to the booze jokes, the girl
jokes, and the double entendres." He and Dean together would
uphold tastelessness. "He's like a brother," Garrison said. "I love
him and I'll fight right to the end of the show for him." Soon,
Garrison revealed, a new concept would be added to the show:
woman as trained animal. As Kay Gardella of the *Daily News* explained it: "Lloyd Bridges, for instance, will walk on with a St.
Bernard, Fess Parker a camel, someone else a seal, or a kangaroo,
and so forth, while Dean will always have the same one. It's a
voluptuous gal in a tiger's outfit. She'll be on Dean's leash." While
Gardella foresaw "a furor with women's lib," Garrison said, "We
hope to get a lot of mileage out of it." And there would be another
innovation: "We've come up with a station-break idea involving a
female impersonator," Garrison explained. "A beautiful voluptuous
girl will be telling Dean at every break that she's really not a girl,
she's a fellow."

On "The Tonight Show" in October, Johnny Carson asked Dean if the gossip was true, that his divorce from Jeannie would cost him millions of dollars. "Ah," Dean dismissed the matter with a wave. "I'll still have enough left over to go back and take care of all the hookers in Steubenville." Several years before, the Steubenville city fathers had named a desolate stretch of ugly highway on the eastern outskirt of town Dean Martin Boulevard in his honor. The day after his comment on the Johnny Carson show, the local WSTV "Phone Party" radio program received a flurry of calls demanding that his name be removed from the highway.

Showdown was finally completed. Dean threw a wrap party for everybody at the Chama Hotel. Susan Clark was thrilled when he asked her to dance. He was a good dancer, she said, "kind of old-fashioned." He sang "That's Amore" as they moved across the room.

"Oh, that's great, Dean. I used to listen to you sing that when I was"—the words *little girl* almost slipped out, but she caught herself: "I used to listen to you sing that song when I was younger."

Dean caught the faltering in her sentence, and he laughed. Clark was thirty-two years old; she had been thirteen when "That's Amore" was a hit. Kathy Hawn was twenty-four; she had been six when "That's Amore" was a hit.

On December 12, pending property-settlement and alimony litigation, Dean's petition for divorce was granted in Los Angeles County Superior Court by Judge Jack T. Ryburn. Drawn up by the law firms of Irell & Manella, representing Dean, and Wyman, Bautzer, Rothman & Kuchel, representing Jeannie, the Marital Dissolution and Property Settlement Agreement of January 1, 1973, listed Dean's living expenses for the past month as $10,497.05; Jeannie's, as $17,479.58. Together, their known and contingent liabilities totaled $6,182,495.03, most of it in notes payable to the City National Bank. While they had only $137,633.91 in their bank accounts, their marketable securities and properties, ranging from an assortment of cars—a 1957 Thunderbird, a 1972 Jaguar 2 + 2, a 1972 Stutz Blackhawk—to extensive real-estate holdings, represented many millions more. In all, the settlement would cost Dean over $6,500,000.

On March 29, 1973, in Judge Ryburn's court, the divorce became final. By then, Dean and Kathy Hawn were living in their new home at 363 Copa de Oro, a Bel-Air estate for which Dean had laid down $500,000 in January. On April 20, barely three weeks after the divorce, Dean and Kathy Hawn applied for their marriage license. Five days later, on April 25, the Reverend S. Mark Hogue, a Congregational minister, pronounced them man and wife.

With an altar and mahogany pews borrowed from the property departments of Warner Bros. and Twentieth Century-Fox, the living-room of the Copa de Oro mansion was transformed into a chapel seating eighty-five. There were gilt cages of fluttering doves. Two hundred dozen white lilacs and ninety-two dozen white tulips flown in from Paris were interspersed throughout the room with sprays of colorful California blossoms. The floral bill alone, from Harry Finley's Flower Fashions in Beverly Hills, came to $50,000. The reception afterward at the Crystal Room of the Beverly Hills Hotel cost nearly as much. There was Beluga caviar and Moët et Chandon Dom Pérignon, beef Wellington and galantine of pheasant, mountain trout stuffed with lobster mousse, pâtés of hare and foie gras, an oyster bar and more booze than could be drunk. The new Mrs. Martin, in a peach-colored French chiffon satin gown, with lilies of the valley in her upswept hair, wore another fifty grand on her wrist: the diamond-and-sapphire bracelet Dean had given her as a wedding-gift. Frank Sinatra, the best man, got a diamond-studded golden cigarette lighter with an obscene inscription.

In one of those books that Dean had never read, Emily Brontë had observed that men in their prime "seldom cherish the delusion of being married for love, by girls: that dream is reserved for the solace of our declining years." But, of course, Emily had never managed to snag herself a sucker worth the winning.

And in the world apart from books, from the font of dago wisdom from which Dean had drunk, long ago had come a saying: *Nessuno è più stolto di un vecchio innamorato.* There is no greater fool than an old man in love.

"The Dean Martin Show" 's eighth season was disastrous. It never placed above twenty-fourth in the ratings. The problem could not be blamed solely, or perhaps even primarily, on the touchiness of women who no longer shaved their legs and of the men who loved them. Cultural fashion, the changing galvanic sensibilities of the times, had a lot to do with it. But the ultimate reality of Dean's divorce from Jeannie and marriage to Kathy had as much, or more, to do with it. As his ex-partner, the monkey, put it: "The public is a strange duck. They'll turn on you." Dean had shattered America's comforting image of him as a man who at heart hewed to the traditional values. His long marriage to Jeannie, the family Christmas shows, the illusion of the old-fashioned family man that dwelt beneath the rogue—these, as much as his *menefreghismo* and as much as what gifts God gave him, were what had endeared him to his fans. Now he had betrayed them. Through the sundering sin of illusion-deprivation, he had abandoned them as surely as he had abandoned Jeannie. Even the easy-listening charts now were closed to his lying songs of love. His last, barely noticeable gasp of a pop hit, "Get On with Your Livin'," released in July, appeared only at the very bottom of the easy-listening charts, and only for two weeks. In August, when the National Organization for Women announced "The Dean Martin Show," along with *Last Tango in Paris,* as winners of its Keep-Her-in-Her-Place awards, it was almost anticlimactic. The show already lay castigated and castrated, barely renewed for another season.

But he could still draw the masses of the faithful to Vegas; that much was certain. At the end of August, as the new MGM Grand Hotel neared completion, Dean signed a three-year contract to perform there six weeks a year at $200,000 a week. There were still seven months to run on Dean's contract with the Riviera, but, with the stipulation that he do two shows a night at the MGM Grand, the Riviera waived its rights and allowed Dean to perform at the opening of the new hotel in December.

Moved by NBC to Friday nights after eight years of Thursdays, Dean's show began its ninth season, as "The Dean Martin Comedy Hour," on September 24. A new feature, the "Roast of the Week," patterned after the Friars Club roasts, was introduced with Ronald Reagan as the first guest of honor. A duet Dean sang with Kris Kristofferson would in retrospect seem a fitting choice for the opening program of what would prove to be the show's final season: "We've Been Around Too Long."

A month later, columnist Joyce Haber of the *Los Angeles Times* received a personal call from Dean. Even Sinatra did not receive calls from Dean. No one did.

But Haber was special. She had once written that Dean was "the latest big star to sneak in and out of Los Angeles' Midway Hospital for some kind of minor cosmetic surgery." Now she had written that Dean's long success on television had been Greg Garrison's doing. It was a brief call.

"Martin," she said in her column a few days later, "used language I've never heard from any star or man of stature or just plain gentleman."

Showdown came and went in November. On December 5, he inaugurated the Celebrity Room of the MGM Grand. "Charisma he has," said the *Los Angeles Times;* "new material he hasn't." He was, the *Times* reviewer concluded, "the world's laziest superstar."

In addition to his six weeks a year at the Grand, the three-year MGM deal called for a picture a year, at $500,000 a shot. Only one would come to pass.

Mr. Ricco was the story of a San Francisco lawyer who successfully defended an accused killer only to discover during a later case that his client, now unjustly implicated in a rash of cop-killings, had in fact been guilty of the earlier crime. There were racial overtones: the acquitted killer was black, his victim white; a white man masqueraded as black to seek his revenge on the law; the murder of a young black by a crooked white detective was made to look like a black-on-black killing. Dean played the lawyer, Joe Ricco. Thalmus Rasulala played his client, Frankie Steele.

"Dean was in a strange place," Rasulala recalled. "I don't know what kind of space he was in. Very closed-off to himself. Very noncommunicative. He just seemed to be very closed. There was very little talk between us. He wasn't unfriendly, just detached. I felt all the time that he was not into the movie. Which made it very difficult to get a rapport going with him. He just seemed to come in, do what he had to do, with very little gusto, and split. It seemed like old hat to him. His interest had just gone. His energy was gone. He was sleepwalking through it. He seemed a little melancholy, a little down."

Paul Bogart, the film's director, found Dean to be "a very kind of sweet, low-key man who wanted to do the picture well. Very reserved, very friendly, and not the least bit difficult. A really nice man. He never made us wait. He was always the first one there. He never pulled any star shit." But again Dean's memory seemed to fail him. "He had trouble retaining his lines," Bogart recalled.

In the end, Bogart said, *Mr. Ricco* was "a failure. It was a stepchild. It didn't get the best of everything. It didn't get the best attention from the studio. It didn't get the best money. We made a little money go a long way. It was a very modest and honest picture of its own kind. But that doesn't cut any ice when it comes to theaters."

Dino Jr. had started collecting guns—a pair of Civil War pistols —at the age of twelve, a year after he had begun taking tennis lessons from Pancho Segura, a year before he had formed his pubescent rock-'n'-roll band. The collection, heavy on assault weapons, was by now valued at about $30,000. Like most collectors, he sold as well as bought. On January 17, 1974, while Dean was in Tucson for the golf tournament that bore his name, young Dino sold two combat rifles, an M-16 and an AK-47, for $625. The buyers turned out to be two Treasury agents from the Bureau of Alcohol, Tobacco and Firearms. They arrested him for unlawful possession of firearms at the Beverly Hills home he shared with Olivia Hussey, where they also seized a .30-caliber carbine, a .45-caliber Thompson submachine gun, two Belgian machine guns, and an antitank cannon. Released on $5,000 bail by United States Magistrate James J. Peene, Dino was indicted by a federal grand jury on February 11. He pleaded not guilty, changed his plea, and was sentenced by Judge William P. Gray on July 1 to a year's probation and a fine of $200.

"The whole thing was innocent," his father said. "Dino's a good kid. He's studying hard to be a doctor. He never asks for money."

A few weeks after Dino was sentenced, Olivia Hussey filed for legal separation from him.

By then, *Mr. Ricco* was finished. It was Dean's fifty-first picture, and with it, his movie-star days, begun a quarter of a century before, came to their virtual end.

He returned to the MGM Grand in September. By now, he had managed to work the word "fuck" into the lyrics of "Tie a Yellow Ribbon (Round the Old Oak Tree)."

In November, he recorded a new album's-worth of songs. With them, his recording-star days came to their virtual end as well.

For the most part, they were ghosts from long ago, those songs; gray hauntings from those Steubenville days that lingered not so much in memory anymore as in the wisps of certain breezes. "That Old Gang of Mine" and "If I Had You" were from the twenties. "Love Thy Neighbor" had been a hit by Bing Crosby in 1934. "Without a Word of Warning" had been recorded by Crosby with the Dorsey Brothers in 1935. "Twilight on the Trail" was from 1936. Reprise, which had released neither a single nor an album by him since the fall of last year, would not bother to release these recordings for almost four years more.

On December 14, Kathy drove Dean's $64,000 Stutz Blackhawk into a tree in Beverly Hills. Everybody in Los Angeles County knew that license plate by now: DRUNKY.

Mr. Ricco was previewed at the MGM Grand in January 1975, the month of the Dean Martin–Tucson Open. *Variety* called it a "total waste of money," a "dreary crime potboiler" that was "lower-case fodder from square one." And so *Variety*, which a quarter of a century earlier had given Dean his first notice as an actor, now gave him his last: "Except for Martin, whose non-acting is getting worse, the rest of the cast is rather good."

Someone at the preview asked Dean if Las Vegas had changed much since the forties.

"Yeah," he said. "About ninety percent of my friends are dead. But the money's better."

Jack Entratter had died of a cerebral hemorrhage in March 1971. He had been fifty-seven, as old as Dean was now. Entratter's *padrone* from the New York days, old Frank Costello, had died two years later, of a heart attack, at the age of eighty-two.

Not long after his new marriage, Dean had filed papers to become the adoptive father of Kathy's eight-year-old daughter, Sasha. A superior-court judgment on February 6 rendered the adoption final and legally binding.

The last of Dean's weekly television shows had been broadcast the previous April. In February 1975, there were two "Dean Martin Celebrity Roast" specials, the first with Lucille Ball, the second with Jackie Gleason. In March 1975, he signed a new multimillion-dollar deal with NBC to host more roasts and a number of one-hour variety specials. The deal was for three years, with an option on another two.

In June, a few days after Dean opened at the MGM Grand, his daughter Gail and her husband, attorney Paul Polena, filed for joint bankruptcy in San Bernardino County Court. Dean's own financial situation drew attention in the press later in the month, when it was revealed at a House Government Operations subcommittee hearing that the Intelligence Gathering and Retrieval System of the Internal Revenue Service maintained a master list of organizations and individuals to be kept under special scrutiny. Dean's wealth and the shadiness of many of those with whom he had been involved were such that he had been placed on the master list, along with the American Civil Liberties Union, the Black Panthers, the Gay Liberation Front, Armand Hammer, and others.

For years, Dean had said that he would retire when his NBC contract expired, but now, after re-signing with the network, he changed his line. "I'll never retire," he told Kay Gardella of the *Daily News*. "A man has to get up to something."

He was in an expansive mood that day. He expounded upon the subtleties of his craft: "I just ask where is the chalk mark, where do I stand and what do I say, and I do it." And upon his love for humanity: "I love the women and I love the men." Then he elucidated: "But I'm no fag."

The first of Dean's new NBC specials was taped in July at a Beverly Hills club called Caves de Roy. His guests were Ronald and Nancy Reagan, Robert Mitchum, and Angie Dickinson. The show was broadcast, as "Dean's Place," on September 6. By then, he had also taped a holiday special, "Dean Martin's California Christmas," with Dionne Warwick and Freddy Fender. "Dean's

Place" would prove a failure. Except for the Christmas specials, a two-part special called "Dean Martin's Red Hot Scandals," and increasingly rare appearances on other people's shows, Dean's presence on television after 1975 would be represented by "The Dean Martin Celebrity Roast."

It was a dais of despair. They sat at banquet tables at either side of the podium: the undead of dreamland and the fleeting stars of the television seasons, each rising in turn, at the beckoning of Dean or his bloated sidekick, Orson Welles, to deliver the moribund jokes consigned to him for the occasion. Taped in part at the NBC studio in Burbank and partly at the Ziegfeld Room of the MGM Grand in Vegas, guests often delivered their lines to empty chairs or pretended spontaneous laughter at words that had been uttered in another state. As many as a thousand cut-and-paste edits were done to give each show the illusion that everyone was together in the same place at the same time. But no amount of editing could vanquish the pervasive air of hollow artificiality that came through. The forced attempts at humor came from a ten-writer assembly line; only Jonathan Winters and Don Rickles were ever allowed to write their own material. The jokes were so bad and the canned laughter so false, and that pervading hollow artificiality so funereal, that the shows had the quality of a relentlessly monotonous but vaguely disquieting dream. There were those who found "The Dean Martin Celebrity Roast" entertaining. There were those who lived canned lives, who found release through canned laughter. *"Time* cries and lets you care," the commercial said. Canned sadness, canned happiness: a wasteland full of empty cans. And there slouched Dean boozily at the dais—perhaps alone among the empty chairs, perhaps with the ghosts of others nearby—laughing forlornly at God only knew what. That image of him, presiding abstractedly at this *convivium* of artificial life, would be the one that America retained, a final remembrance, as he faded from the prime-time heartland of mediocrity to the realm of myth.

He looked at Kathy Hawn, and he looked at himself; and he began to see himself for the fool that he was: a fool not even of love, but worse, a fool of senseless vanity.

On June 25, 1976, they moved from the Copa de Oro mansion to a new home by the sea in Malibu, at 23544 Malibu Colony Drive. Two weeks later, on July 9, Dean walked out on Kathy and Sasha. He went to Mort Viner's home on the Pacific Coast Highway. There, while fooling with a nine-millimeter automatic that Viner kept on a shelf, Dean shot himself in the hand. He was taken to Los Angeles New Hospital, where a surgeon sewed the wound with twenty stitches. Six days later, on July 15, he quietly filed for divorce. Eleven days later, he just as quietly withdrew his petition. The wise man and the fool now were both lost within him.

He stood onstage at the MGM Grand in August, and he threw his scraps of songs languidly to those who had gathered. "Now ain't that better," he said, "than a guy singin' sixteen straight songs, sweatin', and veins stickin' out and hittin' a lot of bad notes?"

By then, he was living at 270 Palisades Walk in Santa Monica. On August 19, he filed a second petition for divorce. At the end of the month, while his lawyers had their pens out, he filed a suit against Warner Brothers Records for $1,500,000, claiming that the company had not allowed him to make the full ten albums it had contracted for in January 1971. Warner Brothers could not prove that Dean's own lethargy had been as much to blame for the contractual lapse as the company's disinterest, and the suit would be settled out of court in February 1978. Later that year, Reprise would finally release the recordings he had made in the autumn of 1974.

Over the last twenty years, since their breakup, the organ-grinder and the monkey had kept their distance. There had been encounters. The two had run into each other on a Palm Springs golf course in February 1957. Bing Crosby had brought Dean onstage during an appearance by Lewis on Eddie Fisher's NBC-TV show in September 1958. While Dean was performing at the Sands in March 1960, Lewis had returned the surprise. Later that year, when Dean was making *All in a Night's Work*, they were both on the Paramount lot. "I'd see him tooling around the lot in his little golf cart with his name on it in lights," Dean said. "When he saw me, he'd duck around a corner." Dean had brought him to his dressing-room for a drink. "I said, 'Now, isn't this better than ducking me?' He said, 'Yep,' and I felt pretty good about it. Then he left. And the next time he saw me, he ducked me again."

To that day, Dean had few kind words for Jerry. "Jerry's trying hard to be a director," he had said the previous year. "He couldn't even direct traffic." But now, sixteen years after they had last seen each other, Frank Sinatra wanted to bring them together again on national television. He talked Dean into it. The occasion would be Lewis's muscular-dystrophy telethon in Las Vegas on September 5, 1976. The secret was kept from Lewis for four days: His production staff, security crew, and orchestra all knew it was coming. Dean was brought in disguised as a waiter. Sinatra went onstage, as scheduled; he sang two songs and presented Lewis with a check for $5,000. "I have a friend," he said, "who loves what you do every year and who just wanted to come out and—would you bring my friend out please?"

Lewis at the time was addicted to Percodan. Lewis himself had been introduced to the drug long ago by Mack Gray, but had not grown dependent on it until after injuring his spine in a fall in 1965. Now he took as many as thirteen of the little yellow Du Pont pills each day. The years between 1973 and 1977, he would later say, were a blur. Only three moments in those years stood out clearly in his mind. One was when he found himself in a London street, "like in a fuckin' B-movie," alone and desperate, waiting to pay $1,000 for ten Percodans. Another was when, in 1977, he stuck a .38-caliber Smith-and-Wesson pistol into his mouth and sat there with his finger on the trigger. The third was when Dean walked out onstage that September night. "That I can remember," he said. "He walked out like a fucking champ, like a gladiator. It was something. A hundred twenty million people watching."

The grins that lighted both their faces as they embraced were brighter and more real than any they had shown in their ten long years as a team. They were the grins of two aging men—the one half-loaded, the other doped to the precipice of unconsciousness; the both of them drifting through desolations of their own doing— the grins of two men who had forgotten more of fame and wealth and venery than most ever dreamed of knowing; two men reminding one another, if only for a glint in the passing night, of a salty sweet breeze and the sound of waves at dawn, and of something that had died long ago.

Dean and Sinatra sang awhile. "So long, Jer!" Dean called, throwing a kiss, as he left the stage.

"Before going to bed," Jerry recalled, "I wrote Dean a letter and had it hand-delivered to his hotel. No reply. A few weeks passed and I sent off another letter, enclosing a twenty-dollar gold piece with the telethon symbol embossed on one side, a love inscription composed especially for him and Frank on the other. Frank responded immediately. As for Dean, not a word.

"The following August, when Dean was working Vegas, I picked up a phone and called his hotel. The operator said he wasn't in. I left a message, waited, waited some more. Finally, I asked Joey Stabile to go see him. 'Just tell Dean he's invited back on the telethon, and remind him we're getting close to Labor Day. But whatever he decides, make sure he knows I want a meeting.'

"So Joey drove to the MGM Grand. Dean greeted him pleasantly; as charming as ever. Everything worked out fine, and Joey set a date for the next day. 'Jerry will come to your hotel,' he said.

" 'No, no,' Dean insisted. 'I'll come and meet Jerry at the Sahara at four o'clock.' "

"I'm still waiting," Jerry would say years later.

On October 22, 1976, Dean and Kathy entered into an agreement whereby Kathy would receive $5,000 a month for three years. An additional $1,000 a month would be paid for the support of ten-year-old Sasha for a period of five years, and $500 per month for three years following. Dean would also pay all tuition, clothing, medical, and dental costs for his adopted daughter through her eighteenth birthday. Dean failed to appear in court for the divorce decree on November 10, claiming he had sprained his back playing golf. An interlocutory judgment of dissolution of marriage was granted nine days later, after he showed up in court, on November 19.

By then, he already had a new broad. The supermarket tabloid *Star* made the revelation sound vaguely fatal: DEAN MARTIN, 59: I'VE FALLEN IN LOVE WITH BING CROSBY'S DAUGHTER-IN-LAW. Thirty-eight-year-old Peggy Crosby was working as a hostess at a private Beverly Hills club called Pips when Dean met her. Her marriage to Bing Crosby's son Phillip had lasted only four months. "She seemed nice enough at the time," the young master Crosby had said, but "my entire experience with her has been a nightmare." His reaction to her romance with Dean was: "I hope they get married and he takes her off my back. She's been taking me to court for two and a half years trying to get one thing or another out of me."

Dean's divorce from Kathy became final on February 24. By then, Peggy Crosby was forgotten; but Dean had found winged love yet again. This one, Andre Boyer, was a nineteen-year-old economics student at UCLA. He had met her on the golf course at the Riviera Country Club in Pacific Palisades. She brought him home to Rolling Hills to meet her mother, with whom she lived. And in May, after NBC renewed its option for two more years of Dean's *convivi di morti*, he took her with him to Tarrytown, New York, to meet his pallies.

The shifting figures of shadowland were no longer so familiar to Dean. Mickey Cohen, upon his release from prison in 1972, had denounced the new *malavita* as a collection of "freaks." Doctors had removed Mickey's stomach in the fall of 1975; nine months later, he had gone to the grave. Sam Giancana had been murdered in the spring of 1975, soon after being ordered to testify before a Senate committee investigating his and Johnny Rosselli's roles in an alleged Central Intelligence Agency plot to assassinate Fidel Castro in the early sixties. The committee, predictably, was headed by a presidential aspirant, Senator Frank Church of Idaho.

After Giancana's killing, seventy-year-old Johnny Rosselli had begun to talk about forbidden things: the CIA, the Kennedys, the ways of the world that few men knew. He himself was called to testify in the summer of 1976 before the same Senate Intelligence Committee that had summoned, and perhaps thereby doomed, Giancana. On August 7, 1976, after Rosselli met with the committee in secret session in Washington, a fifty-five-gallon oil drum, punctured and bound with heavy chains, was found floating in Biscayne Bay, Florida, brought to the surface by gases of decomposition. Inside

the drum, legs and torso sawn apart, were the remains of Johnny
Rosselli.

In New York, old Vito Genovese had gone to the grave in 1969,
twelve years after seizing ultimate rule from Costello. Seventy-four-
year-old Carlo Gambino, whose forces had risen to supersede the
powers that Genovese had left behind, had passed away peacefully
in his Brooklyn apartment in October 1976, leaving Paul Castellano
as the heir of his domain and Johnny and Rosario Gambino, Carlo's
young nephews, as its blooded guardians beneath him. One of the
Gambino group's enterprises was the Westchester Premier Theatre
in Tarrytown, New York. It had begun as a garbage-dumping operation on sixteen acres of marsh in 1973. Two of Carlo's vassals,
Gregory DePalma and Richie Fusco, had come up with the idea of
building a theater on the landfill. They had brought in a Wall Street
broker, Eliot Weisman, to serve as a corporate front and to set up a
public stock offering through the Securities and Exchange Commission. They had opened with Diana Ross in March 1975. But the
stock never took off, and the cost of bringing in big-money acts had
driven DePalma and Fusco into the arms of shylocks to keep the
operation going. It was a losing proposition: there were too many
thieving hands grasping for too little money. One of those hands
belonged to Tommy Marson, a Palm Springs promoter who, it
seemed, knew everybody, from Johnny Rosselli to Frank Sinatra to
Dean Martin. Sinatra had gone east to sing at Tarrytown in April
and September 1976. He had even had his picture taken there,
during the April trip, with old Carlo, who, though smiling benignly,
looked as if he were already dead. Now, in the spring of 1977, the
Westchester Premier Theatre was facing bankruptcy. The big guns,
the old warhorses of cool, had been prevailed upon to save the day.
In January, Dean and Frank had agreed to perform together in
Tarrytown for twelve nights in May. The tickets, priced from fifteen
to thirty dollars a seat, had gone on sale in February and were
almost sold out. Dean and Frank were to be paid $400,000 each,
over the table. While appearing in Tarrytown, Dean stayed with
Andre at the Rye Town Hilton Inn.

Gregory DePalma explained in telephone calls to Tommy Marson how profits from the Sinatra-Martin shows would be hidden from

any eventual bankruptcy officials. At the time, Marson's line in
Palm Springs was being tapped by federal investigators pursuing
the unrelated matter of a suspected criminal conspiracy involving
the Alfa Chemical Corporation, another of Marson's wayward investments. DePalma's calls aroused the investigators' interest, and soon
there was a wiretap on his line in New York as well. It was in place
when he called Eliot Weisman on the early evening of May 19, two
nights after Dean and Sinatra opened in Tarrytown. He was in wop
heaven, sharing tales of the gods. He told Weisman about his dinner
the previous night with Sinatra. Maybe tonight Dean would join
them. He quoted what Sinatra had said last night: "Greg, you've got
to get him out of his fucking shell." Weisman hung on every word.

"I'm supposed to play golf tomorrow with Dean Martin,"
DePalma said. "But he's drunk as a fucking log. He wanted to play
today. He can't. He wanted to play the other day—forget about it.
Frank says, 'Wait, let's wait until next week. I'll take him with me
and you. We got to get him out of his shell.'"

"What's wrong with this guy?" Weisman asked.

"The broad. He's gone, this guy. He's fucking gone. He came in
the dressing-room, he says, 'Greg, what's the password?' I says,
'What password?' He says, 'Don't you know the password?' I says,
'No.' He says, 'It's *swordfish* tonight.' This is a sick fuck."

The next evening, after golf with Frank and Dean, DePalma
called Weisman again.

"We only played nine holes," DePalma said with disappointment. "He's awful. Both of them are awful."

"I thought Dean Martin was supposed to be pretty good."

"Ah, he's fucked up. This guy's on pills. Forget about it. He's
got the shakes. His fucking head's gone. He played horrible. He hit
a fucking house."

"Who did?"

"Dean Martin. Frank says, 'Uh-oh.' But Frank can't play at all.
Dean, you could see at one time he could play. He started the last
two, three holes, he parred. But the guy is junked up though. Definitely, definitely."

"He sure as hell looks it."

"Definitely. I don't know, I can't figure it. I feel so sorry for him. Fuck it."

It was true. By now, Dino was a junkie, washing down Percodan with Scotch.

Gregory DePalma, however, should have been worrying about himself. He and others involved in the Westchester Premier Theatre ended up in federal court the following year on charges of violating Securities and Exchange Commission rules and pillaging their corporation into bankruptcy. Eliot Weisman would be sentenced to six years in prison; DePalma, to four and a half; Richard Fusco, two and a half; and Tommy Marson, a year and a day.

From New York, Dean and Andre, Frank and Barbara Sinatra flew to Chicago, where Dean and Sinatra performed together at the Sabre Room. The twelve-hundred-seat nightclub, which paid the pair $600,000 for the week, charged $100 a head at the door for the dinner show, $90 for the late show. "Sinatra and Martin," *Variety* observed, "are a contrast in styles. Martin is casual, easygoing and seemingly effortless. His voice has also held up over the years and is still rich, deep and controlled. Sinatra, on the other hand, is more formal." And, "more than Martin, Sinatra needs that big orchestra to carry his vocals."

Dean turned sixty in Chicago with his nineteen-year-old *ragazza*. In mid-June, the two couples returned east to appear at the Latin Quarter in Cherry Hill, New Jersey, the town where Rosario Gambino made his home.

One of Gambino's Brooklyn henchmen drunkenly tried to ingratiate himself. "I have so much respect for you," he said, moving in to kiss Dean with his slobbering lips; "so much respect." Dean wiped disgustedly at his cheek where the tough guy had kissed him. "Keep a little for yourself, huh, pallie?"

"Do you know who that was?" somebody said to him.

"Whada you want, a kiss too?"

Elvis died in August, Crosby died in October. Dean, the missing link, lived on.

Ray Ryan, Ricci Martin's godfather, was gone now too. Ryan's activities had wandered too far from his oil wells. He had been convicted in 1971 of manipulating membership records of the Mount Kenya Safari Club, which he held in partnership with the actor William Holden. The club's members had included Crosby, Prince Bernhard of the Netherlands, Dwight Eisenhower, and Winston Churchill. Through his ownership of the El Mirador in Palm Springs and other enterprises, he had gotten far too involved in the shadowland affairs of the new *malavita*. On October 19, in the parking-lot of an Evansville, Indiana, health spa, he had turned the ignition key of his 1977 Lincoln Continental and had been blown to hell. The blast was so powerful that it had knocked out electricity in an entire section of the city.

With his opening at the MGM Grand on December 13, Dean finally got what he had wanted out of Vegas. From this date on, he would do only one show a night. His act was essentially the same as it had been for years, with one notable exception: a dead-serious version of "Brother, Can You Spare a Dime?" It was the song that had pervaded the air in 1932, the year that he had entered Wells High. *Variety* found it "his best and most forceful song of the entire hour."

On December 18, the night NBC broadcast "Dean Martin's Christmas in California," Dean flew into Los Angeles from Vegas to attend his daughter Gina's twenty-first birthday party at the Bistro. He embraced Jeannie that night for the first time since their breakup. It had been twenty-nine Decembers ago: those blue eyes, and that blond hair in the Miami wind, and that sweet, unknowing smile.

Jeannie was still involved with SHARE. In May, Dean brought Sinatra and Sammy Davis, Jr., with him to perform at the SHARE Boomtown benefit at the Santa Monica Civic Auditorium. By then, he had a new broad living with him: a young actress, Phyllis Elizabeth Davis, who would be costarring in the fall in the new ABC-TV crime-drama series "Vegas." Dean would make a guest appearance as himself at the start of the show's second season.

The lady from *Esquire* had been trying for a long time to set up an interview with Dean. Greg Garrison explained to her that in sixteen years, he had gotten only two calls from Dean. Finally, Mort Viner returned her many calls to his office.

"Dean just doesn't do interviews," he explained. "Why don't you take me to lunch, ask me any questions you would ask Dean, I'll answer them, and you can quote me as if I were Dean."

He was back for his nightly hour at the MGM Grand in January 1979. *Variety* said it well: "Dean Martin, in living ennui, presents a better caricature of himself than any other impressionist."

Spring, when a young man's fancy turned to—what was it? A song, something. A new broad: Joni Anderson. She had blue eyes. He thought she had blue eyes, anyway. A new deal: three more years with NBC. Ten, twenty million, whatever. Why even bother to look?

Ronald Reagan, he was all right. He had been on the show three times. Now he wanted to be president. Why the fuck not? Dean and Sinatra sang for him at the Boston Music Hall on November 2. Those *guaglioni* there in Kennedy-land, they paid fifty and a hundred bucks a ticket. Those who wanted to attend the "Golden Circle" reception afterward paid $1,000. At a press conference at the Colonnade Hotel, Dean, flustering both Reagan and a dead-serious Sinatra, threw his own answers at the reporters' questions to Reagan. "I don't think that's any of your business," he said to one woman who asked Reagan about his fund-raising plans. The room filled with laughter. Another woman wanted to know if Reagan expected to win the Massachusetts primary. The governor began to answer her, but Dean cut him off: "Why do you think we're here? Because he's never been here before?"

Nineteen-fucking-eighty. He had outlived Crosby. He had outlived Elvis. He had outlived Terry's Wonder Dogs. He would outlive them all. He had discovered the secret of happiness.

"How's it going?" someone asked him at the Riviera Country Club one day.

"Beautiful," he said. "It's great. I wake up every morning. Massive bowel movement. The Mexican maid makes me some breakfast.

Down to the club here. At least nine holes. A nice lunch. Go home, sit by the TV. The Mexican maid makes me a nice dinner. A few drinks. Go to bed. Wake up the next morning. Another massive bowel movement. Beautiful. This is my life."

Ricci, his youngest boy, was fucking Tippi Hedren's daughter, Melanie Griffith. Dino Jr.—he was in pictures now; *Players,* some shit like that, the last one was called—he had that ice-skater girl, that Dorothy Hamill. Nice girls. Everybody loved somebody sometime. He himself had that new one now, that—what the fuck was her name?

They were still *shports,* him and Frank. Even their tips made the papers. "Who is Hollywood's biggest tipper?" asked the *New York Post* on April 30, when many other papers were wondering about the qualifications of America's new secretary of state. "It's got to be a toss-up between Frank Sinatra and Dean Martin, says Joe Scott, a private club operator who has seen both stars hand out $100 bills for tabs that didn't come to half that amount."

Dean had never done a television commercial, and his last personal use of a telephone had been to make an obscene call to *Los Angeles Times* columnist Joyce Haber. But on August 19, Cunningham & Walsh, the agency that handled advertising for the American Telephone and Telegraph Company, announced that Dean would be paid several million dollars to serve as the AT&T spokesman in a new campaign promoting the company's public telephones and credit cards. Eldon Hanes, AT&T's assistant vice president of public services, explained that "Dean's delivery is easy and relaxed, and his overall manner puts people at ease. That's the message we're trying to deliver to our audience about public telephones and using them." As Dean himself explained, with a shit-eating grin on his face: "The telephone is something that is needed."

At the West Hollywood hotel where he lived, Leonard Barr, seventy-seven, suffered a stroke on October 28 and was taken to Saint Joseph's Hospital in Burbank. There old Bananas died.

On September 30, at the International Ballroom of the Beverly Hilton, Dean, serving as host, had slurred his way through "Prelude to Victory," a live closed-circuit broadcast that originated from Reagan banquets in New York, Oklahoma City, and Beverly Hills, and was transmitted by satellite to grand-a-plate Reagan dinners in nineteen cities across America. Five weeks later, on November 4, Ronald Reagan was elected president.

If Dean had a friend—though many, because of the drugs, saw him as an enemy—it was Mack Gray, the trusted famulus who had stood for almost thirty years between him and the world. Gray, at the age of seventy-five, had fallen ill; and now, on January 17, 1981, he was gone, leaving behind nothing but a stash of white and yellow pills.

Dean was to appear two nights later at the inaugural-eve gala that ABC was broadcasting live from the Capital Center in Landover, Maryland, on January 19. Thousands of people had paid from $100 to $1,000 for seats to see him and Sinatra and the rest of the performers that Johnny Carson would be introducing that night. He even showed up for the rehearsal that afternoon. But when he did, he scared the hell out of everybody. Charley Pride, the black country singer, was running through a song when Dean, seemingly disoriented, wandered onstage with a glass in his hand.

"What the fuck is he doing up there?" Marty Passetta, the show's director, wondered aloud in the control room, his confusion booming inadvertently through the hall's speakers.

Dean stood there, looking around. Big joint. He took a sip. Frank Sinatra came out to lead him off. Dean stumbled a few times on his way to a chair. Then he was gone. When he returned that night for the show, he was so drunk he could barely stand. As George Bush took the stage, Passetta was told that Dean would not be able to sing as planned. He was placed instead to wilt in a seat near the Reagan family.

The password was—why were they showing him this magazine? Oh, Dino, his boy, he was marrying the ice skater. Nice. He had his pilot's wings now, the kid: a lieutenant. He was something.

"Dean was always the guy we wanted for the part," said producer Albert S. Ruddy. "I wasn't sure we'd get him. You always make up a dream list, y'know. It took a little while to get him, I must say, because Mort Viner said, 'Hey, Al, he doesn't need a job. But let me wait for the right moment.' Mort gaffed it for us, and when he finally approached Dean, we got him.

"He had a terrific time. He probably worked a total of two weeks on the film. Got paid about a hundred, a hundred-something. If you wanted to find where Dean was on the set, shit, just hear where people were laughing, and he'd be sitting around telling stories. He had a real good time."

The Cannonball Run was a nonsensical concoction about a cross-country race, a multimillion-dollar variation on Roger Corman's 1976 *Cannonball,* itself a quick rip-off of that year's *Gumball Rally.* It starred Burt Reynolds. Dean played a fake priest. Jimmy the Greek, Dean's boyhood friend from Steubenville, was also in it. So were Sammy Davis, Jr., Bianca Jagger, Dom DeLuise, country singer Mel Tillis, and divers other characters. Ruddy and Twentieth Century-Fox refused to preview the picture for critics prior to its release; their response was foreseen. *The Cannonball Run* "seems to evaporate onscreen right before your eyes," *Variety* said; it "just goes to show you what's possible when the only thing anyone's interested in is making money."

And that is what *The Cannonball Run* did: It made money. Though *Variety* predicted that "Fox will undoubtedly have many of the record 1,682 prints back on its hands within a few weeks," *The Cannonball Run* took in nearly $37,000,000 at the box office. Only five other pictures released in 1981 made more. And they were meatballs too.

The password was—look at this shit: no respect; a month before his sixty-fifth birthday, a fucking senior citizen—and this fucking—he wasn't even a fucking spic: *Mustaffa,* a fucking swami or some shit—this fucking swami highway-patrol cop was busting his fucking ass. No, he didn't want to take a fucking blood-alcohol test. Didn't this fucking creep know who he was? Hadn't he seen "Dean Martin at the Wild Animal Park" the other week? "Weaving at the wheel," *shit.* Yeah, he was in a hurry, that was it. He was delivering a pizza to Bing and Elvis. Pepperoni, anchovies, every fucking thing. What the fuck, he wanted to frisk him now too? Jesus fucking Christ. Yeah, it was a gun, a fucking thirty-eight; what the fuck did he think it was? No, he didn't have a fucking permit to carry it. He was Tom Mix, he didn't need a fucking permit. The pizza was getting cold. Fuck it: Bring on that blood-alcohol test.

Cedars-Sinai Medical Center, then two fucking hours in the drunk tank at the West Hollywood sheriff's station. Nothing: He didn't need booze. He had love, massive bowel movements, things these fucking punks would never understand. And he had a prescription for that shit they found in his blood too.

He was charged with possession of a concealable firearm, entered a plea of nolo contendere, and on August 5 was fined $120 and placed on a year's probation by Judge Andrew J. Weisz of Beverly Hills Municipal Court.

Jimmy Bowen talked him into it: his first recording session in more than eight years. Bowen had been the vice-president of the Nashville office of Elektra/Asylum Records since 1978. Now, in January 1983, Elektra/Asylum merged with Warner Brothers, and Bowen became the head of the Warner group's Nashville division. During the week of January 17, at the Masterfonics studio in Nashville, Dean recorded ten songs, all of which were country except for Ivory Joe Hunter's "Since I Met You Baby," which qualified insofar as Freddy Fender had turned it into a country hit for himself in 1975. Conway Twitty sang with Dean on "My First Country Song," which Twitty's daughter had recorded a few years back under the name of Jessica James; Merle Haggard sang with him on "Everybody's Had the Blues," which had been a hit for Haggard ten years before.

In February, he joined Sinatra, Sammy Davis, and others for a Valentine Love-In benefit for Desert Hospital in Palm Springs. Sonny King, his old roommate from the Bryant, was there as well. The last time Sonny had seen him was nearly twenty years ago, when they were making *Robin and the Seven Hoods.* Dean looked sickly to Sonny now.

Sinatra liked to reminisce. "Sinatra, you talk about yesterday, you've got an audience," Sonny would say. "He loves to remember.

But Dean doesn't." Sonny told Sinatra about the old days, the cof-
fee-and-doughnut days, when he and Dean had shared the fifteen-
cent breakfast special at the Times Square Nedicks.

"Sinatra took me over to Dean, he said, 'Look who's here.'
Dean: 'Um, how ya doin'?' 'Good.' I joked, I said, 'You know, we
gotta have coffee sometime.' We hadn't spoken in years. He looked
at me, he said, 'Oh, yeah, we'll have coffee.' I said, 'You know
something? I'd like to break your fuckin' jaw.' And I walked away.
That was the last time I spoke to him."

Thirty years ago in June, the organ-grinder and the monkey had
sailed together across the sea. Dean had sworn he would never
return to England. Now there he sat on June 7 in the banquet hall of
the Mayfair Hilton in London, while Princess Anne joined the members of the Variety Guild in singing "Happy Birthday" to him.

He opened two nights later at the Apollo Victoria. Though the
promoter had priced the tickets high at £20, all twenty-eight hundred seats had been sold out for all ten nights. BBC-TV and the
Showtime network were taping the event for later broadcast in the
United Kingdom and America.

Warner Brothers released *The Nashville Sessions* album while
he was in London. A single from it, "My First Country Song," appeared on the *Billboard* country charts in July. That summer, Ricci
Martin produced and directed his father's one and only music video,
a $20,000 production of the album's second single, "Since I Met
You Baby."

Then came the culmination in ignominy of a long career of
splendor and sleaze, glory and tastelessness in the moving pictures:
Cannonball Run II.

"How come no one ever asks me to do these kinds of things?"
Sinatra had said to Dean after the first *Cannonball Run.* "Soon as
we heard that," Albert S. Ruddy said, "we got on the telephone and
called up Sinatra's agent. Sinatra wanted to do it because Dean was
gonna be in it and Sammy was gonna be in it, and he just thought it
was a chance for the boys to get back together." Shirley MacLaine
also came along for the ride, as a fake nun, while Dean shed his

fake-priest's collar—"I'll never get laid in this outfit"—to imper-
sonate a cop.

Not only would there once again be no previews for critics. This
time around, the picture would not even be shown in the United
States until six months after opening in Japan. "This film," *Variety*
would say when *Cannonball Run II* finally premiered in America, in
June 1984, "is so inept that the best actor in the pic is Jilly Rizzo.
But he has a great advantage: he's only on screen five seconds and
he doesn't have to talk." Unlike its predecessor, the sequel was an
immense failure in its native land.

They had legalized casino gambling in Atlantic City in 1977.
The first of the casinos, Resorts International, had opened in the
spring of the following year. By April 1983, when Dean performed
at Resorts, it was only one of nine hotel-casinos with yearly revenues of close to $2,000,000,000.

Forty-one-year-old Steve Wynn had gained control of the
Golden Nugget in Las Vegas in 1973, and had opened the Golden
Nugget in Atlantic City a little less than two years ago. Wynn had
thrived in Atlantic City, and though the Golden Nugget showroom
seated less than six hundred, a third of Resorts International's capacity, Wynn was intent on signing the biggest names, no matter
what the price. He was not looking, as Resorts was, to break even
on ticket sales. Most of the Golden Nugget show tickets would be
given to big-money gamblers as a stroke. To Wynn, it was worth
losing $10,000,000 in the showroom to make twice that in the ca-
sino. And that is what he had agreed to pay Sinatra: $10,000,000
for three years. Now he had gotten Dean as well. Sinatra publicized
his price; Dean did not, but it was said to be over $1,500,000 a
year. Sinatra's price was for an exclusive deal with the Golden
Nugget in Las Vegas as well as in Atlantic City. Dean's was for
Atlantic City alone. And Dean, unlike Sinatra, had not agreed to do
television commercials for Wynn.

The Bally Manufacturing Company, the old slot-machine firm
that had grown into a vast shadowland power, had opened its Park
Place casino in late 1979. In April 1986, the Bally organization
would take over the MGM Grand in Las Vegas, rechristening it

Bally's Grand; and not long after that, it would take over the Golden Nugget in Atlantic City as well.

Dean played the MGM Grand in Vegas in mid-September. After all these years, there was really nothing new that one could say. He was a part of the territory. It changed, he did not. "Martin's croon can't be mistaken for any other performer's," *Variety* remarked on the occasion of his latest opening. "It is both lazy and authoritative, a star's delivery." There was one new and strange note: the Golddiggers, who preceded him onstage, now opened with "I Am Woman," the Helen Reddy hit that *Variety* described as the "militant theme" of "femme libbers."

After closing at the Grand, Dean flew east for a benefit with Sinatra for the Retinitis Pigmentosa Foundation at the Waldorf-Astoria on September 20. Steve Wynn, who suffered from the disease, had sold out the affair at $300 a ticket before it was known that Dean and Sinatra would appear there on their way to open at the Golden Nugget together the following night.

They returned to Atlantic City on November 30 to perform at the Golden Nugget's third-anniversary party, an exclusive affair for the casino's biggest suckers. After the show, in the first hour of December—it was Skinny D'Amato's seventy-fifth birthday; they would throw him a surprise party later—Dean and Frank, along with Barbara Sinatra and Mort Viner, strolled into the gambling-hall. Dean walked up to a blackjack table and began fooling with the cards that the dealer had spread out in a fanned arc in readiness for play. The dealer, a Korean woman named Kyong Kim, meekly admonished him. He ignored her. Frank and Barbara drew closer to the table. Sinatra took out a roll of bills and bought twenty-two hundred-dollar chips, with which the three of them began to gamble. Sinatra asked that Kim deal to them by hand from a single deck, rather than from the mechanical, eight-deck shoe. She was hesitant and unnerved.

"If you don't want to do it, go back to China," Sinatra told her.

A Golden Nugget shift manager and a Casino Control Commission inspector approved the request for a one-deck game. Kim, however, went further, and dealt the cards by hand as Sinatra wanted, and not from the shoe as required by law. She also dealt several cards face-down and allowed the players to cut the deck by hand instead of with the plastic cutting-card—both violations of state gaming laws.

Doing it their way, Sinatra and Dean lost about $20,000 in fifteen minutes, then were gone. By eleven o'clock that morning, a report of the violations was brought to the attention of the Casino Control Commission; and on December 2, dealer Kyong Kim and three other Golden Nugget employees—a shift manager, Robert Barnum; a pit boss, Maxwell Spinks; a floor supervisor, Joyce Caparele—were suspended for up to two weeks without pay. Thomas O'Brien, the executive director of the Division of Gaming Enforcement in Trenton, ordered an investigation, while the state attorney general, Irwin Kimmelman, charged that Sinatra and Martin had "intimidated" the casino workers into violating the law. Routine surveillance tapes of the incident were studied. The four Golden Nugget employees were interrogated. James F. Flanagan, the deputy director of the DGE, took statements from Dean, Viner, and the Sinatras. Flanagan described Dean as jovial; the whole uproar seemed ridiculous to him. Sinatra was more serious about it. Both men claimed that they were used to Nevada regulations, which allowed the style of playing they had sought. They had not been aware, they said, that New Jersey casino laws were so much stricter. Dean said they wanted to pay the lost wages of the four suspended employees.

A Casino Control Commission hearing was set for August 1, 1984. At that hearing, Commissioner Joel Jacobson said the four employees "fell prey to the intimidation, the threats, and the fear of reprisals from the two celebrities who precipitated the violation." The Golden Nugget was fined $25,000—$15,000 for dealing by hand, $5,000 for dealing cards face-down, and $5,000 for allowing cards to be freely handled by players.

By then, Skinny D'Amato was dead. His heart had been faltering since the seventies. Some said it was the cigarettes and coffee; others laid the blame on the FBI, which had hounded him relentlessly for more than fifteen years before finally and fruitlessly closing its case in the spring of 1976. In the end, eight years later, on the morning of June 5, it was a heart attack that had taken him.

The end of Skinny was the end of Atlantic City's fabled past, which had lingered on only in his aura. Without him, Atlantic City was merely what it was: a decayed and dreary slum surrounding a few cold-towering corporate casinos that forbade the touching of cards.

As Dean had sworn he would never return to England, so he had sworn he would never return to France. But on July 3, he made his Parisian debut at the Moulin-Rouge, at a charity performance for the Franco-American Volunteer Service to Aid the Mentally Handicapped. At last, as one publication proclaimed, Parisians would be able to experience firsthand "Dean Martin, avec sa gouaille, sa moue et son regard irrésistible"—with his waggish jeer, wry look, and irresistible glance.

Dean and Sinatra were scheduled to open at the Golden Nugget on September 5. But Sinatra was still brooding over Joel Jacobson's characterization of him as "an obnoxious bully," and on September 1, Milton Rudin announced that Sinatra had "decided he will not perform in a state where appointed officials feel the compulsion to use him as a punching-bag." Governor Kean called Sinatra's decision "a loss for New Jersey." Steve Wynn, who had defended Sinatra and Martin since the outset of the controversy last December, booked Kenny Rogers in their stead.

On September 13, the Friars Club, celebrating its eightieth anniversary, honored Dean as Man of the Year. The banquet in the Grand Ballroom of the Waldorf-Astoria drew a crowd of thirteen hundred, who had paid from $250 to $1,000 to attend, with Sinatra, the Friars' Abbot, serving as *conférencier* and toastmaster. President Reagan, who could not attend in person, sent words of tribute on White House stationery.

"In paying tribute to you, Dean, the Friars Club has chosen one of its own, an individual who has time and again honored its tradition of reaching out to those in need," wrote the distinguished former bozo of "The Dean Martin Celebrity Roast," which NBC had revived this year for three specials. Thus far, Joan Collins and Mr. T. had joined the hallowed pantheon that had begun with Reagan eleven years before. "To you, Dean, to Francis Albert, and to all Friars, I send my heartfelt appreciation and congratulations."

Dean's movie career was behind him now. In 1985, his television career came to a virtual close as well. He played himself in the two-hour premiere of Joe Pesci's NBC series, "Half Nelson," broadcast in March. Through May, he appeared with Pesci in six episodes of the short-lived series. There would be a few rare, brief glimpses of him on television in the years to come—on an "All-Star Party for 'Dutch' Reagan," hosted by Sinatra on CBS in December 1985; on an ABC Dom DeLuise special in the spring of 1986; and so on—but there would be no more shows of his own, no more singing for the cameras; and finally there would be nothing. He made his last recordings in 1985 as well. In May of the previous year, Jimmy Bowen had become vice-president of MCA Records and the president of its Nashville division. Once again, Bowen prevailed upon Dean, and the result was one final single, recorded a few weeks after Dean's sixty-eighth birthday and released by MCA in late July.

In September 1986, he put one of his homes up for sale: the Hidden Valley estate in Ventura County, a ten-room Spanish-colonial mansion on sixty-three acres. Sotheby International Realty of Beverly Hills, the appointed broker, placed a price on it of $5,900,000.

His son Dino and Dorothy Hamill had divorced in December 1983. Like his marriage to Olivia, it just was not meant to be. Now thirty-five, he was still his father's pride and joy. The kid was a go-getter and he had kept his nose clean. Tennis, football, that pipsqueak rock-'n'-roll band; the college, a couple pictures, the television—he went for it all. He was a good father too. Dean could see that in his grandson Alexander's eyes. And no hernia for him, either; out there flying every month as a captain in the Air National Guard. It made Dean proud just to look at him.

Dean did not know what it was. He knew he had ulcers, he knew he had kidney problems, he knew a lot of things. *La vecchiaia è carogna.* He knew that too. When he went to Cedars-Sinai Medical Center, the croakers told him it was only a stomach flu. Whatever it was, they kept him there longer than he wanted to be there. That was in the middle of January 1987. Two months later, he still was not feeling right.

It was late on the Saturday afternoon of March 20 when he got the call. Dino and his weapons officer had left March Air Force Base at a quarter to two that afternoon in an F4-C Phantom jet for maneuvers near the San Bernardino mountain range. The plane had vanished from radar screens about ten minutes later, amid a blizzard near Mount San Gorgonio in the San Bernardino National Forest. Major Steve Mensik of the 163d Tactical Fighter Group described Dino as "one of the best pilots in this unit," and expressed optimism that he and the weapons officer, thirty-year-old Captain Ramon Ortiz, may have bailed out before a crash. Both men, he said, had extensive survival training and "quite a bit of survival gear with them."

After four days, searchers still had not found any trace of either the men or the jet. On the fifth day, they told Dean what he already knew.

The wreckage containing the remains of Dino and the weapons officer was found on the east side of Wood Canyon in Riverside County. An investigation later revealed that Dino's last words had been a request for a course change, which a Federal Aviation Administration air-traffic controller at Ontario International Airport had already given him. The blizzard and heavy air traffic had prevented his hearing the transmission. The Phantom jet had plunged almost four thousand feet from its last altitude reading of over nine thousand feet, and had crashed into the side of the mountain at four hundred miles an hour. Both men had perished instantly.

Dean and Jeannie had spent the past five days close together. When it came time to receive what was left of their son, there were no words that could express the blackness they felt.

"It was an unbelievable thing," Jeannie would say four years later; and there still would be disbelief in her voice. "We, as a matter of fact, never speak of it."

For Dean, the idea of a father watching his son go to the grave before him had always seemed the saddest of things that could befall any man. Now he knew it. The darkness would lift, but it would leave the heart forever changed. He would live with it, *la comare secca*, death like a bride of constant mourning, in the breeze of every day, in the black-velvet unraveling of every falling night.

· · ·

Four days after the remains of Dino Jr. were found, Dean's oldest son, Craig, lost his wife. Carole Costello, only forty-eight, died of a stroke at Valley Presbyterian Hospital.

On December 8, in Las Vegas, Dean's youngest daughter, twenty-one-year-old Gina, married Carl Wilson of the Beach Boys. Ten days later, there was another funeral. Old Herman Citron, hospitalized with a brain tumor at Cedars-Sinai Medical Center, had contracted pneumonia and gone to his end at the age of eighty-two.

More than thirteen years ago, in the summer of 1974, Dean and Sinatra had entertained the idea of making an extended concert tour of America, traveling from city to city in a chartered train of their own private cars. The idea had been Dean's as much as Sinatra's. "How much longer have we got?" he had asked Frank. But nothing had come of it. Now Sinatra had revived the notion as something he, Dean, and Sammy Davis could do together.

"There's a lot of people who never get to Vegas," he told them. "We could get a train, live on it, each of us have a private car, plus a dining-car and a bar car."

Later Sinatra told Davis in private, "I think it would be great for Dean. Get him out. For that alone it would be worth doing." Both of them knew that Dean's withdrawal from the world had taken a grievous turn since the death of his son.

"The train is out," he told them a few weeks later during dinner at his Beverly Hills home. "We'd be traveling for a week to play two dates. We'd be carrying forty musicians and a tech crew of another twenty-five or thirty. Then I've got a staff of six. Dean's got two, and Sammy's got three. Besides ourselves, that's eighty-one people. We can't afford to house and feed that many for almost a week between each performance. We'll have to fly. I'll use my plane and we can charter another G-2 for you guys."

As Frank saw it, they would play indoor stadiums and large theaters, places with a capacity of from fifteen to twenty thousand.

"You think we can draw that much?" Dean said. His heart was not in it, but he went along. On December 1, they held a noon reception for the press at Chasen's to announce their plans. The tour would take them to twenty-nine cities in the spring and fall of the coming year. American Express had agreed to be a supporting sponsor; rights had been sold to the Home Box Office network. The tour's producers were Mort Viner and Eliot Weisman—the broker who had been sentenced to six years in prison for his involvement in the Westchester Premier Theatre scandal.

At the start of the press conference, Dean mumbled incoherently for a moment, then said, "Go 'head, Frank, take it away. I can't talk."

A reporter asked Dean a question, which he had difficulty hearing. "We're happy to be doing this thing," he maundered. "What the hell."

Someone wanted to know if any of them had tried to quit smoking. Sinatra, conscious of his image, explained that it was exceptional for him to be smoking at this time of day. Normally, he smoked only after dinner. Dean, still quick with his hands, tossed a cigarette into his mouth. "I smoke during dinner," he said.

Another reporter pursued the matter. Did they feel that their smoking onstage might be a problem in this age when there was so much effort to prevent children from smoking?

"We don't care who smokes," Dean said.

He talked about their style of performing together. They never planned what they would do. "That's like doin' a Broadway play. Which I hate." He spat. "Broadway plays. Ya gotta say the same thing every goddamn night."

"He's diplomatic, I'll tell ya that," Sinatra said.

"Well," said Davis, "I guess the Winter Garden is out."

A British journalist asked Sinatra if he intended to sue Kitty Kelley over the book she had written about him.

"That's not a question for here."

Did they have any qualms about going into arenas that even some of the big rock-music acts had trouble filling?

"This country has not seen us," Dean said. "They've seen rock 'n' roll and all this other—not that I . . ." He seemed to be in good spirits, but he was having trouble finishing sentences.

Somebody asked them if they kept abreast of developments in rock 'n' roll, if they had been to any concerts lately.

Sammy said he had been to see Michael Jackson and the Jacksons.

"Aren't they black?" Dean asked.

When someone mentioned the Rat Pack, Sinatra dismissed the allusion as "that stupid phrase." Press releases for the tour would refer to it as the Together Again Tour; but for the most part the press itself would take up "that stupid phrase" and call it the Rat Pack Tour.

The tour opened to a full house of sixteen thousand at the Oakland Coliseum Arena on March 13, 1988.

"Will someone tell me why we're here?" Dean wondered aloud backstage to Sinatra and Sammy. Neither of them answered him.

Dean went on first. There were problems with the sound system, cries of "Can't hear you!" and "Louder!" He sang seven songs. Davis came out and did thirty-five minutes, announcing to the crowd that he was celebrating "three years of sobriety. For me, it's one day at a time now." After an intermission, Sinatra did his half hour, then the three of them closed together with a twenty-minute medley. Dean fell behind the others by a few bars. "Don't worry, he'll catch up to us," Sinatra said.

"I wanna go home," Dean hollered, and laughter swept through the crowd; but it was more than a joke.

At one point, his mood seemed suddenly to change. He looked long and hard at the faceless sea beyond the stage. What the fuck was he doing here, and who the fuck were these people? He took a final drag from his cigarette and flicked the burning butt into the crowd.

Sinatra confronted him about it after the show. Dean told him to fuck off.

Six days later, they were in Chicago. Sinatra was upset that the three of them had not been given suites on the same floor of the Omni Ambassador East Hotel. He had his valet complain to the manager, but when the manager called Dean's suite to arrange for his things to be moved, Dean told him that he wanted to stay where he was, *lontano*. He told the manager to tell Sinatra that the hotel did not have three empty suites on the same floor. When the manager did as asked, Sinatra threw a fit. "Don't unpack," he yelled to his valet. "We're going to get the hell out of this dump. Get Dean and Sammy in here." Sammy came as summoned, but Dean did not.

At the Chicago Theater the next night, Sinatra complained to Mort Viner that Dean was not singing as well as he should be singing. It was more than a comment, it was a tirade. Viner told Dean about it.

"I can't take this," Dean said. "I'm getting out of here."

He had Viner charter a plane, and the two of them flew back to Los Angeles that midnight. To avoid problems, he checked into Cedars-Sinai Medical Center. It was announced that he had been forced to quit the tour due to a flare-up of his "old kidney problem" and was undergoing a complete diagnosis by his personal physician, Dr. Charles Kivowitz.

Dean had lasted only a week. Sinatra and Sammy went on alone to Bloomington, Minnesota. It was obvious that Dean had no intention of rejoining them. Producer George Schlatter canceled the scheduled taping of the April 6 Radio City Music Hall show that had been planned for the HBO special. On April 15, Liza Minnelli took Dean's place, and the tour went on anew as the Ultimate Event. Dean did not tarry long in the hospital, and it was soon announced that he would be opening—alone—at Bally's Grand in Vegas on April 28.

On June 18, Dean showed up with Jeannie for Sammy Cahn's seventy-fifth-birthday party at the St. James Club. The death of their son was not the source of their renewed closeness. It was strange, really. After almost forty years, they were becoming friends.

In mid-August, at Bally's Grand, he celebrated his two-hundredth Las Vegas engagement. From Vegas, he went to Lake Tahoe, to open at the High Sierra. "Martin has become as close to a self-parody performer as anybody can," *Variety* mused. "There are a few minutes done straight, but they're almost impossible to catch." He ruined every song, either purposely for humor or merely in passing. "Longtime accompanist-conductor Ken Lane joins in, playing to the balconies while Martin plays to the front tables, himself, the boards, anywhere an inebriated gaze could reach.

"It's an act that is, of course, terribly dated, but it has to be allowed to Martin; he's been doing it so long that no amount of social consciousness over the unfunny aspects of intoxication can take it away from him."

The reviewer was new. The world was new. Social consciousness. And worse than that: "un-hip." Him, Dino. That is what the new guy called him: "un-hip."

He knew where he was, and he knew who that was, wheeling out the big birthday cake toward him on the stage of Bally's Grand. The monkey looked good, God bless him, since he'd gotten off the shit. Open-heart surgery agreed with him.

A wish, a wish.

"Here's to seventy-two years of joy you've given the world," Jerry said; "and why we broke up, I'll never know."

Yes. Seventy-two. He knew. Seventy-two years ago today. The little house on Sixth Street. The feast of St. Anthony. He knew.

"You surprised me," he said. It was true. "I love you," he said, "and I mean it." He felt as if he was about to cry, and he did not know why. Is that what old men did, they cried? He should never cry. His mother told him that.

Oh, yes. Hal Wallis was dead. He knew that too. A cocksucker even in death. They were all dead. Not them, though. They were here. The little house on Sixth Street. Nobody made gravy like her. All dead. Even Betty was gone now.

In one of those cowboy pictures—yes, that long ago—the guy told him to die. He could ride, he could shoot, he could do this, that, the other thing, but he couldn't croak good. It looked stupid the way he did it. They did it over and over; it still looked stupid. It was supposed to be the end, the violins, the sunset, the boots on, everything. But the way he did it, it just wouldn't come out right. Maybe that was his problem, he didn't know how to die.

Now Sammy with the throat thing. The doctors said it looked good after the operation. But Dean knew those doctors. They were having the big tribute for him at the Shrine. Sinatra told Dean he had to go. Dean knew he had to go too. He wanted to go. But, Christ, he was getting bad himself, going through hell trying to kick the shit. Look at this: He was shaking even when he drank.

He would have to get on and get off, he told them. He would go on and read the mock telegrams they wanted him to read, and that would be it. He didn't know most of these people—Jesse Jackson, Michael Jackson; where was Shoeless Joe?—but he knew Sammy. And he hated to see him like this: no voice, no nothing, just a lot of guts; *coglion*'s like a fucking lion, this little bastard.

A lot of people thought he looked worse than Sammy that night. Even the papers spoke of "a frail-looking Martin." He had Mort Viner keep it from those papers when he went to the hospital a few days later. Tests. They liked tests, those doctors.

He did not make it to Sinatra's birthday party. Frank would understand. If he didn't, fuck him.

Then Christmas. Then the pointed *cappelini*, the champagne. The Vogue Room. Fifty years, yes. Who was it who had told him that? The Hollenden, it wasn't there anymore. They tore it down. Sammy Watkins, he was long gone. Twenty years and more now, sure. That breeze through the curtains in that room upstairs. Betty. Everything: gone.

His kidney. His prostate. His liver. One of them fucking things. Whatever it was, it hurt. Deana wanted to get married again. He would wait until after that. Then he would let them cut him.

It was the prostate. They put him on the same floor as Sammy. There was a chill. Three grand a day and they play cheap with the heat.

Sammy went in May.

He liked it like this. There was nothing out there.

"He wasn't well," Jeannie said.

"What was wrong with him?"

"That you're just going to have to find out someplace else." She would never mention the drugs. "But, for the children and the grandchildren, and when I saw what condition he was in and how ill he was, I just decided that in spite of his ennui or his disinterest, I was just not going to let it end that way."

He was wasting away. Mort Viner saw it too, she said. "Mort realized that he was not long for this world if we did not step in there."

He did two nights at Resorts in Atlantic City in early June. After his birthday, he did a few nights at Bally's in Vegas. He had trouble standing. Someone brought him a chair. He had trouble moving the microphone to him.

It didn't even sound real: 1991. It sounded like something out of one of them fucking Buck Rogers things.

He could hear them: Alzheimer's. Old-timers' disease: that's what he thought they were saying at first.

"You don't get Dean to do anything," Jeannie said. "Dean does only what he wants to do, when he wants to do it. That has never changed."

She and Mort Viner drew him out for dinner. Jeannie on Saturday nights, Mort during the week. Always the same place, La Famiglia, on North Cañon Drive.

"He's a bit frail now," Jeannie said, as his seventy-fourth birthday approached. "He's gotten a bit frailer, only because he doesn't play golf anymore."

He did nothing. And, as Jeannie said, "Dean can do nothing better than anyone in the world. He can literally do nothing. All he needs is a television set and a Western. The older, the better. He was always content in a void. To tell you the truth, he's content today."

It was her. He recognized the voice. He remembered that blissom heat between her legs, and the golden, sweet heat of that summer. June Allyson. It was her voice on the radio. She was advertising diapers for old people. Yes. Diapers for old people. That's what they were now: old people. From here to eternity, lambskin scum-bags to Depend fitted briefs. It was the best laugh he'd had all year.

"Anyway, we're friends, Dean and I," Jeannie said. And she was one of the very few, maybe the only one, who could say that in truth.

God, he loved the way he sang that song. He could hear himself singing it now, not sound, but the colors of sound; he could hear it.

> *Guarda il mare com'è bello!*
> *Spira tanto sentimento*
> *Come il tuo soave accento*
> *Che me, desto, fa sognar.*

The record was around here somewhere. It was on that new thing they'd sent him, that compact disc, whatever the hell they called it. But it was better this way: just the colors that he could hear.

Of his own life, what errant rays he remembered of it, Dean would say nothing. "You would not learn anything from Dean," Jeannie said. "Quite honestly. He's so distanced himself from his own past, his own life."

Che me, desto, fa sognar.

*T*his was a good one. He had seen it before. The guy on the left, the one on the roan: he was the one. *"The way I see it"*—what the fuck was his name?—*"a man ain't got but two choices."* Look at those clouds, the way they rolled, real slow. The way that guy thumbed his hat back before he talked: They all did that. He himself had done it different; he had drawn it forward, downward, sort of shading one eye. But he was all right, this one. The broad too, she was something. *"You don't know what love is."* Pretty hair, pretty lips. *"You've lived too long with a gun as your only friend."*

The last kiss. *Il bacio finale.* Now back on the roan. *La comare secca.* Those clouds. That song he loved, it was like that. It ended with death's dark breeze: *non farmi morir.* So beautiful a song, so dark an ending. He had felt it, even as a child, long before he had understood it. He had seen it in the eyes of the old ones from the other side when they heard it. He had crept among them, moving through their shadows with his toy gun and his cowboy hat and his imaginings. He was Tom Mix, *nevvero?* And this was, after all, *l'America.* But then there were only the shadows. Even of the imaginings, only shadows remained. *L'America:* shadowings in the breeze. Life, death. Joy, sadness. After seventy-five years, it was all a rerun.

But this was a good one. The wine was good too. Shadow-wine. That's what it was. *Vino Nobile della Morte.* He bought it by the case now. Every swallow brought breath that bore neither memory nor meaning nor even deliverance from them—he no longer needed that deliverance—but rather the strange sweetness of something that may or may not have ever been, except in a dream of faint sea breezes through darkening pines.

Those clouds again. This was where he got it. One through the heart. Now they bring the broad his holster and gun. A few tears, the thing with the face. "Show emotion." That's what those cock-suckers always told him. Some people don't, he'd told them. But they always wanted the monkey faces. Now she takes the gun, gets on her horse. *"Lady, you better get back to where you belong."* Some more with the face. Back and forth with the eyes, the rifle on the wall. He'll never make it. Both hands on the gun. She's got him. *"You ain't got the nerve, lady."* Bang. The next day, the next week, whatever the fuck it is. Two, three minutes, the happy shit, and that's that: THE END.

*N*OTES

I

Emigration: Arpea, *Alle origini dell' emigrazione;* Foerster, *The Italian Emigration of Our Times;* Jarach, "Le cause e gli effetti. . . ."; Mammarella, *La vita quotidiana in Abruzzo;* Morison, *The Oxford History of the American People,* Vol. 3; Nelli, *From Immigrants to Ethnics;* Smith, *Italy;* Stella, *Some Aspects of Italian Immigration.* The Foerster and Smith books, separated by forty years, are especially valuable, and the latter is probably the best history of modern Italy available in English.

The Old Bismark: Herman Bernstein, *New York Times,* 3 April 1910, p. V-2. **The Five Points:** Asbury, *The Gangs of New York.* Black Hand: see under Chapter 3. *Guappu* and *vappu:* Giuseppe Biundi, *Dizionario siciliano-italiano* (Palermo: Fratelli Pedone Lauriel, 1857; reprinted Palermo: Edizioni "Il Vespro," 1978). The Jack London quote is from *John Barleycorn* (1913), XXV.

Steubenville: Brady, *Steubenville Sesqui-Centennial;* Doyle, *20th Century History of Steubenville;* Hunter, "The Pathfinders"; "Steu-

ben, Fort"; "Steubenville"; *Steubenville City Directory,* 1900–17; *Steubenville, Ohio;* Writers Program, *The Ohio Guide.*

Steel: "Iron and Steel Industry"; May, *Principio to Wheeling;* Morison, Vol. 3, pp. 72, 103; "Open-Hearth Process"; "Railroad"; "Steel Manufacture"; Wheeling Steel, *Annual Report.* Also the works cited above under Steubenville. The Stanton quote is from Morison, Vol. 2, p. 496. **Carnegie:** Joseph Frazier Wall, *Andrew Carnegie* (New York: Oxford University Press, 1970; paperback ed., Pittsburgh: University of Pittsburgh Press, 1989).

Data on the Crocetti brothers: Birth Records, State of Ohio; Death Records; interview, Vecchione; Marriage Records, Probate Court, Jefferson County; Parish Records, Church of St. Anthony; Registro degli Atti di Nascita. Guy Crocetti usually gave 1894 or 1895 as the year of his birth, but the record in Montesilvano places his birth precisely at 3:15 A.M., December 5, 1893.

Immigration records of the U. S. Department of Justice, Immigration and Naturalization Service: Certificate of Naturalization No. 612753; Petition for Naturalization No. 3135; *Passenger and Crew Lists of Vessels Arriving at New York, N.Y., 1897–1942.* Immigration records of the U. S. Department of Labor, Naturalization Service: Declarations of Intention Nos. 4051 and 8215, Petition for Naturalization No. 1395; Certificate of Citizenship No. 4274388. **S.S. Madonna, Berlin, Hamburg:** Michael J. Anuta, *Ships of Our Ancestors* (Menominee, Mich.: Ships of Our Ancestors, Inc., 1983), pp. 27, 118, 183; Eugene W. Smith, *Passenger Ships of the World, Past and Present* (Boston: G. H. Dean, 1963), pp. 31, 114, 157.

La Belle: Brady, *Steubenville Sesqui-Centennial;* May, *Principio to Wheeling; Steubenville City Directory,* 1900–17; *Steubenville, Ohio;* Wheeling Steel, *Annual Report;* Writers Program, *The Ohio Guide.* La Belle's parent company, La Belle Iron Works of Wheeling, was founded in 1852. **Holy Name Church, St. Anthony's:** Steubenville Area Chamber of Commerce, *Walking Tour; Steubenville City Directory,* 1904–11. **Crocetti marriages and births; Gaetano Crocetti's arrival:** see above under **Data on the Crocetti brothers.** The train route is documented in editions of the *Railroad Map of Ohio* (Columbus: Commissioners of Public Printing, Columbus Lithograph Co., 1910 and 1914).

Italian barbers: Foerster, *The Italian Emigration,* pp. 333, 336. **Steubenville barbershops and saloons:** *Steubenville City Directory,* 1908. **Saloons closed:** Doyle, *20th Century History.* **DiBacco:** interview, Vecchione; *Steubenville City Directory,* 1906–15.

Barra: Administrative Records; Birth Records, State of Ohio; interview, Dettore; interview, Vecchione; letter, Mehaffey; letters, Milton; Marriage Records, Probate Court, Jefferson County; Obituaries, Leonard Barr; "New Cumberland Memories." **Insanity, institutions:** interview, J. Martin; Writers Project, *The Ohio Guide.* **St. Vincent's Orphanage:** Willson, "St. Vincent's Puts Teamwork First"; Pat Hall, Columbus Metropolitan Library, 29 June 1990. **"She would remember":** interview, J. Martin.

Crocetti moves: interview, Vecchione; *Steubenville City Directory,* 1913–17. The following maps were used throughout: Steubenville Chamber of Commerce, *City of Steubenville* (1976) and *Steubenville, Ohio* (1938); *Steubenville, Ohio* (1946).

Historical background on St. Anthony (1195–1231) and his feast day can be found in "Anthony of Padua, St.," *The New Catholic Encyclopedia,* Vol. I (New York: McGraw Hill, 1967). Background on the feast of St. Anthony in Steubenville came from interviews with Mary Crocetti Vecchione; Dora V. Iacuone and Eugene M. Saggio, secretary and cantor, respectively, of the Church of St. Anthony of Padua; and other Steubenville residents. **Dino Crocetti:** Birth Records, State of Ohio; Parish Records, Church of St. Anthony.

Camillo Crocetti: *The Official Roster of Ohio Soldiers, Sailors and Marines in the World War 1917–18,* Vol. IV (Columbus: F. J. Heer Printing Co., 1926).

Gaetano Crocetti's citizenship application: U. S. Department of Labor. La Belle reorganization: May, *Principio to Wheeling;* Wheeling Steel, *Annual Report;* "Wheeling-Pittsburgh Steel Corp."

Julia Crocetti: Death Records, State of Ohio; interview, Vecchione. Visit of Giovanni and Maria Crocetti: interview, Vecchione; *Passenger and Crew Lists of Vessels Arriving at New York, N.Y., 1897–1942.* Quote ("...all...I spoke..."): Fallaci, "Dean Martin." Grant School: clippings and file in the collection of the Jefferson County Historical Association Museum, Steubenville; Hunter, "The Pathfinders"; interview, Monaco; *Steubenville, Ohio.* Mulliman: interview, Mavromatis. Antonucci: The Antonucci Bros. grocery was located at 529 South Street. Tom Mix (1880–1940): Miller, *The Great Cowboy Stars;* Mix, *The Life and Legend of Tom Mix.* Grand and Capital theatres: file, Jefferson County Historical Association. Quote ("I didn't have to peddle newspapers . . ."): P. Martin, "I Call on Dean Martin." Ten-story building (1924) and Fort Steuben Suspension Bridge (1929): *Steubenville, Ohio;* Writers Program, *The Ohio Guide.* Grant School rebuilt, Stanton School: files, Jefferson County Historical Association; interview, Monaco; *Steu-*benville, Ohio. Communication and confirmation: Parish Records, Church of St. Anthony.

Nick Norcio: interview, Vecchione. (Norcio later operated both a barbershop at 216 South Fourth Street and a restaurant at 162 South Sixth Street: *Steubenville City Directory,* 1933.) Pete Gillette: interview, Vecchione. (Gillette and his wife, Elizabeth, later took over the quarters and barbershop at 331 South Sixth Street, where Ambrogio DiBacco, Guy Crocetti's first American employer, had lived and worked in 1906: *Steubenville City Directory,* 1933.) E. J. Sickler: interview, Vecchione; *Steubenville City Directory,* 1926. Move to Brady Avenue: *Steubenville City Directory,* 1930. Harding Junior High School: Mary Crocetti Vecchione obtained the date of her cousin's transfer to Harding (27 January 1930) from an acquaintance in the school system, 22 May 1989.

Depression: Morison, Vol. 3, pp. 286–93. The Mellon quotations are from Herbert C. Hoover, *The Memoirs of Herbert Hoover* (New York: Macmillan, 1951–52), Vol. III, p. 30. Mellon's theories are discussed in Lawrence Leo Murray III, "Andrew W. Mellon, Secretary of the Treasury, 1921–1932: A Study in Policy" (Dissertation: Michigan State University, 1970). Gambling: Blosser and Regan, "Dean Martin's Wild Childhood"; Fenske, who lived at 901 Franklin Avenue when he taught at Grant, could not be located to confirm these quotations. **Fenske:** interview, Christ.

Boy Scouts: files, Fort Steuben Area Council, Boy Scouts of America, Steubenville; file, Jefferson County Historical Association; "Helping Hand in England Key to Scout Move"; interview, DeLuca; interview, Pompa; interview, Simmons (Fort Steuben Area Council); *St. Anthony's Troop 10* (the Troop 10 photograph appears there, as well as in "Helping Hand in England Key to Scout Move").

Crocetti family moves: *Steubenville City Directory,* 1926–31. **McKinley School:** Mary Crocetti Vecchione obtained the date of her cousin's departure from McKinley (8 February 1931) from an acquaintance in the school system, 22 May 1989. **Santucci:** According to the 1926–27 *Steubenville City Directory,* the family of Osidio Santucci, a fruiterer, lived at 344 South Fifth Street. The Holy Name Church, which later (1944) became the Holy Name Cathedral, was at 411 South Fifth Street.

II

The material for this chapter was harvested from notes taken over a span of years, notes taken for no reason other than that, in each case, an encountered scrap of data seemed at the time to raise some vaguely enticing historical question, or to shed a bit of light on some long-established misconception, or merely—maybe most of all—to testify to the strangeness of what America with a straight face calls her native art forms. In this chapter, those notes have found a reason of sorts. It is now beyond recall where, among those encountered scraps, it was discovered, for instance, that Carrie Finnell was known as the Remote-Control Girl, but had it not been for some long-ago note-taking, the fact itself would now be beyond recall as well.

The source listings that follow were used with the reason for this chapter more immediately to mind; but, in general, while they often confirmed, illuminated, and inspired new questions, none of them, it was discovered, could be taken as gospel. It was odd, for example, that a book about Jews in Hollywood (Gabler, *An Empire of Their Own)* should make no mention of Bugsy Siegel; that neither of two histories of Paramount should make a passing note of the earliest Paramount copyrights. So, once again, odd scraps of old paper in the end proved to be more valuable than books all too often written with too few of those scraps at hand. The clipping files of the Billy Rose Theatre Collection of the New York Public Library at Lincoln Center were used to settle and set aright the contradictions and misinformation encountered in books.

Other than the scraps themselves, the most useful sources here are the most basic: the old record catalogues, the wonderful *Early Motion Pictures* (Niver), the *New York Times Encyclopedia of Film* (a thir-

Tosches, *Country*, rev. ed. (New York: Scribner's, 1985), pp. 218–24; Victor catalogues: 1911, 1920; Raymond R. Wile, "The Development of Sound Recording at the Volta Laboratory," *ARSC Journal*, Vol. 21, No. 2 (Fall 1990); Wile, "Etching the Human Voice: The Berliner Invention of the Gramophone," *ARSC Journal*, Vol. 21, No. 1 (Spring 1990). For early Italian recordings, in addition to the Columbia and Victor catalogues cited above: Kelly, *His Master's Voice;* Spottswood, *Ethnic Music on Records.* Many of the recordings mentioned were located through *The Rigler and Deutsch Record Index* at the Rodgers & Hammerstein Archives of Recorded Sound of the New York Public Library at Lincoln Center.

"Torna a Surriento": Venci, *La canzone napolitana*, pp. 158–59. Author's translation: "See how beautiful the sea is! / It breathes forth so much feeling / like your sweet, soft accent / that, awake, leads me to dream."

Moving pictures: Brown, *The New York Times Encyclopedia of Film;* Conot, *Thomas A. Edison;* Dickson, *Edison's Invention of the Kineto-Phonograph;* files, Billy Rose Theatre Collection, New York Public Library at Lincoln Center; files, Margaret Herrick Library, Academy of Motion Picture Arts and Sciences; Gabler, *An Empire of Their Own;* Hanson, *The American Film Institute Catalog;* Irwin, *The House That Shadows Built;* MacCann, *The First Tycoons;* Niver, *Early Motion Pictures;* U. S. Copyright Office, *Catalogue of Copyright Entries: Performing Arts; "Variety" Music Cavalcade.*

Radio and television: Barnouw, *A History of Broadcasting*, Vols. I and II; Barnouw, *Tube of Plenty;* Buxton and Owen, *The Big Broadcast;* Dunning, *Tune in Yesterday;* files, Billy Rose Theatre Collection, New York Public Library at Lincoln Center; Terrace, *Radio's Golden Years; "Variety" Music Cavalcade.*

Eliot, "ugly": *The Music of Poetry* (1942). **Eliot, "habitual":** "The Television Habit," London *Times*, 20 December 1950. Eliot made his first recording in 1933 (Harvard University Phonograph Records). **James at the movies:** Adeline R. Tintner, *The Museum World of Henry James* (Ann Arbor: U.M.I. Research Press, 1986).

III

Mafia in New Orleans: Herbert Asbury, *The French Quarter: An Informal History of the New Orleans Underworld* (New York: Alfred A. Knopf, 1936), pp. 406–22; "New Orleans," *Encyclopaedia Britannica*, 11th ed. (1902); Peterson, *The Mob*, pp. 458–60.

The earliest writings on the true Sicilian Mafia are still among the best. The first extensive study of the subject was by Leopoldo Franchetti (1847–1917), whose *Condizioni politiche e amministrative della Sicilia*, originally published in Florence in 1877, was reissued in a second edition as *La Sicilia nel 1876: condizioni politiche e amministrative* (Flor-

teen-volume collection of nothing but scraps), and so on. *The First Tycoons* (McCann), an anthology of historical pieces on aspects of the early film industry, is an exceptional book. But the most valuable book here, long out of print, is *"Variety" Music Cavalcade*, a work that weaves together the history of America with that of its culture in a year-by-year chronicle, 1620–1950. (The revised edition of 1962, also hard to find, updates the chronicle through 1961.) It alone is in a class with the scraps.

The Kingfish quotation is from the *Amos 'n' Andy* television episode "The Boarder" (1952).

Lorenzo Da Ponte: April Fitzlyon, *The Libertine Librettist: A Biography of Mozart's Librettist Lorenzo da Ponte* (London: J. Calder, 1955); Joseph Louis Russo, *Lorenzo Da Ponte: Poet and Adventurer* (New York: Columbia University Press, 1922); Da Ponte's own *Memorie di Lorenzo da Ponte da Ceneda scritte da esso* (New York: Gray & Bunce, 1823) has been translated by Elisabeth Abbott as *Memoirs of Lorenzo Da Ponte* (Philadelphia: J. B. Lippincott, 1929; reprinted New York: Orion Press, 1959). The first American edition of *Democracy in America* was published by J. & H. G. Langley of New York. The quote is from Vol. II, Chap. 11. "Reign of mediocrity": *The Bostonians* (1886).

George Washington Johnson, the first recording star, began his career making Edison tinfoil cylinders in 1877. His recordings of "The Laughing Song" and "The Whistling Coon" for Columbia and other labels remained remarkably popular throughout the 1890s. *Popular culture* and *culturology: Oxford English Dictionary.* Juvenal: *Satires,* X, 81.

Phonograph: American Graphophone Company, *The American Graphophone Company;* Billboard, 23 May 1953 (jukebox issue); D. E. Boswell Company, *Phonograph and Graphophone Records* (Chicago: J. Harry Bickley, 1898); Columbia catalogues: 1890, [Spring] 1891, 1892, [August] 1896 *(Catalogue of the Famous "Columbia Records" Manufactured by the Columbia Phonograph Company),* 1898, 1910, 1911, [September] 1917; Robert Conot, *Thomas A. Edison: A Streak of Luck* (New York: Da Capo Press, 1979); Ted Fagan and William R. Moran, *The Encyclopedic Discography of Victor Recordings* (Westport, Conn.: Greenwood Press, 1983 [Vol. 1: "Pre-Matrix Series," 1900–3] and 1986 [Vol. 2, 1903–8]); Gelatt, *The Fabulous Phonograph;* Allen Koenigsberg, *Edison Cylinder Records, 1889–1912* (New York: Stellar Productions, 1969); Bill Randle, *The American Popular Music Discography: 1920–1930,* Vol. 3: *The Columbia 1-D Series, 1923–1929* (Bowling Green, Ohio: Bowling Green University Popular Press, 1974); Brian Rust, *The American Record Label Book* (New Rochelle, NY: Arlington House, 1978); Brian Rust, *Discography of Historical Records on Cylinders and 78s* (Westport, Conn.: Greenwood Press, 1979); Nick

ence: Valecchi, 1925). The other important early sources are: Giuseppe Alongi, *La maffia nei suoi fattori e nelle sue manifestazioni* (Turin: Fratelli Bocca, 1886); Cesare Bruno, *La Sicilia e la Mafia* (Rome: E. Loescher, 1900); Antonino Cutrera, *La mafia e i mafiosi* (Palermo: A. Reber, 1900); Angelo Umilta, *Camorra & Mafia: Notes sur l'Italie* (Neuchâtel: J. Attinger, 1878); and A. Vizzini, *La Mafia* (Rome: Artero, 1880). *I Mafiusi della Vicaria,* the often-mentioned but seldom-quoted 1863 play by Giuseppe Rizzotto of Palermo (1828–95), which contains the first known use of the word itself, was published as *I Mafiusi* (Rome: Perino, 1885) and appears in Loschiavo, below. The word's first definition as a *unione* of persons operating in their own interests *"senza rispetto nè a legge nè a morale"* was in Policarpo Petrocchi's two-volume *Novo dizionàrio universale della lingua Italiana* (Milan: Fratèlli Tréves, 1892), under *maffia.* A wealth of lore was brought together in the chapter "La Mafia e l'omertà" in Vol. XV of the *Biblioteca delle tradizioni popolari siciliane* of the great scholar of Sicilian folklore Giuseppe Pitrè (1841–1916). The original seventeen-volume edition (Palermo, 1870–1913) has been reprinted in a four-volume edition (Bologna: Forni, 1969), in which the Mafia chapter appears in Vol. II, pp. 285–337. In modern times the subject has inspired a vast literature in Italy. The most valuable studies include: Pino Arlacchi, *Mafia, Contadini e Latifondo nella Calabria Tradizionale* (Bologna: Società Editrice il Mulino, 1980), which concentrates on the Calabrian equivalent of the Mafia, the *'ndrangheta;* Giuseppe Guido Loschiavo, *Cento Anni di Mafia* (Roma: Vito Bianco, 1962); and the works of Michele Pantaleone, who was born (1911) and raised in the infamous Mafia stronghold of Don Calò Vizzini's Villalba. The intimacy of Pantaleone's knowledge offsets the flaws of an awkward writer whose observances are often skewed by outbursts of emotion. His landmark study, *Mafia e politica* (Turin: Einaudi, 1962), was published in English as *The Mafia and Politics* (New York: Coward-McCann, 1966). The key Mafia books of the Trieste-born poet and scholar Danilo Dolci have appeared in English as well: *Banditi a Partinico* (Bari: Laterza, 1955) as *Outlaws* (New York: Orion Press, 1961); *Chi gioca solo* (Turin: Einaudi, 1966) as *The Man Who Plays Alone* (New York: Pantheon, 1968). Saverio Di Bella, *Mafia ndranghita e camorra: guida bibliografica* (Soveria Mannelli: Rubbettino, 1983), is a useful if somewhat shoddy bibliography. The best work on the Mafia written in English, and one of the best in any language, is Norman Lewis, *The Honored Society* (New York: G. P. Putnam's Sons, 1964). Luigi Barzini's observations on the Mafia, in *The Italians* (New York: Atheneum, 1964) and *From Caesar to the Mafia* (New York: Library Press, 1971), together with Gaetano Mosca's "Maffia" essay in the *Encyclopaedia Britannica,* 11th ed.

(1902), perhaps provide the most balanced and concise introductory overviews in English. Both Mosca and Barzini eloquently affirm the purely Sicilian nature of the Mafia.

On organized crime in America, Virgil W. Peterson, *The Mob,* is by far the best study, though it suffers from fed-think. Jay Robert Nash, *Bloodletters & Badmen* (New York: M. Evans, 1973), and Carl Sifakis, *The Mafia Encyclopedia* (New York: Facts on File, 1987), are sometimes useful but strewn with errors and misknowing, and should be approached with care. Wise but flawed and overdone is John Scarne's diatribe against the American-Mafia myth, *The Mafia Conspiracy.*

Mussolini, AMGOT, Poletti: "Col. Poletti Decorated," *New York Times,* 13 September 1945, p. 13; Lewis, *The Honored Society;* Pantaleone, *The Mafia and Politics;* Peterson, *The Mob;* "Poletti," *Current Biography,* 1943 ed. (New York: H. W. Wilson, 1944); "Poletti Decorated by Pope," *New York Times,* 24 September 1945, p. 4; "Poletti Discharged from Army," *New York Times,* 15 November 1945, p. 8; "Poletti Discounts Revolts in Italy," *New York Times,* 2 October 1945, p. 3; "Rome Medal for Poletti," *New York Times,* 5 April 1945, p. 8.

Hanna, Ohio Gang: Thomas Beer, *Hanna* (New York: Alfred A. Knopf, 1929); Herbert Croly, *Marcus Alonzo Hanna: His Life and Work* (New York: Macmillan, 1912; reprinted Hamden, Conn.: Archon, 1965); Messick, *The Silent Syndi-*

cate: Morison, *The Oxford History of the American People.* **McKinley:** Messick, *The Silent Syndicate;* Morison, *The Oxford History of the American People.* The Roosevelt quote is from James D. Hart, *The Oxford Companion to American Literature,* 3rd ed. (New York: Oxford University Press, 1956), p. 653.

Purple Gang: Messick, *The Silent Syndicate;* Nash, *Bloodletters & Badmen;* Peterson, *The Mob;* Reid and Demaris, *The Green Felt Jungle,* pp. 63, 66–67. **Prohibition:** Oscar Getz, *Whiskey* (New York: David McKay, 1978); Messick, *The Silent Syndicate;* Morison, *The Oxford History of the American People;* Peterson, *The Mob.* **"Gangster":** *Columbus Evening Dispatch,* 10 April 1896, p. 4. **Harding, Means, et al.:** Randolph C. Downes, "President Making: The Influence of Newton M. Fairbanks and Harry M. Daugherty on the Nomination of Warren G. Harding for the Presidency," *Northeast Ohio Quarterly,* Vol. 31, No. 4 (Fall 1957), pp. 170–78; Will Hays, *The Memoirs of Will H. Hays* (Garden City, N.Y.: Doubleday, 1955); Messick, *The Silent Syndicate;* Morison, *The Oxford History of the American People.* **Edick:** Murray Teigh Bloom, *Money of Their Own: The Great Counterfeiters* (New York: Scribner's, 1957), p. 97.

The Strange Death of President Harding by Gaston B. Means and May Dixon Thacker (New York: Guild Publishing Corp., 1930) sold three hundred thousand copies, according to Alice Payne Hackett and

James Henry Burke, *80 Years of Best-sellers: 1895–1975* (New York: R. R. Bowker, 1977), p. 110.

Auerbachs: "Allege $15,000,000 Profit in Alcohol," *New York Times*, 1 November 1922, p. 32; Messick, *The Silent Syndicate*. Million Dollar Tonic ad: *Barbers' Journal*, various issues, 1920–21 (e.g., March 1921, p. 65). Cincinnati Federal Products: *Barbers' Journal*, October 1920.

IV

Churches: Steubenville Area Chamber of Commerce, *Walking Tour*. **Sin as an industry:** interview, Costanzo; interview, DeSarro; interview, Mavromatis; interview, Monaco; interview, Pavlovich; interview, Torcasio; Nygaard, *Twelve Against the Underworld;* "Reform: Sin on the Ohio." The still explosion was recounted by Costanzo.

Wells High: clippings and file in the collection of the Jefferson County Historical Association Museum, Steubenville; *Wells High Bulletin*, 1932–33. In March 1939, after a fire at Wells, it was renamed Steubenville High School and reopened in 1940. Pittsburgh Steelers: Roger Treat, *The Official Encyclopedia of Football*, 11th rev. ed. (Cranbury, N.J.: A. S. Barnes, 1973).

Isaly's, Green Mill, Donvito's: ads, *Wells High Bulletin*, December 1932. **Capitol Ball Room, Catholic Community Center:** interview, Christ; interview, Costanzo; interview, L. D'Anniballe.

Poolrooms and cigar stores: *Steubenville City Directory*. **Checker tournament:** *Wells High Bulletin*, 30 March 1933, p.2.

Rizzo brothers, bootlegging: Fallaci, "Dean Martin"; Lewis, *Jerry Lewis in Person;* P. Martin, "I Call on Dean Martin."

Nolan, Alexander, etc.: interview, Costanzo; interview, Monaco; interview, Pavlovich. *Steubenville City Directory*, 1930–44. **Lias:** interview, Costanzo; *New York Times*, 3 October 1952, p. 9. **White slavery:** Nygaard, *Twelve Against the Underworld;* "Reform: Sin on the Ohio."

Col. Bradley: "Col. E. R. Bradley, Turf Leader, Dies," *New York Times*, 16 August 1946; Scarne, *Scarne's Complete Guide*.

Sasso: interview, Sasso; interview, Torcasio; Snyder, *Jimmy the Greek*.

Schiappa, Barber, Walker, Brogan, Cooper, etc.: interview, Costanzo; interview, Mavromatis; interview, Monaco; interview, Pavlovich; Nygaard, *Twelve Against the Underworld;* Steubenville City Directory, 1932–40.

Tripodi: Death Records, State of Ohio; interview, Costanzo; interview, Monaco; Marriage Records, Probate Court, Jefferson County.

"Those with whom he would run": interview, Costanzo; interview, DiNovo; interview, Kayafas; interview; Mavromatis; interview, Monaco; interview, Pompa; interview, Sperduti; interview, Synodinos; interview, Torcasio; interview, Vecchione. *Steubenville City Directory*, 1926–36.

Synodinos: interview, Kayafas; interview, Synodinos; Snyder, *Jimmy the Greek.*

Quote ("It was for singin' . . ."): Fallaci, "Dean Martin." **Black Beauty** (Anna Sewell): Marx, *Everybody Loves Somebody,* p. 11. **Basketball:** interview, Christ; interview, L. D'Anniballe.

Picnic movie: interview, J. Martin.

Steubenville Pure Milk: interview, Vecchione. *Steubenville City Directory,* 1930–38. **D&R Service Station:** interview, L. D'Anniballe. **Boxing:** "Band Profiles"; Condon, "They Remember Dino"; "Cover Feature"; Fallaci, "Dean Martin"; interview, Julian; item, "In Short," *Billboard,* 10 June 1944; G. Martin, "My Father the Swinger"; P. Martin, "I Call on Dean Martin"; V. Scott, "Dean Martin Is the Total Entertainer"; Zolotow, "The Martin and Lewis Feud."

Weirton Steel: Condon, "They Remember Dino"; Fallaci, "Dean Martin"; interview, Julian; interview, Yannon; P. Martin, "I Call on Dean Martin."

California trip: interview, Costanzo; interview, DiNovo; interview, J. Martin; interview, Monaco.

Half Moon, Jimmy the Greek: interview, Costanzo; interview Kayafas; interview, Synodinos; Snyder, *Jimmy the Greek; Steubenville City Directory,* 1934–38.

Rex, Quattrone, etc.: Condon, "They Remember Dino"; Fallaci, "Dean Martin"; interview, Costanzo; interview, DeSarro; interview, Mavromatis; interview, Monaco; interview, Sperduti; interview, Synodinos; interview, Torcasio; P. Martin, "I Call on Dean Martin"; Nygaard, *Twelve Against the Underworld; Steubenville City Directory,* 1934–38. **Stogie:** interview, Costanzo; interview, DeSarro; interview, Monaco. **Annenberg:** obituary (Annenberg). **Simera quote:** Condon, "They Remember Dino." **Quote ("I never cheated")**: Fallaci, "Dean Martin." **Silver dollars:** Blosser and Regan, "Dean Martin's Wild Childhood"; interview, Costanzo; interview, Monaco; interview, Torcasio; P. Martin, "I Call on Dean Martin." The loop-the-loop story is from Monaco. **Ordinances:** City of Steubenville. *Revised Ordinances: City of Steubenville, Ohio* (Steubenville: H. C. Cook Co., 1931).

After-hours joints: interview, Costanzo; interview, Monaco.

Miller's: interview, Christ; *Steubenville City Directory,* 1936–38. **Del's:** interview, Sperduti. **Cunningham Stables:** interview, Costanzo; interview, Mavromatis; interview, Pavlovich; interview, Pompa. **Golf:** interview, Pavlovich; interview, Torcasio; Steubenville Chamber of Commerce, *Steubenville, Ohio;* Writers Program, *The Ohio Guide.* **Body of Beautiful:** ad, *Steubenville Herald-Star,* 21 October 1938.

Irma DiBenedetto: interview, Costanzo; interview, D'Aurora; interview, Monaco; interview, Sperduti; interview, Torcasio; interview, Vecchione; interview, Yannon. *Steubenville City Directory,* 1932–46.

V

Craig Beach: interview, Monaco. **"Oh, Marie":** Basso, *Dizionario;* Kelly, *His Master's Voice;* Marzo, *Songs of the People;* Robbins *Collection;* Robbins, *Neapolitan Songs;* Solmi, *Encyclopedia;* U. S. Copyright Office, Library of Congress, *Catalogue of Copyright Entries: Musical Compositions;* Venci, *La canzone.*

Crosby, etc.: Associated Press, "Bing Crosby, 73, Dies"; Bookbinder, *The Films of Bing Crosby;* Bruyninckx, *60 Years of Recorded Jazz;* Buxton and Owen, *The Big Broadcast;* Crosby and Martin, *Call Me Lucky;* "Crosby, Bing," in Hitchcock and Sadie, *The New Grove Dictionary of American Music;* Dunning, *Tune in Yesterday;* Friedwald, *Jazz Singing;* S. Green, *Encyclopedia of the Musical Film;* Jepsen, *Jazz Records;* Kernfeld, *The New Grove Dictionary of Jazz;* obituary (Crosby); Pleasants, *The Great American Popular Singers;* Rust, *Jazz Records;* Rust and Debus, *The Complete Entertainment Discography;* Shapiro, *Popular Music;* Terrace, *Radio's Golden Years;* Whitburn, *Pop Memories.* **Quotes ("discreet use of appoggiaturas"):** Henry Pleasants, "Crosby, Bing," in Hitchcock and Sadie, *The New Grove Dictionary of American Music.* **"A bel-canto baritone":** Henry Pleasants, "Bing Crosby: A Bel Canto Baritone Whose Art Disguises Art," *New York Times,* 5 December 1976. **Quote ("When a**

Bing Crosby movie . . ."): Fallaci, "Dean Martin."

WLW: National Broadcasting Corporation, *Radio Stations of the United States* (May 1937). **Mills Brothers:** Hitchcock and Sadie, *The New Grove Dictionary of American Music* ("Mills Brothers"); Jepsen, *Jazz Records;* Whitburn, *Pop Memories.*

Minstrel show: interview, Crocetti. **Dances, Capitol Ball Room, etc.:** interview, Christ; interview, L. D'Anniballe. **Red Horse Tavern:** interview, Christ; interview, Costanzo; interview, Monaco. **Glenn Miller:** interview, Crocetti. **Venetian:** interview, Costanzo. **Hy-Hat:** interview, Costanzo; interview, Monaco; interview, J. D'Anniballe. **Scrima, Marmarosa:** Bruyninckx, *60 Years of Recorded Jazz;* interview, J. D'Anniballe.

Rainbow Gardens, Half Moon, O'Connell: clipping file ("O'Connell, Helen"), Billy Rose Theatre Collection, New York Public Library; interview, Costanzo; interview, L. D'Anniballe; interview, Mavromatis; interview, Monaco; interview, Paolisso.

Mayfield Road Gang: interview, Downtown Joe; Reid and Demaris, *The Green Felt Jungle;* Messick, *The Silent Syndicate.* **Mounds Club, etc.:** *New York Times,* 3 October 1952, p. 9; Reid and Demaris, *The Green Felt Jungle;* Messick, *The Silent Syndicate.* **Jungle Inn job:** interview, Costanzo.

McKay, Club Gloria, Columbus: ad, *Columbia Evening Dispatch,*

5 May 1939; Condon, *Yesterday's Columbus;* Writers Program, *The Ohio Guide* ("Columbus"). Watkins, Neil House: ad, *Columbus Evening Dispatch*, 28 May 1939. **McKay:** *Columbus City Directory*, 1938; letter, Columbus & Ohio Division.

The published accounts of Martin's leaving the Rex to join McKay are all unreliable: Davidson, "Anything for a Laugh," brings McKay to Walker's; Edwards, "Martin and Lewis: Tops in Comedy," is vague, mentioning only "a visiting band leader"; P. Martin, "I Call on Dean Martin," has Martin incredibly saying that "a bandleader named Sammy Watkins heard me [at Walker's] and offered me fifty bucks a week. . . . He [Watkins] changed my name to Dino Martini" (nine years earlier, however, in Wallace, "Dean Martin Remembers," Martin plainly recalls Columbus); Zolotow, "The Martin and Lewis Feud," has Martin singing with McKay at Walker's and "the hoods" at the Rex offering to "make up the difference" in pay while he was with McKay "in return for 'pieces' of his future"; Sansoni, "The Bawdy, Boozing Life of Dean Martin," takes this to the scandal-sheet extreme, claiming that "he [Martin] paid out plenty before he (like Sinatra) got rid of the 'boys' "; Marx, *Everybody Loves Somebody*, plagiarizing Davidson in passing and embellishing on Zolotow, offers the most ludicrous version, replete with the fabricated names of "Izzy McGregor, a freckle-faced Scottish lad who worked in the casino with him

[Martin]" and "the three small-time hoods who ran the Rex Cigar Store" and decided Martin's future "in the usual manner, by knocking their automatics on the green felt tabletop" (p. 16).

Como: "Como, Perry," in Hitchcock and Sadie, *The New Grove Dictionary of American Music;* "Como, Perry," in Anna Rothe, ed., *Current Biography Yearbook 1947* (New York: H. W. Wilson, 1948); **Martini:** clipping file ("Martini, Nino"), Billy Rose Theatre Collection, New York Public Library; Green, *Encyclopedia of the Musical Film.* **Dino Martini:** "Last Football Party."

Little Italy Night Club, Ritz, Arabian Supper Club, Valley Dale: ads, *Columbus Evening Dispatch*, 1939. **State, Yee brothers:** *Columbus City Directory*, 1938. **"Smart":** ad, *Columbus Evening Dispatch*, 3 February 1939. **Ad ("New Singing Sensation"):** advertisement, Ernie McKay's " 'Band of Romance.' " **Christmas shows:** *Columbus Evening Dispatch*, 20 December 1939, p. B-3; **New Year's Eve:** "New Year's Eve Week-end Entertainers of Note."

Wylie, Golden Pheasant: *Columbus City Directory*, 1920–36; interview, Jacobs; obituary (Austin Wylie).

Watkins: *Cleveland City Directory*, 1910–40; Cook, unidentified *Cleveland Press* clipping; Death Records, State of Ohio, Department of Vital Statistics, Cleveland; Flanagan, "Sammy Watkins Would Reform

Rough World with Melody"; Gartner, *History of the Jews of Cleveland;* interview, Jacobs; interview, Kenaga; letter, Becker; letter, Columbus & Ohio Division; letter, George; letter, Sibits; letter, Sindelar; Marriage Records, Probate Court, Cuyahoga County; obituary (Sammy Watkins), *Cleveland Plain Dealer;* obituary (Sammy Watkins), *Variety;* Preston, "A Great Guy to Have Around"; Pullen, "Dancers Find What Makes Sammy Run"; review, Otis; review, Pull.; reviews, Pullen; "Sammy Watkins Dies Here at 65"; Seltzer; "Son of Cantor at 23 Is Jazz Virtuoso Here"; Spaeth, "Mr. Music Music Music"; "Today's Bio . . . Here's Sammy Watkins." **Quote ("Dean sent me a record"):** Preston, "A Great Guy to Have Around." **Blakstone:** Pullen, review, *Variety,* 12 June 1940.

Cleveland: *Cleveland City Directory,* 1936–40; Condon, *Cleveland* and *Yesterday's Cleveland.* **Whores:** interview, Downtown Joe; interview, Stueve. **Roxy:** ad, *Cleveland Plain Dealer,* 6 October 1940; **Thistledown:** Messick, *The Silent Syndicate.* **East Side Drive-In:** ad, *Cleveland Plain Dealer,* 6 October 1940. **Quote ("ultra-modernistic"):** review, Pullen, *Variety,* 6 October 1937. **Hollenden:** Cleveland Picture File, Western Reserve Historical Society, Cleveland; Condon, *Cleveland* and *Yesterday's Cleveland;* Messick, *The Silent Syndicate.* **Sterling:** interview, Stueve. **Theatrical Grill, Vincent Avenue:** Condon, *Cleveland;* interview, Downtown Joe; interview,

Stueve; Messick, *The Silent Syndicate.* **Quote ("Besides being a hangout"):** Pullen, review, *Variety,* 24 August 1938. **November 1, 1940:** Pullen, review, *Variety,* 6 November 1940.

"Watkins was paid": interview, Jacobs. **"By February 1941":** ad, *Cleveland Plain Dealer,* 2 February 1941, p. 11-B.

Zorita: ad, *Cleveland Plain Dealer,* 30 March 1941.

Betty McDonald: Birth Records, State of Ohio, Department of Vital Statistics, City Health Department, Steubenville, Ohio (Barbara Gail Martin); *Cleveland City Directory,* 1941; Marriage Records, Probate Court, Cuyahoga County; Marx, *Everybody Loves Somebody.* (Though Marx's book is often shoddy and unreliable, it does include quotations drawn from an interview with Betty McDonald Martin; and those quotations of the late Mrs. Martin, and the information they contain, have been used here. Obvious misrememberances have been amended. For example, Marx quotes Betty Martin's reference to *Governor* Lausche in the context of 1941. In reality, Frank John Lausche did not become governor of Ohio until later; he was the mayor of Cleveland in 1941–46.)

L'Araldo: cited in Blum, *V Was for Victory,* p. 150. **Draft:** Fallaci, "Dean Martin"; interview, J. Martin; interview, Vecchione. **Cigarette drive:** Flanagan, "Sammy Watkins Would Reform Rough World with Music." **Stephan Craig Martin:** Birth Records, State of Ohio, Department of Vital Statistics, Cleveland. *Fitch Bandwagon:* Flanagan, "Sammy Watkins Would Reform Rough World with Melody"; Spaeth, "Mr. Music Music Music." **Baptism:** Parish Records, St. Ann's Parish.

Caricature: *Cleveland Plain Dealer,* 2 May 1943. **Contract:** *Sammy Watkins v. Dino Crocetti,* Exhibit A.

Sinatra: Kelley, *His Way.* Sinatra at Riobamba: *Variety,* 17 May 1943. **Riobamba, Kean:** Mortimer, "Nightlife" [column], *New York Sunday Mirror,* 26 September 1943.

VI

New contract: *Sammy Watkins v. Dino Crocetti,* Exhibit B. Wilson: "The Midnight Earl." Mortimer: "Nightlife," *New York Sunday Mirror. Variety:* Kahn., "New Acts." **Subsequent *Variety* quote:** Mori., "Night Club Reviews." **Mortimer quote:** advertisement, *New York Daily Mirror,* 3 October 1943. **Other quotes:** advertisement, *Billboard,* 11 December 1943.

Songs in Martin's Riobamba repertoire: Siegel, "Dean Martin Starting to Click"; Mori., "Night Club Reviews." **Sobol:** advertisement, *Billboard,* 11 December 1943.

Radio shows: "Cover Feature." **London Terrace, Thanksgiving, etc.:** interview, Baylos; Marx, *Everybody Loves Somebody;* Stephen W. Plumb, *The Streets Where They Lived: A Walking Guide to the Residences of Famous New Yorkers* (St. Paul, Minn.: MarLor Press, 1989); Earl Wilson,

"Last Night with Earl Wilson" ("Gene Cops a Roll"), *New York Post,* 16 August 1982. **Sherwood:** "Dodge Weds Gregg Sherwood"; Farrell, "The Story of Three Cinderellas"; Goldstein, "Gregg Sherwood."

Billboard **cover:** 15 January 1944. **Statler tour:** advertisement, *Billboard,* 15 January 1944.

Steubenville visit: Bankruptcy No. 84544; interview, Sperduti. **Dick Richards:** Item ("In Short"), *Billboard,* 10 June 1944; "Band Profiles"; B. Smith, "Case History (1)." **La Martinique:** advertisement, *Billboard,* 10 June 1944; "La Martinique to Close—Tax!"; Mortimer, "Nightlife," *New York Daily Mirror,* 23 July 1944. **Cabaret tax:** "Spots Emerging from Tax Blitz," *Billboard,* 8 July 1944. **Harlequin:** B. Smith, "Follow-Up Review"; B. Smith, "Case History (1)." **Incident:** interview, J. Martin. **London Terrace lien:** Marx, *Everybody Loves Somebody.* **Cash payments:** B. Smith, "Case History (1)."

Perry: Bankruptcy No. 84544; interview, Baylos; interview, King; interview, J. Martin; interview, Military; Marx, *Everybody Loves Somebody;* Mortimer, "It Could Only Happen on Broadway"; B. Smith, "Case History (1)"; obituary (Perry), *New York Post;* obituary (Perry), *Variety;* M. Williams, "The Inside Story"; Wilson, *The Show Business Nobody Knows.* **Costello:** Gosch and Hammer, *The Last Testament of Lucky Luciano;* Mulholland, *The Abbott and Costello Book;* Pullen, "Lou Costello"; B. Smith, "Case History (1)";

Thomas, *Bud and Lou.* **"A few things":** Bankruptcy No. 84544.

Nosejob: Bankruptcy No. 84544; Pullen, "Lou Costello"; M. Williams, "The Inside Story." **"Schnozzola Sinatra":** Mortimer, "Nightlife," *New York Daily Mirror,* 23 July 1944. **Advertisement:** "Plastic Surgery," *Manhattan Classified Telephone Directory,* Fall–Winter 1943. Gene Baylos affirms that Costello helped pay for Martin's nosejob, though Jeanne Martin disputes this, and, in P. Martin, "I Call on Dean Martin," Martin himself is purportedly quoted as saying: "There are so many stories about that [the nosejob] that I'm almost tempted to tell you, 'Take your pick.' The real story is this: a friend of mine, a bookie, lent me $500 so I could have the job done in New York." Frank Military confirms that Martin spent the money given him by Costello, then got additional money from the bookmakers Buff and Peppi. **"A big success":** Kenny, "Nick Kenny: Speaking."

WMCA, "Songs by Dean Martin": advertisement, *The Billboard 1944 Music Year Book;* Alicoate, *The 1944 Radio Annual* and *The 1945 Radio Annual;* letter, T. Martin; "New York's Own Radio Station: WMCA," *Who's Who in Radio;* radio listings, *New York Times,* August 1944–January 1945; B. Smith, "Case History (1)." **Sears percentage:** B. Smith, "Case History (1)."

Richards suit (1946): Bankruptcy No. 84544; B. Smith, "Case History (1)." **MCA buy-out:** B.

Smith, "Case History (1)"; Williams, "The Inside Story." *Billboard* **suit:** Bankruptcy No. 84544.

Glass Hat: B. Smith, "Night Club Reviews," 9 September 1944; "Editorial: Muddy Showcase," *Billboard,* 9 September 1944, p. 26, gives background on the faulty sound system and other problems at the Glass Hat. Though Jerry Lewis misremembers the year he first saw Martin as 1946, *Jerry Lewis in Person,* p. 116, recounts his engagement at the Glass Hat in the summer of 1944.

VII

Jerry Lewis: interview, Lewis; Lewis, "I've Always Been Scared"; Lewis, *Jerry Lewis in Person;* Mrs. J. Lewis, "I Married a Madman!"; B. Smith, "Case History (1)"; Wilde, *The Great Comedians Talk.* **Greshler:** interview, Greshler. **"Jerry had this genius for mugging":** Zolotow, "The Martin and Lewis Feud." **"Mamalu"** (Premier 20168): ad, *Billboard,* 26 August 1944.

In his accounts, Lewis confuses elements of the two Glass Hat engagements. It is obviously to the first, in the summer of 1945, that his earliest memory of Martin refers: they were both on the same bill, and Lewis remembers the scar from Martin's "recent" plastic surgery and mentions Martin's radio show. But he also remembers Martin wearing a winter coat when he first saw him, referring to the winter of 1946, when he says, Sonny King introduced them. It seems likely that his memory of the second encounter, when they came to know one another, has subsumed the memory of their earlier meeting, when their paths merely crossed. This would be corroborated by Lewis's comment (interview, Lewis) that when they played the Havana-Madrid in March 1946—the month given for their first meeting in *Jerry Lewis in Person*—they "had known one another for about six months at the time." **Dorsey session:** Bruyninckx, *60 Years of Recorded Jazz.* **Return to Glass Hat:** *Variety,* 21 March 1945.

Costello: B. Smith, "Case History (1)"; Thomas, *Bud and Lou.* **Hippodrome:** ad, *Baltimore Sun,* 21 September 1944, p. 10. **Baylos there:** *Variety,* 30 October 1946. **Loew's State:** listing, *Variety,* 13 December 1944; Doan., "House Reviews." **WMCA:** letter, T. Martin; radio listings, *New York Times,* December 1944–January 1945.

Barbara Gail Martin: Birth Records, State of Ohio, Department of Vital Statistics, City Health Department, Steubenville, Ohio.

Chanticleer: ad, *Go: The Weekly Magazine of Baltimore Life,* August 1945, in file ("Martin, Dean"), Billy Rose Theatre Collection, New York Public Library.

Havana-Madrid, Lopez: obituary (Lopez). *Variety:* "Nitery Followups." **Five percent:** B. Smith, "Case History (2)." **Bankruptcy:** Bankruptcy No. 84544. **Sonny King there:** *Variety,* 7 February 1945. **Robbery:** "Burglar Suspects

Seized," *New York Times,* 24 January 1946, p. 40; "5 Held Prisoner by Safe-Crackers," *New York Times,* 22 January 1946, p. 42; *Billboard:* "Follow-Up Reviews." **Rio Cabana opening:** Gene Morgan, "Chicago Night Life."

Pickman, Columbia: Marx, *Everybody Loves Somebody;* B. Smith, "Case History (1)."

Rio Cabana, etc.: *Chicago Daily News,* 23 March 1946, p. 7; B. Smith, "Case History (1)"; *Variety* listing, 15 May 1946. **Average American:** "Wages and Hours," "Wealth and Income, U.S. Distribution of," *1947 Britannica Book of the Year* (Chicago: Encyclopedia Britannica, Inc., 1947). **Cumberland:** interview, Lewis.

Pasternak, MGM: Green, *Encyclopedia of the Musical Film;* Marx, *Everybody Loves Somebody; Music Views,* May 1953, p. 21; B. Smith, "Case History (1)." **Gayety:** *Variety,* 18 May 1946. **Perry story:** obituary (Perry), *Variety.* The July 19 contract is reproduced in M. Williams, "The Inside Story."

VIII

Atlantic City, D'Amato, 500 Cafe, etc.: Demaris, *The Boardwalk Jungle;* Gosch and Hammer, *The Last Testament of Lucky Luciano;* Jones, "Skinny D'Amato Dies"; Peterson, *The Mob;* Schwartz, "Greats and Near-Greats Alike: They All Called Him 'Skinny' "; U. S. Department of Justice, Federal Bureau of

Investigation File No. 92-5044, Vol. 1.

Manners: James G. Colbert, "Spicy Act Brings Floor Show Ban." *Boston Post,* 27 March 1946; "Jayne Manners Regains Portraits, Pays Ex $259," *New York Daily Mirror,* 20 June 1952; William H. Rudy, "6 Foot 3 Jayne Jibes at John Bull but Gives Him Lots of Leg to Pull," *New York World-Telegram and the Sun,* 17 April 1952; United Press International, "Film Man Divorced by Jayne," *New York Daily Mirror,* 25 September 1935. **Lewis, second billing:** ad, *Atlantic City Press,* 15 July 1946, p. 11.

Autobiography: Lewis, *Jerry Lewis in Person.* **"Randall 'got sick' ":** interview, Lewis. **Greshler's version, Perry's version:** B. Smith, "Case History (1)." **Contract:** M. Williams, "The Inside Story of Dean Martin and Jerry Lewis."

Diamond: ads, *Billboard,* 13 April, 1 June, 1 July 1946; Gart, *ARLD.* **"Irvin Wolf Presents":** ad, *Atlantic City Press,* 25 July 1946, p. 7. Photo with legend: *Atlantic City Press,* 25 July 1946, p. 7. **"A brief piece":** "Dean Martin Joined Revue at 500 Cafe."

"Dean would be quoted": P. Martin, "I Call on Dean Martin." **"Even Lewis in his autobiography":** *Jerry Lewis in Person,* pp. 138–42, where D'Amato, not Wolf, threatens. **Tucker:** Davidson, "Anything for a Laugh." **August 8:** ad, *Atlantic City Press,* 8 August 1946, p.

10. **Records:** ad, *Billboard,* 31 August 1946, p. 11.

Greshler-Perry: Bankruptcy No. 84544; "Dean Martin Walks Out on Agent Pact with Perry"; interview, Greshler; Lewis, *Jerry Lewis in Person;* B. Smith, "Case History (1)"; M. Williams, "The Inside Story of Dean Martin and Jerry Lewis"; Wilson, *The Show Business Nobody Knows.* **Havana-Madrid:** Stal., "Night Club Reviews." **"Alphabetically right":** interview, Lewis. **Constantino:** interview, Military.

Loew's State: Bankruptcy No. 84544 (Capitol pay); Wood., "New Acts." **Evans:** interview, Lewis; obituary (Evans); B. Smith, "Case History (2)." New York Life: Policy No. 20-721-098 (Martin), issued 20 January 1947. **Latin Casino:** Shal., "Night Club Reviews." **Capitol:** Stal., "House Reviews." **Insurance:** New York Life Policy No. 20-796-917 (Martin), issued 1 May 1947. **Rio Cabana:** Loop., "Night Club Reviews." **Stanley:** listing, *Variety,* 11 June 1947. **Earle:** Shal., "House Reviews." **Creditors' meeting:** Bankruptcy No. 84544. **Loew's State:** listing, *Variety,* 30 July 1947. **"Scout About Town":** recording. **Capitol:** Lowe., "House Reviews." **Smuggs:** interview, Sperduti.

North Jersey mob: Demaris, *The Boardwalk Jungle;* interviews, anon.; Peterson, *The Mob;* Prall and Mockridge, *This Is Costello;* Scarne, *The Mafia Conspiracy.*

Riviera: clipping, *New York Herald-Tribune,* 18 April 1937; Hy Gardner, "Broadway Newsreel,"

Brooklyn Daily Eagle, 9 June 1937; Gosch and Hammer, *The Last Testament of Lucky Luciano; New York Times,* 11 March 1937, p. 43; *New York Times,* 9 June 1937, p. 31; *New York Times,* 17 August 1939, p. 42; *New York Times,* 22 August 1939, p. 20; *New York Times,* 29 August 1939, p. 13; *New York Times,* 12 September 1939, p. 27; *New York Times,* 30 August 1944, p. 14. "Night Club Reviews," *Variety,* 26 June 1946; Scarne, *Scarne's Complete Guide to Gambling.* **Opening:** Jose., "Night Club Reviews." **Threats, arguing, offer to sell:** B. Smith, "Case History (2)."

Apollo: interview, Jerome; listing, *Billboard,* 8 November 1947. **Option:** "Martin Loses Suit to Apollo." **Chez Paree:** Baxt., "Night Club Reviews"; interview, Lewis. **Fischetti:** Brashler, *The Don;* "Fischetti Dies"; Gosch and Hammer, *The Last Testament of Lucky Luciano;* interview, Lewis; obituary (C. Fischetti); obituary (R. Fischetti); Peterson, *The Mob;* Prall, *This Is Costello on the Spot;* B. Smith, "Case History (2)." **Per-capita income:** "Wealth and Income, U.S. Distribution of," *1949* and *1950 Britannica Book of the Year* (Chicago: Encyclopedia Britannica, Inc., 1949 and 1950).

Riverside Drive: Lewis, *Jerry Lewis in Person;* Marx, *Everybody Loves Somebody.* **Capitol:** Jose, "House Reviews" (Capitol, N.Y.); B. Smith, "Case History (2)"; B. Smith, "Vaudeville Reviews."

Saratoga: Peterson, *The Mob;* Scarne, *The Mafia Conspiracy;* Scarne, *Scarne's Complete Guide to Gambling.* **Copacabana:** "Actual Ownership of Night Clubs Is Goal of Investigation by City"; "Adonis Depicted as Resort's Guest"; "Copacabana, City Reach Compromise"; "Copacabana Faces Trial for License"; Eisenberg, Dan, and Landau, *Meyer Lansky;* Katz, *Uncle Frank;* letter, Wright; "Night Club Hearing Defied by Gambler"; "Night Club Owner Denies City Charge"; obituary (Costello); obituary (Entratter); obituary (Podell); Prall, *This Is Costello on the Spot;* "Rents Restaurant at 10 East 60th Street"; "650 Night Clubs Put on Probation Pending Inquiry"; "Victim of Shooting Held"; Walker, *The Night Club Era;* Walter Winchell, "On Broadway," *New York Daily Mirror,* 2 November 1940; "Witness Admits Link to Gambler"; Wright, *The History of the Copacabana.*

Copa debut: Abel., "Night Club Reviews" (Copacabana, N.Y.); interview, Lewis; Lewis, *Jerry Lewis in Person;* P. Martin, "I Call on Dean Martin"; B. Smith, "Case History (2)." **Lester and Condos:** *Variety,* 31 March 1948. **Podell, Davis, Ray:** Wayne Newton, *Once Before I Go* (New York: William Morrow, 1989), p. 62. **Lambs:** Laurie, "Mimics." **Roxy:** Dash, "Ice Show and Vaudeville"; Jose., "House Reviews" (Roxy, N.Y.); Lewis, *Jerry Lewis in Person.*

TV: Barnouw, *The Golden Web;* Barnouw, *Tube of Plenty;* McNeil, *Total Television; Milton Berle;* Stal., "Television." **Bloch:** obituary, *Vari-*

ety, 7 April 1982. **Audition record:** B. Smith, "Case History (2)."

Return to 500 Cafe: ad, *Atlantic City Press;* "Martin and Lewis Hit at 500 Cafe"; Walk., "Night Club Reviews." **"Texaco Star Theatre":** "Television Followup."

Devore: "Hollywood Haberdasher"; obituary (Devore). **Cohen:** Cohen, *Mickey Cohen: In My Own Words;* **Rosenbloom:** Fleischer, *Nat Fleischer's Ring Record Book;* obituary (Rosenbloom). **Slapsy Maxie's:** Fischler, "Night Club Reviews"; interview, Lewis; Kap., "Night Club Reviews" (Slapsy Maxie's, L.A.). **Stabile:** Associated Press, "Stabile to Wed Today"; Bral., "House Reviews"; Cohen., "House Reviews"; Cohen., "Night Club Reviews"; Cohen., "Radio Reviews"; " 'Local Boy Makes Good' "; obituary (Stabile). Quote: Stabile, "Style Is Dick Stabile's 'Corny' Poison Antidote."

Goldstein, Pasternak: obituary (Goldstein), *Variety,* 10 April 1974; B. Smith, "Case History (2)." **Wallis:** McCann. *The First Tycoons;* obituary (Hal Wallis); Wallis and Higham, *Starmaker.* **Hazen:** file, Billy Rose Theatre Collection, New York Public Library of Lincoln Center. **Nervous collapse, NBC, ABC:** B. Smith, "Case History (1)."

Capitol: Bennett, "Capitol Research"; *Billboard,* 14 and 21 August 1948; Gart, *ARLD;* "Martin and Lewis Bow on Discs"; Grendysa, "West Coast R&B"; Nick Tosches, *Unsung Heroes of Rock 'n' Roll,* 2nd rev. ed. (New York: Harmony, 1991). **Capitol signing:** "Martin, Lewis

Inked to 1-Year Pact by Cap." **Deana Martin:** N.Y. Birth Certificate No. 31680. **Wallis deal:** "Martin-Lewis' Film Deal with Hal Wallis Worth $1,250,000"; "Martin-Lewis Signed by Hal Wallis"; B. Smith, "Case History (2)." **Guild cards:** Cohen, *Mickey Cohen: In My Own Words;* interview, Lewis.

Allyson: interview, Lewis. **Adoption:** Allyson, *June Allyson.* **Little Women:** Leigh, *There Really Was a Hollywood.* **Hopper:** Eells, *Hedda and Louella.* **Elgin, Bob Hope:** *Bob Hope: A Half Century on Radio and Television* (New York: Museum of Broadcasting, 1986); B. Smith, "Case History (2)." The Elgin and Hope shows are on file at the Motion Picture, Broadcasting and Recorded Sound Division of the Library of Congress, Washington, D.C. (Elgin: Record Nos. 84080, 88793-98 [Box 48-18]; Hope: Record Nos. 84063 and 84078 [Box 48-18]). **Latin Casino:** "Latin Casino, Philly, Sets Advance Bookings." **Allyson, De Haven, etc.:** interview, Lewis; Marx, *Everybody Loves Somebody.* **"Welcome Aboard":** Doan., "Television Reviews," *Billboard* review: 18 December 1948. **Blackstone:** "Martin-Lewis Stand to Forfeit 18G by Chi Walk." **Copa City:** "Martin-Lewis Tiff with Miami Copa"; Solloway, "Chatter"; Solloway, "Miami's Mad Scramble."

My Friend Irma: Green, *Encyclopedia of the Musical Film;* interview, DeFore; obituary (Lynn); obituary (Marshall); obituary (Wilson); Lewis, *Jerry Lewis in Person;* B.

Smith, "Case History"; *Variety*, 26 April 1947 (radio show); Wallis and Higham, *Starmaker.*

First solo Capitol record: *Billboard*, 15 January 1949; Woods, "Jocks, Jukes and Disks."

NBC deal: Barnouw, *Tube of Plenty;* "NBC Fretting over Bing Deal with Chesties"; "NBC Puts 100G in Martin-Lewis"; "New Voices, Old Gags"; "Radio and Television: Dean Martin and Jerry Lewis Comedy Team to Start NBC Show on Sunday"; B. Smith, "Case History (2)." Preview show: recording.

IX

Beachcomber,   Orange Bowl: Bellamy, "250,000 (Plus) Thrilled at Salute to New Year"; Burns, "60,000 to See Georgia, Texas Gridiron Classic"; Burns, "250,000 Thrilled by Jamboree Parade"; interview, J. Martin; Mike Meserole, ed., *The 1990 Information Please Sports Almanac* (Boston: Houghton Mifflin, 1989); Smilky, "Dream World Alive Heats Shivering Parade Crowd"; B. Smith, "Case History (2)." Solloway, "Chatter." Solloway, "Miami's Mad Scramble"; Wing, "Copy Girl Now Bowl Queen."

Slapsy Maxie's: Kap., "Night Club Reviews" (Slapsy Maxie's, L.A.); "Slapsy Maxie's, L.A., Shutters Temporarily." **Lee duet:** *Billboard*, 5 February 1949.

Elizabeth Anne Martin v. *Dean Paul Martin*, Superior Court, Los Angeles County; Parsons, " 'Mad Love' for Model Costly to Dean Mar-

tin"; Parsons, "Wife Will Sue Dean Martin." *Sammy Watkins* v. *Dino Crocetti.* **Divorce:** "Dean Martin to Face Divorce Suit."

My Friend Irma: interview, DeFore; Wallis and Higham, *Starmaker;* Zukor, *The Public Is Never Wrong.* **NBC show:** Crosby, "Radio in Review"; "NBC Puts 100G in Martin-Lewis"; "New Voices, Old Gags"; "Radio and Television: Dean Martin and Jerry Lewis Comedy Team to Start NBC Show on Sunday, April 3"; Rose., "Radio Reviews." **Telethon:** *Milton Berle.* **"The word itself":** e.g., *San Francisco Examiner*, 10 April 1949, p. 22. A complete collection of *"The Martin and Lewis Show"* transcriptions is on file at the Motion Picture, Broadcasting and Recorded Sound Division of the Library of Congress, Washington, D.C.

Copacabana: B. Smith, "Night Club Reviews" (Copacabana, N.Y.); Sylvester, "Two Young Clowns Arrive." **Rock 'n' roll:** Tosches, *Unsung Heroes of Rock 'n' Roll*, 2nd rev. ed. (New York: Harmony, 1991).

My Friend Irma **preview:** Brog., *Variety*, 17 August 1949. **Renewed contracts:** *Dean Martin and Jerry Lewis* v. *Abner J. Greshler.* **Divorce:** *Elizabeth Anne Martin* v. *Dean Paul Martin*, Clark County, Nevada. **Marriage license:** Marriage Records, Registrar-Recorder, County of Los Angeles, Calif., Registrar's No. 21603; United Press International, "Dean Martin to Wed Cover Girl." **Ciro's:** "Ciro's in H'wood, Dark Since Dec., Sold for 286G"; interview, Hover. **Wedding:** interview, Hover; interview, Lewis; interview, J. Martin; *Los Angeles Times,* 2 September 1949.

Flamingo, Siegel, etc.: Eisenberg, Dan, and Landau, *Meyer Lansky;* Friedrich, *City of Nets;* Gosch and Hammer, *The Last Testament of Lucky Luciano;* Jennings, *We Only Kill Each Other;* Katz, *Uncle Frank;* Messick, *The Beauties & the Beasts;* Messick, *Lansky;* "Night Club Owner Denies City Charge"; Reid and Demaris, *The Green Felt Jungle;* Scarne, *Scarne's Complete Guide to Gambling;* Sifton, "Las Vegas"; Turner, *Gamblers' Money;* Earl Warren, *The Memoirs of Earl Warren* (Garden City, N.Y.: Doubleday, 1977); G. Edward White, *Earl Warren: A Public Life* (New York: Oxford University Press, 1982); Yablonsky, *George Raft.* Mildred Cram's *Forever* was a sixty-page novel, first published, by Knopf, in April 1935. **Desert Inn:** Joseph Franco with Richard Hammer, *Hoffa's Man* (New York: Prentice Hall, 1987; reprinted New York: Dell, 1989); interview, Torcasio; Messick, *The Silent Syndicate;* James Neff, *Mobbed Up* (New York: Atlantic Monthly Press, 1989; reprinted New York: Dell, 1990); Turner, *Gamblers' Money.*

New York Times: Hill, "The Borscht Belt's Latest Gift to the Movies." **Cold-war quote:** *New York Times,* 17 April 1947, p. 21. **Cohen quotes:** Cohen, *Mickey Cohen: In My Own Words.* Interview, Lewis.

Ryan, York: Demaris, *The Last Mafioso;* interview, J. Martin; B. Smith, "Case History (2)"; "Stolkin Quits as RKO President"; United Press International, "Millionaire Oilman Killed by Bomb Blast in His Car."

Paramount: Kahn., "House Reviews." *New York Times* **review:** Crowther, "The Screen in Review: Jerry Lewis, New Comedian, a Bright Spot in Silly Film." **Steubenville:** interview, Vecchione. **Gross:** Wallis's claim, in *Starmaker,* is suspect; the film is not listed in L. Cohen, "All-Time Film Rental Champs," which includes films of lesser grosses in its tabulations. **"Texaco Star Theatre":** *Milton Berle;* interview, Lewis; Lewis, *Jerry Lewis in Person.* **Chez Paree:** Zabe., "Night Club Reviews." **Costello suit:** "Costello's 100G Suit vs. Dean Martin Spurs AGVA"; Thomas, *Bud and Lou.* ***At War with the Army:*** "Martin, Lewis Get 'At War with Army.'"

X

Evans: obituary (Evans). **Granoff, Keller:** Kelley, *His Way.* **Calvet:** Calvet, *Has Corinne Been a Good Girl?* **NBC-TV:** Lewis, *Jerry Lewis in Person;* "Radio and Television: Team of Dean Martin and Jerry Lewis Is Signed"; B. Smith, "Case History (2)." **Ciro's:** Hanna, "Night Club Reviews."

Apollo suit: "Martin Loses Suit to Apollo." **AGVA hearing:** "Martin & Lewis Must Play Philly Nitery or Forfeit 12 G"; *Dean Martin and Jerry Lewis* v. *Abner J. Greshler* 58217 (Exhibit B: copy of AGVA statement).

Amendatory agreement: *Dean Martin and Jerry Lewis* v. *Abner J. Greshler;* B. Smith, "Case History (2)." *My Friend Irma Goes West:* Brog., review; review, *Los Angeles Times;* review, *Newsweek;* Wallis and Higham, *Starmaker.*

MCA, Greshler letter, SAG, NBC, etc.: *Dean Martin and Jerry Lewis* v. *Abner J. Greshler* (Exhibit A: Statement of Claim [AGVA] and letter to Greshler [6 July 1950]; Exhibit B: copy of AGVA statement [26 June 1950]); *Dean Martin and Jerry Lewis* v. *Violet Greshler, et al.;* interview, Greshler; Lewis, *Jerry Lewis in Person;* "Martin & Lewis' Switch to MCA Cues $1,000,000 Suit by Greshler"; E. Thompson, "There's No Show Business Like MCA's Business"; S.M.C. 2645; B. Smith, "Case History (2)." **Screen Associates, Stolkin, etc.:** "Common Interest in Philanthropic Venture"; "Martin and Lewis Sued for 2 Million by Studio"; "RKO Pictures' New Chairman"; "RKO Radio Pictures Reveal Fourth Major Resignation"; "Stolkin Quits as RKO President."

Court petition: "Dean Martin Loses in Court." *At War with the Army: Capitol News,* July 1950; "Paramount Closes Deal for 'At War with Army' "; B. Smith, "Case History (2)." **Harvest Moon Ball:** J. Smith, "Martin-Lewis Antics to Enliven Ball Finals."

"Colgate Comedy Hour": Gould, "Martin and Lewis Score on TV"; interview, Lewis; Lewis, *Jerry Lewis in Person;* Marx, *Everybody Loves Somebody;* Mishkin, "Martin,

Lewis Run Riot on Colgate Video Show"; press release, "Dean Martin and Jerry Lewis"; Rose., "Television Reviews." **Public apology:** *Daily Variety,* 25 September 1950. **"Songs with Most TV Performances" chart:** *Billboard,* 23 September 1950. **Stanley Theatre:** *Steubenville Herald-Star,* 6 October 1950, p. 10. **Subpoenas, demurrer:** *Dean Martin and Jerry Lewis* v. *Violet Greshler, et al.* (Notice of Taking Deposition [filed 5 October 1950]; Affidavit of Service [filed 5 October 1950]; Demurrer to Complaint [filed 13 October 1950]).

Dean Martin Day: interview, L. D'Anniballe; interview, M. D'Anniballe; interview, Kayafas; interview, Lewis; interview, J. Martin; interview, Mavromatis; interview, Sperduti; "Local Boy Makes Good"; "Martin, Lewis Welcomed by Steubenville"; "Steubenville Gets Ready for Dean Martin Day Friday." **Average steel pay:** "Wages and Hours" (1950 figures), *1952 Britannica Book of the Year* (Chicago: Encyclopaedia Britannica, Inc., 1952). *TV Guide:* 11 November 1950. **Watkins case:** Associated Press, "Dean Martin Sued by Agent"; "Dean Martin's Debt, $12,880, Court Decides"; *Sammy Watkins* v. *Dino Crocetti* (Answer [filed 28 September 1949]; Judgment [filed 8 February 1951]). **"Friendly suit":** Spaeth, "Mr. Music Music Music." **Chicago Theatre:** Mel., "House Reviews." **Distribution deal:** "Paramount Closes Deal for 'At War with Army.' " **Amended complaint:** *Dean Martin* and *Jerry Lewis* v. *Violet Greshler, et al.* (Amended Complaint for Accounting and Money Had and Received" [filed 6 November 1950]). **"Greshler maintained":** *Dean Martin and Jerry Lewis* v. *Abner J. Greshler* (Exhibit B: Answer to Claim and Counterclaim [AGVA]). **Greshler refusal:** *Dean Martin and Jerry Lewis* v. *Abner J. Greshler* (Affidavit of Clore Warne [filed 19 January 1951]). **AGVA judgment:** "AGVA Orders M&L Pay Greshler 10G." Interview, Greshler. **Garnishment:** Case No. 568556 and Answer [filed 15 December 1950].

Annual rankings: *Billboard,* 7 October 1950. **David-Livingston:** "Telechatter," *Daily Variety,* 5 July 1950, p. 31. *New York Times:* Gould, "Martin and Lewis Score on TV." *Variety:* Mel., "House Reviews." *At War with the Army* **reviews:** Brog., review *(Variety);* Weiler, "Martin and Lewis in the Army" *(Times);* Scheuer, "Comedy Pair Gold-Brick in 'At War with Army' "; Hale, "Martin, Lewis in Comedy at the Paramount" *(Daily News).*

"Wallis Welcomes Newcomer to Debut in 'The Stooge.' " **Sid Silvers:** Eileen Creelman, "Sid Silvers Explains What Is a Stooge and Why, with Comments on His Career," *New York Sun,* 24 March 1934; Frederick James Smith, "The World's Most Unknown Comedian," *Liberty,* 21 November 1936. **Fischetti:** "Fischetti Dies." **Giancana:** Brashler, *The Don;* Giancana, *Mafia Princess.*

Television: *Milton Berle.* **Yorkin, Lear, etc.:** Marx, *Every-*

body Loves Somebody. **Paramount:** "Comedy Team of Martin and Lewis Keeps Ticket Booths of Paramount Plenty Busy" (unidentified clipping, July 1951, in *New York Daily News* library files); "Free Show"; "Martin & Lewis' 98G Share from N.Y. Par.," *Variety,* July 1951; "Of Local Origin"; "Paramount Busts Record with B.G., Hits 135G," *Billboard,* 16 March 1946, p. 45; Sylvester, "Theatre Survives 2 Comics"; Weiler, "By Way of Report."

Collapse in Chicago: United Press International, "Jerry Lewis Ordered to Rest." **Screen Associates suit** (Superior Court, Los Angeles County, No. 589172): "Martin and Lewis Sued for 2 Million by Studio"; Pryor, "Mel Ferrer Plans Film Life of Bard." *At War with the Army,* **German release:** *Illustrierte Film-Bühne,* No. 2716. *At War with the Army* **gross:** L. Cohen, "All-Time Film Rental Champs."

Danny Lewis: *Variety,* 8 August 1951. *Life:* 13 August 1951. *Sailor Beware:* Brog., review; Calvet, *Has Corinne Been a Good Girl?;* Herndon, *James Dean,* p. 96, which mistakenly states that none of Dean's lines remained in the film; " 'Sailor' Troupe Back." **Dean Paul, Jr.:** Birth Records, Registrar-Recorder, County of Los Angeles.

"Torna a Surriento": Venci, *La canzone napolitana,* pp. 158–59. Author's translation: See how beautiful the sea is! / It breathes forth so much feeling / like your sweet, soft accent / that, awake, leads me to dream.

XI

Faulkner quote: Joseph Blotner, *Faulkner: A Biography* (New York: Random House, 1974; 1-vol. rev. ed., New York: Vintage, 1991 [p. 656]). **"Crime in America":** ad, *Hollywood Reporter*, 23 November 1951, p. 8. Many of the other odd data are from "What That Was: A Chronology of the Coming of Rock 'n' Roll" in Nick Tosches, *Unsung Heroes of Rock 'n' Roll*, 2nd rev. ed. (New York: Harmony, 1991). **Lewis quote:** interview, Lewis. **Martin quote:** Wallace, "Dean Martin Remembers When Cleveland Applauded Politely."

Lewis home: Lewis, *Jerry Lewis in Person;* Mrs. J. Lewis, "I Married a Madman." **Martin home:** V. Scott, "The Improbable Private Life of Mrs. Dean Martin." **New radio show:** Rose., "Radio Reviews," 10 October 1951.

Sailor Beware: Brog., review; Cameron, "Martin, Lewis at Mayfair in Laugh Maker"; Crowther, "The Screen in Review: Dean Martin and Jerry Lewis Seen in 'Sailor Beware' "; I. Hoffman, "Sock Martin-Lewis Fare from Wallis."

Telethon: Gould, "Martin-Lewis Team Reveals Patience, Dignity and Understanding"; interview, Lewis; "Martin & Lewis Marathon"; "Martin & Lewis Telethon"; "Martin, Lewis Plan Hospital Telethon"; "Million for Heart Fund"; obituary, Arthur H. Konvitz, *New York Times*, 6 February 1991; "$1,148,419 Pledged to Heart Hospital."

Scared Stiff, **new Wallis deal:** "Martin and Lewis Return to Work"; Pryor, "Martin and Lewis Shun Movie Roles"; *Music News*, July 1952, p. 27; "Wallis Inks M-L to Straight Salary Pact." **Copacabana:** "AGVA Wants Martin & Lewis in N.Y. to Gab on Their Powder of Copa"; "Martin & Lewis Given to June 1 to Answer Copa"; "Martin & Lewis Seek Shift to Coast for Hearing of N.Y. Copa 'Breach' Charge"; *Music News*, 1 August 1952, p. 25. **Chez Paree:** "M&L Setting 20-Year Record at Chi Chez." **Flamingo:** *Music Views*, November 1952, p. 26. **Golf bag:** *Music Views*, November 1952, p. 27. **Texas State Fair:** Bark., "If Big Time Vaude Is Dead, How Come M&L Kill 'Em in Tex.?"; *Music Views*, December 1952, p. 25; *Music Views*, January 1953, p. 28. **Tour:** "M&L Pull 200G in 10-Day Tour"; *Music Views*, November 1952, p. 30 (itinerary). **Cleveland reporter:** Wallace, "Dean Martin Remembers When Cleveland Applauded Politely."

The Caddy, **York, etc.:** Arnold, "Are Martin and Lewis Breaking Up?"; "Martin and Lewis Start 'The Caddy' "; Pryor, "Martin to End Tie to Lewis Company"; "Common Interest in Philanthropic Venture Maintains Ex-RKO Officers Stolkin, Koolish Tie with Hollywood"; "RKO Pictures' New Chairman Says Losses Are About $100,000 a Week"; "RKO Radio Pictures Reveals Fourth Major Resignation This Week"; "RKO's President: How Mr. Stolkin Won a $3 Million Fortune in Eight Busy

Years"; "Stolkin Quits as RKO President." **Income:** interview, Lewis; Schuyler, "Who's Trying to Break Up Dean Martin and Jerry Lewis?"; "To the Rescue." **The Stooge:** Borg., review; file, Margaret Herrick Library, Academy of Motion Picture Arts and Sciences; Hale, "Martin-Lewis Film"; "Martin and Lewis Cut Up at Preview"; review, *Los Angeles Examiner*, 5 February 1953; review, *Saturday Review*, 7 February 1953.

Sands: interview, Lewis; obituary (Entratter); obituary (Freedman); Reid and Demaris, *The Green Felt Jungle*. **Separation:** *Hollywood Citizen-News*, 11 February 1953; unidentified clipping, *Los Angeles Examiner*; United Press International, "Dean Martins Part."

Wives: interview, Lewis; interview, J. Martin; Mrs. J. Lewis, "I Married a Madman." Interview, J. Martin, with quotes from: Fallaci, "Dean Martin"; Scott, "The Improbable Private Life of Mrs. Dean Martin." **Raft:** Yablonksky, *George Raft*. **Gray:** obituary; Yablonsky, *George Raft*. **Gerard:** Scott, "Dean Martin Is the Total Entertainer." **Percodan:** interview, Cahn; *Physicians' Desk Reference*, 43rd ed. (Oradell, N.J.: Medical Economics Company, 1989). "I'm telling you. I was a witness to it. Mack addicted him to Percodan," Cahn said. "Mack was the kind of guy who was able to get these things when he needed them, you know? He was the supplier. And that's what did Dean in."

Quote ("dearest friend"): D. Lewis, "Dean Martin Really Met the Press." Interview, Lewis. **Quote ("I don't even believe in television"):** Fallaci, "Dean Martin." **La Rue:** *Hollywood Reporter*, 26 March 1953. **Reconciliation:** Associated Press, "Actor Martin, Wife Reunited"; Parsons, " 'Baby on Way' Kept from Dean Martin"; Parsons, "Dean Martin, Wife Reunited."

Passage: J. Smith, "Martin, Lewis at Harvest Ball Finals." **Queen Elizabeth casino:** *Hollywood Reporter*, 12 June 1953. **Scotland:** United Press International, "Scot Not Amused by Martin, Lewis"; Gord., review. **HUAC, McCarthy, Cohn, Schine, etc.:** Barnouw, *Tube of Plenty*; "British Press Cool to McCarthy Aides," *New York Times*, 18 April 1953, p. 8; "British Press Pokes Fun at M'Carthy Investigators," *New York Times*, 26 April 1953, p. IV-9; "Cohn and Schine Return," *New York Times*, 22 April 1953, p. 26; Gabler, *An Empire of Their Own*; Morison, *The Oxford History of the American People*; "Mr. Cohn and Mr. Schine," London *Times*, 21 April 1953, p. 8; "Senator McCarthy's Inquiries," London *Times*, 16 April 1953, p. 11. **Palladium:** "Brit Press Boo as Big 'Boo-Boo' for M&L Abroad"; "Brit Scribe's 'Dry Your Tears, M&L' "; Holt, "Cheers, Then Boos, Puzzle Dean and Jerry"; "London Palladium"; "M&L, Viv Blaine Hecklers Turn Out to Be 2 Youths Who Read Daily Worker"; Watts, "Martin, Lewis and English Critics." **Angeli:** Douglas, *The Ragman's Son*. **Jeanne left behind:** *Hollywood Reporter*, 12

June 1953. **France:** "Brit Press Boo as Big 'Boo-Boo' for M&L Abroad"; Buchwald, "Europe's Lighter Side"; "M&L, Viv Blaine Hecklers Turn Out to Be 2 Youths Who Read Daily Worker." **Return to America:** Mosby, "Dean Is Firm on Criticism"; United Press International, "Dean Martin Got 'Insults' for Whisky."

Herald Tribune **review of** *Scared Stiff*: Guernsey, "Good Humor and Bad." **Warren-Brooks, "That's Amore":** Green, *Encyclopedia of the Musical Film*. **Albany, Paramount:** "Martin & Lewis' 98G Share from N.Y. Par." *The Caddy* **commercial:** audiotape; Meade, "What Happened When the DA Caught Dean and Jerry in a Pornographic Trap"; Thaw, "The Dean Martin and Jerry Lewis Record Scandal." **Ricci James Martin:** Birth Records, Registrar-Recorder, County of Los Angeles. **Sally Mae adoption:** Ritson, "The Nightly Whirl." *The Caddy*: Masters, "Martin-Lewis Film at Mayfair Theatre." **"That's Amore" review:** *Billboard*, 3 October 1953. **Full-page ad:** *Billboard*, 31 October 1953, p. 29. **"Christmas Blues" review:** *Billboard*, 7 November 1953. **"That's Amore"** chart entry: *Billboard*, 14 November 1953. **Scharf:** Scharf and Freedland, *Composed and Conducted by Walter Scharf*. ABC "Thanksgiving Party": Chan., "Television Reviews"; "M&L's 3-Hour ABC Dystrophy TVthon with NBC's Okay"; videotape.

Herald Tribune **review:** Guernsey, "Good Humor and Bad."

Jerry's backyard movies: Bailey, "Mayhem, Unlimited"; "Jerry Lewis Directs a Home Made Movie"; Lewis, *Jerry Lewis in Person;* Lewis, Mrs. J., "I Married a Madman"; "Martin and Lewis' Backyard Movies"; Marx, *Everybody Loves Somebody;* Ritson, "The Nightly Whirl." **McGuire:** Marx, *Everybody Loves Somebody.* *Three Ring Circus:* " 'Big Top' Tuners Set"; interview, Pevney; "Irving Kaye in 'Big Top' "; "Joanne Dru in 'Big Top' "; Lewis, *Jerry Lewis in Person;* Marx, *Everybody Loves Somebody;* "Wallis, Pevney to Phoenix." **"Blind fighter":** Curtis played a deaf boxer in Pevney's *Flesh and Fury* (1952). **Vista Vision:** *Hollywood Reporter*, 9 September 1954. **Wallis art collection:** *Los Angeles Times,* 28 March 1989, p. IV-1. *Sailor Beware* **world gross:** interview, Lewis. **Movie profits:** L. Cohen, "All-Time Film Rental Champs." **Crowther review of** *Money from Home*: *New York Times,* 27 February 1954.

Sperduti: interview, Sperduti. **"Psychological warfare":** Lewis, *Jerry Lewis in Person.* Interview, Dru. Scharf and Freedland, *Composed and Conducted by Walter Scharf.* **MCA meeting:** Marx, *Everybody Loves Somebody;* Schuyler, "Who's Trying to Break Up Dean Martin and Jerry Lewis?" **McKinley Home for Boys:** "Shooting 'Big Top' Scene in Boys Home." **Statement:** "Martin and Lewis Give 'Inside' on Their 'Feud.' " **Lewis recording career:** Bob Furmanek, liner notes, *Jerry Lewis: Collector Series* (Capitol CDP

7 93196 2 [1990]). *Capitol Presents Dean Martin* and *Capitol Presents Jerry Lewis:* LC 6590 and LC 6591 (April 1953); *Capitol Numerical Catalogue* (London: September 1953).

IRS: United Press International, "Filmdom's Elite Given Star Billing, for Taxes." **Martin-Lewis Day, Atlantic City:** ads, *Atlantic City Press,* 15 July 1954, p. 15, and 17 July 1954, p. 13; "Entire Resort 'Lives It Up' in Observing Martin-Lewis Day"; "Martin and Lewis Day"; "Martin and Lewis Film, Resort Draw Praise from Critics"; "Martin and Lewis in A.C."; "Resort Welcomes Back Martin and Lewis"; Ritson, "The Nightly Whirl," 15 and 16 July 1954; Schor, "Resort Bestows Royal Welcome on Martin and Lewis"; Villers, "Dean, Jerry Give Anniversary Act to Cap Their Day"; Watson, "Living It Up with Martin and Lewis." **Ciro's:** ad, *Hollywood Reporter,* 19 August 1954, p. 5, and 30 August 1954, p. 10; Guild, "Night Club Reviews"; interview, Hover; Zolotow, "The Martin and Lewis Feud."

Interview, Foch. D. A. Doran was a Paramount production executive, 1948–60. *Variety:* Holl., review. **"A stranger":** Lewis, *Jerry Lewis in Person. New York Times* review of *Three Ring Circus:* 25 December 1954. *Artists and Models:* interview, Lewis; interview, Malone. *Photoplay:* Arnold, "Are Martin and Lewis Breaking Up?" *Top Secret:* Schuyler, "Who's Trying to Break Up Dean Martin and Jerry Lewis?" *Hollywood Reporter:* 6 April 1953. *Private Lives:* "Dean & Jerry: So Who's Laughing?" (also published in *Private Story,* April 1955).

Catskills premiere: "It's Not Love, Chum"; "Jerry Lewis in N.Y."; Lewis, *Jerry Lewis in Person;* "Martin & Lewis Reviving Original 'Single' Turns"; "Martin and/or Lewis"; " 'Never Too Young' Junket Nets 6 Radio, 2 TV Shows: Jerry Lewis Scores at Press Preview"; "The Pay's the Thing: Dean, Jerry Sign Truce"; " 'Unknown' Catskills Tell Off Dean Martin"; Wilson, "Martin & Lewis ½-Split, Dean Wants to Solo." **Freeman:** Lewis, *Jerry Lewis in Person;* obituary (Freeman). *Photoplay:* Arnold, "The Big Split-Up?" **United Press reporter:** United Press International, "Martin Wants to End Lewis Feud." **Freeman meeting:** Gardella, "Martin & Lewis Stick"; Green, "Bottom-Line Expert Balaban Dies at 83"; "The Pay's the Thing: Dean, Jerry Sign Truce"; Pryor, "Martin and Lewis to Remain a Team." *New York Daily News* **review:** Cameron, "Martin & Lewis Team Take Over Criterion." **August 31:** "Martin and Lewis 'Back in Business.' " *The Hollywood Reporter:* Guild, "Reviews of New TV Shows."

Break-up with Jeanne: Hopper, "Dean Martin Left by Wife, Children"; interview, Cahn; Parsons, "Dean Martin, Wife Decide to Separate"; "Same Old Trouble; Dean Just Won't Whiz." **Freeman:** Lewis, *Jerry Lewis in Person.* **Nelson:** interview, Nelson. *Billboard* **ad:** 19 November 1955. **NBC deal:** "Martin and Lewis Sign Pact"; "Martin and Lewis Sue N.B.C. over Pact"; "To the Rescue." **Crowther review:** *New York Times,* 22 December 1955. **Photoplay:** " 'I Was Wrong,' " January 1956, p. 8. **Motion Picture:** D. Williams, " 'It's My Fault!' "

Hollywood or Bust: interview, Lazarus; interview, Lewis; Lewis, *Jerry Lewis in Person.* **McGuire script:** P. Martin, "I Call on Dean Martin"; Marx, *Everybody Loves Somebody;* Parsons, "Martin and Lewis Again Decide to Go Their Separate Ways in Show Business." **Pardners preview:** "Martin & Lewis Get Par Okay to Split Up Team; Ask Same of Wallis, NBC." **Variety review:** Brog., review.

Break-up, Paramount meeting, etc.: Associated Press, "Martin, Lewis at Odds"; Gardner, "Coast to Coast"; Godbout, "Comedians to Do Separate Turns"; Godbout, "Martin and Lewis Sign as Solo Acts"; Graham, "Hollywood"; interview, Lewis; Lewis, "I've Always Been Scared"; Lewis, *Jerry Lewis in Person;* Bergman, "M&L Return to NBC, Apart"; "M&L Unite to Sue Paramount"; "Martin & Lewis Get Par Okay to Split Up Team; Ask Same of Wallis, NBC"; "Martin & Lewis Nix Hal Wallis' Offer to Release 'Em from Pact for $1,500,000"; "Martin-Lewis Apart for Only One Film"; "Martin, Lewis Breaking Up"; Godbout, "Martin, Lewis Sue N.B.C. over Pact"; P. Martin, "I Call on Pete Martin"; Parsons, "Martin and Lewis Again Decide to Go Their Separate Ways in Show Business"; Pryor, "Martin to

End Tie to Lewis Company"; B. Smith, "Night Club Reviews" (Copacabana, N.Y.), *Show Business;* Wilson, *The Show Business Nobody Knows.*

XII

"**Reign of mediocrity**": *The Bostonians* (1886). "**You ain't heard nothin' yet**": *The Jazz Singer* (1927).

Ten Thousand Bedrooms: Gardner, "Coast to Coast"; interview, Alberghetti; interview, Thorpe; "Martin & Lewis Nix Hal Wallis' Offer to Release 'Em from Pact for $1,500,000"; "Richard Thorpe Directs MGM's '10,000 Bedrooms.' " **Enquirer:** "After I'm Gone I Hope They Say: 'Dean Martin? He Was a Good Guy!' " **Gina Martin:** Birth Records, Registrar-Recorder, County of Los Angeles. "**Rock-a-Bye Your Baby**": Bob Furmanek, liner notes, *Jerry Lewis: Collector Series* (Capitol CDP 7 93196 2 [1990]). **Look:** Lewis, "I've Always Been Scared." **Reaction:** Skolsky, "Dean Martin Puts the Blast on Jerry."

Deana hurt: unidentified clipping, file (Martin, Dean), Margaret Herrick Library of the Academy of Motion Picture Arts. **Confidential:** Morrison, "Memo to Dean Martin: Better Check on Your Ex-Wife!" "**Tonight!**," **etc.:** Gray, "Barry Gray" (column); Kilgallen, "Dean Martin Hits the Gong"; O'Brian, "Come Back, Steve Allen." **Jeanne Martin quote:** Kaufman, "On All Channels." **TV Guide:** Jenkins,

"Dean Martin Blasts Away at Jerry Lewis." *Rave:* "Jerry Lewis' 'Other Wife.' " *Uncensored:* DePlane, "Why Jerry Lewis and Dean Martin Are Playing 'Do You Trust Your Wife?' " *On the QT:* Korst, "Why Martin and Lewis Split."

Ten Thousand Bedrooms reviews: Brog., review *(Variety);* Cameron, "Martin Minus Lewis in New Musical Film *(New York Daily News);* Crowther, "Screen: Solo by Martin"; McCarten, review (the *New Yorker);* Quinn, "Dean Martin Solos in Film at State" *(New York Daily Mirror);* Zinsser, *"Ten Thousand Bedrooms" (New York Herald Tribune).* **Sands:** Schb., "New Acts." **Ken Lane:** L. Kaye, untitled article on Ken Lane.

The Young Lions: Bosworth, *Montgomery Clift;* Dmytryk, *It's a Hell of a Life but Not a Bad Living;* Graham, "Hollywood"; Higham, *Brando;* interview, J. Martin; B. Kaye, "How Dean Martin Muscled Tony Randall out of a Job"; LaGuardia, *Monty;* E. Thompson, "There's No Show Business Like MCA's Business"; *Variety,* 20 October 1948, p. 2.

City of Hope, "Parade of Stars": ad, 25 May 1957, in file ("Martin, Dean"), Billy Rose Theatre Collection, New York Public Library; Baer, "Stars Boost Martin Telethon"; "Dean Martin's Terrif City of Hope Telethon Job; $804,000 in Pledges"; Gardner, "Hy Gardner Calling"; Levenstein, *Testimony for Man;* "Preparing for Telethon Benefit" (photo and legend), *New York Daily Mirror,* 18 April 1957. **Twin Coaches:** Co-

hen., "Night Club Reviews" (Twin Coaches); Condon, "They Remember Dino"; interview, J. D'Anniballe; interview, L. D'Anniballe; interview, Costanzo; interview, Mavromatis; interview, Monaco; interview, Pestian; letter, Pestian.

La Scala dinner with Cahn: interview, Cahn. **France, Brando, Clift, etc.:** Berg, *Goldwyn;* Dmytryk, *It's a Hell of a Life but Not a Bad Living;* Fallaci, "Dean Martin"; Graham, "Gay Paree Not Dean's Cup of Tea"; Henshaw, "Dean Martin Hits Out"; Higham, *Brando;* Hyams, "Dean Martin's 7 Weeks in Paris"; LaGuardia, *Monty;* V. Scott, "Dean Martin a Serious Actor Now"; Sobol, "A Chat with Dean Martin." **Lewis:** LaBarthe, "Lewis au pays de Carroll"; Madsen, "L'Oncle d'Amérique."

Subpoena: Muir, "Filmland Bigs Hiding Out to Duck Subpena." *Confidential* **case:** "Actor Must Testify at Magazine Trial," *New York Times,* 1 August 1957, p. 20; "Agreement Set on Confidential," *New York Times,* 8 November 1957, p. 25; "Counsel Appears for Confidential," *New York Times,* 20 August 1957, p. 53; "Jury Told Family Ran Confidential," *New York Times,* 11 September 1957, p. 30; "Magazine Draws Scorn and Praise," *New York Times,* 8 August 1957, p. 21; "Magazine Trial Put Off on Coast," *New York Times,* 30 July 1957, p. 21; "Mistrial Verdict for Confidential," *New York Times,* 2 October 1957, p. 18; "Police Here Cited at Scandal Trial," *New York Times,* 13 August 1957, p. 53; "Publisher Is Arraigned," *New York Times,* 12 June 1957, p. 56; "2 Magazines Chided for Shunning Trial," *New York Times,* 7 September 1957, p. 12; "2 Magazines Guilty in Obscenity Case," *New York Times,* 19 December 1957, p. 19.

"Dean Martin Show": "A Delightful Surprise," ad, *TV Guide,* 5 October 1957, p. A-15; Gross, "Dean Martin in 'Solo' Bow on Own TV Show"; O'Brian, "Jack O'Brian's TViews: Dean Martin Is Great Alone"; Rose., "Television Reviews"; Torre, "Week End Reviews."

Custody: *Dean Martin* v. *Elizabeth Anne Martin,* Superior Court, Los Angeles County. Also: Associated Press, "Dean Martin in Custody Suit"; "Dean Martin Asks Court for Children"; "Dean Martin Gets Custody of Children"; "Dean Martin Granted Custody of Children"; "Dean Martin Seeks Custody of Children" (unidentified clipping, 19 November 1957, file ["Martin, Dean"], Margaret Herrick Library of the Academy of Motion Picture Arts); "Dean Martin Wins Custody"; interview, J. Martin; United Press International, "Singer Asks Custody of 4 Kids by Ex-Wife."

"Just Kiss Me" ad: *Billboard,* 15 December 1956. **Americana:** Grevatt, "Dean Martin Stretches Miami Single to Homer"; Lary., "Night Club Reviews." *Young Lions* **review:** Abel., review. **"Barely more money":** Cohn, "All-Time Film Rental Champs." **Cocoanut Grove:** Friedman, "Smash Tee-off for Dean Martin." **Dino's Lodge:**

Associated Press, "Dean Martin Sues Cafe Partners"; "Dean Martin Sues over Use of Name"; *Daily Variety,* 10 June 1959; *Daily Variety,* 29 August 1961; *Hollywood Citizen,* 29 August 1961; D. Martin, "Cafe News: Dino Does Column—about Dino's Lodge"; "Make-a-Million Martin." The Rheingold ad was published in many magazines, c. November 1958; the Hemingway ad was published in *Life* and other magazines in 1952. New York reviewer: O'Brian, "Jack O'Brian's TViews: 'The Bell Tolls' Pretty Tinnily."

Some Came Running: Cameron, "Film of Jones Novel on Music Hall Screen"; obituary (Minnelli); obituary (Siegel); Powe., review; Ringgold and McCarty, *The Films of Frank Sinatra;* Winsten, "Reviewing Stand." Crowther review: *New York Times,* 23 January 1958. **Quote ("a snap"):** "$1 Million a Year."

Rio Bravo: Beronius, "Weary Dino Faces Career Test"; interview, Dickinson; interview, J. Martin; Masters, "Newcomers Share Honors with Wayne"; McBride, *Hawks on Hawks;* obituary (Hawks); "$1 Million a Year"; Joel Selvin, *Ricky Nelson: Idol for a Generation* (Chicago: Contemporary Books, 1990), p. 91; Weiler, "Texas Border Town"; Whit., review. **Quote ("I just played myself"):** Gehman, "Dean Martin: Crown Prince of the Clan."

Las Vegas: Reid and Demaris, *The Green Felt Jungle.* **Bogart, Rat Pack, Clan, Kennedy, etc.:** Davis, *Yes I Can;* Davis, *Hollywood in a Suitcase;* Davis, *Why Me?;* Gehman,

"Dean Martin: Crown Prince of the Clan"; Gehman, *Sinatra and His Rat Pack;* interview, J. Martin; Kelley, *His Way;* Lawford, *The Peter Lawford Story;* Lewis, *Jerry Lewis in Person;* Wilson, *The Show Business Nobody Knows.* Theodore C. Sorensen, *Kennedy* (New York: Harper & Row, 1965) is the standard biography. Also of some interest in this context is Joseph P. Berry, *John F. Kennedy and the Media: The First Television President* (Lanham, Md.: University Press of America, 1987).

Career: Beckley, "Movie Review"; Crowther, "Screen: Frustrations in Young Actor's 'Career' "; "Dean Martin's Coin Climb; $200,000 a Pic"; "Dean Martin with Wallis"; Gene., review; interview, Franciosa; Masters, " 'Career' Rates Top in Loew's State Debut."

Van Horne, "Dean Martin Fails to Charm." **Rio Bravo reviews:** Masters, "Newcomers Share Honors with Wayne"; Weiler, "Texas Border Town." **Scholarly study:** Clark Branson, *Howard Hawks: A Jungian Study* (Santa Barbara: Capra Press, 1987), p. 233.

May 3 "Dean Martin Show": Rose., "Dean Martin Show"; Slocum, "Saloonatic Wit." **SHARE:** audiotape of 1959 benefit; "Ciro's in H'wood, Dark Since Dec., Sold for 286G"; Leigh, *There Really Was a Hollywood;* Skolsky, "Hollywood Is My Beat," 12 May 1959. **Who Was That Lady?:** "Dean Martin's Coin Climb; $200,000 a Pic"; Leigh, *There Really Was a Hollywood.* **Bells Are Ringing:** Carey, *Judy Holliday;*

Holtzman, *Judy Holliday;* Lawrence, *The MGM Years.* **Career reviews:** Beckley, "Movie Review"; Crowther, "Screen: Frustrations in Young Actor's Career"; Masters, " 'Career' Rates Top in Loew's State Debut." **"Frank Sinatra Timex Show":** videotape recording. The Durante project is detailed in Frank Capra, *The Name above the Title* (New York: Macmillan, 1971). **Friars Club:** press release, Friars Club Tribute. **Special lyrics:** copies of typescripts from the files of Sammy Cahn.

XIII

Variety quote: Duke, "Night Club Reviews" (Sands, Las Vegas), 9 December 1959. **Sands ownership:** Associated Press, "Dean Martin Buys into Nevada Hotel"; obituary (Abrams); Reid and Demaris, *The Green Felt Jungle;* State of Nevada, Gaming Control Board, Application, 7 June 1961. **Ocean's Eleven, Summit, etc.:** Davis, *Hollywood in a Suitcase;* Davis, *Why Me?;* Davis, *Yes I Can;* Duke, "Summit at the Sands"; Duke, "Vegas' Zillion-$ Five"; interview, Dickinson; interview, Slaughter. **Quote ("Work my ass"):** Gehman, *Sinatra and His Rat Pack.* **Hernia operation:** Associated Press, "Dean Martin Has Surgery"; United Press International, "Dean Martin Leaves Hospital." **Bells Are Ringing:** Hale, "Cheers for Hall's 4th of July Show."

Bobby Kennedy, McClellan committee, Giancana, etc.: Brashler, *The Don;* Joseph Franco and Richard Hammer, *Hoffa's Man* (New York: Prentice Hall, 1987; reprinted New York: Dell, 1989); Giancana, *Mafia Princess*. **Cal-Neva Lodge:** "Nevada Gaming Board Weighs Sinatra Group's Cal-Neva Lodge Buy-in"; Reid and Demaris, *The Green Felt Jungle;* "Sinatra Group's Cal-Neva Buy Gets Nev. Okay"; "Sinatra, Martin & A.C.'s D'Amato Teaming for Buyup of Cal-Neva Club"; United Press International, "Sinatra, Dean Martin Apply to Buy a Casino." **Sands:** Duke, "Night Club Reviews" (Sands, Las Vegas), 20 July 1960.

Ocean's Eleven **reviews:** *Los Angeles Examiner,* 11 August 1960; *The New Yorker,* 20 August 1960; Tube., review. **Nevada Gaming Control Board recommendation:** "Sinatra Group's Cal-Neva Buy Gets Nev. Okay." *All in a Night's Work:* Tube., review; Wallis and Higham, *Starmaker*. **Giancana, D'Amato quotes:** Kelley, *His Way*, p. 307. **Reprise Records:** "Sinatra Label Ready for February Debut"; "Sinatra Label Tag: 'Reprise Records.'" **Inaugural gala:** Kelley, *His Way*. **Lewis, Campbell, Meredith:** Summers, *Goddess*. **Lewis quote:** Angeli, "God's Biggest Goof."

FBI, D'Amato: U. S. Department of Justice, Federal Bureau of Investigation. **Martin Cal-Neva pullout:** Associated Press, "Dean Martin Buys into Nevada Hotel." **Luciano film deal:** Gosch and Hammer, *The Last Testament of Lucky Luciano*. **Sands:** Duke, "Night Club Review" (Sands, Las Vegas), 5 April

1961. *Ada:* interview, Mann; LaGuardia and Arceri, *Red*. **Quote ("There's nothing left to do on TV"), *Guns of Navarone*:** United Press International, "No Appeal for Him in Filming Abroad." **"Giuggiola":** Capitol, "Single-Record News" (Hollywood), 19 May 1961. *Sergeants 3:* interview, Lee; review, Tube. **D'Amato, Pucci, DiMaggio, etc.:** Summers, *Goddess;* U. S. Department of Justice, Federal Bureau of Investigation. **Red Cross Ball:** Leigh, *There Really Was a Hollywood;* United Press International, "Grace Throws Gala and It's a Beauty." *Ada* **reviews:** Hale, Tube., "Susan Hayward Star of Political Drama"; review. **Dino's Lodge suit:** Associated Press, "Dean Martin Sues Cafe Partners"; "Dean Martin Sues over Use of Name"; "Dean Loses Round in Law Suit." **Sands:** Duke, "Night Club Reviews" (Sands, Las Vegas), 4 October 1961. **Jeanne Martin hospitalized:** United Press International, "Martin's Wife Ails"; **Armory Lounge:** Brashler, *The Don;* Giancana, *Mafia Princess*. *Who's Got the Action?:* interview, Mann. **Citron, MCA, Claude, etc.:** press kit, Dean Martin/*Bells Are Ringing* (Los Angeles: MGM, 1959); obituary (Citron); obituary (J. Stein). **Sands:** Duke, "Night Club Reviews" (Sands, Las Vegas), 11 April 1962.

Something's Got to Give, **Monroe, etc.:** "Alleging 'Bad Faith' by Dean Martin, 20th Sues for Damages; MCA 'Shocked'"; Associated Press, "Dean Martin Quits Movie over Monroe Dismissal"; Associated

Press, "Dean Martin Willing to Do Canceled Film"; Associated Press, "Martin Countersues Studio in Rift on Monroe Ouster"; "Dino Counters with $6,885,500 Claim vs. 20th"; Gelman, "Sued for $5 Million, Dean Martin Sleeps"; Graham, "Dean Firm on Not Working without MM"; Hendricks, "MM Out, Dean Out—Film Out"; "Revolt of Film Employers: $2-Mil Disaster with Marilyn"; Schumach, "Film Starring Marilyn Monroe and Dean Martin Shelved by Fox"; Schumach, "Fox Aide Assails 'Whims' of Stars"; Schumach, "Fox Dismisses Marilyn Monroe and Files a Suit for $500,000"; Schumach, "Hollywood Encore: Old Farce Is Reshaped for Marilyn Monroe"; Schumach, "Hollywood Warfare"; Schumach, "Lee Remick Gains by Shelved Movie"; Schumach, "Weakness Seen in Film Industry"; Stein, "Reasons for Action on Martin"; Summers, *Goddess;* United Press International, "Dean Martin and Fox Drop Lawsuits on Monroe Movie"; United Press International, "Dean Martin Sued in Rift on Miss Monroe's Ouster."

D'Amato, Cal-Neva, Monroe, etc.: Summers, *Goddess;* U. S. Department of Justice, Federal Bureau of Investigation. **"Two sleazy little books":** Frank A. Capell, *The Strange Death of Marilyn Monroe* (Herald of Freedom, 1964), and Thomas G. Buchanan, *Who Killed Kennedy?* (London: Secker & Warburg, 1964). **Atlantic City:** "Crowd Waits Two Hours for Frankie, Dino"; "Dean's Here for Week at 500

Club"; Shenfeld, "What Impressed Dean Martin about City?"; U. S. Department of Justice, Federal Bureau of Investigation. *Toys in the Attic:* Horton, *The Films of George Roy Hill;* interview, Mirisch; Schumach, "Slant on Hollywood." **Hancock Raceways:** "Mass. Legislature May Subpoena Both Sinatra, Martin in Racetrack Probe"; "Sinatra, Dean Un-Harnessed, Attys. Report"; United Press International, "Track Stock Countersuit Hits Singers." **Giancana, Villa Venice, etc.:** Brashler, *The Don;* Giancana, *Mafia Princess; The Sinatra Society of America,* No. 39 (September 1991). *Who's Got the Action?* **reviews:** Gene., review; Mishkin, "Screen Review: 'Who's Got the Action?'"

Sands, FBI teletype: Duke, "Night Club Reviews" (Sands, Las Vegas), 30 January 1963; U. S. Department of Justice, Federal Bureau of Investigation. *Who's Been Sleeping in My Bed?:* interview, Mann; Gene., review. **Claudia Martin, *For Those Who Think Young,* marriage:** *Los Angeles Herald-Examiner,* 26 January 1964; Parsons, "It's Rumored Dino's Daughter Not Married"; Scott, "The Improbable Private Life of Mrs. Dean Martin." **Giancana, D'Amato, Cal-Neva, etc.:** Associated Press, "Sinatra Is Accused of Hosting Mobster; D'Amato Under Fire"; Brashler, *The Don;* Giancana, *Mafia Princess;* Kelley, *His Way;* U. S. Department of Justice, Federal Bureau of Investigation. **Sands:** Duke, "Night Club Reviews" (Sands, Las Vegas), 11 September

1963; Leigh, *There Really Was a Hollywood.* **Warner Brothers-Reprise:** Schumach, "Warner Buys Reprise Records, but Sinatra Retains One-third." *Toys in the Attic* **reviews:** Crowther, *New York Times,* 1 August 1963; Hale, " 'Toys in the Attic' Is Major Film"; Kauffmann, review; *New York Journal-American* review quoted in ad, *Hollywood Reporter,* 30 January 1961; Rand, review. **"Tastelessness":** Gene., review. *What a Way to Go!:* Anby., review; interview, Thompson; obituary (Jacobs). *Robin and the Seven Hoods:* Davis, *Why Me?* **Sinatra, Jr., kidnapping, Sands anniversary:** Associated Press, "Pop Sinatra Pops Up at Casino"; United Press International: " 'World Gone Nuts': Dean."

Sands: Duke, "Night Club Reviews" (Sands, Las Vegas), 29 January 1964. **"Maybe a sleeping-pill":** P. Martin, "I Call on Dean Martin." **John Crocetti:** Administrative Records, Probate Court, Jefferson County, Ohio, Vol. 25. **"Guy from *Billboard*":** B. Smith, "Follow-Up Review." **"Everybody Loves Somebody":** L. Kaye, Untitled article on Ken Lane. *Kiss Me, Stupid:* Associated Press, "They Call Sellers Rat Fink"; Dick, *Billy Wilder;* interview, Walston; Kleno, *Kim Novak on Camera;* "Ray Walston Replaces Sellers in 'Kiss Me' "; Schumach, "Hollywood Team: Peter Sellers, Dean Martin Have Fun in Wilder's 'Kiss Me, Stupid' "; Scott, "Dean Martin Has Wacky 'Lunch' ";

Wood, *The Bright Side of Billy Wilder.*

Beatles, "Everybody Loves Somebody": Butler and Osborne, "Dean Martin: The Crooning Croupier." **Sands:** Duke, "Night Club Reviews" (Sands, Las Vegas), 22 July 1964. **Warner-Reprise convention:** Tiegel, "Dino Mixes Act—A Shot of Humor with Song Chasers." **Harrah's:** Long., "Night Club Reviews" (Harrah's, Lake Tahoe). **El Capitan, *"Jerry Lewis Show"*:** interview, Lewis; Lewis, *Jerry Lewis in Person.* Martin's introduction of the Rolling Stones on *Hollywood Palace* is included in the videotape documentary *25 × 5: The Continuing Adventures of the Rolling Stones* (New York: CBS Music Video Enterprises, 1989). **NBC:** Messina, "Dean Martin TVer Planned." *The Sons of Katie Elder:* obituary (Hathaway); Samuel Marx and Joyce Vanderveen, *Deadly Illusions: Jean Harlow and the Murder of Paul Bern* (New York: Random House, 1990); Wallis and Higham, *Starmaker.* *The Silencers:* Crist, "Bond Leads Dino Down a Dirty Alley"; *Hollywood Reporter,* 10 July 1964; *Hollywood Reporter,* 22 March 1965. *Kiss Me, Stupid:* Dick, *Billy Wilder;* Gardiner, *Catholic Viewpoint on Censorship;* Hale, "Sex, Smut, Little Else in 'Kiss Me, Stupid' "; interview, Walston; Pry., review; reviews, file *("Kiss Me, Stupid"),* Margaret Herrick Library of the Academy of Motion Picture Arts; Wood, *The Bright Side of Billy Wilder.* **Real-estate consortium:** "Dean Martin

Group Buys Airport Land"; "Dean Martin Group Buys San Diego Tract."

XIV

The Sons of Katie Elder: Heffernan, "Horse Brings Crisis." **Deana Martin:** clipping, file ("Martin, Dean"), Margaret Herrick Library of the Academy of Motion Picture Arts. **Claudia Martin:** *Hollywood Reporter,* 23 June 1965. *The Silencers:* interview, Stevens; obituary (Karlson). **"The Dean Martin Show":** "Another Variety Show"; "Dean Martin Snags 142 Stars"; Gardella, "Martin Turns Comedian for New Fall NBC Series"; J.M.C., " 'Dean Martin' "; Maksian, "Dean Martin's Opener Set"; review, *New York Post;* videotape. **Sands:** Duke, "Night Club Reviews" (Sands, Las Vegas), 10 November 1965.

The Silencers: Gill, review; Weiler, "Dean Martin and (Shapely) Company Arrive in 'The Silencers.' " **Nielsen rating, Henry Miller:** "Old Moderately"; S. E. Gontarski, "Dionysus in Publishing: Barney Rosset, Grove Press, and the Making of a Countercanon," *The Review of Contemporary Fiction,* Vol. XI (Fall 1990, Grove Press Number). **Miller's meeting with Dean:** Mary V. Dearborn, *The Happiest Man Alive: Henry Miller* (New York: Simon & Schuster, 1991). *Texas Across the River:* "Dean Martin: He Cools It and Makes It"; Muir, "Hollywood," 16 February 1966. *Murderers' Row:* Carroll, "Dean Plays It Boozy and Breezy." Graham, "Thought of

Retiring Makes Martin Wince." **Quotes ("This Jimmy Bowen"):** audiotape, *The National Guard Sessions* radio program (1965). **Polo Lounge:** Bart, "Sinatra Involved in Brawl in Bar"; Fallaci, "Dean Martin"; Muir, "New Sinatra Brawl: Exec in Coma"; Muir, "Too Hurt to Tell of Sinatra Bout."

Treasury bond trailers: *Hollywood Reporter,* 20 July 1966. **"I don't even breathe hard":** Thomas, "Martin Makes It Seem So Easy." **Obscenity protest:** Gardella, "Martin Named by Viewers NBC's New Language Dean." **Gail Martin:** Adil., "Night Club Reviews"; Dale., "New Acts"; Fields, "Without a Helping Hand"; Gross, "Stars' Sons & Daughters Beginning to Take Over." Deana Martin appeared on "The Dean Martin Show" 8 December 1966; Claudia Martin, 9 March 1967. **Engagement to Hutton:** *New York Post,* 10 February 1966. Hutton mentions the engagement in his 1990 book, *From the Beatles to Botham* (London: Lennard), but when questioned (10 January 1992) would say only, "I don't want to talk about it."

Dean Martin Month: "Reprise Records Presents Dean Martin Month: Sales Excitement by America's Best-Selling Vocalist" (Reprise, October 1966).

Texas Across the River: Guarino, "Dean Martin in Funny Western"; Whit., review. *Murderers' Row:* Carroll, "Dean Plays It Boozy and Breezy"; Robe., review. *Rough Night in Jericho:* Graham,

"Thought of Retiring Makes Martin Wince"; interview, Laven; interview, Peppard.

Death of Angela Crocetti: clippings, file ("Martin, Dean"), Margaret Herrick Library of the Academy of Motion Picture Arts; Death Records, Registrar-Recorder, County of Los Angeles.

Bookmakers: Associated Press, "Dean Martin Tells of Losing Bets"; *United States* v. *Mastrippolito* (CRC-11 [12 October 1966], Federal Records Center Accession Number 021-73-A-327, Federal Records Center Location Number RB042460, Agency Box Number 1 [Laguna Niguel, Cal.]). *How to Save a Marriage:* interview, Stevens; obituary (Shapiro); Thomas, "Is There a Real Dean Martin?" *Newsweek:* "Funny-Side Up." **Sands:** Duke, "Night Club Reviews" (Sands, Las Vegas), 22 March 1967. *The Ambushers:* interview, Rule; Thomas, "Is There a Real Dean Martin?" **Land purchases:** "Actor Becoming Large Ventura Landowner"; *Los Angeles Times,* 11 March 1966. **Beverly Hills Country Club:** Becker, "Prospectors Discover That There's Golf in Beverly Hills"; Shirley, "Beverly Hills to Get Lavish Golf Course"; Thomas, "Dean Martin Now Starting Exclusive Country Club." **Income for 1967:** Hellman, "Dean Martin's 4-Ply Performing Parlayed into $5 Mil-a-Year Harvest." **New NBC deal:** "New Dean Martin 3-Year NBC Pact a $34,000,000 Wow." The catalogue of real-estate and other holdings is derived from *Dean Mar-*

tin v. *Jeanne Martin,* Exhibits A-2, B-2, B-3, C, D, and H.

Death of Guy Crocetti: "Dean Martin's Father Dies"; Death Records, Registrar-Recorder, County of Los Angeles. *Bandolero!:* interview, McLaglen; obituary (Hough). **Christmas show:** Gross, "The Martins & Sinatras Joyously Hail Christmas"; Humphrey, "Dino's Christmas Show Puts Rowdy Image in Cold Storage." *Look:* Fallaci, "Dean Martin."

Interview, J. Martin. **Maharishi ad:** *Billboard,* 13 April 1968. **Gold albums:** "Byrds, Dean Martin, Hendrix Nab Goldisks." Jerry Schilling, Elvis's aide from 1964 to 1976, later told Jeanne Martin of Elvis's bashful visits to the Martin property. **Sinatra, Sands, etc.:** Duke, "Night Club Reviews" (Sands, Las Vegas), 8 May 1968; Graham, "Dean & Frankie's Palship on Rocks"; "It's Official on Dino Exit from Sands to Riviera"; obituary (Entratter); "Sinatra Joins Rival of the Sands Hotel in Las Vegas Rift."

Airport **deal:** "Dean Martin Sues Studio for $1 Million." Gail Martin, managed by Bob Crystal, and Deana Martin, managed by Bill Howard, are listed as Reprise artists in *Billboard,* December 1967. **"The Monkees":** 4 March 1968 (episode: "Some Like It Lukewarm"). **Persian Room:** Fields, "Without a Helping Hand." **Gail Martin marriage:** "Bridal Sweet." **Death of Bill Crocetti:** Death Records, Registrar-Recorder, County of Los Angeles.

Torres, Riviera, etc.: *Dean*

Martin v. *Jeanne Martin* (con-
sultancy retainer); "Deano Part
Owner of Vegas Riviera?"; Demaris,
The Boardwalk Jungle; Demaris, *The
Last Mafioso;* "It's Official on Dino
Exit from Sands to Riviera"; Mes-
sick, *The Beauties and the Beasts;*
Reid and Demaris, *The Green Felt
Jungle;* State of Nevada, Gaming
Control Board; Wilson, *The Show
Business Nobody Knows.* **Roselli,
Friars Club:** Associated Press, "Six
to Be Tried in Rigging," *New York
Times,* 16 January 1968, p. 22;
Demaris, *The Last Mafioso;* United
Press International, "Sirhan's Lawyer
Pleads Guilty to Contempt in Cheat-
ing Trial," *New York Times,* 26 Au-
gust 1969, p. 20. Roselli, fined
$55,000, was the only member of the
convicted cheating ring not sen-
tenced to serve time.

Death of Nicky Hilton: obitu-
ary (Hilton). **Craig Martin mar-
riage:** "Singer's Boy Weds Dancer"
(UPI photo and legend), *New York
Daily News,* 9 March 1969. **Carole
Costello:** *Los Angeles Times,* 3 April
1987; obituary (Costello); *Variety,* 1
August 1962. **Claudia Martin mar-
riage:** Haber, "The 'Casual' Dean
Martin Family." **Keil Martin:** Lydia
Encinas and Michael Glynn, " 'Hill
St. Blues' Curse Strikes Again as 7th
Member of Show Dies," *National En-
quirer,* 22 January 1991, p. 36; Alvin
Grimes, "Dean Martin Shattered as
Hill Street 'Son' Dies at Age 46,"
Star, 22 January 1991; obituary, *Va-
riety,* 7 January 1991, p. 107. **Deana**

Martin marriage: "Dean's Daugh-
ter in Duet" (clipping in file, "Mar-
tin, Dean," Billy Rose Theatre Col-
lection, New York Public Library at
Lincoln Center). **Riviera debut:**
Will., "Night Club Reviews" (Rivi-
era, Las Vegas). **Entratter ("Get
that fag out of here"):** Wayne
Newton, *Once Before I Go* (New York:
William Morrow, 1989), p. 99. **Terry
Melcher:** Miller, "Enraged Dean
Martin Takes Daughter from Doris
Day's Son."

Kathy McKee: McKee with
Rudy Maxa, "My Secret Life with
Sammy Davis," *Penthouse,* Septem-
ber 1991, p. 162.

**". . . announced through
Herman Citron":** "Reprise Surprised Martin Has Waxed Last Disk
There." **Nine writers:** Mor., "Television Reviews." **Quote ("as if he
were someone impersonating
Dean Martin"):** Duke, "Night Club
Reviews" (Riviera, Las Vegas), 8 October 1969.

Gail Renshaw: "Dino & His
Wife Are Divorcing"; *Hollywood Cit-
izen,* 27 December 1969; Shearer,
"Dean Martin—He's Going through a
Change of Wife"; United Press Inter-
national, "Dean Martin's Wife to Sue
for Divorce"; Wilson, "For Now, It'll
Be Dino, His Girl and a Chaperone";
Wilson, "Introducing Dino's Choice";
Wilson, *The Show Business Nobody
Knows.* Bob Hope's *Roberta* special
was broadcast by NBC on November
11. **Los Angeles Rams:** Haber,
"Dino and Herbie to Buy the Rams?"

XV

Airport: Rick., review. **Canby:** *New York Times,* 6 March 1970, p. 34. **Claude-NBC deal:** *Dean Martin v. Jeanne Martin,* (Property Settlement Agreement, par. 3.20). **Catherine Hawn:** R. Andrews, "The Dean Martins: We're Having a Wonderful Divorce"; *Dean Martin v. Cathy Mae Martin;* Identification Information Report, Checkmate Investigative Services (1991); Marriage Records, Registrar-Recorder, County of Los Angeles, Calif., License No. WE 1120; "The Price of Dean Martin's Extra Marital Madness"; Reilly, "The Dean Martins: How They Live Together but Love Others"; G. Stevens, "Dean Martin Fearful for Sinatra's Health"; R. Thompson, "How Cathy Hawn Is Luring Dean Martin into Marriage." **Joe E. Lewis testimonial:** Wilson, *The Show Business Nobody Knows.*

New Reprise deal: *Billboard,* 16 January 1971, p. 31. **Columbia suit:** " 'Tell Me Not What I Owe You': Martin." *Something Big:* interview, Blackman; interview, McLaglen; Murf., review. **Retirement plans:** *National Enquirer,* 30 May 1971.

Dean Martin, Jr., marriage: *International Herald Tribune,* 19 April 1971. **Quote ("I don't know him very well"):** Smilgis, "This Swinger Is Dean Martin's Son." **Quote ("He's a funny guy"):** Guerin, "Dino Jr."

Reagan campaign: Reuters, "Dean Martin Deserts, Too"; Turner, "Reagan Beats Foe at Raising Funds"; United Press International, "Martin Joins Sinatra in Supporting Reagan." Jesse Jackson called for a ban in 1978 of "Some Girls."

Jesse Jackson: Chet Flippo, *Rolling Stone,* 27 July 1978, p. 8. **"Klanspersons":** "Klans to Gather in Buna Today," *Beaumont Enterprise,* 24 September 1977, p. 3-A. **Removal of bar:** Mackin, "Martin Gets Dis-barred." **Ding-a-Ling Sisters, etc.:** Bill., review; Maksian, "Martin's Show Revamped." **Dean Martin-Tucson Open:** Werden, "Barber Triumphs at 21st Extra Hole." *Something Big:* Murf., review. **Boston Garden:** Livingston, "Bombing of Dean Martin Concert Points Up Boston's Yen for Rock." **Quote ("I hate guys that sing serious"):** Wilson, "Dean Martin—A Star Who Glows on You."

Divorce: *Dean Martin v. Jeanne Martin.* **Quote ("I'm no gentleman"):** Sawyer, "Cathy & Dean." **Riviera:** "Dean Martin in Show Hassle"; "Riviera Buys Dino's Stock in Facility." *Showdown,* **Universal suits, etc.:** "Dean Martin Sues Studio for $1 Million"; interview, Clark; LeBlanc, "In Dino Veritas"; *New York Times,* 13 May 1972. **NBC censorship:** "Cleaned-up Look for Dino in Sept. Detailed in memo from Garrison"; Gardella, "Defense of Dean Martin Brings a Flood of Mail"; Gardella, "Will NBC Censors Take the Zing Out of Dean Martin?"; "NBC's Move to Launder Some of Dino's Indigo"; *New York Daily News,* 10 May 1972. *Variety* quote: Bill., review. *Life* quote:

Cyclops, "The Witless Reign of King Leer."

Marriage announcement: Gardella, "Dino: Will Marry Again in Fall." **Dyed hair:** Gardella, "Dean Martin Talks Candidly about Dean Martin." **Garrison announcement:** Gardella, "Dino's TV Producer Says Booze and Broads Are In." **Steubenville response to "Tonight Show" comment:** interview, Costanzo. *Showdown* **wrap party:** interview, Clark. **Divorce:** *Dean Martin* v. *Jeanne Martin; New York Times,* 12 December 1972. **Marriage license:** Marriage Records, Registrar-Recorder, County of Los Angeles, Calif.; "That's Amore!" (photo and legend), *New York Daily News,* 21 April 1973. **Marriage:** Gardett, "Dino Weds: Drink Up"; Hoffman, "Dean & Cathy"; item ("Newsmakers"), *Newsweek,* 7 May 1973; Kinnard, "Florist Is a Full-Fledged Entrepreneur"; Marriage Records, Registrar-Recorder, County Of Los Angeles, Calif.; "Dean Martin Marries in Cinema Style"; "Wedding Toast" (photo and legend), *New York Post,* 26 April 1973.

The Brontë quote is from Chapter 2, *Wuthering Heights* (1847). **Twenty-fourth in ratings:** Laurent, "Next Season Doesn't Look Good for Dean's 'De-sexed' TV Show." **NOW award:** Johnston, " 'Women Power' Protests"; Kramer, "Time to Duck!"; "Natl. Org for Women's Show Biz 'Enemy' List." **MGM Grand:** Hilburn, "Martin Set to Open New Hotel"; Scott, "Dino Inaugurates the Grand"; Will, "Night Club Reviews" (MGM Grand), 12 December 1973. **Haber call:** "Exposed! Dean Martin's Visits to That Youth Doctor!"; Haber, "Laundering Dean Martin's Language"; Hurok, "Dean's Cathy Answers Rumors of Romance with James Darren."

Mr. Ricco: interview, Bogart; interview, Rasulala. **Dino Jr. arrest:** W. Burke, "Dean Martin's Son Escapes Jail!"; "Dino Martin Busted: Gun Possession"; Happel, "Dean Martin Speaks Out on His Son's Arrest"; item ("Notes on People"), *New York Times,* 2 July 1974; Smilgis, "This Swinger Is Dean Martin's Son"; United Press International, "Arraign Dino Jr. on Gun Rap"; United Press International, "Dean Martin Jr. Indicted"; United Press International, "Dean Martin's Son Faces Gun Charges." **Legal Separation:** *Hollywood Citizen-News,* 26 July 1974. **"Tie a Yellow Ribbon":** Will., "Night Club Reviews" (MGM Grand), 11 September 1974.

Car wreck: *Los Angeles Herald,* 15 December 1974. *Variety* **review of** *Mr. Ricco:* Murf., review. **Quote ("my friends are dead"):** D. Lewis, "That's Dino!" **Entratter, Costello:** obituary (Entratter); "Frank Costello Dies of Coronary at 82." **Adoption:** Superior Court, Los Angeles County, Calif., Adoption No. AD-86808. **New NBC deal:** *Los Angeles Times,* 26 March 1975, p. IV-24; press release, "The Dean Martin Specials" (New York: NBC Television News, Fall 1975). **Gail Martin bankruptcy:** *Los Angeles Times,* 17 June 1975. **IRS master**

list: Shanahan, "Inquiry Reveals I.R.S. Master List." **Quote ("I'll never retire"):** Gardella, "New Look at Dino Martin." **New NBC specials:** Lewis, "Dean Martin Really Met the Press"; Maksian, "More 'Roasts' for Martin"; Bob Williams, "Dean Martin to Uncork a New Image." The best account of the making of "The Dean Martin Celebrity Roast" shows is in Vallely, "Dean Martin's Closest Friend Is Frank Sinatra (He Sees Him Twice a Year)." See also Gardella, "Dean's 'Roasts': Where the Jokers Are."

 Divorce: *Dean Martin* v. *Cathy Mae Martin.* **Gunshot wound:** *Los Angeles Times,* 11 July 1976; United Press International, "Dean Martin Wounds Self." **MGM Grand:** Will., "Night Club Reviews," (MGM Grand), 18 August 1976. **Warner-Reprise suit:** *Los Angeles Times,* 1 September 1976; *Variety,* 22 February 1978. **Martin-Lewis encounters:** Baer, "Martin and Lewis End Feud After Meeting on Golf Links"; interview, Lewis; Kern, "Bing Helps Dean End Feud with Jerry Lewis"; P. Martin, "I Call on Dean Martin." **Quote ("Jerry's trying hard"):** D. Lewis, "That's Dino!" **Telethon reunion:** Delson, "Penthouse Interview"; interview, Lewis; item ("Newsmakers"), *Newsweek,* 20 September 1976; item, ("Notes on People"), *New York Times,* 7 September 1976; Lewis, *Jerry Lewis in Person.* Maksian "Jerry's Big Day Capped by Dean"; videotape. **Divorce:** *Dean Martin* v. *Cathy Mae Martin;* item ("Notes on People"),

New York Times, 12 November 1976. **Interlocutory judgment:** *Dean Martin* v. *Cathy Mae Martin* (Interlocutory Judgment of Dissolution of Marriage [19 November 1976]); Superior Court, Los Angeles County, Judgment Book No. 7193, p. 274 (24 November 1976). **Peggy Crosby:** Jacques, "Dean Martin, 59: 'I've Fallen in Love with Bing Crosby's Daughter-in-Law' "; *New York Daily News,* 17 November 1976. **Divorce finalized:** *Dean Martin* v. *Cathy Mae Martin* (Request and Declaration for Final Judgment of Dissolution of Marriage [24 February 1977]). **Andre Boyer:** Dworkin and Wilk, "Dean Martin's Girlfriend, 19: 'We're Both Very Much in Love' "; *Los Angeles Herald-Examiner,* 21 June 1977. **NBC renewal:** Maksian, "Dean Is Special in 2-Yr. NBC Deal."

 Cohen, Giancana, Roselli, etc.: Brashler, *The Don;* Giancana, *Mafia Princess;* "Mickey Cohen, Once a Leader of West Coast Rackets, Dead"; *New York Times,* 12 April 1976, p. 1; *New York Times,* 13 April 1976, p. 1; *New York Times,* 14 August 1976, p. 1. **Genovese:** *New York Times,* 15 February 1969, p. 1; Rappleye and Becker, *All American Mafioso.* **Gambinos, etc.:** Nick Tosches, *Power on Earth* (New York: Arbor House, 1986). **DePalma, Fusco, Westchester Premier Theatre, etc.:** Demaris, *The Last Mafioso;* Dworkin and Wilk, "Dean Martin's Girlfriend, 19: 'We're Both Very Much in Love' "; *Los Angeles Herald-Examiner,* 21 June 1977;

press release, "Frank Sinatra & Dean Martin to Co-Star at Westchester Theatre May 17–29" (New York: Solters & Roskin, Inc., 1 February 1977); program, Westchester Premier Theatre, 17–29 May 1977. The Westchester Premier Theatre case was covered in the *New York Times:* 13 November 1977, p. 75; 15 November 1977, p. 33; 18 March 1978, p. 26; 7 June 1978, p. 11; 15 November 1978, p. II-3; 5 January 1979, p. II-3; 23 May 1979, p. II-3; 7 July 1979, p. 20; 16 August 1979, p. II-2. **Sabre Room, Chicago:** Hege., review. **Latin Quarter, Cherry Hill, N.J.:** *Los Angeles Herald-Examiner,* 21 June 1977. **Death of Ray Ryan:** United Press International, "Millionaire Oilman Killed by Bomb Blast in His Car," *New York Times,* 20 October 1977, p. 18.

MGM Grand: Will., "Night Club Reviews" (MGM Grand), 21 December 1977. **Phyllis Davis:** *National Enquirer,* 15 July 1980. **"The lady from *Esquire":* Vallely, "Dean Martin's Closest Friend Is Frank Sinatra (He Sees Him Twice a Year)." **MGM Grand:** Will., "Night Club Reviews" (MGM Grand), 24 January 1979. **Joni Anderson:** clipping, 20 March 1979, file ("Martin, Dean"), Margaret Herrick Library of the Academy of Motion Picture Arts. **Boston Music Hall:** United Press International, "Reagan to Raise Funds with a Sinatra Concert." **Press conference:** videotape.

The golf-course encounter was related by actor Jim Backus to actor Mike McGreevy: interview, McGreevy. **Melanie Griffith:** *National Enquirer,* 15 July 1980. **Dorothy Hamill:** Smilgis, "This Swinger Is Dean Martin's Son." *Players,* produced by Bob Evans and directed by Anthony Harvey, was released in June 1979; Ali McGraw, Evans's ex-wife, co-starred. Dean Paul had previously starred in John Derek's *A Boy . . . A Girl* (1969) and would later star in *Heart Like a Wheel* (1983). **New York Post:** "Biggest Tippers: Frank & Dean."

AT&T deal: "Dean Martin to Be New Bell Spokesman"; "Dino Hears a Bell." **Death of Leonard Barr:** obituary (Barr). **"Prelude to Victory":** videotape; also item captioned "Fund Raising in New York," in Douglas E. Kneeland, "Reagan Pledges Not to End Price Support for Farmers," *New York Times,* 1 October 1980, p. B-6. **Death of Mack Gray:** obituary (Gray). **Inaugural-eve gala:** "Dino Is There . . . Unnoticed"; "Dino Never Got to the Stage"; "Gala Director Says: Dean Martin 'Inebriated.' " **Dino Jr. marriage to Dorothy Hamill:** Adelson, "Move Over, Charles and Di—Dorothy Hamill and Dean Paul Martin Plot a Royal Wedding L.A.-Style"; item ("Notes on People"), *New York Times,* 31 December 1981. **The Cannonball Run:** Cart, review; interview, Ruddy. The five films that made more in 1981, in descending rank: *Raiders of the Lost Ark, Superman II, On Golden Pond, Arthur, Stripes.*

Gun charge: Associated Press, "Dean Martin Arrested"; "Concealed

Gun Rap"; Associated Press, "Dean Wasn't Loaded but He Had Gun That Was"; "Dino Fined $120 over Gun"; "Dino Pays $192 and Packs in the Pistol"; "Martin Fined on Gun Rap"; "Nab Dino for Drunk Driving"; *People of the State of California* v. *Dean Paul Martin;* United Press International, "Dean Martin Accused." **Valentine Love-In:** interview, King.

London: "Dean Martin Gigs Fill London Hall"; "King Dino Faces Royal Treatment"; O'Connor, review; "Royal Welcome for Dean." **"Since I Met You Baby" video (Warner Bros. 760 220-1797):** *Hollywood Reporter,* 29 September 1983.

Atlantic City, Golden Nugget, etc.: Demaris, *The Boardwalk Jungle;* Janson, "Top Two Casinos Gambling Profits in Battle of Stars." **Dean at Resorts International:** Furmanek, "Talent in Action." **MGM Grand:** Will., "Night Club Reviews" (MGM Grand), 14 September 1983. **Waldorf benefit:** "Dino & Frank Will Duet Here"; "Godfather Sinatra"; Roura and Posier, "People: Dino-Frank Duet Here All Sold Out." **Golden Nugget:** "Sinatra, Dean Martin Team on Fall A.C. Date." **Blackjack incident:** Associated Press, "Sinatra Drops Casino Shows, Citing Insult by a Jersey Aide"; Associated Press, "Casino Officials Probing Sinatra Blackjack Flap"; Jankowski, "Casino Fined for Illegal Blackjack Game"; Janson, "Casino May Be Fined for Letting Sinatra and Martin Set Own Rules"; Schwaneberg, "Casino Admits Violation in Celebrity Card Game"; United Press International, "Violations Admitted by Casino." George Henningson, deputy director of investigations for the New Jersey Division of Gaming Enforcement in Trenton, declined to respond to requests for further information. **Death of Skinny D'Amato:** Jones, "Skinny D'Amato Dies"; Schwartz, "Greats and Near-Greats Alike: They All Called Him 'Skinny' "; Zatwaska, "They Mourn for D'Amato."

Paris debut: Curt., "Dean Martin in Paris Moulin Rouge Debut"; J.C., "Dean Martin au Moulin-Rouge." **Golden Nugget cancellation:** Associated Press, "Sinatra Drops Casino Shows, Citing Insult by a Jersey Aide." **Friars tribute:** Joe Cohen, "Friars' Bash for Martin Pulls a Huge Turnout"; *Friars Club Tribute to Dean Martin.* **New NBC "Roast" specials:** "Heating Up Dino's Roasts." **"Half Nelson":** Maksian, "A Role for Dino." **Sale of home:** ad, *Daily Variety,* 19 September 1986.

Death of Dean Martin, Jr.: Associated Press, "Actor's Son Is Missing as Fighter Goes Down"; Associated Press, "Air Controller Blamed in Dino's Crash Death"; Associated Press, "Dean Martin's Son Dead in Jet"; Associated Press, "Dean Martin's Son Is Dead in Jet"; Schermerhorn, "Dean Martin's Son Missing in Crash"; Associated Press, "Effort Is Disclosed to Rescue Jet Flown by Dean Martin Jr."; interview, J. Martin; Schermerhorn, "Dean Martin's Son Missing in Crash."

Death of Carole Costello Martin: *Los Angeles Times,* 3 April 1987; obituary (Costello). **Death of Herman Citron:** obituary (Citron).

Proposed 1974 rail tour: Archerd, "Chartered Train Tour for Sinatra, Martin." **Together Again Tour:** Davis, *Why Me?;* "Dino out of Tour"; "Frank, Sammy & Liza Too!"; item, *New York Daily News,* 22 April 1988; Michelson, " 'Rat Pack' Tour Gets Underway"; " 'Rat Pack' Reunion"; "Reunited Rat Pack"; Schermerhorn, "Dino's Ailing, He Quits Tour by Rat Pack"; "Schlatter Gets Last Laugh"; Stapely, "Sinatra the Hell-Raiser"; videotapes of Chasen's press conference and Oakland concert.

Sammy Cahn party: "Dean & Ex Bring Smiles to L.A. Do." **Bally's Grand:** *Los Angeles Times,* 12 August 1988. **High Sierra:** Shie., "Nightclub Reviews." **Sammy Davis, Jr., tribute:** Grein, "Toasting a Song-and-Dance Man." **Death of Sammy Davis, Jr.:** Flint, "Sammy Davis Jr. Dies at 64"; " 'Mr. Entertainment,' Versatile Sammy Davis Jr., Dies at 64."

There was a surfeit of reports concerning Martin's ill health in the tabloid press during the spring and summer of 1990: Encinas and Fitz, "Dean Martin Fights Pain—Delays Surgery for Daughter's Wedding"; Duffy, Braham, and Aiello, "Dean Martin Shocker; "Dino Joins Sammy Davis Jr. in Hospital"; "Friends Alarmed as Ailing Dean Martin Struggles to Finish Songs on Stage." **Quotes throughout closing section:** interview, J. Martin. June Allyson's radio commercials for Depend fitted briefs were broadcast in 1991–92. **"Torna a Surriento," author's translation:** See how beautiful the sea is! / It breathes forth so much feeling / like your sweet, soft accent / that, awake, leads me to dream.

$\mathcal{S}$OURCES

Interviews

Alberghetti, Anna Maria. 14 November 1989.

Barton, Mrs. De Arv G. 19 September 1989.

Baylos, Gene. 20 February 1991.

Blackman, Honor. 15 December 1989.

Bogart, Paul. 2 November 1989.

Cahn, Sammy. 3 May 1991.

Christ, Christopher. 9 June 1989.

Clark, Susan. 30 October 1989.

Costanzo, Mindy [Emmanuel M.]. 23 May and 2 June 1989.

Crocetti, Archie. 27 February 1991.

D'Anniballe, Joe. 23 May 1989.

D'Anniballe, Leo. 23 and 31 May 1989.

D'Anniballe, Martha Jane McClelland. 31 May 1989.

D'Aurora, Irma DiBenedetto. 7 June 1989.

DeFore, Don. 14 November 1989.

DeLuca, Agon. 3 and 7 June 1989.

DeMarco, Dum-Dum [Rafaello]. 8 May 1989.

DeSarro, John [Stogie]. 22 May and 24 June 1989.

Dettore, Carolyn Cisario. 28 June 1990.

Dickinson, Angie. 17 November 1989.

DiNovo, Michael A. 22 May 1989.

Downtown Joe. 20 September 1989.

Dru, Joanne. 6 November 1989.

Foch, Nina. 27 October 1989.

Franciosa, Anthony. 6 November 1989.

Greshler, Abby. 16 May 1991.

Hover, Herman Douglas. 17 and 18 November 1989.

Jacobs, Merle. 5 July 1989 and 20 February 1991.

Jerome, Jerry. 4 June 1989.

Julian, Emilio [Kid Ketchel]. 9 June 1989.

Kayafas, Angie. 20 May 1989.

Keller, Mrs. Harry. 3 November 1989.

Kenaga, Joan. 18 September 1989.

King, Sonny. 27 and 28 February 1991.

Laven, Arnold. 6 November 1989.

Lazarus, Erna. 7 November 1989.

Lee, Ruta. 7 November 1989.

Lewis, Jerry. 20 December 1990.

Malone, Dorothy. 7 November 1989.

Mann, Daniel. 21 December 1989.

Martin, Jeanne Biegger. 20 January and 18 April 1991.

490 SOURCES

Mavromatis, George. 21 May and 7 June 1989.

McGreevy, Mike. 15 November 1989.

McLaglen, Andrew V. 5 January 1990.

Military, Frank. 23 April and 3 May 1991.

Mirisch, Walter. 3 November 1989.

Monaco, Ross A. 23 May 1989.

Nelson, Lori. 3 November 1989.

Paidousis, Tim. 9 June 1989.

Paolisso, Paul J. 23 and 31 May 1989.

Pavlovich, Mike. 22 May 1989.

Peppard, George. 16 April 1990.

Pestian, Gina Simera. 10 January 1991.

Pevney, Joseph. 7 November 1989.

Pompa, Beans [William J.]. 23 May 1989.

Rasulala, Thalmus. 6 November 1989.

Ruddy, Albert S. 6 November 1989.

Rule, Janice. 6 November 1989.

Sasso, Bob. 21 May 1989.

Schlatter, George. 18 April 1991.

Simmons, Helen. 23 May 1989.

Sperduti, Bernice Del Villan. 20 September 1989.

Stevens, Stella. 1 November 1989.

Stueve, Mark. 21 September 1989.

Synodinos, Agnes. 20 May 1989.

Thompson, J. Lee. 2 November 1989.

Thorpe, Richard. 7 November 1989.

Torcasio, Tony. 8 May 1990.

Vecchione, Mary Crocetti. 22 May and 2 June 1989.

Walston, Ray. 10 November 1989.

Yannon, Anna DeCarlo. 9 June 1989.

Books, Etc.

ADAMS, JOEY. *From Gags to Riches.* New York: Frederick Fell, 1946.

ALICOATE, JACK, ed. *The 1944 Radio Annual.* New York: Radio Daily, 1944.

———. *The 1945 Radio Annual.* New York: Radio Daily, 1945.

ALLYSON, JUNE, with LEIGHTON, FRANCIS SPATZ. *June Allyson.* New York: G. P. Putnam's Sons, 1982.

American Graphophone Company. *The American Graphophone Company: Its Progress and Prospects.* Bridgeport, Conn: American Graphophone Company, 1905.

American Society of Composers, Authors and Publishers. *ASCAP Index of Performed Compositions.* 3 vols. New York: American Society of Composers, Authors and Publishers, 1963.

ARPEA, MARIO. *Alle origini dell'emigrazione abruzzese.* Milan: Franco Angeli, 1987.

Association for Recorded Sound Collections (ARSC) and Associated Audio Archives Committee. *The Rigler and Deutsch Record Index* (RDI). Microfiche. Washington: ARSC, 1983.

BARNOUW, ERIK. *A Tower in Babel: A History of Broadcasting in the United States, Vol. I—to 1933.* New York: Oxford University Press, 1968.

————. *The Golden Web: A History of Broadcasting in the United States, Vol. II—1933 to 1953.* New York: Oxford University Press, 1968.

————. *The Image Empire: A History of Broadcasting in the United States, Vol. III—from 1953.* New York: Oxford University Press, 1970.

————. *Tube of Plenty: The Evolution of American Television.* 2nd rev. ed. New York: Oxford University Press, 1990.

BARTLET, CHUCK, and BERGERON, BARBARA, eds. *"Variety" Obituaries, 1905–1986.* 12 vols. New York: Garland Publishing, 1988–89.

BASSO, ALBERTO, ed. *Dizionario della musica e dei musicisti.* 12 vols. Turin: UTET, 1983–88.

BAWDEN, LIZ-ANNE, ed. *The Oxford Companion to Film.* New York: Oxford University Press, 1976.

BERG, A. SCOTT. *Goldwyn: A Biography.* New York: Alfred A. Knopf, 1989.

BETROCK, ALAN, ed. *The Illustrated Price Guide to Scandal Magazines, 1952–66.* Brooklyn, N.Y.: Shake Books, 1988.

BILLINGS, PAT, and EYLES, ALLEN. *Hollywood Today.* New York: A. S. Barnes, 1971.

BLUM, JOHN MORTON. *V Was for Victory: Politics and American Culture during World War II.* San Diego: Harcourt Brace Jovanovich, 1976.

BOOKBINDER, ROBERT. *The Films of Bing Crosby.* Secaucus, N.J.: Citadel, 1977.

BOSWORTH, PATRICIA. *Montgomery Clift: A Biography.* New York: Arbor House, 1977.

BRADY, MALCOLM J., ed. *Steubenville Sesqui-Centennial Veterans Homecoming.* Steubenville, Ohio: H. C. Cook, 1947.

BRASHLER, WILLIAM. *The Don: The Life and Death of Sam Giancana.* New York: Harper & Row, 1977. *Caveat lector* (let the reader beware).

BROOKS, TIM, and MARSH, EARLE. *The Complete Directory to Prime Time Network TV Shows, 1946–Present.* 4th ed. New York: Ballantine, 1988.

BROWN, GENE, ed. *The New York Times Encyclopedia of Film.* 13 vols. New York: Times Books, 1984.

BRUYNINCKX, WALTER. *60 Years of Recorded Jazz, 1917–1977.* 25 vols. Mechelen, Belgium: W. Bruyninckx, 1978–80.

BUXTON, FRANK, and OWEN, BILL. *The Big Broadcast, 1920–1950.* New York: Viking, 1972.

CAHN, SAMMY. *I Should Care: The Sammy Cahn Story.* New York: Arbor House, 1974.

CALVET, CORINNE. *Has Corinne Been a Good Girl?* New York: St. Martin's Press, 1983.

CANNISTRARO, PHILIP V., ed. *Historical Dictionary of Fascist Italy.* Westport, Conn.: Greenwood Press, 1982.

CAREY, GARY. *Judy Holliday: An Intimate Life Story.* New York: Seaview, 1982.

CLARK, THOMAS L. *The Dictionary of Gambling & Gaming.* Cold Spring, N.Y.: Lexik House, 1987.

Cleveland City Directory. Cleveland: Cleveland Directory Co., 1909–10; 1920–21; 1925; 1928; 1931; 1936; 1937; 1940; 1941.

COHEN, MICKEY, as told to NUGENT, JOHN PEER. *Mickey Cohen: In My Own Words.* Englewood Cliffs, N.J.: Prentice-Hall, 1975. *Caveat lector.*

Columbus City Directory. R. L. Polk & Co., 1935; 1938.

CONDON, GEORGE E. *Cleveland: The Best Kept Secret.* Garden City, N.Y.: Doubleday, 1967.

———. *Yesterday's Cleveland.* Seemann's Historic Cities Series No. 30. Miami: E. A. Seemann, 1976.

———. *Yesterday's Columbus: A Pictorial History of Ohio's Capital.* Seemann's Historic Cities Series No. 31. Miami: E. A. Seemann, 1977.

COURSODON, JEAN-PIERRE, with SAUVAGE, PIERRE. *American Directors.* 2 vols. New York: McGraw-Hill, 1983.

CROSBY, BING, and MARTIN, PETE. *Call Me Lucky.* New York: Simon & Schuster, 1953.

CUPPER, DAN. *Pennsylvania Turnpike: A History.* Lebanon, Pa.: Applied Arts, 1990.

DAVIS, SAMMY, JR.: *Hollywood in a Suitcase.* New York: William Morrow, 1980.

DAVIS, SAMMY, JR.; BOYAR, JANE; and BOYAR, BURT. *Why Me?* New York: Farrar, Straus & Giroux, 1989.

———. *Yes I Can.* New York: Farrar, Straus & Giroux, 1965.

Dean Martin Tucson Open. Official Tournament Program. Tucson, 1975.

DEBENHAM, WARREN. *Laughter on Record: A Comedy Discography.* Metuchen, N.J.: Scarecrow Press, 1988.

DEMARIS, OVID. *The Boardwalk Jungle.* New York: Bantam, 1987.

———. *The Last Mafioso: The Treacherous World of Jimmy Fratianno.* New York: Bantam Books, 1981.

DICK, BERNARD F. *Billy Wilder.* Twayne's Theatrical Art Series. Boston: Twayne, 1980.

DICKSON, ANTONIA and W.K.L. *Edison's Invention of the Kineto-Phonograph.* Los Angeles: Pueblo Press, 1939.

DIXON, WHEELER W. *The "B" Directors: A Biographical Directory.* Metuchen, N.J.: Scarecrow Press, 1985.

DMYTRYK, EDWARD. *It's a Hell of a Life But Not a Bad Living.* New York: Times Books, 1978.

DOUGLAS, KIRK. *The Ragman's Son.* New York: Simon & Schuster, 1988.

DOYLE, JOSEPH B. *20th Century History of Steubenville and Jefferson County, Ohio, and Representative Citizens.* Chicago: Richmond-Arnold, 1910.

DUNNING, JOHN. *Tune in Yesterday: The Ultimate Encyclopedia of Old-Time Radio, 1925–1976.* Englewood Cliffs, N.J.: Prentice-Hall, 1976.

EAMES, JOHN DOUGLAS. *The Paramount Story.* New York: Crown, 1985.

EDMONDS, I. G., and REIKO, MIMURA. *Paramount Pictures and the People Who Made Them.* San Diego: A. S. Barnes, 1980.

EELLS, GEORGE. *Hedda and Louella.* New York: G. P. Putnam's Sons, 1972.

EINSTEIN, DANIEL. *Special Edition: A Guide to Network Television Documentary Series and Special News Reports, 1955–1979.* Metuchen, N.J.: Scarecrow Press, 1987.

EISENBERG, DENNIS; DAN, URI; and LANDAU, ELI. *Meyer Lansky: Mogul of the Mob.* New York & London: Paddington Press, 1979.

ELLIS, JACK C.; DERRY, CHARLES; and KERN, SHARON. *The Film Book Bibliography, 1940–1975.* Metuchen, N.J.: Scarecrow Press, 1979.

EWEN, DAVID. *American Popular Songs.* New York, Random House, 1966.

———. *American Songwriters.* An H. W. Wilson Biographical Dictionary. New York: H. W. Wilson, 1987.

FAITH, WILLIAM ROBERT. *Bob Hope: A Life in Comedy.* New York: G. P. Putnam's Sons, 1982.

FALLACI, ORIANA. *The Egotists: Sixteen Surprising Interviews.* Chicago: Regnery, 1968.

FAVARA, ALBERTO. *Canti della terra e del mare di Sicilia.* 4 vols. Milan: G. Ricordi, 1907–59.

FERRELL, ROBERT H. *The Twentieth Century: An Almanac.* New York: Bison, 1984.

FISHER, EDDIE. *Eddie: My Life, My Loves.* New York: Harper & Row, 1981.

FLEISCHER, NAT. *Nat Fleischer's Ring Record Book and Boxing Encyclopedia.* 1st ed. New York: Ring Book Shop, 1941.

FOERSTER, ROBERT F. *The Italian Emigration of Our Times.* Cambridge: Harvard University Press, 1919.

FREDERICKS, VIC. *Who's Who in Rock 'n Roll.* New York: Frederick Fell, 1958.

Friars Club Tribute to Dean Martin, September 13, 1984. New York: Friars Club, 1984.

FRIEDRICH, OTTO. *City of Nets: A Portrait of Hollywood in the 1940's.* New York: Harper & Row, 1986.

FRIEDWALD, WILL. *Jazz Singing: America's Great Voices from Bessie Smith to Bebop and Beyond.* New York: Scribners, 1990.

GABLER, NEAL. *An Empire of Their Own: How the Jews Invented Hollywood.* New York: Doubleday, 1988.

GAMBACCINI, PAUL; RICE, TIM; and RICE, JO. *British Hit Singles.* 6th ed. Enfield, Middlesex: Guinness Books, 1987.

GARDINER, HAROLD C., S.J. *Catholic Viewpoint on Censorship.* Garden City, N.Y.: Hanover House, 1958.

GART, GALEN. *ARLD: The American Record Label Directory and Dating Guide, 1940–1959.* Milford, N.H.: Big Nickel Publications, 1989.

GARTNER, LLOYD P. *History of the Jews of Cleveland.* 2nd ed. Cleveland: Western Reserve Historical Society and the Jewish Community Federation of Cleveland [Cranford, N.J.: Associated University Presses], 1987.

GEHMAN, RICHARD. *Sinatra and His Rat Pack.* New York: Belmont, 1961.

———. *That Kid–The Story of Jerry Lewis.* New York: Avon, 1964.

GELATT, ROLAND. *The Fabulous Phonograph: From Edison to Stereo.* Rev. ed. New York: Appleton-Century, 1965.

GIAMMARCO, ERNESTO. *Dizionario Abruzzese e Molisano.* 4 vols. Rome: Edizioni dell'Ateneo & Bizzarri, 1968–79.

GIANCANA, ANTOINETTE, and RENNER, THOMAS C. *Mafia Princess: Growing Up in Sam Giancana's Family.* New York: William Morrow, 1984.

GOSCH, MARTIN A., and HAMMER, RICHARD. *The Last Testament of Lucky Luciano.* Boston: Little, Brown, 1975.

GREEN, ABEL, and LAURIE, JOE, JR. *Show Biz from Vaude to Video.* New York: Henry Holt, 1951.

GREEN, STANLEY. *Encyclopedia of the Musical Film.* New York: Oxford University Press, 1981.

HALLIWELL, LESLIE. *Halliwell's Filmgoer's Companion.* 9th ed. London: Grafton, 1988.

HARRIS, STEVE. *Film, Television and Stage Music on Phonograph Records.* Jefferson, N.C.: McFarland & Co., 1988.

HERNDON, VENABLE. *James Dean: A Short Life.* Garden City, N.Y.: Doubleday, 1974.

HIGHAM, CHARLES. *Brando: The Unauthorized Biography.* New York: New American Library, 1987.

HIRSCH, PHIL. *Hollywood Uncensored: The Stars—Their Secrets and Their Scandals.* New York: Pyramid, 1965. *Caveat lector.*

HITCHCOCK, H. WILEY, and SADIE, STANLEY. *The New Grove Dictionary of American Music.* 4 vols. New York: Grove's Dictionaries of Music, 1986.

HOLTZMAN, WILL. *Judy Holliday.* New York: G. P. Putnam's Sons, 1982.

HORTON, ANDREW. *The Films of George Roy Hill.* New York: Columbia University Press, 1984.

JAQUES CATTELL PRESS, comp. *ASCAP Biographical Dictionary.* 4th ed. New York: R. R. Bowker, 1980.

JENNINGS, DEAN. *We Only Kill Each Other: The Life and Bad Times of Bugsy Siegel.* Englewood Cliffs, N.J.: Prentice-Hall, 1967.

JEPSEN, JORGEN GRUNNET. *Jazz Records, 1942–1965.* 11 vols. Holte, Denmark: K. E. Knudson, 1963–70.

JOSEFSBERG, MILT. *The Jack Benny Show.* New Rochelle: Arlington House, 1977.

RUST, BRIAN. *Jazz Records, 1897–1942.* 5th rev. ed. 2 vols. Chigwell, Essex: Storyville Publications, 1982.

———, and DEBUS, ALLEN G. *The Complete Entertainment Discography.* 2nd ed. New York: Da Capo, 1989.

St. Anthony's Troop 10 50th Anniversary. Steubenville, Ohio: Tri-State Publishing Co., 1977.

SCARNE, JOHN. *The Mafia Conspiracy.* North Bergen, N.J.: Scarne Enterprises, 1976.

———. *Scarne's Complete Guide to Gambling.* New York: Simon & Schuster, 1961.

SCHARF, WALTER, and FREEDLAND, MICHAEL. *Composed and Conducted by Walter Scharf.* London: Vallentine, Mitchell & Co., 1988.

SCHUSTER, MEL, comp. *Motion Picture Performers: A Bibliography of Magazine and Periodical Articles, 1900–1969.* Metuchen, N.J.: Scarecrow Press, 1971.

———. *Motion Picture Performers: A Bibliography of Magazine and Periodical Articles, Supplement No. 1, 1970–1974.* Metuchen, N.J.: Scarecrow Press, 1976.

SHAPIRO, NAT, ed. *Popular Music.* 6 vols. New York: Adrian Press, 1967–73.

———, and POLLACK, BRUCE. *Popular Music, 1920–1979.* 3 vols. Detroit: Gale Research, 1985.

SHIPMAN, DAVID. *The Great Movie Stars.* 2nd rev. ed. 2 vols. London: Macdonald, 1989.

SMITH, DENIS MACK. *Italy: A Modern History.* Ann Arbor: University of Michigan, 1959.

SMITH, RONALD L. *Comedy on Record: The Complete Critical Discography.* New York: Garland, 1988.

SNYDER, JIMMY, with HERSKOWITZ, MICKEY, and PERKINS, STEVE. *Jimmy the Greek by Himself.* Chicago: Playboy Press, 1975.

SOLMI, ANGELO, ed. *Enciclopedia della musica.* 6 vols. Milan: Rizzoli, 1972–74.

SPADA, JAMES. *Peter Lawford: The Man Who Kept the Secrets.* New York: Bantam, 1991.

SPOTTSWOOD, RICHARD K. *Ethnic Music on Records: A Discography of Ethnic Recordings Produced in the U.S., 1893 to 1942.* Vol. 1: Western Europe. Urbana and Chicago: University of Illinois Press, 1990.

STELLA, ANTONIO. *Some Aspects of Italian Immigration to the United States.* New York: G. P. Putnam's Sons, 1924.

Steubenville Area Chamber of Commerce. *Walking Tour of Downtown Historic Churches.* Steubenville, Ohio: Chamber of Commerce, [n.d., c. 1983].

Steubenville Chamber of Commerce. *City of Steubenville.* Map. Steubenville, 1976.

KATZ, EPHRAIM. *The Film Encyclopedia.* New York: Crowell, 1979.

KATZ, LEONARD. *Uncle Frank: The Biography of Frank Costello.* New York: Drake, 1973.

KELLEY, KITTY. *His Way: The Unauthorized Biography of Frank Sinatra.* New York: Bantam, 1987. *Caveat lector.*

KELLY, ALAN. *His Master's Voice/La Voce del Padrone.* Westport, Conn.: Greenwood Press, 1988.

KERNFELD, BARRY, ed. *The New Grove Dictionary of Jazz.* 2 vols. New York: Grove's Dictionaries of Music, 1988.

KINKLE, ROGER D. *The Complete Encyclopedia of Popular Music and Jazz, 1900–1950.* 4 vols. New Rochelle, N.Y.: Arlington House, 1974.

KLENO, LARRY. *Kim Novak on Camera.* San Diego: A. S. Barnes, 1980.

LaGUARDIA, ROBERT. *Monty: A Biography of Montgomery Clift.* New York: Harcourt Brace Jovanovich, 1978.

———, and ARCERI, GENE. *Red: The Tempestuous Life of Susan Hayward.* New York: Macmillan, 1985.

LANGMAN, LARRY. *A Guide to American Film Directors.* 2 vols. Metuchen, N.J.: Scarecrow Press, 1981.

LAWFORD, PATRICIA SEATON. *The Peter Lawford Story.* New York: Carroll & Graf, 1988.

LAWRENCE, THOMAS B. *The MGM Years.* New Rochelle, N.Y.: Columbia House, 1972.

LAX, ROGER, and SMITH, FREDERICK. *The Great Song Thesaurus.* 2nd ed. New York: Oxford University Press, 1989.

LEIGH, JANET. *There Really Was a Hollywood.* New York: Doubleday, 1984.

LEVENSTEIN, AARON. *Testimony for Man: The Story of the City of Hope.* Los Angeles: City of Hope, 1968.

LEWIS, JERRY, with GLUCK, HERB. *Jerry Lewis in Person.* New York: Atheneum, 1982.

LIMBACHER, JAMES L. *Film Music: From Violins to Video.* Metuchen, N.J.: Scarecrow Press, 1974.

Long Beach Directory. Long Beach, Cal., 1945; 1948; 1951–52; 1953.

LONSTEIN, ALBERT I., and MARINO, VITO R. *The Revised Compleat Sinatra.* New York: Musicprint Corp., 1979.

Los Angeles City Directory. Los Angeles, Cal., 1948.

LUPINETTI, DONATANGELO. *Canto popolare abruzzese.* Pescara: Centro Studi Abruzessi, 1973.

LYNCH, RICHARD CHIGLEY. *Movie Musicals on Record.* Westport, Conn.: Greenwood Press, 1989.

Lynn Farnol Group, Inc., ed. *ASCAP Biographical Dictionary.* New York: American Society of Composers, Authors and Publishers, 1966.

MACCANN, RICHARD DYER. *The First Tycoons*. Metuchen, N.J.: Scarecrow Press, 1987.

MALTIN, LEONARD, ed. *Leonard Maltin's TV Movies and Video Guide*. 1990 ed. New York: New American Library, Signet, 1989.

———. *Movie Comedy Teams*. Rev. ed. New York: Plume, 1985.

MAMMARELLA, LUIGI. *La vita quotidiana in Abruzzo alla fine del Secolo XIX*. I Tascabili d'Abruzzo, 15. Cerchio, Aquila: Adelmo Polla, 1986.

MARTIN, PETE. *Pete Martin Calls On . . .* New York: Simon & Schuster, 1962.

MARX, ARTHUR. *Everybody Loves Somebody Sometime (Especially Himself)*. New York: Hawthorn, 1974. *Caveat lector.*

MARX, KENNETH S. *Star Stats: Who's Who in Hollywood*. Los Angeles: Price/Stern/Sloan, 1979.

MARZO, EDUARDO. *Songs of the People: Neapolitan Songs*. New York: G. Schirmer, 1905.

MASON, WILEY, and BONA, DAMIEN. *Inside Oscar: The Unofficial History of the Academy Awards*. New York: Ballantine, 1987.

MATTFELD, JULIUS, comp. *"Variety" Music Cavalcade, 1620–1950*. New York: Prentice-Hall, 1952.

MAY, EARL CHAPIN. *Principio to Wheeling, 1715–1945: A Pageant of Iron and Steel*. New York: Harper & Brothers, 1945.

MCBRIDE, JOSEPH. *Hawks on Hawks*. Berkeley: University of California Press, 1982.

MCNEIL, ALEX. *Total Television: A Comprehensive Guide to Programming from 1948 to the Present*. 2nd ed. New York: Viking Penguin, 1984.

MESSICK, HANK. *The Beauties & the Beasts: The Mob in Show Business*. New York: David McKay, 1973. *Caveat lector.*

———. *Lansky*. New York: Putnam, 1971.

———. *The Silent Syndicate*. New York: Macmillan, 1967.

MILLER, LEO O. *The Great Cowboy Stars of Movies & Television*. New Rochelle, N.Y.: Arlington House, 1979.

Milton Berle: Mr. Television. New York: Museum of Broadcasting, 1985.

MIX, PAUL E. *The Life and Legend of Tom Mix*. New York: A. S. Barnes, 1972.

MORELLA, JOE, and EPSTEIN, EDWARD Z. *Lana*. New York: Citadel, 1971.

MORISON, SAMUEL ELIOT. *The Oxford History of the American People*. New York: Oxford University Press, 1965. Source references are to the paperback edition: 3 vols. New York: New American Library, Mentor, 1972.

MORITZ, CHARLES, ed. *Current Biography Yearbook 1964*. New York: H. W. Wilson, 1965.

MULHOLLAND, JIM. *The Abbott and Costello Book*. Popular Library Film Series. New York, Popular Library, 1977.

NELLI, HUMBERT S. *From Immigrants to Ethnics: The Italian Americans*. N York: Oxford University Press, 1983.

NIVER, KEMP R. *Early Motion Pictures: The Paper Print Collection in t Library of Congress*. Washington, D.C.: Motion Picture, Broadcasting, a Recorded Sound Division, Library of Congress, 1985.

NOLAN, WILLIAM F. *Sinners and Supermen*. North Hollywood: All Star Book 1965.

NYGAARD, NORMAN E. *Twelve Against the Underworld*. New York: Hobson Bo Press, 1947.

PARISH, JAMES ROBERT. *Actors' Television Credits, 1950–1972*. Metuchen, N. Scarecrow Press, 1973.

———, with TROST, MARK. *Actors' Television Credits: Supplement I*. Metuche N.J.: Scarecrow Press, 1978.

———, and TERRACE, VINCENT. *Actors' Television Credits: Supplement I 1982–1985*. Metuchen, N.J.: Scarecrow Press, 1986.

PETERSON, VIRGIL W. *The Mob*. Ottawa, Ill.: Green Hill, 1983.

PITTS, MICHAEL R., and HARRISON, LOUIS H. *Hollywood on Record: The Fil Stars' Discography*. Metuchen, N.J.: Scarecrow Press, 1978.

PLEASANTS, HARRY. *The Great American Popular Singers*. London: Gollanc 1974; New York: Simon & Schuster, 1985.

PRALL, ROBERT H., and MOCKRIDGE, NORTON. *This Is Costello on the Spo* Greenwich, Conn.: Fawcett, 1951.

RAPPLEYE, CHARLES, and BECKER, ED. *All American Mafioso: The Johnny Ros selli Story*. New York: Doubleday, 1991.

RAYMOND, JACK. *Show Music on Record*. New York: Frederick Ungar, 1982.

REID, ED, and DEMARIS, OVID. *The Green Felt Jungle*. New York: Trident Press 1963.

RICE, TIM; RICE, JO; GAMBACCINI, PAUL; and READ, MIKE. *Guinness British Hi Albums*. 2nd ed. Enfield, Middlesex: Guinness Books, 1986.

RICHARDS, DICK. *A Gospel Fan Letter to Dean Martin*. New York; World Mis sion to Religions, n.d.

RINGGOLD, GENE, and MCCARTY, CLIFFORD. *The Films of Frank Sinatra*. Se caucus, N.J.: Lyle Stuart, Citadel Press, 1973.

RIPLEY, R., ed. *Everlast Boxing Record Book*. New York: Everlast, 1923.

ROBBINS, EDWARD. *Neapolitan Songs Everyone Loves*. New York: Bibo, Bloede & Lang, 1927.

Robbins Collection of Neapolitan Songs. New York: Robbins Music Corp. 1953.

ROUSE, SARAH, and LOUGHNEY, KATHERINE, comps. *Three Decades of Television A Catalog of Television Programs Acquired by the Library of Congress, 1949–1979*. Washington, D.C.: Library of Congress, 1989.

————. *Steubenville, Ohio.* Map. Steubenville: H. C. Cook, 1946.

Steubenville City Directory. Biennial vols. Akron, Ohio: Burch Directory Co., 1902–44. [Vols. 4–6 (1902–6), 9–14 (1912–24), 17–21 (1930–38), 23–24 (1942–44): Schiappa Library, Steubenville; Vols. 5–9 (1904–10), 15–18 (1926–34): New York Public Library; Vol. 22 (1940): Jefferson County Historical Association.]

Steubenville, Ohio. Map. Steubenville: H. C. Cook, 1938.

————. Steubenville [?], Ohio: Compton Engraving & Printing Co., 1937.

SUMMERS, ANTHONY. *Goddess: The Secret Lives of Marilyn Monroe.* New York: New American Library, Onyx Books, 1986.

TAYLOR, JANE RUSSELL, and JACKSON, ARTHUR. *The Hollywood Musical.* New York: McGraw-Hill, 1971.

TAYLOR, THEODORE. *Jule: The Story of Composer Jule Styne.* New York: Random House, 1979.

TERESA, VINCENT, with RENNER, THOMAS C. *My Life in the Mafia.* Garden City, N.Y.: Doubleday, 1973. *Caveat lector.*

TERRACE, VINCENT. *Encyclopedia of Television Series, Pilots and Specials, 1937–1984.* 3 vols. New York: New York Zeotrope, 1985–86.

————. *Radio's Golden Years: The Encyclopedia of Radio Programs, 1930–1960.* San Diego: A. S. Barnes, 1981.

THOMAS, BOB. *Bud and Lou.* New York: J. B. Lippincott, 1977.

TURNER, LANA. *Lana.* New York: E. P. Dutton, 1982.

TURNER, WALLACE. *Gamblers' Money: The New Force in American Life.* Boston: Houghton Mifflin, 1965.

UEBERHORST, HORST. *Friedrich Wilhelm von Steuben.* Munich: Heinz Moos, 1981.

U. S. Copyright Office, Library of Congress. *Catalogue of Copyright Entries: Musical Compositions.* Washington: Government Printing Office, 1900–46.

————. *Catalogue of Copyright Entries: Music,* 1947–77.

————. *Catalogue of Copyright Entries: Performing Arts.* Washington: Government Printing Office, 1978.

————. *Motion Pictures, 1940–1949.* Washington: Government Printing Office, 1953.

————. *Motion Pictures, 1950–1959.* Washington: Government Printing Office, 1960.

————. *Motion Pictures, 1960–1969.* Washington: Government Printing Office, 1971.

"Variety" Radio Directory, 1937–1938. New York: Variety, Inc., 1937.

VENCI, ANTONIO. *La canzone napolitana nel tempo, nella letteratura, nell'arte.* Naples: Alfredo Guida, 1955.

WALKER, STANLEY. *The Night Club Era.* New York: Frederick A. Stokes, 1933.

WALLIS, HAL, and HIGHAM, CHARLES. *Starmaker.* New York: Macmillan, 1980.

Wheeling Steel Corporation. *Annual Report of the Wheeling Steel Corporation, Wheeling, W. Va., for the Year Ended December 31, 1920.* Wheeling, W. Va.: Wheeling Steel Corporation, 1921.

WHITBURN, JOEL. *The "Billboard" Book of Top 40 Albums.* New York: Billboard Publications, 1987.

———. *Bubbling Under the Hot 100, 1959–1981.* Menomonee Falls, Wis.: Record Research, 1982.

———. *Pop Memories, 1890–1954.* Menomonee Falls, Wis.: Record Research, 1986. This book should be approached with special care, as most of the "hits" listed in it reflect no historical chart positions.

———. *Top Country Singles, 1944–1988.* Menomonee Falls, Wis.: Record Research, 1989.

———. *Top Easy Listening Records, 1961–1974.* Menomonee Falls, Wis.: Record Research, 1975.

———. *Top LP's, 1945–1972.* Menomonee Falls, Wis.: Record Research, 1973.

———. *Top Pop Albums, 1955–1986.* Menomonee Falls, Wis.: Record Research, 1985.

———. *Top Pop Singles, 1955–1986.* Menomonee Falls, Wis.: Record Research, 1987.

———. *Top R&B Singles, 1942–1988.* Menomonee Falls, Wis.: Record Research, 1988.

Who's Who in Radio. New York: Radio Publications Co., 1935.

WILDE, LARRY. *The Great Comedians Talk about Comedy.* New York: Citadel, 1968.

WILLIAMS, JOHN R. *This Was "Your Hit Parade."* Camden, Me.: J. R. Williams, 1973.

WILSON, EARL. *The Show Business Nobody Knows.* Chicago: Cowles, 1971.

WOOD, TOM. *The Bright Side of Billy Wilder, Primarily.* Garden City, N.Y.: Doubleday, 1970.

WRIGHT, HARRIET. *The History of the Copacabana.* New York: World Famous Copa Girls, Inc., 1984.

Writers Program of the Works Projects Administration. *The Ohio Guide.* New York: Oxford University Press, 1940.

YABLONSKY, LEWIS. *George Raft.* San Francisco: Mercury House, 1989.

ZUKOR, ADOLPH, with KRAMER, DALE. *The Public Is Never Wrong.* New York: G. P. Putnam's Sons, 1953.

Articles, Etc.

ABEL [ABEL GREEN]. "Night Club Reviews" (Copacabana, N.Y.). *Variety,* 14 April 1948.

————. "Night Club Reviews" (Slapsy Maxie's, L.A.). *Variety,* 22 September 1948.

————. Review of *The Young Lions. Variety,* 19 March 1958.

"Academy Awards Telecast Great Show: Jerry Lewis Turns in Outstanding Performance." *Hollywood Reporter,* 22 March 1956, p. 4.

ACE, GOODMAN. "TV and Radio: Adult Delinquents." *Saturday Review,* 3 September 1955, p. 21.

"Actor Becoming Large Ventura Landowner." *Los Angeles Times,* 8 March 1967, p. 22.

"Actual Ownership of Night Clubs Is Goal of Investigation by City." *New York Times,* 8 September 1944, p. 26.

ADAIR, LINCOLN. "Movie-of-the-Month: *The Young Lions* at the Paramount Theatre." *What's Cookin' in New York,* 1958, p. 10.

ADAMS, VAL. "2 Guest Singers off Crosby Show: Sinatra and Martin Canceled from C.B.S. Program." *New York Times,* October 1963.

————. "Sinatra to Join 2d Crosby Show." *New York Times,* 20 October 1963.

ADELSON, SUZANNE. "Couples: Move Over, Charles and Di—Dorothy Hamill and Dean Paul Martin Plot a Royal Wedding L.A.-Style." *People,* 11 January 1982, p. 64.

ADIL. "Night Club Reviews" (King Edward, Toronto [Gail Martin]). *Variety,* 8 June 1966, p. 53.

Advertisement: Ernie McKay's " 'Band of Romance' starring Dino Martini." *Columbus Evening Dispatch,* 14 December 1939, p. 14-B.*

Advertisement: Sammy Watkins and His Orchestra with Dean Martin. *Cleveland Plain Dealer,* 2 February 1941, p. 11-B. [Also all subsequent advertisements for the Vogue Room, Hotel Hollenden, published in the *Plain Dealer* through 3 October 1943.]

Advertisement: Martin ("The Newest Fashion in Song Style") at the Riobamba, N.Y. *New York Sunday Mirror,* 26 September 1943, p. 33.

Advertisement: Martin at the Riobamba ("sings and looks like Sinatra—only healthier"—Lee Mortimer, *Mirror). New York Daily Mirror,* 3 October 1943, p. 37.

Advertisement: Martin "Held over by our demand" at the Riobamba. *New York Daily Mirror,* 31 October 1943.

Advertisement: Martin at the Riobamba. *Billboard,* 11 December 1943, p. 19.

Advertisement: Martin at the Statler Hotel, Buffalo. *Billboard,* 15 January 1944.

Advertisement: "Introducing the Dean of the 'Voices,' La Martinique." *Billboard,* 10 June 1944, p. 23.

Advertisement: "America's Newest Singing Sensation." *Billboard 1944 Music Year Book,* October 1944, p. 245.

* Advertisement entries are listed chronologically.

Advertisement: Martin and Lewis at the 500 Cafe. *Atlantic City Press,* 25 July 1946, p. 7.

Advertisement: "The Country's Newest Singing Sensation—Exclusive on Diamond [Records]!" *Billboard,* 31 August 1946, p. 24.

Advertisement: Martin & Lewis at the Havana-Madrid ("New York's Greatest Laugh Show"). *New York Daily Mirror,* 19 September 1946, p. 23.

Advertisement: Martin's opening at the New Chanticleer, Baltimore, August 9, 1949. Unidentified publication, August 1949.

Advertisement: Martin & Lewis, "The Colgate Comedy Hour." *TV Guide,* 19 September 1952, p. 19.

Advertisement: Macy's (Father's Day)/"Colgate Comedy Hour." *New York Times,* 31 May 1953.

Advertisement: Macy's (Catalina Swimsuits)/*Pardners. New York Times,* 8 July 1956.

Advertisement: American Airlines (DC-7 Nonstop Mercury from Los Angeles [leaves New York 10 A.M. E.D.T., arrives Los Angeles 3:30 P.M. P.D.T.]). *New York Times,* 10 July 1956.

Advertisement: Martin & Lewis, Copacabana. *New York Daily Mirror,* 16 July 1956.

Advertisement: "The Dean Martin Show" (5 October 1957). *TV Guide,* 5 October 1957, p. A-15.

Advertisement: Rheingold beer (" 'Better than a hole in one!' says DEAN MARTIN"). *Cue for Passion,* 24 November 1958.

Advertisement: "Former Dean Martin Estate," Sotheby's International Realty, *Daily Variety,* 19 September 1986.

"After I'm Gone I Hope They Say: 'Dean Martin? He Was a Good Guy!' " *New York Enquirer,* 20 August 1956.

"AGVA Orders M&L Pay Greshler 10 G or Not Work Vaude." *Daily Variety,* 15 February 1951, p. 1.

"AGVA Wants Martin & Lewis in N.Y. to Gab on Their Powder of Copa." *Variety,* 14 May 1952, p. 55.

"Alleging 'Bad Faith' by Dean Martin, 20th Sues for Damages; MCA 'Shocked.' " *Variety,* 20 June 1962, p. 3.

"All That Glamour and a Hug from the Boss, Too." *TV Guide,* 18 April 1970, p. 15.

AMORY, CLEVELAND. "Review" ("The Dean Martin Show"). *TV Guide,* 9 April 1966, p. 26.

ANBY. Review of *What a Way to Go! Variety,* 1 April 1964.

ANDREWS, PHILLIP. "Exclusive! Dean Martin to Adopt Cathy Hawn's Child?" *Photoplay,* December 1971, p. 83.

ANDREWS, ROBERT. "The Dean Martins: We're Having a Wonderful Divorce . . . with a Little Help from Our Friends." *Photoplay,* April 1971, p. 50.

ANGELI, MICHAEL. "God's Biggest Goof." *Esquire,* February 1991, p. 98.

"Another Variety Show: It's Good" ("The Dean Martin Show," 16, 23, 30 September 1965.) *New York Herald Tribune,* 1 October 1965.

ARCHERD, ARMY. "Chartered Train Tour for Sinatra, Martin." *Variety,* 26 June 1974, p. 62.

ARDMORE, JANE. "Pop, Where Are You?" *Photoplay,* December 1967, p. 32.

ARMSTRONG, GEORGE. "Time to Part?" *Photoplay,* May 1953, p. 31.

ARNOLD, MAXINE. "Are Martin and Lewis Breaking Up?" *Photoplay,* July 1954, p. 50.

———. "Are They Heading for the Big Split-up?" *Photoplay,* September 1955, p. 31.

———. "The More the Merrier." *Photoplay,* January 1954, p. 38.

Associated Press. "Actor Martin, Wife Reunited." *New York Daily News,* 20 March 1953.

———. "Actor's Son Is Missing as Fighter Goes Down." *New York Times,* 24 March 1987, p. 24.

———. "Air Controller Blamed in Dino's Crash Death." *New York Post,* 10 May 1988.

———. "Bing Crosby, 73, Dies in Madrid at Golf Course." *New York Times,* 15 October 1977, p. 1.

———. "Bob Hope Joins Inaugural Gala." *New York Times,* 31 December 1980, p. C-13.

———. "Casino Officials Probing Sinatra Blackjack Flap." *New York Daily News,* 14 December 1983, p. 4.

———. "Dean Martin Arrested." *New York Daily News,* 10 May 1982.

———. "Dean Martin Buys into Nevada Hotel." *New York Journal-American,* 20 July 1961.

———. "Dean Martin Has Surgery." *New York Times,* 16 June 1960.

———. "Dean Martin in Custody Suit." *New York Journal-American,* 19 November 1957.

———. "Dean Martin Quits Movie over Monroe Dismissal." *New York Times,* 10 June 1962, p. 56.

———. "Dean Martin Quits over MM Firing." *New York Daily Mirror,* 10 June 1962, p. 4.

———. "Dean Martins Have Daughter." *New York Times,* 21 December 1956, p. 19.

———. "Dean Martin's Son Dead in Jet." *New York Times,* 26 March 1987, p. D-18.

———. "Dean Martin Sued by Agent." *New York Herald Tribune,* 14 July 1950.

———. "Dean Martin Sues Cafe Partners." *New York Post,* 29 August 1961.

———. "Dean Martin Tells of Losing Bets." *New York Post,* 5 January 1967.

————. "Dean Martin under Knife." *New York Daily News,* 5 January 1964.

————. "Dean Martin Willing to Do Canceled Film." *New York Post,* 18 June 1962.

————. "Dean Wasn't Loaded but He Had Gun That Was: DA Aide." *New York Daily News,* 3 June 1982.

————. "Effort Is Disclosed to Rescue Jet Flown by Dean Martin Jr." *New York Times,* 12 June 1987, p. B-8.

————. "Jerry, Dean Make Up." *New York Daily News,* 14 March 1960.

————. "Martin Countersues Studio in Rift on Monroe Ouster." *New York Times,* 26 June 1962, p. 25.

————. "Martin, Lewis at Odds." *New York Times,* 19 June 1956, p. 25.

————. "Mrs. Dean Martin Has 2nd Child." *New York Times,* 22 September 1953.

————. "Pop Sinatra Pops Up at Casino." *New York Daily News,* 16 December 1963, p. 3.

————. "Sinatra Drops Casino Shows, Citing Insult by a Jersey Aide." *New York Times,* 2 September 1984, p. 54.

————. "Sinatra Is Accused of Hosting Mobster; D'Amato Under Fire." *Atlantic City Press,* 12 September 1963, p. 1.

————. "Stabile to Wed Today: Grace Barrie Will Be Bride of Orchestra Leader." *New York Herald Tribune,* 27 December 1937.

————. "They Call Sellers Rat Fink." *New York Daily News,* 19 June 1964.

BACON, JAMES. "Dean Martin Is in His Toughest Test: Screen Role with Nary a Drink." *Louisville Courier-Journal,* 5 March 1961.

BAER, ATRA. "Martin and Lewis End Feud After Meeting on Golf Links." *New York Journal-American,* 18 February 1958.

————. "Stars Boost Martin Telethon" ("Parade of Stars," 24–25 May 1958). *New York Journal-American,* 26 May 1958.

BAILEY, CORINNE. "Mayhem, Unlimited." *Photoplay,* October 1953, p. 46.

"Band Leader Sues Singer for $32,590." *Cleveland Plain Dealer,* 1 July 1950.

"Band Profiles." *Billboard 1944 Music Year Book,* October 1944.

BARK. "If Bigtime Vaude Is Really Dead, How Come M&L Kill 'Em in Tex.?" (Texas State Fair, Dallas, 4–10 October 1952). *Variety,* 8 November 1952.

Barbers' Journal. Various issues, 1920–21.

BARSTOW, JAMES S., JR. "Evolution of Martin & Lewis, Comedians." *New York Herald Tribune,* 7 August 1949.

BART, PETER. "Sinatra Involved in Brawl in Bar." *New York Times,* 11 June 1966.

BASCOMBE, LAURA. "The Dean Martin Marriage—'I Bore the Hell out of My Husband.' " *Photoplay,* February 1969, p. 68.

BAXT. "Night Club Reviews" (Chez Paree, Chicago). *Variety,* 10 December 1947.

BECKER, BILL. "Prospectors Discover That There's Golf in Beverly Hills." *New York Times*, 2 July 1967, p. V-7.

BECKER, WILLIAM. *The Cleveland Press* Collection, Cleveland State University Archives, Cleveland, Ohio. Letter. 24 October 1989.

BECKLEY, PAUL V. "Movie Review" *(Career)*. *New York Herald Tribune*, 9 October 1959.

BELLAMY, JEANNE. "250,000 (Plus) Thrilled at Salute to New Year." *Miami Herald*, 1 January 1949, p. 1.

BENNETT, BILL. "Capitol Research." *Record Research*, July 1981; October 1981; December 1981; March/April 1982; July 1982; October 1982; June 1987; October 1987; February 1988; June 1988; November 1988; April 1989; September/October 1989.

BERGMAN, RUDY. "M&L Return to NBC, Apart." *New York Daily News*, 21 November 1956.

BERONIUS, GEORGE. "Weary Dino Faces Career Test." *Los Angeles Times*, 22 June 1958, p. 1.

BIER. "Television Reviews" ("Dom DeLuise and Friends, Part 4," 17 May 1986). *Variety*, 11 June 1986.

"Biggest Tippers: Frank & Dean." *New York Post*, 30 April 1980, p. 6.

" 'Big Top' Tuners Set." *Hollywood Reporter*, 19 March 1954, p. 3.

BILL. "Television Reviews" ("The Dean Martin Show"). *Variety*, 22 September 1971, p. 27.

"Bill Miller Sells Riverside, Reno in $5-Mil. Deal." *Variety*, 20 June 1962.

"Birthday Gift." Photograph and legend (Associated Press): Claudia Martin and Lord Timothy Hudson to wed. *New York Post*, 10 February 1966.

BLOSSER, JOHN, and REGAN, JUDITH. "Dean Martin's Wild Childhood." *National Enquirer*, 7 May 1985, p. 24.

BOK. "Television Reviews" ("All-Star Party for 'Dutch' Reagan," 8 December 1985). *Variety*, 25 December 1985.

———. "Television Reviews" ("Dean Martin Celebrity Roast," 23 February 1984). *Variety*, 29 February 1984, p. 82.

———. "Television Reviews" ("Dean Martin's Christmas at Sea World," 10 December 1981). *Variety*, 16 December 1981, p. 4.

———. "Television Reviews" ("Dean's Place," 6 September 1975). *Variety*, 10 September 1975, p. 62.

———. "Television Reviews" ("Dom DeLuise and Friends," *Part 2*, 23 February 1984). *Variety*, 29 February 1984.

———. "Television Reviews" ("Half Nelson," 24 April 1985). *Variety*, 3 April 1985.

BOYAR, BURT. "Beau Broadway" [column]. Unidentified clipping, April 1957.

BRAL. "House Reviews" (Dick Stabile: State, N.Y.). *Variety*, 16 September 1936.

Brenna, Tony. "Crippled Midget with Muscular Dystrophy Charges . . . Jerry Lewis Roughed Me Up and Threatened to Kill Me!" *National Enquirer,* 10 July 1990, p. 17.

"Bridal Sweet." *New York Sunday News,* 8 September 1968, p. 4.

"Brightspot" [column]. *New York Daily Mirror,* 30 June 1944, p. 24.

"Brit. Press Boo as Big 'Boo-Boo' for M&L Abroad." *Variety,* July 1953, p. 1.

"Brit. Scribe's 'Dry Your Tears, M&L'; Scot Sends 'Em Dollar for Drink." *Variety,* 5 August 1953, p. 2.

Brog. Review of *Artists and Models,* 9 November 1955.

———. Review of *At War with the Army. Variety,* 13 December 1950.

———. Review of *The Caddy. Variety,* 5 August 1953.

———. Review of *Hollywood or Bust. Variety,* 5 December 1956.

———. Review of *Jumping Jacks. Variety,* 4 June 1952.

———. Review of *Living It Up. Variety,* 5 May 1954.

———. Review of *Money from Home. Variety,* 2 December 1953.

———. Review of *My Friend Irma. Variety,* 17 August 1949.

———. Review of *My Friend Irma Goes West. Variety,* 31 May 1950.

———. Review of *Pardners. Variety,* 27 June 1956.

———. Review of *Road to Bali. Variety,* 19 November 1952.

———. Review of *Sailor Beware. Variety,* 5 December 1951.

———. Review of *Scared Stiff. Variety,* 15 April 1953.

———. Review of *The Stooge. Variety,* 8 October 1952.

———. Review of *Ten Thousand Bedrooms,* 20 February 1957.

———. Review of *That's My Boy. Variety,* 13 June 1951.

Buchwald, Art. "Europe's Lighter Side: 'Gargoyle, My Foot,' Say Martin, Lewis." *New York Herald Tribune,* 19 July 1953, p. II-5.

Burke, Nat. "Off Booze, On Blondes." *Photoplay,* July 1970, p. 50.

Burke, Wally. "Dean's Son Escapes Jail!" *Photoplay,* September 1974, p. 38.

Burns, Jimmy. "60,000 to See Georgia, Texas Gridiron Classic." *Miami Herald,* 1 January 1949, p. 1.

———. "250,000 Thrilled by Jamboree Parade." *Miami Herald,* 1 January 1948, p. 1.

Butler, Dale, and Osborne, Jerry. "Dean Martin: The Crooning Croupier." *DISCoveries,* August 1989, p. 132.

"Byrds, Dean Martin, Hendrix Nab Goldisks." *Variety,* 27 March 1968.

Cameron, Kate. "Film of Jones Novel on Music Hall Screen" *(Some Came Running). New York Daily News,* 23 June 1959.

———. "Martin and Lewis Cavort at the Mayfair" *(Pardners). New York Daily News,* 26 July 1956.

———. "Martin & Lewis Team Take Over Criterion" *(You're Never Too Young). New York Daily News,* 26 August 1955.

————. "Martin, Lewis at Mayfair in Laugh Maker" *(Sailor Beware). New York Daily News*, 1 February 1952.

————. "Martin, Lewis in a New One at Paramount" *(Jumping Jacks). New York Daily News*, 24 July 1952.

————. "Martin Minus Lewis in New Musical Film" *(Ten Thousand Bedrooms). New York Daily News*, 4 April 1957.

Capitol News [Capitol Records, Hollywood]. All issues, November 1948 through January 1952.

Capitol Record Catalogues: *Capitol Records* (1946–47); *New Capitol Records* (1946–47); *Capitol Records Numerical Catalog* (1947); the weekly *New Records* and *New Releases* sheets (1951–58); the *Capitol's "400"* LP catalogue (1960).

CARROLL, KATHLEEN. "Dean Plays It Boozy and Breezy" *(Murderers' Row). New York Daily News*, 22 December 1966.

————. "Innocuous Sex Farce Opens at Music Hall" *(How to Save a Marriage and Ruin Your Life). New York Daily News*, 19 January 1968.

————. " 'Sons of Katie Elder' Really Good Western." *New York Daily News*, 26 August 1965.

CART. Review of *The Cannonball Run. Variety*, 24 June 1981.

CHAN. "Television Reviews" ("Martin & Lewis Thanksgiving Party," 25 November 1953). *Variety*, 2 December 1953.

"Ciro's in H'wood, Dark Since Dec., Sold for 286G." *Variety*, 6 August 1958.

"Cleaned-up Look for Dino in Sept. Detailed in Memo from Garrison." *Variety*, 14 June 1972, p. 31.

CLEMENT, HAL. "Dean Martin-Jerry Lewis: Reconciliation in the Making?" *Top Secret*, January 1963, p. 20.

CLEMENT, HAROLD A. "Dean and Jerry (Nearly) Broke the Bank at Las Vegas!" *Top Secret*, April 1956, p. 11.

"Co-Boss of 500 Club Looks with Regret at Lack of Conventions." *Atlantic City Press*, 5 August 1962, p. 6.

COHEN. "House Reviews" (Dick Stabile: Stanley, Pittsburgh). *Variety*, 22 September 1937.

————. "Night Club Reviews" (Dick Stabile: Italian Terrace, Pittsburgh). *Variety*, 20 October 1937.

————. "Night Club Reviews" (Twin Coaches, Pittsburgh). *Variety*, 12 June 1957, p. 73.

————. "Radio Reviews" (Dick Stabile: WCAE, Pittsburgh). *Variety*, 21 April 1937.

COHEN, JOE. "Friars' Bash for Dean Martin Pulls a Huge Turnout." *Variety*, 19 September 1984, p. 2.

COHN, LAWRENCE, comp. "All-Time Film Rental Champs." *Variety*, 6 May 1991, p. 82.

"Col. E. R. Bradley, Turf Leader, Dies." *New York Times,* 16 August 1946, p. 21.

Columbus & Ohio Division, Public Library of Columbus and Franklin County, Columbus Ohio. Letter. June 1989.

"Comedy Team of Martin and Lewis Keeps Ticket Booths at Paramount Plenty Busy." *New York Times,* 6 July 1951, p. 14.

"Common Interest in Philanthropic Venture Maintains Ex-RKO Officers Stolkin, Koolish Tie with Hollywood." *Wall Street Journal,* 28 October 1952, p. 12.

"Concealed Gun Rap: Follows Traffic Nab of Dean Martin on Coast." *Variety,* 9 June 1982, p. 4.

CONDON, MAURICE. "They Remember Dino." *TV Guide,* 18 September 1965, p. 8.

COOK, ALTON. "Martin and Lewis Sure-Fire in West" *(Pardners). New York World Telegram,* 26 July 1956, p. 22.

COOK, ARTHUR. Unidentified *Cleveland Press* clipping, 9 December 1929, *Cleveland Press* Collection, Cleveland State University Archives.

"Copacabana, City Reach Compromise." *New York Times,* 1 October 1944, p. 40.

"Copacabana Faces Trial for License." *New York Times,* 1 September 1944, p. 15.

"Costello's 100G Suit vs. Dean Martin Spurs AGVA to Probe Mgt. Pacts." *Variety,* 30 November 1949, p. 2.

"Cover Feature." *Billboard,* 15 January 1944.

CRIST, JUDITH. "Bond Leads Dino Down a Dirty Alley" *(The Silencers). New York Herald Tribune,* 27 March 1966, *New York* magazine section, p. 27.

CROSBY, JOHN. "Radio in Review" ("The Martin & Lewis Show," 3, 10, 17, 24 April 1949). *New York Herald Tribune,* 2 May 1949.

"Crowd Waits Two Hours for Frankie, Dino." *Atlantic City Press,* 24 August 1962, p. 22.

CROWTHER, BOSLEY. "Screen: Frustrations in Young Actor's 'Career' " *(Career). New York Times,* 9 October 1959, p. 24.

———. "The Screen in Review: Jerry Lewis, New Comedian, a Bright Spot in Silly Film 'My Friend Irma.' " *New York Times,* 29 September 1949, p. 39.

———. "The Screen in Review: Dean Martin and Jerry Lewis Seen in 'Sailor Beware' at the Mayfair Theatre." *New York Times,* 1 February 1952.

———. "Screen: Solo by Martin" *(Ten Thousand Bedrooms). New York Times,* 4 April 1957.

CURT. "Dean Martin in Paris Moulin Rouge Debut at Fund-Raising Gala." *Variety,* 11 July 1984, p. 2.

CYCLOPS. "The Witless Reign of King Leer" ("The Dean Martin Show"). *Life,* 7 April 1972.

DAKU. "Television Reviews" ("Las Vegas: An All-Star 75th Anniversary," 16 February 1983). *Variety*, 23 February 1983.

DALE [DALE OLSON]. "New Acts" (Gail Martin, Ye Little Club, L.A.). *Variety*, 20 April 1966, p. 61.

DASH, THOMAS R. "Ice Show and Vaudeville, Both on Stage and Screen, Mark Gala Roxy Occasion." Unidentified clipping, 1948.

DAVIDSON, BILL. "Anything for a Laugh." *Collier's*, 10 February 1951, p. 31.

"Dean & Ex Bring Smiles to L.A. Do." *New York Daily News*, 20 June 1988.

"Dean and Jeanne Break It Up." *New York Daily News*, 25 January 1956.

"Dean & Jerry at Mayfair Theatre to Welcome Newsmen at Sneak Preview of 'Pardners.'" *Daily Variety*, 28 June 1956, p. 1.

"Dean & Jerry: So Who's Laughing?" *Private Lives*, April 1955, p. 60.

"Dean and Jerry Warned by Studio: Get Down to Biz." *New York Enquirer*, 11 July 1955, p. 19.

"Dean Desperately Ill! Jeanne Flies to His Side!" *TV Radio Talk*, July 1968, p. 54.

"Dean Loses Round in Law Suit." *Citizen-News* [Los Angeles], 23 January 1962.

"Dean Martin Accused." *New York Times*, 3 June 1982, p. B-6.

"Dean Martin Asks Court for Children." *Los Angeles Mirror-News*, 19 November 1957.

"Dean Martin Day Ceremonies, Parade Scheduled for Friday." *Steubenville Herald-Star*, 4 October 1950, p. 2.

"Dean Martin Gets Custody of Children." *Los Angeles Examiner*, 12 December 1957.

"Dean Martin Gigs Fill London Hall." *Variety*, 15 June 1983, p. 2.

"Dean Martin Granted Custody of Children." *Los Angeles Times*, 12 December 1957.

"Dean Martin Group Buys Airport Land." *Los Angeles Times*, 31 December 1964.

"Dean Martin Group Buys San Diego Tract." *Variety*, 13 January 1965.

"Dean Martin: He Cools It and Makes It." *Look*, 17 May 1966, p. 55.

"Dean Martin in Show Hassle." *Billboard*, 4 March 1972, p. 16.

"Dean Martin Joined Revue at 500 Cafe." *Atlantic City Press*, 27 July 1946, p. 11.

"Dean Martin: 'Kid Crochett' Took to Crooning." *Billboard*, 15 January 1944.

"Dean Martin Loses in Court." *Los Angeles Times*, 11 July 1950.

"Dean Martin Loves Being Apart, but Not on That Dystrophy Fund 'Credit.'" *Variety*, October 1958.

"Dean Martin Marries in Cinema Style." *Times* [London], 27 April 1973.

"Dean Martin's Coin Climb; $200,000 a Pic." *Variety*, December 1959.

"Dean Martin's Debt, $12,880, Court Decides." *Los Angeles Times*, 15 November 1950.

"Dean Martin's Father Dies." *New York Times*, 31 August 1967, p. 33.

"Dean Martin Signs for NBC Specials." *Variety*, 27 September 1978, p. 62.

"Dean Martin Snags 142 Stars." *Hollywood Reporter*, 10 June 1965.

"Dean Martin's Terrif City of Hope Telethon Job: $804,000 in Pledges." *Variety*, 29 May 1957.

"Dean Martin Sues over Use of Name." *Los Angeles Times*, 13 January 1962.

"Dean Martin Sues Studio for $1 Million." *Los Angeles Times*, 21 April 1972, p. I-4.

"Dean Martin: The Total Entertainer." Special section, *Billboard*, 20 September 1969, p. DM-1.

"Dean Martin to Be New Bell Spokesman." *New York Times*, 20 August 1980, p. D-13.

"Dean Martin to Face Divorce Suit." *Los Angeles Examiner*, 10 March 1949.

"Dean Martin Unhappy with Present Pattern." *Variety*, 23 April 1958.

"Dean Martin Walks Out on Agent Pact with Perry." *Variety*, 11 September 1946, p. 53.

"Dean Martin Wins Custody." *New York Times*, 11 December 1957, p. 40.

"Dean Martin 'Withdraws' from York Prod'ns; Only Future Deals to Be Own." *Daily Variety*, 10 January 1957, p. 10.

"Dean Martin with Wallis." *Variety*, November 1958.

"Deano Part Owner of Vegas Riviera?" *Variety*, 25 December 1968.

"Dean's Daughter in Duet." Photograph and legend (Associated Press): Deana Martin and Terence Mathew Guerin, wedding. *New York Daily News*, 15 March 1969.

"Dean's Here for Week at 500 Club." *Atlantic City Press*, 18 August 1962, p. 10.

"Decide on Divorce." Photograph and legend. *New York Journal-American*, 25 January 1956.

"A Delightful Surprise." *New York Times*, 7 October 1957.

DELSON, JAMES. "Penthouse Interview: Jerry Lewis." *Penthouse*, May 1984, p. 109.

DENI, LAURA. "Dino Calling Right Business Tune." *Billboard*, 6 June 1970, p. 18.

DePLANE, HENRY. "Why Jerry Lewis and Dean Martin Are Playing 'Do You Trust Your Wife?'" *Uncensored*, July 1957, p. 42.

DEXTER, GEORGE. "Open Letter to Martin and Lewis." *Whisper*, December 1956, p. 36.

"Dino & Frank Will Duet Here." *New York Daily News*, 13 August 1983.

"Dino & His Wife Are Divorcing." *New York Daily News*, 11 December 1969, p. 4.

FIELDS, SIDNEY. "Without a Helping Hand." *New York Daily News,* 7 March 1968.

"Fischetti Dies and Leaves Few to Mourn Him: Heart Attack Kills Gang Chieftain at 50." *Chicago Daily Tribune,* 12 April 1951, p. VI-6.

FISCHLER, ALAN. "Night Club Reviews" (Slapsy Maxie's). *Billboard,* 21 August 1948, p. 40.

FLANAGAN, JAMES B. "Sammy Watkins Would Reform Rough World with Melody." *Cleveland Plain Dealer,* 11 December 1966, p. 7-I.

FLINT, PETER B. "Sammy Davis Jr. Dies at 64; Top Showman Broke Barriers." *New York Times,* 17 May 1990, p. 1.

FOB. "Television Reviews" ("The Dean Martin Celebrity Roast," 27 February 1976). *Variety,* 3 March 1976, p. 66.

"Follow-Up Reviews" (Havana-Madrid, N.Y.). *Billboard,* 16 March 1946, p. 45.

FORD, FRANK. "How Dean Martin Was Taken for 40 Grand." *Confidential,* September 1955.

"Frank Costello Dies of Coronary at 82; Underworld Leader." *New York Times,* 19 February 1973, p. 1.

"Frank, Sammy & Liza Too!" *New York Daily News,* 27 April 1988.

"Free Show." *The New Yorker,* 28 July 1951, p. 16.

FRIEDMAN, JOEL. "Smash Tee-off for Dean Martin." *Billboard,* 21 April 1958, p. 7.

"Friends Alarmed as Ailing Dean Martin Struggles to Finish Songs on Stage." *Star,* 1 May 1990, p. 43.

"Funny-Side Up." *Newsweek,* 20 March 1967, p. 97.

FURMANEK, BOB. "Talent in Action" (Resorts International, Atlantic City). *Billboard,* 9 April 1983, p. 27.

"Gala Director Says: Dean Martin 'Inebriated.' " *New York Daily News,* 21 January 1981.

GARDELLA, KAY. "Dean Martin Talks Candidly about Dean Martin." *New York Sunday News,* 6 August 1972, p. III-1.

———. "Dean's 'Roasts': Where the Jokers Are." *New York Daily News,* 5 February 1978, Leisure section, p. 11.

———. "Defense of Dean Martin Brings a Flood of Mail." *New York Daily News,* 10 May 1972.

———. "Dino's TV Producer Says Booze and Broads Are In." *New York Daily News,* 30 August 1972.

———. "Dino: Will Marry Again in Fall." *New York Daily News,* 29 July 1972, p. 6.

———. "Jerry Talks about Critics While Dean Sings for 'Em." *New York Daily News,* 13 January 1960.

———. "Martin & Lewis Stick." *New York Daily News,* 9 August 1955.

————. "Martin Named by Viewers NBC's New Language Dean." *New York Daily News,* 22 October 1966.

————. "Martin, Rooney & Sinatra Make Beautiful Music" ("Startime: The Dean Martin Show," 3 November 1959). *New York Daily News,* 4 November 1959.

————. "Martin's Solo Number Sweetest Melody Yet." *New York Daily News,* 21 April 1959.

————. "Martin Turns Comedian for New Fall NBC Series." *New York Daily News,* 12 June 1965.

————. "Newhart & Martin to Be TV's New Comedy Team?" *New York Daily News,* 12 July 1967, p. 92.

————. "New Look at Dino Martin: An Easy-Going Dynamo." *New York Daily News,* 7 July 1975, p. 74.

————. "There'll Be Some Changes on the Dean Martin Show." *New York Daily News,* 8 August 1970.

————. " 'A Thousand Times No,' Sings Dean about Jerry." *New York Daily News,* 1 August 1967.

————. "Two TV Martins Mix a Good Musical Martini" ("The Dean Martin Show," 25 April 1961). *New York Daily News,* 26 April 1961.

————. "What's On" ("Rawhide," 30 October 1964). *New York Daily News,* 31 October 1964.

————. "Will NBC Censors Take the Zing out of Dean?" *New York Daily News,* 14 June 1972, p. 22.

GARDETT, CAMPBELL. "Dino Weds: Drink Up." *New York Post,* 26 April 1973.

GARDNER, HY. "Coast to Coast" [column]. *New York Herald Tribune,* 24 July 1956.

————. "Hy Gardner Calling" [column]. *New York Herald Tribune,* 29 May 1957.

GARRISON, ED. "Martin & Lewis: Why Their Togetherness Had to Go Phfft!" *Uncensored,* January 1958, p. 16.

GARRISON, GREG. "Dealing with Dino." *New York Daily Mirror,* 1971.

GEHMAN, RICHARD. "Dean Martin: Crown Prince of the Clan." *American Weekly,* 30 August 1959, p. 4.

GELMAN, DAVID. "Sued for $5 Million, Dean Martin Sleeps." *New York Post,* 19 June 1962.

GENE. Review of *Career. Variety,* 30 September 1959.

————. Review of *Who's Been Sleeping in My Bed? Variety,* 4 December 1963.

————. Review of *Who's Got the Action? Variety,* 12 December 1962.

GEORGE, HENRY S. President, Local No. 4, American Federation of Musicians, Cleveland, Ohio. Letter. 12 June 1989.

GILBERT, JUSTIN. "Dean and Jerry Still 'Pardners' in Picture" *(Pardners). New York Daily Mirror*, 26 July 1956.

GILL, BRENDAN. Review of *The Silencers. The New Yorker*, 27 March 1966.

———. Review of *Texas Across the River. Saturday Review*, December 1966.

GODBOUT, OSCAR. "Comedians to Do Separate Turns." *New York Times*, 20 June 1956, p. 28.

———. "Martin and Lewis Sign as Solo Acts." *New York Times*, 21 November 1956, p. 54.

———. "Martin, Lewis Sue N.B.C. over Pact." *New York Times*, 15 August 1956, p. 59.

"Godfather Sinatra." *New York Daily News*, 22 September 1983.

GOLDSTEIN, KITTY. "Gregg Sherwood: Why Don't You Give Up?" *On the QT*, June 1955, p. 18.

GORD. "House Reviews" (Empire, Glasgow). *Variety*, 24 June 1953.

GOTRAM, MIKE. "What's Really Behind All This Dean Martin-Jerry Lewis Name-Calling!" *Top Secret*, December 1959, p. 26.

GOULD, JACK. "Martin and Lewis Score on TV Show." *New York Times*, 18 September 1950, p. 42.

———. "Martin-Lewis Team Reveals Patience, Dignity and Understanding on Benefit TV Marathon." *New York Times*, 17 March 1952, p. 27.

———. "TV: New Crosby Crown" ("The Bing Crosby Show," 1 October 1958). *New York Times*, 2 October 1958.

GRAHAM, SHEILAH. "Dean & Frankie's Palship on Rocks." *New York Post*, 9 April 1968, p. 58.

———. "Dean Gets New Kind of Role." *New York Daily Mirror*, 24 June 1957.

———. "Dean Martin 'Relaxes' in Hard Work." *New York Post*, 24 September 1966, p. 54.

———. "Dean Firm on Not Working without MM: Chemistry Is Why." *New York Daily Mirror*, 11 June 1962, p. 8.

———. "Gay Paree Not Dean's Cup of Tea." *New York Daily Mirror*, 3 May 1959.

———. "Hollywood" [column]. *New York Daily Mirror*, 11 November 1956; 13 April 1957.

———. "Thought of Retiring Makes Martin Wince." *Newark Evening News*, 24 September 1966.

GRAY, BARRY. "Barry Gray" [column]. *New York Post*, 1 February 1957.

GREEN, ABEL. "Bottom-Line Expert Balaban Dies at 83." *Variety*, 10 March 1971.

GREIN, PAUL. "Toasting a Song-and-Dance Man." *Los Angeles Times*, 13 November 1989, p. F-1.

GRENDYSA, PETER. "West Coast R&B: Gold under the Palms." *Goldmine*, 12 April 1985, p. 28.

GREVATT, REN. "Dean Martin Stretches Miami Single to Homer" (Americana, Miami). *Billboard*, 24 February 1958, p. 7.

GRIMES, ALVIN. "Dean Martin Shattered as Hill Street 'Son' Dies at Age 46." *Star*, 22 January 1991.

GRIS, HENRY. "Dean Martin at 57: Why I'm Not About to Retire." *National Enquirer*, 1975.

GROS. "Television Reviews" ("The Dean Martin Show," 22 November 1958). *Variety*, 26 November 1958.

GROSS, BEN. " 'All-Time Favorite' Hits Heard on a TV Special" ("Your All-Time Favorite Songs," 26 November 1964). *New York Daily News*, 27 November 1964.

———. "Dean Martin in 'Solo' Bow on Own TV Show" ("The Dean Martin Show," 5 October 1957). *New York Daily News*, 7 October 1957.

———. "Dean and Jerry Should Heed Comedienne Coca." *New York Daily News*, 25 July 1955.

———. "The Martins & Sinatras Joyously Hail Christmas" ("The Dean Martin Show," 21 December 1967). *New York Daily News*, 22 December 1967.

———. "Stars' Sons & Daughters Beginning to Take Over" ("The Dean Martin Show," 26 October 1966). *New York Daily News*, 29 October 1966.

GUARINO, ANN. "Bland Crime Drama" *(Mr. Ricco)*. *New York Daily News*, 30 January 1975.

———. "Dean Martin in Funny Western" *(Texas Across the River)*. *New York Daily News*, 24 November 1966.

———. "Dean Martin in Spy Romp" *(The Silencers)*. *New York Daily News*, 17 March 1966.

GUERIN, TERRY. "Dino Jr." *Interview*, November 1972, p. 29.

GUERNSEY, OTIS L., JR. "Good Humor and Bad: Two Movies: 'Stalag 17,' 'Scared Stiff.' " *New York Herald Tribune*, 12 July 1953, IV-1.

GUILD, LEO. "Night Club Reviews" (Ciro's, L.A., 19 August 1954), *Hollywood Reporter*, 23 August 1954, p. 4.

———. "Reviews of New TV Shows" ("Colgate Variety Hour": *Martin & Lewis*, 18 September 1955). *Hollywood Reporter*, 19 September 1955, p. 9.

HABER, JOYCE. "The 'Casual' Dean Martin Family." *New York Post*, 17 June 1969, p. 80.

———. "Dino and Herbie to Buy the Rams?" *Los Angeles Times*, 3 December 1969, p. IV-22.

———. "Laundering Dean Martin's Language." *Los Angeles Times*, 15 October 1973, p. IV-14.

HALE, WANDA. "Cheers for Hall's 4th of July Show" *(Bells Are Ringing)*. *New York Daily News*, 24 June 1960.

———. "Martin and Lewis on Mayfair Screen" *(Scared Stiff)*. *New York Daily News*, 4 July 1953.

———. "Martin-Lewis Film" *(The Stooge)*. *New York Daily News*, 5 February 1953.

———. "Martin, Lewis in Comedy at the Paramount" *(At War with the Army)*. *New York Daily News*, 25 January 1951.

———. "Movies: Frank & Dean Overdo Lines in Texas Tale" *(Four for Texas)*. *New York Daily News*, 26 December 1963.

———. "New Comedy Stars Dean and Shirley" *(All in a Night's Work)*. *New York Daily News*, 23 March 1961.

———. "Sex, Smut, Little Else in 'Kiss Me, Stupid.' " *New York Daily News*, 23 December 1964.

———. "Susan Hayward Star of Political Drama" *(Ada)*. *New York Daily News*, 26 August 1961.

———. " 'Toys in the Attic' Is Major Film." *New York Daily News*, August 1963.

HALL, CLAUDE. "Dino in Dandy Show" *Billboard*, 2 October 1965, p. 48.

HANNA, DAVID. "Night Club Reviews" (Ciro's, L.A., 17 April 1950). *Hollywood Reporter*, 21 April 1950, p. 4.

HAPPEL, JASON. "Dean Martin Speaks Out on His Son's Arrest." *Photoplay*, April 1974, p. 38.

"Heating Up Dino's Roasts." *New York Post*, 16 February 1984, p. 102.

HEFFERNAN, HAROLD. "Horse Brings Crisis: Dean Martin Gets a Double in Mexico." *Newark Evening News*, 12 February 1965.

———. "Jeanne Martin Still Carries Hot Torch for Hubby Dean." *Long Island Press*, 18 February 1970, p. 28.

HEGE. "Night Club Reviews" (Sabre Room, Chicago). *Variety*, 15 June 1977, p. 79.

HELLMAN, JACK. "Dean Martin's 4-Ply Performing Parlayed into $5 Mil-a-Year Harvest." *Daily Variety*, 26 April 1967, p. 1.

"Helping Hand in England Key to Scout Move." *Steubenville Herald-Star*, 11 June 1977, p. 79; February 1982, p. 3-A.

HENDRICKS, ALFRED T. "MM Out, Dean Out—Film Out." *New York Post*, 12 June 1962, p. 3.

HENSHAW, LAURIE. "Dean Martin Hits Out." *Melody Maker*, 13 July 1957, p. 3.

HERM [HERM SHOENFELD]. "Radio Reviews" ("Elgin Holiday Star Time," 25 November 1948). *Variety*, 1 December 1948.

———. "Television Reviews" ("The Dean Martin Show," 1 February 1958). *Variety*, February 1958.

HILBURN, ROBERT. "Martin Set to Open New Hotel." *Los Angeles Times*, 30 August 1973, p. IV-15.

HILL, GLADWIN. "The Borscht Belt's Latest Gift to the Movies." *New York Times,* 18 September 1949, p. II-5.

"History of the Immaculate Conception Roman Catholic Church of New Cumberland, W. Va." Unidentified photocopy, Office of the Chancellor, Diocese of Wheeling-Charleston, W. Va.

HOBSON, DICK. "This Man Earns More Money in a Year than Anyone in the History of Show Business." *TV Guide,* 28 September 1968, p. 20.

HOFFMAN, ASHLEY. "Dean & Cathy: Why They Had to Marry." *Photoplay,* July 1973, p. 33.

HOFFMAN, IRVING. "Sock Martin-Lewis Fare from Wallis" *(Sailor Beware). Hollywood Reporter,* 29 November 1951, p. 3.

HOLL. Review of *You're Never Too Young. Variety,* 15 June 1955.

"Hollywood Haberdasher: Dressing the Stars." *Newsweek,* 18 July 1960.

HOLT, PAUL. "Cheers, Then Boos, Puzzle Dean and Jerry." *Daily Herald* [London], 23 June 1953, p. 3.

HOPPER, HEDDA. "Dean Martin Left by Wife, Children." *Los Angeles Times,* 14 October 1955.

———. "Hollywood" [column]. *New York Daily News,* 19 April 1950.

———. "New Comedy Team 'Fresh': Martin and Lewis Spell Box Office." *New York Daily News,* 24 June 1951.

HOVER, HERMAN. Letter. January 1990.

"How Do They Ever Get on the Air?" *TV Guide,* 28 May 1955, p. 18.

HUMPHREY, HAL. "Dino's Christmas Show Puts Rowdy Image in Cold Storage." *The Courier-Journal & Times* [Louisville], 1 October 1967.

HUNTER, W. H. "The Pathfinders of Jefferson County." *Ohio Archaeological and Historical Quarterly,* Vol. 6 (1898), p. 95.

HUROK, WALLACE. "Dean's Cathy Answers Rumors of Romance with James Darren." *Photoplay,* July 1974, p. 57.

HYAMS, JOE. "Dean Martin's 7 Weeks in Paris." *New York Herald Tribune,* 1957.

———. "Some Answers from Dean Martin." *New York Herald Tribune,* 21 October 1959.

"Iron and Steel Industry." *Academic American Encyclopedia.* Vol. 11. Danbury, Conn.: Grolier, 1987.

"Irving Kaye in 'Big Top.'" *Hollywood Reporter,* 15 March 1954, p. 2.

"Is Booze Ruining Dean?" *Foto-Rama,* October 1960, p. 94.

Item. *Atlantic City Press,* 25 July 1946, p. 7.

Item. *Billboard,* 16 January 1971, p. 31.

Item. *Columbus Evening Dispatch,* 29 December 1939, p. A-8.

Item. ("Hollywood"). *New York Daily News,* 3 October 1971.

Item. ("In Short"). *Billboard,* 10 June 1944, p. 21.

Item. ("In Short"). *Billboard,* 1 May 1948, p. 43.

Item. *Los Angeles Times*, 5 August 1973.

Item ("Married"). *New York Herald Tribune*, 19 April 1971.

Item ("The New Show: Be Nice to Your Set"). *TV Guide*, 19 September 1952, p. 24.

Item ("Newsmakers"). *Newsweek*, 7 May 1973, p. 60.

Item ("Newsmakers"). *Newsweek*, 20 September 1976, p. 64.

Item. *Newsweek*, 22 December 1969, p. 58.

Item. *New York Daily Mirror*, 27 May 1957, p. 18.

Item. *New York Daily News*, 27 February 1976, p. 12.

Item. *New York Times*, 13 May 1972, p. 15.

Item. *New York Times*, 12 December 1972, p. 57.

Item. *New York Times*, 12 June 1974, p. 51.

Item ("Notes on People"). *New York Times*, 15 February 1972, p. 30.

Item ("Notes on People"). *New York Times*, 5 August 1973, p. 54.

Item ("Notes on People"). *New York Times*, 27 April 1973, p. 43.

Item ("Notes on People"). *New York Times*, 2 July 1974, p. 27.

Item ("Notes on People"). *New York Times*, 7 September 1976, p. 66.

Item ("Notes on People"). *New York Times*, 12 November 1976, p. 15.

Item ("Notes on People"). *New York Times*, 5 January 1977, p. C-52.

Item ("Notes on People"). *New York Times*, 14 October 1980, p. B-12.

Item ("Notes on People"). *New York Times*, 31 December 1981, p. B-4.

Item ("Page Six"). *New York Post*, 30 April 1980, p. 6.

Item ("Page Six"). *New York Post*, 12 August 1982, p. 6.

Item ("Signings"). *Billboard*, 16 January 1971, p. 16.

Item ("Zipcode U.S.A."). *New York Herald Tribune*, 8 August 1965.

"It's Not Love, Chum." *Newsweek*, 15 August 1955, p. 81.

"It's Official on Dino Exit from Sands to Riviera." *Variety*, 22 January 1969.

JACQUES, STEVE. "Dean Martin, 59: I've Fallen in Love with Bing Crosby's Daughter-in-Law." *Star*, 30 November 1976, p. 3.

JANKOWSKI, LINDA. "Casino Fined for Illegal Blackjack Game: Sinatra, Martin Blamed for Incident." *Courier-Post* [Southern N.J.], 2 August 1984, p. 1.

JANSON, DONALD. "Casino May Be Fined for Letting Sinatra and Martin Set Own Rules." *New York Times*, 8 January 1984, p. 38.

———. "Top Two Casinos Gambling Profits in Battle of Stars." *New York Times*, 28 October 1983, p. B-1.

JARACH, CESARE. "Le cause e gli effetti dell'emigrazione negli Abruzzi e nel Molise." *Revista di Emigrazione*, Vol. III, Nos. 3–4 (March–April 1910), p. 1.

J. C. "Dean Martin au Moulin-Rouge." *France-Soir*, 3 July 1984.

JENKINS, DAN. "The Birth of Jerry Lewis' New Career." *TV Guide*, 19 January 1957, p. 17.

————. "Dean Martin Blasts Away at Jerry Lewis." *TV Guide,* 13–19 April 1957, p. 17.

"Jerry Lewis Directs a Home Made Movie." *Look,* 29 January 1952, p. 78.

"Jerry Lewis: Hollywood's Greatest Ingrate." *Uncensored,* April 1963, p. 25.

"Jerry Lewis in N.Y." *Hollywood Reporter,* 10 June 1955, p. 3.

"Jerry Lewis' 'Other Wife.' " *Rave,* June 1957, p. 16.

J. M. C. " 'Dean Martin.' " ("The Dean Martin Show," 16 September 1965). *Christian Science Monitor,* 18 September 1965.

"Joanne Dru in 'Big Top.' " *Hollywood Reporter,* 8 February 1954, p. 2.

JOHNSTON, LAURIE. " 'Women Power' Protests 'Male Domination' of Wall Street." *New York Times,* 24 August 1973, p. 39.

JONES, BARTON. "Skinny D'Amato Dies." *Press* [Atlantic City], 6 June 1984, p. 1.

JOSE [JOE COHEN]. "House Reviews" (Capitol, N.Y.). *Variety,* 10 March 1948.

————. "House Reviews" (Roxy, N.Y.). *Variety,* 30 September 1948.

————. "Night Club Reviews" (Riviera, N.J.). *Variety,* 10 September 1947.

Just Dino [Dean Martin Association, Croydon, England]. Various issues, 1960–91.

KAHN. "House Reviews" (Paramount, N.Y.). *Variety,* 5 October 1949.

————. "New Acts" (Dean Martin). *Variety,* 29 September 1943.

————. "Night Club Reviews" (Riobamba, N.Y.). *Variety,* 29 September 1943.

KAP [MIKE KAPLAN]. "Night Club Reviews" (Slapsy Maxie's, L.A.). *Variety,* 18 August 1948.

————. "Night Club Reviews" (Slapsy Maxie's, L.A.). *Variety,* 26 January 1949.

————. "Night Club Reviews" (Ciro's, L.A.). *Variety,* 26 April 1950, p. 60.

KAUFFMANN, STANLEY. Review of *Toys in the Attic. New Republic,* 17 August 1963.

KAUFMAN, DAVE. "On All Channels." *Daily Variety,* 19 February 1957.

KAYE, BERYL. "How Dean Martin Muscled Tony Randall out of a Job." *Confidential,* October 1960, p. 36.

KAYE, LORETTA. Untitled article on Ken Lane. *DISCoveries,* August 1989, p. 142.

KENNY, NICK. "Nick Kenny: Speaking" [column]. *New York Daily Mirror,* 19 August 1944, p. 12.

KERN, JANET. "Bing Helps Dean End Feud with Jerry Lewis." *Chicago American,* 1 October 1958, p. 31.

KILGALLEN, DOROTHY. "Dean Martin Hits the Gong" ("Tonight!," 28 January 1957). *New York Journal-American,* 31 January 1957.

"King Dino Faces Royal Treatment." *New York Daily News,* 27 May 1983, p. 9.

KINNARD, JUDITH. "Florist Is a Full-Fledged Entrepreneur." *New York Times,* 5 August 1973, p. 54.

KORST, CHARLES. "Why Martin and Lewis Split." *On the QT,* September 1957, p. 34.

KRAMER, MARCIA. "Time to Duck! Feminists Give Their Awards." *New York Daily News,* 21 August 1978.

LABARTHE, ANDRÉ S. "Lewis au pays de Carroll." *Cahiers du Cinema,* June 1962, p. 1.

LADER, LAWRENCE. "The Slapsy Twins." *Pageant,* April 1951, p. 142.

"La Martinique to Close—Tax!" *Billboard,* 10 June 1944.

LAND. "Martin & Lewis: An Unbelievable Saga Made Real." *Variety,* 30 October 1974, p. 4.

LANG, CHARLES. "Mom's the Word . . . Ask Dean Martin." *Confidential,* January 1958, p. 32.

LARDINE, BOB. "Dino's Very High Year." *New York Sunday News,* 26 March 1967, p. 4.

LARY [LARRY SOLLOWAY]. "Night Club Reviews" (Americana, Miami). *Variety,* 26 February 1958, p. 53.

"Last Football Party." *Columbus Evening Dispatch,* 24 November 1939, p. 16-A.

"Latin Casino, Philly, Sets Advance Bookings." *Variety,* 13 October 1948.

LAURENT, LAWRENCE. "Next Season Doesn't Look Good for Dean's 'De-sexed' TV Show." *Courier-Journal & Times* [Louisville]; [reprinted from *Washington Post*], June 1973.

LAURIE, JOE, JR. "Followup Comment." *Variety,* 6 April 1949, p. 33.

———. "Mimics." *Variety,* 19 May 1948, p. 52.

LEBLANC, JERRY. "In Dino Veritas." *New York Sunday News,* 9 July 1972, p. 8.

LES. "Television Reviews" ("The Dean Martin Show" ["Lincoln-Mercury Startime"], 12 January 1960). *Variety,* January 1960.

LEWIS, DAN. "Dean Martin Really Met the Press." *Sunday Record* [Bergen County, N.J.], 3 August 1975, p. B-21.

———. "That's Dino! Despite TV and Films, There's Time for Potshots at an Ex-Pal." *Sunday Record* [Bergen County, N.J.], 2 February 1975, p. B-19.

LEWIS, JERRY. "That's My Boy." *Hollywood Reporter,* 29 October 1951, Section 2.

———. "What I Really Think of Dean Martin: A Fine Actor with a Sharp Wit." *New York Journal-American,* c. June 1956.

LEWIS, JERRY; as told to BILL DAVIDSON. "I've Always Been Scared." *Look,* 5 February 1957, p. 51.

LEWIS, MRS. JERRY [PATTI PALMER LEWIS]. "I Married a Madman!" *American* magazine, January 1952, p. 23.

LITTLE, AMY. "Cathy: 'I Can't Keep Dean Home!'" *Photoplay*, December 1973, p. 43.

LIVINGSTON, GUY. "Bombing of Dean Martin Concert Points Up Boston's Yen for Rock." *Variety*, 13 October 1971, p. 45.

"'Local Boy Makes Good': Dick Stabile, Appearing at Chatterbox, Is Famous Leader." *Newark Evening News*, 26 April 1941.

"Local Boy Makes Good: Martin, Lewis Receive Gala Welcome in City." *Steubenville Herald-Star*, 7 October 1950, p. 1.

"London Palladium: Martin and Lewis." *Times* [London], 23 June 1953, p. 2.

LONG. "Night Club Reviews" (Harrah's, Lake Tahoe). *Variety*, 9 September 1964.

LOOP. "Night Club Reviews" (Rio Cabana, Chicago). *Variety*, 28 May 1947.

LOWE. "House Reviews" (Capitol, Washington, D.C.). *Variety*, 13 August 1947.

LOYN. Review of *Cannonball Run II*. *Variety*, 11 July 1984.

MACDONALD, ELIZABETH. "Letter to a Star." *Silver Screen*, May 1952, p. 36.

MACKIN, TOM. "Martin Gets Dis-barred." *Newark Evening News*, 29 July 1970, p. 59.

MADSEN, AXEL. "L'Oncle d'Amérique: entretien avec Jerry Lewis." *Cahiers du Cinema*, February 1966, p. 30.

"Make-a-Million Martin." *Life*, 22 December 1958, p. 109.

MAKSIAN, GEORGE. "Dean Is Special in 2-Yr. NBC Deal" [column: "News around the Dials"]. *New York Daily News*, 16 May 1977, p. 57.

———. "Dean Martin's Opener Set" [column: "News around the Dials"]. *New York Daily News*, 1 September 1965.

———. "Jerry's Big Day Capped by Dean." *New York Daily News*, 19 September 1976.

———. "Martin's Show Revamped" [column: "News around the Dials"]. *New York Daily News*, 21 April 1971.

———. "More 'Roasts' for Martin" [column: "News around the Dials"]. *New York Daily News*, 5 April 1976, p. 59.

———. "A Role for Dino." *New York Daily News*, 28 February 1985.

———. "Vegas Special Might Reunite Martin & Lewis." *New York Daily News*, 15 October 1987.

"M&L Pull 200G in 10-Day Tour." *Variety*, 5 November 1952.

"M&L Set 20-Year Record at Chi Chez." *Variety*, 13 August 1952.

"M&L's 3-Hour ABC Dystrophy TVthon with NBC's Okay." *Variety*, October 28, 1952, p. 1.

"M&L, Viv Blaine Hecklers Turn Out to Be 2 Youths Who Read Daily Worker." *Variety*, July 1953, p. 1.

MANNERS, DOROTHY. "Nix Rumor Martins Patching Things Up." *New York Daily Mirror*, 9 June 1971.

MARCHESE, JOHN. "Frank's Place." *7 Days,* 10 May 1989, p. 22.

"Marilyn Monroe Dead, Pills Near." *New York Times,* 6 August 1962, p. 1.

"Martin & Lewis." Photographs from "The Colgate Comedy Hour." *Look,* 19 June 1951.

"Martin and Lewis in A.C." *Atlantic City Press,* 17 July 1954, p. 4.

"Martin and Lewis 'Back in Business.'" *Hollywood Reporter,* 1 September 1955, p. 2.

"Martin and Lewis' Backyard Movies." *TV Guide,* 5 June 1953, p. 4.

"Martin and Lewis Bow on Discs." *Capitol News,* November 1948, p. 3.

"Martin and Lewis Cut Up at Preview." *New York Herald Tribune,* 31 December 1952.

"Martin and Lewis Day: Comedy Team Prepared for Busy Schedule Today." *Atlantic City Press,* 15 July 1954, p. 1.

"Martin and Lewis Film, Resort Draw Praise from Critics." *Atlantic City Press,* 17 July 1954, p. 13.

"Martin & Lewis Get Par. Okay to Split Up Team; Ask Same of Wallis, NBC." *Daily Variety,* 18 June 1956, p. 1.

"Martin and Lewis Give 'Inside' on Their 'Feud.'" *Hollywood Reporter,* 19 March 1954, p. 5.

"Martin & Lewis Given to June 1 to Answer Copa." *Variety,* 28 May 1952.

"Martin and Lewis Hit at 500 Cafe." *Atlantic City Press,* 22 July 1948, p. 9.

"Martin and Lewis Hit Road in May." *Hollywood Reporter,* 30 March 1954, p. 2.

"Martin and Lewis in A.C." *Atlantic City Press,* 17 July 1954, p. 4.

"Martin and Lewis in Movie Comedy." *New York Times,* 1 November 1951.

"Martin & Lewis Marathon." *TV Guide,* 14–20 March 1952, p. 6.

"Martin & Lewis Must Play Philly Nitery or Forfeit 12 G, Sez AGVA." *Variety,* 12 October 1949, p. 50.

"Martin & Lewis' 98G Share from N.Y. Par," *Variety,* September 1953, p. 1.

"Martin & Lewis Nix Hal Wallis' Offer to Release 'Em from Pact for $1,500,000." *Daily Variety,* 25 June 1956, p. 1.

"Martin and Lewis Return to Work." *New York Herald Tribune,* 21 May 1952.

"Martin & Lewis Reunite." *New York Daily News,* 9 June 1989.

"Martin & Lewis Reviving Original 'Single' Turns." *Hollywood Reporter,* 6 June 1955, p. 3.

"Martin & Lewis Seek Shift to Coast for Hearing of N.Y. Copa 'Breach' Charge." *Variety,* 21 May 1952.

"Martin & Lewis Set for Tex. State Fair," *Variety,* 28 May 1952.

"Martin and Lewis Sign Pact." *New York Times,* 12 December 1955.

"Martin and Lewis Start 'The Caddy.'" *New York Herald Tribune,* 27 December 1952.

"Martin and Lewis Sued for 2 Million by Studio." *New York Herald Tribune,* 5 August 1951.

"Martin & Lewis' Switch to MCA Cues $1,000,000 Suit by Greshler." *Variety,* 12 July 1950, p. 45.

"Martin & Lewis Telethon" ("The New York Cardiac Hospital Telethon," 15 March 1952). *Variety,* 19 March 1952, p. 1.

"Martin & Lewis Together!" *New York Daily News,* 1 May 1988.

"Martin and/or Lewis." Unidentified clipping, 7 August 1955.

MARTIN, DEAN. "Cafe News: Dino Does Column—about Dino's Lodge." *Los Angeles Examiner,* 7 April 1961.

———. "It Wasn't My Idea." *Silver Screen,* July 1954, p. 38.

———. "Memories Are Made of This." *Hit Parader,* March 1956.

———. "That's My Boy." *Hollywood Reporter,* 29 October 1951, Section 2.

———, and LEWIS, JERRY. "A Joint Statement." *See,* January 1953, p. 34.

MARTIN, MRS. DEAN [JEANNE]. "How I Trained My Husband." *Photoplay,* March 1953, p. 52.

"Martin Fined on Gun Rap." *Variety,* 11 August 1982, p. 2.

"Martin for Lewis." *New York Herald Tribune,* 9 January 1961.

MARTIN, GAIL. "My Father the Swinger." *Coronet,* May 1967.

"Martin-Lewis Apart for Only One Film." *Hollywood Reporter,* 19 June 1956, p. 1.

"Martin, Lewis Breaking Up." *New York World Telegram,* 19 June 1956.

"Martin-Lewis' Film Deal with Hal Wallis Worth $1,250,000." *Variety,* 1 September 1948, p. 2.

"Martin, Lewis Get 'At War with Army.' " *Variety,* 2 December 1949.

"Martin, Lewis Inked to 1-Year Pact by Cap." *Billboard,* 28 August 1948.

"Martin, Lewis Plan Hospital Telathon." *New York Herald Tribune,* 27 December 1952.

"Martin-Lewis Signed by Hal Wallis for 'My Friend Irma.' " *Paramount News,* 13 September 1948.

"Martin-Lewis Stand to Forfeit 18G by Chi Walk." *Variety,* 3 November 1948.

"Martin-Lewis Tiff with Miami Copa." *Variety,* 17 November 1948, p. 50.

"Martin, Lewis Welcomed by Steubenville." *Steubenville Herald-Star,* 6 October 1950, p. 1.

"Martin Loses Suit to Apollo." *Billboard,* 27 May 1950.

MARTIN, PETE. "I Call on Dean Martin." *Saturday Evening Post,* 29 April 1961, p. 16.

"Martin Show." *New York Herald Tribune,* 19 October 1964.

MARTIN, TED. Letter. 3 July 1992.

"Martin's Hub Gig Pulls Poor 70G." *Variety,* 13 October 1971, p. 45.

MARTIN, TED. Letter. 3 July 1992.

MARX, ARTHUR. "The Inside Story of Dean Martin's Fantastic Climb to Super-Stardom." *National Enquirer,* 12 November 1974.

"Mass. Legislature May Subpoena Both Sinatra, Martin in Racetrack Probe." *Daily Variety,* 7 March 1963, p. 3.

MASTERS, DOROTHY. "As TV Doctor, Martin Shuns Adoring Fans" *(Who's Been Sleeping in My Bed?). New York Daily News,* 26 December 1963.

———. " 'Career' Rates Top in Loew's State Debut." *New York Daily News,* 9 October 1959.

———. "Martin & Lewis Film above Par" *(Hollywood or Bust). New York Daily News,* 23 December 1956.

———. "Martin-Lewis Film at Mayfair Theatre" *(The Caddy). New York Daily News,* 19 September 1953.

———. "Newcomers Share Honors with Wayne" *(Rio Bravo). New York Daily News,* 19 March 1959.

———. "A Newcomer Steals Martin, Lewis Film" *(That's My Boy). New York Daily News,* August 1951.

"Mayris Chaney Is Married." *New York Times,* 19 August 1943, p. 24.

McFADDEN, WILLIAM. "Just Call Him Dandy Jack Lindsay." *New York Daily News,* 3 January 1967, p. 10.

McCARTEN, JOHN. Review of *Ten Thousand Bedrooms. The New Yorker,* 1957.

McCLAIN, LAURIE. "2 Bonus Interviews with Dean's Ex-Loves." *Photoplay,* July 1973, p. 36.

MEADE, HARLAN. "What Happened When the DA Caught Dean and Jerry in a Pornographic Trap." *Top Secret,* October 1958, p. 40.

MEHAFFEY, JANE. Librarian, Swaney Memorial Library Association, New Cumberland, W. Va. Letter. June 1989.

MEL. "House Reviews" (Chicago, Chicago). *Variety,* 22 November 1950.

MERRON, FRANCES. "Bright Spot" [column]. *New York Daily Mirror,* 20 September 1946, p. 29.

MESSINA, MATT. "Dean Martin TVer Planned." *New York Daily News,* 23 September 1964.

MICHELSON, HERB. " 'Rat Pack' Tour Gets Underway; Could Gross $20-Mil by Autumn." *Variety,* 16 March 1988, p. 97.

"Mickey Cohen, Once a Leader of West Coast Rackets, Dead." *New York Times,* 30 July 1976, p. IV-13.

MILLER, TOM. "Enraged Dean Martin Takes Daughter from Doris Day's Son." *Photoplay,* October 1971, p. 72.

"Million for Heart Fund." *New York Daily News,* 16 March 1952.

MILTON, JEAN. New Cumberland, W. Va. Letters. 7 August 1989 and May 1991.

MISHKIN, LEO. "Martin, Lewis Run Riot on Colgate Video Show." *New York Morning Telegraph,* 19 September 1950.

―――. "Screen Review: 'Who's Got the Action?' Has Univac as 'Star.'" *Morning Telegraph* [New York], 25 December 1962.

"'Mr. Entertainment,' Versatile Sammy Davis Jr., Dies at 64." *Variety*, 23 May 1990, p. 86.

MOR. "Television Reviews" ("The Dean Martin Show"). *Variety*, 24 September 1969.

MORGAN, GENE. "Chicago Night Life" [column]. *Chicago Daily News*, 13 March 1946, p. 18.

MORI. "Night Club Reviews" (Riobamba, N.Y.). *Variety*, 27 October 1943, p. 40.

MORRIS, A. "'I'm Embarrassed to Be Dean Martin's Son!'" *Photoplay*, April 1968, p. 3.

MORRISON, E. H. "Memo to Dean Martin: Better Check on Your Ex-Wife!" *Confidential*, November 1956, p. 26.

MORTIMER, LEE. "It Could Only Happen on Broadway." *New York Sunday Mirror Magazine*, 15 October 1950, p. 21.

―――. "Nightlife" [column]. *New York Sunday Mirror*, 26 September 1943, p. 33.

―――. "Nightlife" [column]. *New York Daily Mirror*, 28 June 1944, p. 25.

―――. "Nightlife" [column]. *New York Daily Mirror*, 23 July 1944, p. 26.

MOSBY, ALINE. "Dean Is Firm on Criticism." *New York World Telegram*, 5 August 1953, p. 1.

MUIR, FLORABEL. "Behind Hollywood's Silken Curtain." *New York Daily News*, 26 March 1956, p. 30.

―――. "Filmland Bigs Hiding Out to Duck Subpena." *New York Daily News*, 11 August 1957, p. 3.

―――. "Hollywood" [column]. *New York Daily News*, 16 February 1966.

―――. "New Sinatra Brawl: Exec in a Coma." *New York Daily News*, 11 June 1966, p. 2.

―――. "Too Hurt to Tell of Sinatra Bout." *New York Daily News*, 12 June 1966.

MURF. Review of *The Ambushers*. *Variety*, 20 December 1967.

―――. Review of *Bandolero*. *Variety*, 5 June 1968.

―――. Review of *How to Save a Marriage and Ruin Your Life*. *Variety*, 24 January 1968.

―――. Review of *Mr. Ricco*. *Variety*, 29 January 1975.

―――. Review of *Something Big*. *Variety*, 10 November 1971.

―――. Review of *The Wrecking Crew*. *Variety*, 25 December 1968.

MUSEL, ROBERT. "What Ever Happened to Yesterday?" *TV Guide*, 18 July 1970, p. 28.

"Musicians Sue N.B.C. on Reruns." *New York Times*, 3 December 1973, p. 53.

Music News [Capitol Records, Hollywood]. All issues, March 1952 through August 1952.

Music Views [Capitol Records, Hollywood]. All issues, September 1952 through August 1959.

MYDANS, SETH. "Friends Mourn Sammy Davis Jr., Eulogized as 'the Only of a Kind.' " *New York Times,* 19 May 1990, p. 30.

"Nab Dino for Drunk Driving." *New York Daily News,* 10 May 1982.

NARVAEZ, ALFONSO A. "Morris Dalitz, 89, Ex-Bootlegger and Owner of Las Vegas Casinos" [obituary]. *New York Times,* 1 September 1989.

NASH, REV. ROBERT C. Chancellor, Diocese of Wheeling-Charleston, Wheeling, West Va. Letter. 23 May 1989.

"Natl. Org for Women's Show Biz 'Enemy' List: Dino, 'Tango,' Soapvideo." *Variety,* 1973.

"NBC Eyes Tues. Night Boost via Martin & Lewis." *Billboard,* 9 April 1949.

"NBC Fretting over Bing Deal with Chesties." *Variety,* 26 February 1949, p. 3.

"NBC Puts 100G in Martin-Lewis; Show Still in Air." *Variety,* 26 February 1949, p. 3.

"NBC's Move to Launder Some of Dino's Indigo." *Variety,* 10 May 1972, p. 1.

"NBC's New Talent Splurge." *Variety,* 26 February 1949, p. 3.

"Nevada Gaming Board Weighs Sinatra Group's Cal-Neva Lodge Buy-in." *Variety,* 20 July 1960.

" 'Never Too Young' Junket Nets 6 Radio, 2 TV Shows: Jerry Lewis Scores at Press Preview." *Hollywood Reporter,* 13 June 1955, p. 3.

"New Cumberland Memories." *Panhandle Press* [New Cumberland, W. Va.], 8 August 1972, p. 7.

"New Dean Martin 3-Year NBC Pact a $34,000,000 Wow." *Variety,* 14 June 1967, p. 27.

"New Martin-Lewis Feud over Fisher Show." *Los Angeles Examiner,* 24 December 1958.

"New Martin-NBC Pact." *Variety,* 26 March 1975, p. 38.

"New Voices, Old Gags." *Newsweek,* 18 April 1949, p. 61.

"New Year's Week-end Entertainers of Note." *Columbus Evening Dispatch,* 29 December 1939, p. A-8.

"Night Club Hearing Defied by Gambler: Costello Refuses to Testify in Copacabana Case." *New York Times,* 16 September 1944, p. 15.

"Night Club Owner Denies City Charge." *New York Times,* 12 September 1944, p. 21.

"Nitery Followups" (Havana-Madrid). *Variety,* 19 December 1945, p. 40.

Obituary (Hy Abrams). *Variety,* 5 February 1975.

Obituary (Moses Annenberg). *New York Times,* 21 July 1942.

Obituary (Leonard Barr). *Hollywood Reporter,* 28 November 1980.

Obituary (Leonard Barr). *Steubenville Herald-Star,* 22 November 1980.

Obituary (Barbara Bates). *Variety,* 21 May 1969.

Obituary (Ray Bloch). *Variety,* 7 April 1982.

Obituary (Veda Ann Borg). *Variety,* 19 September 1973.

Obituary (Nat Brandwynne). *Variety,* 15 March 1978.

Obituary (Herman Citron). *Variety,* 18 November 1987.

Obituary (Richard Conte). *Variety,* 23 April 1975.

Obituary (Carole Costello). *Variety,* 8 April 1987, p. 95.

Obituary (Norma Crane). *Variety,* 3 October 1973.

Obituary (Bing Crosby). *Variety,* 19 October 1977.

Obituary (Sy Devore). *New York Times,* 13 July 1966.

Obituary (Theo DeWitt). *Variety,* 5 July 1944.

Obituary (Jack Entratter). *New York Times,* 12 March 1971.

Obituary (Jack Entratter). *Variety,* 17 March 1971.

Obituary (George Evans). *Variety,* 8 February 1950.

Obituary (Charles Fischetti). *New York Times,* 12 April 1951.

Obituary (Rocco Fischetti). *New York Times,* 7 July 1964.

Obituary (Arthur Freed). *Variety,* 18 April 1973.

Obituary (Jake Freedman). *Variety,* 22 January 1958.

Obituary (Y. Frank Freeman). *Variety,* 12 February 1969.

Obituary (Robert Goldstein). *Variety,* 10 April 1974.

Obituary (Mack Gray). *Variety,* 11 February 1981.

Obituary (Henry Hathaway). *Variety,* 20 February 1985.

Obituary (Howard Hawks). *Variety,* 28 December 1977.

Obituary (Susan Hayward). *Variety,* 19 March 1975.

Obituary (Nicky Hilton). *Variety,* 12 February 1969.

Obituary (Judy Holliday). *Variety,* 9 June 1965.

Obituary (Stanley Hough). *Variety,* 7 March 1990.

Obituary (Arthur P. Jacobs). *Variety,* 4 July 1973.

Obituary (Phil Karlson). *Variety,* 26 February 1986.

Obituary (Nick Kenny). *Variety,* 3 December 1975.

Obituary (A. E. Lichtman). *Variety,* 1 September 1965.

Obituary (Angel Lopez). *New York Times,* 13 July 1968.

Obituary (Diana Lynn). *Variety,* 22 December 1971.

Obituary (George Marshall). *Variety,* 19 February 1975.

Obituary (Dean Paul Martin, Jr.). *Variety,* 1 April 1987.

Obituary (Jimmy McHugh). *Variety,* 28 May 1969.

Obituary (Vincente Minnelli). *Variety,* 30 July 1986.

Obituary (Carmen Miranda). *Variety,* 10 August 1955.

Obituary (Lee Mortimer). *Variety,* 6 March 1963.

Obituary (Lou Perry). *New York Post,* 14 August 1981, p. 69.

Obituary (Lou Perry). *Variety,* 19 August 1981, p. 69.

Obituary (Jules Podell). *Variety*, 3 October 1973.

Obituary (Glenn Pullen). *Variety*, 9 March 1983.

Obituary (Martin Rackin). *Variety*, 21 April 1976.

Obituary (Renato Rascel). *Variety*, 14 January 1991, p. 126.

Obituary (Donna Reed). *Variety*, 22 January 1986.

Obituary (Maxie Rosenbloom). *Variety*, 10 March 1976.

Obituary (George Seaton). *Variety*, 1 August 1979.

Obituary (Moe Sedway). *New York Times*, 5 January 1952.

Obituary (Stanley Shapiro). *Variety*, 25 July 1990, p. 67.

Obituary (Sol Siegel). *Variety*, 5 January 1983.

Obituary (Dick Stabile). *Variety*, 1 October 1980, p. 127.

Obituary (Jules Stein). *Variety*, 6 May 1981.

Obituary (Inger Stevens). *Variety*, 6 May 1970.

Obituary (Robert Strauss). *Variety*, 26 February 1975.

Obituary (Frank Tashlin). *Variety*, 10 May 1972.

Obituary (Norman Taurog). *Variety*, 15 April 1981.

Obituary (Richard Thorpe). *Variety*, 13 May 1991.

Obituary (Hal Walker). *Variety*, 19 July 1972.

Obituary (Hal Wallis). *Variety*, 15 October 1986.

Obituary (Sammy Watkins). *Cleveland Plain Dealer*, 27 June 1969, p. 4-Z.

Obituary (Sammy Watkins). *Variety*, 30 July 1969.

Obituary (Lawrence Weingarten). *Variety*, 12 February 1975.

Obituary (Marie Wilson). *Variety*, 29 November 1972.

Obituary (Austin J. Wylie). *Variety*, 10 December 1947.

O'BRIAN, JACK. "Come Back, Steve Allen." *New York Journal-American*, 29 January 1957, p. 16.

———. "Jack O'Brian's TViews: 'The Bell Tolls' Pretty Tinnily" ("The Dean Martin Show," 19 March 1959). *New York Journal-American*, 20 March 1959, p. 26.

———. "Jack O'Brian's TViews: Dean Martin Is Great Alone" ("The Dean Martin Show," 5 October 1957). *New York Journal-American*, 7 October 1957, p. 20.

———. "Twice as Good Half as Long" ("The Bing Crosby Show," 1 October 1958), *New York Journal-American*, 2 October 1958, p. 28.

O'BRIEN, FRED. "Papas Sinatra & Martin: Why They Help Their Daughters! Why They Hurt Their Sons!" *Photoplay*, July 1968, p. 50.

———. "What They're Doing to Their Daughters: Why Sinatra Has Nancy Trailed! Why Martin's Daughters Trail Him!" *Photoplay*, March 1968, p. 41.

O'CONNOR, JOHN J. Review of "Dean Martin in London," 8 November 1983. *New York Times*, 5 November 1983, p. 55.

"Of Local Origin." *New York Times*, 10 July 1951, p. 30.

"Old Moderately." *Time,* 11 March 1966, p. 60.

"$1 Million a Year." *Newsweek,* 9 February 1959, p. 94.

"$1,148,419 Pledged to Heart Hospital." *New York Times,* 16 March 1952, p. 71.

"Open-Hearth Process." *New Encyclopedia Britannica.* 15th ed. Vol. 8. Chicago: University of Chicago Press, 1988.

"Opening Night Concert Riles Martin's Fans." *Cleveland Plain Dealer,* 24 September 1965.

OTIS. "Radio Reviews" (Sammy Watkins, WHKC, Columbus). *Variety,* 19 January 1938.

"Paramount Closes Deal for 'At War with Army.'" *Paramount News,* 4 December 1950.

"'Pardners' a Good Comedy Sparked by Martin & Lewis." *Hollywood Reporter,* 25 June 1956, p. 3.

PARSONS, LOUELLA O. "'Baby on Way' Kept from Dean Martin." *Los Angeles Examiner,* 19 March 1953.

———. "Dean Martin: Happy in Solo Role." *Pictorial TView,* 12 May 1957, p. 3.

———. "The Dean Martins—All Nine of 'Em." *Pictorial TView,* 7 September 1958, p. 5.

———. "Dean Martin, Wife Decide to Separate." *Los Angeles Examiner,* 14 October 1955, p. 2.

———. "Dean Martin, Wife Reunited." *Los Angeles Examiner,* 20 March 1953.

———. "It's Rumored Dean Martin's Daughter Not Married." *Los Angeles Herald-Examiner,* 2 August 1963.

———. "'Mad Love' for Model Costly to Dean Martin." *Los Angeles Examiner,* 29 March 1949.

———. "Martin and Lewis Again Decide to Go Their Separate Ways in Show Business." *New York Journal-American,* 20 June 1956.

———. "Wife Will Sue Dean Martin." *Los Angeles Examiner,* 21 February 1949, p. 3.

"The Pay's the Thing: Dean, Jerry Sign Truce." *New York Post,* 9 August 1955, p. 3.

"Perry Likes to Sing; Dean Has a Comedy Fling." *Billboard,* 19 September 1970.

PESTIAN, GINA SIMERA. Letter. 14 January 1991.

Photograph and legend: Martin & Lewis, *My Friend Irma. New York Herald Tribune,* 20 November 1948.*

Photograph and legend (Associated Press): Martin with Jeanne Martin and son Ricci. *New York Daily News,* 25 November 1953.

* Photograph entries are listed chronologically.

Photograph and legend: Martin with Jeanne Martin, Cocoanut Grove. *New York Journal-American*, 15 May 1954.

Photograph and legend: Martin & Lewis onstage. *Cue*, 11 June 1955.

Photograph and legend: Martin with Jeanne Martin, separation. *New York Journal-American*, 14 October 1955, p. 20.

Photograph and legend: Martin with Jeanne Martin. *Motion Picture*, December 1955.

Photograph and legend: Martin with Jeanne Martin, SHARE benefit. *New York Journal-American*, 9 June 1956.

Photograph and legend: Martin with parents, Ciro's testimonial. *New York Daily News*, 7 July 1956.

Photograph and legend: Martin with Jeanne Martin. *New York Journal-American*, 18 August 1956.

Photograph and legend: Martin juggling oranges. *New York Journal-American*, 27 October 1956, p. 13.

Photograph and legend: Martin with Gloria Kreiger, Hungarian Relief benefit. *Photoplay*, November 1956.

Photograph and legend (Associated Press): Martin with Jeanne and daughter Gina. *New York Daily Mirror*, 21 December 1956.

Photograph and legend: Martin with Jeanne, London Palladium. *Silver Screen*, February 1957.

Photograph and legend: Martin with George Jessel, Arthur Konvitz, and Martin Tannenbaum; "Parade of Stars" telethon. *New York Daily Mirror*, 18 April 1957.

Photograph and legend: Martin, "Parade of Stars" telethon. *New York Post*, 25 May 1957.

Photograph and legend: Martin with Martin Tannenbaum and Mike Durso, "Parade of Stars." *New York Daily Mirror*, 27 May 1957, p. 18.

Photograph and legend: Martin with Arthur Konvitz, "Parade of Stars" telethon. *New York Daily Mirror*, 30 May 1957.

Photograph and legend: Martin with Jeanne Martin, Club Mocambo party. *New York Journal-American*, 12 October 1957.

Photograph and legend (United Press): Martin with Jeanne Martin and daughter Gina. *New York World-Telegram*, 21 August 1957.

Photograph and legend: Martin with Bing Crosby, "The Dean Martin Show." *Sunday News* [New York], 16 November 1958, p. 16.

Photograph and legend: *Some Came Running*. *New York Times Magazine*, 4 January 1959.

Photograph and legend: Martin with Gisele MacKenzie and Donald O'Connor, "The Dean Martin Show" (19 March 1959). *New York Daily News*, 15 March 1959.

Photograph and legend: Martin with Bob Hope and Mae West, "The Dean Martin Show" (3 May 1959). *New York Daily News*, 3 May 1959.

Photograph and legend: Martin and Gail Martin, "The Dean Martin Show" (25 May 1967). *Newsday*, 25 May 1967.

Photograph and legend: Martin with Minnie Pearl, "The Dean Martin Show" (6 March 1969). *Newsday*, 6 March 1969.

Photograph and legend (Associated Press): Martin and Catherine Mae Hawn, wedding. *New York Post*, 26 April 1973.

POWE. Review of *Some Came Running. Variety*, 24 December 1958.

———. Review of *Who Was That Lady? Variety*, 13 January 1960.

Press biography: "Jimmy Bowen." Nashville: Universal Records, December 1988.

Pressbook: "Hollywood at Play: A Columbia 'Screen Snapshots' Special." Los Angeles: Columbia Pictures, 1951.

Press kit: Dean Martin/*Bells Are Ringing*. "Biographical Information" and profile of Martin with quotes. Los Angeles: MGM, 29 October 1959.

Press release: "Dean Martin and Jerry Lewis" ("The Colgate Comedy Hour"). New York: NBC Television News, WNBT New York, August 1950.

Press release: Dean Martin Friars Club Tribute. Beverly Hills: Rogers & Cowan, Inc., 8 November 1959.

Press release: "The Dean Martin Specials." New York: NBC Television News, Fall 1975.

Press release: "Frank Sinatra & Dean Martin to Co-Star at Westchester Premier Theatre May 17–29." New York: Solters & Roskin, Inc., 1 February 1977.

PRESTON, HOWARD. "A Great Guy to Have Around." *Cleveland Plain Dealer*, 2 October 1968.

"The Price of Dean Martin's Extra Marital Madnesses." *Confidential*, November 1970, p. 34.

Program: Westchester Premier Theatre, 17–29 May 1977.

PRY. Review of *Kiss Me, Stupid. Variety*, 16 December 1964.

PRYOR, THOMAS M. "Martin and Lewis Shun Movie Roles." *New York Times*, 2 April 1952.

———. "Martin and Lewis to Remain a Team." *New York Times*, 9 August 1955, p. 28.

———. "Martin to End Tie to Lewis Company." *New York Times*, 16 April 1957, p. 38.

———. "Mel Ferrer Plans Film Life of Bard." *New York Times*, 4 August 1951, p. 7.

PULL [GLENN C. PULLEN]. "Night Club Reviews" (Sammy Watkins, Vogue Room, Cleveland). *Variety*, 6 October 1937.

PULLEN, GLENN C. "Dancers Find What Makes Sammy Run." *Cleveland Plain Dealer,* 24 January 1960.

———. "Lou Costello Plans a Movie Build-up for Ohio Singer." *Cleveland Plain Dealer,* 13 August 1944.

———. "Night Club Reviews" (Sammy Watkins, Vogue Room, Cleveland). *Variety,* 30 March 1938.

———. "Night Club Reviews" (Sammy Watkins, Vogue Room, Cleveland). *Variety,* 18 May 1938.

———. "Night Club Reviews" (Sammy Watkins, Vogue Room, Cleveland). *Variety,* 24 August 1938.

———. "Night Club Reviews" (Sammy Watkins, Vogue Room, Cleveland). *Variety,* 18 January 1939.

———. "Night Club Reviews" (Sammy Watkins, Vogue Room, Cleveland). *Variety,* 27 March 1940.

———. "Night Club Reviews" (Sammy Watkins, Vogue Room, Cleveland). *Variety,* 12 June 1940.

———. "Night Club Reviews" (Sammy Watkins with Martin, Vogue Room, Cleveland). *Variety,* 6 November 1940, p. 42.

QUINN, FRED. "Dean Martin Solos in Film at State" *(Ten Thousand Bedrooms). New York Mirror,* 4 April 1957.

RADDATZ, LESLIE. "It's 12 o'Clock, and Nobody's Opened the Peanut Butter Yet." *TV Guide,* 18 February 1967, p. 15.

"Radio and Television: Dean Martin and Jerry Lewis Comedy Team to Start NBC Show on Sunday, April 3." *New York Times,* 11 March 1949.

"Radio and Television: Team of Dean Martin and Jerry Lewis Is Signed by N.B.C. for Video Series." *New York Times,* 14 February 1950.

"Railroad." *Academic American Encyclopedia.* Vol. 16. Danbury, Conn." Grolier, 1987.

RAND, CHRISTOPHER. Review of *Toys in the Attic. The New Yorker,* 10 August 1963.

" 'Rat Pack' Reunion." *New York Daily News,* 2 December 1987.

"Ray Walston Replaces Sellers in 'Kiss Me.' " *Hollywood Reporter,* 13 April 1964, p. 2.

"RCA's 'Rush Act' on Disking: Others Bide Time in Post-Ban Rush." *Variety,* 29 December 1948, p. 39.

"Reform: Sin on the Ohio." *Newsweek,* 25 September 1946, p. 33.

REILLY, NAIDA. "The Dean Martins: How They Live Together but Love Others." *Photoplay,* February 1971, p. 62.

"Rents Restaurant at 10 East 60th Street." *New York Times,* 17 September 1940, p. 41.

"Reprise Surprised Martin Has Waxed Last Disk There." *Daily Variety,* 11 July 1969.

"Resort Welcomes Back Martin and Lewis." *Atlantic City Press,* 15 July 1954, p. 10.

"Reunited Rat Pack." *Los Angeles Times,* 15 March 1988, p. VI-1.

REUTERS. "Dean Martin Deserts, Too." *New York Daily News,* 17 July 1970.

Review of "The Dean Martin Show," 16 September 1965. *New York Post,* 17 September 1965.

Review of *Hollywood or Bust. Hollywood Reporter,* 4 December 1956.

Review of *Hollywood or Bust. New York Times,* 24 December 1956.

Review of *My Friend Irma Goes West. Los Angeles Times,* 30 June 1950.

Review of *My Friend Irma Goes West. Newsweek,* 14 August 1950.

Review of *Ocean's Eleven. Los Angeles Examiner,* 11 August 1960.

Review of *Ocean's Eleven. The New Yorker,* 20 August 1960.

Review of *Ocean's Eleven. Observer* [London], 28 August 1960.

Review of *The Stooge. Los Angeles Examiner,* 5 February 1953.

Review of *The Stooge. Saturday Review,* 7 February 1953.

"Revolt of Film Employers: $2-Mil Disaster with Marilyn." *Variety,* 13 June 1962, p. 3.

RICH. Review of *The Road to Hong Kong. Variety,* 4 April 1962.

"Richard Thorpe Directs MGM's '10,000 Bedrooms.'" *Hollywood Reporter,* 25 June 1956, p. 1.

RICK. Review of *Airport. Variety,* 18 February 1970.

"The Riot Started in Atlantic City." *TV Guide,* 11 November 1950, p. 8.

RITSON, RED. "The Nightly Whirl" [column]. *Atlantic City Press,* 16 July 1954, p. 18.

———. "Welcome Dean & Jerry!" [column: "The Nightly Whirl"]. *Atlantic City Press,* 15 July 1954, p. 12.

"Riviera Buys Dino's Stock in Facility." *Los Angeles Times,* 22 February 1972, p. IV-9.

"RKO Pictures' New Chairman Says Losses Are About $100,000 a Week, Sees Red Ink for Two More Years." *Wall Street Journal,* 21 October 1952, p. 5.

"RKO Radio Pictures Reveals Fourth Major Resignation This Week." *Wall Street Journal,* 25 October 1952, p. 1.

"RKO's President: How Mr. Stolkin Won a $3 Million Fortune in Eight Busy Years." *Wall Street Journal,* 20 October 1952, p. 1.

ROBE. Review of *Murderers' Row. Variety,* 14 December 1966.

ROSE. "Dean Martin Show" ("The Dean Martin Show"). *Variety,* 6 May 1959.

———. "Radio Reviews" ("The Martin and Lewis Show"). *Variety,* 6 April 1949, p. 33.

———. "Radio Reviews" ("The Martin and Lewis Show"). *Variety,* 10 October 1951, p. 27.

————. "Television Reviews" ("The Colgate Comedy Hour," 17 September 1950). *Variety,* 20 September 1950, p. 31.

————. "Television Reviews" ("The Dean Martin Show," 5 October 1957). *Variety,* 9 October 1957.

ROSE, JACK. Santa Monica, Cal. Letter. 7 November 1989.

ROSS, RIC. "Frank Sinatra: Fifty Years of Unusual Songs, Part Two (1949–1959)." *DISCoveries,* September 1989, p. 108.

ROURA, PHIL, and POSTER, TOM. "People: Dino Doing a Solo." *New York Daily News,* 18 April 1988.

————. "People: Dino-Frank Duet Here All Sold Out." *New York Daily News,* 18 September 1983.

————. "People: Hottest Ticket in Town? Frankie & Dino at the Friars." *New York Daily News,* 11 July 1984.

" 'Sailor' Troupe Back." *Hollywood Reporter,* 25 September 1951, p. 6.

"Same Old Trouble; Dean Just Won't Whiz." *New York Post,* 14 October 1955.

"Sammy Watkins Dies Here at 65." *Cleveland Plain Dealer,* 27 July 1969, p. 1.

"Sammy Watkins Is Bandwagon Contest Victor." *Cleveland Press,* 27 June 1942.

SANSONI, JOHN. "The Bawdy, Boozing Life of Dean Martin." *Inside Story,* January 1962, p. 42.

SARGENT, MICHAEL J. Coordinator, Applicant Services, Gaming Control Board, Carson City, Nevada. Letter. 11 January 1990.

SAWYER, DAVID. "Cathy & Dean: Passion & Quarrels." *Photoplay,* May 1972, p. 54.

SCHB. "New Acts" (Martin, Sands, Las Vegas). *Variety,* 13 March 1957, p. 54.

SCHERMERHORN, JACK. "Dean Martin's Son Missing in Crash." *New York Post,* 24 March 1987, p. 4.

————. "Dino's Ailing, He Quits Tour by Rat Pack." *New York Post,* 22 March 1988, p. 3.

SCHEUER, PHILIP K. "Comedy Pair Gold-Brick in 'At War with Army.' " *Los Angeles Times,* 2 February 1951.

"Schlatter Gets Last Laugh." *New York Daily News,* 30 March 1988.

SCHOR, SAM. "Resort Bestows Royal Welcome on Martin and Lewis." *Atlantic City Press,* 16 July 1954, p. 28.

SCHREIBER, CHARLES J. "Did Dean Martin Pull a Boo-Boo?" *New York World Telegram,* 16 August 1958.

SCHUMACH, MURRAY. "Film Starring Marilyn Monroe and Dean Martin Shelved by Fox." *New York Times,* 12 June 1962, p. 42.

————. "Fox Aide Assails 'Whims' of Stars." *New York Times,* 11 June 1962, p. 38.

————. "Fox Dismisses Marilyn Monroe and Files a Suit for $500,000." *New York Times*, 9 June 1962, p. 19.

————. "Hollywood Encore: Old Farce Is Reshaped for Marilyn Monroe." *New York Times*, 3 June 1962, p. B-5.1.

————. "Hollywood Team: Peter Sellers, Dean Martin Have Fun in Wilder's 'Kiss Me, Stupid.'" *New York Times*, 5 April 1964.

————. "Hollywood Warfare." *New York Times*, 17 June 1962, p. B-9.

————. "Lee Remick Gains by Shelved Movie." *New York Times*, 14 June 1962, p. 23.

————. "Slant on Hollywood." *New York Times*, 30 October 1962.

————. "$10,000,000 Pact for Jerry Lewis." *New York Times*, 8 June 1959, p. 32.

————. "Warner Buys Reprise Records, but Sinatra Retains One-third." *New York Times*, 8 August 1963, p. 19.

————. "Weakness Seen in Film Industry." *New York Times*, 8 June 1962, p. 38.

SCHUYLER, DICK. "Who's Trying to Break Up Dean Martin and Jerry Lewis?" *Top Secret*, October 1954, p. 6.

SCHWANEBERG, ROBERT. "Casino Admits Violation in Celebrity Card Game." *Newark Star-Ledger*, 13 July 1984, p. 27.

SCHWARTZ, SONNY. "Greats and Near-Greats Alike: They All Called Him 'Skinny.'" *Press* [Atlantic City], 11 June 1984, p. 5.

SCOTT, JOHN L. "Dino Inaugurates the Grand." *Los Angeles Times*, 7 December 1973.

SCOTT, VERNON. "Dean Martin a Serious Actor Now." *New York Morning Telegraph*, 3 September 1957.

————. "Dean Martin Has Wacky 'Lunch.'" *Newark Evening News*, 25 June 1964.

————. "Dean Martin Is the Total Entertainer." *Billboard*, 20 September 1969, p. DM-1.

————. "The Improbable Private Life of Mrs. Dean Martin." *Ladies' Home Journal*, November 1968, p. 97.

SEE, CAROLYN. "The Matter of Dean Martin's Mail." *TV Guide*, 1 March 1969, p. 15.

SHAL. "House Reviews" (Earle, Philadelphia). *Variety*, 18 June 1947.

————. "Night Club Reviews" (Latin Casino, Philadelphia). *Variety*, 26 March 1947.

SHANAHAN, EILEEN. "Inquiry Reveals I.R.S. Master List." *New York Times*, 21 June 1975, p. 1.

SHAW, MANUEL. "The Untold Story of Dean Martin." *Inside Story*, February 1957, p. 38.

SHEARER, LLOYD. "Dean Martin—He's Going through a Change of Wife." *Parade,* December 1969.

SHENFELD, GARY. "What Impressed Dean Martin about City? . . . Patter of Rain." *Atlantic City Press,* 22 August 1962, p. 21.

SHEPARD, RICHARD F. "Jack Benny, 80, Dies of Cancer on Coast." *New York Times,* 28 December 1974, p. 1.

SHIE. "Nightclub Reviews" (High Sierra, Lake Tahoe). *Variety,* 17 August 1988, p. 45.

SHIRLEY, LIZ. "Beverly Hills to Get Lavish Golf Course." *Los Angeles Times,* 26 April 1967.

"Shooting 'Big Top' Scene in Boys Home." *Daily Variety,* 19 March 1954, p. 4.

SIBITS, JEAN. Membership Services, Local No. 4, American Federation of Musicians, Cleveland, Ohio. Letter. 8 June 1989.

SIEGEL, NORMAN. "Dean Martin Starting to Click as This Season's Newest Manhattan Cafe Crooner." *Cleveland Press,* 5 November 1943.

SIFTON, SAMUEL. "Las Vegas: An Oasis." *American Heritage,* May/June 1990, p. 38.

SIMMONS, FOSTER L. "Dean Martin & Jerry Lewis: Who's Sorry Now?" *Inside Story,* August 1957, p. 11.

"Sinatra & Martin Team in New York." *Billboard,* 12 February 1977, p. 20.

"Sinatra, Dean Martin Team on Fall A.C. Date; High Rollers to Benefit." *Variety,* 10 August 1983, p. 1.

"Sinatra, Dean Un-Harnessed, Attys. Report." *Daily Variety,* 8 March 1963.

"Sinatra Group's Cal-Neva Buy Gets Nev. Okay." *Variety,* 14 September 1960.

"Sinatra Is Guest" ("The Dean Martin Show," 1 November 1960). *New York Times,* 2 November 1960.

"Sinatra Joins Rival of the Sands Hotel in Las Vegas Rift." *New York Times,* 12 September 1967.

"Sinatra Label Ready for February Debut." *Billboard,* 5 December 1960.

"Sinatra Label Tag: 'Reprise Records.' " *Billboard,* 26 December 1960, p. 4.

"Sinatra, Martin & A.C.'s D'Amato Teaming for Buyup of Cal-Neva Club." *Variety,* 29 June 1960.

SINDELAR, ANN K. Reference Supervisor, Western Reserve Historical Society, Cleveland, Ohio. Letter. 3 October 1989.

"Singer's Boy Weds Dancer." Photograph and legend (United Press): Craig Martin and Kami Stevens, wedding. *New York Daily News,* 9 March 1969.

"650 Night Clubs Put on Probation Pending Inquiry." *New York Times,* 2 October 1944, p. 1.

"64Gs Up in Arms." *New York Daily News,* 22 September 1955.

Skolsky, Sidney. "Dean Martin Hits Jerry Lewis for Naming Wife in Mag Article." *New York Post*, 1957, p. 4.

————. "Dean Martin Puts the Blast on Jerry." *New York Post*, 22 January 1957, p. 4.

————. "Crazy for Money." *New York Post*, 17 February 1952, p. M-5.

————. "Hollywood Is My Beat" [column]. *New York Post*, 6 November 1949, p. M-10.

————. "Hollywood Is My Beat" [column]. *New York Post*, 5 May 1957, p. M-3.

————. "Hollywood Is My Beat" [column]. *New York Post*, 1958.

————. "Hollywood Is My Beat" [column]. *New York Post*, 12 May 1959.

————. "Hollywood Is My Beat" [column]. *New York Post*, 5 June 1960, p. M-3.

"Slapsy Maxie's, L.A., Shutters Temporarily; No Name Talent Available." *Variety*, 16 February 1949.

Sloan, Robin Adams. "The Gossip Column." *New York Daily News*, 7 July 1974, p. 2.

————. "The Gossip Column." *New York Daily News*, 21 September 1975, p. 2.

————. "The Gossip Column." *New York Daily News*, 5 October 1976, p. 56.

Slocum, Bill. "Saloonatic Wit" ("The Dean Martin Show," 3 May 1959). *New York Mirror*, 10 May 1959, p. 63.

"S'Martin-Ed Up." *Billboard*, 13 September 1947.

Smilgis, Martha. "On the Move: This Swinger Is Dean Martin's Son, Dorothy Hamill's Man and Maybe the Next Robert Redford." *People*, 6 November 1978, p. 115.

Smilky, Nixon. "Dream World Alive Heats Shivering Parade Crowd: Mob Riot Aftermath to Parade." *Miami Herald*, 1 January 1949, p. 1.

Smith, Bill. "Case History (1): Too Many Cooks Didn't Kill Martin and Lewis." *Billboard*, 10 March 1951, p. 3.

————. "Case History (2): Big Dough, Big Aches Wind Up M&L Story." *Billboard*, 17 March 1951, p. 2.

————. "Follow-up Review" (Harlequin, N.Y.). *Billboard*, 8 July 1944.

————. "Night Club Reviews" (Copacabana, N.Y.). *Billboard*, 30 April 1949.

————. "Night Club Reviews" (Copacabana, N.Y.). *Show Business*, 23 July 1956.

————. "Night Club Reviews" (Glass Hat, N.Y.), *Billboard*, 10 June 1944.

————. "Night Club Reviews" (Glass Hat, N.Y.). *Billboard*, 9 September 1944, p. 26.

————. "Vaudeville Reviews" (Capitol, N.Y.). *Billboard*, 13 March 1948, p. 41.

SMITH, JACK. "Martin-Lewis Antics to Enliven Ball Finals." *New York Daily News,* 11 September 1950.

———. "Martin, Lewis at Harvest Ball Finals." *New York Daily News,* 30 August 1953.

SOBOL, LOUIS. "A Chat with Dean Martin." *New York Journal-American,* 19 September 1957.

SOLLOWAY, LARRY. "Chatter." *Variety,* 17 November 1948, p. 62.

———. "Chatter." *Variety,* 24 November 1948, p. 54.

———. "Miami's Mad Scramble for Nitery $$; Copa City, Beachcomber in Openings." *Variety,* 29 December 1948, p. 47.

"Son of Cantor at 23 Is Jazz Virtuoso Here." Unidentified Cleveland newspaper clipping, c. 1927, *Cleveland Press* Collection, Cleveland State University Archives.

SPAETH, ARTHUR. "Mr. Music Music Music." *Cleveland in Full Face,* 1954.

STABILE, DICK. "Style Is Dick Stabile's 'Corny' Poison Antidote: Dance Band Leader Strives for 'Hallmark' of Originality." Unidentified newspaper clipping, 17 July 1938.

STAL. "House Reviews" (Capitol, N.Y.). *Variety,* 16 April 1947.

———. "Night Club Reviews" (Havana-Madrid, N.Y.). *Variety,* 25 September 1946, p. 56.

———. "Television" ("Toast of the Town," 20 June 1948). *Variety,* 23 June 1948.

STAPELY, BILL. As told to Diane Albright. "Sinatra the Hell-Raiser." *Enquirer,* 8 May 1990, p. 28.

"Steel Manufacture." *McGraw-Hill Encyclopedia of Science & Technology.* Vol. 17. New York: McGraw-Hill, 1987.

STEIN, HERB. "Reasons for Action on Martin." *New York Morning Telegraph,* 16 June 1962.

STERBA, JAMES P. "Howard Hughes Dies at 70 on Flight to Texas Hospital." *New York Times,* 28 December 1974, p. 1.

"Steuben, Fort." *Dictionary of American History.* Rev. ed. Vol. 6. New York: Charles Scribner's Sons, 1976.

"Steubenville." *Encyclopaedia Britannica.* 11th ed. Vol. 25. New York: Encyclopaedia Britannica Co., 1911.

"Steubenville Gets Ready for Dean Martin Day Friday." *Steubenville Herald-Star,* 5 October 1950.

STEVENS, GEORGE. "Dean & Cathy's Honeymoon Cottage!" *Photoplay,* March 1972, p. 24.

———. "Dean Martin Fearful for Sinatra's Health." *Photoplay,* September 1971, p. 65.

STEVENS, JERRY. "Why Dean Martin Calls Himself a 'Bum.'" *Top Secret,* June 1958, p. 24.

"Stolkin Quits as RKO President; He and 2 Others Leave Board." *Wall Street Journal*, 23 October 1952, p. 1.

STONE, WALTER. "Dean & Jeanne Finally Battle It out in Public over Cathy." *Photoplay*, January 1973, p. 75.

STORRICK, B. E. "Dean Martin's Wife Talks about Her Husband's Other Women." *Photoplay*, March 1969, p. 56.

SYLVESTER, BOB. "Dream Street: Purely Personal" ("The Dean Martin Show"). *New York Daily News*, 10 January 1967.

SYLVESTER, ROBERT. "Theatre Survives 2 Comics." *New York Daily News*, 18 July 1951.

———. "Two Young Clowns Arrive; Worth All the Adjectives." *New York Daily News*, 23 April 1949.

"The Talk of Show Business." *Time*, 23 May 1949, p. 57.

TAUROG, NORMAN. "It Really Happened." *Photoplay*, April 1954, p. 36.

TAYLOR, GENE. "Are Dean Martin's Movie Capers Shocking the TV Fans?" *Whisper*, September 1966, p. 18.

"Television Followup" ("Texaco Star Theatre"). *Variety*, 11 August 1948, p. 35.

"Television Reviews" ("The Dean Martin Show"). *Variety*, p. 56.

" 'Tell Me Not What I Owe You': Martin." *Variety*, 10 March 1971, p. 5.

"That's Amore!" Photograph and legend (United Press); Martin and Catherine Mae Hawn, applying for marriage license. *New York Daily News*, 21 April 1973.

THAW, TERRY. "The Dean Martin and Jerry Lewis Record Scandal." *Lowdown*, October 1955, p. 16.

THOMAS, BOB. "Dean Martin Now Starting Exclusive Country Club." *Herald-News* [Passaic, N.J.], 22 May 1967.

———. "Is There a Real Dean Martin?" *Good Housekeeping*, November 1967, p. 96.

———. "It's a Synch, Martin Will Be Singing." *New York Post*, 16 December 1977, p. 61.

———. "Lou Costello Sponsored an Unknown $50-a-Week Singer Named Dean Martin—& Then Dumped Him." *National Enquirer*, March 1977.

———. "Martin & Lewis: A Clash of Ego." *New York World Telegram*, 23 June 1956.

———. "Martin Makes It Seem So Easy." *New York Post*, 23 August 1966.

THOMPSON, CHARLES. "Lowdown on the Boozin', Ballin' Dean of the Clan." *Uncensored*, December 1962, p. 25.

THOMPSON, EDWARD T. "There's No Show Business Like MCA's Business." *Fortune*, July 1960, p. 114.

THOMPSON, HOWARD. "Screen: Romantic Farce: Criterion Offers 'Who Was

That Lady?' " *(Who Was That Lady?)*. *New York Times*, 16 April 1960, p. 10.

THOMPSON, ROBERT. "How Cathy Hawn Is Luring Dean Martin into Marriage." *Photoplay*, November 1971, p. 78.

"3 Guilty of Passing Sammy Davis Slur." *Variety*, 27 June 1962, p. 3.

TIEGEL, ELIOT. "Dino Mixes Act—a Shot of Humor with Song Chasers." *Billboard*, 1 August 1964, p. 14.

"Today's Bio . . . Here's Sammy Watkins." Unidentified Cleveland newspaper clipping, c. 1927, *Cleveland Press* Collection, Cleveland State University Archives.

TONE. "Television Reviews" ("All-Star Party for Lucille Ball," 9 December 1984). *Variety*, 12 December 1984.

———. "Television Reviews" ("Dom DeLuise and Friends," 16 February 1983). *Variety*, 23 February 1983.

TORRE, MARIE. "Dean Martin Show" ("The Dean Martin Show," 22 November 1958). *New York Herald Tribune*, 24 November 1958.

———. "Week End Reviews: 'Dean Martin Show' " ("The Dean Martin Show," 5 October 1957). *New York Herald Tribune*, 7 October 1957, p. III-4.

TOSCHES, NICK. "God Created Dean Martin in His Own Image, Then Stood Back." *Waxpaper*, October 1978, p. 9.

"To the Rescue." *Time*, 9 January 1956, p. 74.

TRAU. "Television Reviews" ("The Dean Martin Show," 19 March 1959). *Variety*, March 1959.

TUBE. Review of *Ada*. *Variety*, 26 July 1961.

———. Review of *All in a Night's Work*. *Variety*, 22 March 1961.

———. Review of *Bells Are Ringing*. *Variety*, 8 June 1960.

———. Review of *Ocean's Eleven*. *Variety*, 10 August 1960.

———. Review of *Sergeants 3*. *Variety*, 24 January 1962.

———. Review of *Toys in the Attic*. *Variety*, 26 July 1963.

TURNER, WALLACE. "Reagan Beats Foe at Raising Funds." *New York Times*, 11 October 1970, p. 52.

"$12,500,000 Merger of Film Companies." *New York Times*, 29 June 1916.

"20 Policemen Face Grand Jury Action in Vice 'Frame-ups.' " *New York Times*, 6 December 1930, p. 1.

"250G Damage Suit Thrown at M&L." *Variety*, c. 1952.

Unidentified clippings. Files [Copacabana (N.Y.); Desert Inn (Las Vegas); Five Hundred Club (Atlantic City, N.J.); Leon & Eddie's (N.Y.); Lewis, Jerry; Martin, Dean; Martin & Lewis; Martini, Nino; O'Connell, Helen; Perry, Lou; Riobamba (N.Y.); Riviera (Fort Lee, N.J.); Riviera (Las Vegas); Sands (Las Vegas); Stabile, Dick; Watkins, Sammy], Billy Rose Theatre Collection, New York Public Library.

Unidentified clippings. Files [Citron, Herman; Martin, Dean; Martin & Lewis; Martin films by title], Margaret Herrick Library of the Academy of Motion Picture Arts, Beverly Hills.

United Press International. "Arraign Dino Jr. on Gun Rap." *New York Daily News*, 19 January 1974.

———. "Dean Martin Accused." *New York Times*, 4 June 1982, p. B-6.

———. "Dean Martin and Fox Drop Lawsuits on Monroe Movie." *New York Times*, 5 June 1963, p. 32.

———. "Dean Martin Got 'Insults' for Whisky." *Los Angeles Daily News*, 23 July 1953.

———. "Dean Martin Jr. Indicted." *New York Times*, 12 February 1974, p. 42.

———. "Dean Martin Leaves Hospital." *New York Times*, 24 June 1960.

———. "Dean Martins Part; She Says It's 'to Clear Air.' " *New York Daily News*, 11 February 1953.

———. "Dean Martin's Son Faces Gun Charges." *New York Times*, 19 January 1974, p. 20.

———. "Dean Martin Sued in Rift on Miss Monroe's Ouster." *New York Times*, 19 June 1962, p. 27.

———. "Dean Martin's Wife to Sue for Divorce." *New York Times*, 11 December 1969, p. 71.

———. "Dean Martin to Wed Cover Girl." *New York Daily News*, 28 August 1949.

———. "Dean Martin Wounds Self." *New York Daily News*, 10 July 1976.

———. "Filmdom's Elite Given Star Billing, for Taxes." *New York Daily News*, 23 April 1954.

———. "Grace Throws Gala and It's a Beauty." *New York Daily News*, 12 August 1961.

———. "Jerry Lewis Ordered to Rest." *New York Times*, 3 August 1951, p. 10.

———. "Martin and Lewis Win Film Poll." *New York Times*, 29 September 1950, p. 32.

———. "Martin Joins Sinatra in Supporting Reagan." *New York Times*, 16 July 1975, p. 35.

———. "Martin's Wife Ails." *New York Daily News*, 7 October 1961.

———. "Martin Wants to End Lewis Feud." Unidentified newspaper clipping, 4 August 1955.

———. "Millionaire Oilman Killed by Bomb Blast in His Car." *New York Times*, 20 October 1977, p. 18.

———. "No Appeal for Him in Filming Abroad, Claims Dean Martin." *New York Morning Telegraph*, 9 August 1961.

———. "Reagan to Raise Funds with a Sinatra Concert." *New York Times,* 1 October 1979, p. 11.

———. "Scot Not Amused by Martin, Lewis." *New York Herald Tribune,* 11 June 1953.

———. "Sinatra, Dean Martin Apply to Buy a Casino." *New York Times,* 14 July 1960, p. 42.

———. "Singer Asks Custody of 4 Kids by Ex-Wife." *New York Daily News,* 20 November 1957.

———. "Studio Sues Dean Martin for 5 Million." *New York Herald Tribune,* 19 June 1962.

———. "Track Stock Countersuit Hits Singers." *Los Angeles Citizen-News,* 12 October 1962.

———. "Violations Admitted by Casino." *New York Times,* 14 July 1984, p. 28.

———. " 'World Gone Nuts': Dean." *New York Daily News,* 11 September 1963.

" 'Unknown' Catskills Tell Off Dean Martin." *New York Post,* 8 June 1955, p. 5.

VALLELY, JEAN. "Dean Martin's Closest Friend Is Frank Sinatra (He Sees Him Twice a Year)." *Esquire,* 4 July 1978, p. 61.

VAN HORNE, HARRIET. "Dean Martin Fails to Charm" ("The Dean Martin Show," 19 March 1959). *New York World Telegram,* 20 March 1959.

"Variety Bills." *Variety,* 9 April 1947–7 July 1948.

"Victim of Shooting Held." *New York Times,* 2 July 1929, p. 13.

VILLERS, RALPH. "Dean, Jerry Give Anniversary Act to Cap Their Day." *Atlantic City Press,* 17 July 1954, p. 12.

WALK. "Night Club Reviews" (500 Club, Atlantic City). *Variety,* 28 July 1948.

WALLACE, INEZ. "Dean Martin Remembers When Cleveland Applauded Politely." *Cleveland Plain Dealer,* 16 November 1952.

"Wallis Inks M-L to Straight Salary Pact." *Daily Variety,* 20 May 1952, p. 1.

"Wallis Newcomer to Debut in 'The Stooge.' " *Paramount News,* 24 July 1950.

"Wallis, Para. Sued over '3 Ring Circus' Script." *Hollywood Reporter,* 17 August 1955, p. 2.

"Wallis, Pevney to Phoenix." *Hollywood Reporter,* 3 February 1954, p. 2.

WALSH, BRIDGET. "Billy Graham Converting Dean Martin?" *Photoplay,* August 1971, p. 96.

Warner Bros. Artist Performance Records (Dean Martin: Artist Code A-8759): February 1962–January 1983.

WATSON, ARTHUR. "Living It Up with Martin and Lewis." *New York Daily News,* 18 July 1954, p. 64.

WATTS, RICHARD, JR. "Martin, Lewis and English Critics." Unidentified newspaper clipping, 12 August 1953.

WEILER, A. H. "By Way of Report." *New York Times,* 15 July 1951, p. II-3.

———. "Martin and Lewis in the Army" *(At War with the Army). New York Times,* 25 January 1951.

———. "Dean Martin and (Shapely) Company Arrive in 'The Silencers.' " *New York Times,* 17 March 1966.

———. "Texas Border Town" *(Rio Bravo). New York Times,* 19 March 1959, p. 40.

Wells High Bulletin [Steubenville]. Various issues, 1932–33.

WERDEN, LINCOLN A. "Barber Triumphs at 21st Extra Hole." *New York Times,* 25 January 1972, p. 29.

"Wheeling-Pittsburgh Steel Corp." *Moody's Industrial Manual.* 1989 ed. Vol. 2. New York: Moody's Investment Services, 1989.

WHIT. Review of *Five Card Stud. Variety,* 17 July 1968.

———. Review of *Marriage on the Rocks. Variety,* 22 September 1965.

———. Review of *Rio Bravo. Variety,* 18 February 1959.

———. Review of *Robin and the Seven Hoods. Variety,* 24 June 1964.

———. Review of *Rough Night in Jericho. Variety,* 9 August 1967.

———. Review of *Showdown. Variety,* 23 May 1973.

———. Review of *The Silencers. Variety,* 9 February 1966.

———. Review of *The Sons of Katie Elder. Variety,* 30 June 1965.

———. Review of *Texas Across the River. Variety,* 14 September 1966.

———. Review of *Three Ring Circus. Variety,* 27 October 1954.

WHITNEY, DWIGHT. "Life Is Just a Laugh." *TV Guide,* 10 April 1976, p. 21.

"Why Dean's the Lover Who Can't Stay Up Late." *Photoplay,* May 1970, p. 45.

WILL. "Night Club Reviews" (MGM Grand, Las Vegas). *Variety,* 12 December 1973, p. 55.

———. "Night Club Reviews" (MGM Grand, Las Vegas). *Variety,* 11 September 1974, p. 73.

———. "Night Club Reviews" (MGM Grand, Las Vegas). *Variety,* 11 December 1974, p. 51.

———. "Night Club Reviews" (MGM Grand, Las Vegas). *Variety,* 18 August 1976, p. 68.

———. "Night Club Reviews" (MGM Grand, Las Vegas). *Variety,* 21 December 1977, p. 71.

———. "Night Club Reviews" (MGM Grand, Las Vegas). *Variety,* 24 January 1979, p. 91.

———. "Night Club Reviews" (MGM Grand, Las Vegas). *Variety,* 14 September 1983, p. 99.

———. "Night Club Reviews" (Riviera, Las Vegas). *Variety,* 25 June 1969.

WILLIAMS, BOB. "Dean Martin to Uncork a New Image" [column: "On the Air"]. *New York Post,* September 1975.

————. "On the Air" [column]. *New York Post,* 29 March 1959.

————. "On the Air" [column]. *New York Post,* 28 June 1967.

WILLIAMS, BRIAN, and HITCHENS, NEAL. "Jerry Lewis Bombshell as Son Charges Comic Was a Cruel Tyrant Who Beat and Terrified His 6 Sons." *National Enquirer,* 9 May 1989, p. 40.

WILLIAMS, DAVID. " 'Why I Let Dean Love Another Woman.' " *Photoplay,* February 1972, p. 68.

WILLIAMS, DICK. "Dean Martin Doesn't (and Needn't) Fret." *Los Angeles Mirror News,* 3 March 1959, p. II-6.

————. " 'It's My Fault!' " *Motion Picture,* June 1956, p. 14.

WILLIAMS, MATT. "The Inside Story of Dean Martin and Jerry Lewis . . . Broadway's $5,000,000 Brush-off!" *Confidential,* November 1955, p. 41.

WILLSON, BRAD. "St. Vincent's Puts Teamwork First." *Columbus Sunday Dispatch Magazine,* 26 June 1949, p. 22.

WILSON, EARL. "Dean Martin and the Mrs. Are Back Together Again." *New York Post,* 5 March 1956.

————. "Dean Martin—A Star Who Glows on You" [column: "On Broadway"]. *New York Post,* December 1971.

————. "Dean's Gail Goes Home" [column: "It Happened Last Night"]. *New York Post,* 21 March 1970.

————. "Dino: New Show Business?" [column: "It Happened Last Night"]. *New York Post,* 16 August 1971.

————. "A Few Words from Dean" [column: "It Happened Last Night"]. *New York Post,* 25 May 1970.

————. "For Now, It'll Be Dino, His Girl and a Chaperone." *New York Post,* 13 December 1969.

————. "Four on a Honeymoon" [column: "It Happened Last Night"]. *New York Post,* 23 April 1973.

————. "Honest Man." *New York Post,* 8 March 1958.

————. "Introducing Dino's Choice." *New York Post,* 12 December 1969.

————. "It Happened Last Night" [column] (Sands, Las Vegas). *New York Post,* 21 November 1957.

————. "Martin & Lewis ½-Split, Dean Wants to Solo." *New York Post,* 7 June 1955, p. 5.

————. "The Midnight Earl" [column: "It Happened Last Night"]. *New York Post,* 25 September 1943, p. 20.

————. "The Phenomenal Dean Martin" [column: "Earl Wilson on Broadway"]. *New York Post,* 10 June 1967.

————. "That's Our Dino" [column: "It Happened Last Night"]. *New York Post,* 6 August 1968.

WING, GRACE. "Copy Girl Now Bowl Queen." *Miami Daily News,* [c. December 1947].

WINSTEN, ARCHER. "Reviewing Stand" *(Some Came Running)*. *New York Post*, 23 January 1959, p. 46.

———. "Reviewing Stand" *(Ten Thousand Bedrooms)*. *New York Post*, 4 April 1957, p. 36.

———. "Reviewing Stand" *(The Young Lions)*. *New York Post*, 3 April 1958, p. 16.

"Witness Admits Link to Gambler." *New York Times*, 15 September 1944, p. 21.

WOOD. "New Acts" (Martin & Lewis). *Variety*, 22 January 1947, p. 54.

———. "Night Club Reviews" (Dick Stabile, Essex House, N.Y.). *Variety*, 24 January 1940.

WOOD, STAN. "Dean Martin Denies Loss of 40 Gs in Golf Match." *Los Angeles Mirror-News*, 10 August 1955.

WOODS, BERNIE. "Jocks, Jukes and Disks." *Variety*, 29 December 1948, p. 41.

WRIGHT, HARRIET. Letter. 5 April 1990.

ZABE. "Night Club Reviews" (Chez Paree, Chicago). *Variety*, 23 November 1949.

ZATWASKA, STEPHANIE. "They Mourn for D'Amato." *Press* [Atlantic City], 9 June 1984.

ZEITLIN, IRA. "Behind the Riot Act." *Photoplay,* September 1952, p. 56.

ZINSSER, WILLIAM K. *"Ten Thousand Bedrooms."* *New York Herald Tribune*, 4 April 1957, p. 17.

ZOLOTOW, MAURICE. "The Martin and Lewis Feud." *Cosmopolitan,* October 1955, p. 62.

Court Records, Government Archives, Etc.

Administrative Records, Probate Court, Jefferson County, Ohio. Vol. 17, p. 246: James V. Crocetti.

Administrative Records, Probate Court, Jefferson County, Ohio. Vol. 25, p. 321: John Crocetti.

Administrative Records, Probate Court, Jefferson County, Ohio. Guardian Vol. 4, p. 352: File No. 10.458 [guardianship of Angelina Barr], January 1910.

Bankruptcy No. 84544: Martin (filed 23 January 1946; discharged 27 December 1947), U.S. District Court, Southern District of New York. Accession No. 57A136, Federal Records Center Location 24891.

Birth Records, Registrar-Recorder, County of Los Angeles, Calif. Certificate of Birth: Dean Paul Martin, Jr., 17 November 1951.

Birth Records, Registrar-Recorder, County of Los Angeles, Calif. Certificate of Birth: Ricci James Martin, 20 September 1953.

Birth Records, Registrar-Recorder, County of Los Angeles, Calif. Certificate of Birth: Gina Carolyn Martin, 20 December 1956.

Birth Records, State of Ohio, Department of Vital Statistics, City Health Department, Steubenville, Ohio. Certificate of Birth: Angela Barra, 18 December 1897.

Birth Records, State of Ohio, Department of Vital Statistics, City Health Department, Steubenville, Ohio. Certificate of Birth: Alico [sic] Crocetti, 7 May 1917 [and Affidavit, 24 October 1969 correcting name to Archie John Crocetti].

Birth Records, State of Ohio, Department of Vital Statistics, City Health Department, Steubenville, Ohio. Certificate of Birth: Guglielmo Crocetti, 21 June 1916.

Birth Records, State of Ohio, Department of Vital Statistics, City Health Department, Steubenville, Ohio. Certificate of Birth: Dino Crocetti, 7 June 1917 [and Affidavit, 26 January 1953, of name missing from original certificate].

Birth Records, State of Ohio, Department of Vital Statistics, City Health Department, Steubenville, Ohio. Certificate of Birth: John Crocetti, 20 June 1915.

Birth Records, State of Ohio, Department of Vital Statistics, City Health Department, Steubenville, Ohio. Certificate of Birth: Maria Crocetti, 15 June 1913.

Birth Records, State of Ohio, Department of Vital Statistics, City Health Department, Steubenville, Ohio. Certificate of Birth: Robert Crocetti, 17 November 1915.

Birth Records, State of Ohio, Department of Vital Statistics, City Health Department, Steubenville, Ohio. Certificate of Birth: Barbara Gail Martin, 11 April 1945.

Birth Records, State of Ohio, Department of Vital Statistics, Cleveland, Ohio. Certificate of Birth: Stephan Craig Martin, 29 June 1942.

Death Records, Registrar-Recorder, County of Los Angeles, Calif. Certificate of Death 7097-051774: Angela Crocetti, 25 December 1966.

Death Records, Registrar-Recorder, County of Los Angeles, Calif. Certificate of Death 7097-035415: Guy Crocetti, 29 August 1967.

Death Records, Registrar-Recorder, County of Los Angeles, Calif. Certificate of Death 7097-041973: William Anthony Crocetti, 20 October 1968.

Death Records, State of Ohio, Department of Vital Statistics, City Health Department, Steubenville, Ohio. Certificate of Death: Julia Porreca Crocetti, 25 September 1920.

Death Records, State of Ohio, Department of Vital Statistics, City Health Department, Steubenville, Ohio. Certificate of Death: Vincenzo Tripodi, 17 December 1987.

Death Records, State of Ohio, Department of Vital Statistics, Cleveland, Ohio. Certificate of Death: Sammy Watkins, 26 July 1969.

Marriage Records, Probate Court, Cuyahoga County, Ohio. License No. 59144: Sam B. Watkovitz [Sammy Watkins] and Lillian P. Curry, 8 April 1939.

Marriage Records, Probate Court, Cuyahoga County, Ohio. License No. 88761: Dino Crocetti and Elizabeth A. McDonald, 2 October 1941.

Marriage Records, Probate Court, Jefferson County, Ohio. Vol. 22, p. 364: Giuseppe Crocetti and Julia Porreca Schiappa, 14 September 1912.

Marriage Records, Probate Court, Jefferson County, Ohio. Vol. 23, p. 304: Vincenzo Crocetti and Maria Biandoria Febo, 8 March 1914.

Marriage Records, Probate Court, Jefferson County, Ohio. Vol. 23, p. 483: Gaetano Crocetti and Angela Barra, 25 October 1914.

Marriage Records, Probate Court, Jefferson County, Ohio. Vol. 29, p. 612: Vincenzo Tripodi and Amelia Buffone, 1926.

Marriage Records, Probate Court, Jefferson County, Ohio. Vol. 40, p. 643: Robert A. Crocetti and Katherine Sullivan, 2 April 1946.

Marriage Records, Registrar-Recorder, County of Los Angeles, Calif. Registrar's No. 21603: Dean Martin and Jeanne Biegger, 1 September 1949.

Marriage Records, Registrar-Recorder, County of Los Angeles, Calif. License No. WE 1120: Dean Martin and Catherine Mae Hawn, 25 April 1973.

Parish Records, Church of St. Anthony of Padua, Steubenville, Ohio. Certificate of Baptism: Dino Crocetti, 16 September 1917.

Parish Records, Church of St. Anthony of Padua, Steubenville, Ohio. Record of Confirmation, Rectory Ledger, p. 22: Dean Crocetti, 30 April 1928.

Parish Records, St. Ann's Parish, Cleveland, Ohio. Certificate of Baptism: Stephen Craig Crocetti, 16 August 1942.

Registro degli Atti di Nascita, Comune di Montesilvano, Provincia di Pescara. Anno 1893, Parte I, No. 32: Gaetano Crocetti.

State of Nevada, Gaming Control Board, Carson City. Application for State Gaming License: Dean P. Martin, 7 June 1961.

State of Nevada, Gaming Control Board, Carson City. Application for State Gaming License: Dean P. Martin, 14 January 1969.

U.S. Department of Justice, Federal Bureau of Investigation, Washington, D.C. File No. 92-5044: Paul Emilio D'Amato.

U.S. Department of Justice, Immigration and Naturalization Service, Cleveland, Ohio. Petition for Naturalization No. 3135 and Amendment of Petition: [James] Vincenzo Crocetti.

U.S. Department of Justice, Immigration and Naturalization Service, Cleveland, Ohio. Certificate of Naturalization No. 6127538: James Vincenzo Crocetti, 8 March 1944.

U.S. Department of Justice, Immigration and Naturalization Service. *Passenger and Crew Lists of Vessels Arriving at New York, N.Y., 1897–1942* (Washington, D.C.: National Archives Microfilm Publication T-715). May 17,

1907 [Vol. 2018; National Archives Roll 897]: list 43, p. 44, no. 26 [Giuseppe Crocetti]. March 3, 1910 [Vol. 3123; N.A. Roll 1419]: list 44, p. 76, no. 12 [Vincenzo Crocetti]. September 11, 1913 [Vol. 4940; N.A. Roll 2173]: list 215, p. 78, no. 29 [Gaetano Crocetti]. March 22, 1921 [Vol. 6731; N.A. Roll 2940]: list 213, p. 55, no. 30 [Giovanni Crocetti].

U.S. Department of Labor, Naturalization Service. Declaration of Intention No. 4051 [Common Pleas Court, Jefferson County, Ohio]: Guy Crocetti, 31 February 1919.

U.S. Department of Labor, Naturalization Service. Declaration of Intention No. 8215 [Common Pleas Court, Jefferson County, Ohio]: Guy Crocetti, 25 April 1932.

U.S. Department of Labor, Naturalization Service. Petition for Naturalization No. 1395: Guy Crocetti, 4 March 1937.

U.S. Department of Labor, Naturalization Service. Certificate of Citizenship No. 4274388: Guy Crocetti, 7 September 1937.

Trial Transcripts and Files

Dean Martin v. *Cathy Mae Martin.* Superior Court, Los Angeles County, Calif. No. D 896123: 15 July 1976.

Dean Martin v. *Cathy Mae Martin.* Superior Court, Los Angeles County, Calif. No. D 89899: 19 November 1976.

Dean Martin v. *Elizabeth Anne Martin.* Superior Court, Los Angeles County, Calif. No. S.M.D. 16571: 18 November 1957.

Dean Martin v. *Jeanne Martin.* Superior Court, Los Angeles County, Calif. No. D 803030: 14 February 1972.

Dean Martin and Jerry Lewis v. *Abner J. Greshler.* Superior Court, Los Angeles County, Calif. [Before the Arbitration Tribunal of Screen Actors Guild, Inc.]. No. 582187: 19 January 1951.

Dean Martin and Jerry Lewis v. *Violet Greshler, et al.* Superior Court, Los Angeles County, Calif. No. S.M.C. 2645: 5 October 1950.

Elizabeth Anne Martin v. *Dean Paul Martin.* Clark County, Nevada. Case No. 46103: 24 August 1949.

Elizabeth Anne Martin v. *Dean Paul Martin.* Superior Court, Los Angeles County, Calif. No. D 375286: 14 February 1949.

People of the State of California v. *Dean Paul Martin.* Municipal Court, Beverly Hills Judicial District, County of Los Angeles, Calif. No. M 70102: 2 June 1982.

Screen Associates v. *Dean Martin.* Superior Court, Los Angeles County, Calif. No. 589172: 3 August 1951.

Sammy Watkins v. *Dino Crocetti.* Superior Court, Los Angeles County, Calif. No. 555747: 15 February 1949.

DISCOGRAPHY

The number preceding the title is the master number. Following the title is the original single-release number, if any, and the original album-release number, if any.

DIAMOND RECORDS
July 1946

2035A	Which Way Did My Heart Go?	2035	Diamond D-7
2035X	All of Me	2035	Diamond D-7
2036A	I Got the Sun in the Morning	2036	
2036X	The Sweetheart of Sigma Chi	2036	

APOLLO RECORDS
October 1947

3142	Oh, Marie	1088	EP 705
3143	Walkin' My Baby Back Home	1088	EP 705

November 1947

3229	Santa Lucia	1116	EP 705
3230	Hold Me	1116	EP 705
3231	Memory Lane		Audition 33-5936
3232	Louise		Audition 33-5936

EMBASSY RECORDS
November 1947 [?]

124A	One Foot in Heaven	124
124B	The Night Is Young and You're So Beautiful	124

CAPITOL RECORDS
September 13, 1948

| 3494 | The Money Song
[w/ Jerry Lewis] | 15249 | |
| 3495 | That Certain Party
[w/ Jerry Lewis] | 15249 | CDP 7 91633 2 |

Note: These were vocal tracks. The music tracks, by the Mario R. Armengol Orchestra, were recorded on September 9.

November 22, 1948

| 3550 | Tarra Ta-larra Ta-Lar | 15329 | |
| 3600 | Once in Love with Amy | 15329 | Pickwick 3057 |

December 14, 1948

| 3587 | You Was! *[w/ Peggy Lee]* | 15349 |

December 17, 1948

| 3805 | Powder Your Face with Sunshine
(Smile! Smile! Smile!) | 15351 | CDP 7 91633 2* |
| 3806 | Absence Makes the Heart Grow Fonder
(for Somebody Else) | 15351 | Pickwick 3136 |

Note: Music tracks, by the Paul Weston Orchestra, were recorded December 15.
*Previously released in the 1966 LP anthology Camp *(Capitol T-2472).*

January 26, 1949

| 3906 | Have a Little Sympathy | 15395 |
| 3907 | Johnny, Get Your Girl | 15395 |

March 9, 1949

| 4089 | Dreamy Old New England Moon | 549 |
| 4090 | Three Wishes | 549 |

June 20, 1949

| 4520 | Just for Fun | 691 |
| 4558 | My Own, My Only, My All | 691 |

August 12, 1949

| 4873 | That Lucky Old Sun | 726 | Pickwick 3057 |
| 4874 | Vieni Su (Say You Love Me Too!) | 726 | |

March 3, 1950

5604	Rain	937	Pickwick 3136
5605	Zing-a Zing-a Zing Boom	937	
5606	I'm Gonna Paper All My Walls with Your Love Letters	948	Tower 5036
5607	Muskrat Ramble	948	CDP 7 94306 2

March 28, 1950

5662	I Don't Care if the Sun Don't Shine	981	CDP 7 94306 2
5699	Choo'n Gum	981	
5800	Be Honest with Me	1002	2212
5801	I Still Get a Thrill	1002	Pickwick 3057

April 27, 1950

| 5919 | Bye Bye Blackbird | 1052 | CDP 7 94306 2 |
| 5920 | Happy Feet | 1052 | CDP 7 94306 2 |

April 28, 1950

5923	Baby, Obey Me	1028	
5924	I'll Always Love You (Day After Day)	1028	Tower 5036
5925	The Darktown Strutters' Ball		CDP 7 94306 2
5926	Rock-a-Bye Your Baby with a Dixie Melody		

July 6, 1950

| 6311 | I'm in Love with You [w/ Margaret Whiting] | 1160 | |
| 6312 | Don't Rock the Boat, Dear [w/ Margaret Whiting] | 1160 | |

July 31, 1950

| 6467 | Tonda Wanda Hoy | 1358 | |
| 6468 | Who's Sorry Now? | 1458 | Pickwick 3057 |

| 6469 | Wham! Bam! Thank You, Ma'am! | 1139 | |
| 6470 | The Peddler's Serenade | 1139 | |

December 2, 1950

6886	If	1342	Pickwick 3057
6887	Beside You	1458	Tower 5059
6888	I Love the Way You Say Goodnight	1342	Tower 5036
6889	You and Your Beautiful Eyes	1358	

April 9, 1951

7324	We Never Talk Much, We Just Sit Around [w/ Helen O'Connell]	1575	
7325	How D'ya Like Your Eggs in the Morning? [w/ Helen O'Connell]	1575	
7326	In the Cool, Cool, Cool of the Evening	1703	Pickwick 3136
7327	Bonne Nuit	1703	

June 20, 1951

7254	Luna Mezzo Mare	1724	EP 481
7255	Pennies from Heaven		Tower 5018
7256	Go Go Go Go	1724	

August 29, 1951

7478	Aw C'mon	1797	
7479	Hangin' Around with You	1797	
7480	Solitaire	1817	2815
7481	My Heart Has Found a Home Now	1938	

September 15, 1951

7973	(Ma Come Bali) Bella Bimba	1811	
9020	The Sailors' Polka	1901	
9021	I Ran All the Way Home	1817	Tower 5059
9022	Meanderin'	1811	

November 5, 1951

9282	As You Are	1921	
9292	Blue Smoke (Kohu-Auwahi)	1885	
9293	Night Train to Memphis	1885	

November 19, 1951

9318	Until	1938	Tower 5036
9319	Oh Boy! Oh Boy! Oh Boy! Oh Boy! Oh Boy!	1921	
9320	Come Back to Sorrento (Torna a Surriento)	2140	401
9321	Never Before	1901	Tower 5059

January 21, 1952

9625	When You're Smiling	1975	401
9626	Won't You Surrender	2001	
9627	All I Have to Give You	1975	Tower 5036
9628	Pretty as a Picture	2001	

April 8, 1952

9871	Oh, Marie	2140	401
9937	I Passed Your House Tonight	2071	
9938	Bet-I-Cha	2071	

June 12, 1952

10272	You Belong to Me	2165	CDP 7 91633 2
10273	Kiss	2319	
10274	What Could Be More Beautiful	2319	Tower 5059
10275	Little Did We Know	2378	Tower 5018

July 2, 1952

10173	Susan		
10174	The Peanut Vendor		
10352	I Know a Dream When I See One	2240	
10353	Second Chance	2240	Tower 5059
10354	Hominy Grits	2165	CDP 7 94306 2

November 20, 1952

| 10836 | Just One More Chance | | H-401 |
| 10837 | I'm Yours | | H-401 |

10838	With My Eyes Wide Open I'm Dreaming		H-401
10839	There's My Lover	2378	Tower 5059
10840	A Girl Named Mary and a Boy Named Bill		H-401
10841	Louise		H-401
10842	Who's Your Little Who-Zis!		H-401
10843	I Feel Like a Feather in the Breeze		H-401
10844	I Feel a Song Comin' On		H-401

May 4, 1953

11532	'Til I Find You	2485	Tower 5059
11533	Don't You Remember?	2555	EP 939, 1047
11534	If I Could Sing Like Bing	2555	
11535	Love Me, Love Me	2485	2815

August 13, 1953

11693	I Want You		
11694	That's Amore	2589	EP 481, 401
11695	You're the Right One	2589	
11697	I'd Cry Like a Baby		

September 3, 1953

20187	Where Can I Go Without You?		
20188	If I Should Love Again	2640	Tower 5036

October 5, 1953

11943	The Christmas Blues	2640	CDP 7 9 31152

December 23, 1953

12132	Hey, Brother, Pour the Wine	2749	2212
12133	Money Burns a Hole in My Pocket	2818	EP 533
12134	Moments Like This		
12135	That's What I Like	2870	EP 533, 2815

December 24, 1953

11696	I Want You		
11697	I'd Cry Like a Baby	2749	CDP 7 91633 2

April 20, 1954

12811	How Do You Speak to an Angel?		EP 533
12813	Ev'ry Street's a Boulevard in Old New York [w/ Jerry Lewis]		EP 533
12841	Money Burns a Hole in My Pocket		EP 533
12842	That's What I Like		EP 533

Note: Capitol purchased these masters from Paramount.

April 22, 1954

12571	Belle from Barcelona (O-o-lé, Mu-cha-cha)	3011	
12572	Sway	2818	2601
12573	Under the Bridges of Paris	3036	
12574	The Peddlar Man (Ten I Loved)	2870	2815
12608	I Never Had a Chance		

August 12, 1954

12908	Confused	3011	
12909	One More Time	2911	Tower 5059
12910	Try Again	2911	2815
12911	I'll Gladly Make the Same Mistake Again	3988	

September 7, 1954

13011	Open Up the Doghouse (Two Cats Are Comin' In) [w/ Nat King Cole]	2985
13012	Long, Long Ago [w/ Nat King Cole]	2985

*Note: These duets were released on a Cole album in England (*Music for Pleasure *1432) in 1971. The Official label of Denmark later released them as well, on the 1990 album* Havin' Fun with Nat King Cole *(LP 12003; CD 812003).*

September 30, 1954

12705	Mississippi Mud	576
12717	When It's Sleepy Time Down South	576
13029	Carolina Moon	576

13030	'Way Down Yonder in New Orleans		576

October 7, 1954

13050	Just a Little Bit South of North Carolina		576
13051	Georgia on My Mind		576
13056	Waiting for the Robert E. Lee		576
13057	Carolina in the Morning		576

November 26, 1954

13208	Let Me Go, Lover		EP 9123
13209	The Naughty Lady of Shady Lane		EP 9123
13210	Mambo Italiano		EP 9123
13211	That's All I Want from You		EP 9123

December 28, 1954

13387	Young and Foolish	3036	2212

February 4, 1955

13548	Basin Street Blues		576
13549	Is It True What They Say About Dixie?		576
13550	Dinah		576
13551	Alabamy Bound		576

April 20, 1955

13722	Chee Chee-oo Chee (Sang the Little Bird)		
13723	In Napoli	3238	Tower 5018
13724	The Lady with the Big Umbrella	3352	
13725	I Like Them All	3238	EP 701

April 25, 1955

13741	Chee Chee-oo Chee (Sang the Little Bird)	3133	Tower 5018
13742	Love Is All That Matters	3153	Tower 5036
13743	Simpatico	3153	
13744	Ridin' into Love	3133	EP 701

April 27, 1955

13749	Relax-Ay-Voo *[w/ Line Renaud]*	3196	
13750	Two Sleepy People *[w/ Line Renaud]*	3196	
13751	I Know Your Mother Loves You		

October 28, 1955

14643	Memories Are Made of This	3295	EP 701, 2601
14658	Change of Heart	3295	EP 701
14668	When You Pretend		
14669	The Lucky Song		EP 702

November 18, 1955

14707	When You Pretend		EP 702
14708	You Look So Familiar		EP 702
14709	Innamorata (Sweetheart)	3352	EP 702, CDP 7 91633 2

February 8, 1956

15026	*Children's Songs from Italy— Part 1*		
15027	*Children's Songs from Italy— Part 2*		

March 7, 1956

15176	The Look	3577	1047
15177	Mississippi Dreamboat	3521	2212
15178	Standing on the Corner	3414	2815
15179	Street of Love (Rue de Mon Amour)		Tower 5036
15180	Watching the World Go By	3414	2212

May 15, 1956

15474	Pardners *[w/ Jerry Lewis]*		EP 752

May 22, 1956

15481	The Test of Time	3521	1047
15482	Me 'n' You 'n' the Moon		EP 752
15483	The Wind, the Wind		EP 752
15484	I'm Gonna Steal You Away	3468	

August 20, 1956

15850	Bamboozled	3680	
15851	Give Me a Sign	3577	
15852	Captured	3648	
15853	I Know I Can't Forget	3604	1047

November 26, 1956

16026	I Never Had a Chance	3718	Tower 5006
16027	It Looks Like Love		EP 806
16028	Let's Be Friendly		EP 806
16029	Just Kiss Me	3604	

December 6, 1956

16227	A Day in the Country		EP 806
16228	Hollywood or Bust		EP 806
16229	The Man Who Plays the Mandolino	3648	2815

January 28, 1957

16531	Nevertheless (I'm in Love with You)		849
16532	I Can't Give You Anything but Love	3718	849
16533	It's Easy to Remember		849
16534	Pretty Baby		849
16539	Sleepy Time Gal		849
16540	For You		849

January 30, 1957

16527	Maybe		849
16528	Once in a While		849
16529	I Don't Know Why (I Just Do)		849
16530	The Object of My Affection		849
16545	Only Forever		849
16546	You've Got Me Crying Again		849

February 5, 1957

16567	Money Is a Problem		EP 840
16570	You I Love		EP 840
16571	Ten Thousand Bedrooms		EP 840
16572	Only Trust Your Heart	3680	EP 840

May 22, 1957

17023	Beau James	3752	
17074	Promise Her Anything	3787	1047
17075	The Tricche Tracche	3787	
17076	Write to Me from Naples	3752	1047

October 24, 1957

17707	Good Mornin', Life	3841	
17708	Makin' Love Ukulele Style	3841	1047
17716	Cheatin' on Me		1047

January 23, 1958

18250	Return to Me (Ritorna a Me)	3894	EP 939, 1047
18252	Buona Sera		1047
18253	Forgetting You	3894	2212
18283	Tu Sei Bella, Signorina	4518	
18290	Angel Baby	3988	1047

March 1958

| | It's 1200 Miles from Palm Springs to Texas | HB-2160 | |

Note: Promotional recording for Texas Desert Week in Palm Springs, April 16–20, 1958.

June 20, 1958

19438	You Were Made for Love	4124	Tower 5036
19439	Once Upon a Time (It Happened)	4065	
19440	Outa My Mind	4028	
19441	The Magician	4065	

July 14, 1958

| 19593 | Volare (Nel Blu, Dipinto di Blu) | 4028 | EP 1027, 1047 |

September 15, 1958

30113	Rio Bravo	4174	Tower 5006
30114	It Takes So Long (to Say Goodbye)	4124	Tower 5006
30115	On an Evening in Roma (Sott'er Celo de Roma)	4222	

30116	My Rifle, My Pony and Me	4174

Note: This was Martin's first stereo (three-track) session.

October 13, 1958

30354	Dream	1150
30355	Dream a Little Dream of Me	1150
30356	Good Night Sweetheart	1150
30357	Cuddle Up a Little Closer	1150

October 14, 1958

30400	Sleep Warm	PRO-987	1150
30401	Let's Put Out the Lights		1150
30402	Brahms' Lullaby		1150
30403	Goodnight, My Love		1150

October 15, 1958

30147	Sleepy Time Gal		1150
30148	Wrap Your Troubles in Dreams		1150
30149	All I Do Is Dream of You	PRO-987	1150
30150	Hit the Road to Dreamland		1150

January 1959 (Warner Bros.)

	My Rifle, My Pony and Me [w/ Ricky Nelson]	Warner Bros. JB-2262

Note: Promotional recording for the film Rio Bravo; *released as a one-sided single in February 1959.*

May 13, 1959

31662	Sogni d'Oro	4472	
31663	Napoli		
31664	You Can't Love 'Em All	4222	Pickwick 3057
31665	How Sweet It Is	4472	Tower 5018
31678	Off Again, On Again		Tower 5006

May 15, 1959

31691	Humdinger	4420	
31692	I Ain't Gonna Lead This Life No More	4287	Pickwick 3057
31693	Love Me, My Love		Tower 5006
31694	Buttercup of Golden Hair	4391	

July 29, 1959

32147	The Things We Did Last Summer	1285	
32148	Winter Wonderland	1285	
32149	White Christmas	1285	
32150	Canadian Sunset	1285	

August 4, 1959

32161	A Winter Romance	1285	
32162	June in January	1285	
32163	It Won't Cool Off	1285	
32164	I've Got My Love to Keep Me Warm	1285	

August 6, 1959

32191	Out in the Cold Again	1285	
32192	Baby, It's Cold Outside	1285	
32193	Rudolph the Red-Nosed Reindeer	1285	
32194	Let It Snow! Let It Snow! Let It Snow!	1285	

August 31, 1959

32304	Professor! Professor!	4361	
32305	Napoli	4361	
32306	(Love Is a) Career	4287	Tower 5006
32307	Who Was That Lady?	4328	Tower 5018

May 9, 1960

33702	Do It Yourself	1435	
33704	Better Than a Dream [w/ Judy Holliday]	1435	
33705	I Met a Girl	1435	
33706	Just in Time [w/ Judy Holliday]	1435	
	My Guiding Star*	SPO-145	

Note: Capitol purchased these masters from MGM.

*Deleted from the soundtrack of Bells Are Ringing, *this recording was released as a bootleg single in 1976.*

May 9, 1960

33744	Someday		1442
33745	On the Street Where You Live		1442
33746	I've Grown Accustomed to Her Face		1442
33747	Imagination		1442

May 10, 1960

33804	Until the Real Thing Comes Along		1442
33805	Please Don't Talk About Me when I'm Gone		1442
33806	You're Nobody 'til Somebody Loves You		1442
33807	Ain't That a Kick in the Head	4420	Pickwick 3057
33808	Mean to Me		1442

May 17, 1960

33847	Just in Time	4391	1442
33848	True Love		1442
33849	Heaven Can Wait		1442
33850	I Can't Believe That You're in Love with Me		1442

December 12, 1960

35075	The Story of Life		
35076	Bella Bella Bambina		
35077	Giuggiola	4570	
35078	Sparklin' Eyes	4518	Tower 5018

December 13, 1960

35083	Let Me Know	
35084	Be an Angel	
35085	Hear My Heart (Sente le Coure)	

February 10, 1961

35351	All in a Night's Work	4551	Pickwick 3089
35352	The Story of Life	4570	Tower 5006
35353	Giuggiola		
35354	Hear My Heart (Sente le Coure)		Tower 5006

February 15, 1961

35404	Be an Angel		Tower 5006
35405	Bella Bella Bambina	4551	
35406	Let Me Know		Tower 5018

September 6, 1961

36411	Arrivederci, Roma	1659
36428	There's No Tomorrow	
	(O Sole Mio)	1659
36436	Return to Me	1659
36443	Non Dimenticar	1659
36444	I Have but One Heart	
	(O Marenariello)	1659

September 7, 1961

36449	You're Breaking My Heart	
	(Mattinata)	1659
36450	On an Evening in Roma	
	(Sott'er Celo de Roma)	1659
36451	Pardon (Perdoname)	1659
36452	Just Say I Love Her	
	(Dicitencello Vuie)	1659

September 8, 1961

36453	Take Me in Your Arms (Torna	
	a Surriento)	1659
36454	My Heart Reminds Me	1659
35455	Vieni Su	1659

December 18, 1961

36853	Love, Your Spell Is	
	Everywhere	1702
36854	Cha Cha Cha d'Amour	
	(Melodie d'Amour)	1702
36879	Amor	1702
36887	Two Loves Have I	1702

December 19, 1961

36898	I Love You Much Too Much	1702
36899	Let Me Love You Tonight	1702
36921	My One and Only Love	1702
36922	I Wish You Love	1702

December 20, 1961

36946	If Love Is Good to Me	1702
36947	(I Love You) for Sentimental Reasons	1702
36948	Somebody Loves You	1702
36949	A Hundred Years from Today	1702

REPRISE RECORDS
February 13, 1962

857	Senza Fine	20140
858	Dame Su Amor	20082
859	Baby-O	20082
860	Just Close Your Eyes	20058
861	Tik-a-Tee, Tik-a-Tay	20058

February 26, 1962

912	Ç'est Si Bon	20072	6021
913	The Poor People of Paris	20072	6021
914	The River Seine		6021
915	I Love Paris		6021
916	The Last Time I Saw Paris		6021
917	Mimi		6021
918	April in Paris	40016	6021
919	Darling, Je Vous Aime Beaucoup		6021
920	Gigi		6021
921	La Vie en Rose		6021
922	Ç'est Magnifique	40019	6021
923	Mam'selle	40019	6021

August 28–30, 1962

1428	Mañana		6054
1429	South of the Border		6054
1430	Tangerine		6054
1431	In a Little Spanish Town	20116	6054
1432	El Rancho Grande		6054
1433	What a Difference a Day Made		6054
1434	Always in My Heart		6054
1435	Magic Is the Moonlight		6054
1436	Bésame Mucho		6054
1437	From the Bottom of My Heart (Dammi, Dammi, Dammi)	20116	

| 1438 | Who's Got the Action? | 20140 | |
| 1439 | La Paloma | | 6054 |

October 22, 1962

| 1510 | Sam's Song [w/ Sammy Davis, Jr.] | 20128 | 6188 |

December 1962

1605	Any Time		6061
1606	Room Full of Roses		6061
1607	My Heart Cries for You		6061
1608	I'm So Lonesome I Could Cry		6061
1609	Shutters and Boards		6061
1610	Singing the Blues		6061
1611	Ain't Gonna Try Anymore	20150	6061
1612	Face in the Crowd	20150	6061
1613	Things		6061
1614	Blue, Blue Day		6061
1615	Hey, Good Lookin'		6061
1616	I Walk the Line		6061

April 22, 1963

2011	My Sugar's Gone	20194	6085
2012	Candy Kisses		6085
2013	Take Good Care of Her		6085
2014	I Can't Help It		6085

April 23, 1963

2015	I'm Gonna Change Everything		6085
2016	Bouquet of Roses	0466	6085
2017	From Lover to Loser		6085
2018	Rockin' Alone		6085

April 24, 1963

2019	Second Hand Rose		6085
2020	Corrine, Corrina		6085
2021	The Middle of the Night Is My Cryin' Time	20194	6085
2022	Just a Little Lovin'		6085

August 13, 1963

2149	We Open in Venice		
	[w/ Sinatra & Davis]		2017
2155	Bianca		2017
2159	If This Isn't Love		
	[w/ the Hi-Lo's]		2015

August 1963

2184	Fugue for Tinhorns		
	[w/ Sinatra & Crosby]	20217	2016
2185	The Oldest Established		
	(Permanent Floating Crap		
	Game in New York)		
	[w/ Sinatra & Crosby]	20217	2016
2188	Guys and Dolls [w/ Sinatra]		2016
2196	Guys and Dolls (Reprise)		
	[w/ Sinatra]		2016
2224	Peace on Earth/Silent Night		50001

October 6, 1963

2299	Via Veneto	20215	
2300	Mama Rosa	20215	

December 17, 1963

2476	Grazie, Prego, Scusi	0252	
2477	Marina		
2478	Take Me		6140
2479	La Giostra (The Merry-Go-		
	Round)	0252	

March 12–15, 1964

2662	My Melancholy Baby		6123
2663	Smile		6123
2664	I'm Confessin'		6123
2665	Baby, Won't You Please Come		
	Home?		6123
2666	I Don't Know Why (I Just Do)		6123
2667	Fools Rush In		6123
2668	I'll Buy That Dream		6123
2669	Blue Moon		6123
2670	If You Were the Only Girl		6123
2671	Gimme a Little Kiss		6123

| 2672 | Everybody Loves Somebody | | 6123 |
| 2673 | Hands Across the Table | | 6123 |

April 10, 1964

2631	Style [w/ Sinatra, Crosby & Davis]		2021
2632	Mr. Booze [w/ Sinatra, Crosby & Davis]		2021
2633	Don't Be a Do-Badder (Finale) [w/ Sinatra, Crosby & Davis]		2021
2634	Any Man Who Loves His Mother		2021

April 16, 1964

2703	Everybody Loves Somebody	0281	6130
2704	Your Other Love		6130
2705	Siesta Fiesta		6130
2706	A Little Voice	0281	6130

August 7, 1964

2914	So Long, Baby		6140
2915	The Door Is Still Open to My Heart	0307	6140
2916	You're Nobody 'til Somebody Loves You	0333	6140
2917	Every Minute, Every Hour	0307	6140

August 24, 1964

2932	We'll Sing in the Sunshine		6140
2933	Clinging Vine		6140
2934	Always Together		6140
2935	In the Misty Moonlight	0640	6140

November 3, 1964

3035	Have a Heart		6146
3036	You'll Always Be the One I Love	0333	6146
3037	Wedding Bells		6146
3038	Sophia	PRO-200	

December 22, 1964

3140	Send Me the Pillow You Dream On	0344	6146
3141	I'll Be Seeing You	0344	6146
3142	Send Me Some Lovin'		6146
3144	In the Chapel in the Moonlight	0601	6146
3145	I'll Hold You in My Heart		6146
3146	My Heart Is an Open Book		6146

March 13–16, 1965

H-3308	(Remember Me) I'm the One Who Loves You	0369	6170
H-3309	Here Comes My Baby		6170
H-3310	Welcome to My World	0601	6170
H-3311	The Birds and the Bees		6170
H-3312	I Don't Think You Love Me Anymore		6170
H-3313	My Shoes Keep Walking Back to You		6170
H-3314	Born to Lose		6170
H-3315	King of the Road		6170
H-3316	Take These Chains from My Heart		6170
H-3317	Walk On By		6170
H-3318	Bumming Around	0393	6170
H-3319	Red Roses for a Blue Lady		6170

July 2, 1965

H-3622	Love, Love, Love		6181
H-3623	Houston	0393	6181
H-3624	Little Lovely One		6181

September 15, 1965

H-3740	I Will	0415	6181
H-3741	Down Home		6181
H-3742	Old Yellow Line		6181

September 20, 1965

H-3743	The First Thing Ev'ry Morning		6181
H-3744	Everybody but Me		6181
H-3745	You're the Reason I'm in Love	0415	6181

October 5, 1965

H-3746	Hammer and Nails		6181
H-3747	Snap Your Fingers		6181
H-3748	Detour		6181

January 11, 1966

J-3966	Somewhere There's a Someone	0443	6201
J-3967	That Old Clock on the Wall	0443	6201
J-3968	Leave a Light in Your Window		

January 26–27, 1966

J-3991	South of the Border		6211
J-3992	Empty Saddles in the Old Corral		6211
J-3993	Red Sails in the Sunset		6211
J-3994	On the Sunny Side of the Street		6211
J-3997	The Glory of Love	0640	6211
J-3999	Side by Side		6211
J-4000	If You Knew Susie		6211
J-4001	The Last Round-Up		6211

March 26, 1966

J-4158	Come Running Back	0466	6213
J-4159	Shades	0500	6213
J-4160	One Lonely Boy	0765	6213
J-4161	Terrible, Tangled Web		6213

April 11, 1966

J-4196	Don't Let the Blues Make You Bad		6213
J-4197	Nobody but a Fool (Would Love You)		6213
J-4198	I'm Living in Two Worlds		6213
J-4199	Today Is Not the Day		6213

June 30, 1966

| J-4409 | A Million and One | 0500 | 6213 |
| J-4411 | A Marshmellow World | 0542 | 6222 |

August 17, 1966

J-4472	Nobody's Baby Again	0516	6242
J-4473	It Just Happened That Way	0516	6242
J-4474	White Christmas		6222

September 20, 1966

J-4512	Winter Wonderland		6222
J-4513	Let It Snow, Let It Snow, Let It Snow		6222
J-4514	Jingle Bells		6222
J-4515	The Things We Did Last Summer		6222
J-4516	Blue Christmas	0542	6222
J-4517	Silent Night		6222
J-4518	I'll Be Home for Christmas		6222
J-4519	Silver Bells	PRO-247	6222

October 19, 1966

J-4573	The One I Love (Belongs to Somebody Else)		6233
J-4574	Baby, Won't You Please Come Home		6233
J-4775	If I Had You		6233
J-4576	I've Grown Accustomed to Your Face		6233
J-4577	It's the Talk of the Town		6233
J-4578	Just Friends		6233
J-4579	S'posin'		6233
J-4580	What Can I Say After I Say I'm Sorry		6233
J-4581	Home		6233

December 11, 1966

J-4611	I'm Not the Marrying Kind	0538	6242
J-4614	Thirty More Miles to San Diego		6242
J-4616	(Open Up the Door) Let the Good Times In	0538	6242
J-4617	Pride		6250

March 13, 1967

| K-4860 | You've Still Got a Place in My Heart | | 6242 |

K-4861	Sweet, Sweet Lovable You		6242
K-4862	Think About Me	0571	6242
K-4863	Lay Some Happiness on Me	0571	6242
K-4864	He's Got You		6242
K-4865	If I Ever Get Back to Georgia		6242

June 23, 1967

K-6043	Little Ole Wine Drinker Me	0608	6250
K-6056	Turn to Me		6250
K-6057	Release Me		6250
K-6058	I Can't Help Remembering You	0608	6250
K-6059	The Green Green Grass of Home		6250
K-6060	A Place in the Shade		6250
K-6061	Wallpaper Roses	0640	6250

September 20, 1967

| K-6161 | Things *[w/ Nancy Sinatra]* | | 6277 |

Note: Nancy Sinatra overdub of existing master 1613 (December 1962).

February 13, 1968

| L-6446 | You've Still Got a Place in My Heart | 0672 | |

Note: Instrumental overdub of existing master K-4860 (March 1967).

June 27, 1968

L-6652	By the Time I Get to Phoenix		6330
L-6653	Gentle on My Mind	0812	6330
L-6654	Rainbows Are Back in Style	0780	6330
L-6655	Honey		6330

June 28, 1968

L-6656	That's When I See the Blues	0812	6330
L-6657	Welcome to My Heart		6330
L-6658	Drowning in My Tears	0841	6330
L-6659	Not Enough Indians	0780	6330
L-6660	That Old Time Feelin'	0761	6330
L-6661	April Again	0761	6330

July 23, 1968

L-6739	Five Card Stud	0765	

June 11–12, 1969

M-7323	Do You Believe This Town		6338
M-7324	Where the Blue and Lonely Go		6338
M-7372	Make It Rain		6338
M-7373	The Sneaky Little Side of Me		6338
M-7377	Crying Time	0857	6338
M-7378	I Take a Lot of Pride in What I Am	0841	6338
M-7379	If You Ever Get Around to Loving Me		6338
M-7380	One Cup of Happiness (and One Peace of Mind)	0857	6338
M-7381	Little Green Apples		6338
M-7382	The Sun Is Shining (on Everybody but Me)		6338

January 8–9, 1970

N-17990	Down Home	0893	
N-17991	For the Love of a Woman	0915	
N-17992	The Tracks of My Tears	0915	
N-17993	Come On Down	0893	

May 27–28, 1970

N-18647	Make the World Go Away		6403
N-18648	Together Again		6403
N-18649	Detroit City		6403
N-18650	Once a Day		6403
N-18651	Heart over Mind		6403
N-18652	Turn the World Around	0955	6403
N-18653	Here We Go Again	0934	6403
N-18654	Tip of My Fingers		6403
N-18655	It Keeps Right On A-Hurtin'		6403
N-18656	My Woman, My Woman, My Wife	0934	6403

August 18, 1970

N-18954	I'm Gonna Sit Right Down and Write Myself a Letter		
N-18957	Come Live with Me		

N-18958	Smoke		
N-18959	Bidin' My Time		

September 29–30, 1970

N-19136	Invisible Tears		6428
N-19137	Raindrops Keep Fallin' on My Head		6428
N-19138	For Once in My Life		6428
N-19139	Raining in My Heart	1004	6428
N-19140	Sweetheart		6428
N-19145	Georgia Sunshine	0973	6428
N-19146	A Perfect Mountain		6428
N-19147	Marry Me		6428
N-19148	For the Good Times	0973	6428
N-19149	She's a Little Bit Country	1004	6428

April 12, 1971

PCA-0293	The Right Kind of Woman	1060	2053
PCA-0294	Do You Think It's Time		
PCA-0295	I Can Remember		

November 16–17, 1971

PCA-0907	I Don't Know What I'm Doing		2053
PCA-0908	The Small Exception of Me		2053
PCA-0909	Party Dolls and Wine		2053
PCA-0910	Blue Memories		2053
PCA-0911	I Can Give You What You Want Now	1085	2053
PCA-0912	Kiss the World Goodbye		2053
PCA-0913	Just the Other Side of Nowhere		2053
PCA-0914	Guess Who	1085	2053
PCA-0915	The Right Kind of Woman		
PCA-0916	What's Yesterday	1060	2053

December 21–22, 1972

QCA-3655	I'm Sitting on Top of the World		2113
QCA-3656	Smile	1166	2113
QCA-3657	When the Red, Red Robin Comes Bob, Bob, Bobbin' Along		2113
QCA-3658	Ramblin' Rose		2113

QCA-3659	Get On with Your Livin'	1166	2174
QCA-3660	I Wonder Who's Kissing Her Now		2113
QCA-3661	It's a Good Day		2113
QCA-3662	At Sundown		2113
QCA-3663	You Made Me Love You (I Didn't Want to Do It)	1141	2113
QCA-3664	Almost Like Being in Love		2113
QCA-3665	I'm Forever Blowing Bubbles		2113
QCA-3666	Amor Mio	1141	2174

July 25–26, 1973

RCA-4136	Gimme a Little Kiss (Will Ya, Huh!)		2174
RCA-4137	Baby, Won't You Please Come Home		2174
RCA-4138	I'm Confessin' (That I Love You)		2174
RCA-4139	I Don't Know Why		2174
RCA-4140	Free to Carry On	1178	2174
RCA-4141	Tie a Yellow Ribbon ('Round the Old Oak Tree)		2174
RCA-4142	You Better Move On		2174
RCA-4143	You're the Best Thing That Ever Happened to Me	1178	2174

August 10, 1973

RCA-4172	I'll Hold Out My Hand		

November 22, 1974

SCA-5183	Twilight on the Trail		2267
SCA-5184	Love Thy Neighbor		2267
SCA-5185	Without a Word of Warning		2267
SCA-5186	That Old Gang of Mine		2267

November 25, 1974

SCA-7825	If I Had You		2267
SCA-7826	It's Magic		2267
SCA-7827	I Cried for You		2267
SCA-7828	The Day You Came Along		2267
SCA-7829	Only Forever		2267
SCA-7830	Once in a While		2267

WARNER BROS. RECORDS
January 17–21, 1983

BTN-1711	My First Country Song [w/ Conway Twitty]	7-29584	1-23870
BTN-1712	Love Put a Song in My Heart		1-23870
BTN-1713	Old Bones		1-23870
BTN-1714	Drinkin' Champagne	7-29480	1-23870
BTN-1738	Everybody's Had the Blues [w/ Merle Haggard]		1-23870
BTN-1739	Don't Give Up on Me		1-23870
BTN-1740	Shoulder to Shoulder		1-23870
BTN-1741	Since I Met You Baby	7-29480	1-23870
BTN-1742	In Love up to My Heart		1-23870
BTN-1846	Hangin' Around	7-29584	1-23870

MCA RECORDS
July 1985

| MC-18550 | LA Is My Home | 52662 |
| MC-18551 | Drinking Champagne* | 52662 |

Warner Bros. master BTN-1714 (January 1983).

Albums

Manhattan at Midnight
Diamond D-7 (October 1946) *78-rpm album*

Dean Martin
Apollo EP 705 (1951) *45-rpm EP (extended-play) album*

Dean Martin Sings
Capitol H-401 (January 1953) *33-rpm ten-inch album*

Sunny Italy
Capitol EAP-1-481 (December 1953) *45-rpm EP*

Living It Up
Capitol EAP-1-533 (June 1954) *45-rpm EP*

Dean Martin
Capitol EAP-1-9123 (December 1954) *45-rpm EP*

Dean Martin Sings
Capitol T-401 (April 1955) *33-rpm LP (long-play) album*

Swingin' Down Yonder
  Capitol T-576 (July 1955) *33-rpm LP*

Memories Are Made of This
  Capitol EAP-1-701 (December 1955) *45-rpm EP*

Artists and Models
  Capitol EAP-1-702 (December 1955) *45-rpm EP*

Pardners
  Capitol EAP-1-752 (June 1956) *45-rpm EP*

Hollywood or Bust
  Capitol EAP-1-806 (December 1956) *45-rpm EP*

Ten Thousand Bedrooms
  Capitol EAP-1-840 (February 1957) *45-rpm EP*

Pretty Baby
  Capitol T-849 (June 1957) *33-rpm LP*

Return to Me
  Capitol EAP-1-939 (April 1958) *45-rpm EP*

Volare
  Capitol EAP-1-1027 (August 1958) *45-rpm EP*

This Is Dean Martin
  Capitol T-1047 (September 1958) *33-rpm LP*

Dean Martin Sings—Nicolini Lucchesi Plays
  Audition 33-5936 (1959)

Sleep Warm
  Capitol T/ST-1150 (March 1959)

A Winter Romance
  Capitol T/ST-1285 (November 1959)

Bells Are Ringing
  Capitol W/SW-1435 (June 1960)

This Time I'm Swingin'!
  Capitol T/ST-1442 (September 1960)

Dino: Italian Love Songs
  Capitol T/ST-1659 (February 1962)

Cha-Cha de Amor
  Capitol T/ST-1702 (April 1962)

French Style
Reprise R/R9-6021 (April 1962)

Dino Latino
Reprise R/R9-6054 (October 1962)

Dean "Tex" Martin: Country Style
Reprise R/R9-6061 (January 1963)

Dean "Tex" Martin Rides Again
Reprise R/R9-6085 (April 1963)

The Reprise Musical Repertory Theatre Presents "Finian's Rainbow"
Reprise F/FS-2015 (November 1963)

The Reprise Musical Repertory Theatre Presents "Guys and Dolls"
Reprise F/FS-2016 (November 1963)

The Reprise Musical Repertory Theatre Presents "Kiss Me, Kate"
Reprise F/FS-2017 (November 1963)

Robin and the Seven Hoods
Reprise F/FS-2021 (May 1964)

Dream with Dean
Reprise R/RS-6123 (June 1964)

Everybody Loves Somebody
Reprise R/RS-6130 (June 1964)

The Door Is Still Open to My Heart
Reprise R/RS-6140 (November 1964)

Dean Martin Hits Again
Reprise R/RS-6146 (January 1965)

The Lush Years Album
Tower T/DT-5006 (April 1965)

(Remember Me) I'm the One Who Loves You
Reprise R/RS-6170 (September 1965)

Houston
Reprise R/RS-6181 (October 1965)

Somewhere There's a Someone
Reprise R/RS-6201 (February 1966)

Relaxin'
Tower T/DT-5018 (February 1966)

You Can't Love 'Em All
Pickwick PC/SPC-3057 (1966)

Dean Martin Sings Songs from "The Silencers"
Reprise R/RS-6211 (March 1966)

The Hit Sound of Dean Martin
Reprise R/RS-6213 (September 1966)

The Dean Martin Christmas Album
Reprise R/RS-6222 (October 1966)

The Dean Martin TV Show
Reprise R/RS-6233 (November 1966)

I Can't Give You Anything but Love
Pickwick PC/SPC-3089 (1966)

Happiness Is Dean Martin
Reprise R/RS-6242 (April 1967)

Young and Foolish
Pickwick PC/SPC-3136 (1967)

Welcome to My World
Reprise R/RS-6250 (July 1967)

Gentle on My Mind
Reprise RS-6330 (November 1968)

I Take a Lot of Pride in What I Am
Reprise RS-6338 (August 1969)

My Woman, My Woman, My Wife
Reprise RS-6403 (July 1970)

For the Good Times
Reprise RS-6428 (January 1971)

Dino
Reprise MS-2053 (January 1972)

Sittin' on Top of the World
Reprise MS-2113 (May 1973)

You're the Best Thing That Ever Happened to Me
Reprise MS-2174 (November 1973)

Once in a While
Reprise MSK-2267 (August 1978)

The Nashville Sessions
Warner Bros. WB-1-23870-1 (June 1983)

Dean Martin: The Capitol Collector's Series
Capitol CDP 7 91633 2 (December 1989) *CD (compact-disc) album*

A Winter Romance
Capitol CDP 7 93115 2 (January 1990) *CD*

Swingin' Down Yonder
Capitol CDP 7 94306 2 (June 1991) *CD*

ILMS

My Friend Irma (Paramount)
September 1949
Produced by Hal Wallis and Cy Howard; © Wallis-Hazen, Inc., 14 July 1949.
Directed by George Marshall. Screenplay by Cy Howard and Parke Levy;
based on the CBS radio program "My Friend Irma," created by Cy Howard.
Edited by Leroy Stone. Score by Roy Webb. Songs by Jay Livingston and Ray
Evans. B&W, 102 minutes.

My Friend Irma Goes West (Paramount)
August 1950
Produced by Hal Wallis; © Wallis-Hazen, Inc., 18 May 1950. Directed by Hal
Walker. Screenplay by Cy Howard and Parke Levy; based on characters cre-
ated by Cy Howard for the CBS radio program "My Friend Irma." Edited by
Warren Low. Songs by Jay Livingston and Ray Evans. B&W, 90 minutes.

At War with the Army (Paramount)
January 1951
Produced by Abner J. Greshler and Fred F. Finklehoffe; © York Pictures
Corp. & Screen Associates, Inc., 23 January 1951. Directed by Hal Walker.
Screenplay by Fred E. Finklehoffe; based on a play by James B. Allardice.
Songs by Mack David and Jerry Livingston. B&W, 92 minutes.

That's My Boy (Paramount)
August 1951
Produced by Hal Wallis and Cy Howard; © Wallis-Hazen, Inc., 1 August
1951. Directed by Hal Walker. Screenplay by Cy Howard. Edited by Warren
Low. New song by Jay Livingston and Ray Evans. B&W, 98 minutes.

Hollywood at Play (Columbia)
September 1951
One-reel, 35-mm, black-and-white "Screen Snapshot"; © Columbia Pictures
Corp., 17 September 1951.

Sailor Beware (Paramount)
February 1952

Produced by Hal Wallis; © Wallis-Hazen, Inc., 4 December 1951. Directed by Hal Walker. Screenplay by James Allardice and Martin Rackin, with additional dialogue by John Grant; adapted from a play by Kenyon Nicholson and Charles Robinson. Edited by Warren Low. Musical direction by Joseph J. Lilley. Songs by Mack David and Jerry Livingston. B&W, 104 minutes.

Jumping Jacks (Paramount)
July 1952

Produced by Hal Wallis; © Wallis-Hazen, Inc., 9 July 1952. Directed by Norman Taurog. Screenplay by Robert Lees, Fred Rinaldo, and Herbert Baker, with additional dialogue by James Allardice and Richard Weil; from a story by Brian Marlow. Edited by Stanley Johnson. Songs by Mack David and Jerry Livingston. B&W, 96 minutes.

The Stooge (Paramount)
February 1953

Produced by Hal Wallis; © Wallis-Hazen, Inc., 1 February 1953 [in notice 1951]. Directed by Norman Taurog. Screenplay by Fred F. Finklehoffe and Martin Rackin, with additional dialogue by Elwood Ullman; from a story by Fred F. Finklehoffe and Sid Silvers. Edited by Warren Low. Musical direction by Joseph J. Lilley. New song by Mack David and Jerry Livingston. B&W, 100 minutes.

Road to Bali (Paramount)
January 1953

Produced by Harry Tugend; © Bing Crosby Enterprises & Hope Enterprises, 1 January 1953 [in notice 1952]. Directed by Hal Walker. Technicolor, 91 minutes.

Martin & Lewis had a cameo appearance in this Hope-Crosby film.

Scared Stiff (Paramount)
July 1953

Produced by Hal Wallis; © Wallis-Hazen, Inc., 1 June 1953 [in notice 1952]. Directed by George Marshall. Screenplay by Herbert Baker and Walter DeLeon, with additional dialogue by Ed Simmons and Norman Lear; based on a play by Paul Dickey and Charles W. Goddard. Edited by Warren Low. Musical direction by Joseph J. Lilley. New songs by Mack David and Jerry Livingston. B&W, 106 minutes.

The Caddy (Paramount)
September 1953
Produced by Paul Jones; © York Pictures Corp., 4 September 1953. Directed by Norman Taurog. Screenplay by Edmund Hartman and Danny Arnold, with additional dialogue by Ken Englund; from a story by Danny Arnold. Edited by Warren Low. Musical direction by Joseph J. Lilley. Songs by Harry Warren and Jack Brooks. B&W, 95 minutes.

Money from Home (Paramount)
February 1954
Produced by Hal Wallis; © Hal B. Wallis & Joseph H. Hazen, 1 February 1954 [in notice 1953]. Directed by George Marshall. Screenplay by James Allardice and Hal Kanter; from a story by Damon Runyon. Edited by Warren Low. Songs by Jack Brooks and Joseph J. Lilley, Burton Lane and Frank Loesser. Technicolor, 99 minutes.

Living It Up (Paramount)
July 1954
Produced by Paul Jones; © York Pictures Corp., 1 August 1954. Directed by Norman Taurog. Screenplay by Jack Rose and Melville Shavelson; from the musical comedy *Hazel Flagg* (book, Ben Hecht; music, Jule Styne; lyrics, Bob Hilliard), based on a story by James Street. Edited by Archie Marshek. Music arranged and conducted by Walter Scharf. Technicolor, 94 minutes.

Three Ring Circus (Paramount)
December 1954
Produced by Hal Wallis; © Hal B. Wallis & Joseph H. Hazen, 22 December 1954. Directed by Joseph Pevney. Screenplay by Don McGuire. Edited by Warren Low. Music by Walter Scharf. Technicolor, 103 minutes.

You're Never Too Young (Paramount)
August 1955
Produced by Paul Jones; © York Pictures Corp., 2 August 1955. Directed by Norman Taurog. Screenplay by Sidney Sheldon; suggested by a play by Edward Childs Carpenter, from a story by Fannie Kilbourne. Edited by Archie Marshek. Music arranged and conducted by Walter Scharf. Songs by Sammy Cahn and Arthur Schwartz. Technicolor, Vistavision, 102 minutes.

Artists and Models (Paramount)
December 1955
Produced by Hal Wallis; © Hal B. Wallis & Joseph H. Hazen, 21 December 1951. Directed by Frank Tashlin. Screenplay by Frank Tashlin, Hal Kanter,

and Herbert Baker; adapted by Don McGuire from a play by Michael David-
son and Norman Lessing. Edited by Walter Low. Music by Walter Scharf.
Vocal arrangements by Norman Luboff. New songs by Harry Warren and Jack
Brooks. Technicolor, Vistavision, 108 minutes.

Pardners (Paramount)
July 1956

Produced by Paul Jones; © York Pictures Corp., 25 July 1956. Directed by
Norman Taurog. Screenplay by Sidney Sheldon; screen story by Jerry Davis;
from a story by Mervin J. Houser. Edited by Archie Marshek. Music conducted by Frank De Vol. Songs by Sammy Cahn and James Van Heusen.
Technicolor, 86 minutes.

Hollywood or Bust (Paramount)
December 1956

Produced by Hal Wallis; © Hal B. Wallis & Joseph H. Hazen, 1 December
1956. Directed by Frank Tashlin. Screenplay by Erna Lazarus. Edited by
Howard Smith. Music arranged and conducted by Walter Scharf. Songs by
Sammy Fain and Paul Francis Webster. Technicolor, 94 minutes.

Ten Thousand Bedrooms (Metro-Goldwyn-Mayer)
April 1957

Produced by Joe Pasternak; © Loew's, Inc., 12 February 1957. Directed by
Richard Thorpe. Screenplay by Laslo Vadnay, Art Cohn, William Ludwig, and
Leonard Spigelglass. Edited by John McSweeney, Jr. New songs by Nicholas
Brodszky and Sammy Cahn. Metrocolor, 113 minutes.

The Young Lions (20th Century-Fox)
April 1958

Produced by Al Lichtman; © 20th Century-Fox, 18 March 1958. Directed by
Edward Dmytryk. Screenplay by Edward Anhalt, from the novel by Irwin
Shaw. Edited by Dorothy Spencer. Music composed by Hugo Friedhofer; con-
ducted by Lionel Newman. B&W, Cinemascope, 167 minutes.

Some Came Running (Metro-Goldwyn-Mayer)
January 1959

Produced by Sol C. Siegel; © Loew's, Inc., & Sol C. Siegel Productions, Inc.,
9 December 1958. Directed by Vincente Minnelli. Screenplay by John Patrick
and Arthur Sheekman; from the novel by James Jones. Edited by Adrienne
Fazan. Music by Elmer Bernstein. Color, Cinemascope, 137 minutes.

Rio Bravo (Warner Bros.)
March 1959
Produced by Howard Hawks; © Armada, 4 April 1959 [in notice 1958].
Directed by Howard Hawks. Screenplay by Jules Furthman and Leigh Brackett; from a short story by B. H. McCampbell. Edited by Folmar Blangsted.
Music by Dimitri Tiomkin. Technicolor, 140 minutes.

Career (Paramount)
October 1959
Produced by Hal Wallis; © Hal B. Wallis & Joseph H. Hazen, 8 October 1959. Directed by Joseph Anthony. Screenplay by James Lee, from his play. Edited by Warren Low. B&W, 105 minutes.

Who Was That Lady? (Columbia)
April 1960
Produced by George Sidney and Norman Krasna; © Ansark-George Sidney Productions, 1 January 1960 [in notice 1959]. Directed by George Sidney. Screenplay by Norman Krasna, from his play *Who Was That Lady I Saw You With?* Edited by Viola Lawrence. Music by André Previn. B&W, 116 minutes.

Bells Are Ringing (Metro-Goldwyn-Mayer)
June 1960
Produced by Arthur Freed; © Metro-Goldwyn-Mayer, Inc., & Arthur Freed Productions, Inc., 23 May 1960. Directed by Vincente Minnelli. Screenplay by Betty Comden and Adolph Green, from their musical play. Edited by Adrienne Fazan. Music by Jule Styne. Color, Cinemascope, 126 minutes.

Ocean's Eleven (Warner Bros.)
August 1960
Produced by Lewis Milestone; © Dorchester Productions, 4 August 1960. Directed by Lewis Milestone. Screenplay by Harry Brown and Charles Lederer; from a story by George Clayton Johnson and Jack Golden Russell. Edited by Philip W. Anderson. Music by Nelson Riddle. Color, Panavision, 127 minutes.

Pepe (Columbia)
December 1960
Produced by George Sidney; © George Sidney International Pictures, 1 March 1961 [in notice 1960]. Directed by George Sidney. Technicolor, Cinemascope, 195 minutes [later cut to 157 minutes].

    Martin had a cameo appearance in this overblown Cantinflas fiasco.

All in a Night's Work (Paramount)
March 1961

Produced by Hal Wallis; © Hal B. Wallis & Joseph H. Hazen, Inc., 31 December 1960. Directed by Joseph Anthony. Screenplay by Edmund Beloin, Maurice Richlin, and Sidney Sheldon; from a story by Margit Veszi and a play by Owen Elford. Edited by Howard Smith. Music by André Previn. Technicolor, 94 minutes.

Ada (Metro-Goldwyn-Mayer)
August 1961

Produced by Lawrence Weingarten; © MGM, Avon Productions, & Chalmar, 16 June 1961. Directed by Daniel Mann. Screenplay by Arthur Sheekman and William Driskill; from the novel *Ada Dallas* by Wirt Williams. Edited by Ralph E. Winters. Music by Bronislau Kaper. Metrocolor, 109 minutes.

Sergeants 3 (United Artists)
February 1962

Produced by Frank Sinatra; © Essex-Claude Productions, 9 February 1962. Directed by John Sturges. Screenplay by W. R. Burnett. Edited by Ferris Webster. Music by Billy May. Technicolor, 113 minutes.

The Road to Hong Kong (United Artists)
June 1962

Produced by Melvin Frank; © Melnor Films, Ltd., 23 May 1962. Directed by Norman Panama. B&W, 91 minutes.

Martin had a cameo appearance in this British Hope-Crosby film.

Who's Got the Action? (Paramount)
December 1962

Produced by Jack Rose; © Paramount, Amro Productions, Mea Productions, & Claude Productions, 21 December 1962. Directed by Daniel Mann. Screenplay by Jack Rose; from a novel by Alexander Rose. Edited by Howard Smith. Music by George Duning. Technicolor, Panavision, 93 minutes.

Come Blow Your Horn (Paramount)
June 1963

Produced by Norman Lear and Bud Yorkin; © Essex Productions & Tandem Enterprises, 6 June 1963. Directed by Bud Yorkin. Technicolor, Panavision, 112 minutes.

Martin had a cameo appearance as a bum in this Sinatra picture.

Toys in the Attic (United Artists)
August 1963
Produced by Walter Mirisch; © Mirisch & Claude, 17 June 1963. Directed by
George Roy Hill. Screenplay by James Poe; from the play by Lillian Hellman.
Edited by Stuart Gilmore. Music by George Duning. B&W, Panavision, 88
minutes.

Who's Been Sleeping in My Bed? (Paramount)
December 1963
Produced by Jack Rose; © Paramount, Amro Productions, Mea Productions,
& Claude Productions, 17 October 1963. Directed by Daniel Mann. Screen-
play by Jack Rose. Edited by George Tomasini. Music by George Duning.
Technicolor, Panavision, 103 minutes.

Four for Texas (Warner Bros.)
December 1963
Produced and directed by Robert Aldrich; © Sam Co., 4 January 1964.
Screenplay by Teddi Sherman and Robert Aldrich. Edited by Michael Lu-
ciano. Music by Nelson Riddle. Technicolor, 115 minutes.

What a Way to Go! (20th Century-Fox)
May 1964
Produced by Arthur P. Jacobs; © Apjac-Orchard Productions, Inc. & 20th
Century-Fox Film Corp., 14 May 1964. Directed by J. Lee Thompson. Screenplay by Betty Comden and Adolph Green; from a story by Gwen Davis. Edited
by Marjorie Fowler. Music by Nelson Riddle. Songs by Jule Styne. DeLuxe
color, Cinemascope, 111 minutes.

Robin and the Seven Hoods (Warner Bros.)
August 1964
Produced by Frank Sinatra; © P.C. Productions, 27 June 1964. Directed by
Gordon Douglas. Screenplay by David R. Schwartz. Edited by Sam O'Steen.
Music by Nelson Riddle. Songs by Sammy Cahn and James Van Heusen.
Technicolor, Panavision, 123 minutes.

Kiss Me, Stupid (Lopert)
December 1964
Produced by Billy Wilder; © Phalanx Productions, Inc., Mirisch Corporation
of Delaware, & Claude Productions, Inc., 22 December 1964. Directed by
Billy Wilder. Screenplay by Billy Wilder and I. A. L. Diamond; from the play
L'Ora della Fantasia by Anna Bonacci. Edited by Daniel Mandell. Music by
André Previn. Songs by George and Ira Gershwin. B&W, 126 minutes.

The Sons of Katie Elder (Paramount)
August 1965
Produced by Hal Wallis; © Paramount Pictures Corp., Hal B. Wallis, Joseph H. Hazen, & John Wayne, 24 June 1965. Directed by Henry Hathaway. Screenplay by William H. Wright, Allan Weiss, and Harry Essex; from a story by Talbot Jennings. Edited by Warren Low. Music by Elmer Bernstein. Technicolor, Panavision, 120 minutes.

Marriage on the Rocks (Warner Bros.)
September 1965
Produced by William H. Daniels; © A-C Productions & Warner Bros., 2 October 1965. Directed by Jack Donohue. Screenplay by Cy Howard. Edited by Sam O'Steen. Music by Nelson Riddle. Technicolor, Panavision, 109 minutes.

The Silencers (Columbia)
March 1966
Produced by Irving Allen; © Meadway-Claude Productions Co., 1 March 1966. Directed by Phil Karlson. Screenplay by Oscar Saul; based on the books *The Silencers* and *Death of a Citizen,* by Donald Hamilton. Edited by Charles Nelson. Music by Elmer Bernstein. PatheColor, 103 minutes.

Texas Across the River (Universal)
November 1966
Produced by Harry Keller; © Universal Pictures, 22 October 1966. Directed by Michael Gordon. Screenplay by Wells Root, Harold Greene, and Ben Starr. Edited by Gene Milford. Music by DeVol. Technicolor, Techniscope, 100 minutes.

Murderers' Row (Columbia)
December 1966
Produced by Irving Allen; © Meadway-Claude Pictures No. 2, 1 December 1966. Directed by Henry Levin. Screenplay by Herbert Baker; based on the novel *Murderers' Row* by Donald Hamilton. Edited by Walter Thompson. Music by Lalo Schifrin. Songs by Tommy Boyce and Bobby Hart, Lalo Schifrin and Howard Greenfield. Technicolor, 108 minutes.

Rough Night in Jericho (Universal)
November 1967
Produced by Martin Rackin. Directed by Arnold Laven. Screenplay by Sydney Boehm and Marvin H. Alpert; based on the novel *The Man in Black* by

Marvin H. Alpert. Edited by Ted J. Kent. Music by Don Costa. Technicolor, Techniscope, 102 minutes.

The Ambushers (Columbia)
December 1967
Produced by Irving Allen; © Meadway-Claude Films No. 3, 1 December 1967. Directed by Henry Levin. Screenplay by Herbert Baker; based on the novel by Donald Hamilton. Edited by Harold F. Kress. Music by Hugo Montenegro. Title song by Herbert Baker. Color, 101 minutes.

How to Save a Marriage—and Ruin Your Life (Columbia)
January 1968
Produced by Stanley Shapiro; © Columbia Pictures Corp., 31 December 1967. Directed by Fielder Cook. Screenplay by Stanley Shapiro and Nate Monaster. Edited by Philip Anderson. Music by Michel Legrand. Song lyric by Mack David. PatheColor, Panavision, 102 minutes.

Bandolero! (20th Century-Fox)
July 1968
Produced by Robert L. Jacks; © 20th Century-Fox Film Corp., 18 June 1968. Directed by Andrew V. McLaglen. Screenplay by James Lee Barrett; from a story by Stanley L. Hough. Edited by Folmar Blangsted. Music by Jerry Goldsmith. DeLuxe color, Panavision, 107 minutes.

Five Card Stud (Paramount)
August 1968
Produced by Hal Wallis; © Paramount Pictures Corp., Hal B. Wallis, & Joseph H. Hazen, 12 July 1968. Directed by Henry Hathaway. Screenplay by Marguerite Roberts; from a novel by Ray Gaulden. Edited by Warren Low. Music by Maurice Jarre. Technicolor, 101 minutes.

The Wrecking Crew (Columbia)
February 1969
Produced by Irving Allen; © Meadway-Claude Films No. 4, 1 February 1969 [in notice 1968]. Directed by Phil Karlson. Screenplay by William McGivern; based on a novel by Donald Hamilton. Edited by Maury Winetrobe. Music by Hugo Montenegro. Song by Mack David and Frank DeVol. Technicolor, 105 minutes.

Airport (Universal)

March 1970

Produced by Ross Hunter; © Universal Pictures & Ross Hunter Productions, Inc., 5 March 1970 [in notice 1969]. Directed by George Seaton. Screenplay by George Seaton; from the novel by Arthur Hailey. Edited by Stuart Gilmore. Music by Alfred Newman. Technicolor, Todd-AO, 137 minutes.

Something Big (National General)

January 1972

Produced and directed by Andrew V. McLaglen; © Stanmore Productions & Penbar Productions, Inc., 23 September 1971. Screenplay by James Lee Barrett. Edited by Robert Simpson. Music by Marvin Hamlisch. Song by Burt Bacharach and Hal David. Technicolor, 107 minutes.

Showdown (Universal)

November 1973

Produced and directed by George Seaton. Screenplay by Theodore Taylor; from a story by Hank Fine. Edited by John W. Holmes. Music by David Shire. Technicolor, Todd-AO 35, 90 minutes.

Mr. Ricco (United Artists)

January 1975

Produced by Douglas Netter; © MGM, 29 January 1975. Directed by Paul Bogart. Screenplay by Robert Hoban; from a story by Ed Harvey and Francis Kiernan. Edited by Michael McLean. Music by Chico Hamilton. Metrocolor, 98 minutes.

The Cannonball Run (20th Century-Fox)

June 1981

Produced by Albert S. Ruddy; © 1981. Directed by Hal Needham. Screenplay by Brock Yates. Edited by Donn Cambern and William D. Gordean. Music supervision by Snuff Garrett. Technicolor, 93 minutes.

Since I Met You Baby (Warner Bros.)

September 1983

Music video. Warner Bros. No. 760 220-1797. Produced and directed by Ricci Martin; © Sasha Corp./Warner Bros. Records, 1 September 1983. 2:44 minutes.

Cannonball Run II (Warner Bros.)

June 1984

Produced by Albert S. Ruddy; © 1983. Directed by Hal Needham. Screenplay by Harvey Miller, Hal Needham, and Albert Ruddy; based on characters by Brock Yates. Edited by William Gordean. Music by Al Capps. Animation by Ralph Bakshi. Technicolor, 106 minutes.

$\mathcal{I}$NDEX

Photo: Noni Watters

NICK TOSCHES has written for *The New York Times,*
Esquire, Vanity Fair, and *Rolling Stone.* He is the au-
thor of *Hellfire,* the landmark biography of Jerry Lee
Lewis, and of *Cut Numbers,* which won France's Prix
Calibre .38 for the best first novel of 1990. He lives in
New York City.